American Government

IN **BLACK** AND **WHITE**
DIVERSITY AND DEMOCRACY

Fourth Edition

Paula D. McClain

Steven C. Tauber

New York   Oxford
OXFORD UNIVERSITY PRESS

Oxford University Press is a department of the University of Oxford.
It furthers the University's objective of excellence in research, scholarship,
and education by publishing worldwide. Oxford is a registered trade mark of
Oxford University Press in the UK and certain other countries.

Published in the United States of America by Oxford University Press
198 Madison Avenue, New York, NY 10016, United States of America.

© 2020, 2018, 2015, 2014, 2010 by Oxford University Press

For titles covered by Section 112 of the US Higher Education
Opportunity Act, please visit www.oup.com/us/he for the latest
information about pricing and alternate formats.

Library of Congress Cataloging-in-Publication Data

CIP data is on file at the Library of Congress
978-0-19-092851-3

9 8 7 6 5 4 3 2 1
Printed by LSC Communications, Inc., United States of America

To my husband, Paul C. Jacobson, daughters Kristina and Jessica, and grandsons, Jackson, Sterling and Braxton, whose love and support continued to sustain me through this long and long and continuing project.

Paula D. McClain

Dedicated to my wife Meghan and the memory of her sister Kathleen Hogan (1971–2013)

Steven C. Tauber

Brief Contents

Contents

To the Student

Alexis de Tocqueville, who was an early French visitor to the United States and wrote *Democracy in America* (1835), believed that the essence of America was in the uniquely free and egalitarian ideas that abounded at its founding. Yet, Tocqueville noted that the treatment and situation of Blacks and Indians in the United States contradicted the American passion for democracy. He saw slavery and the denial of constitutional rights and protections to Blacks as the principal threat to the American democratic system. From his perspective, Blacks would never be included in America's democracy; even the American Revolution's egalitarian principles would never change Whites' negative views of Blacks. Indians, he felt, would resist being civilized, and in so doing would be wiped out. Tocqueville believed that the institution of slavery should be abolished, but he also felt that the aftermath would be catastrophic because Blacks, Whites, and Indians would not be able to live together, so White genocidal violence against Blacks and Indians would follow.

For much of the history of the United States, the issues of race and the place of Blacks and American Indians, and later other racial or ethnic minority groups such as Asians and Latinos have been enduring threads in the American political fabric. Although they are still threads that can be pulled to generate angst and divisions, a great deal has changed since Tocqueville made his observations in 1835.

In 2008, Senator Barack Obama (D-IL) became the Democratic nominee for President of the United States and the first Black person to represent a major political party in the presidential race in the history of the United States. On November 4, 2008, Obama was elected the first African American president of the United States, with a wide margin in both the popular and electoral votes. He was reelected to a second term in 2012 by a substantial, albeit somewhat reduced, margin in the popular and electoral votes.

Many Americans view the historic election of a Black as president as a signal that issues of racism and inequality have been resolved and that there is no need for more or new public policies to address racial inequalities. They assert that any remaining inequalities are the result of a lack of individual initiative, not societal barriers. On the contrary, we believe that the election of Barack Obama brought into sharp relief the centrality of issues of race to American politics. In fact, President Obama's success made it more difficult, not less, to address some of the issues of inequality that continue to exist in the United States. Issues that have emerged since the Trump Administration, such as the president's reaction to the violence in Charlottesville, Virginia and the policy of separating Latino children from their families at the border, demonstrate that race and ethnicity are still central to American politics.

In this book, we are concerned with the complexities of the American political system and inequalities that continue to exist within it. If you read and understand the text, we believe you will benefit in four ways.

First, government is more than just a set of institutions, rules, and procedures by which those institutions operate. Government exists also in our perceptions about and our experiences with government. Every American might perceive government differently, and each of us behaves somewhat differently based on these perceptions. Describing government in this sense is not something that is feasible here, but we can report on the perceptions of different peoples grouped by shared characteristics. The United States is not "one nation . . . indivisible" but, instead, something different to each of us based on our citizenship status, socioeconomic class, religion, age, place of residence, race, ethnicity, gender, and many other factors.

Second, we offer a practical view of American government supported by empirical analysis. By using hard evidence to support our views, we hope to avoid a naive "how government should work" approach and give you a firm base for developing informed opinions. For example, we list the powers of the president, but in reality these powers are limited and the president is much less powerful than a simple list of official powers would suggest.

Third, you will have a sense of how race has played out in the American governmental system and its politics. Although some historical events present a sad and painful look at the American system, recent events such as the election of President Obama show a more hopeful albeit cautious look at the American political system and its politics.

Finally, reading this book will give you a more holistic and realistic perspective on American government. You will have a sense of what government can do and what American citizens must do to help government achieve its objectives. Regardless of whether that help comes through social movements, voting, or participation in other types of political activity, people—individually and collectively—are central to the American governmental system.

New to the Fourth Edition

- Updates and analysis place the 2018 election and its results into political and cultural context for students.
- Expanded coverage of issues of race and ethnicity that have emerged since the election of President Donald Trump
- Expanded coverage of the #MeToo Movement
- Enhanced discussion of political science research in relevant chapters provides insights into both the scholarly debates and consensus of the discipline. Many of the tables in the chapters have been updated with the most recent data available.

Revisions to the Fourth Edition

- Fully updated to reflect the results of the 2018 midterm elections, with revised figure and table data throughout, in addition to deep-dive discussion of what these changes could mean for policy, partisanship, and the current administration
- Updated discussion of legalized marijuana following former Attorney General Sessions' threatened reversal
- Chapter Four (Civil Liberties) opening vignette rewritten to discuss Charlottesville protests and attack
- Updated discussions about freedom of the press and the current administration's stance on the media
- Chapter Five (Civil Rights) opening vignette rewritten to focus on DACA and the related executive order and court cases, as well as immigration
- Sections added discussing the Women's March and #MeToo
- Revised and updated discussion of LGBTQ rights and the current administration's policies
- Discussion of Hurricanes Irma, Harvey, and Maria accompany an examination of the government response to each
- Updated oversight discussion of the Robert Mueller's investigation, Russian collusion, and obstruction of justice
- Chapter Seven (Executive) opening vignette rewritten to focus on John Kelly and the importance of the Chief of Staff position as it relates to race and gender. Discussions include his lies about Rep. Frederica Wilson, his stance on immigration, and his response to domestic abusers on his staff in the wake of the #MeToo movement
- Updated to include Congress and the President's attempts to end Obamacare, and the tax bill
- Added discussions of FCC and net neutrality as it pertains to independent regulatory commissions, especially how these changes affect civil rights groups and disenfranchised Americans
- Chapter Nine (The Judiciary) updated with discussions of the Gorsuch and Kavanaugh appointments, Kavanaugh's rape accusations, the subsequent investigation and hearing, and his confirmation in spite of these. Additional discussion of the Senate's failure to consider Merrick Garland.
- Chapter Eleven (The Media) opening vignette changed to address Russian interference in the 2016 Presidential election through social media, especially how race and ethnicity have been used to stoke tensions across the nation
- Expanded social media discussion to include Trump's use of Twitter as a means of communication with the media, his opponents, and his supporters

Organization of This Book

Chapter 1, "American Government and Politics in a Racially Divided World," introduces the concept of government in its general and various forms. It also shows that the choices the Framers of the Constitution made in structuring the new governments were neither accidental nor unconnected. The structures of these governments had theoretical and philosophical foundations in classical liberalism, republicanism, and a tradition of exclusion.

Chapter 2, "The Constitution: Rights and Race Intertwined," introduces the basic government documents—the Declaration of Independence and the Constitution. It addresses the events and problems under the Articles of Confederation that led to the drafting of the 1787 Constitution and focuses on the overt and tacit role that slavery played throughout the constitutional process.

Chapter 3, "Federalism: Balancing Power, Balancing Rights," explains the concept of federalism—the balance of power between the national government and the states. It also discusses how that power has ebbed and flowed since the founding of the republic.

Chapter 4, "Civil Liberties: Freedom and Government Authority in Tension," addresses the tension between government authority and the civil liberties afforded citizens under the Bill of Rights. We pay particular attention to how each amendment also offers protections against state governments.

Chapter 5, "Civil Rights: Inequality and Equality," focuses on the increased legal protection afforded various racial and ethnic minorities and women over time and how the reality of this protection has varied across levels of government. We also discuss the differences in timing of the extensions of these protections to the various groups, including the LGBT community, the elderly, and disabled people.

Chapter 6, "Congress: Representation and Lawmaking," outlines the general functions of and influences on Congress, as well as the nature of representation in our democratic system.

Chapter 7, "The Presidency: Conventional Wisdom Redefined," looks at the Office of the President. We outline the roles, powers, and limitations of the president of the United States and the Office of the President, with the purpose of presenting a realistic view of what can and cannot reasonably be expected of presidents. We pay particular attention to the presidential selection process.

Chapter 8, "The Bureaucracy: Career Government Employees, Accountability, and Race," addresses the important topic of government agencies. We examine and assess the relative size and range of functions of the national bureaucracy, and the racial, ethnic, and gender composition of these bureaucracies.

Chapter 9, "The Judiciary: Blending Law and Politics," describes the structure, selection processes, and decision-making dynamics of the national courts. The influence of these factors on the operation of these important institutions highlights the differences among various levels of courts.

Chapter 10, "Public Opinion: Divided By Race?" listens to the voice of the people. We explore the complexities of public opinion by examining the views of the many publics that exist in the American political system, including their racial, gender, and regional differences. A second focus is the role public opinion plays in the American political process.

Chapter 11, "The Media: Reinforcing Racial Stereotypes?" focuses on the role of the media in the American political process. We examine the media's influence on the formation of public opinion, policy agenda setting, and campaigns. We also consider the importance of symbols and symbolism and the "parallel press."

Chapter 12, "Social Movements: Civil Rights as a Movement Model," looks at how opinions are mobilized into efforts to address grievances. Preconditions and timing are of key interest. Drawing from illustrations of several populations, we examine why groups coalesce into social movements at certain points in time and not at others when conditions are perhaps even worse.

Chapter 13, "Interest Groups: Good Outcomes with Few Resources," flows from the discussion of social movements. This chapter distinguishes between social movements and interest groups and examines the ways in which interest groups affect the policy process and influence political outcomes. We note that interest groups are not only those organizations or racial and ethnic minorities and women who have been excluded from the political process, but also are far more likely to include strong majority-dominated organizations whose influence and access are generally much greater than those of the so-called special interests of disadvantaged groups.

Chapter 14, "Political Parties: Linking Voters and Governing Institutions," provides a history of the development of the national two-party system in the United States. We discuss the pros and cons of a two-party system as well as the strengths and weaknesses of the current Democratic and Republican parties. The history of the experiences of Blacks, Latinos, American Indians, and Asian Americans is discussed to provide a context for the current placement of these groups within the two political parties.

Chapter 15, "Voting and Elections: From Obama to Clinton," discusses the voting behaviors of the American public. Voting at the national level for the president commands the most attention. We also consider the factors of race and gender in the examination of voting patterns.

Chapter 16, "The Making of Domestic and Foreign Policy," outlines the public policymaking process, summarizing how all institutions and processes converge to help explain what government does and does not do. It focuses on the differences and the relationship between both domestic and foreign policy.

Note about Terminology

Before proceeding, it is important to define the terms used throughout the book.[1] First, the terms *Black* and *African American* are used interchangeably. Recent research suggests that among Americans of African descent, slightly more than 1 percent difference exists in those who prefer to be called Black (48.1 percent) and those who prefer to be called African American (49.2 percent).[2] Our own preference is for the term *Black* because it concisely describes an identity and a status in American society that are based on color. The Black experience in the United States differs markedly from that of White ethnics, and the use of *African*

American might convey the impression that Blacks are just another ethnic group similar to Italian Americans, Irish Americans, or Polish Americans.

Similarly, we use *Latino* and *Hispanic* interchangeably as umbrella terms when we cannot distinguish among subgroups of the nation's Spanish-origin population. Many academics reject the term *Hispanic* because it was devised by the U.S. Census Bureau to classify individuals and is devoid of any connection to the people to which it refers in the United States. The term comes from the Latin word for Spain and is associated with people from the Iberian Peninsula in Europe. It refers to people of Spain, Portugal, Gibraltar, and Andorra, and clearly does not technically include individuals of Mexican, Puerto Rican, Cuban, and Central and South American descent. We most often use *Latino* in recognition of this distinction because this term refers more exclusively to persons of Mexican and Latin American origin.

Third, we use the term *Indian peoples* or *American Indians* rather than the population term *Native American*. Scholars of American Indian politics dislike the term *Native American* because it can be applied literally to any person born in the Americas. Although the terms *Indian peoples* and *American Indians* ignore geographical differences and cultural diversity among Indian groupings, they are the preferred terms of scholars working in the area.[3]

Fourth, the term *Asian American* is an umbrella term for a number of ethnic origin groups—Japanese, Koreans, Chinese, Filipinos, Southeast Asians, and East Indians. We use the term when we or the data we use do not allow us to differentiate among these various ethnic origin groups.

At times, we use the term *ethnicity* in a specific sense of the term—generally meaning the groupings of people on the basis of learned characteristics, often associated with national origin. Issues of ethnicity are particularly pertinent in the Latino, Asian, and Indian groups and are becoming more important in the Black population as the number of Black immigrants from Africa and the Caribbean increases.

We also use the terms *racial minority* or *racial and ethnic minorities* as a shorthand method of identifying Blacks, Latinos, Asian Americans, and American Indians collectively based on their proportion of the population vis-à-vis the majority White population.

We also use the generic term *women* at times, but most often we specify which group of women to which we are referring. Women as a category have been excluded from participation in many segments of American society, but we do not consider the generic category of women as a numerical minority of the population.

Significantly, we use the capitalized form for all of the various racial and ethnic groups—White, Black, Asian American, American Indian, and Latino—as well as for the various ethnic origin groups, such as Mexican American.

Finally, a word about the concept of *equality* that we examine and apply throughout this book. There are many ongoing debates about the kinds of equality and which should be embraced and pursued by governmental policies. Political philosophers pitch "equality of opportunity" against "equality of outcome" and weigh in on their relative benefits. Measures of fairness or justice are overlaid on top of these categories in an attempt to moderate their disparate results. In this book, we look at all these values through the lens of racial and ethnic disparity. Thus, some of the measures and evaluations of equality we suggest apply only to those who have suffered or benefited from racial and ethnic inequality. Other lessons we draw about equality can be applied across the spectrum of public policy—to the poor White woman in Appalachia, the auto worker who just lost his job, the gay person being taunted at work, or the disabled person who cannot go where she wants because there is no wheelchair access. We do not take on these inequalities in as great a depth as we do racial and ethnic inequality, but many of the measures and evaluations of equality we make can be extended to them as well—and we encourage students to read the text with that in mind.

Chapter Features

Each chapter has a set of features that highlight the main themes of the chapter and provide information important to understanding many of the points raised in the chapter. Each feature plays a specific role in the text in support of our approach to American government:

- Chapter opening **vignettes**, drawn from actual events, that highlight the theme of complex inequalities. These vignettes are intended to help make concrete concepts that might appear abstract.
- **Glossary** definitions in the text when the term is first encountered, making it easier to find the definitions and understand their meaning in context.
- **Measuring Equality boxes** provide empirical, quantitative data that support a conclusion or underscore an argument we make to provide you with information on a topic that might be unfamiliar.
- **Our Voices boxes** contain excerpts from the writings of important people or organizations to allow you to "hear" their voices and excerpts from original documents important to the development and workings of the American political system.
- **Evaluating Equality boxes** contain a scenarios that ask you to use the central points of the chapter as a basis for thinking critically about aspects of our political system. These are framed in terms of questions for debate or discussion.
- **Chapter conclusions** tie the chapter content into the opening vignette and draw the themes together.
- **Review questions** at the end of each chapter that are also tied to the theme. By focusing on the review questions, you will be able to distill the main issues from each chapter.
- **Additional readings** with short annotations for each reference.

In all, we hope these features add to your interest in the story of American government that we tell through the lens of race and ethnicity.

Teaching and Learning Support

Oxford University Press offers instructors and students a comprehensive teaching and learning package of support materials for adopters of *American Government in Black and White 4e.*

Ancillary Resource Center

The Ancillary Resource Center (ARC) at https://oup-arc.com is a convenient destination for all teaching and learning resources that accompany this book. Accessed online through individual user accounts, the ARC provides instructors with up-to-date ancillaries while guaranteeing the security of grade-significant resources. In addition, it allows OUP to keep users informed when new content becomes available. The ARC for *American Government in Black and White, 4e* contains a variety of materials to aid in teaching:

- **Instructor's Resource Manual with Test Item File**—The Instructor's Resource Manual includes chapter objectives, detailed chapter outlines, lecture suggestions and activities, discussion questions, video resources, and Web resources. The Test Item File includes more than two thousand five hundred test questions including multiple-choice, short-answer, and essay questions.
- **Computerized Test Bank**—Using the Diploma test authoring and management tool, the computerized test bank that accompanies this text is designed for both novice and advanced users. Diploma enables instructors to create and edit questions, create randomized quizzes and tests with an easy-to-use drag-and-drop tool, publish quizzes and tests to online courses, and print quizzes and tests for paper-based assessments.
- **PowerPoint-Based Slides**—Each chapter has two slide decks to support your lectures. One deck includes the chapter outline and content; the other includes just the artwork included in the text.
- **CNN** and other video resources—Offering recent clips on timely topics, clips are approximately 5-10 minutes in length providing a great way to launch your lectures about key concepts with real world issues and examples.

Digital Learning Tools

American Government in Black and White, 4e comes with an extensive array of digital learning tools to ensure your students get the most out of your course. Developed exclusively to support OUP American Government titles, these activities have been extensively reviewed by users of similar digital content in their classrooms. Several assignment types provide your students with various activities that teach core concepts, allow students to develop data literacy around important contemporary topics and issues, and to role play as decision makers to engage with problems that simulate real world political challenges. Each activity includes an auto-graded assessment so students can immediately see their level of knowledge of the content under study and are optimized to work on any mobile device or computer. For users of learning management systems, results can be recorded to the gradebooks in one of several currently supported systems. Access to these activities are free with purchase of a new print or electronic textbook. These and additional study tools are available at www.oup.com/us/McClain, through links embedded in the enhanced ebook, and within course cartridges. Each activity is described below:

Interactive Media Activities

Interactive Media Activities are simulations of real world events, problems, and challenges developed to connect text and classroom topics to everyday life. Designed to be assigned as homework, each activity takes approximately 15 to 20 minutes to complete and produces unique results for each student. Students are put into the role of a political actor or decision maker and get to experience how various aspects of politics works, seeing the trade-offs required to produce meaningful policies and outcomes. Topics include:

Individualism vs. Solidarity	*Election Reform*
Passing Immigration Reform	*Fact-checking the Media*
Electing Cheryl Martin	*Passing the Thirteenth Amendment*
Building the USS Relief	*Negotiating with China*
Intervening in Bhutan	*NEW—Healthcare and Federalism*
The Fight Against Warrantless Wiretapping	*NEW—The Changing Face of Affirmative Action*
Balancing the Budget	*NEW—Surveys, Bias & Fake News*
Redistricting in "Texachusetts"	*NEW—Free Speech on Campus*
Saving the Electric Car	*NEW—The People vs. the Pipeline*

Media Tutorials

These animated videos are designed to teach key concepts taught in the course, as well as address important contemporary issues. Each tutorial runs 2-4 minutes in length and ends with an assessment for students to test what they know. Topics include:

The Constitution: A Brief Tour	*The Judiciary: How do judges interpret the Constitution?*
Civil Rights: How does the Fourteenth Amendment ensure equal rights for all Citizens?	*Polling: How do we know what people know?*
Federalism: What does it mean to Incorporate the Bill of Rights?	*Campaigns and Elections: How does gerrymandering work?*
Political Participation: What affects voter turnout?	*NEW: Democracy vs. Republic*
Media: How is the news shaped by agenda setting, framing, and profit bias?	*NEW: Freedom of Religion*
	NEW: Executive Orders
Interest Groups: What is a Political Action Committee (PAC), and what makes some PACs Super PACs?	*NEW: Political Culture Across States*
	NEW: Party Organization
	NEW: Bureaucracies
Congress: Why do we hate Congress but keep electing the same representatives?	*NEW: Discretionary and Mandatory Spending*

NEW Issue Navigators

These *new* features offer students an interactive way to explore data related to major issues in American politics today, and allow students to reflect on the sources of their own views and opinions. Each activity will improve your students' abilities to think through their political opinions by using compelling and vetted information to raise the level of classroom debate. Students will analyze several data sources and positions for each topic. They'll then get to answer questions that indicate their own beliefs and values on these issues, and compare themselves to national polling data. The exercises include assessments around the data to ensure students can interpret the data presented and understand what it means. Issues include:

Climate change	*Free trade and tariffs*
Immigration	*Healthcare reform*
Gerrymandering/redistricting	*Social Security solvency*
Gun Control and federalism	*Tax Reform*

Online Study Tools. Many additional online study tools are available at www.oup.com/us/McClain for student's self-paced learning and assessment. For each chapter, these include interactive flashcards, chapter review Power-Point slides, key terms quizzes, chapter quizzes, chapter exams, short answer essay tests, videos, web activities and web links.

Enhanced ebook. The enhanced ebook provides students with a versatile, accessible, online version of the textbook, with all of the above resources integrated on the appropriate pages via clickable icons that connect to each study tool. The ebook reader also provides functionality that will help students be more effective in their study time—for instance, bookmarking, highlighting, note taking, and search tools. Every new copy of the print text includes access to the ebook. The eBook is also available for separate purchase, either online or through campus bookstores.

Learning Management System integration

OUP offers the ability to integrate OUP content into currently supported versions of Canvas, D2L, or Blackboard. Contact your local rep or visit oup-arc.com/integration for more information.

Format Choices

Oxford University Press offers cost-saving alternatives to meet the needs of all students. This text is offered in a Loose-leaf format at a 30% discount off the list price of the text; and in an eBook format, through Redshelf for a 50% discount. You can also customize our textbooks to create the course material you want for your class. For more information, please contact your Oxford University Press representative, call 800.280.0280, or visit us online at www.oup.com/us/Morone.

Packaging Options

Adopters of *American Government in Black and White* can package *any* Oxford University Press book with the text for a twenty percent savings off the total package price. See our many trade and scholarly offerings at www.oup.com, then contact your local OUP sales representative to request a package ISBN. Below are additional suggestions to package with the text:

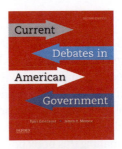

STAY CURRENT

Package with Emenaker and Morone's *Current Debates in American Government*, Second Edition, and **save 20 percent** on accessible, contemporary readings in American government.

GET SPECIALIZED

Package with a *What Everyone Needs to Know* paperback **for only $5!** Written by leading experts, each volume in this acclaimed series offers a balanced and authoritative primer on complex issues and countries.

WRITE AND RESEARCH BETTER

Package with *Writing in Political Science* **for only $5** or *Research and Writing Guide for Political Science* for free!

KNOW YOUR RIGHTS

Package with *The United States Constitution: What It Says, What It Means* **for free!**

BECOME AN EXPERT IN NO TIME

Package one of Oxford's *Very Short Introductions* **for free!**

Acknowledgments

This text has been long in the making even though it was published at an auspicious time in U.S. political history. Many reviewers, editors, colleagues, and friends have given advice and offered help while we developed the text. It is impossible to thank everyone individually who contributed to our efforts, but it is important to acknowledge the vast collective effort that resulted in such a mold-breaking text. We accept responsibility for any errors and shortcomings reflected in the text but share full credit for its strengths with the people who joined us in making this book possible.

The reviewers for the first edition deserve special credit for combining content expertise with pedagogical concern and an eye on late-breaking 2008 election developments:

Russell G. Brooker, *Alverno College*
Michael S. Rodriguez, *Richard Stockton College of New Jersey*
Bilal Dabir Sekou, *University of Hartford*
Sherri L. Wallace, *University of Louisville*

We would also like to thank the reviewers of the second edition:
Damien Arthuer, *West Virginia State University*
Robert Ballinger, *South Texas College*
Geoff Bowden, *Savannah State University*
Meigan M. Fields, *Fort Valley State University*
Nicole Krassas, *Eastern Connecticut State University*
Anthony A. Maalouf, *Delaware County Community College*
Linda McKinstry, *Delaware County Community College*
Nathan K. Mitchell, *Prairie View A&M University*
Billy Monroe, *Prairie View A&M University*
Megan Ostbur, Xavier *University of Louisiana*
Mordu Serry-Kamal, *Winston-Salem State University*
James Daniel Steele, *North Carolina Agricultural and Technical State University*
Richard W. Waterman, *University of Kentucky*
S. Ife Williams, *Delaware County Community College*
Zaphon Wilson, *Saint Augustine's University*
Ahmed Y. Zohny, *Coppin State University*

We would also like to thank the reviewers of the third edition:
Rosalind Blanco Cook, *Tulane University*
Jeffrey Bloodworth, *Gannon University*
Joseph Romance, *Fort Hays State University*
Alec Ewald, *University of Vermont*
Edward Larsen, *Delaware County Community College*
Lenore VanderZee, *State University of New York at Canton*
Raymond Sandoval, *Dallas County Community College*
Ervin Kallfa, Hostos *Community College*
We would also like to thank the reviewers of the fourth edition:
Jennifer Sacco, *Quinnipiac University*
Richard Waterman, *University of Kentucky*

On the fourth edition we are deeply indebted to the excellent staff at Oxford University Press. In particular, we would like to thank Patrick Keefe and Alison Ball for expert photo research, marketing, and editorial assistance. We would also like to thank Jana MacIsaac and Holly Haydash for their outstanding editorial notes, which have undoubtedly improved this text. We are also grateful to Jennifer Carpenter for her guidance and leadership in our revisions. Finally, we would like to thank the thousands of students we have taught over the years.

—**Paula D. McClain and Steven C. Tauber**

The fourth edition has also been a collective effort. Duke University graduate students, Gloria Ayee and Nura Sediqe spent countless hours gathering new data and updating older material. Jessica Johnson Carew completed the Instructor's Manual and Test Bank and I am appreciative that she agreed to take on that arduous task. I also want to thank Steve Tauber for signing on as a coauthor on a project that had many fits and starts, and lots of twists and turns. It has been a pleasure working with Steve on the first, second and third editions of this book, and I anticipate that this will be a long-term co-authorship.

On a personal note, I could not have achieved much of what I have accomplished professionally without the love and support of my husband, Paul C. Jacobson. We have developed into quite a team over the decades, pursuing both our careers (Paul is a lawyer) while raising two daughters—Kristina and Jessica. We are now the proud grandparents of three grandsons, Jackson B. -Ragland Sterling A. Ragland and Braxton Landis Ragland (Kristina's sons), and find that we enjoy being grandparents almost as much as we enjoy being parents. Paul has been involved in this project in more ways than he had anticipated, or appreciated. I thank him for his unconditional support and continuing love. This book is dedicated to them with much love and appreciation.

—**Paula D. McClain**

Numerous conversations with my colleagues in the School of Interdisciplinary Global Studies (formerly the Department of Government & International Affairs) at the University of South Florida, especially Mark Amen, Cheryl Hall, Rachel May, Susan MacManus, Bernd Reiter, Cheryl Rodriguez, and Scott Solomon, have been invaluable. I would also like to thank Paula McClain, one of my mentors from graduate school, for inviting me to be a coauthor. I have enjoyed working with her on multiple editions of this book and look forward to future collaborations.

On a personal level, I would like to thank my friends in the Tampa Bay area, as well as those scattered throughout the nation, for their support and friendship. I am thankful for the love and support of my in-laws Red and Ellen Hogan. I am especially grateful to my parents, Richard and Barbara Tauber, for their love, support, and encouragement throughout my life. Finally and most important, I am indebted to my wife, Meghan Tauber. I would not have been able to complete this book without her love, support, humor, and friendship through all the ups and downs that come with a project of this magnitude.

—**Steven C. Tauber**

About the Authors

Paula D. McClain is professor of political science and public policy and Dean of the Graduate School and Vice Provost for Graduate Education at Duke University. She directs the American Political Science Association's Ralph Bunche Summer Institute, hosted by Duke University and funded by the National Science Foundation and Duke University. She was formerly the cofounding director of the Center for the Study of Race, Ethnicity and Gender in the Social Sciences at Duke University. A Howard University PhD, her primary research interests are in racial minority group politics, particularly minority political and social competition, and urban politics. Her articles have appeared in numerous journals, and she is author of many books, including the popular, award-winning classroom supplement, *"Can We All Get along?": Racial and Ethnic Minorities in American Politics*, co authored with Joseph Stewart, Jr., and the seventh edition will be published in early 2017. Jessica Johnson Carew will be joining her as a new co-author. Professor McClain has won many awards for scholarship and teaching and has served the discipline in many capacities. She was elected to the American Academy of Arts and Sciences in 2014. She is currently President-elect of the American Political Science Association. She is particularly valued for her commitment to mentoring students from every background.

Steven C. Tauber entered the University of California–San Diego with the goal of becoming a doctor and then a lawyer. By his junior year, however, he found his political science courses so intellectually stimulating that he decided to pursue a career as a political science professor. He entered the PhD program in government at the University of Virginia, receiving his PhD in 1995, and started teaching at the University of South Florida in Tampa, where he is now an associate professor with tenure. He is also currently serving a stint as department chair. Professor Tauber enjoys teaching classes in introduction to American government, constitutional law, judicial politics, research methods and statistics, and American political thought. He has published refereed journal articles and book chapters on interest group use of the federal judiciary, minority group politics, and the effect of animal advocacy groups. In 2016 he published *Navigating the Jungle: Law, Politics, and the Animal Advocacy Movement* (Routledge). His current research focuses primarily on animal rights in a global context. Just as some of his undergraduate political science classes sparked his interest in political science, he hopes that this book will have the same effect on the current generation of undergraduate students.

American Government and Politics in a Racially Divided World

In 2016, Governor Jack Markell signed a long-awaited resolution officially apologizing for the state's role in slavery. The apology for slavery illustrates the long and sometimes painful history of the United States' struggle with race, from the time of Thomas Jefferson, a slave owner to President Barack Obama, the first Black president of the United States to President Donald Trump.

December 6, 2015, marked the 150th anniversary of the abolishment of slavery, when the U.S. Congress ratified the Thirteenth Amendment to the Constitution. There were numerous events recognizing the end of slavery, including an official White House event presided over by President Barack Obama. On February 11, 2016, Delaware joined eight other states to formally apologize for slavery when Governor Jack Markell (D) signed the state's joint resolution. Delaware's resolution acknowledged its participation in 226 years of slavery first of both Native Americans and Africans in the mid-1600s; by the close of the 1700s its entire slave population was of African descent. The resolution also included acknowledgments that Delaware criminalized humanitarian attempts to assist slaves and that in later times Delaware passed and enforced Jim Crow laws to deny the rights of African American citizens for much of the twentieth century.[1]

On July 29, 2008, the U.S. House of Representatives passed a nonbinding resolution, introduced and championed by Representative Steven Cohen (D-TN), that offered a formal apology for the government's participation in African American slavery and the establishment of Jim Crow laws. The resolution said, in part, "African Americans continue to suffer from the consequences of slavery and Jim Crow—long after both systems were formally abolished—through enormous damage and loss, both tangible and intangible, including the loss of human dignity and liberty, the frustration of careers and professional lives, and the long-term loss of income and opportunity."[2]

On June 18, 2009, the U.S. Senate unanimously passed a similar resolution apologizing to African Americans for slavery and Jim Crow. The Senate resolution said explicitly that the apology could not be used in support of reparations (or compensation for past wrongs).[3]

intro

*The story of apologies for slavery is a complex one that highlights some of the underlying dilemmas that face the U.S. political system—how to reconcile its stated principles of how individuals should be treated with how the government actually treats and has treated individuals. The apologies are intended to acknowledge the nation's complicity in a destructive and immoral institution, at the same time avoiding any discussion of **reparations** for the descendants of those enslaved.*

Reparations A concept or tool for providing monetary payments to members of aggrieved groups based on past wrongful actions against them or their ancestors.

Both sides criticize the apologies for slavery. Arkansas Governor Mike Beebe (D) questioned whether Arkansas should join the other Southern states in apologizing for slavery: "I think Arkansas has as good a feel for folks working together as any Southern state or any other state, so I think we've moved past that."[4] In Georgia, which also debated the issue, former speaker of the house Glen Richardson (R) expressed the views of many of his constituents when he said, "I'm not sure what we ought to be apologizing for. I think slavery was wrong—absolutely. But no one here was in office then."[5]

On the other side, John Hope Franklin (now deceased), a prominent historian of African American history, was also not a fan of apologies. Referring to North Carolina's issuance of an apology on April 12, 2007, by a unanimous vote of the House and the Senate, Franklin said:

> It's going to become an epidemic now. People are running around apologizing for slavery. What about that awful period since slavery—Reconstruction, Jim Crow and all the rest? What about the enormous wealth that was built up by Black labor? If I was sitting on a billion dollars that someone had made when I sat on them, I probably would not be slow to apologize, if that's all it takes. I think that's little to pay for the gazillions that Black people built up—the wealth of this country—with their labor, and now you're going to say I'm sorry I beat the hell out of you for all these years? That's not enough.[6]

On May 31, 2007, Alabama governor Bob Riley (R) signed a resolution expressing the state's "profound regret" for Alabama's participation in slavery and apologizing for slavery's wrongs and their lingering aftereffects.[7] With his signature, Alabama became the fourth Southern state to issue an apology for slavery, following apologies issued by the legislatures of Maryland, Virginia, and North Carolina. Riley said, "Slavery was evil and is a part of American history. I believe all Alabamians are proud of the tremendous progress we have made and continue to make."[8] Florida issued an apology in March 2008. In the North, New York was the first state to issue an apology, in June 2007, followed by New Jersey in January 2008, and Tennessee and Connecticut in 2009.

Despite apologies by several states, apologies by the federal government and on behalf of the American people for mistreatment of a segment of its population are rare. It was not until 1988 that Congress passed legislation issuing an apology and providing reparations for Japanese Americans interned during World War II. In 1993, the United States apologized to native Hawaiians for providing military assistance to the White businessmen who in 1893 had overthrown Queen Liliuokalani, placed her under house arrest, and seized the islands of Hawaii for the United States.

These actions and the controversy surrounding them raise several questions and concerns about the American political system. Why did a government founded on the concepts of freedom and equality engage in actions and put in place policies that were inequitable and unjust? Why is it so difficult for this government to make amends for the inequities and inequalities it created? Who benefits from inequalities? When inequalities are created, those who have access to an arena such as voting, employment, political office, and education gain at the expense of those who are denied

In 1893, the United States military, at the behest of White businessmen, overthrew Queen Liliuokalani and seized the islands of Hawaii for the United States. On July 4, 1894, the Republic of Hawaii was declared with Sanford B. Dole as president. Queen Liliuokalani was eventually arrested in 1895 and held until 1896.

opportunities. When government moves to correct the inequalities it created, those who have gained a privileged position might perceive a lessening of opportunities for themselves. Is it possible to correct inequalities for those aggrieved without creating the belief that the government is reducing opportunities for others? These are difficult questions, but ones that the American political system has struggled with since its inception.

The U.S. government is built on a foundation with values that are expressed in phrases such as "All men are created equal"; "life, liberty, and the pursuit of happiness"; and "government by the people." These phrases, many Americans believe, convey the essence of the United States. Yet these simple phrases do not convey the complexities of government, the reality that government treats people differently, or the continual struggle necessary to ensure that the values expressed in those phrases apply equally to all Americans.

All of these questions illustrate the complicated and conflicted nature of American government and politics in our time. Yet the sources of these complexities and conflicts are rooted in the history of government in general and of the United States in particular. Only by exploring that history can we understand these issues more fully. To that end, this opening chapter begins by examining what government is, what it does, and what forms it can take. This information serves as the context for understanding the ideas that influenced the creation of the American political system and continue to this day to shape its political debates.

The Nature of Government

Can you imagine a situation in which all people could do whatever they wanted without regard for how their actions could affect others? If you wanted to drive 100 miles per hour through your neighborhood streets, or launch a rocket from your backyard, you could do so without concern for the safety of your neighbors or airline passengers overhead. It is difficult to imagine living in a country without some mechanism for controlling the behaviors and managing the conflicts that arise when people interact. The mechanism that does this is government.

When you think of government, some of you might think of the president and the White House, others think of senators and representatives and the U.S. Capitol, and still others think of the Internal Revenue Service, the people down at city hall, or the postal service. Each of these thoughts recognizes a part of government. In the simplest sense, **government** is a social institution that controls the behavior of people. It does this by managing conflicts, establishing order, and devising rules and regulations. More concretely, government is the entity that has the authority to make decisions for you and all those who live in a political unit, such as a country, a state, or a city. When we speak of the government, we refer to those individuals who make up that political and administrative hierarchy.

Government A social institution that controls the behavior of people; the political and administrative hierarchy of an organized state.

The Functions of Government

Government serves several essential functions, including providing security, serving the public good, managing and resolving conflicts, and offering services. A first function of government is the provision of security. National governments maintain armed forces to protect their countries from attack from other countries; for example, the United States maintains an armed force that consists of the U.S. Army, Navy, Air Force, Marines, and Coast Guard. The United States is estimated to have from 700 to 1,000 bases around the world that range from small drone sites in Afghanistan to large permanent military bases, such as Ramstein Air Force Base in Germany.[9]

Government provides security in other ways as well. It tries to protect citizens from such harms as unfair business practices, discrimination, and denial of constitutional rights. In the United States laws have been passed to correct those harms, such as the 1968 Fair Housing Act aimed at protecting African Americans and other racial minorities from discrimination in the purchase of a home and the renting of an apartment or house. In addition, Title IX of the Education Amendments of 1972, as amended, prohibits discrimination on the basis of sex in federally assisted education programs. The latter has had a tremendous effect on the ability of women to participate in sports. In 1971, women made up 7 percent of high school athletes; in 2008, women made up 41 percent of all high school athletes. At the university level, women were 15 percent of all college athletes in 1971, but 43 percent of all college athletes by 2008.[10] In 2012, at the collegiate level, there were 8.73 women's varsity teams per school, up from 2.5 in 1970.[11]

A second function of government is to provide for the **public good**, a policy or action that benefits society as a whole rather than a specific individual. Government has the responsibility to address issues and problems in terms of how they affect the well-being of the larger society. Even though you also might think about issues and problems that affect society, you, like most individuals, are likely to make decisions for your own benefit. Thus, government is the entity charged with making decisions that will reflect broad, rather than narrow, interests in society.

Public Good A government policy or action that benefits society as a whole rather than a specific individual.

One way government ensures the public good is through laws and regulations. For example, legislation to protect the environment, such as the Clean Air Act of 1963, and its amendments over the years, has the broader interests of society as its objective and is therefore a public good. National defense is also a public good because it provides security for the entire nation, not a particular individual. The Civil Rights Act of 1964 made it illegal to discriminate against African Americans and other racial minorities in the use of public accommodations, such as restaurants, movie theaters, and hotels, thereby outlawing segregation and serving the interests of all citizens.

The process of determining what is best for the well-being of society, however, generates debate and controversy, which leads to a third function of government: managing and resolving conflict. The give-and-take in a

Title IX has expanded opportunities for female athletes and has resulted in the development of major women's sports teams. Chelsea Gray (12) of Duke University drives to the basket against Dawnn Maye of Georgia Tech in an NCAA women's college basketball game on December 6, 2012. Duke won the game 85–52.

Politics The conflict, competition, and compromise that occur within a political system.

governmental system, and the resolution of the problems that arise in that system through the process of discussion, bargaining, and competition, are called **politics**. Bargaining could occur among groups that want different outcomes on the same issue or among individuals who want to occupy positions in government. Government serves as the arbitrator of this compromise process. Congress balances the arguments from groups of people who will be affected by specific legislation and tries to balance those interests in compromises struck in the final bill.

Governments also offer services, a fourth function, many of which would not be had if government did not provide them. In the United States, our government supports the postal system, education, hospitals, transportation, and Social Security for elderly citizens, among other things. Although some private entities might build a toll highway, it is unlikely that the national interstate highway system that runs from east to west and north to south in the country would have been built without the federal government. Likewise, large public universities, such as the University of California–Berkeley, Ohio State University, or the University of Maryland–College Park, would not have been established without the land grants of the federal government's Morrill Acts of 1862 and 1890.[12]

Although most governments participate in these functions, not all governments do so in the same way. For example, in Denmark health care is universal and basically free to patients. In the United States, despite the passage of the Affordable Care Act of 2010 that will provide health care for many of the currently uninsured, people must pay something for physician and hospital services.[13] The differences in how governments approach these functions are rooted in the type of government in question, its philosophical foundations, and its source of authority.

The Types of Government

Democracy A system of government in which political power is exercised by the people.

Direct Democracy A democracy in which the people are able to participate directly in decision making.

Some form of government oversees every country in the world, but those governments differ in form and structure. The United States is a **democracy**, a system of government in which the people exercise political power. The word *democracy* derives from the Greek words *demos* (the people) and *kratos* (authority). The way in which people participate in a democracy may be direct or indirect (representative). **Direct democracy** exists when people make decisions themselves rather than electing individuals to make decisions on their behalf. The democracy of the ancient Greeks was direct in that everyone who was eligible to participate in government had a say in the decision-making process in an open forum. In the United States, the town meeting format found today in some New England towns serves as a form of direct democracy. Every resident of the town is eligible to participate in the town meeting and to vote on the resolution of issues taken up in the meeting.

Indirect (or representative) democracy exists when people do not make governmental decisions themselves but elect individuals to represent their interests. Indirect, or representative, democracy is the most common form of government found in the world today; individuals elect officials to represent them in the political process and to participate on their behalf. The United States is a representative democracy. Americans elect people to represent them at all levels of government—U.S. Congress, state legislatures, city councils, school boards, and mayors' offices, among others. Most countries that are democracies are representative; no pure direct democracies exist among the governments of the world today.

Most democracies derive their governmental authority from a written **constitution**, which is a set of formal written rules and principles governing the country. In a **constitutional democracy**, authority for government stems from the constitution. In such democracies, all actions by government must conform to the constitution, and officials who make and enforce the law are themselves subject to the law.

Constitutional democracies share several characteristics.

1. There are free elections in which candidates compete with each other, and the political opposition (those not in power) is free to criticize the government.
2. The press and other media are free, meaning they operate independently of the government, and censorship is rare.
3. Elections are held at regular intervals; elected officials serve for a prescribed length of time, never for life; and the transition of power from one elected official to the next is a peaceful process.
4. Personal and civil rights, such as freedom of speech and religion, are protected.[14]

The United States, Great Britain, Canada, Australia, Iceland, the Netherlands, South Africa, and a host of other countries that exhibit these characteristics are constitutional democracies. Although Great Britain does not have a single written constitution similar to that of the United States, its governing principles stem from numerous legislative acts, common law, and conventions that provide a constitutional framework.

Principles of Constitutional Democracies

Even though the structures of constitutional democracies may differ—for instance, certain countries have presidents and other countries have prime ministers and parliaments—they all share several common principles. These principles provide a common basis for understanding some of the values

Indirect (or Representative) Democracy A democracy in which people do not participate directly in decision making and instead elect individuals to represent their interests.

Constitution A set of formal written rules and principles governing a state.

Constitutional Democracy A government that derives its authority from a constitution.

present in constitutional democracies. These principles are the rule of law, natural law, and natural rights. Understanding the principles common to constitutional democracies provides a window through which to view the essential features of the American political system.

The Rule of Law

Rule of Law The predominance of law over discretionary authority.

A first element of constitutional democracy is a belief in the **rule of law**, the idea that laws should take precedence over the arbitrary governance of people. According to the rule of law, all citizens, including the government and government officials, must obey the law. This principle prohibits constitutional democracies from acting in an arbitrary and capricious manner. For example, the U.S. government cannot take your property without following a prescribed legal process. By law and constitutional authority, the government cannot detain you without telling you the charges and allowing you to obtain legal counsel. Government's actions must adhere to authority granted in a constitution or in laws passed by the legislature.

The rule of law is a core principle of the American political system. Laws passed by a legislative body such as the U.S. Congress, a state legislature, or a city council are intended to bring order and fairness to the political system. By the rule of law, everyone is supposed to be equal before the law, and the law is supposed to apply equally to all. No person—rich, poor, official, or ordinary—is supposed to be above the law. In reality, the United States has a history of treating its citizens differently based on race, gender, and sexual orientation. Paula D. McClain and Joseph Stewart, Jr. argue that for much of the nation's history, Blacks were subject to a "separate system of laws."[15]

Natural Law

Natural Law Law that comes from nature and is superior to statutory law.

A second principle underlying a constitutional democratic government is **natural law**, law that comes from nature and is superior to written law passed by legislatures. The theory of natural law holds that a system of right or justice comes from nature rather than from rules of society and that it applies to all persons. Human beings have the ability to reason ("right reason") and through the use of reason are able to determine the proper and correct thing to do. Cicero (106–43 BCE), a political philosopher in ancient Rome and one of the earliest to discuss the concept, provided a definition of natural law:

> There is in fact a true law—namely, right reason—which is in accordance with nature, applies to all men, and is unchangeable and eternal. By its commands this law summons men to the performance of their duties; by its prohibitions it restrains them from doing wrong. Its commands and prohibitions always influence good men, but are without effect on the bad. To invalidate this law by human legislation is never morally right, nor is it permissible ever to restrict its operation, and to annul it wholly impossible.[16]

Statutory Law A type of law pertaining to rules made by legislatures, especially Congress.

Natural law theory argues that if **statutory law**, or the laws passed by legislative bodies, conflicts with natural law—for example, the correct thing to do—it need not be obeyed. The U.S. Declaration of Independence invokes natural law in its first paragraph:

> When in the course of human events it becomes necessary for one people to dissolve the political bands which have connected them with another, and to assume among the powers of the earth, the *separate and equal station to which the Laws of Nature and of Nature's God entitle them*, a decent respect to the opinions of mankind requires that they should declare the causes which impel them to the separation.

The clause emphasized here in italics argues that natural law entitled the colonists to break away from Great Britain.

Natural Rights

A third and last common principle of constitutional democratic governments is that of **natural rights**, those rights to which every person is entitled and that exist apart from and are not dependent on government, such as life and liberty. Natural rights stem from natural law and belong to individuals from birth. The concept of natural rights is drawn primarily from the work of John Locke (1632–1704), an English political theorist. Locke argued that natural law endowed people with natural rights, which for Locke were "life, liberty, and property." In the Declaration of Independence, Thomas Jefferson adapted Locke's natural rights of life, liberty, and property to "Life, Liberty, and the pursuit of Happiness."

Natural Rights Rights to which every person is entitled, such as life and liberty; rights that are not dependent on government.

Foundations of American Government

Given that constitutional democracies share similar principles of government, yet might differ in structure, why does the United States have the political system that it does? What are the theoretical and philosophical underpinnings of the system, and from where did they come?

The American system of government draws on several theories of government and governing in Western European political thought and is the product of multiple political traditions. These traditions include (1) **classical liberalism**, a name now applied to a body of Western European political philosophy that is concerned with the freedom of the individual and the role of government in protecting that freedom; (2) **classical republicanism**, a theory that says rule by the people ought to be indirect through representatives; and (3) **inegalitarianism**, a tradition of excluding large segments of the American population from participation in the political system despite the universal language of equality, liberty, and freedom.[17] These traditions are central to an understanding of the American political system.

Classical Liberalism A body of Western European political philosophy that is concerned with the freedom of the individual and the role of government in protecting that freedom.

Classical Republicanism A theory that rule by the people ought to be indirect through representatives.

Inegalitarianism A tradition of excluding large segments of the American population from participation in the political system despite the language of equality, liberty, and freedom.

Classical Liberalism

The founders of American government, particularly Thomas Jefferson, author of the Declaration of Independence, were familiar with contemporary Western European political thought. They were especially influenced by the ideas of classical liberalism, a body of thought aimed at liberating the individual from the oppressive restraints of feudalism and monarchial rule.

Feudalism A system of landholding involving a network of allegiances and obligations.

Under **feudalism**, a system of landholding practiced widely in Medieval Europe, peasants, called serfs, pledged their loyalty and a portion of their income to a lord in exchange for protection. Rather than protect the serfs, however, lords too often abused their power over their dependents.

By the fifteenth century, feudalism had begun to die out in England, France, and other countries in Western Europe, only to be replaced by monarchical rule. Although the change brought serfdom to an end, people in these countries were still subject to the seemingly arbitrary authority of their rulers. In time, political thinkers began to challenge this authority and collectively their ideas came to define what we now call classical liberalism.

Thomas Hobbes (1588–1679), a British political philosopher, believed, as expressed in his work *Leviathan* (1651), that by nature men are aggressive and, therefore, are afraid of being attacked. To protect themselves from attack, men contract with each other to form a civil society and to create a mechanism, government, for resolving these fears. Men create government by entering into a **social contract** in which people give up a little bit of their independence for the safety and peace that government creates. Hobbes stated that without government, life would be extremely difficult and possibly very "nasty, brutish, and short," to use his oft-quoted words.

Social Contract Individuals creating government by entering into a contract with it.

The work of English political theorist John Locke best exemplifies classical liberalism, particularly his *Two Treatises of Government* (1689). In these works, Locke argued that the responsibility of government is to protect an individual's right to own property. If the government fails in this responsibility, then the people have the right to overturn the government and establish a new one.

Locke proposed several mechanisms for limiting government's power. First, the powers of government should be divided among several branches. Locke distrusted executive power (the monarch) and believed that the executive should be subordinate and accountable to the legislature (parliament). But he believed that controls needed to be placed on the legislature as well. These controls include a belief in the rule of law, a view that laws should not be arbitrary but should be designed for the good of the people, and an argument that taxes should not be raised without the consent of the people or their representatives.

Although liberal theorists might differ on some key ideas, such as their notions of natural law, individualism, and self-interest, all liberal theories share these four characteristics:[18]

1. *Liberalism is optimistic.* This optimism is expressed in the belief that society works better if individuals are left to themselves without government interference. Liberalism places great faith in the behavior and motivations of individuals unrestrained by coercive restrictions.

2. *Liberalism favors the individual over the group*. Liberalism gives individual self-determination or individualism priority over societal good. Individual freedom is paramount, and government should not infringe on that freedom.

3. *Liberalism supports free-market economics*. Liberalism holds that the role of government is to protect and facilitate economic development. Government should not enact legislation or regulations that hamper economic development. This tenet is exemplified in the work of eighteenth-century Scottish philosopher Adam Smith (1723–1790), whose book *An Inquiry into the Nature and Causes of the Wealth of Nations* (1776) is considered the first modern work of economics and the primer for free-market economics, what he called self-interested competition. He argued against the development of monopolies.

4. *Liberalism places reason before faith*. Liberalism seeks to "liberate" the human mind from unquestioned acceptance of religious dogma by focusing on those things that can be proved or demonstrated. The widespread belief at the time, known as the divine right of kings, held that the monarch derived his or her right to rule from the will of God. Thus, the monarch was not subject to any authority other than that of God.

The influence of classical liberalism is evident in the early documents of the nation—the Declaration of Independence, the state constitutions developed after independence, and the U.S. Constitution. Thomas Jefferson drew substantially from John Locke in writing the Declaration of Independence. Locke's natural rights—"life, liberty, and property"—became Jefferson's "Life, Liberty, and the pursuit of Happiness." Jefferson adapted Locke's statement on equality—"men being by nature all free, equal, and independent"—to "All men are created equal." According to the Declaration, "To secure these [natural] rights, Governments are instituted among Men."

Classical liberal theory is also prominent in *The Federalist Papers* (1787)—essays written by Alexander Hamilton of New York, James Madison of Virginia, and John Jay of New York—in support of ratification of the Constitution. One fundamental liberal principle central to several of the essays is government's responsibility to protect private property and to provide an environment in which people can use private property as a basis for commerce. Arguing in favor of limited government, the authors stated that the political system of the new United States would be one in which the national government and state governments shared power, but that the powers given to the national government would be "few and defined." The writers also wanted to assure the states that the scope of the national government's role would be limited primarily by a checks-and-balances system that would prevent any one of the three branches of the national government from acquiring too much power.

Classical liberal theory has exerted other influences as well. The American political values of religious toleration, separation of church and state, freedom of expression, restrictions on police behavior, free elections, and an economic policy aimed at sustained growth on the basis of private ownership derive from the theory of classical liberalism.[19]

It would be a mistake to confuse classical liberalism with the way we use the term *liberal* (political liberalism) in our contemporary political world. In contemporary politics, a **liberal** is someone who believes that government has a role to play in the lives of individuals and that government should be looked to for solutions to problems. Political liberals support programs aimed at job creation, universal health care, elimination of discrimination in American society, and support for the poor, among others. Liberals are also interested in protecting individual civil rights and liberties and believe that government has a responsibility to protect citizens' rights.

We juxtapose this definition of contemporary political liberalism against the definition of the contemporary political term *conservative*. **Conservatives** are individuals who believe in a limited role for government and do not believe that government should be turned to for solutions to some problems. Conservatives believe that too much government regulation hinders the ability of the free market to function unfettered; conservatives are strong believers in a free-market economy. They are not in favor of governmental expansion of individual rights and liberties. Conservatives do believe, however, that the government has a major role to play in defense, and they are more likely to support increases in defense spending while opposing spending in social program areas. In many ways, contemporary conservatism resembles classical liberalism more than today's political liberalism does.

Classical Republicanism

Whereas classical liberalism emphasizes individualism and self-interest, classical republicanism concerns itself with **civic virtue**, the subordination of individualism and individual self-interest to the interest of society. Civic virtue is demanded both of those who govern and those who are governed. Classical republicanism, with its origins in ancient Rome, views government as divided into different branches with a checks-and-balances system preventing any one branch from gathering too much power.[20] Direct democracy is unworkable, in this view, because it is unwieldy to have everyone participating in government's decision-making process. Thus, republicans argue for representative democracy—individuals elect other individuals to represent them in government's affairs.

English political theorists such as James Harrington and Algernon Sidney and French jurist Baron de Montesquieu wrote on aspects of republicanism. James Harrington (1611–1677) in *The Commonwealth of Oceana* (1656) argued that, although the government is accountable to the people, direct democracy is impossible because it is chaotic, with everyone trying to participate in decision making. Thus, government should be a representative democracy in which the people elect officials to represent them. Algernon Sidney (1622–1683) also

Liberal An individual who believes that government has a role to play in the lives of individuals and that government can provide solutions to policy problems.

Conservative Individual who believes that government should play a limited role in the lives of individuals and that government is not the source of solutions for problems.

Civic Virtue The subordination of individualism and individual self-interest to the interest of society.

Test your knowledge of civics.

rejected direct democracy and argued in *Discourses Concerning Government* (1698, published after his death) that people would delegate their authority to the legislature.

Charles-Louis de Secondat, Baron de Montesquieu (1689–1755), a French observer of British government, in his work *Spirit of the Laws* (1748), further refined the idea of the division of power among several branches of government in what he called the balanced constitutions. Montesquieu believed that if legislative, executive, and judicial powers were all held by the same person or body it would signal the end of liberty. He saw the principle of separation of powers as a guarantee on the restraint of government and the assurance that individuals would retain their liberty.[21]

Five characteristics, common to all republican theories, define the essence of classical republicanism:

Thomas Hobbes (1588–1679), a British political philosopher, believed that government was necessary, but that individuals enter into a social contract with government in which they give up a little bit of their independence for the safety and peace that government creates.

1. *Republicanism believes in a virtuous citizenry.* Classical republicanism defines a virtuous citizenry as a public-spirited, self-sacrificing people devoted to the general good of the community. Both leaders and followers will subordinate private interests to the public good. Virtuous citizens will participate in government with the public good in mind.

2. *Republicanism is concerned with property.* Like classical liberalism, classical republicanism is concerned with property. In classical republicanism, property ownership is a primary criterion for holding political office and for voting for those who run for office.

3. *Republicanism sees the people as the ultimate authority but believes they must be kept at a distance.* Government governs with the consent of the people. The people, however, delegate their authority to representatives who then run the government on behalf of the people. Government works best when the masses of people are kept far from the levers of power.

4. *Republicanism advocates a distribution of power across branches of government.* No one person should be able to control all the levers of power. To avoid such singular control, power must be distributed among the branches of government. This arrangement has become known as the doctrine of separation of powers. Also, a system of checks and balances exists to prevent any one branch from garnering too much power.

5. *Republicanism believes that the rights of individuals must be protected.* Even though individuals delegate their authority to elected

John Locke (1632–1704), an English philosopher, argued that government's responsibility is to protect an individual's right to own property, and if government fails, then the people have the right to overturn the government and establish a new one.

Charles-Louis de Secondat de Montesquieu (1689–1755), a French philosopher and jurist, was considered a classical republican theorist. He saw the principle of separation of powers as a guarantee on the restraint of government and the assurance that individuals would retain their liberty.

representatives, they must have their rights protected from the government. This protection occurs through a bill of rights.

The influence of classical republicanism is evident in the state constitutions and the U.S. Constitution, particularly in the government values associated with republicanism: the rule of law, a sovereign people, elected representatives, separation of powers, and a system of checks and balances on the branches of government. As with liberal ideas, republican ideas also ran throughout *The Federalist Papers*. In the papers, the authors discussed in detail the reasons that the new government would be a **republican form of government** rather than a direct democracy. Citizens would elect people to represent them in government, and the views of the people would be filtered through these individuals. Those elected individuals would administer the government. Yet, other voices spoke out at the time, voices arguing that classical republicanism required the abolition of slavery. See the remarks of the Reverend Lemuel Haynes in "Our Voices: Lemuel Haynes—Republicanism and Slavery" on page 17.

How have our ideas about democracy and republics shaped our government?

Republican Form of Government A government whose powers are exercised by elected representatives who are directly or indirectly accountable to the people governed.

It is important not to confuse classical republicanism with the contemporary Republican Party. In some ways, contemporary Democrats (who are often liberals) espouse philosophies and support policies closer to those of classical republicanism than to those of classical liberalism. Both the Democratic and Republican parties, although differing in philosophy and policy preferences, are grounded in the classical liberal and classical republican foundations undergirding the U.S. political system.

Tradition of Exclusion (Inegalitarianism)

The American Founders created a system based on liberal and republican ideals. They believed that individual freedoms and liberties were fundamental values. They were passionate in their arguments defending these beliefs. Despite the inclusive and egalitarian principles embodied in such words as *equality*, *liberty*, and *freedom*, however, the Founders did not intend for such principles to be universally applied. Instead, they followed a **tradition of exclusion** (or inegalitarianism) that denied to large segments of the American population the protections promised in the Declaration of Independence and the Constitution. This exclusionary tradition, which many would argue is consistent with some of the tenets of liberalism, accepted the notion that not all people are equal and that inequalities are acceptable and need not be corrected. Moreover, the Founders did not see this tradition of exclusion as being inconsistent with the notion that "all men are created equal." In other words, liberalism provides room for the development of inegalitarianism. The inequality of treatment under this tradition was often based on characteristics such as race, gender, ethnicity, and religion.[22] (Table 1.1 provides a comparison of the elements of classical liberalism, classical republicanism, and the tradition of exclusion.)

Tradition of Exclusion A tradition that excludes groups from the political system based on their ascribed traits, such as race, gender, and religion.

The origins of this tradition are many and varied. In some instances, the origins are rooted in practice and culture. In others, they are anchored in the works of political philosophers. At the time of the founding of the United States, gender, ethnic, racial, and religious hierarchies were worldwide phenomena.

White Women. Many of the attitudes toward women and their place in society can be traced to a global or philosophical context, but some aspects of the attitudes were uniquely American. The subordination of White women during colonial times created cultural and economic discrimination against them.[23]

In addition, Western political philosophy during the Enlightenment (the Age of Reason in the eighteenth century), with which the Founders were familiar, rarely considered the role of women in the civic and political arenas. When political philosophers did mention women, they were considered in subservient roles to men in not only physical but mental and moral capabilities as well. French philosopher Jean-Jacques Rousseau (1712–1778) argued that the world of women was separate from the empire of men. Women were

TABLE 1.1 Key Points of Comparison of Classical Liberalism, Classical Republicanism, and the Tradition of Exclusion

Classical Liberalism Optimism	Classical Republicanism Pessimism	Tradition of Exclusion Oppression
Government by consent	Government based on popular sovereignty	Government based on the consent of White males
Direct democracy	Elected representatives	People defined narrowly in terms of race (White), gender (male), and religion (Protestant)
Limited government	Separation of powers and checks and balances	Limited government, but force of government used to exclude non-Whites and White women
Majority rule but with minority protection	Barriers to majority rule	Minority rights nonexistent
Market economy	Market economy	Non-Whites and White women excluded from economy
Individual/equal rights paramount	Property ownership/ natural rights central	Property ownership rights denied to most, but not all, non-Whites and some women; a majority of Blacks were considered property
Rule of law	Rule of law	Law used to oppress non-Whites and, to a lesser extent, White women
Religious freedom	Religious freedom	White Protestants considered superior to all others

not to be members of the political world.[24] Rousseau wrote in *Emile* (1762): "In the union of the sexes each alike contributes to the common end, but in different ways. From this diversity springs the first difference which may be observed between man and woman in their moral relations. The man should be strong and active; the woman should be weak and passive; the one must have both the power and the will; it is enough that the other should offer little resistance."[25]

Aspects of English common law—law derived from custom and practice rather than legislative statutes—that governed the relations between husbands and wives also played a major role in defining the role of women in the new nation. That law included the doctrine of **coverture**, which transferred a woman's civic identity to her husband at marriage, giving him use and direction of her property. Thus, married women had no identity apart from that of their husbands.[26] Coverture's influence on the role of women carried over to the American colonies.

Coverture A doctrine and system in British common law according to which marriage merged a woman's legal identity with that of her husband.

our voices

Lemuel Haynes—Republicanism and Slavery

Between 1776 and 1820, Lemuel Haynes, a Black New England Congregational minister and patriot of the Revolution, wrote a series of essays and sermons setting his opposition to slavery and his insistence on equal rights for Black Americans in the context of the two great influences on his thinking: republican ideology and New Divinity theology, a movement away from the Calvinist theology of the New England Puritans. Drawing from republican ideology, Haynes argued that because liberty was a natural right, slavery was unlawful. Republican liberty, he continued, was threatened by slavery and oppression, which undermined the virtue that led individuals to promote and defend liberty.

Here are excerpts from "Liberty Further Extended: Or Free thoughts on the illegality of Slave-keeping; Wherein those arguments that Are used in its vindication Are plainly confuted. Together with a humble Address to such as are Concearned in the practise" (1776):

It is not my Business to Enquire into Every particular practise, that is practised in this Land, that may come under this Odeus Character; But, what I have in view, is humbly to offer som[e] free thoughts, on the practise of Slave-keeping. Opression, is not spoken of, nor ranked in the sacred oracles, among the Least of those sins, that are the procureing Caus of those signal Judgments, which god is pleas'd to bring upon the Children of men. Therefore let us attend. I mean to white [write] with freedom, yet with the greatest Submission.

And the main proposition, which I intend for some Breif illustration is this, Namely, That an *African, or, in other terms, that a Negro may Justly Chalenge, and*

has an undeniable right to his ["freed(om)" is blotted out] *Liberty: Consequently, the practise of Slave-keeping, which so much abounds in this Land is illicit.*

Why do you think that Haynes felt that slavery threatened the republican notion of liberty?

Lemuel Haynes (1753–1833) was an influential African American religious leader who argued against slavery. Haynes's arguments were grounded in classical republican theory.

Blacks. In the case of Blacks, American colonists' views stemmed not from English common law, but from attitudes and behaviors the colonists had brought with them. For the English, Blacks' skin color set them apart from White colonists. Because Blacks were from a continent that was not Christian, they were also, in this view, defective in religion. For many Whites, these two aspects made Blacks something less than human beings. Therefore, many Whites did not consider owning Blacks as slaves to be wrong.[27]

The first Africans arrived at Jamestown, Virginia, in 1619 as indentured servants, individuals who contracted themselves to work as servants for a specified period of time for people who often had paid their passage to the American colonies. By 1641, Massachusetts had incorporated slavery into colonial law. Slavery was instituted on a broad scale in Virginia in 1661 as the need for labor increased and Whites found Indian servitude and slavery inadequate and the supply of White indentured servants insufficient. The permanent enslavement of Africans and African Americans became the answer to the labor problem. The supply of Blacks appeared to be endless, and their color made them easily identifiable.[28]

Rogers Smith, a University of Pennsylvania political theorist, argues that these negative attitudes toward Blacks were given a uniquely American character when political figures at the time of the founding began to use a fascination with the science of the Enlightenment to explain the differences between Blacks and Whites.[29] Thomas Jefferson was one of those individuals. Jefferson's original draft of the Declaration of Independence included an indictment of King George for his participation in the Black slave trade, but the language was struck from the final version. Jefferson, while a member of the Virginia House of Burgesses, also pushed for the abolition of slavery in Virginia.

Jefferson, however, did not believe that Blacks should be citizens. Nor did his antislavery sentiments prevent him from owning slaves himself (see "Evaluating Equality: Thomas Jefferson and Sally Hemings"). In his *Notes on the State of Virginia* (1785), a book in which Jefferson sought to use the scientific methodology of the Enlightenment to study everything from foliage to Blacks, Jefferson was uncompromising in his belief that Blacks were innately inferior to Whites. He advocated removing free Blacks from the nation and colonizing them somewhere away from the United States.[30] Some scholars argue that Jefferson helped to inaugurate the historical tendency in America to legitimize racial prejudice with the gloss of pseudoscience—fake science utterly lacking supporting evidence.[31]

Race is a prominent thread in the American political fabric and is part of the original tapestry of the American political system. Yet race is a social and political, rather than a biological, construction. The **social construction of race** in the United States evolved directly from government's interest in defining and expanding the boundaries of Blackness for purposes of enslavement initially and for purposes of exclusion later. Many states went to great lengths to define the amount of "Negro" blood (e.g., one-eighth, one-sixteenth, "any ascertainable amount of Negro blood") that legally classified an individual as Black.[32] The state-supported and legally codified definition of who was Black resulted in the construction of a group that varied widely in phenotype, skin color, and physical characteristics.

Social Construction of Race The construction of a group of people of various phenotypes, skin colors, and physical characteristics for political and social purposes such as enslavement and exclusion.

American Indians. The arguments used for the inferiority of Blacks were applied to American Indians as well. Many colonists felt that because American Indians, like Blacks, were not Christian and their skin color was dark, they

evaluating equality

Thomas Jefferson and Sally Hemings

Is it possible to reconcile Thomas Jefferson's views on slavery with his actions?

Thomas Jefferson is often characterized as being opposed to slavery. Yet he continued to own slaves. Is it possible to reconcile these seemingly contradictory elements?

Jefferson's Views

Jefferson's original draft of the Declaration of Independence contained a sharp attack on King George III for his support and facilitation of the slave trade and the enslavement of Africans. This attack, however, was unacceptable to both Northern and Southern delegates and was removed from the final document. In later years, Jefferson would write passionately of the evils of slavery and the need to abolish the institution.

Despite his antislavery views, Jefferson did not believe that the United States should attempt to incorporate Blacks into the nation. In his *Notes on the State of Virginia*, Jefferson was uncompromising in his belief that Blacks were innately inferior to Whites. He advocated removing free Blacks from the nation and colonizing them outside the United States. He also found Blacks physically offensive and argued against the intermixing of White and Black blood.

Jefferson's Actions

Despite Jefferson's writings on the evils of slavery, he did not free his own slaves. Even on his death, he freed only five of his approximately 130 slaves. In addition, during his life, Jefferson was said to have fathered

In June 2018, Monticello, Thomas Jefferson's mountaintop plantation, opened an exhibit on the life of Sally Hemings, Jefferson's slave and the mother of at least six of his children. Historical research and DNA evidence showed that Jefferson was the father of her children. Yet, some of Jefferson's White descendants refuse to accept this and continue to try to disprove the scientific and historical evidence. On the other hand, many others accept the evidence and have welcomed the Black descendants of Jefferson's and Sally Hemings's children as part of the Jefferson extended family.

children by his slave Sally Hemings, although Jefferson and his supporters denied that this was true. Some Jefferson historians have pointed to his disdain for Blacks as proof that he would not have fathered children with his slave.

In 1998, however, DNA testing confirmed, within a certain degree of probability, that Thomas Jefferson had fathered at least one of Hemings's children.[1] Meticulous research by Annette Gordon-Reed, a law professor at Harvard University, is now acknowledged to provide additional proof that Jefferson indeed fathered all of Sally Hemings's children.[2] In June 2018, the Thomas Jefferson Foundation, which owns

and runs Monticello, opened an exhibit on "The Life of Sally Hemings" in a room that they suggest would be similar to the one that Sally Hemings might have had. This room is next to one that contains the oral histories of the descendants of slaves that were owned by Jefferson and lived on Monticello. The Sally Hemings room and the attention to the exhibit finally acknowledges her and that she was the mother of six of Jefferson's children.[3]

- Is it possible to reconcile Jefferson's public pronouncements and his belief in liberal and republican ideals with his private behavior of owning slaves,

(Continued)

evaluating equality *(Continued)*

including his own children? Why or why not?

- Does the contradiction between Jefferson's public writings and private behavior have any parallels with contemporary politicians and government or public figures? Explain your answer.

[1] Foster, E. A., Jobling, M. A., Taylor, P. G., Donnelly, P., de Knijff, P., Mieremet T., . . . Tyler-Smith, C. (1998). Jefferson fathered slave's last child. *Nature, 196,* 27–28.

[2] Gordon-Reed, A. (1997). *Thomas Jefferson and Sally Hemings: An American controversy.* Charlottesville: University of Virginia Press.

[3] Stockman, F. (2018, June 18). Monticello is done avoiding Jefferson's relationship with Sally Hemings. *New York Times.* Retrieved from https://www.nytimes.com/2018/06/16/us/sally-hemings-exhibit-monticello.html.

were not quite human and were culturally and intellectually inferior to Europeans. The colonists felt that if Indians were to live near or among White settlements, they needed to be transformed into "civilized" human beings.[33] Massachusetts divided its Indian population into wild tribes and converted tribes.[34]

Because the colonists perceived Indians to be unfamiliar with European ways of thinking and to have vastly different conceptions of property than they themselves did, the colonists developed the notion that Indians were similar to children and needed to be directed in all aspects of life. The colonists then decided that Indian lands should be sold to settlers at reduced prices as an exercise in the colonists' trusteeship of Indians and their lands.[35] With the takeover of their lands, many tribes went to war with settlers as they moved west. Whites came to look on Indians as alien enemies who should be and needed to be destroyed.[36]

The tradition of exclusion and denial of rights and privileges to certain groups shaped the definition of who was an "American" in the new nation.[37] "True" Americans were those who possessed morally and intellectually superior traits often associated with race and gender. Thus, many Americans believed that non-Whites and women should be governed as subjects or second-class citizens and be excluded from participation in the nation.[38] The tradition of exclusion was based on several assumptions:

Men were naturally suited to rule over women. Women were inferior to men in physical as well as mental and moral capabilities. Therefore, women were not suited to participate in public life.

White northern Europeans were superior, culturally and biologically, to southern, darker-skinned Europeans, African Americans, American Indians, and all other races and civilizations. Non-White peoples were inferior in every aspect, and many Whites questioned whether darker-skinned people were even human.

Protestant Christianity was superior to any other form of religion. Protestant Christians were superior to those who practiced other religions.

Exclusion and the Founding

Under the tradition of exclusion, groups of Americans were excluded from full participation in the new nation, and that exclusion was hierarchical. It ranged from the initial denial of the vote to unpropertied White males, to the denial of the vote and participation in the formal structures of government to White women, to the denial of citizenship and suffrage to African Americans and American Indians (see "Measuring Equality: Who Was Eligible to Be Included in 'We the People'?" on page 22).

Although the Founders intended the rights and guarantees of the Constitution to extend to all free White males, not all free White males were eligible to participate in the affairs of government. In the early days of the nation, only propertied White males were eligible to vote. Property ownership was thought to give people a stake in the political system and allow them to have a say in how it was run. Those who owned no property, therefore, had no stake in the system and thus no right to a voice in government decision making.

It is true that White women were citizens of the United States from the beginning of the new nation,[39] but the relationship of White women to the new nation was different in substantial and important respects from the relationship of White males to their nation. The political exclusion of White women from the Constitution did not originate with that document. State constitutions written after 1776 explicitly or implicitly denied White women the limited political rights they had enjoyed before the Revolution, such as the ability to vote in local elections. None of the new state constitutions, except that of New Jersey, granted women the right to vote.

Portrait of Mrs. John Stevens (Judith Sargent, later Mrs. John Murray) 1751–1820, by John Singleton Copley. Judith Sargent, like Lemuel Haynes, was a voice of those excluded from the original conception of those eligible to participate in the new nation. White women—like slaves, freed Blacks, and American Indians—were not originally considered a part of the political system.

The primary reasoning behind not giving the vote to women was the continued reliance, present since colonial times, on coverture, which (as explained earlier) held that on marriage a woman's legal identity merged into that of her husband. Thus, to give women in the new nation the right to vote would be synonymous with giving their husbands two votes.

The Founders did not intend the Constitution to apply to Blacks and Indians.[40] Following the ratification of the Constitution, Congress passed the Naturalization Act of 1790 in response to its new constitutional power to legislate a uniform rule to deal with the process by which foreigners could be "admitted to the rights of citizens." The act stated, as did all naturalization legislation from 1790 through 1854, that only a "free White person" was eligible to become a citizen of the United States. Because, according to prevailing belief, Indians and slaves did not understand the European way of life

measuring equality

Who Was Eligible to Be Included in "We the People"?

Figure 1.1 provides a visual illustration of the number of people present at the founding of the United States and, of those, how many were eligible to participate in the new nation. Indians were not counted, so the population number was actually greater than the 3.9 million shown here. The chart shows that 20.7 percent of the population were White males over the age of sixteen. The actual number of people eligible to participate in the new nation was even smaller than 20.7 percent because the requirements were "a White male, twenty-one years of age and over, and a property owner." According to National Archives estimates, as few as 6 percent of the counted population were White male property owners. What picture of the new nation do these data present? Who was included in the phrase "We the People"?

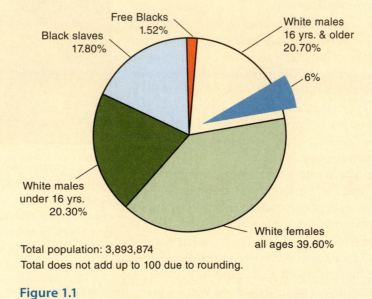

Free Blacks 1.52%

Black slaves 17.80%

White males 16 yrs. & older 20.70%

6%

White males under 16 yrs. 20.30%

White females all ages 39.60%

Total population: 3,893,874
Total does not add up to 100 due to rounding.

Figure 1.1

and political system, they were not free and were, therefore, not suited to be members of the political system or to exercise the duties and responsibilities of citizenship, and they were justifiably excluded from all this legislation.[41]

The issue of what to do with Black slaves in the new nation was central to several of the compromises struck on the Constitution. In the end, an African American's right to liberty conflicted with a White master's right to property. In keeping with the classical liberal foundations of the nation, the right of property took precedence.[42] Many of the Founders viewed Blacks as property, not citizens of the new republican nation.

Under the Articles of Confederation, the country's first constitution, the Continental Congress established a committee to address the question of

Indian inclusiveness. The initial committee report recommended that Congress urge the states to make it easy for Indians to become citizens. Most American Indians traded with, protected, and supported European settlers until conflict erupted over control of land. This report, however, was tabled by the Congress. A subsequent report by a different committee "referred to Indians, not as potential citizens, but as possible allies."[43] This categorization meant that Indians were not to be included as citizens in the new nation. They were foreign aliens outside the nation despite their living physically within it.

Despite the Founders' notions about the place of American Indians in the new nation, they drew on many of the concepts practiced by them. American Indians exercised democratic norms and behaviors before contact with Europeans. The most famous Indian confederation was the League of the Iroquois, located in what is now upper New York State. Although there is disagreement over the date of the establishment of the League of the Iroquois, it existed prior to contact with Europeans. Many scholars suggest that the League of the Iroquois influenced the shaping of the U.S. Constitution. Benjamin Franklin used the league as the basis for the Albany Plan of Union in 1754.[44] In October 1988, the U.S. Congress passed Concurrent Resolution 331 to recognize the influence of the Iroquois Constitution on the U.S. Constitution and Bill of Rights.

The Iroquois Confederacy initially consisted of five tribes—the Mohawk, Onondaga, Oneida, Cayuga, and Seneca—with the Tuscarora joining in 1722. This loose group of tribes formed an organized government based on several

The map shows the land of the six Iroquois nations that covered what is now the states of New York and Pennsylvania.

democratic principles. The league was governed by a constitution, the Great Law of Peace. Under the constitution, the chiefs of the tribes were appointed by the female leaders of the tribes, who also had the authority to remove the chiefs for misconduct, sickness, or other reasons causing them to be ineffective. When a chief died, the women chose a new one.[45]

The governing council of the initial Five Nation Confederation consisted of fifty representatives divided proportionally among the tribes, with the Onondagas having fourteen delegates; the Cayugas, ten; the Mohawks and Oneidas, nine delegates each; and the Senecas, eight. (Initially, the Tuscarora had no voting rights.) Warriors were prohibited from being council representatives because they might adopt warlike positions and attempt to promote warlike policies. All delegates were chosen by their tribes in accordance with tribal governance rules. The council was obliged to meet every five years, more often if necessary.[46]

The Great Law of Peace was initially recorded with beads on wampum belts, as were records of meetings and decisions reached by the Council of the Five Nations. Concern about possible loss or destruction of the belts prompted translation of the document into English in 1880 by Seth Newhouse, a Mohawk.[47]

Conclusion

The opening vignette about the various apologies for slavery and later segregation illustrates how central race was to the development of the American political system. As was demonstrated throughout the chapter, race intertwined intimately with the liberal and republican theories at the foundation of this system.

Aspects of classical liberalism include the notion of limited government, the rule of law, and the primacy of private property. Concepts associated with the classical republican tradition include a sense of civic virtue, a belief that institutions derive their authority from the people, and support for elected representation. The tradition of exclusion subscribes to the notion of inequality among people. According to this tradition, true Americans are drawn only from a certain group of people, a group that excludes non-Whites and women. The Founders of the American system of government blended inegalitarian beliefs with the principles of classical liberalism and classical republicanism.[48]

The classical liberal and republican foundations of the American political system remain embodied in American government. Strains of the traditions of exclusion endure as well. Inequalities abound in our political system, many stemming directly from this tradition. We still struggle with the paradox of a commitment to democratic and egalitarian principles and a continued conflict between these principles and the experiences of many citizens who have been and are treated differently by the American government.

review
REVIEW QUESTIONS _____

1. What are the three principles underlying constitutional democracy?

2. How and where are these three principles evident in the American system of government?

3. What were the three theoretical traditions at the foundation of the American political system?

4. How did elements of the tradition of exclusion influence who was covered by the Constitution?

5. Please explain this statement: One cannot truly be a student of American government and politics without understanding the role that race played in the development of the American political system.

Check your understanding of Chapter 1.

terms
KEY TERMS _____

Civic Virtue p. 12

Classical Liberalism p. 9

Classical Republicanism p. 9

Conservatives p. 12

Constitution p. 7

Constitutional Democracy p. 7

Coverture p. 16

Democracy p. 6

Direct Democracy p. 6

Feudalism p. 10

Government p. 4

Indirect (or Representative) Democracy p. 7

Inegalitarianism p. 9

Liberal p. 12

Natural Law p. 8

Natural Rights p. 9

Politics p. 6

Public Good p. 5

Reparations p. 2

Republican Form of Government p. 14

Rule of Law p. 8

Social Construction of Race p. 18

Social Contract p. 10

Statutory Law p. 8

Tradition of Exclusion p. 15

Need to review key ideas in greater depth? Click here.

readings
ADDITIONAL READINGS _____

Johansen, B. E. (1982). *Forgotten Founders: How the American Indian helped shape democracy.* Boston: Harvard Common Press.

> This study investigates the use of democratic principles by American Indians prior to contact with Europeans and how Indian use of these principles helped shape the American democratic system.

Gibson, A. R. (2009). *Interpreting the founding: Guide to the enduring debates over the origins and foundations of the American republic* (2nd ed., revised and expanded). Lawrence: University Press of Kansas.

> This book provides summaries and analyses of the leading interpretive frameworks that have guided the study of the Founding.

Sellers, M. N. S. (1994). *American republicanism: Interpretation of the Constitution of the United States.* New York: New York University Press.

> This book examines the influence of the Roman republic on the U.S. Constitution.

Kerber, L. K. (1980). *Women of the republic: Intellect and ideology in revolutionary America.* Chapel Hill: University of North Carolina Press.

> This book studies the political views of American women during the founding of the nation.

Kaplan, S. (1973). *The Black presence in the era of the American Revolution, 1770–1800.* Washington, DC: National Portrait Gallery, Smithsonian Institution.

> This book chronicles Black American speaking and writing during the Revolutionary period.

Flashcard review.

2

The Constitution: Rights and Race Intertwined

Roseanne Barr (left) sent a tweet comparing Valerie Jarrett (right), a former advisor to President Barack Obama, to an ape. The dehumanization of African Americans by comparing them to apes has a very long and racist history. ABC made the decision to cancel Barr's show, *Roseanne*, because of her racist comments. But the show was resurrected as *The Conner's*, killing of Barr's character.

On May 29, 2018, the American broadcast television network ABC, abruptly canceled the hit sitcom *Roseanne* after the show's co-creator, star, and namesake, Roseanne Barr, went on a vitriolic and racist rant on the social networking platform Twitter.[1] The hit sitcom had returned to television only two months earlier, in March 2018, after a twenty-one-year hiatus. Barr's offensive Twitter post was about Valerie Jarrett, who had served as a senior advisor to President Barack Obama and was one of his most influential aides.[2] In the tweet, in which Jarrett was identified by her initials, Barr compared her to an ape and linked her to the Muslim Brotherhood. Jarret, an African American woman, was born in Shiraz, Iran.

Barr's twitter posts were in response to an online claim that President Obama had spied on French presidential candidates, and that Jarrett, specifically, who had also served as assistant to the president for intergovernmental affairs in the Obama administration, had helped President Obama "hide a lot" of questionable political activities.[3] Earlier that same day, Barr had posted other inexplicable tweets including false conspiracy theories about billionaire George Soros being a Nazi and war criminal who had turned in fellow Jews to German officials during the Holocaust. Soros was actually fourteen years old when his home country, Hungary, was under German occupation, and he was forced to hide his Jewish identity from the government.[4] Barr also accused Soros of wanting to "overthrow… [the U.S.] constitutional republic."[5]

Barr, who has a large fan base that includes staunch Trump supporters, is known to regularly retweet conservative memes and post stories that are in line with Republican political ideologies.[6] Roseanne Conner, the character portrayed by Barr in the TV sitcom, is a Trump supporter. Indeed, the show is about a working-class family, and Barr had even commented that she believed that it was working-class people who had elected Donald Trump.[7] After the show's premier, President Trump had even called Roseanne to thank her for her support and to congratulate her on the reboot's "huge" ratings.[8]

After receiving considerable backlash for her comments about Jarrett, Roseanne deleted the tweet and later claimed that it was a joke that was in "bad taste," which she regretted making. Although the comedian later issued a longer apology, in which she claimed that she had posted the offensive tweets when she was under the influence of prescription sleep medication, the damage from her inflammatory comments was already done.[9] Channing Dungey, the president of ABC Entertainment Group, released a statement shortly after Barr's bizarre social-media rant, saying, "Roseanne's Twitter statement is abhorrent, repugnant and inconsistent with our values, and we have decided to cancel her show." Barr's talent agency, ICM Partners, also dropped her as a client, remarking that her Twitter posts were "antithetical to [their] core values, both as individuals and as an agency."

ABC's decision to cancel Barr's show, despite the fact that *Roseanne* was the top-rated television program of the season, was widely applauded. Many people backed ABC's decision, while others claimed that the network showed double standards when it came to the issue of free speech.[10] President Trump also commented on the show's cancelation, but instead of denouncing the racist tweets, he instead expressed anger at the television network. President Trump was unhappy that Robert A. Iger, the chairman of Disney, which is the parent company of ABC, had called Jarrett to apologize for Barr's comments. The White House press secretary, Sarah Huckabee Sanders, also noted that President Trump disapproved of what he viewed as the media's "hypocrisy" when it came to their response to what he viewed as attacks against him and his administration.[11] Some of Barr's supporters have criticized ABC's decision to fire the comedian on the basis that it violates her right to free speech, but their arguments are based on an incorrect understanding of the guarantees and protections under the Constitution. While it is true that even speech that may be considered to be hateful or racist is protected under the First Amendment—that is, the government cannot punish individuals for making hateful or racist comments—employers, on the other hand, are under no constitutional obligation to permit free speech that they deem to be against their organization's values.[12]

intro *This vignette highlights one aspect of the U.S. Constitution that is central to our system of government—freedom of speech. It also highlights that while people are free to say things, it does not mean that there are no consequences for what people say.*

This chapter examines how the Founders of the nation went about making the Constitution the basic governing document of the United States. The story of the

Constitution is one that describes guarantees of liberty and freedom for some, while simultaneously excluding large segments of the population that were present in the new United States at the time of ratification. Moreover, issues of race were central to the debates about the Constitution and played a major role in the distribution of power in the new nation. Race and the construction of the new nation were intertwined and woven into the political fabric of the United States.

What does the Constitution do? Get a brief tour.

A Revolution for Independence

The path to the American Revolution was long and winding. The buildup to the Revolution consisted of many events, some that pushed the colonists away from Britain and others that gave the colonists pause and pulled them back. The decision to declare independence and go to war was not an easy one, and it was carefully considered by all those involved.

The Road to Revolution

The issues of colonial autonomy and monarchial rule were central questions that fueled the American Revolution. The colonists were upset with what they perceived to be unfair acts by King George III and Parliament. Between 1739 and 1763, Great Britain engaged in several wars in Europe and in the Americas that generated a tremendous debt. Faced with this debt and the expense of maintaining troops in the Americas, Great Britain decided to raise revenue from the colonies. Up to that point, the colonies had not been expected to generate revenue, and they historically paid very little tax to the Crown.

In 1764, Parliament passed the American Revenue Act, commonly referred to as the Sugar Act, which required the colonies to pay a heavy tariff on sugar and other raw materials and on manufactured products imported to the colonies from foreign countries. That act was followed in the same year by the Currency Act, which prohibited the colonies from issuing currency. In 1765, Parliament passed the Quartering Act, which required local governments in the colonies to provide barracks and supplies for British troops. In the same year, it also passed the Stamp Act, which placed a tax on everything printed or written on paper—newspapers, pamphlets, insurance policies, playing cards, legal documents, ships' documents, licenses, and so forth.

The Stamp Act was the first legislation to impose a direct tax on the colonists themselves, and they feared that this would be the first of many direct taxes to come.[13] The colonists had resented earlier legislation, but now they organized to protest the latest act. The Massachusetts Assembly called for a general meeting on Britain's revenue-raising tactics. Nine colonies sent representatives to this meeting, the Stamp Act Congress, which met in New York City in October 1765. The congress declared that taxation without representation was a violation of the colonists' rights as British subjects and argued that only the colonial government, not Parliament, could levy taxes on the colonists. The colonists backed up their protests with a boycott against goods made in Britain.

On December 16, 1773, the Sons of Liberty boarded ships in Boston Harbor and threw three crates of tea overboard in protest of the British government and the East India Company's tax policy on tea and the Tea Act, which the colonists considered unfair.

Faced with the dramatic drop in exports to the colonies, Parliament eventually repealed the Stamp Act in 1766, but at the same time it passed the Declaratory Act, which stated that Parliament had supremacy over the colonies "in all cases whatsoever." Another series of acts in 1767, named the Townshend Acts after Charles Townshend, the British chancellor of the Exchequer, instituted heavy taxes on all vessels entering colonial ports and placed duties on all manufactured goods. Colonial resentment and opposition continued to mount as pamphleteers and newspapers fanned the fires of protest against Parliament's actions.[14]

In 1773, Parliament passed the Tea Act as a means of bailing out the East India Company, which was on the verge of bankruptcy. The act not only imposed a tax on tea imported into America, but also gave the East India Company exclusive rights to sell tea to the colonies. Protests against the Tea Act took place in several colonies, but the most dramatic incident occurred in Boston. On the night of December 16, 1773, colonists disguised as American Indians boarded ships docked in Boston harbor and threw chests of tea overboard. The infamous Boston Tea Party destroyed 340 chests of tea worth nearly £10,000. Parliament responded with the Coercive Acts, which closed Boston Harbor, revoked Massachusetts' colonial charter, sent British officials charged with crimes to England or Canada for trial, and again legalized the housing of British troops in unoccupied buildings in the colonies.

Opposition to Britain continued to build, particularly in Massachusetts. In May 1774, participants in a Boston town meeting called for a general colonial congress to deal collectively with the colonies' problems with Britain. In September 1774, twelve colonies sent delegates, fifty-six in all, to the meeting of the First Continental Congress in Philadelphia. The Congress denounced the Coercive Acts as cruel and illegitimate, arguing that Parliament had no authority over the colonies because the colonies owed allegiance to the king only. The delegates drafted a resolution addressed to King George and the British and American peoples stating their opposition to the acts and calling for another boycott of British goods.[15] Before the Congress dispersed at the end of the month, it laid plans for the Second Continental Congress to meet in May 1775.

Learn about the Framers.

To King George III, the actions and resolution of the First Continental Congress meant that the colonies were now in a state of rebellion. The winter of 1774–1775 passed without major incidents, but on April 18, 1775 (some sources say April 19), British troops and Massachusetts militiamen exchanged gunfire at the battles of Lexington and Concord, two small farm villages in eastern Massachusetts. The American Revolution had begun. The Second Continental Congress, meeting in May 1775, in Philadelphia, took control of the war and in June, named George Washington as chief of the Continental Forces and charged him with raising an army to fight the British.

Declaring Independence

Although the Second Continental Congress authorized the raising of an army to fight the British, it issued no formal call for independence from Britain. The congress believed that Massachusetts and the rest of the colonies had the right to resist Britain's oppressive behavior, but it was not yet convinced that severing ties with Britain was the correct step. As the fighting continued, however, many colonists began to consider independence from Britain. Thomas Paine, a British journalist and political philosopher who came to the colonies in 1774 at the request of Benjamin Franklin, helped sway that opinion. In January 1776, Paine wrote *Common Sense*, a pamphlet that argued strongly for the immediate declaration of independence for the colonies. *Common Sense* was wildly popular, selling between 300,000 and 500,000 copies.

By the spring of 1776, sentiment was running high for breaking with Britain.[16] North Carolina was the first colony to authorize its delegates to the Second Continental Congress to vote for independence, with Virginia a close second. Richard Henry Lee of Virginia, a representative to both Continental Congresses and an ardent advocate of independence, offered a resolution that the colonies declare themselves independent of Great Britain.

After much debate, the Second Continental Congress decided to appoint a committee to draft a declaration of independence. The committee consisted of Thomas Jefferson of Virginia, Benjamin Franklin of Pennsylvania, John Adams of Massachusetts, Robert R. Livingston of New York, and Roger Sherman of

Crispus Attucks (c. 1723–1770), a former slave, merchant and seaman, was the first person killed on March 5, 1770, by British soldiers in what has become known as the Boston Massacre. The British soldiers who fired the fatal shots were tried and defended by John Adams, who used Attucks's race and supposed terrifying looks as a justification for the soldiers killing him. The soldiers were acquitted.

Connecticut. Jefferson drafted the document, which cataloged the abuses of King George and drew on several Western European political traditions, principally liberalism and republicanism (see Chapter 1), as justification for the colonies to declare their independence. (See Table 2.1 for a list of selected events leading up to the Declaration of Independence.)

Although he was a slave owner himself, Jefferson's original draft of the Declaration of Independence included an indictment of King George for engaging in and perpetuating slavery: "violating the most sacred rights of life and liberty in the persons of a distant people who never offended him, captivating and carrying them into slavery in another hemisphere or to incur miserable death in their transportation hither to." Both Southern and Northern delegates objected to the clause. Southerners argued that slavery was fundamental to the economy of the new nation, and Northerners viewed slavery merely as a business that needed regulating.[17] The debate over removing this indictment foreshadowed the difficulties that the issue of slavery would present the new nation and for the nation moving forward. The way the nation handled issues of race at the beginning continues to influence how the nation deals with issues of race today.

TABLE 2.1 Selected Legislation/Events Leading to the Declaration of Independence

Legislation/Events	Date	Provisions	Colonial Reaction
Sugar Act	April 5, 1764	Revises duties on sugar, coffee, tea, wine, other imports; expands jurisdiction of vice-admiralty courts	Protest in several assemblies of taxation for revenue
Stamp Act	March 22, 1765; repealed March 18, 1766	Requires that printed documents (deeds, newspapers, marriage licenses, etc.) be issued only on special stamped paper purchased from stamp distributors	Riots in cities; collectors forced to resign; Stamp Act Congress (October 1765)
Quartering Act	May 1765	Requires colonists to supply British troops with housing and other items (candles, firewood, etc.)	Protest in assemblies; New York Assembly punished for failure to comply (1767)
Declaratory Act	March 18, 1766	Declares Parliament's sovereignty over the colonies "in all cases whatsoever"	Celebration over repeal of the Stamp Act, blotting its effect
Townshend Revenue Acts	June 26, June 29, July 2, 1767; all repealed except duty on tea	Imposes new duties on glass, lead, paper, paints, tea; tightens customs collections in America	Nonimportation of British goods; protest in assemblies; newspaper attacks on British policy
Boston Massacre	March 1770	Five men were killed by British soldiers. Crispus Attucks, a runaway slave from Framingham, MA, and subsequent sailor, was the first to die in the attack and thus became the first person to die in the American Revolution	The British soldiers were defended by John Adams, the future second president of the United States, who used Attucks's race in his defense of the British soldiers, referring to Attucks as "a stout Molatto fellow, whose very looks, was enough to terrify any person"; the soldiers were acquitted
Tea Act	May 10, 1773	Gives East India Company right to sell tea directly to Americans; reduces some duties on tea	Protests against favoritism shown to monopolistic company; tea destroyed in Boston (December 16, 1773)
Coercive Acts (Intolerable Acts)	March–June 1774	Closes port of Boston; restructures Massachusetts government; restricts town meetings; quarters troops in Boston; sends British officials accused of crimes to England or Canada for trial	Boycott of British goods; convening of First Continental Congress (September 1774)
Prohibitory Act	December 22, 1775	Declares British intention to coerce Americans into submission; imposes embargo on American goods; seizes American ships	Movement of Continental Congress closer to decision for independence

Thomas Jefferson, third president of the United States, was the author of the Declaration of Independence and a slaveholder. He fathered six children with his slave, Sally Hemings, freeing the children in his lifetime but not freeing their mother in his will. His children were the only slaves that Jefferson ever freed.

On July 4, 1776, the Continental Congress voted on a declaration of independence and announced, with these words, the colonies' independence from Britain:

> We, therefore, the Representative of the United States of America, . . . do, in the Name, and by the Authority of the good People of these Colonies, solemnly publish and declare, That these United Colonies are, and of Right ought to be Free and Independent States; that they are Absolved from all Allegiance to the British Crown, and that all political connection between them and the State of Great Britain, is and ought to be totally dissolved.

The story of the road to independence can be placed under the broad category of inequitable treatment. The colonists felt that Britain was not treating them fairly on a number of dimensions—taxing the colonies to pay debts in Britain when the colonists were not allowed to have representatives in Parliament, removing power from the colonial governments, and trampling on what the colonists perceived to be their rights to govern themselves. Debates about equality and inequality were central to the concerns that brought about independence from Britain and the founding of the United States of America.

The meaning of equality was posited within their colonial experiences and the influence of the Enlightenment, and was within the context of the basic principle of freedom. Scholars have argued that the equality spoken of in the Declaration of Independence was not one of human equality as we think about it now, but the position of man in the state of nature.[18] The Founders held no illusions that all people were born with equality of intellect or virtue; in fact, Thomas Jefferson and John Adams, in a series of letters, both identified a group of individuals who were to be entrusted with running the new nation and the common man. They saw no conflict between the idea that all men are created equal and what they saw as natural inequalities between human beings.[19]

Given the belief in inequalities among human beings, the Founders made assumptions about who was and who was not to be included in this new government. Despite the language of equality and inclusion, many people who lived in the new nation—White women, free Blacks, enslaved Blacks, and American Indians—were not to be included as participants in the new nation.

Unitary Form of Government
A system in which the central government exercises complete control and authority over subunits of government, which means that states or other governmental units do not have autonomous powers.

First Attempt at National Government: The Articles of Confederation

When Richard Henry Lee offered his resolution for independence, he also proposed a plan for a new form of government for the nation. Britain, with which the colonies were now at war, had a **unitary form of government**, a system in which the central government exercises complete control and authority over its states or governmental units. Lee proposed a **confederation**, a system in which states or other types of government units organize a weak central government with limited scope and powers while reserving ultimate power for themselves. In such a government, each state retains its power, sovereigty, and independence.

A Limited National Government

Shortly after the appointment of the committee to draft the Declaration of Independence, another committee was established, chaired by John Dickinson of Delaware, to devise a plan for the new governmental structure.[20] On July 12, 1776, Dickinson's committee submitted the "Articles of Confederation and Perpetual Union" to the Second Continental Congress. Whereas the Continental Congress had swiftly passed the Declaration of Independence, the delegates debated for more than a year before voting on the Articles of Confederation. On November 15, 1777, the Congress formally adopted the Articles and sent them to the thirteen states for ratification. Final ratification of the Articles of Confederation did not occur until 1781 when Maryland, the last of the states to do so, finally ratified.[21]

The Articles of Confederation set up a central government with very limited powers. The states were used to operating independently and were not keen on ceding power to a central government. The Articles established a **unicameral form of government**, a system with a legislative body of one house only, and named their legislature the Congress. As the central government, Congress could enact legislation, but it had little power to enforce the laws it passed. Real power resided in the states. Members of Congress were appointed annually by the state legislatures, which also paid their salaries. Each state, regardless of population size, had one vote in Congress. There was also no executive branch and no national judicial system.

Congress was given the authority to declare war and to negotiate peace, to coin and borrow money, to make treaties and alliances, to regulate trade with American Indians, and to appoint military officers. Congress also could not enact taxes or control trade among the states. States were free to compete with each other for trade with foreign countries, and the competition was fierce.

Weaknesses of the Articles of Confederation

Economic conditions in the new nation were depressed during the early years of the new republic. Imports from and exports to Britain had dropped significantly, and farm income had fallen. Under the Articles, each state issued its own currency, and the shortage of revenue led residents in many states to call on their state governments to issue more currency so that people could pay their debts.

In Massachusetts, many farmers faced the loss of their property or imprisonment because they were unable to pay their debts and taxes. In 1786–1787, dissident farmers, who attempted to shut down courthouses, clashed several

Confederation A system in which states or other types of government units organize a weak central government with limited scope and powers while reserving ultimate power for themselves.

Unicameral Form of Government A government system that consists of only one legislative body (rather than two or more).

times with local militias, which were defending the courts. The most serious rebellion was led by Daniel Shays, a Revolutionary War veteran. In September 1786, Shays and his followers marched on Springfield, where the state supreme court was meeting, and surrounded the courthouse, thereby forcing the court to adjourn. In December, Shays and his forces again marched on Springfield in an attempt to capture an arsenal (see "Our Voices: Prince Hall [1748–1807]"). Although their attempt to take the arsenal was unsuccessful and Shays's forces were eventually defeated, the uprising highlighted the level of discontent with state government, particularly the legislature and the courts.

Shays's Rebellion exposed the weakness of the Articles of Confederation. The national government was unable to support Massachusetts during the rebellion. Congress authorized the raising of troops, but it had no authority to raise money to support them. Under the Articles, Congress could only ask states for the money it needed to carry out its functions. Clearly, Congress required revenue to send and receive ambassadors, manage domestic and foreign affairs, establish post offices, staff and equip military forces, and handle the few other limited functions delegated to the national government. Lacking the authority to force either the states or the people to pay taxes (a power reserved solely to the states) led to predictable and devastating results.

The mechanisms for adopting and changing the Articles presented problems. Both processes required all thirteen states to agree. Thus, it was not until four years after the national Congress adopted the Articles in 1777 that the last state, Maryland, finally ratified them. Changes were also unlikely under the rule of unanimity; each state, in effect, had the power of veto. Thus, any revision or alteration of the Articles could have been blocked by the disapproval of one state. In all, the problems manifested in the Articles of Confederation seemed to suggest that the people who had successfully revolted against the world's greatest military power might not be able to figure out how to govern themselves. It was against this backdrop that the Congress, in February 1787, called a convention to meet in Philadelphia to revise the Articles of Confederation.

Second Attempt at National Government: The Constitution

Go online to view The 10-Minute Guide to the Constitution from Cornell University.

When the fifty-five men we now know as the Framers of the Constitution met in Philadelphia in the summer of 1787, their purpose was to deal with an economic and political crisis and to address problems with the governmental system established by the Articles of Confederation. The convention delegates faced a balancing problem. The most obvious course of action was to shift some power from the state governments to the national government. But if they gave too much power to the national government, they would create a unitary form of government. Most delegates wanted to avoid this solution because such a government might too closely resemble the system under the British. Thus, the convention delegates established a government in which

our voices

Prince Hall (1748–1807)

In September 1786, during the uprising known as Shays's Rebellion, Governor James Bowdoin issued a call for volunteers to head west to help put down the rebellion. Prince Hall, a former slave who, having been initially denied membership in White Freemason organizations, founded the African American Freemasons, the African Lodge No. 1, in Boston, wrote a letter to Governor Bowdoin offering the services of seven hundred Black troops. Historians contend that Hall made this offer in an effort to show the loyalty of Black Americans to the state of Massachusetts and, although they were denied citizenship, to demonstrate the desire of Blacks to be citizens of the state and, by extension, citizens of the United States. Historians also suggest that Bowdoin rejected the offer because, although slavery had been abolished in Massachusetts, hostility to Blacks in general and fear of armed Black men in particular were high.

In his letter, Hall drew on his group's organization as Freemasons to make his argument for the willingness of these men to volunteer on behalf of the state of Massachusetts.

Here is an excerpt from Hall's letter to Governor James Bowdoin in November 1786:

We, by the Providence of God, are members of a fraternity that not only enjoins upon us to be peaceable subjects to the civil powers where we reside, but it also forbids our having any concern in any plot of conspiracies against the state where we dwell; and as it is the unhappy lot of this state at the present date, and as the meanest of its members must feel that want of a lawful and good government, as we have been protected for many years under this once happy Constitution, so we hope, by the blessing of God, we may long enjoy that blessing; therefore, we, though unworthy members of this Commonwealth, are willing to help and support, as far as our weak and feeble abilities may become necessary in this time of trouble and confusion, as you in your wisdom shall direct us. That

Prince Hall, a former slave, founded the African American Freemasons. During Shays's Rebellion in 1786, Hall wrote to Massachusetts' Governor Bowdoin to volunteer seven hundred Black troops to fight on behalf of the State of Massachusetts.

we may, under just and lawful authority, live peaceable lives in all godliness and honesty, is the hearty wish of your humble servants, the members of the African Lodge.

Sources: Walker, C. D. B. (2008). *A noble fight: African American Freemasonry and the struggle for democracy in America.* Urbana: University of Illinois Press, 77–79; Kaplan, S. (1973). *The Black presence in the era of the American Revolution, 1770–1800.* Greenwich, CT: New York Graphic Society.

Concurrent Powers
Powers shared by the national government and state governments, such as the power to tax and borrow money.

National Government
A system of government in which powers are distributed between the central government (federal government) and subunits, such as states.

some powers remained at the state level, some were vested in the national government, and some were shared, an arrangement also known as **concurrent powers**. In so doing, the delegates established a **national government**, the central government under a federal system.

The Convention Delegates

The idea of a federal government did not appear out of thin air to the convention delegates as they sat sweating through the summer heat of Philadelphia. The Framers drew on the political philosophies of liberalism and republicanism as they set about revising the government. They also drew on their own experience. More than 70 percent of the members of the convention held high state offices. Many of these men had participated in the formation of a government at the state level. Three of the twelve states represented at the Constitutional Convention sent their governors. (Rhode Island's legislature, controlled by those sympathetic to Shays, did not send any delegates.) Four-fifths of the delegates had served in the Continental Congress established under the Articles; eight others had signed the Declaration of Independence.[22]

In addition to their government experience, the Framers shared other characteristics. All of the delegates who convened in Philadelphia were male and White, as White males were the only ones with political power in the early republic. They were well educated; more than half of them had attended college. They were also wealthy. Although the forms of wealth varied—including land, businesses, slaves, cash, credit, or bonds—most of the delegates had amassed sizable fortunes. Thus, the Framers were hardly representative of the new nation's overall population (see "Measuring Equality: Whom did the Framers Represent?").

Forming a New Government

The delegates to the Philadelphia convention quickly made three procedural decisions that would ultimately prove crucial to the success of their efforts. First, they chose George Washington to preside over the sessions. It is hard to overestimate Washington's stature at the time. He had headed the army that had defeated the British for the new country's independence and had taken no pay for his efforts. He had paid the revolutionary soldiers who served under him out of his own pocket. One-fifth of the attendees had served as officers under Washington's command. In addition, he owned a good bit of the country—thousands of acres of land in Kentucky, Maryland, the Northwest Territory (the area between the Ohio and Mississippi Rivers that eventually became the states of Ohio, Indiana, Illinois, Michigan, Wisconsin, and part of Minnesota), Pennsylvania, and Virginia.

Second, the group decided to hold secret sessions. No information emerged from the meetings until the final announcement. This secrecy was important because the third major decision the conventioneers quickly reached was to scrap their mandate merely to "revise the Articles of Confederation." They decided instead to draft a new document. Thus, the Constitution came into being

measuring equality

Whom Did the Framers Represent?

The language of the Constitution guarantees equality and freedom to all men. Yet we know that the Framers of the Constitution intended the guarantees and protections to apply only to a small segment of the population in the United States at the time. Who were the Framers really (see Table 2.A)? How representative of the rest of the population were they (see Table 2.B)? What do the data here on the characteristics of the Framers suggest to you about the strata of the population that they represented?

TABLE 2.A Characteristics of the Fifty-Five Framers[a]

White: 100% (55)
Male: 100% (55)

Education Level
University educated: 56.4% (31)

Institutions attended
Princeton University (10)
University of Pennsylvania (2)
Columbia College (2)
William and Mary College (3)
Harvard University (3)
Scottish universities (3)
Yale University (4)
Middle and Inner Temple, London (6)

Occupation
Lawyer only: 47.3% (26)
Lawyer and another profession: 16.3% (9)

Government Experience
Colonial/military official: 94.5% (52)
Member of Continental Congress: 74.5% (41)

Property Ownership
Owned their residences: 100% (55)
Owned lands used for farming: 56.4% (31)
Owned slaves: 31% (17)

Economic Level[b]
Wealthy: 10.9% (6)
Middle class/comfortable: 76.3% (42)
Poor: 12.7% (7)

TABLE 2.B Characteristics of the General Population According to the 1790 Census[c]

Race
White: 80.40% (3,140,531)
Slave Black: 17.83% (694,207)
Free Black: 1.52% (59,196)

Gender (White population only)
Male: 50.92% (1,599,213)
Female: 49.08% (1,541,318)

Education Level[d]
"Most" White male children in the North attended school for 4 to 6 months a year from age 4 to 14.
"Substantial amount" of White male children in the South attended school for 4 to 6 months a year from age 4 to 14.
"Few" White male children in the West attended school or were literate.
"Very few" White male children attended college or university.[e]
"Very few" White female children received any formal classroom instruction.

Significant Colonial Occupations[f]
Farming
Lumbering
Fishing
Iron mining
Trading in furs and skins
Producing naval stores

(Continued)

measuring equality (*Continued*)

TABLE 2.B (*Continued*)

Property Ownership
White slave-owning families: 11.6% (47,664)
Land owners: 13% (of 1774 population)
People associated with slave owning: 7.2% (of White population in 1790); 6.13% (in 1774)

Economic Level (in 1774) (category classifications determined from the distribution of wealth)[g]
High wealth: Top 2% held 24.6% of the wealth.
Middle wealth: Top 20% held 73.2% of the wealth.
Low wealth: 70% held only 28.6% of the wealth.
Very low wealth: Bottom 10% owned 1.7% of the wealth (in other words, they were in debt).
No wealth: 81.53% had no measurable wealth.

[a] The U.S. Constitution: The Delegates. *National Archives and Records Administration. Retrieved from http://www.gov/exhall/charters/constitution/confath.html;* McDonald, F. (1958). We the people: The economic origins of the Constitution. *Chicago: University of Chicago Press, chaps. 1–3.*

[b] Information on economic levels was drawn from the "Biographical Index of Our Founding Fathers," National Archives and Record Administration, Washington, DC. The category classifications were determined from language in the biographies. Actual dollar figures of wealth and income are not readily available.

[c] Unless otherwise indicated, data are taken from the 1790 census, which mainly surveyed population characteristics.

[d] Kaestle, C. F. 91983). Pillars of the republic. *New York: Hill & Wang, 1983; Genealogical Publishing Company. (1989). A century of population growth. Baltimore: Author.*

[e] The 1790 census indicated that there were 807,312 White males over the age of sixteen in the country. A listing of the most prominent colleges and universities at the same time shows a combined enrollment of 1,122 students (White males).

[f] Sutherland, S. H. (1936). Population distribution in Colonial America. *New York: Columbia University Press, p. xi.*

[g] Jones, A. H. (1980). Wealth of a nation to be. *New York: Columbia University Press; Jones, A. H. (1977). American colonial wealth. New York: Arno Press.*

Virginia Plan Drafted by James Madison of Virginia at the 1787 Constitutional Convention; a proposal for a system of government that called for the establishment of a strong central government with three branches: a bicameral legislature, a chief executive chosen by the legislature, and a powerful judiciary.

Bicameral Legislature A legislature with two bodies, usually referred to as the upper and lower chambers, or, as is most common in the United States, the House and the Senate.

only because the Framers chose to ignore the instructions they had been given by their state legislatures and to draft a new national governing document.

In one sense, this decision was as revolutionary as the decision to break from England, but in this case the Framers were, quite literally, revolting against themselves. In essence, the Framers were threatening their own privileged status by deciding to replace the government in which many of them served and to shift power away from the states they represented. Nevertheless, without the secrecy, the opposition to creating a new national government would have had the chance to mobilize.

The Great Compromise

Edmund Randolph of Virginia introduced the plan that proposed adopting a new national government rather than amending the Articles of Confederation. The **Virginia Plan**, drafted by fellow Virginian James Madison, called for the establishment of a strong central government with three branches: legislative, executive, and judicial. The legislature would consist of two houses—that is, it would be a **bicameral legislature**—with the number of representatives for each state based on population size or money contributions to the national government.

Representatives to the lower house would be elected by the people, and members of the upper chamber would be elected by the lower house from nominations submitted by the state legislatures. The legislature would select the national chief executive. The judicial branch would consist of a supreme court and subordinate national courts whose judges would be selected by the legislature. The plan also proposed the creation of a committee of revision to consist of a chief executive and several members of the judiciary. This committee would have veto power over legislative acts.

The Virginia Plan's proposal for proportional representation in the legislature favored the more populous states of the time—Virginia, Massachusetts, and Pennsylvania. Needless to say, the smaller states of New Jersey and Georgia were opposed to the Virginia Plan. Under the Articles of Confederation, each state had equal representation. Proportional representation of the Virginia Plan would give more power to the more populous states.

William Paterson of New Jersey introduced an alternative plan that aimed to amend the Articles of Confederation. The **New Jersey Plan** sought to maintain the confederation's unicameral legislature wherein each state was represented equally with one representative per state. Representatives would be elected by state legislatures. The plan also called for the creation of a supreme court. To address problems that had surfaced under the Articles of Confederation, Congress would be given more power. The New Jersey Plan proposed shifting the power to tax and regulate foreign and interstate commerce from the individual states to the national legislature. Congress could also name more than one person to a chief executive committee—a plural executive that would have no veto power.

The delegates debated differences between the Virginia and New Jersey plans but decided to move in the direction suggested by the Virginia Plan, because they wanted to create a new national government, not merely amend the Articles of Confederation. A committee was appointed to resolve the differences between the two plans and forge them into one document. The most significant problem continued to be the issue of equal versus proportional representation. Finally, Roger Sherman of Connecticut offered a compromise.

Sherman's plan, known as the **Connecticut Compromise**, or the **Great Compromise**, proposed that each state would have equal representation in the upper house of the legislature, the Senate, and proportional representation in the lower House of Representatives. Representation in the House would be based on a state's population, with one elected representative for every thirty thousand persons. There would be a total of fifty-six representatives. The lower house would have the power to originate legislation for raising and spending money. In the Senate, each state would have equal representation, with two senators for each state selected by the state's legislature.[23] (In the end, the size of the House of Representatives was set at sixty-five in the original Constitution from 1787 until the first census in 1790, at which point the size of the House grew to 105.[24])

New Jersey Plan Drafted by William Paterson of New Jersey at the 1787 Constitutional Convention; a proposal for a system of government that called for the maintenance of a confederation with a unicameral legislature in which all states were represented equally, a multimember executive without the power to veto legislation, and a supreme court.

Great Compromise (or Connecticut Compromise) Worked out by a committee at the 1787 Constitutional Convention, a compromise that called for membership in the House of Representatives based on population, with states having equal representation in the Senate.

Slavery was a cruel and harsh institution that paid little to no attention to familial relations. This woodcut from the 1800s is a rarity in that it depicts the auctioning of an entire family. Nevertheless, there was no guarantee that a family would be able to stay together.

The question of how to determine the population base for representation in the lower house required additional debate and compromise. Slavery was at the heart of the debate, although the issue was not the abolition of slavery. Delegates from slaveholding states considered slaves property, not people. Nevertheless, for the sake of greater power in the national government, they wanted slaves counted as free persons to determine representation in the lower house. This would give the slaveholding states added votes in the House of Representatives, despite the fact that the slaves being counted for purposes of representation would not be represented by those who were elected. Delegates from nonslaveholding states, however, did not want the slaves counted.

Three-Fifths Compromise
A compromise reached at the Constitutional Convention over how state populations were to be counted for purposes of allocating seats in the House of Representatives; each slave was to be counted as three-fifths of a person for representational purposes.

The debate was resolved, at least until the Civil War, by the **Three-Fifths Compromise**, which counted each slave as three-fifths of a person for representational purposes in the House of Representatives (see "Evaluating Equality: The Effect of the Three-Fifths Compromise on the Political Power of the South" on page 44). The delegates finally voted on and passed the Great Compromise, and the document was given to a committee charged with organizing and refining the draft constitution. Members of the committee included Alexander Hamilton of New York and James Madison of Virginia.

Debate over Ratification

On September 17, 1787, the convention passed the draft constitution and forwarded it to the Continental Congress to be passed on to the states. For the

Constitution to become the new national governing document, it had to be ratified by three-fourths of the states, or nine of the thirteen. Ratification was not an easy process, as there was significant opposition to the Constitution. Those in favor of ratification called themselves **Federalists**, leaving those against it to identify themselves as Antifederalists. The Federalists favored a strong central government with a bicameral national legislature, whereas the **Antifederalists** preferred a weaker federal government with a unicameral national legislature.

Federalists Proponents of the Constitution during the ratification process.

Antifederalists Opponents of the Constitution during the ratification process.

On September 28, 1787, the Continental Congress sent the Constitution to the states without making any specific recommendation for or against ratification. Several states were not pleased with the new document, especially New York, which was concerned about an erosion of state authority. To counter opposition, the Federalists decided to conduct a concerted campaign for ratification. Three of the signers of the proposed Constitution—James Madison of Virginia and Alexander Hamilton and John Jay of New York—wrote a series of anonymous letters to the public laying out the arguments in favor of immediate ratification. Many leaders of the thirteen states were terrified that a strong national government would infringe on their sovereign powers. *The Federalist Papers*, as the letters became known when they were collected and published as a volume, sought to show that the states and the national government would share powers and that most of the powers already held and exercised by the states would remain as such.

The Federalist Papers A collection of the eighty-five articles written by James Madison, Alexander Hamilton, and John Jay in support of the ratification of the Constitution.

Prominent opponents of the Constitution were Richard Henry Lee, Patrick Henry, and George Mason of Virginia; Sam Adams of Massachusetts; and George Clinton of New York. The Antifederalists, who believed the proposed Constitution would fail and anarchy and despotism would ensue, insisted on the addition of a bill of rights, feared a consolidated government, opposed unlimited taxing power, and were opposed to standing armies in peacetime.[25]

Ratification took some time because many states had specific concerns. The absence of a bill of rights to protect civil liberties troubled many states, especially North Carolina. Delaware was the first state to ratify, on December 7, 1787, but the Constitution was not finally approved until New Hampshire, the ninth state to do so, ratified on June 21, 1788. Rhode Island, which refused to send a delegation to the Philadelphia convention, rejected the Constitution in March 1788, and stayed out of the new nation until 1790, when it ratified the Constitution by just two votes at a state convention. (Rhode Island's state legislature was so fractionalized that it could not function.) (See Table 2.2 for a comparison of the Articles of Confederation with the Constitution.)

The Bill of Rights

The new government took office in January 1789. Presidential electors were chosen in the states as they were electing their representatives to the House and as the state legislatures were appointing senators. The Constitution provided for the president to be elected by electors, rather than by popular vote.

evaluating equality

The Effect of the Three-Fifths Compromise on the Political Power of the South

This congressional compromise, which counted each slave as three-fifths of a person for representational purposes in the House of Representatives, resolved the debate on how to apportion representatives in the House. Although not what the Southern delegates wanted, the Three-Fifths Compromise never-theless tilted political power in the House of Representatives and in the new government to the South. Table 2.C,

TABLE 2.C 1790 CENSUS POPULATION STATISTICS33*

	Total Population	White Males 16 Years and Over	White Males Under 16 Years	All Other White Females	Free Persons	Slaves
Connecticut	237,655	60,739 [25.56%]	54,289 [22.84%]	117,208 [49.32%]	2,771 [1.17%]	2,648 [1.11%]
Delaware	59,096	11,783 [19.94%]	12,143 [20.55%]	22,384 [37.88%]	3,899 [6.60%]	8,887 [15.04%]
Georgia	82,548	13,103 [15.87%]	14,044 [17.01%]	25,739 [31.18%]	398 [0.48%]	29,264 [35.35%]
Maryland	319,728	55,915 [17.49%]	51,339 [16.06%]	101,395 [31.71%]	8,043 [2.52%]	103,036 [32.23%]
Massachusetts	378,556	95,433 [25.21%]	87,279 [23.06%]	190,475 [50.32%]	5,369 [1.42%]	0
New Hampshire	141,899	36,074 [25.42%]	34,855 [24.56%]	70,183 [49.46%]	630 [0.44%]	157 [0.11%]
New Jersey	184,139	45,251 [24.57%]	41,416 [22.49%]	83,287 [45.23%]	2,762 [1.50%]	11,423 [6.20%]
New York	340,241	83,815 [24.63%]	78,258 [23.00%]	152,293 [44.76%]	4,682 [1.38%]	21,193 [6.23%]
North Carolina	395,005	70,172 [17.76%]	77,653 [19.66%]	141,356 [35.79%]	5,041 [1.28%]	100,783 [25.51%]
Pennsylvania	433,611	110,559 [25.50%]	106,928 [24.66%]	205,886 [47.48%]	6,531 [1.51%]	3,707 [0.85%]
Rhode Island	69,112	16,506 [23.23%]	15,745 [22.78%]	32,869 [47.56%]	3,484 [5.04%]	958 [1.39%]
South Carolina	249,073	35,576 [14.28%]	37,722 [15.14%]	66,880 [26.85%]	1,801 [0.72%]	107,094 [43.00%]
Virginia	747,550	110,936 [14.84%]	116,135 [15.54%]	215,046 [28.77%]	12,866 [1.72%]	292,627 [39.13%]

*The facts and assertions listed here are attributable to Gary Wills and are taken from his text as well as lec-tures and roundtable discussions conducted at the Hoover Institute at Stanford University. Both video and audio files as well as a transcript of the latter discussion can be found at http://www.hoover.org/multimedia/uk/2993311.html.

derived from the 1790 census (the first census after ratification of the Constitution), shows the population distributions in the thirteen original states.

Here are some of the effects of the Three-Fifths Compromise:

- In 1793, the size of the House of Representatives was 105 members; Southern states received forty-seven seats, rather than the thirty-three they would have received if slaves had not been counted.

- In 1812, the size of the House of Representatives was 143 members and slaveholding states had seventy-six seats, instead of the fifty-nine they would have had.

- In 1833, the size of the House was 240 members and Southern states had ninety-eight seats, instead of the seventy-three they would have had.

- By 1850, the North had twice the population of the South, but Southerners had held the presidency for fifty of sixty-two years and had occupied eighteen of thirty-one Supreme Court seats.

Source: U.S. Census, 1790; http://www .hoover.org/multimedia/uk/2993311.html.

How states chose their electors was up to them, with most electors chosen by the state legislatures, but a small number chosen through an election. The first Congress met in New York in March, and in April, the Senate counted the presidential electors' ballots for president. George Washington was elected unanimously with 69 electoral votes, but each elector had two votes and John Adams received the second highest number of votes and was chosen as vice president. One of Congress's first acts was to send to the states twelve amendments to the Constitution that had grown out of the state-ratifying conventions. Of these, the last ten were ratified by the states and, in 1791, they became a part of the U.S. Constitution. These first ten amendments are called the **Bill of Rights**. The two amendments that were not ratified dealt with establishing a ratio of the number of people to be represented by one member of the House of Representatives and forbidding the Senate and House from raising their own salaries.

Bill of Rights The first ten amendments to the Constitution, which focus primarily on individual liberties and basic rights.

The Bill of Rights, pushed by the Antifederalists and proposed by James Madison of Virginia, spells out individual rights and liberties. As with other elements of the Constitution, the Bill of Rights was not original to that document. Many state constitutions, in particular the Constitution of Virginia (1776), had such protections. The language of the Virginia Declaration of Rights, written by George Mason and adopted by the Virginia Constitutional Convention on June 12, 1776, became the basis for the Bill of Rights.

National Government Under the Constitution

Government under the Articles of Confederation had been in existence for only seven years when the Framers decided to replace it with something else. For these men to repudiate so quickly a system that many of them had participated in creating indicated that the problems with the system were numerous and widespread.

TABLE 2.2 The Articles of Confederation versus the Constitution

Political Challenge	Articles of Confederation	Constitution
Process for ratification or amendment	Consent of every state legislature	Consent of three-fourths of state conventions or legislatures
Number of houses in legislature	One	Two
Type of representation	One to seven delegates for each state; each state with only one vote in Congress	Two senators for each state in upper house (Senate); each senator with one vote. One representative to lower house (House of Representatives) for every 30,000 people (in 1788) in a state; each representative with one vote
Process of election and term of office	Delegates appointed annually by state legislatures	Senators chosen by state legislatures for six-year term (direct election after 1913); representatives chosen by vote of citizens for two-year term
Executive	No separate executive; delegates annually electing one president, who possesses no veto, no power to appoint officers or to conduct policy; administration of government carried out by a committee of states	Separate executive branch; president elected by electoral college to four-year term; president granted veto, power to conduct policy and to appoint ambassadors, judges, and officers of executive departments established by legislation
Judiciary	Most adjudication left to state and local courts; Congress the final court of appeal in disputes between states	Separate branch consisting of Supreme Court and inferior courts established by Congress to enforce federal law
Taxation	Taxes levied only by states; congressional funding of the Common Treasury through requests for state contributions	Federal government granted powers of taxation
Regulation of commerce	Foreign commerce regulated by treaty made by Congress but with no check on conflicting state regulations	Regulation of all foreign commerce by Congress through treaty; congressional consent required for all state regulations
Slavery	Makes no specific reference to slavery, but refers to "free inhabitants" in various sections; also, the notion of counting slaves as three-fifths of a person actually originated during debates about how to establish a property foundation for taxation purposes of the new states; the measure was never passed, but the assumption is that slavery was to be allowed	Slavery was to be allowed, although not stated explicitly, prohibited Congress from outlawing slave trade for twenty years, slaves were to count as three-fifths of a person for representation purposes, and runaway slaves were to be returned to their masters

National Supremacy

An important part of the Constitution that separates it so fundamentally from the Articles of Confederation is the **supremacy clause**, which states that the Constitution and the laws of the United States are the law of the land and supreme to all other laws passed by state and local governments. By this assertion the Framers dealt with the overarching problem of the Articles. As long as a national law was made under authority granted in the Constitution, it superseded state law when the two came into conflict.

The Legislative Branch

Under the Articles, state legislatures had appointed delegates to Congress and the appointees were expected to vote as their states' legislatures wished. Delegates who violated their instructions could be recalled. This arrangement allowed state legislatures to exercise power in the national government. The new Constitution set fixed terms of office for members of Congress and provided that at least some members of Congress would be directly elected by the people. These provisions allowed national legislators to act independently of their states' legislatures.

The Framers also assigned the legislative branch responsibility for dealing with specific problems denied it under the Articles. Table 2.3 lists the **enumerated powers**, which consist of seventeen specific grants of power to Congress. This was the first time our national government granted power in this way. With the supremacy clause and the listing of the enumerated powers, the Framers were changing how the new nation was governed because they were granting supreme power to the national government but also clearly specifying, and thereby limiting, its power.

Under the Articles of Confederation, the national government did not have the power to levy taxes. Only the states had the power to tax. Thus, the first power they granted the new Congress dealt with the power to tax. Congress could "lay and collect taxes, duties, imposts and excises."

Supremacy Clause A clause in Article 6 of the Constitution stipulating that the Constitution and national laws are "supreme," meaning that when state laws are in conflict with national laws, the latter supersede and take precedence.

Enumerated Powers Powers of the federal government specifically stated in the Constitution.

TABLE 2.3 Enumerated Powers of Congress in Article 1, Section 8, of the Constitution

Congress has the following powers:
1. To collect taxes, duties, imposts, and excises
2. To provide for defense and general welfare
3. To borrow money
4. To regulate commerce with foreign nations, states, and Indian tribes
5. To establish naturalization and bankruptcy laws
6. To coin money and determine standards of weights and measures
7. To provide for punishment of securities and money counterfeiting
8. To establish post offices and post roads
9. To devise copyright and patent laws
10. To define and punish pirates and felonies committed on the high seas and crimes against the law of nations
11. To declare war
12. To raise and support armies
13. To provide and maintain a navy
14. To make rules for governing and regulating land and naval forces
15. To organize, arm, and discipline the militia
16. To exercise exclusive control of the seat of government of the United States
17. To make laws necessary to carry out the other sixteen powers

The Constitution grants Congress explicit powers to regulate the instruments of commerce. Such authority includes:

- The power to borrow money
- The power to regulate interstate and foreign commerce and trade with Indian tribes
- The power to establish bankruptcy laws, standards of weights and measures, post offices and post roads, and patent and copyright laws
- The power to coin money
- The power to punish counterfeiters and pirates

The Framers also gave Congress a set of powers of authority for a national military. Congress is explicitly empowered to declare war, to provide for and regulate an army and a navy, and to do the same for the militia.

The Framers could not anticipate every situation that might call for a response from national government. Rather than try to specify every power Congress might need, they added a clause dealing with **implied powers**—those powers exercised by the government that are not specifically mentioned in the Constitution. The first clause of Article 1, Section 8, of the Constitution states that Congress shall have the power "to make all Laws which shall be necessary and proper for carrying into execution the foregoing powers, and all other powers vested by this Constitution in the government of the United States, or in any Department or officer thereof."

Implied Powers Government powers that are inferred from the powers expressly enumerated in the Constitution.

This clause, known as the **necessary and proper clause**, gives Congress the authority to make whatever laws are necessary and proper to carry out its enumerated responsibilities. The clause is sometimes called the elastic clause because it allows the meaning of the Constitution to be stretched. It is the basis of the implied powers of the national government. For example, nowhere in the Constitution does it say that Congress should establish an internal revenue service. But Congress is empowered to collect taxes and, after the Sixteenth Amendment, to do so on the basis of income. Thus, the necessary and proper clause of the Constitution allows Congress to create an agency to execute its expressed power to tax. How the courts interpret the necessary and proper clause determines the scope of the national government's authority. In 1819, Chief Justice of the Supreme Court John Marshall articulated a broad interpretation of the word *necessary* in the context of the necessary and proper clause. In the landmark case of *McCulloch v. Maryland* (1819), Marshall ruled that the Bank of the United States was constitutional under the "necessary and proper clause" even though the bank was not imperative for Congress to carry out its enumerated powers.[26]

Necessary and Proper Clause A clause in Article 1 of the Constitution giving Congress the authority to make whatever laws are necessary and proper to carry out its enumerated responsibilities (sometimes called the elastic clause).

The Executive Branch

Under the Articles, there was only one branch of government, the legislative branch, that had no concrete power to execute any of the decisions it made. For example, if Congress asked the states to contribute troops to a national army and one state decided not to do so, who would enforce Congress's request? The Articles did not specify. The Framers addressed this problem by creating an executive branch of government. In so doing, they vested "the executive Power" in a president, elected indirectly by the voters, whose job, among other duties, was to "take Care that the Laws be faithfully executed."

The decision to have a president was a compromise. The Virginia Plan proposed a single executive, whereas the New Jersey Plan provided for a plural executive. The Founders decided on a single executive called a president, having already explicitly ruled out any possibility of the use of titles of nobility and having prohibited any person holding any office in the new nation from accepting, without the consent of Congress, any title or office from "any King, Prince or Foreign State."

The Judicial Branch

Just as there had been no executive under the Articles, there had been no judicial system. Laws passed by the national Congress were enforced in state courts by judges selected in the individual states. This arrangement led to a great deal of variation in how laws were enforced across states.

To resolve this issue, the Framers created a third branch of government. Article 3, Section 1, of the Constitution states that the judicial power of the United States is to be vested in "one Supreme Court and in such inferior courts as the Congress may from time to time ordain and establish." This article established a federal court system with the U.S. Supreme Court at the top of the system having final authority over all lower courts, and with Congress granted the power to create lower-level national courts.

Liberalized Amendment Rules

The requirement under the Articles that all states agree to an amendment gave each state a veto power over any change in government. Attaining unanimity on any nontrivial proposal was virtually impossible. Thus, the Framers relaxed the rules on formally amending the Constitution. Article 5 specifies that three-fourths of the states must ratify a proposed amendment to the Constitution before it can become law. By giving the power to block fundamental changes to a small minority of states rather than to any one state, the Framers made changing the Constitution difficult enough to ensure stable government, but not so difficult as to completely thwart improvement or modification.

Since the passage of the first ten amendments, the Constitution has been amended seventeen times. These amendments have dealt with a variety of issues. For instance, the Twelfth Amendment (ratified in 1804) established the mechanism for presidential elections, the Thirteenth Amendment (ratified in 1865) abolished slavery, the Nineteenth Amendment (ratified in 1920) granted voting rights to women, and the Twenty-Sixth Amendment (ratified in 1971) lowered the voting age to eighteen. Many of the amendments have extended constitutional protections to segments of the American population left out of the original Constitution. It has been estimated that more than 10,000 amendments to the Constitution have been proposed in Congress, many of them several times, since ratification in 1789.[27] (See Table 2.4 for a complete listing and description of the amendments.)

TABLE 2.4 Amendments to the Constitution

Amendment 1 (1791)
Freedom of religion, speech, the press, assembly, and petition

Amendment 2 (1791)
Right to bear arms

Amendment 3 (1791)
Right of a person not to have to house (quarter) soldiers without the person's consent

Amendment 4 (1791)
Right of a person to not be subject to unreasonable searches and seizures; no warrants without probable cause

Amendment 5 (1791)
Right to a grand jury for capital and infamous crimes, to avoid double jeopardy, against self-incrimination, to due process, and to compensation for public appropriation of private property

Amendment 6 (1791)
Right to a speedy and public trial, to a jury, to be informed of the nature of one's crime, to be confronted with the witnesses against one, to aid in obtaining witnesses, and to assistance of counsel

Amendment 7 (1791)
Right to a jury in common lawsuits if controversy exceeds $20 and the right not to have the facts of a jury trial reexamined by any court other than according to the rules of the common law

Amendment 8 (1791)
Right to be free of cruel or unusual punishment or excessive bail

Amendment 9 (1791)
Right to all fundamental rights in addition to those listed in first eight amendments

Amendment 10 (1791)
The powers not delegated to the federal government by the Constitution, or prohibited by it to the states, reserved for the states or the people

Amendment 11 (1798)
Limitation of jurisdiction of the federal judiciary: does not extend to suits brought by citizens of one state against another state or foreign citizens against a state within the United States

Amendment 12 (1804)
Electoral College and process of electing the president and vice president

Amendment 13 (1865)
Abolition of slavery

Amendment 14 (1868)
Definition of a citizen of the United States and right to due process of law and to equal protection; prevention of states from interfering in the rights of citizens
Representation in House according to all persons in each state
Loss of right to run for office if one has engaged in insurrection or rebellion
Public debt of the United States

Amendment 15 (1870)
Extension of the right to vote to Black males; no denial of this right based on "race, color, or previous condition of servitude"

Amendment 16 (1913)
Income tax

Amendment 17 (1913)
Popular election of senators

Amendment 18 (1919)
Prohibition

Amendment 19 (1920)
Women's suffrage

Amendment 20 (1933)
Beginning and end of the terms of president, vice president, and Congress
What transpires if president dies before inauguration, if no one gets enough votes to be president by time new term should begin, and if there is neither a president nor a vice president

Amendment 21 (1933)
Repeal of Prohibition

Amendment 22 (1951)
Term limits of presidency

Amendment 23 (1961)
Appointment of Washington, DC, electors to Electoral College

Amendment 24 (1964)
Right to vote without being subjected to a poll or any other tax

Amendment 25 (1967)
Succession and process for removal of the president

Amendment 26 (1971)
Right to vote lowered to eighteen years of age

Amendment 27 (1992)
Congressional compensation/renumeration

Planning for Potential Pitfalls

Just because the Framers thought the national government should be stronger than it was under the Articles of Confederation does not mean that they were in favor of a powerfully centralized government. In fact, the federal form of government they adopted attempted to balance powers evenly between the national and state governments rather than concentrate powers at any one level. The Framers went to extraordinary lengths to try to prevent any one part of government, any one group, or any one official from wielding too much power. The general rule seems to have been this: When in doubt, divide power.

Separating Powers

The possibility of an all-powerful chief executive, legislature, or judiciary that could exercise unlimited power was an essential concern of the Framers. To prevent such a possibility, they decided on a **separation of powers** among the branches of government. (See Chapter 1 discussion on classical republicanism, which advocated dispersing power among several branches of government.)

Separation of Powers
The manner in which the Constitution divides power among the three branches of government—the legislature, the executive, and the judiciary.

Varying Terms of Office

The Constitution sets the terms of office for members of each branch of the national government. Terms of office vary to prevent any one person from gathering unlimited power by being able to stay in office indefinitely. Members of the House of Representatives serve two-year terms, and all members of the House come up for reelection at the same time. Senators are elected for six-year terms, with one-third of the Senate up for reelection every two years. The president and vice president are elected for four-year terms, and, since the ratification of the Twenty-Second Amendment in 1951, no person can be elected more than twice or serve for more than ten years as president of the United States. Judges of national courts are the only officials who have unlimited terms once appointed and confirmed.

Selecting National Government Officials

Each national government official originally had, and largely continues to have, a different method of selection. Members of the House of Representatives are directly elected by the people. Under the original Constitution, U.S. senators were selected by the legislatures in their respective states. The Seventeenth Amendment, adopted in 1913, changed the method of selection so that U.S. senators are now directly elected by the people of the state in which they reside.

Passing the 13th Amendment

Although citizens vote for the president every four years, the United States does not have direct election of the president. The president is, in fact, officially selected by the **Electoral College**—a collection of individuals nominated by political parties who are pledged to support the party's candidate in the official presidential election. When voters go to the polls to vote for the president, they are actually voting for a set of electors, whose names, in some states, are listed beside the names of the presidential candidate from each political party.

Electoral College The entity that selects the president and vice president, consisting of 538 electors chosen from the fifty states and the District of Columbia.

The Electoral College consists of 538 electors; their number is equal to the total number of senators and House members from the fifty states plus three electors from the District of Columbia. Forty-eight states have a winner-take-all electoral vote distribution, and two states, Nebraska and Maine, have a system of proportional allocation of their electoral votes. A presidential candidate must receive a majority (270 votes) of the Electoral College votes to be elected. Although Americans usually know which candidate received the majority of the popular vote and Electoral College vote on election night, the president is not officially elected until December when the electors for the winning candidate travel to their respective state capitals to cast the official votes and certify the election. There have been three instances where the individual elected president won the Electoral College vote, but lost the national popular vote—in 1876 Democrat Samuel Tilden won the popular vote but lost the Electoral College vote to Republican Rutherford B. Hayes; in 1880 Democrat Grover Cleveland won the popular vote, but lost the electoral votes to Republican Benjamin Harrison; and in 2000, Democrat Al Gore won the national popular vote, but Republican George W. Bush won the Electoral College vote.

Members of the national judiciary are selected by the president, and their appointments must be approved by the Senate. The two-stage process is another aspect of separation of powers: One branch cannot act unilaterally to appoint individuals to lifetime appointments to the judiciary. The president may nominate judges, but the Senate must actually make the appointments by approving the nominations. Since 1789, of the 160 nominations to the U.S. Supreme Court, twelve were not confirmed by the Senate, eleven nominees withdrew, ten were not acted on by the Senate, and three nominees' hearings were postponed (*http://www.senate.gov/pagelayout/ reference/nominations/-Nominations.htm*).

Qualifying for National Office

The formal qualifications for holding a position in each branch of government differ. Even though these differences might appear small, they are worth noting because they highlight the view the Framers had of the qualities and maturity of the people that could hold office in each branch. Each representative must be at least twenty-five years old, hold U.S. citizenship for at least seven years, and be a resident of the state from which he or she is elected at the time of election. U.S. senators must be at least thirty years of age, have a minimum of nine years of citizenship, and reside in the state from which elected. The president must be a natural-born citizen, at least thirty-five years old, and a resident of the United States for no less than fourteen years. The Constitution prescribes no such age, citizenship, or residential requirements for judges in national courts.

U.S. Vice President Joe Biden (left) takes part in the count of the Electoral College votes for the 2016 presidential election as Speaker Paul Ryan (right) looks on during a joint session at the Capitol in Washington on January 6, 2017. Donald Trump was officially declared the winner of the 2016 presidential election after the counting session—a constitutionally mandated requirement.

Instituting Checks and Balances

In addition to the structural separations of powers, the Framers built a system of functional checks by which each branch can influence outcomes in one or both of the other branches. Congress has certain powers that it can use to check the power of both other branches of government. For example, Congress controls appropriations, "the power of the purse," and thus it determines how much money is available for officials in the other two branches to carry out their duties. Likewise, Congress can impeach, convict, and remove from office both executive and judicial officials. Yet within Congress, checks on its own powers are present. Both houses of Congress must pass legislation before it can become law, thereby providing for a check of one legislative body on the other.

The Supreme Court has the power to review acts of Congress and declare legislation unconstitutional, a power not contained in the Constitution but one that evolved through the process of judicial review. This authority of the Supreme Court means that Congress cannot pass legislation that violates the Constitution. The Court has a check on the authority of the president because the actions of a president can be brought before the Court through suit filed by Congress.

Both the executive and legislative branches have the power to check the judiciary. The president appoints federal judges and justices of the Supreme Court. Congress can then pass legislation or propose constitutional amendments that override Supreme Court decisions. In addition, Congress has the power to impeach federal judges and Supreme Court justices.

The president can veto legislation passed by Congress. This power ensures that legislation passed by Congress must clear an additional hurdle before it becomes law. Congress can override a presidential veto, but the vote required to override—two-thirds of each house—is much higher than the simple majority, or one more than half, required to pass legislation. The president is commander in chief of the armed forces, but only Congress has the power to declare war. The president negotiates treaties with foreign governments and nominates members for the cabinet and other governmental posts; the Senate must approve treaties and confirm the president's nominees.

Conclusion

The opening vignette about actress Roseanne Barr's racist tweet raised the tension between an individual's First Amendment free-speech right to write racist messages and ABC's decision to cancel her top-rated television show. This example is illustrative of how issues about race can become intertwined with constitutional rights and guarantees. Discussions about race and the role it would play in the founding of the new nation were front and center for the Founders and for many of the people who were excluded from the protections and guarantees provided in the governing document, the Constitution, that provides the framework for our system of government.

Check your understanding of Chapter 2.

review
REVIEW QUESTIONS

1. Why did the colonies decide to declare their independence from Britain?

2. What were the reasons the drafters of the Articles of Confederation chose the type of governmental structure that they did?

3. In what ways were the Framers of the Constitution not representative of the population of the United States?

4. What were the differences between the Virginia Plan and the New Jersey Plan? How were these differences reconciled?

5. What did the Three-Fifths Compromise say about the role of slaves in the new nation?

Need to review key ideas in greater depth? Click here.

terms
KEY TERMS

Antifederalists p. 43

Bicameral Legislature p. 40

Bill of Rights p. 45

Concurrent Powers p. 38

Confederation p. 35

Electoral College p. 51

Enumerated Powers p. 47

Federalists p. 43

Great Compromise (or Connecticut Compromise) p. 41

Implied Powers p. 48

National Government p. 38

Necessary and Proper Clause p. 48

New Jersey Plan p. 41

Separation of Powers p. 51

Supremacy Clause p. 47

The Federalist Papers, p. 43

Three-Fifths Compromise p. 42

Unicameral Form of Government p. 35

Unitary Form of Government p. 34

Virginia Plan p. 40

Flashcard review.

readings
ADDITIONAL READINGS

Greene, J. P. (1995). *Understanding the American Revolution: Issues and actors*. Charlottesville: University Press of Virginia.

> This book approaches the American Revolution by examining how the shape and nature of colonial politics and the backgrounds of specific individuals led to the American Revolution.

Frey, S. R. (1991). *Water from the rock: Black resistance in a revolutionary age*. Princeton, NJ: Princeton University Press.

> This book explores the role of slavery and slave resistance during the period of the American Revolution.

Wood, G. S. (1969). *The creation of the American republic*. Chapel Hill: University of North Carolina Press.

> This study focuses on the motives of the Founders and identifies social divisions as the source of opposition to or support for ratification of the Constitution.

Amar, A. R. (2006). *America's Constitution: A biography*. New York: Random House.

> This book examines not only what the Constitution says, but also why it says what it does.

Gordon-Reed, A. (1998). *Thomas Jefferson and Sally Hemings: An American controversy*. Charlottesville: University of Virginia Press.

> This book brings the complicated relationships between slaves and slaveholders to light with a focus on Thomas Jefferson and Sally Hemings.

CHAPTER 3

Federalism: Balancing Power, Balancing Rights

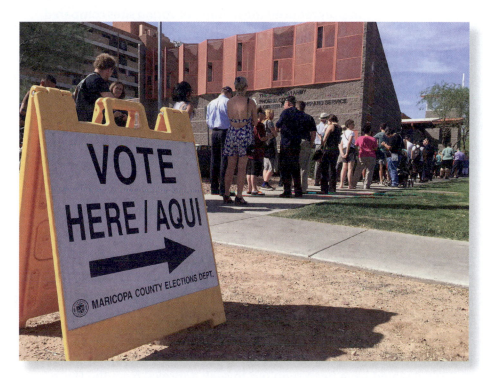

Hopeful voters wait in long lines at a polling place in downtown Phoenix to cast a vote in Arizona's presidential preference election on March 22, 2016. Initially, Maricopa County officials blamed the long lines on more Independents voting than expected, but they eventually conceded that severely slashing the number of polling sites caused the long waits.

O n March 22, 2016, the state of Arizona held its vote for the presidential primary, and although voting proceeded smoothly in most of the state, voters in Maricopa County—the largest county in the state because it contains the Greater Phoenix Metropolitan Area—waited in line for several hours, with many people denied the opportunity to vote. Initially county officials blamed the long lines on the fact that Independent voters were voting in the Democratic and Republican primaries, but they later conceded that the problem was that the county sharply reduced the number of voting sites compared to previous elections. In fact, the number of polling sites in Maricopa County dwindled from 400 in 2008 to 200 in 2012 to 60 in 2016. Maricopa County had 1.25 million eligible voters in 2016, which means that with 60 polling stations, the county provided one polling station for every 20,000 voters. The ratio was nowhere near as stark in other Arizona counties. Pima County, which contains the major city of Tucson, provided one polling station for every 1,200 voters. The rural counties of Navajo and Apache supplied one voting station for about every 1,000 eligible voters. Maricopa County officials justified the severe cutbacks on voting sites as a way to save money.[1]

Although these long lines inconvenienced all voters in Maricopa County, there is a race and ethnicity component to this story because Maricopa County is more than 30 percent Latino,[2] which means that Maricopa County's decision to cut polling places heavily influenced Latinos. In fact, had the county made this decision to cut voting sites prior to 2013, it would have been required to seek approval from the United States government—specifically the Department of Justice—because the *Voting Rights Act of 1965* required the state of Arizona to preclear any changes in voting procedures with the U.S. Department of Justice. Arizona was one of the states designated as having a history of discrimination, which means that its reduction of polling sites would have needed the approval of the federal government, and given the negative impact on Latino voters, it is unlikely that the Justice Department would have allowed the county to cut so many polling places. However, in 2013, the U.S. Supreme Court ruled that the section of the Voting Rights Act

Voting Rights Act of 1965
A federal law that has significantly curtailed disenfranchisement of racial and ethnic minorities by banning literacy tests, empowering the federal government to investigate voting discrimination based on race and ethnicity, and requiring federal supervision of jurisdictions with a history of voting discrimination (the U.S. Supreme Court has sharply limited the last provision).

identifying certain states as having a history of voting discrimination was unconstitutional,[3] which effectively ended the need for Arizona localities to preclear changes in voting procedures, such as closing polling places. Although, the U.S. Department of Justice did announce that it would investigate Maricopa County's actions based on its still intact authority under the Voting Rights Act to investigate any state or local government actions that limit racial and ethnic minorities' right to vote.[4] Interestingly, in the 2016 General Election, Maricopa County Recorder, the position in charge of elections in the county, Helen Purcell (R) lost to Democrat Adrian Fontes after Fontes raised concerns with the primary election problems. Fontes became the first Latino elected to a county-wide position in Maricopa County.[5]

intro

*In addition to describing how Maricopa County's action caused frustration for many voters, this story illustrates the importance of voting as an issue of federalism. **Federalism** refers to the balance of power between the national government and the state and local governments. Each level of government serves a distinct function and affects Americans' daily lives. Central to federalism is the concept of **sovereignty**, which means complete political power and authority. Therefore, the question of federalism concerns the extent to which the national government has sovereignty over the entire nation compared to the state and local governments' sovereignty over their respective regions.*

The issue of control over voting procedures is a prime example of federalism's significance. Specifically, the Constitution and national laws regulate voting to make it fairer, especially for racial and ethnic minorities; yet, states and local governments exercise tremendous discretion over voting procedures, such as where to place polling stations, voter identification requirements, and early voting rules. However, the U.S. Constitution, specifically the Fifteenth Amendment (ratified in 1870) gives the national government control over voting, and under the authority of this amendment Congress passed the Voting Rights Act in 1965 to ensure that racial and ethnic minorities would fully realize the right to vote. In other words, the national government exerted authority over the states to protect voting rights. However, in 2013, the U.S Supreme Court returned much of that power back to the states by effectively ending the preclearance requirement for certain jurisdictions.

The balance of power among the three levels of government, but especially between the national government on one hand and the state and local governments on the other, has been controversial throughout American political history. Recall from Chapter 2 that under the Articles of Confederation virtually all authority resided in the state and local governments, whereas the national government was extremely weak. The ratification of the Constitution, however, represented a major power shift in favor of the national government. Since then, federalism has evolved considerably.

Federalism The balance of power between the national government on one side and the state and local governments on the other side.

Sovereignty Complete political power and authority.

Moreover, as the story of Maricopa County's voting problems shows, the balance of power between the national government and the states significantly affects racial and ethnic minorities.

In this chapter, we examine the role of federalism in American government, paying special attention to how federalism affects racial and ethnic minorities. Before understanding the relationship among the levels of government, one must first understand the structures of and actors in state and local governments; therefore, we begin the chapter with an explanation of state and local governments. We then shift the discussion to federalism under the Constitution, which provides the framework for federalism. Finally, we turn our attention to the development and evolution of federalism over the course of American history.

Federalism and State and Local Governments

Compare federal and state authority.

Federalism concerns state and local governments, so it is important to understand how the state and local governments function. In many significant ways, state and local governments mirror the national government, although there is some variation. In this section, we cover the structure of state legislatures, governors, and courts, focusing on the similarities and differences among the states. We then examine the unique issues involving local government.

State and local governments make policies that affect their residents' daily lives, and so they also influence the politics of race and ethnicity. As a general, albeit not exclusive, rule the higher the concentration of racial and ethnic minority population in a state or local area, the greater the influence racial and ethnic minorities exert on their government. Moreover, the concentration of key minority groups (Blacks, Latinos, Asian Americans, and American Indians) varies throughout the United States. Figures 3.1, 3.2, 3.3, and 3.4 show the population concentrations of Blacks, Latinos, Asian Americans, and American Indians, respectively. We see that African Americans tend to be concentrated in the South and East, whereas Latinos are more concentrated in the Southwest. Asian Americans generally live on the West Coast, and American Indians are more scattered.

State Legislatures

Bicameral Legislature
A legislature with two bodies, usually referred to as the upper and lower chambers, or, as is most common in the United States, the House and the Senate.

Unicameral legislature
A legislature that consists of only one body (rather than two or more).

Similar to the U.S. Congress, state legislatures represent the citizens of the states and make laws governing the states. Forty-nine states have a **bicameral legislature**, which means there are two distinct houses of the legislature. The only exception is Nebraska, which has a **unicameral legislature**, or one-house, legislature. Despite this similarity in structure, state legislatures vary in terms of how frequently they meet. For example, in 2018, the state legislatures in Montana, Nevada, North Dakota, and Texas will not formally meet, and the legislature in New Mexico will formally meet for only one month. Conversely, the legislatures in Illinois, Massachusetts, Michigan, New Jersey, New York, Ohio, Pennsylvania, and Wisconsin will be in session throughout most of the year.[6]

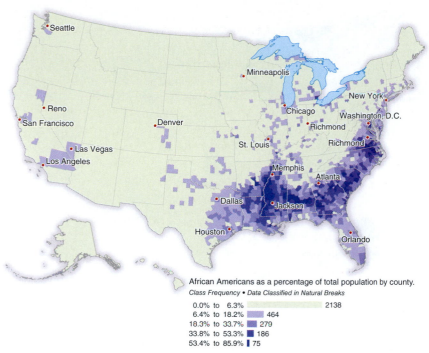

African Americans as a percentage of total population by county.
Class Frequency • Data Classified in Natural Breaks

0.0% to 6.3%		2138
6.4% to 18.2%		464
18.3% to 33.7%		279
33.8% to 53.3%		186
53.4% to 85.9%		75

Figure 3.1 African American Population as a Percentage of County Population: 2014

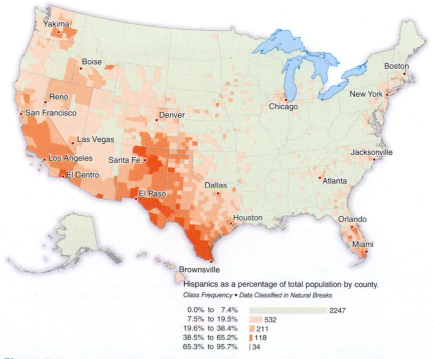

Hispanics as a percentage of total population by county.
Class Frequency • Data Classified in Natural Breaks

0.0% to 7.4%		2247
7.5% to 19.5%		532
19.6% to 38.4%		211
38.5% to 65.2%		118
65.3% to 95.7%		34

Figure 3.2 Latino Population as a Percentage of Total Population by County: 2014

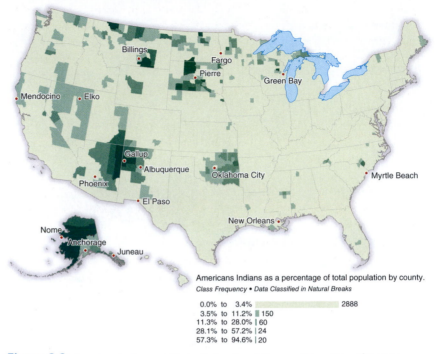

Americans Indians as a percentage of total population by county.
Class Frequency • Data Classified in Natural Breaks

0.0% to 3.4%		2888
3.5% to 11.2%		150
11.3% to 28.0%		60
28.1% to 57.2%		24
57.3% to 94.6%		20

Figure 3.3 American Indian and Alaska Native Population as a Percentage of County Population: 2014

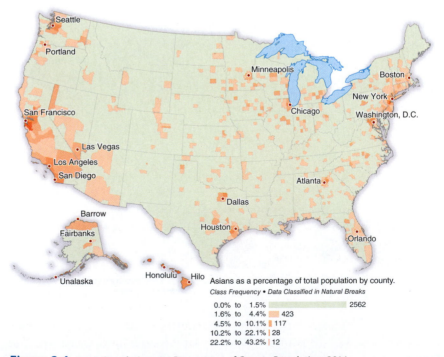

Asians as a percentage of total population by county.
Class Frequency • Data Classified in Natural Breaks

0.0% to 1.5%		2562
1.6% to 4.4%		423
4.5% to 10.1%		117
10.2% to 22.1%		28
22.2% to 43.2%		12

Figure 3.4 Asian Population as a Percentage of County Population: 2014

Given state legislatures' power to make policies within the state, representation is a key issue. After the census every ten years, each state government carves the state into districts representing distinct geographic regions, and each district sends representatives to the state legislature based on population. In most states, only one legislator represents each district, but in a few states, such as Washington, multiple legislators represent a single district. In 2018 West Virginia passed a law requiring the State House of Representatives to switch from multi-member districts to single-member districts after the 2020 Census.[7] Prior to the 1960s, state legislative districts had wild deviations in population within a state, with rural, unpopulated areas having the same number of representatives as heavily populated urban areas, many of which contained large minority populations. Thus, rural interests dominated state legislatures, and urban areas were underrepresented relative to their population. In 1964, the U.S. Supreme Court in *Reynolds v. Sims* ruled that within each state, the legislative districts must be roughly equal in population,[8] which resulted in fairer representation, but minorities remained concentrated in certain districts.

In most states, after each census, the political party that controls the state legislature or governorship redraws legislative districts in ways that maximize its chances of winning seats in the legislature and thus retaining its majority control. This process is known as **gerrymandering**, and we discuss it in more detail in Chapter 6.

Gerrymandering The practice in which a group, usually a political party, uses redistricting to maximize its chances of winning elections.

Gerrymandering can also affect racial and ethnic minorities. After the passage of the Voting Rights Act of 1965—see the opening story—more racial and ethnic minorities were able to vote; therefore, to diminish minorities' electoral power, many state governments, particularly although not exclusively in the South, gerrymandered districts in a way that divided minority populations among multiple districts. This practice had the effect of limiting the number of Blacks and Latinos elected to state legislatures because Whites rarely voted for minority candidates.

How does gerrymandering work?

To prevent states from drawing legislative districts that discriminated against minorities, the U.S. Congress amended the Voting Rights Act in 1982. Then, in 1986 the U.S. Supreme Court ruled that the amended Voting Rights Act prohibited districts that diminished minorities' ability to elect minority legislators, even if the state did not purposely intend to discriminate.[9] As a result of these developments, gerrymandering began in favor of minority interests. Since the 1990s, state legislatures have drawn more **majority-minority districts**, meaning districts in which more than half of the residents belong to a single minority group. With more majority-minority districts, the number of minority legislators, especially Blacks and Latinos, has increased dramatically (see "Measuring Equality: Black and Latino Representation in State Legislatures" on page 63).

Majority-Minority Districts Legislative districts that contain a population made up of more than 50 percent of a racial or ethnic minority group.

Governors

Just as state legislatures are in many ways similar to the U.S. Congress, state executives, known as governors, share similar responsibilities with respect to their states as the U.S. president has with respect to the country as a whole. Governors enforce laws made by the state legislatures, but they vary considerably in terms of their power.

Similar to the president, governors have the power to veto or reject laws passed by state legislatures, but many governors exercise more veto authority than the president enjoys. For example, most governors possess the power of a **line-item veto**, which means that they can reject specific expenditures and taxes, while allowing the remainder of a law to prevail. The line-item veto essentially gives governors the power to change legislation, not just to veto bills. The president of the United States lacks such line-item veto authority.[10]

Additionally, governors exert authority by appointing the leaders of the state agencies that administer laws, including agencies dealing with law enforcement, transportation, prison management, education (including public colleges and universities), financial regulation, and emergency management. By appointing the key agency leaders, governors influence policymaking in these areas. There is variation, however, across states in terms of which positions governors appoint and which are elected separately.

Given the power that governors wield, they can exert a tremendous influence on racial and ethnic minorities within the state, particularly in voting. The story of Maricopa County that we recounted at the beginning of the chapter is only one of numerous examples of voting problems in states and localities that disproportionately affect minorities. For example, during the 2012 election Floridians experienced long lines, which a recent study confirms affected racial and minority voters more than White voters.[11] One of the reasons for the long lines was the reduction of early voting days, in which the government opens poll sites for several weeks before the actual election day. Although Florida's state legislature passed the initial bill to reduce the number of early voting days, Republican Governor Rick Scott signed the legislation—he could have vetoed it. Furthermore, when local election officials petitioned the governor to extend early voting days because of anticipated Election Day turnout, the governor refused. Secretary of State Ken Detzner, an appointee of Governor Scott's, was responsible for certifying the state's official results. Detzner admitted to significant problems with the state's voting procedures and claimed that he would lead the investigation into the problems that occurred.[12] In early 2013, after initially denying the state's responsibility for the election problems, Governor Scott announced his preference for restoring early voting days and increasing the number of early voting sites.[13] In 2014, the state tried to purge ineligible voters, but reversed course after county election officials protested that doing so would mistakenly remove too many eligible minority voters.[14] Although there were isolated reports of individuals intimidating minority voters, Florida experiences far fewer long lines during the 2016 election.[15] Nevertheless, a recent study demonstrates that even though Black and Latino average wait times to vote decreased in 2016 compared to 2012, Blacks and Latinos still waited longer than Whites to vote in 2016–19 minutes for Blacks, 13 minutes for Latinos, and 10 minutes for Whites.[16]

Line-Item Veto Governors' power to reject specific expenditures and taxes, while allowing the remainder of a bill to stand.

measuring equality

Black and Latino Representation in State Legislatures

Black and Latino representation in state legislatures is important to ensure that policies reflect the interests of these groups. The Voting Rights Act and U.S. Supreme Court decisions resulted in state legislatures drawing majority-minority districts, which helped Blacks and Latinos increase their representation in state legislatures, particularly in states that have sizable Black and Latino populations.

Initially, minority representation can be understood as the percentage of each group in the legislature; however, that figure alone is not sufficient because it does not account for the size of the group's population in the state. For example, if Blacks constitute 15 percent of a state legislature, then one would assume that they are well represented, and in many states this figure would demonstrate high representation. However, if the state

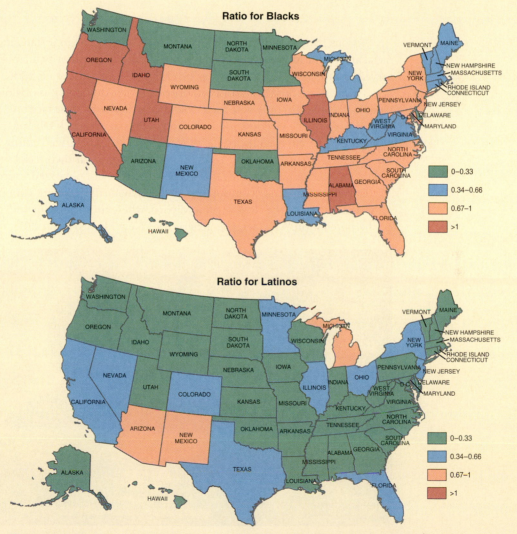

Figure 3.5 Ratio of Black and Latino Representation in State Legislatures Over Population

(Continued)

measuring equality *(Continued)*

is 25 percent Black, then the 15 percent figure would reflect underrepresentation. Therefore, it is useful to consider minority representation as a ratio of the percentage of the group in the state legislature divided by the percentage of the group in the population of the state. A ratio less than one indicates underrepresentation, and a ratio greater than one indicates overrepresentation.

The maps in Figure 3.5 show the ratio of the percentage of Blacks and Latinos in each state legislature over the percentage of Blacks and Latinos in each state.

States in green have a ratio between 0 and 0.33; states in blue have a ratio between 0.34 and 0.66; states in orange have a ratio between 0.67 and 1; and states in red have a ratio over 1.

When evaluating these maps, consider Figures 3.1 and 3.2, which show population concentrations of Blacks and Latinos. Can you see any patterns? Notice that African American ratios are higher than Latino ratios in most states. What are some possible reasons for this discrepancy?

Actions by governors influence the lives of all citizens in a state, including racial and ethnic minorities, and yet few racial and ethnic minority members have served as governors. Governors must be elected by the entire state, which makes it less likely that a racial or ethnic minority can win. Although it is obviously not true that people will only vote for a candidate who shares their race or ethnicity, as evidenced by the election and reelection of President Barack Obama, political science research has established the existence of racially polarized voting; that is, the general tendency of voters to vote for members of their own racial or ethnic group. Yet, there is also research that evidences the lack of polarized voting.[17]

Currently, no minority group constitutes a majority of a state's population, although Latinos come close in New Mexico, where they make up 48.5 percent of the population.[18] In fact, the governor of New Mexico from 2011 through

New Mexico Gov.-elect Michelle Lujan-Grisham waves to supporters following her acceptance speech in Albuquerque, N.M. Tuesday, Nov. 6, 2018. New Mexico has a large Latino population; therefore, it has elected several Latino governors. Lujan Grisham follows Susana Martinez, another Latina, but Lujan Grisham is a Democrat, whereas Martinez is a Republican.

2019, Susana Martinez, is the first Latina female governor in the United States, and in 2019 she was replaced by Michelle Lujan Grisham, who is also Latina. Table 3.1 provides the short list of current and former minority governors. Examine that table in light of the concentrations of Blacks, Latinos, and Asians (see Figures 3.1, 3.2, and 3.3).

State Courts

The third branch of state government is the state judiciary. Both national and state governments have judicial systems, but the bulk of cases that transpire in court on a daily basis, such as most criminal prosecutions and lawsuits for monetary damages, take place in state trial courts. Even most criminal cases that receive national and even international attention, such as the Bill Cosby rape trials, take place in state courts.

State courts are hierarchical systems with different levels ranked in order of authority. At the bottom rung are state trial courts, which decide criminal and civil cases, ranging from petty to major concerns. Juries determine the

TABLE 3.1 Current and Former Minority Governors

Name	State	Race/Ethnicity	Party	Term
Current				
David Ige	Hawaii	Japanese American	D	2014–present
Michelle Lujan Grisham	New Mexico	Mexican American	D	2019–present
Former				
Raul Castro	Arizona	Mexican American	D	1975–1977
Ben Cayetano	Hawaii	Filipino	D	1994–2002
Nikki Haley	South Carolina	South Asian	R	2011–2017
Gary Locke	Washington	Chinese American	D	1996–2005
Robert Martinez	Florida	Cuban American	R	1987–1991
Susana Martinez	New Mexico	Mexican American	R	2011–2019
Romulado Pacheco	California	Mexican American	R	1875
David Paterson	New York	African American	D	2008–2010
Deval Patrick	Massachusetts	African American	D	2007–2015
P.B.S. Pinchback	Louisiana	African American	R	1872–1873
Bill Richardson	New Mexico	Mexican American	D	2003–2011
Brian Sandoval	Nevada	Mexican American	R	2011–2019
John D. Waihe'e	Hawaii	Native Hawaiian	D	1986–1994
Douglas Wilder	Virginia	African American	D	1989–1993

Source: Data adapted from McClain, P. D., & Carew, J. D. J. (2018). "Can we all get along?": Racial and ethnic minorities in American politics (7th ed.). Boulder, CO: Westview Press, p. 183. Updated by the authors.

outcome of most of the more important cases, and the judge acts as a referee to ensure that the trial proceeds fairly. About forty states have intermediate appellate courts that hear appeals, which are reviews of the legal decisions made in lower court cases. All states also have a court of last resort, usually, but not always, called a state supreme court. These courts of last resort have the final say on appeals within their respective states.

Although juries play a key role in state judiciaries, judges are the most important actors in these institutions, and states vary considerably in how they select judges. Recall from Chapter 2 that federal judges are nominated by the president, confirmed by the Senate, and serve for a term of good behavior (i.e., they serve life terms as long as they are not removed from office after impeachment). However, states use a variety of methods for selecting their judges. For example, in Virginia the state legislature selects judges, whereas in two others—New Jersey and California (for appellate judges only)—the governor makes the decision. Many states hold elections, and in some of these states, such as Pennsylvania, Texas, and West Virginia, the judges run with political party labels, whereas in other states, such as Arkansas, Minnesota, and Washington, they run in nonpartisan elections. Since the twentieth century many states, including Alaska, Missouri, Utah, Vermont, and Wyoming, have employed the **merit system**, in which an unelected, nonpartisan commission provides a short list of potential judges to fill a vacancy. The governor (or in South Carolina the legislature) then must select one name from that list to serve a term as a judge. When the term ends in most merit selection states, the voters decide whether to keep the judge in a **retention election**; there is no opponent. If the voters decide to retain the judge, then he or she serves another term; if not, there is a vacancy and the process starts anew.[19]

Political scientists study whether the type of judicial selection system influences legal policy within a state. Many observers are concerned that elected judges act more as politicians than as judges; they worry more about pleasing the voters than serving the law. In fact, scholars have found that judicial elections are beginning to resemble elections for legislative and executive branch offices, with an increased amount of campaign spending, money raising (primarily from attorneys who might appear before the judges), and more negative advertisements. One expert notes that judicial elections have become "nastier, noisier, and costlier."[20] Another criticism of elected judiciaries is that judges will make decisions according to public opinion, instead of what the law requires. Empirical evidence shows that judges facing imminent election do alter their opinions to comport with voters' attitudes.[21] Despite these criticisms of judicial elections, however, some scholars defend elections, arguing that the critics' indictments are overblown and elections preserve accountability by allowing voters to remove unfit judges.[22]

Because state courts have the power to overturn laws that violate the state constitution, establish rules of criminal procedure, and set parameters governing civil suits, they are clearly important policymakers. Therefore, the number of minority state judges is a key issue in racial and ethnic politics. The U.S.

Merit System A system of selecting state judges in which a nonpartisan commission presents the governor with a short list of judicial candidates, out of which the governor selects one name; that judge later appears before the voters in a retention election.

Retention Election A type of judicial election in which voters decide only whether to keep the judge in office; there are no opposition candidates.

Supreme Court ruled in 1991 that the Voting Rights Act requires the drawing of majority-minority districts in judicial elections that occur in districts.[23] The empirical evidence on whether the type of selection system influences minority representation is mixed, however. One study showed that historically states with partisan election systems were among the first states to include a Black justice on the state court of last resort.[24] However, other studies demonstrate that the type of formal selection system does not affect minority representation in state courts.[25] Additionally, despite isolated instances of minority judges losing retention elections, such as Latino California Supreme Court Justice Cruz Reynoso in 1986, empirical evidence shows that race plays no role in retention voting.[26]

Local Governments

Federalism not only involves the relationship between the national government and state governments, it also entails the relationship between state and local governments. The Constitution does not explicitly mention local governments (except for Washington, DC). **Dillon's Rule**, articulated in an 1868 case by Judge John Dillon, stipulates that municipal governments may only draw power from what state governments grant them; they lack independent authority. Dillon's Rule dominated municipal governance until the twentieth century when more states began adopting **home rule** for their local governments to give them more autonomy in carrying out daily operations. The question of home rule is especially complex concerning the status of Washington, DC.

The Constitution created Washington, DC, to be the nation's capital and house the federal government, but it has now evolved into a vibrant city with almost 700,000 residents, 47.7 percent of whom are Black and 10.9 percent of whom are Latino.[27] The Washington, DC, metropolitan area is even larger, extending into southern Maryland and northern Virginia. In many respects, Washington, DC, is like all other major American cities, except for one key difference—it does not belong to a state. Instead, it is controlled by the U.S. Congress and president, although it does possess some home rule. As a result, there are often clashes between Congress and the residents of Washington, DC. For example, in 2015 Washington, DC, officially decriminalized personal possession of marijuana after residents overwhelmingly voted for this policy in 2014. However, Republicans in Congress oppose decriminalization; therefore, they have threatened to use their authority to undermine this policy. In fact, at the time two House members—Jason Chaffetz (R-UT) and Mark Meadows (R-NC)—threatened to imprison Washington, DC's African American mayor Muriel Bowser for defying Congress's authority.[28] Many residents of Washington, DC, are so resentful of living under congressional authority that they want the city to become a state, or at the very least send voting members to the U.S. House of Representatives and Senate, where they currently lack representation. However, at this point, they still remain under Congress's control. In Chapter 6, we discuss Washington, DC's lack of representation in more detail.

All states are divided into political units known as counties (Louisiana refers to them as parishes), and in most states counties have their own

Dillon's Rule A principle of local governance in which municipal governments lack independent authority; they can only draw power from their state governments.

Home Rule A principle of local governance in which local governments can govern themselves independently of the state governments.

County Commissions
Representative bodies that make policies that apply to the county.

Municipalities The incorporated districts, usually cities or towns, that comprise the local government.

School Districts Local government entities that create policies for public schools.

government (only Connecticut and Rhode Island do not).[29] Counties often refer to their governments as **county commissions**, which make policies that apply to the county. **Municipalities** are the incorporated districts—cities and towns—that exist within counties. County and municipal governments handle local issues, such as sewage treatment, waste management, snow removal, neighborhood maintenance, economic development, police and fire protection, and parks and recreation. In some states, county governments share these responsibilities with municipal governments, but in other states the tasks are separated. **School districts** are local government entities that create policies for public schools from kindergarten through high school.

Municipal governments, which are at the heart of local governments, consist of elected legislative bodies, usually known as city councils or city commissions, and executive figures, known as mayors. In some cities the council selects the mayor, but in other cities voters separately elect the mayor. Mayors' powers also vary tremendously across different localities. Some cities have mayors who are essentially figureheads, with no real power, while appointed city managers handle most of the executive functions. Conversely, in other cities mayors exert significant executive authority, similar to the U.S. president and many governors.

Given their vast powers, municipal governments are obviously influential in the daily lives of racial and ethnic minorities, especially in the areas of

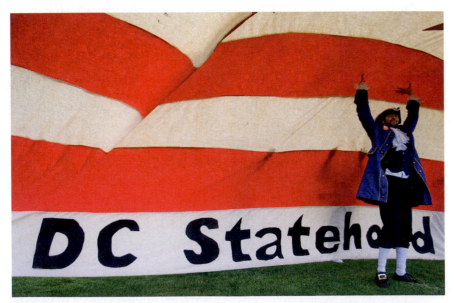

Nikolas Schiller of the DC Statehood Green Party helps fly a giant DC Statehood flag on the West Lawn of the Capitol following the DC voting rights march on Monday, April 16, 2007. Washington, DC, occupies a unique place in American federalism. Although almost 700,000 people, most of whom are racial or ethnic minorities, live in DC, the national government still controls some of the governance of the city, and DC voters have no representation in Congress. Many DC residents believe that DC should achieve full statehood, which would allow it to control its own sovereignty and enjoy representation in Congress.

law enforcement, neighborhood maintenance, and economic development. As a result, minority representation in municipal government is an important factor shaping how the governments affect minorities' lives. At one time, cities with large minority populations lived under White mayors, but since the 1970s, minority mayors have been far more common in cities with high minority populations and even in some cities with substantial White populations. Minority mayors have undoubtedly helped minorities in their cities, but the extent of their influence is a more contested, nuanced story.[30]

Federalism and the Constitution

As the architecture of American government, the Constitution sets the framework for the balance of power between the national and state and local governments. As discussed in Chapter 2, the U.S. Constitution was designed primarily to create a stronger national government in response to the weaknesses of the Articles of Confederation, which placed virtually all power with the states. Therefore, key parts of the Constitution expand the power of the national government, even as other sections protect state authority. In this section, we examine how national power expanded through both the Constitution and its amendments and also how the Constitution preserves state autonomy.

The Constitution and National Government Power

For the most part, Article I, Section 8, of the Constitution enumerates the powers of the national government. As discussed in Chapter 2, Article I, Section 8, powers are vast, giving the national government the power to tax, borrow on the credit of the United States, coin money, conduct foreign affairs, and maintain the armed forces to protect the security of the United States, among many others. Therefore, the national government often controls major issues that face the country, but in times of national disasters, federalism often requires national and state and local governments to work together. For example, after Hurricane Irma struck Florida in September 2017, President Donald Trump worked closely with Florida Republican Governor Rick Scott to address the aftermath of the major storm.[31] However, after Hurricane Maria struck the American Commonwealth of Puerto Rico a couple of weeks later, President Trump criticized San Juan Mayor Carmen Yulín Cruz, despite her heavy engagement in the recovery effort, because the mayor questioned the amount of help her city received from the federal government.[32]

One extremely significant enumerated power is the **commerce clause**, which gives the national government the authority to regulate commerce among the states, foreign nations, and Indian tribes. Under the Articles of Confederation the national government lacked the authority to regulate interstate commerce, which led to economic chaos during that period. The Framers understood that the nation is stronger with a national economy regulated by the national government. As we discuss later in this chapter, the commerce clause was instrumental in expanding national power in terms of economic regulation and also in areas of civil rights.

Commerce Clause A constitutional provision that gives the national government the authority to regulate commerce among the states, foreign nations, and Indian tribes; it has been used to expand the power of the national government.

As chief executives of their municipalities, mayors occupy exceedingly important positions in urban politics and within the American federal system. Pictured here are three significant minority mayors: Vi Lyles (Charlotte, NC), who is African American; Sam Liccardo (San Jose, CA), who is Latino; and Lily Mei (Fremont, CA), who is Asian American.

Necessary and Proper Clause
A clause in Article I of the Constitution giving Congress the authority to make whatever laws are necessary and proper to carry out its enumerated responsibilities (sometimes called the elastic clause).

Another crucial clause in Article I, Section 8, is the **necessary and proper clause** (or elastic clause), which gives the national government the authority to enact laws implied by the enumerated powers, as long as the laws are "necessary and proper" for carrying out one of the enumerated powers. The elastic clause provides the national government with the opportunity to expand its authority as long as it can show that the implied power is plausibly connected to an enumerated power.

Article I also grants Congress the authority to "establish uniform Rule of Naturalization," which has been significant for minority group politics because it gives the national government the power to set immigration and citizenship policy. Under this authority, Congress passed the Naturalization Act of 1790, which limited the possibility of citizenship only to free Whites.[33] Since then, Congress has passed numerous bills that have both restricted and expanded the ability of immigrants, especially racial and ethnic minorities, to become American citizens. In Chapter 5 we discuss in more detail how immigration policy affects racial and ethnic minorities.

The **supremacy clause**, Article VI, stipulates that the Constitution and national laws and treaties created under constitutional authority are "the supreme law of the land." The Constitution authorizes the national government to make laws and treaties and prevents state and local governments from enacting policies that contradict them. If there is a conflict between a state law and a constitutionally legitimate national one, then the national law supersedes the state law every time. For example, because the Constitution and national civil rights laws prohibit racial discrimination, states cannot validly enact laws that allow for such discrimination.

Article IV establishes national rules directing how states must relate to each other. The **extradition clause** (Article IV, Section 2, Clause 2) stipulates that if a person is charged with a crime in one state and flees to another state, then the second state must send the accused criminal back to the first state. The **full faith and credit clause** (Article IV, Section I) requires states to recognize official documents and records from other states. For example, a person with a driver's license issued in New York is allowed to drive in Wyoming.

The **privileges and immunities clause** prevents states from discriminating against citizens of other states. Therefore, if a citizen of North Carolina travels to South Carolina, then South Carolina cannot hold the North Carolinian to a different legal standard simply because he or she is from a different state. However, through their power to grant licenses in certain professions, states can prevent out-of-state residents, such as doctors and lawyers, from practicing their profession in the state. This power emanates from the fact that the nonresidents lack a license, not solely because they are from another state.

Finally, it is worth noting that prior to the end of slavery, Article IV also included the **fugitive slave clause**, which stipulated that if slaves escaped from a slave state to a free state, then they were not considered free. The free state was required to return the escaped slaves to their owners in the slave state.

Article I, Section 10, lists specific powers that the Constitution denies to states. Most notably, states are forbidden from entering into treaties with other nations and coining money. Furthermore, the **interstate compact clause** requires the approval of Congress when states enter into official agreements with one another, for instance to manage transportation facilities, waterways, and environmental concerns that transverse state lines.[34] Other provisions in this section protect individual liberties against state governments. States cannot pass a **bill of attainder**—a law that punishes specific people who have not first been convicted in a court. Moreover, states are forbidden from enacting **ex post facto laws**, which are criminal sanctions that apply retroactively

Supremacy Clause A clause in Article VI of the Constitution stipulating that the Constitution and national laws are supreme, meaning that when state laws conflict with national laws, national laws take precedence.

Extradition Clause A provision in the Constitution stipulating that if a person is charged with a crime in one state and flees to another state, then the second state must send the accused criminal back to the first state.

Full Faith and Credit Clause A constitutional provision requiring states to recognize official documents and records from other states.

Privileges and Immunities Clause A provision in Article IV of the Constitution that prevents states from discriminating against citizens of other states.

Fugitive Slave Clause A clause in the Constitution stipulating if slaves escaped from a slave state to a free state, the free state must return them to their owners in the slave state. The Thirteenth Amendment invalidated this clause.

Interstate Compact Clause A clause in Article I, Section 10, of the Constitution that requires the approval of Congress when states enter into official agreements with one another.

Bill of Attainder A law passed by a legislative body that punishes specific people without convicting them in a court.

Ex Post Facto Law A criminal sanction that applies retroactively and could result in governments charging people for acts committed before they were outlawed.

and could result in governments charging people for acts committed before they were outlawed.

Constitutional Amendments and National Power

The Constitution of 1787 bestows significant authority on the national government, and several amendments have further expanded the national government's power, especially in the area of civil rights. Prior to the Civil War, states determined the civil rights status of their residents. Many states, especially Southern and border states, relegated Blacks to the status of slaves, and even most states that banned slavery denied Blacks basic rights, such as voting, owning property, and serving on juries. A small number of states conferred civil rights on African Americans, but they did not always stop discrimination by private entities.[35]

After the end of the Civil War, however, three major constitutional amendments shifted the balance of power in favor of the national government to determine civil rights policies. The **Thirteenth Amendment** (1865) banned slavery throughout the United States; thus, states were no longer free to decide whether to allow slavery. The **Fourteenth Amendment** (1868) prevented states from denying on the basis of race full citizenship to their residents, and two clauses in this amendment are especially significant for setting national civil rights policy. The **due process clause** requires states to use normal judicial and criminal procedures before denying a citizen the right to life, liberty, or property. The **equal protection clause** prevents states from passing laws that treat citizens differently on the basis of race. Finally, the **Fifteenth Amendment** (1870) prevents states from denying citizens the right to vote because of their race or ethnicity. Of course, as we discuss later in this chapter and in Chapter 5, states circumvented the requirements of these amendments until the middle of the twentieth century.

During the twentieth century, three constitutional amendments expanded national authority over states concerning the question of voter eligibility. The **Nineteenth Amendment** prevents states from denying women the right to vote because of their sex. The Twenty-Fourth Amendment ends the practice of **poll taxes**, which were fees that states charged citizens as a condition of being able to vote. Because many racial and ethnic minorities tended to be poorer than Whites, poll taxes disproportionately hurt racial and ethnic minority voters. Finally, the Twenty-Sixth Amendment set a nationwide voting eligibility age of eighteen. Prior to the ratification of the amendment, many states had set voting eligibility at twenty-one years old.

The Constitution and State Power

Although much of the Constitution expands national power, some provisions preserve state authority. Whereas the national government is restricted solely to powers enumerated in the Constitution or implied by those enumerated powers, state governments enjoy much broader **police powers**—general and unwritten powers to regulate health, safety, and morals. This principle is enshrined in the **Tenth Amendment**, which is part of the Bill of Rights.

Thirteenth Amendment An amendment to the Constitution that prohibits slavery throughout the United States.

Fourteenth Amendment An amendment to the Constitution that prevents states from denying on the basis of race full citizenship to their residents.

Due Process Clause A specific provision of the Fourteenth Amendment that requires states to use normal judicial and criminal procedures before denying a citizen life, liberty, or property.

Equal Protection Clause A specific provision of the Fourteenth Amendment that prevents states from passing laws that treat people differently on account of race or ethnicity.

Fifteenth Amendment An amendment to the Constitution that prevents states from denying the right to vote on the basis of race or ethnicity.

Nineteenth Amendment An amendment to the Constitution that prevents states from denying women the right to vote because of their sex.

Poll Taxes Fees that states charged citizens to vote and that disenfranchised the poor and minority citizens.

Police Power A general, unwritten power to regulate health, safety, and morals.

Tenth Amendment An amendment to the Constitution that guarantees states powers not given to the national government or forbidden to the states.

Specifically, the Tenth Amendment provides that "the powers not delegated to the United States by the Constitution, nor prohibited by it to the States, are re-served to the States respectively, or to the people." In other words, the amend-ment stipulates that the states are the default possessors of power; powers belong to the states unless the Constitution expressly grants them to the na-tional government or expressly denies them to the states.

Although the Tenth Amendment is the most important constitutional guardian of state power, other aspects of the Constitution preserve state au-thority as well. The Eleventh Amendment prevents citizens of one state (or for-eigners) from suing another state in federal court, unless the state consents. Furthermore, the nature of representation in the national government en-hances state authority. Article I establishes that each state, regardless of popula-tion, sends two senators to the U.S. Senate; therefore, the U.S. Senate represents states more than it represents people. For example, Wyoming, which as of 2017 has a population of only 579,315, enjoys the same representation in the Senate as California, which as of 2017 has 39,536,653 people.[36] Similarly, the Elec-toral College selects the president based on results in individual states, which elevates the importance of states in presidential selection (see Chapter 7).

The Evolution of American Federalism

Although the Constitution establishes the balance of power between states and the national government, federalism is not a static concept; it has changed con-siderably over the course of American history. Depending on the dominant ide-ology in the government and varying economic and social concerns, different versions of federalism have emerged as power has shifted between the national government and the states. As we explain this evolution of federalism and the de-bates that surround it, we emphasize Congressional legislation and U.S. Supreme Court decisions that have been instrumental. In addition, we look at how the changing dynamics of federalism have influenced racial and ethnic minorities.

Federalism in the Early Republic and Industrialization

After the ratification of the Constitution, the United States faced a choice be-tween adopting an agricultural economy dominated by local farms and in-terests or an industrial economy promoted by the national government. By the 1790s, the national government embraced industrialization and promoted industrial manufacturing. To accomplish these goals, the U.S. government sought major improvements in roads, railroads, and canals to transport raw materials to manufacturing facilities and the finished products to consumers. These massive projects extended across state lines and thus required a tremen-dous amount of funding, which the national government raised through pri-vate banks and through its power to borrow money, tax, and spend.

McCulloch v. Maryland. To facilitate these financial goals, in 1791 Congress chartered the Bank of the United States, also known as the "national bank." As noted federalism scholar Daniel Elazar observed, the bank "served as the fiscal and banking arm of the federal government and manager of the federal deposits."[37] Given this scope, the bank was able to control a considerable amount of economic activity in the United States. Some political leaders, notably Thomas Jefferson and James Madison, opposed the national bank and argued that the national government lacked the constitutional authority to establish a bank. However, supporters, led by Treasury Secretary Alexander Hamilton, disagreed with that claim, maintaining that the national bank was constitutional and important to achieving economic success. Although the bank charter expired in 1811, it was revived in 1817, which regenerated the controversy.[38]

As a means of opposing the re-chartered Bank of the United States, the Maryland legislature voted to tax the branch of the United States Bank located in Baltimore. When the bank cashier refused to pay the tax, the controversy went to the U.S. Supreme Court. In the 1819 U.S. Supreme Court case *McCulloch v. Maryland*, Chief Justice John Marshall upheld the bank and overruled the tax. Marshall, a fervent nationalist, argued that even though the Constitution does not explicitly grant Congress the power to establish a bank, the bank is a "necessary and proper" way for the national government to carry out its explicit powers to tax, spend, borrow money, and regulate commerce.[39] In addition to upholding the bank, this case established a loose interpretation of the word *necessary* in the necessary and proper clause, so that the **implied power** need only facilitate the execution of an enumerated power, rather than being required for it. Marshall's broad interpretation of *necessary* still stands today and has allowed the national government to expand its power in other areas.[40]

Implied Power Government powers that are inferred from the powers expressly enumerated in the Constitution.

Gibbons v. Ogden. The Marshall Court expanded the power of the national government in other areas as well. In the 1824 *Gibbons v. Ogden* decision, the Supreme Court instituted a broad definition of the commerce clause. The case arose from a conflict between two companies competing for shipping business in the waterways between New York and New Jersey. One company, owned by Aaron Ogden, possessed exclusive rights granted by the national government to the entire area between the two states, whereas the other company, owned by Thomas Gibbons, possessed exclusive rights granted by the state of New York to New York's waterways.

When this dispute arrived at the Supreme Court, Chief Justice John Marshall ruled that the national government controls all stages of commerce that extend across state lines. As a result, even when the instrument of commerce occurs within a state's border at a particular time, the national government retains authority as long as the goods or services extend into another state. Moreover, the Court ruled that commerce is not restricted to the mere trading of goods and services; it also includes navigation across state lines.[41] This case established a precedent of broadly interpreting the commerce clause.[42]

Civil Rights Issues. Despite this expansion of national authority in the service of industrialization and economic growth, states still retained authority when it came to questions about slavery and civil rights for Blacks and American Indians.

When the national government set civil rights policy, it was generally concerned with preserving slavery. In 1793, Congress passed the Fugitive Slave Act, which established the process for capturing and returning slaves who escaped to free states—recall that Article IV of the Constitution protected slave owners' ability to secure their escaped slaves' return. When Pennsylvania, a free state, enacted laws forbidding the return of slaves who escaped to Pennsylvania, the Supreme Court overturned that policy as a violation of Article IV and the Fugitive Slave Act.[43]

The Supreme Court expanded state control over civil rights in the 1857 *Dred Scott v. Sandford* case. This case concerned a slave who had lived in free territory and returned to the slave state of Missouri, where he sued for his freedom. By this time Chief Justice Roger Taney had replaced John Marshall, and Taney did not share Marshall's enthusiasm for the supremacy of national authority. In Chapter 5 we discuss in more detail the renowned civil rights impact of Chief Justice Taney's decision in *Dred Scott*, but Taney's opinion also had bearing on federalism because he declared the Missouri Compromise to be unconstitutional. The Missouri Compromise was a federal law that determined which American territories could allow slavery and which ones could not. Taney ruled that Congress lacked the authority to regulate slavery in the territories; therefore, territories could determine basic civil rights questions for themselves.[44]

Latinos and American Indians also felt federalism's effects. For example, the Treaty of Guadalupe Hidalgo, which settled the Mexican-American War in 1848, granted citizenship to the conquered Mexicans who elected to stay in the newly annexed portions of the United States. However, western states, most notably California, still mistreated Mexican Americans, even taking their property.[45] With respect to American Indians, the Constitution suggests that Indian tribes are separate entities, and the commerce clause includes the national government's power to regulate commerce with them. However, during the early American Republic the national and state governments subjugated Indians by removing them from their tribal lands and in many cases committing genocide against them. See "Our Voices: John Marshall and the Status of Indian Tribes" on page 77 for excerpts from two early 1830s U.S. Supreme Court cases that articulate the status of Indian Tribes in our federal system.

Dual Federalism and the Ascendency of State Autonomy

Although the Civil War represented a victory for national unity over state autonomy, the period after the Civil War is best characterized as one in which state governments enjoyed increased independence from the national government. The type of federalism that dominated during the late nineteenth and early twentieth centuries is known as **dual federalism**, in which state governments and the national government ruled only in their own spheres. Federalism scholar Martin Grodzins referred to dual federalism as "layer cake federalism" because of the clear lines between national and state government authority.[46] The national government was limited to a strict interpretation of the powers granted in the Constitution, and states enjoyed broad police powers to rule within their own territory.[47] Accordingly, states were able to decide for

Dual Federalism A view of federalism in which the national government is limited to a strict interpretation of the powers granted in the Constitution, while states enjoy broad police power to rule within their own territory.

themselves policies concerning economic regulation and civil rights—an idea often referred to as "states' rights."

Monopolies. After the Civil War, a primary economic issue concerned regulating against the excesses of the industrialized economy, including the development of **monopolies**, which exist when one company controls an entire industry. With one dominant company, there is no competition, and without competition workers and consumers suffer. Other economic problems concerned exploiting labor by making workers toil long hours in unsafe and uncomfortable conditions for little pay. Industrial corporations frequently employed children in these positions. Although state governments and the national government allowed many of these economic problems to persist, by the late nineteenth century and early twentieth century the national government attempted to regulate the most severe excesses. However, the U.S. Supreme Court, which was dominated by justices who advocated states' rights, significantly curtailed the national government's authority to regulate the economy.

> **Monopoly** A situation in which one company controls an entire industry.

To address the problem of monopolies, Congress passed the Sherman Antitrust Act of 1890, which gave the national government the authority to break up monopolies into different companies. The national government based its power on the commerce clause, under the view that monopolies are vast, interstate entities that affect the national economy. However, in the 1895 *United States v. E.C. Knight Company* case the Supreme Court limited the national government's authority. In this case, the U.S. government wanted to prevent one company from owning 98 percent of sugar refining in the nation. The Supreme Court ruled, however, that sugar production was manufacturing, which is distinct from commerce, and that the Tenth Amendment gave states the sole authority to regulate monopolies in the manufacturing sector.[48] The Court's creation of this distinction between manufacturing and commerce and its reading of the Tenth Amendment limited the national government's authority to regulate most monopolies.

Child Labor. The Supreme Court also used this commerce versus manufacturing distinction to prevent the national government from addressing the problem of child labor. Many companies exploited poor children by paying them low wages for long hours and dangerous work. The Keating-Owen Child Labor Act of 1916 forbade the interstate shipment of any good that was produced with child labor. The 1918 case of *Hammer v. Dagenhart* overturned this law, however, because a narrow majority of the justices held that it regulated child labor at the manufacturing stage, not the commerce stage; accordingly, the national government lacked the authority to issue regulations under the commerce clause. The Tenth Amendment gave states sole authority to regulate child labor,[49] but few states enacted meaningful regulations, and child labor persisted throughout the early twentieth century.

Grants-in-Aid. Despite these restraints, the national government exerted some limited authority. For example, in the 1860s the national government

our voices

John Marshall and the Status of Indian Tribes

Prior to the ratification of the Constitution in 1787, Indian tribes were considered foreign nations that could individually enter into treaties with colonial governments and states under the Articles of Confederation. The Constitution gave the national government the authority to engage with different tribes, and the Indian Commerce Clause gives the national government the authority to regulate commerce with Indian tribes; however, state governments also sought to exert authority over the tribes located within their borders.

Indians were initially highly independent in their relations with the American government, but the tradition of exclusion dominating American politics during the early nineteenth century produced policies that usurped tribal lands and even led to genocide in many cases. In the early 1830s, the U.S. Supreme Court, particularly Chief Justice John Marshall, settled disputes over the status of Indians in the American federal system. Although Marshall was an ardent nationalist, when it came to the status of Indian tribes his view was more nuanced.

Cherokee Nation v. Georgia, 30 U.S. 1 (1831)

After the state of Georgia sought to seize the Cherokee land within its borders, the Cherokee Nation challenged these actions as a violation of treaties in which the U.S. government formally recognized Cherokee lands as belonging to the tribe. The supremacy clause places the provisions of national treaties over state laws; therefore, the Cherokee petitioned the Court to overturn Georgia's policy. The outcome of this case depended on the status of Indian tribes in the American federal system. If Cherokee were analogous to an independent nation, then they had grounds to seek recompense in federal court. However, if the Cherokee lacked the status of an independent nation, then they could not use the federal judiciary to secure their rights. In patronizing language, Chief Justice Marshall ruled that Indian tribes were not similar to independent nations and that the Indian tribes were subordinate to American government. Marshall wrote:

> Though the Indians are acknowledged to have an unquestionable, and heretofore, unquestioned right to the lands they occupy, until that right should be extinguished by a voluntary cession to our government, yet it may well be doubted whether those tribes which reside within those acknowledged boundaries of the United States can, with strict accuracy, be denominated foreign nations. They may, more correctly, perhaps, be denominated domestic dependent nations. They occupy a territory to which we assert a title independent of their will, which must take effect in point of possession when their right of possession ceases. Meanwhile they are in a state of pupillage. Their relation to the United States resembles that of a ward to his guardian.

> They look to our government for protection; rely upon its kindness and its power; appeal to it for the relief of their wants; and address their President as their Great Father. They and their country are considered by foreign nations, as well as by ourselves, as being so completely under the sovereignty and dominion of the United States that any attempt to acquire their lands, or to form a political connection to them, would be considered by all as an invasion of our territory and an act of hostility.

Worcester v. Georgia, 31 U.S. 515 (1832)

The following year, the Supreme Court decided the case of *Worcester v. Georgia*, which involved Samuel Worcester, a northern White missionary who lived with the Cherokee and supported their struggle against oppression. In response to Worcester's influence with the Cherokee, the state of Georgia enacted a law that banned Whites from living in Cherokee areas unless they secured a license from the state. Worcester was arrested for violating this law and sentenced to four years in prison. He appealed his conviction, arguing that the Constitution, treaties between the U.S. Government and Cherokee, and federal statutes determine who is allowed to reside in Indian tribal lands; therefore, state governments lack the authority to proscribe who could live in Cherokee territory. This time, Chief Justice Marshall sided in favor of tribal authority, ruling that Indian tribes are independent entities that can control their own territory. In this opinion, Marshall more readily accepts the notion that Indian tribes exert sovereignty over their own affairs, and are in

(Continued)

our voices *(Continued)*

many ways equal to other nations, particularly in their dealings with the national government. He wrote:

> The Indian nations had always been considered as distinct, independent political communities, retaining their original natural rights as the undisputed possessors of the soil from time immemorial, with the single exception of that imposed by irresistible power, which excluded them from intercourse with any other European potentate than the first discoverer of the coast of a particular region claimed: and this was a restriction which those European potentates imposed on themselves, as well as on the Indians. The very term "nation," so generally applied to them, means "a people distinct from others." The Constitution, by declaring treaties already made, as well as those to be made, as supreme law of the land, has adopted and sanctioned the previous treaties with the Indian nations, and consequently admits

their rank among those powers who are capable of making treaties. The words "treaty" and "nation" are words of our own language, selected in our diplomatic and legislative proceedings, by ourselves, having each a definite and well understood meaning. We have applied them to Indians, as we have applied them to other nations of the earth. They are applied to all in the same sense.

- Why do you think Justice Marshall ruled so differently in these two cases?
- How has the national government's regard for the status of American Indians changed since the time of these rulings?

Sources: Adapted from *Cherokee Nation v. Georgia*, 30 U.S. 1, 17–18 (1831) and *Worcester v. Georgia*, 31 U.S. 515, 559–560 (1832). See also Sundquist, M. L. (2010–2011). *Worcester v. Georgia*: A breakdown in the separation of powers. *American Indian Law Review, 35*, 239–255.

---

sought to improve education and research in agriculture, mining, and engineering to expand technology and economic growth. It lacked the power, though, even under the commerce clause, to charter national universities or compel states to shift their universities' missions toward these technological fields. To address this problem, Congress passed the Morrill Land Grant Act of 1862, in which the national government donated federally owned property to the states, conditioned on the states establishing agricultural, mining, or technological universities on that property. This law was an early example of a **grant-in-aid**—the national government providing money or property to the states to accomplish a policy goal. In the Second Morrill Land Grant Act, which was passed in 1890, the national government donated property to create technological universities for African Americans because many states denied them admission to their public universities. This law established historically Black colleges and universities (HBCUs), which helped educate millions of African Americans during the height of segregation—and still do today.[50]

Grants-in-Aid National government expenditures that provide money or property to the states to accomplish a policy goal.

Civil Rights Issues. In addition to controlling economic policy, states continued to determine civil rights policies during the late nineteenth and early twentieth centuries. Recall that the Thirteenth, Fourteenth, and Fifteenth Amendments expanded national authority to regulate civil rights policy; however, by the late nineteenth century it became clear that the U.S. Supreme Court's interpretation of the Fourteenth and Fifteenth Amendments allowed states to deny rights and treat people differently because of race. Southern states required that Blacks and Whites be separated in all public facilities, including schools. In *Plessy v. Ferguson* (1896), the U.S. Supreme Court established the legal principle of **separate but equal**, which meant that under the Fourteenth Amendment equal protection clause the states could segregate by race, as long as they provided facilities for both races.[51] Aside from the fact that separate but equal allowed dominant White elites to separate themselves from Blacks in the South and Mexican Americans in the Southwest, the reality is that the facilities were nowhere near equal. For example, White schools in the South received far more funds and had much better facilities compared to Black schools.

Despite the Fifteenth Amendment ban on racial discrimination in voting, states enacted passing literacy tests as a condition for registering to vote. Although literacy tests appear to be race-neutral, they were administered in a way that allowed Whites to pass and Blacks to fail. Recall, as well, that during this period states were allowed to levy poll taxes, which disproportionately affected African Americans. Finally, the U.S. Supreme Court invalidated the national government's ability to prosecute state officials who denied Blacks the

Graduates are pictured at Florida A&M University, which is a historically Black college and university. In the late nineteenth century, the national government provided states with the land to establish universities designed to educate African Americans, who were explicitly denied admission to White state schools in Southern and border states. The creation of HBCUs is an example of the national government using its funding power to influence public policy.

right to vote[52] and to prosecute violent terrorist organizations, such as the Ku Klux Klan, for intimidating Blacks attempting to vote.[53] With these restraints on the national government, it was left to the states to decide whether to prosecute individuals who prevented Blacks from voting, and Southern states and many Northern states refused to do so. In short, during the late nineteenth and early twentieth century, the Fifteenth Amendment provided no real limitations on states' abilities to disenfranchise people on account of race.

Separate but Equal A legal principle that allowed states to segregate the races in public facilities, as long as the state provided each race with basic access to the public facility in question.

Cooperative Federalism and the Growth of the National Government

The period of dual federalism ended in the 1930s when the national government successfully exerted control over the national economy and ushered in a new period known as **cooperative federalism**. Unlike dual federalism, in which there were clear distinctions between state and national authority, cooperative federalism entailed greater shared powers between the national and state governments, and as a result the national government increased its authority. Federalism scholar Martin Grodzins referred to cooperative federalism as "marble cake federalism" because the distinctions between national

Cooperative Federalism A view of federalism in which the national government expands its power and blurs the lines between national and state authority.

and state authority were blurred rather than reflecting separate spheres as in dual federalism.[54]

Incorporation. Since the 1930s, one way the national government's authority has increased relative to the states is through the process of **incorporation**—the application of the Bill of Rights (see Chapter 2) to state and local governments. Before the twentieth century the Supreme Court repeatedly held that the Bill of Rights was intended to apply only to the national government and not the states; therefore, states were free to enact policies that violated the liberties contained in the Bill of Rights, such as freedom of speech, freedom of religion, freedom from warrantless searches, and trial by jury. However, in *Palko v. Connecticut* (1937), the Court announced the principle of selective incorporation, which stipulates that the most important provisions of the Bill of Rights apply to the states as well.[55] Since 1937 virtually all of the provisions in the Bill of Rights have been considered essential and thus incorporated. States are no longer able to deny their residents basic liberties. We discuss incorporation in more detail in Chapter 4.

Incorporation The application of the Bill of Rights to state and local governments.

Economic Regulation. Another way in which the national government has increased its authority relative to the states was in the area of economic regulation. The impetus behind this change in federalism was the Great Depression and President Franklin Roosevelt's New Deal. During the Great Depression, which began in 1929, the economy stagnated, unemployment skyrocketed, financial institutions failed, the agricultural industry declined, and the country experienced a host of other economic and social problems. To combat these economic troubles, the New Deal, which President Roosevelt proposed when he entered office in 1933, consisted of national policies that took unprecedented control over the economy by creating work for the unemployed, regulating banks and the stock market, controlling agricultural production, and protecting labor unions. During President Roosevelt's first term, however, the U.S. Supreme Court overturned New Deal programs, arguing that they exceeded the national government's authority to regulate commerce, again relying on the distinction between manufacturing and commerce as well as the Court's belief that the Tenth Amendment gave states sole authority to regulate the economy.[56]

In 1937, however, Supreme Court Justice Owen Roberts, who voted to overturn New Deal legislation in the past, changed his view and voted to uphold economic regulation. The landmark case *National Labor Relations Board v. Jones & Laughlin Steel Company* concerned the constitutionality of the Wagner Act, which protected workers' rights to unionize. The Court ruled that even though Jones & Laughlin engaged in manufacturing, its vast steel enterprise was interstate and commercial in scope.[57] In 1941, after President Roosevelt replaced anti–New Deal justices, who had retired or died, with New Deal supporters, the Supreme Court unanimously rejected the distinction between commerce and manufacturing, giving the national government the authority to regulate the economy.[58]

Moreover, in the 1942 *Wickard v. Filburn* case, the Supreme Court upheld an even more expansive view of the national government's commerce power.

Under the principle of "separate but equal" the U.S. Supreme Court allowed states to segregate their facilities, including public schools, as long as they provided facilities for both races. They enacted these policies despite the Fourteenth Amendment to the Constitution, which requires that states treat Blacks and Whites equally. As these photos demonstrate, however, the facilities were not remotely equal. The White schoolchildren are in comfortable, spacious facilities, whereas the Black schoolchildren are in substandard, crowded conditions. In 1954 the U.S. Supreme Court overturned the "separate but equal" principle.

This case concerned the Agricultural Adjustment Act of 1938, which sought to stabilize farm prices by setting quotas limiting individual farmers' crop production. Roscoe Filburn was fined under this act because he exceeded his allotted wheat quota, but he claimed that because he used the excess wheat to feed his own livestock, his activity was not interstate and was thus outside the scope of national regulation. The Supreme Court disagreed and unanimously upheld the fine against Filburn, arguing that even if the activity was confined within Filburn's Ohio farm, it still had a "substantial effect" on interstate commerce.[59] Accordingly, the national government could now regulate any economic endeavor, as long as it could show a substantial effect on interstate commerce.

During the 1960s, President Lyndon Johnson's Great Society Program and "War on Poverty" further increased the power of the national government. Johnson sought to combat poverty through government programs designed to improve education, housing, transportation, and health care for the poor. However, the national government lacks the constitutional authority to simply mandate programs to improve the welfare of the poor. Instead, the national government employed **categorical grants**, which are grants-in-aid that contain numerous, detailed provisions on how the states and local governments must use the money. For example, in the Medicaid program the national government gives money to the states with strict regulations dealing with how health care coverage should be provided to poor people, although states enjoy some discretion on how to run their programs.[60] Another example of a categorical grant is Head Start, which was established in the 1960s to provide states with money to create early childhood education programs for poor children. By accepting the money of categorical grants, states agree to numerous requirements dictated by the national government.[61]

The national government has also expanded its power through the use of **unfunded mandates**—directives the national government issues to state and local governments without compensating them for complying. For example, environmental legislation, such as the Clean Air Act (passed in 1970) and the Clean Water Act (passed in 1972), require state and local governments to limit pollution in the air and water, but the states and localities are largely responsible for paying the cost of the environmental cleanup that these laws require.[62] Additionally, in 1974 Congress required states and local governments to pay their employees minimum wage and extra compensation for overtime. In 1976, the U.S. Supreme Court ruled that this unfunded mandate violated states' Tenth Amendment rights,[63] but in 1985 the Court reversed itself and upheld this mandate.[64] Although unfunded mandates have accomplished important policy goals, they place considerable financial burden on states and localities; accordingly, they are quite controversial.[65]

Civil Rights Policies. In addition to economic concerns, changes in civil rights policies since the 1950s have also exerted a strong impact on federalism. In the landmark 1954 *Brown v. Board of Education* case, the U.S. Supreme Court ended the principle of "separate but equal" and ruled that the Fourteenth

Categorical Grants
Grants-in-aid that contain numerous, detailed provisions on how the states and local governments use the money.

Unfunded Mandates
Directives the national government issues to state and local governments without compensating them for complying.

Amendment prevents states from segregating races.[66] In other words, the Court created a national policy that prohibited states from separating races in public facilities. Although Southern states resisted desegregation, by the late 1950s and 1960s Presidents Dwight Eisenhower and John F. Kennedy dispatched the military to forcibly integrate public schools.

Brown v. Board of Education addressed direct discrimination by the states, but it did not address racial discrimination committed by private businesses, which often refused to hire or promote racial minorities (as well as women). Many private businesses, such as restaurants and hotels, refused to serve minorities or forcibly separated them from Whites. In 1964, Congress and President Johnson passed the landmark **Civil Rights Act of 1964**, which addressed private mistreatment of minorities. The national government drew its authority to ban racial discrimination in the private sector from the commerce clause because racial discrimination substantially affected interstate commerce—recall the substantial effect language from the *Wickard v. Filburn* case. Although Southern hotel and restaurant owners challenged the constitutionality of the Civil Rights Act based on the view that regulating racial discrimination exceeds the national government's constitutional authority, in 1964 the Supreme Court unanimously upheld the Civil Rights Act, ruling that racial discrimination substantially affects interstate commerce.[67]

During the 1960s and 1970s, the national government also assumed more authority over voting. The Fifteenth Amendment prevents states from discriminating on the basis of race when it comes to voting, but as we discussed earlier, states used devices such as literacy tests to prevent Blacks from voting. To address these problems, Congress passed the Voting Rights Act of 1965, which banned states from using literacy tests. Moreover, Sections 4 and 5 of the Voting Rights Act nationalized voting procedures. Section 4 identifies states and localities that have a history of voting discrimination against Blacks or Latinos, and these jurisdictions are reported in Table 3.2. Section 5 then stipulates that those covered jurisdictions cannot alter any voting procedure unless the U.S. Justice Department or a federal judge ensures that the change does not negatively affect minority voting rights. However, in early 2013 the U.S. Supreme Court ruled in the case of *Shelby County, AL v. Holder* that the formula used in Section 4 of the Voting Rights Act was unconstitutional, arguing that national government supervision over those jurisdictions is no longer necessary because vestiges of discrimination have been removed. Some justices, such as Justice Ruth Bader Ginsburg, indicated that this provision was still necessary, but Justice Antonin Scalia referred to it as a "racial entitlement."[68] Although Congress could revise Sections 4 and 5 of the Voting Rights Act, it has not done so, and experts indicate that it is unlikely that it will.[69] Amendments to the Voting Rights Act also require states to print bilingual or trilingual ballots in areas that have significant populations of people who are not native English speakers. In sum, the Voting Rights Act represented a major shift in national authority over voting to protect racial and ethnic minorities, although problems still persist in

Civil Rights Act of 1964
A federal law that prevents private businesses from discriminating in service and personnel policies.

many states. In the next Evaluating Equality box we discuss in more detail the controversies over the *Shelby County (AL) v. Holder* decision and its impact on federalism.

The relationship among the national government, state governments, and American Indian tribes has also changed extensively since the early twentieth century. Beginning in the 1930s, the national government expanded tribal sovereignty for the Indians living on reservations. The 1975 Indian Self-Determination and Education Act enhanced tribal governments' ability to govern themselves. Yet federal laws have expanded individual rights of Indians living on tribal land, thus restricting tribal authority. Most notably, the American Indian Civil Rights Act of 1968 granted individual Indians the same constitutional rights vis à vis their tribal governments that other Americans have with respect to their state and local governments. Therefore, tribal governments must respect freedom of speech, freedom of the press, freedom of religion, and procedural guarantees in criminal justice.[70] However, since the late 1980s, the U.S Supreme Court has held that tribal sovereignty outweighs state laws banning gambling; therefore, indigenous tribes have been able to operate lucrative casinos on their tribal land in states that otherwise ban casino gambling.[71]

Additionally, U.S. Supreme Court decisions that have increased the rights of women have also limited state authority. The landmark case *Reed v. Reed* (1971) overturned state policies that arbitrarily favored one sex over the other. This case specifically concerned an Idaho law that explicitly preferred males over females in determining who would control estates in inheritance cases.[72] Another federalism and women's issue relates to abortion. In the 1973 historic *Roe v. Wade* case, the U.S. Supreme Court overturned state laws that banned abortion, ruling that pregnant women have a constitutional right to abortion.[73] We cover abortion in more detail in Chapters 4 and 5, but the fact that the *Roe* decision created a national policy on abortion rights reflects a significant shift in favor of national authority.

The Era of Devolution

By the 1970s, the dominant thinking among political leaders, especially, but not exclusively, Republicans, was that the national government had assumed too much authority during the 1960s. Critics argued that states and local governments better understand their own problems, so they should be able to control their own policies without too much interference from the national government. The national government should set general policies, but state and local governments should decide the details. As a result of this shift in thinking, the national government began to pursue a policy of **devolution**—a partial return of power to state and local governments.

Devolution A view of federalism that advocates partially returning power to state and local governments.

The Role of Presidents and Congress. Devolution began in 1969 under President Richard Nixon, who used the term *New Federalism* to promote his priorities of taking power away from the national government and returning it to the

evaluating equality

Shelby County (AL) v. Holder and Section 4 of the Voting Rights Act

The Voting Rights Act of 1965 and its subsequent amendments have significantly curbed racial discrimination in voting. Section 2 of the act prevents any state or locality from denying someone the right to vote based on race or ethnicity, and it gives the national government and citizens the authority to sue any state or local government that violates the act. Since the passage of the act, federal courts have used Section 2 to expand voting rights for racial and ethnic minorities. Sections 4 and 5 of the Act work differently. Section 4 articulated a formula to identify states and localities with a history of disenfranchising racial and ethnic minorities, and Section 5 requires that these "covered" jurisdictions cannot change any voting procedure without the advanced permission of the United States Justice Department. The Justice Department must make sure that the proposed changes will not depress minority voting. Although Sections 4 and 5 were initially intended to be temporary, Congress actually expanded the range of covered jurisdictions since the Voting Rights Act's passage in 1965.

Students should understand that the Voting Rights Act is not only important for civil rights (see Chapter 5), but it is also important for federalism, particularly Sections 4 and 5. These parts of the act single out specific jurisdictions and place them under the control of the national government. Although all states and localities can be sued under Section 2, only some states and localities must endure the additional supervision of the national government. Most states and localities are permitted to change polling places or the times during which polls are open, but the covered jurisdictions must seek the Justice Department's permission to make the same changes.

Alabama has been covered under Section 4 since the Act was first passed in 1965, and in 2011 Shelby County, in Alabama, challenged the constitutionality of Sections 4 and 5. Specifically, Shelby County argued that this portion of the Act violated state sovereignty because it treated states unequally, whereas the national government argued that the "covered" jurisdictions' history of disenfranchisement necessitated the disparate treatment. In its *Shelby County, AL v. Holder* decision, the U.S. Supreme Court sided with Shelby County and ruled that Section 4 was unconstitutional because the historic voting discrimination that initially justified the formula was no longer present in the "covered" jurisdictions; therefore, Congress lacks the authority to treat states unequally.

The Supreme Court was sharply divided in this decision. Writing for the majority, Chief Justice John Roberts noted that Sections 4 and 5 of the Voting Rights Act represented a radical change in the principles of federalism and that national governments should treat the sovereign states equally. He states, "While one state waits months or years and expends funds to implement a validly enacted law, its neighbor can typically put the same law immediately through the normal legislative process." However, Roberts recognizes that the extensive minority disenfranchisement in the covered areas warranted "these departures from the basic features of our system of government." The problem for Roberts was that "Nearly fifty years later, things have changed dramatically." He cites statistics showing that minority voter registration is just as high in the covered jurisdictions as in the noncovered jurisdictions. The extent of minorities elected to office is also as high, if not higher, in the covered jurisdictions than in the noncovered jurisdictions. Therefore, the infringements on state authority were no longer warranted.

Conversely, Justice Ruth Bader Ginsburg wrote for the four dissenting justices. Justice Ginsburg argues that the Fifteenth Amendment, the constitutional basis of the Voting Rights Act, gives Congress the "power to enforce [the amendment] by appropriate legislation." This authority gives Congress wide discretion to prevent racial disenfranchisement, even if it infringes on state sovereignty. Justice Ginsburg agreed with the majority that there have been tremendous improvements in minority voting rights and access since the passage of the Act. In fact, she credits Sections 4 and 5 for creating these improvements; therefore, Congress should have the authority to keep these provisions in place—to preserve and expand on voting rights success. Justice Ginsburg cited numerous recent examples of the preclearance provision preventing covered jurisdictions from enacting policies that would have depressed minority voting. She stated, "Throwing out preclearance when it has worked and is continuing to work to stop discriminatory

(Continued)

evaluating equality *(Continued)*

changes is like throwing away your umbrella in a rainstorm because you are not getting wet."

Although there is no debate over the importance of protecting minority voting rights, this case presents interesting contrasts on views of federalism—the conflict between state autonomy on one side and the national government's authority on the other side. Review the full opinion from the official U.S. Supreme Court website at *https://www.supremecourt.*

gov/opinions/12pdf/12-96_6k47.pdf. Debate among yourselves the merits of the different arguments, and for the purposes of this chapter, focus the debate on the principles of federalism that this case represents, as well as the intersection between federalism and racial equality.

1. At what point should the national government be allowed to treat states differently based on historic discrimination?

2. Is Justice Ginsburg's umbrella analogy correct—will the covered jurisdictions revert to practices that diminish minority voting?

3. How should the story of the long lines in Maricopa, Arizona in 2016, shape opinions on this issue?

TABLE 3.2 Jurisdictions Previously Covered under Sections 4 and 5 of the Voting Rights Act

States Completely Covered
Alabama
Alaska
Arizona
Georgia
Louisiana
Mississippi
South Carolina
Texas
Virginia
States Partially Covered by County
California: 4 out of 58 counties
Florida: 5 out of 67 counties
New York: 4 out of 62 counties
North Carolina: 40 out of 100 counties
South Dakota: 2 out of 66 counties
States Partially Covered by City/Town
Michigan: 2 towns
New Hampshire: 10 towns

Source: Adapted from the United States Department of Justice. (2015). Jurisdictions previously covered by Section 5. Retrieved May 12, 2018, from https://www.justice.gov/crt/jurisdictions-previously-covered-section-5#note1.

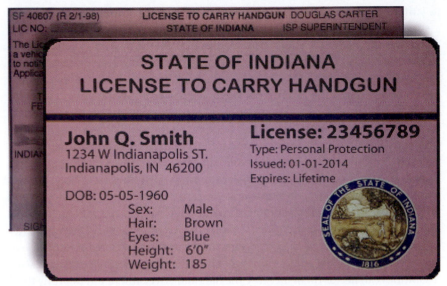

Photo of a license to carry a gun. In many states, such as Texas, a gun license is an acceptable form of identification to be able to vote, but a college student identification, even from a state university, is not acceptable.

state and local governments.[74] President Ronald Reagan expanded devolution in the 1980s,[75] and most presidents since that time, including Democratic President Bill Clinton, have advocated devolution policies in some form or another. In fact, in his 1996 State of the Union Address, President Clinton famously stated, "The era of big government is over. But we cannot go back to the time when our citizens were left to fend for themselves."[76] The primary method of promoting devolution is through **block grants**—grants-in-aid from the national government that are general, contain minimal regulations, and give state and local governments considerable discretion on how the money should be used. Unlike categorical grants, in which the national government strongly controls how states use the money, block grants enable states to spend the money as they best see fit to accomplish a general policy goal.

For example, in 1974 the national government created the Community Development Block Grant Program, which allowed states and local governments to provide housing for the poor and help improve neighborhoods.[77] Another, more controversial, block grant was the Personal Responsibility and Work Opportunity Act of 1996, also known as welfare reform. The Republican-controlled Congress and Democratic President Bill Clinton passed this bill, which replaced categorical grant welfare programs, most notably Aid to Families with Dependent Children (AFDC), with Temporary Assistance for Needy Families (TANF). TANF provides money to states with minimal regulation, except the direction that the states use the money to help recipients find meaningful employment.[78] Critics of TANF argue that it has not provided adequate funds for the poor and has caused many people, especially children and minorities,

Block Grants Grants-in-aid from the national government that are general, contain minimal regulations, and give state and local governments considerable discretion on how the money should be used.

Navigate federal
and state healthcare
policy.

to suffer in extreme poverty.[79] Although the U.S. government has touted it as a success, the National Association of Black Social Workers has argued that TANF has not helped Black families and that, under the law, White recipients have been more likely than Black recipients to find meaningful employment.[80]

Despite the dominance of devolution since 1980, the national government has still exerted its authority over states when it comes to certain policy goals. For example, the national government lacks the constitutional authority to mandate a minimum drinking age, which falls under the state police power. However, when a majority of political leaders desired to establish a national twenty-one-year-old drinking age, Congress passed, and usually pro-devolution president Ronald Reagan signed, the National Minimum Drinking Age Act of 1984, which withholds highway funds to states that do not adopt a twenty-one-year-old drinking age. The U.S. Supreme Court upheld this act, ruling that Congress did not exceed its authority.[81] Furthermore, the Americans with Disabilities Act (ADA) of 1990 (which we discuss in more detail in Chapter 5) requires that businesses and state and local governments update their facilities so that people with disabilities can access them. Because the national government did not fully fund these improvements, the ADA has amounted to an unfunded mandate.[82]

The Obama administration had a mixed record in federalism. On the one hand President Obama promoted policies that limited state autonomy. For example, the Patient Protection and Affordable Care Act of 2010, also known as the Affordable Care Act or ObamaCare, gives the national government a considerable amount of control over states' ability to provide health insurance. The Affordable Care Act also requires that individuals purchase health insurance or pay a penalty, and the U.S. Supreme Court upheld this provision, despite challenges that it exceeds the national government's power.[83] Conversely, the Obama administration has deferred to states in other areas. For example, since 2013 several states have legalized cannabis, even allowing the legal sale of marijuana. Because the national government still bans the sale of marijuana, the Obama administration possesses the authority to use federal law enforcement to arrest marijuana sellers in these states regardless of state law.[84] Nevertheless, the Obama administration announced that it would allow states to operate legalized marijuana sales as long as states regulated them.[85]

Although President Obama's successor Donald Trump is a Republican, which as a party tends to support state autonomy, early evidence shows that the Trump administration also has a mixed record in federalism. Despite campaigning to repeal Obamacare, President Trump did not convince Congress to overturn the law;[86] however, President Trump allowed states to require Medicaid recipients to work or participate in job training programs as a condition of receiving the benefit.[87] However, in other areas, the Trump administration has sought to impose its will on state and local governments. For example, Trump's former Attorney General Jeff Sessions reversed the Obama policy that permitted recreational marijuana sales in states with legalized marijuana,[88] but to date the administration has not actually prosecuted marijuana sales in these states. Additionally, early in his administration, President Trump announced that the federal government would withhold funds from cities that would not assist in capturing undocumented immigrants. However, as of the summer of 2018, the federal judiciary has ruled that this policy is unconstitutional.[89]

The Role of the Supreme Court. Since 1980, the U.S. Supreme Court has been a significant institution in devolving power back to the states. Notably, the Court has restricted the national government's use of the commerce clause to expand its authority. For example, the Gun Free School Zones Act of 1990 criminalized possession of a firearm within 1,000 feet of a school. Normally, states control questions of gun possession and education, but in this instance the national government justified its authority under the commerce clause because guns in schools devalue education and cause additional crime that spreads across state lines, both of which substantially affect interstate commerce. However, in the 1995 case *United States v. Lopez* the U.S. Supreme Court narrowly overturned this law because it did not accept the national government's justification of a "substantial effect." Chief Justice Rehnquist wrote, "To uphold the government's contentions here, we would have to pile inference upon inference in a manner that would bid fair to convert congressional authority under the Commerce Clause to a general police power of the sort retained by the states."[90]

Additionally, in 2000, in *United States v. Morrison*, the U.S. Supreme Court overturned the portion of the Violence Against Women Act of 1994 that allowed victims of gender-based violence to sue their attackers in federal court. Although states normally decide questions of gender-based violent crimes, the national government argued that violence against women costs the national economy over $3 billion per year; therefore, gender-based violence substantially affects interstate commerce. However, the Supreme Court rejected that argument.[91]

Despite the Supreme Court's willingness to reign in the national government, it has upheld the national government's use of the commerce clause to override state authority in particular policy areas. The concept of **preemption**, which is based on the supremacy clause, permits the national government to overturn state and local laws that conflict with national policies, and preemption has been especially controversial in drug enforcement policies. Beginning in the 1990s many states decriminalized marijuana for medicinal use. However, the national government banned any use of marijuana under the Controlled Substances Act, and the Drug Enforcement Agency enforced the law against people who had permission in their states to use marijuana for medical uses. These patients challenged the national government's policy, arguing that the marijuana they used did not cross state lines and so the national government lacked power to regulate it under the commerce clause. In the 2005 *Gonzales v. Raich* case, a majority of the Supreme Court relied on the *Wickard v. Filburn* case to show that marijuana use exerts a "substantial effect" on interstate commerce.[92] As discussed above, despite having the power to enforce marijuana laws in states that have legalized it, the federal government has been restrained in using this power for the past decade, notwithstanding the Trump administration's threats to prosecute marijuana cases in these states.

Preemption A concept that permits the national government to overturn state and local laws.

Although the Supreme Court has upheld preemption in cases related to drug enforcement, it has declined to preempt state laws in other areas. For example, in the 1991 *Gregory v. Ashcroft* case, the Court ruled that a state's Tenth Amendment right to determine qualifications for political office supersedes the federal Age Discrimination in Employment Act, which prohibits employment discrimination based on age (see Chapter 5). In this case, a Missouri state judge unsuccessfully challenged a state law requiring judges to retire at the age of 70.[93]

Since the 1980s, devolution has occurred with respect to the issue of abortion as well. Recall that in 1973 the U.S. Supreme Court declared that women have a right to an abortion, which nationalized the issue. States were no longer able to outlaw the procedure. Since then, the Supreme Court has upheld the general right to an abortion, but it has allowed states to institute restrictions on abortion, such as mandatory waiting periods before an abortion can be performed, requirements that physicians show the patient photographs of the fetus, and parental consent for minors seeking an abortion.[94]

The U.S. Supreme Court has also weighed in on the issue of devolution with respect to civil rights, particularly over how to integrate public schools. By the late 1960s, many public schools were still segregated not because of state government action, but rather because of geography. Blacks, Latinos, and Whites tended to live in different neighborhoods, and therefore went to different schools. In 1971, the U.S. Supreme Court upheld the practice of court-ordered busing White and minority students to schools farther from their home to achieve full integration.[95] However, twenty years later the U.S. Supreme Court gave permission for local areas to cease busing if they could show they made a genuine effort to achieve integration.[96]

Finally, the Supreme Court has reinterpreted the Eleventh Amendment in a way that influences federalism in general and racial politics in particular. Recall that the Eleventh Amendment prevents states from being sued in federal court by citizens of another state, but it is silent on the issue of states being sued by their own citizens. In the 1996 case of *Seminole Tribe of Florida v. Florida*, the Supreme Court expanded the Eleventh Amendment to shield states. Under its power to regulate commerce with Indian tribes, the national government passed the Indian Gaming Regulatory Act of 1988, which recognized tribes' rights to run casinos, even if the state in which they are located bans casino gambling. The law required the state government and tribe to enter into negotiations on establishing casinos, and if the state failed to negotiate in good faith, then the tribe could sue the state in federal court. However, the U.S. Supreme Court ruled that the Eleventh Amendment contains protections for states that extend beyond the strict language of the amendment; therefore, states could be exempt from being sued in federal court by their own citizens.[97]

Since the early republic the U.S. Supreme Court has been instrumental in drawing the lines between state power and national power, ruling in favor of both. Table 3.3 lists the key Supreme Court cases that have expanded the power of the national government at the expense of state and local governments, and Table 3.4 lists the key U.S Supreme Court cases that have given more power to state and local governments.

TABLE 3.3 Key U.S. Supreme Court Cases Expanding the Power of the National Government at the Expense of State and Local Governments in the Areas of Economics and Civil Rights

Case Name	Year	Issue Area
Brown v. Board of Education	1954	Civil Rights
Garcia v. San Antonio Metropolitan Transit Authority	1985	Economics
Gibbons v. Ogden	1824	Economics
Gonzalez v. Raich	2005	Criminal
Heart of Atlanta Motel v. United States	1965	Civil Rights
Katzenbach v. McClung	1965	Civil Rights
McCulloch v. Maryland	1819	Economics
National Federation of Independent Business v. Sebelius	2012	Economics
National Labor Relations Bd. v. Jones & Laughlin Steel	1937	Economics
Reed v. Reed	1971	Civil Rights
Roe v. Wade	1973	Civil Rights
Swann v. Charlotte-Mecklenburg Board of Education	1971	Civil Rights
Thornburg v. Gingles	1986	Civil Rights
United States v. Darby Lumber	1941	Economics
Wickard v. Filburn	1942	Economics

TABLE 3.4 Key U.S. Supreme Court Cases Limiting National Authority and Giving Power to State and Local Governments in the Areas of Economics and Civil Rights

Case Name	Year	Issue Area
Board of Education, Oklahoma City v. Dowell	1991	Civil Rights
Carter v. Carter Coal Company	1936	Economics
Dred Scott v. Sandford	1857	Civil Rights
Gregory v. Ashcroft	1991	Civil Rights
Hammer v. Dagenhart	1819	Economics
National League of Cities v. Usery	1976	Economics
Planned Parenthood v. Casey	1992	Civil Rights
Plessy v. Ferguson	1896	Civil Rights
Prigg v. Pennsylvania	1842	Civil Rights
Schechter Poultry Corporation v. United States	1935	Economics
Seminole Tribe of Florida v. Florida	1996	Civil Rights
Shelby County, AL v. Holder	2013	Civil Rights
United States v. Butler	1936	Economics
United States v. Cruikshank	1875	Civil Rights
United States v. Lopez	1995	Criminal
United States v. Morrison	2000	Civil Rights
United States v. Reese	1876	Civil Rights

Conclusion

The controversies over mishaps during the 2016 presidential primary in Arizona typify the significance of federalism in American government. To ensure fair elections and prevent racial discrimination, the national government exerts considerable control over voting procedures. The Fifteenth Amendment and the Voting Rights Act limit states' abilities to disenfranchise racial and ethnic minorities. However, states still decide questions of where to locate polling places, how long to allow voting, and what kind of authority voting officials have over voters. When Maricopa County slashed the number of polling sites, there were frustratingly long lines, particularly in areas with heavy minority populations.

The U.S. federal government consists of three distinct levels (national, state, and local), and each level performs key policymaking functions and affects people's daily lives in different ways. Moreover, there is tremendous competition for power among the three levels of government, especially between the national government on one side and state and local governments on the other. The balance of power among the levels of government is called federalism, and it is a central component of American government and politics. Federalism influences all aspects of American government, but it plays an especially significant role in minority group politics.

State and local governments are key components of our federal system. Although they share many similarities, individual states and localities structure their governments differently from the legislatures that make the laws, to the governors and mayors that execute them, and the courts that settle disputes. Although racial and ethnic minorities have been traditionally excluded from positions of power in state and local government, since the late twentieth century, many minority groups have been better represented in state legislatures, courts, and even as governors.

The Constitution forms the framework for the balance of power between the national government and the state and local governments. The Framers of the Constitution sought to strengthen the national government; therefore, many constitutional provisions expand national authority. However, parts of the Constitution, most notably the Tenth Amendment, preserve state power. The original Constitution allowed states to determine their own civil rights policies, even to the point of allowing slavery. However, constitutional amendments have restricted states' abilities to deny people rights, especially in voting. The Fifteenth Amendment bars states from denying people the right to vote on account of race; the Nineteenth Amendment prohibits states from denying people the right to vote on account of sex; and the Twenty-Fourth Amendment prevents states from enacting poll taxes, which disproportionately hurt poor and minority populations.

During the early years of the Republic the national government expanded power to promote industrialization and economic development. After the Civil War, the period of dual federalism dominated. State governments and the national government governed within their own spheres, and the Supreme

Court sharply curtailed the authority of the national government. Despite the passage of the post–Civil War constitutional amendments, states were still free to mistreat racial and ethnic minorities until the middle of the twentieth century. States required facilities to be segregated and cleverly circumvented the Fifteenth Amendment.

After the Great Depression, the period of cooperative federalism emerged, and the lines between state and national authority blurred. Cooperative federalism was characterized by significant increases in the power of the national government, often at the expense of state and local governments. Supreme Court decisions such as *Brown v. Board of Education*, and federal statutes such as the Civil Rights Act of 1964 and the Voting Rights Act of 1965, nationalized civil rights policies and advanced equality.

Since the 1970s, a period of devolution has occurred. Although the national government has given some power back to the states, it still retains considerable authority over policymaking. Moreover, although since the early twentieth century Republicans have favored devolution and Democrats have favored national control, the Obama and Trump administrations have demonstrated that federalism is not necessarily a partisan issue, and the policy at stake is more relevant than the balance of power between the national governments and the states.

review REVIEW QUESTIONS

1. To what extent are Blacks and Latinos represented in state legislatures, and how does this minority representation vary by region?

2. How specifically did the original Constitution expand national authority but enable states to maintain slavery?

3. Compare and contrast civil rights outcomes in the eras of dual federalism, cooperative federalism, and devolution. In which era have civil rights advances been most apparent? Why?

4. How did the controversies over access to voting and long lines at the polls during the 2016 election reflect issues of federalism?

5. How has federalism influenced the status of Indian tribes in American government?

Check your understanding of Chapter 3.

terms KEY TERMS

Bicameral Legislature p. 58	Dual Federalism p. 75	Full Faith and Credit Clause p. 71
Bill of Attainder p. 71	Due Process Clause p. 72	
Block Grants p. 87	Equal Protection Clause p. 72	Gerrymandering p. 61
Categorical Grants p. 82	Ex Post Facto Law p. 71	Grants-in-Aid p. 78
Civil Rights Act of 1964 p. 83	Extradition Clause p. 71	Home Rule p. 67
Commerce Clause p. 69	Federalism p. 57	Implied Power p. 74
Cooperative Federalism p. 79	Fifteenth Amendment p. 72	Incorporation p. 80
County Commissions p. 68	Fourteenth Amendment p. 72	Interstate Compact Clause p. 71
Devolution p. 84		
Dillon's Rule p. 67	Fugitive Slave Clause p. 71	Line-Item Veto p. 62

Need to review key ideas in greater depth? Click here.

Flashcard review.

ADDITIONAL READINGS

Banks, C. P., & Blakeman, J. C. (2012). *The U.S. Supreme Court and New Federalism: From the Rehnquist to the Roberts court*. Lanham, MD: Rowman & Littlefield.

> This book offers a thorough account of the Supreme Court's federalism jurisprudence over the past quarter-century, particularly its deference to state governments. Although Banks and Blakeman focus on national security and religious liberty, the book chronicles decisions concerning race and ethnicity.

Bullock III, C. S., Gaddie, R. K., & Wert, J. J. (2016). *The rise and fall of the Voting Rights Act*. Norman: University of Oklahoma Press.

> This book traces Black access to voting from Reconstruction through the present, and their extensive data demonstrate that the Voting Rights Act and its amendments have improved minority voting participation and representation. They also analyze how the politics of the federal judiciary led to the recent landmark decision in *Shelby County (AL) v. Holder*.

Mason, W. D. (2000). *Indian gaming: Tribal sovereignty and American politics*. Norman: University of Oklahoma Press.

> This is one of the leading analyses of how casino gambling on American Indian reservations has influenced the position of tribal governments in the larger context of American federalism.

Meadows, T. K., & Schaller, T. F. (2006). *Devolution and Black state legislators: Challenges and choices in the twenty-first century*. Albany: State University of New York Press.

> As devolution has given more power to state governments, state legislatures have become a more important public policy force. As a result, African American state legislators now play a significant role in shaping policy in the states, and this book offers a thorough analysis of the more than six hundred African Americans who serve in state legislatures.

Provine, D. M., Varsanyi, M., Lewis, P. G., & Decker, S. H. (2016). *Policing immigrants: Local law enforcement on the front lines*. Chicago: University of Chicago Press.

> The national government has increasingly relied on local police to enforce immigration policies, and this book offers a comprehensive study of how the complexities of federalism influence immigration enforcement. The authors uncover significant variation in immigration enforcement among different localities, which ultimately leads to biased and inadequate law enforcement.

Civil Liberties: Freedom and Government Authority in Tension

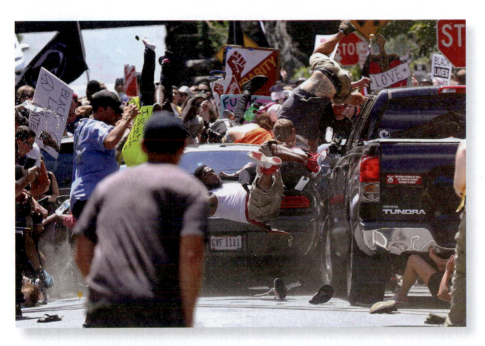

James Fields drives into counterprotesters in Charlottesville, Virginia, on August 12, 2017. Fields is a White supremacist who attended the "Unite the Right" rally, presumably to protest the removal of a statue of Robert E. Lee, and his actions result in one death and numerous injuries. This horrific story starkly illustrates the line between the protected liberty of free expression, even hateful speech, and unprotected actions. Despite Fields's despicable actions, civil liberties still afford him the right to a fair trial.

Charlottesville, where the University of Virginia is located, is a typical college town, with a progressive and diverse population consisting of students and locals. However, it is also in the South; therefore, it has a history of slavery and discrimination. As a way to address its unsavory past, the Charlottesville City Council voted in February 2017 to remove from a public park a statue of Confederate General Robert E. Lee.[1] In reaction to this decision, a group led by former Grand Wizard of the Ku Klux Klan David Duke and well-known White supremacists Richard Spencer and Jason Kessler organized a rally, known as "Unite the Right," presumably to protest the statue removal. On Friday, August 11, 2017—the night before the scheduled rally—a number of White supremacists marched on the grounds of the University of Virginia holding torches, reminiscent of anti-Jewish marches in Nazi Germany, shouting "Jews will not replace us." Fights between these marchers and opponents of bigotry occurred, and police arrested one person.[2]

The actual rally that occurred the next day was even more chaotic. White supremacists clashed violently with counterprotesters, resulting in fighting, throwing objects, and spraying chemicals. There were injuries and arrests, but the events turned especially tragic when 20-year-old White supremacist James Alex Fields, from Maumee, Ohio, drove his car through a crown of counterprotesters. Not only did Fields injure 19 people, some severely, but he also killed 32-year-old counterprotester Heather Heyer. Fields drove away, but authorities captured him. Police soon dispersed both the rally and the counterprotesters, and later that evening the city of Charlottesville voted to empower the police to enact a curfew and prevent people from assembling. In addition to Heyer, two police officers died after their helicopter crashed while they were monitoring events. The Commonwealth of Virginia charged Fields with first-degree murder and a number of lesser crimes. Additionally, three other White supremacists were charged for their actions in Charlottesville—one for shooting a firearm at counterprotesters and two for maliciously beating an African American male. In December 2018 Fields was convicted of first degree murder.[3]

Watch how the nation responded to the events in Charlottesville.

intro

The terrible events in Charlottesville exemplify the politics surrounding **civil liberties**—*the constitutional freedoms that Americans enjoy and on which governments may not encroach. The term* civil liberties *is often confused with the term* civil rights, *which concerns the protections against unequal treatment that the government guarantees all groups. We discuss civil rights in the next chapter. Here we focus on the issue of civil liberties, which concerns individuals' freedom from governmental control.*

The Bill of Rights guarantees a variety of civil liberties, which are shown in Table 4.1, and the story of Charlottesville involves a number of these important liberties. Most notably this story centers on the First Amendment Freedom of Speech and Freedom of Assembly. Although White supremacy is undoubtedly a despicable view, the First Amendment provides people the right to express racial, ethnic, or religious prejudice. It even allows for a group of bigots to assemble and express their views together. The government may not prevent people from or punish people for expressing hatred toward any group. However, as with all civil liberties, the first Amendment has limits. As in the case of Charlottesville, the government possesses the authority to stop an assembly when it threatens public safety, notwithstanding rally organizer Richard Spencer's claim that the police violated his freedom of speech.[4] Moreover, it is equally important to realize that despite the nefarious nature of James Fields's actions, civil liberties also protect him. He had a Sixth Amendment right to a fair trial by jury with effective assistance of counsel, and the Eighth Amendment prevents him from enduring "cruel and unusual punishment" in his sentencing.

This chapter focuses on the politics of civil liberties. Table 4.1 lists a vast number of civil liberties; however, there are too many to discuss in a single chapter. For our purposes, four aspects of civil liberties merit extended discussion: freedom of expression, freedom of religion, criminal justice, and privacy. This chapter also demonstrates that, although the amendments in the Bill of Rights spell out Americans' civil liberties, the language of the amendments is ambiguous; therefore, civil liberties are not absolutes. Often, the ambiguity of the Bill of Rights is manifested in debates between the government's perceived need to exert authority in the name of regulating public morals and safety and those who place a greater value on individual liberty and autonomy.

Additionally, civil liberties controversies have a racial and ethnic component. Civil liberties often protect racial and ethnic minorities, especially in the area of free expression for civil rights activists and in the area of criminal justice. However, as the opening story indicates, civil liberties could also protect the liberties for people who harbor racial, ethnic, or religious prejudice.

Civil Liberties The constitutional freedoms that Americans enjoy and on which the government may not encroach.

Assess current debates on the Second Amendment.

TABLE 4.1   **Liberties Contained in the Bill of Rights**

Amendment	Status of Liberty	Incorporation Status
First	No government establishment of a religion	1947
First	Free exercise of religion	1940
First	Freedom of speech	1927
First	Freedom of the press	1931
First	Freedom to peacefully assemble	1937
First	Freedom to petition the government for redress	1937
Second	Right to bear arms	2010
Third	Protection against quartering of soldiers in private homes during times of peace	Not incorporated
Fourth	Protection against search of a home or business without a warrant issued by a neutral third party and based on probable cause	1949
Fifth	Protection against trial for major crimes without a grand jury indictment	Not incorporated
Fifth	Guarantee of no trial twice for the same offense (double jeopardy clause)	1969
Fifth	Protection against being forced to testify against oneself	1964
Fifth	Protection against denial of life, liberty, or property without due process of law	Specified in the Fourteenth Amendment
Fifth	Protection against taking of private property (eminent domain clause)	1896
Sixth	Right of defendants to have a speedy, public trial	1967
Sixth	Right of defendants to have a trial by jury	1968
Sixth	Right of defendants to be informed of their charges	1965
Sixth	Right of defendants to confront their accusers and compel witnesses to testify on their behalf	1965
Sixth	Right of counsel for criminal defendants	1963
Seventh	Right of defendants to have a trial by jury in civil suits	Not incorporated
Eighth	Protection against the imposition of excessive bail or fines	Not incorporated[a]
Eighth	Protection against imposition of "cruel and unusual punishment"	1962
Ninth	Guarantee of unwritten rights retained by the people	N/A[b]
Tenth	Granting to states powers not reserved to the national government or prohibited to the states	Not incorporated[c]

[a] During the 2018-2019 term, the U.S. Supreme Court will decide the case of Timbs v. Indiana to determine whether the Eighth amendment ban on excessive fines should be incorporated.

[b] The Ninth Amendment itself cannot be incorporated because it does not enumerate a specific right; however, the Ninth Amendment was used to incorporate the unwritten right to privacy in 1965.

[c] Because the Tenth Amendment grants rights to states and not to people, it is not relevant to incorpora-tion.

Source: Adapted from O'Brien, D. M. (2011). Constitutional law and politics: Vol. 2. Civil rights and civil liberties (8th ed.). New York: Norton, pp. 330–332.

The Bill of Rights

As already mentioned, civil liberties are an important part of the Bill of Rights. Before discussing specific civil liberties, let us consider how the Bill of Rights affects American government.

What does it mean to incorporate the Bill of Rights?

Origins of the Bill of Rights

Chapter 2 explained that the Bill of Rights was not part of the original Constitution. After the initial Constitution was drafted, many political leaders contended that a bill of rights was necessary to protect against government encroachments on civil liberties. These leaders feared that a centralized national government would become tyrannical, similar to the tyranny the colonists experienced when ruled by the English king and Parliament, that is, the centralized government in London. Supporters of a bill of rights believed that state governments would protect liberties because, unlike the national government, they were close to the governed. Furthermore, many states already had enumerated protections, such as those in the Virginia Declaration of Rights, which we also discussed in Chapter 2. Supporters of the Bill of Rights maintained that, without similar specified limitations, the national government could become too powerful.

Despite this push for a bill of rights, many Framers, most notably Alexander Hamilton and James Madison, opposed including a bill of rights in the Constitution. This group argued that separation of powers and checks and balances would be sufficient to protect individual liberty and prevent the national government from becoming tyrannical. In "Federalist Paper No. 84," Alexander Hamilton predicted that specifically listing individual rights could actually lessen liberty because the government would adhere only to those rights listed and would not respect any equally important unlisted rights.[5]

Nevertheless, there was enough support for a bill of rights that its absence threatened to prevent the ratification of the Constitution. To increase support for ratification, James Madison agreed to propose a bill of rights as constitutional amendments after the Constitution was ratified. In 1791, the first ten amendments became the Bill of Rights.[6]

Incorporation of the Bill of Rights

Initially, the Bill of Rights applied only to the national government. Although people feared that the national government would trounce civil liberties, they were less concerned about the states and localities. By the early nineteenth century, however, it was clear that state and local governments were violating civil liberties, even those contained in the Bill of Rights. As a result, the question of **incorporation**—whether the Bill of Rights should apply to the states as well as to the national government—arose.

An example of the incorporation problem occurred during the early nineteenth century when the city of Baltimore engaged in construction projects to improve the quality of life in the city. However, this construction made the

Incorporation The application of the Bill of Rights to state and local governments.

Eminent Domain A provision in the Fifth Amendment to the Constitution that requires the government to provide compensation when it takes private property for public use.

Fourteenth Amendment An amendment to the Constitution that prevents states from denying on the basis of race full citizenship to its residents.

Due Process Clause A specific provision in the Fourteenth Amendment to the Constitution that requires states to use normal judicial and criminal procedures before denying a citizen life, liberty, or property.

Selective Incorporation The process by which the Supreme Court has gradually incorporated specific liberties deemed absolutely necessary in a free society.

How does the 14th Amendment apply to different groups?

water surrounding John Barron's wharf so shallow that ships were no longer able to use it. Because Baltimore's construction project cost Barron a considerable sum of money, he sued the city, and the trial court awarded Barron compensation in accordance with the Fifth Amendment **eminent domain** clause, which requires the government to provide compensation when it takes private property for public use. However, in 1833 the U.S. Supreme Court ruled that Baltimore did not need to compensate Barron because the Fifth Amendment did not apply to the states and localities. In other words, the Supreme Court refused to incorporate the Bill of Rights.[7]

The ratification of the **Fourteenth Amendment** in 1868 reinvigorated the question of incorporation. The Fourteenth Amendment was added to the Constitution after the Civil War to ensure that states gave former slaves full citizenship rights. Specifically, the amendment's **due process clause** prevents states from denying any resident life, liberty, or property without following normal criminal and judicial procedures. Many legal thinkers at the time, such as U.S. Supreme Court Justice John Marshall Harlan, argued that the protections contained in the Bill of Rights were inherent in the concept of "due process of law" and therefore the due process clause should incorporate the entire Bill of Rights. However, in the 1884 case of *Hurtado v. California*, the Supreme Court refused to use the due process clause to incorporate the Bill of Rights after the state of California indicted Hurtado for a capital crime without a grand jury, an action that the Fifth Amendment prevents.[8] We discuss the Fourteenth Amendment in more detail in Chapter 5.

In the twentieth century, the Supreme Court moderated its stance on incorporation by adopting the concept of **selective incorporation**, the incorporation of only some of the liberties in the Bill of Rights. The selective incorporation principle was first announced in the 1937 case of *Palko v. Connecticut*. After the state of Connecticut tried Frank Palko twice for the same crime, he argued that the state had violated his Fifth Amendment right against double jeopardy. Although the U.S. Supreme Court ruled that the Fifth Amendment double jeopardy clause should not be incorporated, Justice Benjamin Cardozo established that the due process clause of the Fourteenth Amendment incorporates only those liberties deemed to be essential for a free society.[9] Thus, Cardozo created a distinction within the Bill of Rights between more important liberties, which should be incorporated, and less important liberties, which should not be incorporated. Since 1937, especially during the 1950s and 1960s, the Supreme Court gradually incorporated most of the liberties contained in the Bill of Rights, and currently only a few liberties remain unincorporated. Table 4.1 indicates when each liberty has been incorporated or if it has not been.

Because of selective incorporation, most civil liberties are now uniformly applied throughout the United States. As a result, many of the liberties we discuss throughout this chapter apply at all levels of government: nation, state, and local. Recall from Chapter 3 how incorporation increased the power of the national government and decreased the power of states and localities.

Freedom of Expression

The First Amendment of the Constitution states, "Congress shall make no law . . . abridging the freedom of speech, or of the press; or of the right of the people to peacefully assemble, and to petition the government for redress." Although the language of the First Amendment seems clear, the issue of free expression is quite nebulous. There are a number of instances in which the government has restrained free expression out of concern for security (see the opening vignette), civility, and morality. Moreover, debates over freedom of expression often intersect minority-group politics. This section discusses the key freedom-of-expression topics of political dissent, pornography, and offensive speech, and freedom of the press.

Political Dissent

An essential ingredient of free expression is the right to political dissent, which entails advocating fundamental changes in our form of government, even calling for its overthrow, or joining a group that promotes those subversive ideas. During the early twentieth century, fears of a communist revolution compelled the national and state governments to outlaw views perceived to be anti-American. For example, in 1917, following the entry of the United States into World War I and the communist takeover of Russia, the federal government passed the Espionage Act, which outlawed interference with the nation's war effort. The United States government subsequently investigated thousands of people who actively opposed America's policy in World War I or simply expressed support for communism, socialism, and other left-wing causes, including civil rights for African Americans, and many of these individuals received lengthy prison terms for their expression.[10]

Emma Goldman was a Jewish Russian immigrant anarchist who advocated overthrowing the government in the early twentieth century. Because political dissent was not protected at the time, she was imprisoned and eventually deported for expressing her views, which would be constitutionally protected today.

Despite the First Amendment, the U.S. Supreme Court upheld these laws by using the **clear and present danger test**, which allowed the government to criminalize expression that is "used in such circumstances and are of such a nature as to create a clear and present danger that they will bring about the substantial evils that Congress has a right to prevent."[11] Although the clear and present danger test seemingly protected civil liberties and restricted government control, the Supreme Court from the 1920s through the 1950s usually interpreted the mere advocacy of communism or socialism as a clear and present danger. Therefore, numerous Americans, many of whom were immigrants, were punished for political dissent. For example, Emma Goldman was a Russian immigrant and anarchist who advocated overthrowing the U.S.

Clear and Present Danger Test A guideline that requires the government to demonstrate that banned expression poses a definite and immediate threat to peace or national security.

Protecting freedom of speech

government. She was imprisoned several times throughout her life for advocacy of her ideas, most notably opposing American entry into World War I. She was eventually deported.[12] By the late 1960s, however, the Supreme Court fully protected the right of political dissent by reinterpreting the clear and present danger test to protect dissent unless it directly encourages lawless actions.[13]

Another form of political dissent is flag desecration, in which an individual or group burns or otherwise defiles the American flag. Flag desecration is a method of expressing opposition to American policies and even the American system of government itself, and many people consider it to be extremely offensive. Consequently, most states and the federal government outlawed it. However, in 1989 the U.S. Supreme Court included flag desecration as a form of political dissent protected under the First Amendment.[14] On numerous occasions, Congress has attempted to propose a constitutional amendment to overturn the Supreme Court's decision and allow the government to criminalize flag desecration, but despite always passing comfortably in the House, the proposal has failed to garner the necessary two-thirds vote in the Senate.[15]

Pornography and Offensive Speech

Pornography is a form of expression with limited First Amendment protection. National, state, and local governments contend that to protect the safety and morals of their citizens, they possess the authority to ban sexually explicit material. When deciding the level of protection to afford sexually explicit material, the U.S. Supreme Court has distinguished between obscene material, which is not protected, and nonobscene material, which is protected.

Prior to the 1950s, the federal and state governments heavily regulated explicit material based on a standard of what could be harmful to the most vulnerable in society. Therefore, state and local governments were allowed to ban literature, including classics, because merely a few passages could harm children. In a series of pornography cases between the 1950s and 1970s, the Supreme Court developed a more permissive definition of obscenity. Most important, the *Miller* standard (from the 1973 Supreme Court case *Miller v. California*) stipulates that material is protected under the First Amendment if the work as a whole is not excessively sexual or if it has political, literary, artistic, or scientific value. However, states and local communities have tremendous leeway in defining prurience and determining whether the questionable material possesses redeeming value.[16] Under the *Miller* standard, local communities can regulate the dissemination or display of sexually explicit material, including the sale of pornographic magazines and the establishment of adult entertainment businesses. States and localities, however, can no longer ban literature and cinema.[17]

Other government regulations have limited speech that is offensive even if it is not sexual in nature. In 1942, the Supreme Court established the **fighting words** exception to the First Amendment, which stipulates that some forms of expression can damage other people or create a breach of the peace. Fighting words are essentially not speech; thus, they are not protected under the First Amendment.[18]

Fighting Words Derisive, insulting, or offensive words that inflict damage on other people and are therefore not protected by the First Amendment.

By the late 1960s, however, American culture had become more tolerant of derisive, insulting, and coarse language. This trend was reflected in the Supreme Court's constriction of the fighting words exception, which increased protection for speech that many deem to be offensive. In the 1971 landmark case of *Cohen v. California*, the Supreme Court significantly limited states' ability to criminalize the public display of curse words.[19]

Regulations on offensive speech intersect with minority-group politics in debates over **hate speech**, or expression that is hostile toward racial or ethnic minorities (as well as expression directed toward those of a particular gender, sexual orientation, or religious preference). During the late 1980s and early 1990s, many states, localities, and public universities adopted regulations prohibiting hate speech. However, in 1992, the U.S. Supreme Court struck down bans on hate speech, ruling that, although governments can ban fighting words, they cannot prohibit fighting words specifically directed toward minority groups. By singling out fighting words directed against minority groups, the laws discriminate against people who hold a particular viewpoint, the holding of which the First Amendment protects.[20]

Still, the Supreme Court has upheld restrictions on hate speech. For example, in 1993 the U.S. Supreme Court unanimously upheld state laws that allow for increased criminal penalties when victims are purposely selected because of their race, ethnicity, national origin, gender, religion, or sexual orientation.[21] In addition, states are permitted to ban burning a cross, which is essential to Ku Klux Klan rituals, but only when cross-burning is used explicitly as a form of intimidation against a racial, ethnic, or religious minority.[22] In 2015 the Supreme Court upheld Texas' policy of preventing offensive messages on state-issued specialty license plates. Like many states, Texas allows private organizations to place messages on license plates, which automobile owners can then obtain by paying an additional fee. In 2009 the Texas Division of the Sons of Confederate Veterans applied to create a specialty license

Hate Speech A form of expression that is hostile toward a particular race, ethnicity, gender, religion, nationality, or sexual orientation.

Although the civil liberties protect a considerable amount of hateful speech and usually prevent governments from regulating offensive hate speech, the U.S. Supreme Court ruled in 2015 that Texas was not required to issue this license plate because states possess the authority to prevent the impression that it endorses offensive views.

plate that displayed the Confederate flag, but the state denied the application because the Confederate flag was deemed offensive, particularly to racial and ethnic minorities. The U.S. Supreme court ruled that the state had the authority to prevent the impression that it endorses offensive views.[23]

Freedom of the Press

The First Amendment also explicitly protects freedom of the press, but the press is a broad term that encompasses a variety of media, including print media (newspapers, pamphlets, and magazines), broadcast radio and television, cable and satellite radio and television, and the Internet. The extent of First Amendment protection varies considerably among these media. The First Amendment protects print media by limiting **prior restraint**, which is a government attempt to prevent or impede the publication and distribution of printed material. Consequently, the American government cannot prevent the publication of material that is highly critical of its policies, even during times of war.[24]

Prior Restraint A usually impermissible government regulation that prevents the publication of printed material.

Likewise, protections against prior restraint can protect media outlets that maliciously attack racial and ethnic minorities. During the 1920s, the state of Minnesota closed Jay Near's newspaper, the *Saturday Press*, because its anti-Black, anti-Jewish, and anti-Catholic prejudice violated a state law banning the publication of "malicious, scandalous, or defamatory" material. The state threatened to fine Near if he continued to publish his paper. However, the U.S. Supreme Court overturned this law as a prior restraint in violation of the First Amendment.[25]

Similar to preventing bans on most hate speech, the First Amendment freedom of the press prevents prior restraints on racist publications. It is important to contrast American protection for hate speech with other constitutional democracies that protect civil liberties. For example, as a means of preventing another rise of the Nazi Party, Germany bans neo-Nazi and other hateful publications. In fact, in Germany (and several other European nations) it is illegal to deny the existence of the Holocaust, whereas the United States Constitution protects this view.[26]

Libel The publication of written material that damages a person's reputation.

Another freedom of the press issue concerns **libel**, which is the publication of written material that damages a person's reputation. Individuals who are libeled can sue the publication for monetary damages; thus, libel presents a financial burden on the freedom of the press. Newspapers and magazines would censor themselves from printing controversial stories out of fear that they would have to pay significant damages to victims of libel. However, the U.S. Supreme Court ruled that the First Amendment requires that public figures suing for libel must show not only that the information in question is untrue, but also that the publication deliberately intended to be malicious, false, and damaging.[27] If a public figure suing for libel cannot prove that the publication intended to inflict harm, then the publication is protected under the First Amendment. After receiving negative press coverage, President Donald Trump has complained about libel protections and argued that the law should be changed to allow public figures greater latitude to sue media outlets.[28]

In contrast to the strong First Amendment protection that print media enjoy, broadcast radio and television are subject to considerable government regulation. The different standard results from the availability of outlets for expression. With print media, anyone with enough means can publish and distribute his or her views. But there are a finite number of frequencies on which broadcast radio and television stations can transmit their signal. Therefore, stations may not broadcast unless the federal government, specifically the Federal Communications Commission (FCC), grants a license. Based on its authority to issue these licenses, the FCC can regulate the content of the broadcasts. For example, because children can be easily exposed to radio and television broadcasts, the FCC prohibits the airing of "indecent material," even if that material is protected in other media venues.[29]

Like print media, cable and satellite television and radio, the Internet, and streaming services, such as Netflix, enjoy strong First Amendment protection. Cable and satellite subscribers voluntarily decide to purchase their system and can choose which channels are transmitted into their homes; therefore, cable and satellite subscribers enjoy much more control over what their children could unwittingly watch compared to broadcast radio and television listeners. Because the Internet can be used easily to access pornography, the federal government has sought to regulate sexually explicit material on the Internet; however, the Supreme Court has invalidated these laws as a violation of the First Amendment.[30] The federal judiciary still limits governmental attempts to censor pornography on the Internet.

The cast of the Netflix original series *Orange Is the New Black* receive a Screen Actors Guild Award. The show depicts life in a female federal prison. It emphasizes issues of race, sexual orientation, political corruption, and problems associated with mass incarceration. Because the program is shown on a streaming service, it is able to depict sexually explicit scenes and mature subject matter, which would not be permitted on broadcast television.

Freedom of Religion

The debate over the relationship between religion and government is a critical civil liberties issue. As with freedom of expression, freedom of religion draws on the First Amendment. Specifically, the First Amendment states that "Congress shall make no law respecting an establishment of religion, or prohibiting the free exercise thereof." The establishment clause prevents the government from sponsoring or favoring religion. The free exercise clause ensures that all Americans are free to worship as they choose. Because these clauses are worded so broadly, their interpretation is ambiguous when applied to political controversies surrounding religion. Furthermore, the interpretation of both clauses has affected the politics of race and ethnicity.

Establishment of Religion

Establishment Clause A provision in the First Amendment to the U.S. Constitution that prevents the government from endorsing religion.

Separation of Church and State A constitutional principle that prevents the government (federal, state, or local) from interfering with or advancing religion or religious activity.

The **establishment clause** prohibits state sponsorship of religion, which since 1947 the U.S. Supreme Court has interpreted to mean a separation of church and state.[31] **Separation of church and state** prevents the government (state, federal, or local) from interfering with or advancing any religion or religious activity. For example, since the 1960s the U.S. Supreme Court has consistently ruled that all forms of organized prayer in public schools violate the establishment clause,[32] even though a majority of Americans favor voluntary prayer in public schools.[33]

However, the Supreme Court has recently interpreted the establishment clause to allow some government mixing with religion, especially when a government provides funds that can aid religious institutions. Several states and localities have provided parents of children in poorly performing public schools with vouchers to apply toward tuition at private schools. Because the vast majority of voucher recipients use the money for parochial schools, many people argue that the voucher programs violate the establishment clause, but the Supreme Court has ruled that vouchers do not directly aid religion and are thus constitutional.[34] A similar establishment clause controversy concerns the government collaborating with religious organizations to handle social welfare duties, which has been the practice in the Bush, Obama, and Trump administrations through an office in the Executive Branch dedicated to promoting partnerships between government agencies and religious groups.[35]

Minority-group politics intersects issues of government funding of religious schools and social services because low-income Blacks and Latinos are often the beneficiaries of such policies. Although many racial and ethnic minorities oppose vouchers, a significant number of Blacks and Latinos are willing to overlook the establishment clause concerns and push for any program that addresses poverty in minority communities. A 2015 survey shows that Blacks and Latinos favor school vouchers for low-income families significantly more than the national average—58 percent for Latinos and 66 percent for African Americans versus 42 percent of the national average.[36]

Free Exercise of Religion

Although the **free exercise clause** clearly prevents laws that directly prohibit the practice of religion, it is less clear whether it protects against neutral, secular laws that indirectly and unintentionally hinder religion. Prior to the 1960s, laws that disadvantaged religious worship were permitted as long as they were designed with a neutral, nonreligious intent. As a result, adherents to uncommon religions often suffered unintentional discrimination at the hands of those who adhered to the more mainstream religions.[37]

By the 1960s, the free exercise clause was expanded to emphasize an individual's ability to worship regardless of the intent of a law. If a neutral law adversely affected religious worship, then the government was required to show a compelling reason for enforcing the law. Thus, Americans were exempt from following laws that hindered the practice of their religion, unless the government could show a compelling justification to require obedience to those laws.[38]

Although this standard allowed for religious exemptions from secular laws, the Supreme Court would not exempt religious groups if the government could show a compelling justification for requiring them to adhere to these laws. Two controversial examples of compelling justification involve race and ethnicity. During the 1970s, Bob Jones University, a Christian college, lost its tax-exempt status because its ban on interracial dating and marriage violated federal civil rights laws. The school claimed that the free exercise clause allowed it to discriminate, but the Supreme Court ruled that the government's interest in preventing racial discrimination overrode the free exercise clause.[39] In 1987, the Supreme Court ruled that New Jersey prison security regulations were a compelling justification for denying Islamic prisoners, many of whom were Black, permission to congregate for prayer during a lockdown.[40]

In 1990, the U.S. Supreme Court reinterpreted the free exercise clause in favor of government authority over individual religious liberty. In the landmark case of *Employment Division v. Smith* (1990), two Native American drug counselors were fired for ingesting the hallucinogenic substance peyote as part of an ancient religious ceremony. The state of Oregon denied them unemployment benefits, arguing that the counselors had been dismissed for "disciplinary" reasons, and the U.S. Supreme Court upheld this policy, refusing to overturn neutral, secular laws even if they hinder the practice of religion.[41] By shifting the emphasis back to the intent of the law, this ruling diminished religious liberty for adherents to nontraditional religions, particularly American Indian Peoples. "Our Voices: The Right to Practice Nontraditional Religions (*Employment Division v. Smith*)," on page 110, discusses in more detail the issue of religious liberty for Native Americans.

Despite the Supreme Court's more recent tilt toward government authority in free exercise cases, the free exercise clause has protected Americans, especially racial and ethnic minorities, from laws that directly prevent them from practicing their religion. In 1993, the Supreme Court struck down a city of Hialeah, Florida, ordinance that banned the ritualistic sacrifice of animals

Free Exercise Clause A provision in the First Amendment to the U.S. Constitution that prevents the government from prohibiting people from practicing their religion.

How do we interpret the free exercise and establishment clauses?

within the city limits. This policy was intended to prevent Santeria worshippers,[42] most of whom are Latino or Afro-Caribbean, from practicing their religion. Because the ordinance was specifically directed at Santeria, the Court ruled that it was not a neutral, secular law.[43] In 2006, the U.S. Supreme Court overturned a criminal ban on a hallucinogenic tea used in tribal religious ceremonies because outlawing the sacred tea violated American Indians' free exercise of religion.[44]

Recently, free exercise of religion has become an issue for American Muslims. Unlike some countries, such as France, the United States has not banned certain Muslim practices, such as women wearing a veil (or *hijab*), but there have been conflicts concerning Islamic religious practices. For example, the clothing store Abercrombie & Fitch did not hire Samantha Elauf, a Muslim woman who wears a hijab, because it conflicted with the store's dress code policy. The Equal Employment Opportunity Commission (EEOC), a government agency that protects individuals' civil rights (see Chapter 8), sued Abercrombie & Fitch on Elauf's behalf because the company's religious discrimination violated Title VII of the Civil Rights Act (see Chapter 5). The U.S. Supreme Court ruled overwhelmingly that the company cannot refuse to hire someone for wearing the religious garment, even if that person does not explicitly ask for an accommodation.[45] Similarly, in 2015 the Supreme Court ruled against an Arkansas prison that prevented Muslim inmates from growing beards. The state argued that this regulation was necessary because inmates could hide contraband in their beards, but the U.S. Supreme Court unanimously ruled in favor of Muslim prisoners' religious liberty.[46]

Criminal Justice

Civil liberties are also relevant for criminal justice issues. Several amendments in the Bill of Rights protect individuals and limit government law enforcement at each stage of the criminal justice process: investigation (Fourth and Fifth), trial (Sixth), and punishment (Eighth). Because the language of these amendments is broadly worded, their application to criminal justice issues varies considerably. The unequal application of civil liberties to criminal justice has led to less protection for racial and ethnic minorities, especially as a result of the "War on Drugs" and the "War on Terror."

Investigation

The Fourth Amendment to the Constitution states that "The right of the people to be secure in their persons, houses, papers, and effects, against unreasonable searches and seizures shall not be violated, and no Warrants shall issue, but upon probable cause, supported by oath or affirmation, and particularly describing the place to be searched, and the persons or things to be seized." Therefore, before law enforcement officers search people, homes, or businesses, they are required by the Fourth Amendment to secure a **search warrant**, which is a legal document issued by a judge or a magistrate that

Search Warrant A legal document that allows law enforcement to search someone's person, home, or business.

specifically authorizes police to enter into a private area and search for and seize evidence of criminal activity. The Fourth Amendment stipulates that the judge or magistrate cannot issue a warrant unless the law enforcement officer has shown **probable cause**—the majority of the evidence must support the existence of criminal activity. This amendment protects individuals because the police must prove to a neutral third party—the judge or magistrate—that there is sufficient reason to violate the sanctity of someone's property or person. To enforce the provisions of the Fourth Amendment, the **exclusionary rule** mandates that any evidence gathered in violation of the Fourth Amendment may not be used in court against the defendant unless the law enforcement officers in question are able to demonstrate that they acted in good faith.[47]

Despite these clear civil liberties guarantees embodied in the Fourth Amendment, there have been exceptions to the warrant requirement, especially as technological advancements have allowed law enforcement to uncover evidence inside a person's home or business without physically entering the structure. In 1967, the Supreme Court ruled that law enforcement agents needed a warrant before listening to private telephone conversations with a wiretap device.[48] However, in the name of fighting terrorism since the September 11, 2001, attacks, the U.S. government has conducted electronic wiretap investigations of suspected terrorists without warrants. In 2006, a federal judge ruled that the government needed to get a warrant even for terrorism investigations.[49] However, that decision was overturned on appeal,[50] and the U.S. Supreme Court declined to review that appeal.[51]

Conversely, civil liberties organizations have successfully stopped another data collection process in which the National Security Agency (NSA), an intelligence-gathering agency in the national government, collected everyone's telephone "meta-data," without any suspicion of terrorist activity. The NSA did not record conversations, but it did record who made the calls, who received the calls, and the length of the calls. The American Civil Liberties Union (ACLU) challenged this practice in federal court, arguing that it violated the Fourth Amendment and even the USA PATRIOT Act (this is the acronym for Uniting and Strengthening America by Providing Appropriate Tools Required to Intercept and Obstruct Terrorism), which authorized more extensive surveillance after the September 11 attacks. In 2015 the Second Circuit Court of Appeals sided with the ACLU and invalidated the mass, suspicionless "meta" searches.[52] Soon after this decision, Congress passed the USA Freedom Act, which replaced the expired USA PATRIOT Act, and this new bill explicitly banned these searches of phone records.[53]

The concept of **racial profiling**, or singling out suspects for searches because of their race or ethnicity, also presents important concerns about the application of the Fourth Amendment. The phrase "driving while Black" emphasizes the point law enforcement officers are more likely to stop, search, and even arrest African Americans than they are likely to arrest Whites. A number of studies have shown that with all other circumstances being equal,

Probable Cause A legal requirement that there be more evidence indicating guilt than indicating innocence before a law enforcement officer can act.

Exclusionary Rule A judicially created civil liberties protection that prohibits the use of evidence gathered in violation of the Fourth Amendment.

Racial Profiling A law enforcement technique that singles out suspects on the basis of their race or ethnicity.

our voices

The Right to Practice Nontraditional Religions (*Employment Division v. Smith*)

Although the First Amendment clearly protects an individual's right to pursue a chosen religion, American laws and policies often discriminate against people who adhere to nontraditional religions. Laws are drafted to be neutral and to have no explicit intent to hinder religious practice might still harm nontraditional worshippers. For example, Alfred Smith and Galen Black were two drug and alcohol rehabilitation counselors who belonged to the Native American Church. As part of their religion, Smith and Black participated in a sacred ceremony involving the ingestion of peyote, which is an illegal substance that induces a psychedelic effect. Even though drug laws exempted American Indian religions from prosecution, Smith and Black were still dismissed from their jobs because they had violated a policy forbidding the consumption of a controlled substance. The state of Oregon then denied Smith and Black unemployment benefits because they had been dismissed for disciplinary reasons. They took their case to the Supreme

Court, arguing that Oregon's secular, neutral policy still hindered the practice of their religion in violation of the First Amendment.

The excerpts here come from an exchange between Craig A. Dorsay, who argued Smith and Black's case before the U.S. Supreme Court, and Associate Justice Antonin Scalia. Much of Dorsay's argument focused on the importance of protecting a nontraditional, even unpopular, religious practice. His use of the term *ethnocentric* to describe Oregon's policy is particularly interesting. An ethnocentric view evaluates other cultures according to the preconceived notions of one's own culture. In other words, the dominant Judeo-Christian viewpoint in Oregon was unwilling to go beyond its own religious precepts to understand the importance of peyote in American Indian religion. Note also how Dorsay compared the practice of ingesting peyote to the consumption of sacramental wine. The late Justice Scalia was clearly skeptical and assumed that peyote was necessarily harmful.

Native Americans engage in a peyote ceremony. Although peyote is generally a banned substance, the First Amendment's free exercise clause allows Native Americans to use it as part of a religious ceremony that they have been practicing for thousands of years.

DORSAY: If you looked at this situation and Indian people were in charge of government, and you look at the devastating impact that alcohol has had on Indian people . . . you might well find that alcohol was the Schedule 1 substance and peyote was not listed at all. And we are getting here to the heart of the ethnocentric view . . . of what constitutes religion in the United States. And I think that needs to be looked at very hard before determining what is a dangerous substance and what is not.

SCALIA: Your pointing to the traditional use of wine at religious services would not make any difference. I don't assume that the states would be compelled to allow excessive use of alcohol, drunken parties on grounds of religion. . . . I don't see a correlation between the wine and the peyote. I mean, it is acknowledged that . . . the whole purpose of the ingestion of peyote is its hallucinogenic effect.

DORSAY: I don't disagree with that. What I disagree with is the fact that the ingestion is harmful. There is no documented evidence that the use of peyote in these carefully circumscribed ceremonials has any harm to the individual, to the society . . ., or to . . . law enforcement.

Ultimately, the majority of the Supreme Court did not accept Dorsay's argument and upheld Oregon's policy. In his opinion, Scalia recognized that this ruling "will place at a relative disadvantage those religious practices that are not widely engaged in; but that is an unavoidable consequence of democratic government."*

* *Employment Division v. Smith*, 494 U.S. 872 (1990), 893.

Source: Adapted from Irons, P. (Ed.). (1997). *May it please the court: The First Amendment.* New York: New Press, pp. 91–92. The entire oral argument can be heard at Oyez.org, sponsored by the Illinois Institute of Technology Chicago, Kent School of Law, https://www.oyez.org/cases/1989/88-1213.

Black drivers are more likely than White drivers to be stopped and searched by police. Recently, cases of "driving while Black" culminated in tragic results. For example, in Minnesota in 2016, an African American named Philando Castile was initially stopped because he vaguely resembled a robbery suspect (based on the width of his nose), despite no actual evidence that Castile committed a robbery. The situation quickly escalated and resulted in police shooting and killing Castile.[54] Racial profiling also affects Latinos, especially in immigration enforcement. For example, in 2018 Ana Suda and Mimi Hernandez, who are both American citizens, were speaking Spanish while shopping for food at a Montana gas station. A border patrol agent overheard them speaking Spanish and detained them for more than thirty minutes on the suspicion that they were undocumented immigrants.[55]

Because the September 11, 2001, attacks on the World Trade Center and Pentagon were carried out by people smuggling weapons onto commercial airliners, the federal government has greatly intensified security at airports. All passengers, regardless of suspicion, are subject to hand searches of their luggage and x-ray searches of their person. However, because all the September 11 hijackers were Middle Eastern men, passengers who fit that profile are most likely to be searched, without corroborating suspicion.[56] "Evaluating Equality: Recognizing and Debating Conflicting Values in Political Cartoons on Racial Profiling in Fighting Terrorism" on page 113 explores this controversy in more detail from the perspective of political cartoons.

Among other guarantees, the Fifth Amendment to the Constitution provides that "No person . . . shall be compelled in any criminal case to be a witness against himself." This provision clearly guarantees that defendants cannot be forced to furnish information that could be used against them in a trial. However, the language does not obviously apply to police interrogations, and, before the 1960s, states were able to determine their own police interrogation procedures, which often included physical and psychological means of extracting confessions. In 1964, the U.S. Supreme Court expanded the scope of the Fifth Amendment when it ruled that confessions would not be admissible at trial if the police refused a suspect's request that an attorney be present during the interrogation.[57] With an attorney present, the suspect is able to counter the various confession-inducing techniques that police employ.

The Supreme Court expanded legal protections against forced confessions when it issued its landmark ruling in *Miranda v. Arizona* (1966). In this case, police in Phoenix, Arizona, suspected that Ernesto Miranda, a twenty-three-year-old illiterate indigent, had kidnapped and raped an eighteen-year-old woman. While in police custody and without an attorney, Miranda confessed to the crime, and prosecutors used that confession to convict him of rape and kidnapping. Miranda appealed his conviction, and the U.S. Supreme Court extended its control over the way in which police officers question suspects. In addition to allowing attorneys to be present during interrogation, the ruling stated that law enforcement agents are required to inform suspects of what have come to be called **Miranda rights**.[58] This ruling advanced civil liberties by ensuring that citizens' ignorance of their rights does not preclude enjoyment of those rights.

Miranda Rights The Supreme Court's requirement that law enforcement must inform criminal suspects of the following: (1) that they have the right to remain silent, (2) that anything they say can be used against them in court, (3) that they have the right to the presence of an attorney, and (4) that if they cannot afford an attorney, then the court will appoint one before the interrogation takes place.

Trial

The Sixth Amendment to the Constitution guarantees that "In all criminal prosecutions, the accused shall enjoy the right to a speedy trial, by an impartial jury . . . and to have the Assistance of Council in his defence." Although the Constitution explicitly guarantees both liberties, they are not applied equally throughout the United States. For most of the nation's history, state governments did not provide defense attorneys for defendants who could not afford legal counsel. In the early 1960s, the Supreme Court ruled that the Sixth Amendment requires states to appoint attorneys for defendants who cannot afford them.[59] As a result, states and localities now provide the needy with legal counsel through public defenders, who are government-employed attorneys charged with the task of advocating on behalf of criminal defendants who cannot afford legal fees. The requirement that courts must provide counsel for poor defendants has equalized the application of a critical civil liberty.

Despite the requirement that states and localities appoint counsel for the indigent, class inequities in legal representation for criminal defendants still exist. With limited financial support, public defenders are not able to devote sufficient time and resources to defending their many clients. The indigent might get a defense, but it is probably not the best possible defense. Conversely, wealthy clients are able to afford highly skilled lawyers who can

evaluating equality

Recognizing and Debating Conflicting Values in Political Cartoons on Racial Profiling in Fighting Terrorism

The Fourth Amendment guarantees that law enforcement cannot stop, search, or harass Americans without reasonable suspicion of wrongdoing. However, many Americans, especially in times of crisis, are willing to forgo this right to enhance security.

After the September 11, 2001, attacks, airline passengers surrendered more of their Fourth and Fifth Amendment civil liberties. Everyday items have been banned from airplanes, air travelers are required to submit to x-ray searches, and they and their luggage can be stopped and searched at any time. Because of the threat of terrorism, airline passengers do not enjoy the same rights as if they are in a car, on the street, or in their homes.

The issue of airport searches becomes more complex because searches are not conducted uniformly. Because the September 11 hijackers were all Middle Eastern men, people who appear to be of the same ethnic background are far more likely to be searched. Supporters of this form of racial profiling argue that it is a sensible way to ensure the safety of all Americans. They value security above all else. Conversely, opponents of racial profiling at airports argue that civil liberties need to be applied equally for all people regardless of race or national origin. They emphasize the values of equality and a uniform application of civil liberties.

Through the use of visual and verbal humor, the two political cartoons here typify the values underlying both views. The Wayne Stayskal cartoon from the *Tampa Tribune* (June 10, 2002) (top) endorses the value of security. By ignoring what is "obvious" before their eyes, these security personnel, who refuse to profile, are compromising security, as symbolized by the threat the extraterrestrial being poses. The 2002 Lalo Alcaraz cartoon from the *LA Weekly* (bottom) supports the value that individual liberties must be applied universally if they are to mean anything. This cartoon depicts racial profiling not as a safety measure, but

Source: (Courtesy of Lalo Alcaraz/Los Angeles Times)

(Continued)

evaluating equality (Continued)

instead as an arbitrary and discriminatory practice.

Although the cartoons use humor to illustrate their opinions, racial profiling is a serious issue. Nobody should condone blatant racial or ethnic profiling, but the issue does present important debates about the balance between security and liberty.

- To what extent should airport security use physical appearance in making decisions to investigate terrorist activities?
- Should individuals have less civil liberties protection in airports, which are more vulnerable to a terrorist attack?
- Do more recent terrorist attacks—such as the 2013 Boston Marathon bombing, the 2016 Pulse Nightclub shooting in Orlando, or the 2017 Vehicle attack against pedestrians in New York City—merit additional scrutiny in public (i.e., outside of airports), especially against Muslims?
- Numerous other instances of police shooting unarmed Blacks demonstrate that racial profiling also occurs in everyday law enforcement that is not related to terrorism. To what extent should national, state, and local governments use their authority to prevent this form of racial profiling?

devote full attention to their cases. A recent study of public defenders in New York State found that many low-income defendants never consulted with their court-appointed attorneys until the day of their hearings.[60]

This disparity affects racial and ethnic minorities, who are often in need of public defenders. Recently, evidence has emerged that public defenders exhibit "implicit bias" (i.e. unconscious racial prejudice) against African American defendants. For example, given their limited resources, public defenders are likely to prioritize their effort for clients they believe to be innocent, and their "implicit bias" can lead some public defenders to assume that their Black clients are less likely than their White clients to be innocent.[61]

In addition to mandating the right to counsel, the Sixth Amendment grants an accused person the right to trial by an impartial jury. The size of juries varies across states, ranging from six to twelve members. Whereas a trial judge rules on matters of law, a jury decides whether the evidence proves beyond a reasonable doubt that a defendant is guilty. Although all states are required to try criminal defendants with a jury, the impartiality of juries is less clear. The process of convening juries allows each side to manipulate the type of jury that is empaneled.

Prior to the commencement of a trial, prosecutors and defense attorneys submit questions to a pool of possible jurors to eliminate potentially prejudiced jurors. Judges will dismiss any potential juror deemed unable to decide the case fairly and objectively. Additionally, the prosecution and the defense are each allotted a set number of **peremptory challenges**, which allow them to dismiss a potential juror without providing a reason. Both sides strategically use their given number of peremptory challenges to eliminate people who would be most predisposed against their side.

Peremptory Challenges The right of each side in a legal case to discard a set number of potential jurors without needing to express a reason for doing so.

This jury selection process has led to the underrepresentation of racial and ethnic minorities on juries. Since the end of the Civil War, the U.S. Supreme Court has prevented states from actively prohibiting Blacks from serving on juries.[62] Nevertheless, prosecutors routinely used their peremptory challenges to remove African Americans from specific juries, particularly in cases with an African American defendant.

Although the U.S. Supreme Court in 1986 ruled that it is unconstitutional for prosecutors to use their peremptory challenges to eliminate Blacks or other racial minorities from a specific jury,[63] there is still some controversy over whether discrimination still exists. Legal experts have found that prosecutors are still able to get away with racial discrimination by using racially neutral terms to justify excluding racial minorities. For example, in Alabama 85 percent of Blacks in a jury pool were dismissed for vague reasons, such as they "were unkempt and gruff," "resembled the [Black] defendant," or "were unemployed."[64] However, a recent empirical study has found that peremptory challenges do not affect the racial and ethnic composition of juries throughout the United States, but juries with only six members are less racially diverse than juries with twelve members.[65]

Punishment

The Eighth Amendment to the Constitution states, "Excessive bail shall not be required, nor excessive fines imposed, nor cruel and unusual punishments inflicted"; however, the amendment provides no clear definition of "cruel."

A death-row inmate at the Lieber Correctional Institution near Ridgeville, South Carolina, February 19, 2003. The death penalty is a controversial issue of civil liberties, with some people arguing that it violates the Eighth Amendment ban on cruel and unusual punishment and discriminates against racial and ethnic minorities. However, a majority of the country supports capital punishment.

The Eighth Amendment prevents brutal or wantonly negligent treatment of prisoners. As a result, prisoners who are victims of excessive beatings can sue in federal court on the basis of their Eighth Amendment rights.[66] However, the Eighth Amendment does not apply to questions concerning the magnitude of a criminal sentence or whether the "sentence fits the crime." In fact, in 1991 the U.S. Supreme Court ruled that it was not cruel and unusual for Michigan to sentence a man to life in prison without parole for possessing 672 grams of cocaine, even though murderers in Michigan received the same sentence (Michigan has no death penalty) and the equivalent crime in other states carried significantly lower penalties.[67] Although Michigan has relaxed these mandatory life-without-parole sentences for drug crimes,[68] the Supreme Court's interpretation of the Eighth Amendment persists today.

There is also evidence that criminal sentences are disproportionate according to race and ethnicity. Since the 1970s, African American and Latino incarceration rates have increased at a much faster rate than the incarceration rate of Whites. A 2015 study shows that although Whites and Blacks have equal levels of drug use, Blacks are six times more likely than Whites to be imprisoned for drug crimes. Additionally, although African Americans constitute only one-eighth of people who use illegal drugs, they constitute one-third of people in jail or prison for drug crimes.[69]

Table 4.2 demonstrates that, despite a few exceptions, states with the highest Black incarceration rates relative to White incarceration rates have moderately sized Black populations, and states with the lowest Black incarceration rates relative to White incarceration rates have high Black populations. However, Table 4.3 shows that similar patterns do not exist for Latinos and that the disparities between Latinos and Whites is narrower than the disparity between Blacks and Whites. We discuss racial disparities in sentencing in more detail in Chapter 16, focusing especially on the racial impact of inequities between sentencing for crack cocaine versus powder cocaine.

The Eighth Amendment has been significant in the issue of the death penalty. Although many Americans regard capital punishment as "cruel and unusual," the Eighth Amendment does not prevent death sentences. Each state sets its own policies on capital punishment, including whether to use it at all. The Supreme Court has also upheld states' authority to choose their method of execution, despite claims that they cause immense suffering before killing the inmate.[70] Currently, thirty-one states have the death penalty, and seventeen states plus the District of Columbia do not. Since 2007 seven states that had capital punishment (Connecticut, Illinois, Maryland, Nebraska, New Jersey, New Mexico, and New York) have abolished it. Governors in four states with capital punishment (Colorado, Oregon, Pennsylvania, and Washington) have imposed moratoriums on executions, but capital punishment still exists in those states, and future governors could reinstitute executions.[71]

There is evidence that capital punishment is administered in a racially discriminatory fashion. In the late 1980s, social scientists uncovered

TABLE 4.2 States with the Highest and Lowest Ratios of Black (2016 Data) to White Incarceration Rates and Percent Black Population (2017 Data)

Highest Black Incarceration Rate			Lowest Black Incarceration Rate		
State	Rate	Percent Black	State	Rate	Percent Black
New Jersey	12.2:1	15.0	Hawaii	2.4:1	2.2
Wisconsin	11.5:1	6.6	Mississippi	3.0:1	37.7
Iowa	11.1:1	3.7	Georgia	3.2:1	32.0
Minnesota	11.0:1	6.2	Kentucky	3.3:1	8.3
Vermont	10.5:1	1.3	Alabama	3.3:1	26.8
Connecticut	9.4:1	11.8	West Virginia	3.5:1	3.6
Pennsylvania	8.9:1	11.8	Florida	3.5:1	16.8
California	8.8:1	6.5	Tennessee	3.7:1	17.1
Nebraska	8.4:1	5.1	Arkansas	3.8:1	15.7
Rhode Island	8.3:1	8.1	Alaska	3.8:1	3.8

Sources: Adapted from The Sentencing Project. The facts: State-by-state data. Retrieved May 26, 2018, from https://www.sentencingproject.org/the-facts/#map?dataset-option=SIR; U.S. Census. QuickFacts. Retrieved May 26, 2018, from https://www.census.gov/quickfacts/fact/table/US/PST045216. Washington, DC, was not included in this analysis because of missing data.

TABLE 4.3 States with the Highest and Lowest Ratios of Latino (2016 Data) to White Incarceration Rates and Percent Latino Population (2017 Data)

Highest Latino Incarceration Rate			Lowest Latino Incarceration Rate		
State	Rate	Percent Latino	State	Rate	Percent Latino
Massachusetts	4.3:1	11.5	Louisiana	0.1:1	5.0
Connecticut	3.9:1	15.7	Florida	0.2:1	24.9
Pennsylvania	3.3:1	7.0	Hawaii	0.3:1	10.4
New York	3.4:1	19.0	Michigan	0.4:1	5.0
Minnesota	2.6:1	15.4	Kentucky	0.4:1	3.5
Wisconsin	2.5:1	6.7	Virginia	0.4:1	9.1
Rhode Island	2.5:1	14.9	West Virginia	0.5:1	1.5
North Dakota	2.3:1	3.6	Alaska	0.5:1	7.0
Colorado	2.3:1	21.3	Arkansas	0.6:1	7.3
New Jersey	2.5:1	20.0	Tennessee	0.6:1	5.2

Sources: Adapted from The Sentencing Project. The facts: State-by-state data. Retrieved May 26, 2018, from https://www.sentencingproject.org/the-facts/#map?dataset-option=SIR; U.S. Census. QuickFacts. Retrieved May 26, 2018, from https://www.census.gov/quickfacts/fact/table/US/PST045216. Alabama, Maryland, Montana, Vermont, and Washington, DC, were not included in this analysis because of missing data.

evidence of two specific forms of racial discrimination in capital punishment. With all else held constant, Black defendants were more likely than White defendants to receive capital punishment, and prosecutors were far more likely to seek and receive death sentences in cases where the victim was White than in cases where the victim was Black.[72] However, the U.S. Supreme Court has ruled that statistical evidence of racial discrimination in capital punishment generally is insufficient by itself to invalidate the death sentence of any individual.[73] "Measuring Equality: Discrimination, Death Row Population, and Executions in States with the Death Penalty" addresses this issue in more detail.

Privacy

All the civil liberties discussed up to this point are mentioned specifically in one of the amendments in the Bill of Rights. However, the U.S. Supreme Court has extended protection to a civil liberty that is not explicitly mentioned in the Constitution: the right to privacy. This right refers to an individual's general right to be left alone, and although this right is not specifically mentioned in the Constitution, it is considered just as fundamental as the rights enumerated in the Constitution.

measuring equality

Discrimination, Death Row Population, and Executions in States with the Death Penalty

Many activists and scholars have uncovered evidence of racial disparities in capital sentencing patterns, in which minorities are more likely than Whites to receive a death sentence. These disparities could be the result of different crime patterns, disparate rates of arrest, prosecutorial discretion in seeking the death penalty, and the behavior of juries and judges in deciding sentences. Although we do not conclusively test these competing explanations here, we do address geographical variations in these disparities for Blacks and Latinos. Table 4.4 displays by state the percentage of the overall population that is Black, the percentage of the death row population that is Black, and the ratio of Blacks on death row to Blacks in the population. A ratio greater than 1:1 means that Blacks are sentenced to death in a proportion larger than their presence in the population, and a ratio less than 1:1

demonstrates that Blacks are sentenced to death in a proportion that is lower than their presence in the population. Additionally, Figure 4.1 shows for each region (South, Midwest, and West) the average ratio of Black composition on death row to Black population percentage.

What are some patterns among the different states? Is there significant variation among regions? Considering the regional history of discrimination against Blacks, are you surprised by those results?

We have conducted the same analysis for Latinos (see Table 4.5). Again, examine whether there is significant variation among the states and regions. Considering the regional history of discrimination against Latinos, are you surprised by those results? Do you notice any stark differences between the sentencing disparities for Blacks and the disparities for Latinos?

TABLE 4.4 Blacks on Death Row

State	Percent of State Black	Percent of Death Row Black	Ratio Death Row/Population
North			
New Hampshire	1.5	0.0	0.0:1
Pennsylvania	11.8	53.4	4.53:1
Midwest			
Indiana	9.7	25.0	2.58:1
Kansas	6.2	30.0	4.84:1
Missouri	11.8	33.0	2.80:1
Nebraska	5.0	27.3	5.46:1
Ohio	12.8	55.6	4.34:1
Oklahoma	7.8	45.8	5.87:1
South Dakota	2.0	0.0	0. 00:1
South			
Alabama	26.8	53.4	1.99:1
Arkansas	15.7	54.8	3.49:1
Florida	16.8	38.1	2.27:1
Georgia	32.0	52.5	1.64:1
Kentucky	8.3	15.2	1.83:1
Louisiana	32.6	65.2	2.00:1
Mississippi	37.7	52.1	1.38:1
North Carolina	22.2	52.1	2.35:1
South Carolina	27.5	52.5	1.91:1
Tennessee	17.1	46.8	2.74:1
Texas	12.6	43.6	3.46:1
Virginia	19.8	50.0	2.53:1
West			
Arizona	4.9	13.6	2.78:1
California	6.5	36.3	5.58:1
Colorado	4.6	100.0	21.74:1
Idaho	0.8	0.0	0.00:1
Montana	0.6	0.0	0.00:1
Nevada	9.6	36.6	3.81:1
New Mexico	2.5	0.0	0.00:1
Oregon	2.1	6.3	3.00:1
Utah	1.4	11.1	7.93:1
Washington	4.1	37.5	9.15:1
Wyoming	1.3	0.0	0.00:1

(Continued)

measuring equality *(Continued)*

TABLE 4.5 Latinos on Death Row

State	Percent of State Latino	Percent of Death Row Latino	Ratio Death Row/Population
New Hampshire	3.5	0.0	0. 00:1
Pennsylvania	7.0	8.9	1.27:1
Midwest			
Indiana	6.8	0.0	0.00:1
Kansas	11.6	0.0	0.00:1
Missouri	4.1	0.0	0.00:1
Nebraska	10.7	45.5	4.25:1
Ohio	3.7	1.4	0.38:1
Oklahoma	10.3	4.2	0.41:1
South Dakota	3.7	0.0	0.00:1
South			
Alabama	4.2	1.0	0.24:1
Arkansas	7.3	3.2	0.44:1
Florida	24.9	7.1	0.29:1
Georgia	9.4	4.9	0.52:1
Kentucky	3.5	0.0	0.00:1
Louisiana	5.0	4.2	0.84:1
Mississippi	3.1	2.1	0.68:1
North Carolina	9.2	3.4	0.37:1
South Carolina	5.5	2.5	0.45:1
Tennessee	5.2	1.6	0.31:1
Texas	39.1	27.4	0.70:1
Virginia	9.1	0.0	0.00:1
West			
Arizona	30.9	20.0	0.73:1
California	38.9	25.2	0.65:1
Colorado	21.3	0	0.00:1
Idaho	12.3	0.0	0.00:1
Montana	3.6	0.0	0.00:1
Nevada	28.5	12.2	0.43:1
New Mexico	48.5	0.0	0.00:1
Oregon	12.8	9.4	0.73:1
Utah	13.8	22.2	1.61:1
Washington	12.4	0.0	0.00:1
Wyoming	10.0	0.0	0.00:1

Sources: Adapted from Criminal Justice Project of the NAACP Legal Defense Fund. (2017, October 1). Death Row, USA: Winter 2016, pp. 37–38. Retrieved May 26, 2018, from http://www.naacpldf.org/files/case_issue/DRUSAFall2017_.pdf; U.S. Census. QuickFacts. Retrieved May 26, 2018, from https://www.census.gov/quickfacts/fact/table/US/PST045216.

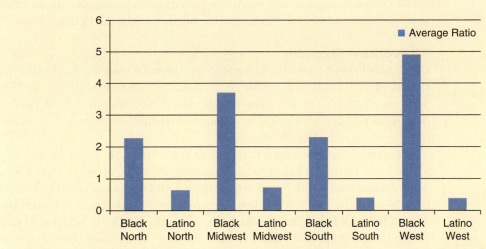

Figure 4.1 Average Ratio of Group Composition on Death Row to Group Composition of Population by Region (North, Midwest, South, and West) and Race/Ethnicity (Black and Latino)

The right to privacy gives Americans a zone of control over personal life decisions, and this zone of control is immune from government intrusion. Because the legal definition of privacy is so vague, however, there is little agreement on how far this zone should extend. The debates over the right to privacy have been most acute regarding decisions affecting a person's own autonomy and reproductive freedom. These debates have also affected minority-group politics.

Personal Autonomy

One aspect of privacy concerns personal autonomy, the ability of individuals to control significant life decisions without government interference. Personal autonomy includes sexual relations between consenting adults, particularly same-sex couples. For most of American history, states were permitted to ban sexual activity between people of the same sex, and in the 1984 case of *Bowers v. Hardwick*, the U.S. Supreme Court upheld these laws as constitutional.[74]

After 1984, many states overturned such laws on their own, and those that kept the laws rarely enforced them. Nevertheless, in 1998 the state of Texas fined two males $200 each for engaging in sexual activity with each other. In the landmark 2003 *Lawrence v. Texas* decision, the U.S. Supreme Court overturned *Bowers v. Hardwick*, holding that laws banning consensual sexual activity between adults infringe on the individual's right to privacy.[75]

Another personal autonomy issue concerns the **right to die**. Most states possess some authority to prevent individuals from taking their own lives, even if those individuals are terminally ill. The Supreme Court has ruled, however, that an individual's right to privacy includes the right to refuse medical treatment either directly, through a spouse, or indirectly, through a living will, which is a legal document that directs doctors to discontinue treatment

Right to Die An extension of the right to privacy that includes an individual's right to refuse life-saving medical treatment but does not include the right to commit suicide.

under certain circumstances when the patient is unconscious. Absent prior approval, the state's interest in preserving life outweighs the right to privacy.[76]

Reproductive Freedom

Challenges to state laws interfering with reproductive choice are crucial to the right to privacy. In the landmark case of *Griswold v. Connecticut* (1965), the U.S. Supreme Court overturned a law banning the dissemination of birth control because it violated an unwritten constitutional right to privacy that allows couples access to birth control.[77]

The right to privacy then extended to the issue of abortion. In the early 1970s, most states, including Texas, outlawed abortion. So when Jane Roe, a poor woman residing in Texas, was pregnant, she could not obtain an abortion. With the help of lawyers interested in legalizing abortion, Roe sued the state of Texas for the right to an abortion, and in the landmark case *Roe v. Wade* (1973) the U.S. Supreme Court extended the unwritten constitutional right of privacy to include a woman's control over her pregnancy. The right to an abortion is segmented into three trimesters (periods of three months each). In the first trimester, states have no authority to regulate abortions, but in the second trimester, states can regulate abortions to protect the mother's health. In the third trimester, when the fetus is most able to live outside the woman's womb, states are free to ban abortions in most instances.[78]

This decision generated tremendous controversy between the "pro-choice" view, which supports extending the right to privacy to a woman's control over her pregnancy, and the "pro-life" view, which believes that the government has the authority to protect the fetus in the womb. Pressured by influential groups that bill themselves as "pro-life," many states enacted laws that restricted abortions and made them more difficult to obtain. For example, many states require women to receive counseling before getting an abortion, impose a waiting period (up to twenty-four hours) before a woman can receive an abortion, and order minors to notify their parents or even seek parental consent before getting an abortion. Although the Supreme Court consistently upheld the right to an abortion, it allowed states to enact restrictions that limit that right.[79] Significant controversy continues to exist over attempts to enact restrictions on abortions. For example, in 2016 Iowa banned abortions after the detection of a heartbeat in the fetus, which occurs approximately six weeks into the pregnancy. It is extremely unlikely that within six weeks women will know that they are pregnant and have time to schedule an abortion; consequently, this law effectively bans abortions in Iowa. However, after pro-choice groups challenged this law, a judge has banned it from going into effect as the litigation proceeds.[80] Moreover, under the auspices of ensuring the safety of the procedures, about half of American states regulate abortion providers by requiring abortions to be performed by clinics that have admitting privileges to hospitals, forcing clinics to be located within a prescribed distance from a hospital, and specifying the length and width of rooms and corridors in abortion clinics. Abortion rights supporters argue that these provisions are

Abortion is a controversial political issue that generates considerable passion on both sides. Many people believe that life begins at conception; therefore, abortion is tantamount to murder. Others believe that the constitutional right to privacy protects a woman's decision to control her pregnancy.

unnecessary for safety and are instead subtle ways to limit or eliminate access to abortion.[81] In late June 2016 the U.S. Supreme Court overturned by a 5–3 vote Texas' restrictions on abortion, including a requirement that doctors have admitting privileges at a nearby hospital and regulations on the building. The majority ruled that these restrictions amounted to an "undue burden" on the right to abortion.[82]

Many of these restrictions accomplished their goals of reducing abortion access within states because they forced abortion providers to close. In fact, as of the beginning of 2018 six states (Kentucky, Mississippi, North Dakota, South Dakota, West Virginia, and Wyoming) had only one abortion provider in the entire state, and some of those facilities are in danger of closing.[83] The lack of abortion access adversely impacts low-income women, many of whom are racial or ethnic minorities, because it is more difficult for them to travel far distances to get an abortion. One study demonstrates that travel distance is more likely to decrease abortion access for Latina women compared to Black and White women.[84]

Attitudes about abortion also differ among different racial and ethnic groups. Slightly over half (51 percent) of women receiving abortions in the United States are White, and about 39 percent of women receiving abortions are African Americans, but these figure vary widely across different states.[85] Moreover, as Figure 4.2 shows, Latinos support abortion far less than do

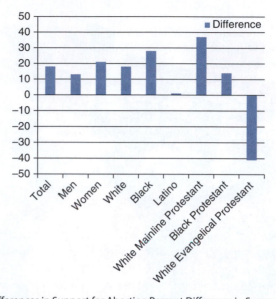

Figure 4.2 Differences in Support for Abortion Percent Difference in Support (should be legal in all or most cases) Versus Opposition (should be illegal in all or most cases) for Abortion
Source: Data adapted from the Pew Research Center: Religion and Public Life. (2017, July 7). Public opinion on abortion: Views on abortion, 1995–2017. *Retrieved May 27, 2018, from http://www.pewforum.org/fact-sheet/public-opinion-on-abortion/.*

Whites and Blacks. The figure also demonstrates that White mainline Protestants are more supportive of abortion rights than are Black Protestants, and men are slightly more supportive of abortions than are women. Additionally, a recent study shows that support for abortion varies among Latinos depends on religious identification. Catholic Latinos support abortion rights more than Fundamentalist Protestant Latinos do.[86]

Conclusion

Civil liberties are the constitutional freedoms that individuals enjoy and on which the government may not encroach, and they are a central component of the relationship between individuals and their government. The Bill of Rights specifies liberties—such as freedom of expression, freedom of religion, and freedom in the criminal justice process—and most provisions of the Bill of Rights apply to all levels of government. Additionally, since the 1960s the U.S. Supreme Court has read a right to privacy into the Bill of Rights.

Although civil liberties are spelled out in the Bill of Rights, their language is vague, ambiguous, and subject to individual interpretation. This chapter examined the specific civil liberties issues of political dissent, pornography and offensive speech, freedom of the press, separation of church and state, freedom to worship, protections for those accused of crimes (including right to counsel and right to jury trial), criminal sentencing policies, personal autonomy, and reproductive freedom.

The politics of race and ethnicity shapes controversies over civil liberties. Racial and ethnic minorities have received less civil liberties protection than have Whites. Undoubtedly, civil liberties have been applied more equally since the founding of the American Republic, but key U.S. Supreme Court rulings, especially since the 1980s, have afforded federal, state, and local governments considerable discretion to decide civil liberties questions. As a result, many government actions have resulted in lower civil liberties for racial and ethnic minorities. For example, although American Indians' religious activities that involve illegal drug use are immune from prosecution, the group's religious practices are not fully protected. States are free to deny unemployment benefits to American Indians who are fired for engaging in religious ceremonies involving illegal drug use. Additionally, in some states the lack of abortion access affects minority women more than it affects White women.

Racial inequality in civil liberties is particularly pronounced in issues of criminal justice. Higher incarceration rates for minorities than for Whites and racial discrimination in capital punishment demonstrate that civil liberties are not uniformly applied across racial and ethnic groups. In many states, racial and ethnic minorities are underrepresented in public defender offices and on juries.

Instances of racial profiling and the police shootings of African Americans clearly illustrate the intersection between race and ethnicity and civil liberties. For the protections of the Fourth and Fifth Amendments to have any meaning, they must be applied equally. Yet, law enforcement officers arbitrarily violated African Americans' civil liberties because of their ethnicity. In short, racial and ethnic politics greatly influences the extent to which civil liberties are fully enjoyed in the United States.

Finally, civil liberties and racial equality can clash. Issues concerning the regulation of hate speech, especially the 2017 White supremacy rally that occurred in Charlottesville, Virginia, demonstrate the complexity of this conflict. Freedom of expression is central to civil liberties; therefore, people are free to expound views that are hateful against racial, ethnic, and religious minorities. However, when these views translate to violent actions, then the protections of the First Amendment do not apply,

review
REVIEW QUESTIONS

1. To what extent does the First Amendment protect hate speech?

2. How does the current interpretation of the free exercise clause affect Native Americans' freedom of worship?

3. What is racial profiling, and what Fourth Amendment questions does it raise?

4. To what extent are the fair trial guarantees of the Sixth Amendment fully applied to racial and ethnic minority groups? Focus specifically on limits on peremptory challenges and the problems that exist with public defenders, especially concerning implicit bias against minority defendants.

5. To what extent are there disproportionate criminal sentences for racial and ethnic minorities? Do those disparities also exist for capital punishment?

Check your understanding of Chapter 4.

Need to review key
ideas in greater
depth? Click here.

Flashcard review.

terms
KEY TERMS

Civil Liberties p. 97

Clear and Present Danger
   Test p. 101

Due Process Clause p. 100

Eminent Domain p. 100

Establishment Clause p. 106

Exclusionary Rule p. 109

Fighting Words p. 102

Fourteenth Amendment
   p. 100

Free Exercise Clause p. 107

Hate Speech p. 103

Incorporation p. 99

Libel p. 104

Miranda Rights p. 112

Peremptory Challenges p. 114

Prior Restraint p. 104

Probable Cause p. 109

Racial Profiling p. 109

Right to Die p. 121

Search Warrant p. 108

Selective Incorporation p. 100

Separation of Church and
   State p. 106

readings
ADDITIONAL READINGS

Gould, J. B. (2005). *Speak no evil: The triumph of hate speech regulation.* Chicago: University of Chicago Press.

> This thorough study provides an empirical analysis of the reasons behind the adoption and continuation of hate speech regulation on college campuses.

Long, C. N. (2000). *Religious freedom and Indian rights: The case of* Oregon v. Smith. Lawrence: University Press of Kansas.

> This is a scholarly analysis of the Supreme Court's landmark ruling limiting religious liberty.

Nguyen, T. (2005). *We are all suspects now: Untold stories from immigrant communities after 9/11.* Boston: Beacon Press.

> This book presents stories of immigrant families who were targeted by law enforcement after the attacks of September 11, 2001.

Tehranian, J. (2009). *Whitewashed: America's invisible Middle Eastern minorities.* New York: New York University Press.

> This book addresses racial profiling and discrimination against Middle Easterners in the United States, especially after the attacks of September 11, 2001.

Zimring, F. E. (2017). *When police kill.* Cambridge, MA; Harvard University Press.

> In the wake of high-profile police killings of unarmed African Americans, this books offers a deep empirical analysis of instances on which law enforcement kills suspects, especially racial and ethnic minorities. Based on this empirical evidence, Zimring offers policy prescriptions to reduce this problem.

Civil Rights: Inequality and Equality

Fernando Espino Casas graduates *magna cum laude* from Harvard University in 2015. When he was a small child, Casas's parents illegally immigrated to the United States; therefore, Casas is technically an undocumented immigrant. Because of President Obama's 2012 executive order Deferred Action for Childhood Arrivals (DACA), Casas was allowed to purse a college education and work in the United States without fear of deportation. However, in 2017 President Trump repealed DACA, and despite being a productive member of the workforce, Casas's future in the United States remains uncertain.

When he was a baby in 1994, Fernando Espino Casas's parents illegally entered into the United States, ultimately settling in Milwaukee, Wisconsin. Casas was extremely successful growing up, ultimately matriculating at Harvard University in 2011. However, as an undocumented immigrant, Casas faced barriers to receiving aid and getting a job, despite the fact that he was not responsible for crossing the border illegally. Fortunately, for Casas, and for hundreds of thousands of similarly situated people, in 2012 President Barack Obama announced an executive order called the Deferred Action for Childhood Arrivals (DACA), which prevented deporting people whose parents brought them illegally to the United States when they were children, as long as they are working or in school. President Obama issued the order after Congress refused to pass the Development, Relief, and Education for Alien Minors (DREAM) Act that would have legislatively created the same policy that DACA did. Additionally, DACA allows people in Casas's circumstances, known as Dreamers, the opportunity to work legally in the United States. As a result of DACA, Casas was able to work while at Harvard and graduate *magna cum laude*.[1]

However, in September 2017, the Trump Administration – Donald Trump campaigned against DACA – announced that he would end the program in March 2018, unless Congress passed a comprehensive immigration bill that included funding for a wall along the border between the United States and Mexico. As a candidate Trump had promised that Mexico would pay for the wall, but after the Mexican government refused to pay, President Trump wanted Congress to appropriate money for it. Congress sought a bipartisan solution. In fact, Senate Minority Whip Richard Durbin (D-IL) mentioned Fernando Casas as an example of a successful Dreamer who contributes significantly to American society and whose life would be completely upended if he were forced to return to Mexico.[2] After President Trump publically opposed a compromise developed in the Senate, Congress was unable to reach an agreement.[3] In April 2018, a federal judge ruled that President Trump's DACA reversal was unconstitutional because his administration provided no legal basis for its decision. However, the Trump administration still has an opportunity to provide a sufficient legal basis. This litigation is still ongoing;

chapter outline

features

Sponsor a bill on
immigration reform
and see if you can
get it passed.

therefore, the ultimate status of Dreamers is still unclear.[4] The level of uncertainty surrounding DACA is extremely stressful for the hundreds of thousands of Dreamers, like Casas, who is currently a business analyst in Chicago.[5] He has spent virtually his entire life in the United States, and he has no connections to Mexico if the United States were to force him to move there. Moreover, Casas is clearly a productive member of society; therefore, preventing him, as well as all other Dreamers, from working in the United States would not only hurt them, but would also hurt the United States as a whole.

intro

The issue of undocumented immigrants has emerged as one of the most controversial civil rights issues in recent years. In 2015, there were an estimated 11 million unauthorized immigrants living in the United States, and less than half of them are from Mexico. While the number of undocumented immigrants had grown from 3.5 million in 1990, it had actually shrunk from a record high of 12.2 million in 2007.[6] Many of these undocumented immigrants work in menial jobs in the hotel, restaurant, construction, and agricultural industries, and although they are valuable to the economy, a considerable number of Americans resent their presence in the United States because of their unauthorized status; they believe illegal immigrants take jobs from legal workers and cause violence. The fact that productive Dreamers like Fernando Espino Casas, who only knows life in the United States, are undocumented immigrants complicates this issue.

*The story of Fernando Casas and controversies over undocumented immigrants typify the politics of **civil rights**, which are the protections against unequal treatment that the government guarantees to all groups. Throughout American history, many people have been, and in many cases still are, treated unfairly because of their race, national origin, gender, or sexual orientation. Improvement in civil rights has been gradual and intermittent for these groups, with some groups receiving more protections than others.*

Civil rights progress is initiated when the victims of discrimination form organizations that actively seek equality through social change, and governments respond by gradually protecting those victims from unfair treatment. The extent of civil rights success varies across different groups. The politics of civil rights is dynamic and complex in terms of defining discrimination and determining the ultimate outcome. Moreover, as this story demonstrates, various institutions of government—the president, Congress, and the federal courts—play a key role in shaping civil rights policy, often in conflict with each other.

Although we address issues of race and ethnicity throughout this book, this chapter focuses specifically on the politics of civil rights. First, we define terms and explain concepts that are essential to understanding civil rights. Then we address the civil rights struggles of African Americans, Latinos, Asian Americans, and American Indians; women; the lesbian, gay, bisexual, transgender and queer or questioning (LGBTQ) community; older adults; and people with disabilities.

Civil Rights The protections against unequal treatment that the government guarantees to all groups.

Civil Rights Terms and Concepts

Prior to our discussion of civil rights, we must first define the terms and concepts that frame civil rights politics. Although many of the terms appear familiar, their meanings are subtle and demand precise explanation. Three concepts especially relevant to civil rights are group designation, forms of inequality, and segregation.

Group Designation

Race A socially constructed classification of people based on their physical characteristics, especially skin color.

Group designation, or the classification of a set of people based on defined criteria, is a fluid concept that is particularly relevant in the examination of civil rights. A significant group demarcation is **race**, which is the classification of people based on physical characteristics, especially skin color. People often mistakenly believe that race is determined biologically, but, in fact, it is socially constructed. The designation of a person's race in the United States has historically been decided by American society's desire to exclude groups of people from participation in the social and political life of the nation. For example, until the middle of the twentieth century, many states wrote laws designating the degree of Black ancestry necessary to be legally classified as Black. Louisiana and North Carolina used the one-sixteenth criterion (one great-great-grandparent), but most states used a one-eighth standard (if at least one great-grandparent was Black, a person was legally considered to be Black).[7]

Determining precise racial classification can be difficult because an increasing number of people identify themselves as belonging to more than one race. For example, former professional wrestler and major movie and television star (and rumored future presidential candidate) Dwayne "The Rock" Johnson has a father who is Afro Canadian and a mother who is Samoan.[8] Table 5.1 demonstrates the fluid categorizations for race used by the U.S. Census throughout American history.

Ethnicity A socially constructed classification of people based on national origin or culture.

Another concept used to indicate group status is **ethnicity**, or classification based on national origin or culture. Although many people use the terms *race* and *ethnicity* interchangeably, the two words are distinct. People of different ethnicities are often members of the same race. For example, Italian Americans and Irish Americans are White in terms of race but are of different ethnicities. Likewise, people of different races may be of the same ethnicity. Some Latinos, a classification based on ethnicity, are White, whereas others are Black, Asian, or American Indian. The 2010 U.S. Census blurred the distinction between race and ethnicity by designating White, Black, Asian American, Indian or Alaskan Native, Chinese, Japanese, and Hawaiian, and other Pacific islanders as different racial categories, but it considered Latino an ethnicity. Some argue that Judaism is an ethnicity because there is a shared immigrant-based culture, and Jewish Americans have experienced discrimination; however, others maintain that Judaism is a religion, not an ethnicity, especially because there are different ethnic groups that adhere to the religion.[9] As with race, classifications based on ethnicity have been a significant basis for unequal treatment throughout American history.

TABLE 5.1 Racial Categories Used by the U.S. Census, 1790–2010

Year	Categories
1790	Free Whites, other free persons, and slaves
1800, 1810	Free Whites, other free persons (except Indians not taxed), and slaves
1820	Free Whites, slaves, free colored persons, and other persons (except Indians not taxed)
1830, 1840	Free White persons, slaves, and free colored persons
1850	White, Black, and mulatto
1860	White, Black, mulatto, and Indian
1870, 1880	White, Black, mulatto, Chinese, and Indian
1890	White, Black, mulatto, quadroon, octaroon, Chinese, Japanese, and Indian
1900	White, Black, Chinese, Japanese, and Indian
1910	White, Black, mulatto, Chinese, Japanese, Indian, and other
1920	White, Black, mulatto, Indian, Chinese, Japanese, Filipino, Hindu, Korean, and other
1930	White, Negro, Mexican, Indian, Chinese, Japanese, Filipino, Hindu, Korean, and other
1940	White, Negro, Indian, Chinese, Japanese, Filipino, Hindu, Korean, and other
1950	White, Negro, Indian, Japanese, Chinese, Filipino, and other
1960	White, Negro, American Indian, Japanese, Chinese, Filipino, Hawaiian, part Hawaiian, Aleut, and Eskimo
1970	White, Negro or Black, American Indian, Japanese, Chinese, Filipino, Hawaiian, Korean, and other
1980	White, Negro, Japanese, Chinese, Filipino, Korean, Vietnamese, American Indian, Asian Indian, Hawaiian, Guamanian, Samoan, Eskimo, Aleut, and other
1990	White, Black, American Indian, Eskimo, Aleut, Chinese, Filipino, Hawaiian, Korean, Vietnamese, Japanese, Asian Indian, Guamanian, other Pacific Islander, and other
2000	White, Black/African American/Negro, American Indian or Alaskan Native, Asian Indian, Chinese, Filipino, other Asian, Hawaiian, Guamanian or Chomorro, Samoan, other Pacific Islander, other, and some other race (individuals who consider themselves multiracial can choose two or more races)
2010	White, Black/African American/Negro, American Indian or Alaskan Native, Asian Indian, Japanese, Native Hawaiian, Chinese, Korean, Guamanian or Chomorro, Filipino, Vietnamese, Samoan, Other Asian, Other Pacific Islander, and some other race

Sources: Adapted from National Research Council. (2000). Measuring racial discrimination: Panel on Methods for Assessing Discrimination. *Washington, DC: National Academies Press, 2004, p. 31; United States Census 2010.* Census Form: Question 6, What is this person's race? *Retrieved May 29, 2018, from* http://www.censusquestions.com/2010-us-census-form.pdf, accessed May 29, 2018.

Gender Social relations between the sexes and attitudes about how the sexes interact and the roles that society assumes they will play.

Another group demarcation is **gender**, which refers to social classifications based on sex. Whereas sex is determined biologically (i.e., most people are born male or female), gender refers to the social ramifications of distinctions between male and female. Students learning a foreign language, such as French or Spanish, are familiar with the concept of gender whereby some words are designated masculine and others are designated feminine. Gender has legal and political connotations because governments and private entities have denied women the same opportunities as men. Additionally, gender identity plays a significant role in civil rights politics because people who are transgender identify with a different gender than what they were assigned at birth. Transgender people can often be subject to humiliating forms of discrimination, which we discuss later in the chapter.

Forms of Inequality

Inequality The extent to which one group enjoys more political, social, or economic benefits than another group.

Inequality of Opportunity A form of inequality in which laws or official actions deny specific groups social, political, or economic benefits that are available to other groups.

Inequality of Outcome A form of inequality in which social and demographic forces, not official laws or policies, cause one group to enjoy more political, social, or economic benefits than another group.

At the core of civil rights politics is the concept of **inequality**—that is, the extent to which one group enjoys more political, social, or economic benefits than another group. **Inequality of opportunity** exists when laws or official government actions deny specific groups social, political, and economic benefits that are available to other groups. With inequality of opportunity a dominant group controls the government and uses that authority to mistreat subordinate groups based on their characteristics. For example, until the twentieth century, many state laws, written by exclusively male lawmakers, discriminated against women by denying them the opportunity to pursue certain professions, vote, or own property. Conversely, **inequality of outcome** is a form of inequality in which social and demographic forces, not laws or official actions, cause one group to enjoy more political and economic benefits than another group. Because the dominant group does not explicitly use governmental authority to discriminate or deny opportunities to the subordinate group, redressing inequality of outcome is murky and controversial. For example, as we discuss later in this chapter, women on average earn less money than men for the same jobs. This inequality does not stem from official government policies; in fact, there are laws that prevent some types of salary discrimination against women.

Segregation

Segregation Physical separation of a dominant group from a subordinate group.

Another concept important for civil rights is **segregation**, in which a dominant group physically separates itself from a subordinate group. Some religious groups, such as the Amish or Hasidic Jews, choose to segregate themselves, but the vast majority of segregation results from the dominant group seeking to separate itself from the subordinate group. For example, when Southern White society insisted on segregating public schools through the 1960s, they operated on the belief that Black children were inferior and should not associate with their White children. Many Southern Whites even expressed fears that Blacks and Whites going to school together could lead to them dating and even procreating with one another. Segregation almost always results in

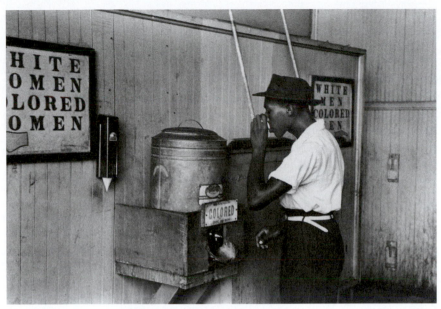

During the era of Jim Crow segregation and before the Civil Rights Act, Blacks and Whites were forced to use different restrooms and drink from different fountains.

unequal enjoyment of political, social, and economic benefits. In the segregated South, Black schools received far less public money and were provided with lower-quality facilities compared to White schools.

Segregation that occurs as the result of law or official government action is known as **de jure segregation**. An example of de jure segregation existed when state laws mandated separate schools for Black children and White children, which, as we explain later in this chapter, wrought terrible hardships on African Americans.

Segregation that occurs through natural forces or results from social practice is called **de facto segregation**. Thus, de facto segregation is neither legally sanctioned nor government imposed. For example, despite the elimination of laws and policies establishing segregated schools, many schools today are still overwhelmingly White, Black, or Latino because vestiges of past discrimination, economic forces, and individual preferences have resulted in housing patterns that separate people by race or ethnicity.

De Jure Segregation Physical separation of groups that results from laws or official government actions.

De Facto Segregation Physical separation of groups that is not legally sanctioned or imposed by the government but instead stems from individual preferences and economic forces.

Race, Ethnicity, and Civil Rights

Although civil rights encompasses a wide variety of groups, the plurality of civil rights issues concern race and ethnicity. A vast number of racial and ethnic groups have experienced discrimination and segregation, but a single chapter cannot adequately cover them all. Therefore, this section focuses on the most significant—African Americans, Latinos, Asian Americans, and

American Indians. Each story involves inequality and segregation, the formation of political movements to improve civil rights, and significant, yet incomplete, civil rights progress.

Blacks

Because Blacks have traditionally suffered the most from discrimination, their struggle has exerted the most significant impact on civil rights throughout the entire course of American history. The story of Black civil rights is one marked by extreme mistreatment with a slow, gradual increase in the enjoyment of civil rights. Currently, de jure discrimination and segregation have vanished, but civil rights issues still remain for African Americans.

Enslavement of Blacks. Africans were first brought to the Western Hemisphere as slaves during the 1600s to meet labor shortages in the burgeoning agricultural industries. Enslaved Africans living in the American colonies enjoyed no civil rights, and although some Blacks did become free, colonial governments did not regard free Blacks as equal to Whites.

Even during the American Revolution, when political leaders espoused principles of liberty and equality for all, the tradition of exclusion, which was based on Whites' views that Blacks were inferior, denied Blacks fundamental rights. An original draft of the Declaration of Independence reprimanded the King of England for his role in the slave trade, but the authors struck this clause from the final document because many of the delegates to the Continental Congress, including Thomas Jefferson, owned slaves.[10]

One of the most despicable aspects of the slave trade was dividing families, even separating parents from their children.

After the establishment of the American Republic, the U.S. Constitution did not give any rights to slaves or free Blacks; each state determined its own policy on civil rights. By the early nineteenth century, Northern states had abolished slavery, and some laws in Northern states actually protected Blacks' civil rights. For example, in the early 1780s courts in Massachusetts no longer recognized the legality of slavery, and as a result slaves successfully sued for freedom. However, it was still the case that free Blacks were denied basic civil rights in Northern states. In fact, free Blacks could vote only in the states of New York, Rhode Island, Massachusetts, Maine, Vermont, and New Hampshire, and even in those states Blacks were subject to segregation and unequal treatment. Because the economies of Southern states still relied heavily on slave labor, their laws explicitly recognized the existence of slavery and the property rights of slaveholders. Blacks had absolutely no civil rights in the South.[11]

Although slavery was not controversial during the founding era, by the early nineteenth century slavery had emerged as a contentious issue. A growing number of people concentrated in the Middle Atlantic and New England states where slavery was not central to the economy, known as **abolitionists**, morally opposed slavery. Abolitionists advocated laws to end or restrict slavery, and many of them actively helped to free slaves.

Nineteenth-century laws in Northern states reflected the abolitionists' hostility toward slavery. For example, many Northern states criminally banned Southern slaveholders from entering their boundaries to capture runaway slaves. However, the U.S. Supreme Court in 1842 ruled in *Prigg v. Pennsylvania* that the U.S. Constitution, federal laws, and slaveholders' property rights superseded the authority of states seeking to protect runaway slaves and punish slave catchers.[12]

As the nation expanded westward during the nineteenth century, debates over slavery in the new territories exacerbated the rancor between pro- and antislavery forces. The Northwest Ordinance of 1787 banned slavery in newly annexed territory, which eventually became the states of Ohio, Indiana, Illinois, Michigan, Wisconsin, and parts of Minnesota.[13] By the early nineteenth century, conflicts between Northerners and Southerners arose over whether to admit new states as slave states or free states. The Missouri Compromise of 1820 allowed Missouri to enter as a slave state as long as Maine could enter as a free state, and the compromise set a latitudinal boundary, north of which slavery was prohibited and south of which slavery was permitted.[14] However, in 1854 the Kansas and Nebraska Act allowed the citizens (i.e., White males) of the territories of Kansas and Nebraska to determine for themselves whether to allow slavery, even though both territories were north of the boundary where slavery should have been prohibited.[15]

By the late 1850s, debates over slavery had become too intractable to reconcile. The 1857 U.S. Supreme Court case of ***Dred Scott v. Sandford*** concerned a Missouri slave (Dred Scott) who tried to sue for his freedom in Illinois—a free state. Chief Justice Roger Taney ruled that Congress had no authority to

Abolitionists Nineteenth-century political activists who sought to end slavery.

See clips from and analysis of The Birth of a Nation.

Dred Scott v. Sandford
A controversial 1857 Supreme Court decision that ruled Congress lacked power to regulate slavery and Blacks had no civil rights.

ban slavery in the territories and that because Blacks were not citizens of the United States, they could not sue in federal court.[16] This controversial decision prevented Congress from regulating slavery, and it denied fundamental civil rights to Blacks. The *Dred Scott* decision was a leading contributing factor to the Civil War.

The Civil War and Reconstruction. The Civil War initiated minor and usually unenforced improvements in civil rights for African Americans. In 1862, President Abraham Lincoln established the **Emancipation Proclamation** as the first federal policy offering civil rights for Blacks. This executive order freed all slaves in the Confederacy as of January 1, 1863.[17] Of course, because the war still raged, the federal government did not have jurisdiction over the rebellious states, and the proclamation did not affect the few Union states that retained vestiges of slavery (Maryland, Delaware, Kentucky, West Virginia, and Missouri). After the South lost the Civil War, the ratification of the **Thirteenth Amendment** to the U.S. Constitution in 1865 officially forbade slavery throughout the United States.

Although the Thirteenth Amendment ended slavery, discrimination against African Americans still existed. Most notably, former Confederate states passed **Black Codes**, which singled out African Americans for mistreatment and discrimination. See "Our Voices: South Carolina's Black Codes" for a more complete discussion of this issue. In response to these codes, Congress proposed the **Fourteenth Amendment**, which was ratified in 1868. This amendment was designed to ensure that states gave former slaves full citizenship rights.

In Chapter 4, we discussed the due process clause of the Fourteenth Amendment, which prevents states from denying any resident life, liberty, or property without following normal criminal and judicial procedures. The Fourteenth Amendment contains an parallel clause: the **equal protection clause**, which requires state laws to treat all people equally regardless of their race or ethnicity. Additionally, to address voting discrimination, the **Fifteenth Amendment**, ratified in 1870, prohibited voting discrimination on account of race.

Immediately following the Civil War, the period of Reconstruction provided hope for supporters of Black civil rights. **Reconstruction** refers to the period from 1865 to 1877 in which a set of policies brought the former rebellious Confederate states back into the Union. Congress directed Reconstruction, and because former abolitionists and Republican supporters of civil rights controlled Congress, Reconstruction initially punished White Southerners and insisted on civil rights for African Americans. For example, Congress sought to ensure a livelihood for former slaves by creating the Freedman's Bureau, which provided former slaves with land, food, and education.[18]

More important, Congress passed the Enforcement Acts of 1870, 1871, and 1875 to enforce the Fifteenth Amendment and the Civil Rights Act of 1875 to ban racial segregation in public places. Because the Union Army

Emancipation Proclamation An executive order issued by President Abraham Lincoln during the Civil War that freed the slaves in the Confederacy.

Thirteenth Amendment An amendment to the Constitution that prohibits slavery throughout the United States.

Black Codes Laws passed in Southern states during the immediate aftermath of the Civil War that singled out African Americans for mistreatment and discrimination.

Fourteenth Amendment An amendment to the Constitution that prevents states from denying on the basis of race full citizenship to their residents.

Equal Protection Clause A specific provision in the Fourteenth Amendment that prevents states from passing laws that treat people differently on account of race or ethnicity.

Fifteenth Amendment An amendment to the Constitution that prevents states from denying the right to vote on the basis of race or ethnicity.

Reconstruction The period from 1865 to 1877 in which former Confederate states were brought back into the Union, often characterized by a military presence in the South and civil rights progress for Blacks.

our voices

South Carolina's Black Codes

Although the Thirteenth Amendment ended slavery throughout the United States, Southern states passed laws, known as Black Codes, to regulate the conduct of newly freed African Americans. Black Codes regulated many aspects of African Americans' lives, including terms of employment and personal relationships, and they were based on the view that the former slaves were inherently inferior to Whites. Specifically, Black Codes mandated that any orphaned, homeless, or unemployed Black person could be forced to work as an apprentice. They required that any African American choosing to own a business or pursue a career as an artisan had to pay a fee, seek a license, and serve as an apprentice.

Supporters of Black Codes claimed that they were necessary to integrate the former slaves into a postwar society, but opponents challenged that claim, arguing that the imposed apprenticeship reestablished a system of servitude. The Fourteenth Amendment to the Constitution overturned all Black Codes.

Below are excerpts from South Carolina's Black Code. Note the difference between the rules for males versus females, which reflect the blatant gender discrimination of the time period.

Be it enacted by the Senate and House of Representatives . . .

VII. . . . Marriage between a white person and a person of color, shall be illegal and void. . . .

IX. The marriage of an apprentice shall not, without consent of the master, be lawful. . . .

XV. A child over the age of two years, born of a colored parent, may be bound by the father, if he is living in the District, or in the case of his death or his absence from the District, by the mother, as an apprentice, to any respectable white or colored person, who is competent, to make a contract—a male until he shall attain the age of twenty-one years and a female until she shall attain the age of eighteen years. . . .

XXIII. The master shall have authority to inflict moderate chastisement and impose reasonable restraint upon his apprentice, and to recapture him if he departs from his service.

XLV. On farms or in out-door service, the hours of labor, except on Sunday, shall be from sun-rise to sun-set, with a reasonable interval for breakfast and dinner. . . . The servant shall be careful of all the animals and instruments used by him, shall protect the same from injury by other persons, and shall be answerable for all property lost, destroyed or injured by his negligence, dishonesty or bad faith. . . .

XLVI. . . . Servants shall be quiet and orderly in their quarters . . . and retire to rest at reasonable hours. . . .

LXXII. No person of color shall pursue or practice the art, trade or business of an artisan, mechanic or shopkeeper, or any other trade of employment or a business (besides that of husbandry, or that of a servant under contract for services or labor) on his own account or for his own benefit . . . until he shall have obtained a license therefore from the Judge of the District Court. . . .

XCVII. . . . The District Judge or a Magistrate shall issue a warrant for the arrest of any person of color known or believed to be a vagrant. . . . On conviction, the defendant shall be liable to imprisonment, and to hard labor. . . .

XCVIII. The defendant, if sentenced to labor after conviction, may, by order of the District Judge or Magistrate, before whom he was convicted, be hired for such wages as can be obtained for his services. . . .

Source: Adapted from Blaustein, A. P. & Zangrando, R. L. (1970). *Civil rights and the Black American: A documentary history.* New York: Clarion, pp. 217–225.

maintained a strong presence in the South during Reconstruction, these laws were strictly enforced. As a result of Reconstruction, African Americans voted, whereas former Confederate soldiers could not. Consequently, many Blacks were elected to local, state, and federal offices.[19]

Jim Crow Laws The Southern practice of racially segregating all public facilities, such as transportation, schools, libraries, hotels, hospitals, theaters, parks, and cemeteries.

Listen to a discussion of the Plessy case.

Plessy v. Ferguson A controversial 1896 Supreme Court decision that ruled that under the Fourteenth Amendment, states were allowed to segregate by race.

Separate but Equal Principle A legal principle that allowed states to segregate the races in public facilities, as long as the state provided each race with basic access to the public facility in question.

Disenfranchisement A government denying a group the right to vote.

Literacy Tests A form of disenfranchisement in which potential voters need to demonstrate the ability to read as a condition for registering to vote.

The Era of Segregation and Discrimination. Despite the promise of Reconstruction, the initial progress toward full civil rights for African Americans was short-lived. The disputed election of 1876 marked the beginning of the end of Reconstruction when Republican presidential candidate Rutherford B. Hayes promised some Southern states that if he received their electoral votes, he would withdraw federal troops from the South. When Hayes assumed office in 1877, he fulfilled his promise to remove troops and effectively ended Reconstruction.[20] Without the military presence enforcing civil rights laws, states were free to discriminate against Blacks. States passed **Jim Crow laws**, which segregated all public facilities, such as transportation, schools, libraries, hotels, hospitals, theaters, parks, and cemeteries. The name Jim Crow came from a figure in a well-known nineteenth-century traveling minstrel show, in which a White actor depicted extremely offensive stereotypes of African Americans.[21]

Black leaders sought to challenge segregation in federal court. In 1892, Homer Plessy, who was one-eighth Black, refused to sit in the "colored only" section of a train leaving New Orleans, Louisiana. He was arrested, convicted, and fined for violating Louisiana's segregation law. Plessy then appealed to the Supreme Court, arguing that Jim Crow laws violated the Fourteenth Amendment. In the infamous *Plessy v. Ferguson* case of 1896, the Court ruled against Plessy and upheld Jim Crow laws, arguing that the Fourteenth Amendment equal protection clause permitted segregation as long as the facilities provided for each race were equal. The Court thereby established the **separate but equal principle**, which sanctioned segregating African Americans as long as they were given the same facilities granted to Whites.[22]

By the beginning of the twentieth century, Blacks were treated as second-class citizens. In addition to living under a strictly segregated system, African Americans suffered severe economic discrimination. Despite the claims of the "equal" in "separate but equal," states spent three times more per capita on education for White students than for Black students, and as a result Black schools were overcrowded, unsanitary, and staffed with poorly trained and underpaid teachers. Only rarely would White-owned companies hire Blacks, and even Black professionals, such as doctors, found limited opportunities. To make matters worse, terrorist organizations such as the Ku Klux Klan intimidated Blacks with violence. Between 1900 and 1920, an average of sixty-seven African Americans were lynched per year.[23]

Another form of discrimination against African Americans concerned **disenfranchisement**, or denial of the right to vote. In 1876, the U.S. Supreme Court ruled that Congress lacked jurisdiction to regulate state and local elections,[24] which allowed states to enact policies intended to disenfranchise African Americans in those elections. Blacks attempting to register to vote in Southern states faced **literacy tests**, which were seemingly race-neutral but were administered in a blatantly discriminatory fashion. For example, Whites would be given simple reading tests, whereas Blacks were required to read and understand complicated provisions in the state constitution. Moreover, White local government officials graded Blacks much more harshly than they graded Whites. **Grandfather clauses** exempted people from literacy tests who had been able to vote at the end of the Civil War, which obviously applied only to Whites and not to Blacks. **Poll taxes**—fees assessed on people registering to vote—contributed to African American disenfranchisement because Blacks were less likely than Whites to be able to afford those fees. African Americans even suffered from Ku Klux Klan terrorist intimidation when they attempted to register to vote.

As a result of these disenfranchisement techniques, Black voter registration in the South was extremely low. As late as 1962, only 13.4 percent of African Americans in Alabama and 6.7 percent in Mississippi were registered to vote, despite the fact that 30.0 percent of the total population of Alabama and 42.0 percent of the total population of Mississippi were Black.[25] Because Blacks made up such a small percentage of the electorate, they could not elect political leaders who would address their political, social, and economic concerns.

The Civil Rights Era. By the middle of the twentieth century, civil rights prospects for Blacks improved. A key turning point in civil rights history was World War II. First, the war highlighted the contradiction between the American war against racial, ethnic, and religious hatred in Europe on the one hand and the atrocious treatment of African Americans in the United States on the other hand.[26] In addition, an economic perspective emphasizes the fact that during the war the government's need for massive increases in industrial production improved Black employment in factories, but Black employees soon clashed with White business leaders and employees. To prevent these conflicts from disrupting the war effort, the government enacted policies that protected African American workers. For example, the government banned defense companies receiving federal money from employment discrimination based on race, and it created the Fair Employment Practices Committee to enforce this order.[27]

Interest groups and social movements were extremely critical in establishing more significant civil rights progress. In the early twentieth century, civil rights activists formed groups to lobby the national government to end de jure segregation, terrorist violence, and inequality of opportunity. The most significant group was the National Association for the Advancement of Colored People (NAACP), which was established in 1909 to pressure national, state, and local governments to increase political and economic equality, end segregation, and ensure voting rights.[28]

NAACP leaders recognized that because legislatures and executives were accountable only to the White electorate, those branches of government would be unreceptive to NAACP claims. Accordingly, the NAACP concentrated its resources on providing the financial and intellectual sponsorship of litigation in the federal judiciary, where legal argument, not the will of the majority, influences outcomes. The organization was successful in the 1915 case of *Guinn and Beal v. United States*, in which the Supreme Court ruled that grandfather clauses violated the Fifteenth Amendment.[29] Sponsoring litigation became

Grandfather Clause A policy designed to disenfranchise Blacks by exempting Whites, but not Blacks, from literacy tests.

Poll Taxes Fees that states charged citizens to vote and that disenfranchised the poor and minority citizens.

such an integral part of the NAACP that in 1940 it formed an entirely separate litigating organization known as the NAACP Legal Defense and Education Fund (LDF) to focus solely on litigating, while the main NAACP would concentrate more on lobbying.[30]

Brown v. Board of Education
A landmark 1954 Supreme Court case that prohibited government-sponsored segregation as a violation of the Fourteenth Amendment equal protection clause.

The most significant of the cases that the LDF litigated is ***Brown v. Board of Education***, the 1954 U.S. Supreme Court decision that overruled the principle of "separate but equal" and prohibited states from segregating schools on account of race. In the Court's opinion, Chief Justice Earl Warren wrote: "We conclude that in the field of public education the doctrine of 'separate but equal' has no place. Separate educational facilities are inherently unequal."[31] For the first time since the 1870s, the national government imposed on the states meaningful civil rights requirements. Despite the significance of the *Brown v. Board of Education* ruling, segregation and discrimination persisted. Most Southern school districts continued to segregate schools until the late 1950s and early 1960s when Presidents Dwight Eisenhower and John F. Kennedy deployed armed forces to ensure the safety of African American students entering formerly segregated schools. The *Brown v. Board of Education* decision was also limited in expanding civil rights because it did not address discrimination by private businesses, such as transportation facilities, hotels, and restaurants.

Civil rights leaders recognized that litigation alone would not be a successful strategy for dealing with those forms of discrimination, and they organized a variety of protest strategies, including boycotts of the facilities that

Rosa Parks sitting on a bus in Montgomery, Alabama. In 1955, Ms. Parks refused to relinquish her seat to a White rider, despite the city rule that Blacks needed to sit in the back of the bus. Her arrest sparked a boycott of the Montgomery bus system, which ultimately was a catalyst for the Civil Rights Movement of the 1950s and 1960s.

discriminated against African Americans. The most notable boycott was the Montgomery bus boycott, which was spawned by the arrest of Rosa Parks for her refusal to relinquish her seat to a White passenger in 1955. Instead of riding the bus, Blacks in Montgomery walked, carpooled, or found other means of transportation in the hopes of depriving the bus company of the critical revenue it earned from African American patrons.[32]

Sit-ins, where Black patrons refused to move from the White section of restaurants and other public accommodations, were another form of nonviolent resistance. The most significant sit-in took place in 1960, when four Black college students refused to disperse from a Whites-only lunch counter in Greensboro, North Carolina. The national press publicized the protest, and over the next month sit-ins were launched throughout the country.[33]

Sit-in A form of protest against segregated restaurants in which Black patrons refused to move from Whites-only sections.

Large marches were another form of nonviolent protest. They enabled civil rights leaders to show the American public and the country's political leaders the extent of intense opposition to discrimination. The most significant march was the August 1963 March on Washington for Jobs and Freedom, which drew more than 250,000 Americans of all races and ethnicities; numerous civil rights organizations, labor unions, and religious groups participated as well. At the culmination of the march, civil rights leader Dr. Martin Luther King, Jr. delivered his famous and inspirational "I Have a Dream" speech.[34] The media covered the event extensively, and although its impact on public opinion was negligible, its peaceful success did nudge policymakers to support greater civil rights protections.[35]

Watch Martin Luther King's "I Have a Dream" speech.

As a result of the protests, increasing public pressure, and the political skills of President Lyndon Johnson,[36] Congress passed the landmark **Civil Rights Act of 1964** to end segregation and discrimination in the private sector. Specifically, the law prohibited discrimination and segregation in public accommodations, even privately owned hotels and restaurants; allowed the president to deny funds to federal agencies, states, and localities that discriminated on account of race or ethnicity; and required the Justice Department to bring legal action against school districts that still resisted desegregation. The law also prevented employers from discriminating on account of race or ethnicity in hiring, firing, or promotion decisions.

Civil Rights Act of 1964 A federal law that prevented private businesses from discriminating in service and personnel policies.

Congress also passed the **Voting Rights Act of 1965**, which empowered the federal government to supervise voting in states and localities to guarantee voting rights for African Americans. As discussed in Chapter 3, the law invalidated voting procedures designed to discriminate, including literacy tests. The law allowed federal officials to assume control over voter registration in jurisdictions where there had been voting discrimination, and the act required any locality with a history of voting discrimination to obtain permission from the U.S. Department of Justice before changing any aspect of their voting practices. The Justice Department would ensure that the changes were not intended to weaken minority voting. However, as we discussed in Chapter 3, the 2013 Supreme Court decision in *Shelby County (AL) v. Holder* invalidated the formula used to determine which jurisdictions were subject to preclearance.[37]

Voting Rights Act of 1965 A federal law that significantly curtailed disenfranchisement of racial and ethnic minorities by banning literacy tests and requiring federal supervision of jurisdictions with a history of voting discrimination.

This photo from the historic 1963 March on Washington exemplifies the goals of the Civil Rights Movement during the 1960s. Media coverage of this march demonstrated to the American public and political leaders the seriousness of racial discrimination and the widespread support to end it.

The Voting Rights Act of 1965 quickly increased Black voting participation. Black voter registration in the South increased from 38 percent in 1965 to 65 percent by 1969, and in Mississippi alone Black voting registration jumped from 7 to 67 percent.[38] The Voting Rights Act was expanded in the 1980s and 1990s to require states to draw legislative districts with more Blacks and Latinos (we discuss this in more detail in Chapter 6). See the Measuring Equality box for a more detailed discussion of the results of the Voting Rights Act.

Busing. Although civil rights progress erased much of the inequality of opportunity facing Blacks since the colonial period, they still encountered inequality of outcome and de facto desegregation. For example, in the late 1960s federal courts required school districts to bus Black students into predominantly White schools and White students into predominantly Black schools to integrate public schools that were de facto segregated. Many White, and even some Black, parents objected strenuously to school district busing of their children to schools often located far away from their homes, but in 1971 the U.S. Supreme Court upheld mandatory busing as an acceptable means of achieving integrated schools.[39]

There is empirical evidence that busing helped to end de facto segregation. During the late 1950s and early 1960s, almost no Black schoolchildren attended majority White schools in the South, but by the middle of the 1980s about 45 percent of Black schoolchildren attended majority White schools in the South.[40]

measuring equality

Voter Registration and the Voting Rights Act of 1965

Voting is crucial to political power, and therefore disenfranchisement is a severe form of discrimination. From the beginning of the American Republic, states solely determined eligibility for voting. At the time, most states, even ones that had abolished slavery, denied Blacks the right to vote. States were even free to disenfranchise Whites who did not own a sufficient amount of property. The Fifteenth Amendment to the Constitution, ratified in 1870, was designed to prevent racial discrimination in voting, but it was unsuccessful in achieving that goal. States, mainly in the South, disenfranchised Blacks through poll taxes, literacy tests (as well as grandfather clauses), and failure to prosecute terrorist intimidation against African Americans attempting to vote. The Voting Rights Act of 1965 sought to end disenfranchisement by banning literacy tests and, more important, placing jurisdictions with a history of racial disenfranchisement under federal supervision.

Although this book focuses on the national government, state government is still important because, as discussed in Chapter 3, it enacts policies on criminal justice, education, welfare, and civil rights. State legislatures generally draw districts for the U.S. House of Representatives. Accordingly, civil rights advocates are extremely concerned about minority representation in state legislatures, and the Voting Rights Act was designed to address this concern.

We compiled data from the eleven states of the former Confederacy, and the results are shown in Figures 5.1 and 5.2. Figure 5.1 illustrates for each year the combined percentage of African Americans in the eleven state legislatures. Figure 5.2 displays the increase (in percentage units) from the previous time. The percentage of Black legislators has consistently increased since the passage of the Voting Rights Act, but the rate of increase has varied considerably. What factors could explain the overall increase in Black legislators?

What factors could explain the different rates of increase?

Figure 5.1   Percentage of Southern State Legislators Who Are Black, from Prior to the Voting Rights Act through 2007. The States are Alabama, Arkansas, Georgia, Florida, Louisiana, Mississippi, North Carolina, South Carolina, Tennessee, Texas, and Virginia

Figure 5.2   Increase (from the Previous Time) in the Percentage of Southern State Legislators Who Are Black, 1971–2007. The States are Alabama, Arkansas, Georgia, Florida, Louisiana, Mississippi, North Carolina, South Carolina, Tennessee, Texas, and Virginia

In 1991, the Supreme Court allowed school districts to end busing even if de facto segregation still existed as long as the school district showed a federal judge that it had made a good-faith effort to integrate schools.[41] During the 1990s, school districts throughout the country ended two decades of busing. However, many communities, such as Seattle, Washington, still made their public school assignments to ensure a racial balance. In 2007, though, the

U.S. Supreme Court ruled that assigning students to public school based on race violates the Constitution, even if the policy is designed to help racial or ethnic minorities.[42]

Empirical evidence shows that since the early 1990s, there have been increases in de facto segregation. Between the middle of the 1980s and the early 2000s, the percentage of Blacks attending majority White schools in the South declined from about 45 percent to about 30 percent.[43] Figure 5.3 demonstrates that after peaking in the early 1990s there was a significant decrease in Black students attending majority white schools (i.e., an increase in segregation). Figure 5.4 reveals a slight increase in Black students attending heavily segregated schools—those containing more than 90 percent minority students— although there is some variation by region. A 2016 study by the Government Accountability Office, a federal government research agency, found not only an increasing number of predominantly Black and Latino schools, but it also found that these schools had higher levels of poverty and offered far fewer classes in math, science, and college preparation than schools with a larger percentage of White students.[44]

Affirmative Action Corrective policies that attempt to help racial and ethnic minorities (as well as women) achieve equality in education and the workforce by providing them with advantages in college admission, hiring, promotion, and the awarding of contracts.

Affirmative Action. Another civil rights controversy is **affirmative action**, which refers to policies that attempt to help racial and ethnic minorities (as well as women) achieve equality in education and employment by providing

Figure 5.3 Percentage of African American Students Who Attend Majority-White Schools in the United States, 1954-2011

Source: Data Adapted from Gary Orfield and Erika Frankenberg, with Jongyeon Ee and John Kuscera, Brown at 60: Great Progress, A Long retreat and an Uncertain Future, *Civil Rights Project, University of California at Los Angeles, May 15, 2014, 10, https://www.civilrightsproject.ucla.edu/research/k-12-education/integration-and-diversity/brown-at-60-great-progress-a-long-retreat-and-an-uncertain-future/Brown-at-60-051814.pdf, accessed June 13, 2018*

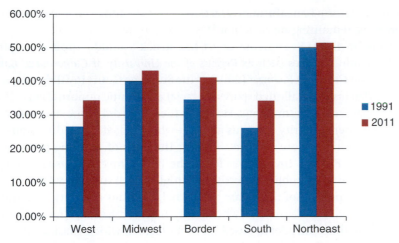

Figure 5.4 Figure 5.4 Percentage of Black Students Attending Schools with More than 90 percent Minority Students, 1991 and 2011, by Region

Source: Data Adapted from Gary Orfield and Erika Frankenberg, with Jongyeon Ee and John Kuscera, Brown at 60: Great Progress, A Long retreat and an Uncertain Future, *Civil Rights Project, University of California at Los Angeles, May 15, 2014, 18, https://www.civilrightsproject.ucla.edu/research/k-12-education/integration-and-diversity/brown-at-60-great-progress-a-long-retreat-and-an-uncertain-future/Brown-at-60-051814.pdf, accessed June 13, 2018*

them with advantages in college admission, hiring, promotion, and the awarding of contracts. Although controversial when applied to women and Latinos, affirmative action is especially contentious for Black civil rights. During the 1960s and early 1970s, public and private universities reserved a number of undergraduate and graduate admission slots for minorities. Many private companies gave hiring and promotion advantages to minorities, and recipients of federal, state, and local government contracts were required to subcontract to a minimum number of minority-owned businesses.

Supporters of affirmative action argue that it helps to remedy past discrimination because the preferences give racial and ethnic minorities opportunities they previously lacked. Additionally, supporters contend that affirmative action increases minorities in universities and businesses, which ensures diversity in education and the workplace. Opponents of affirmative action maintain that the preferences amount to discrimination against Whites, which violates the prohibition against racial inequality embodied in the equal protection clause of the Fourteenth Amendment. African American law professor Stephen Carter, who received some benefits from affirmative action, criticizes racial preferences because they stigmatize minority professionals as being admitted to universities or hired for jobs solely because of affirmative action. Carter also maintains that affirmative action mainly helps middle- and upper-class minorities and allows the government to ignore expensive policies that genuinely address problems experienced by poor minorities.[45] Currently, eight states (Arizona, California, Colorado, Florida, Michigan, Nebraska, New Hampshire,

Apply affirmative action laws.

and Washington) ban affirmative action in their public university system, whereas the remaining states do not.[46]

Thus far, the U.S. Supreme Court has struck a middle ground on affirmative action. In cases such as *Regents of the University of California v. Bakke* (1978)[47] and *Grutter v. Bollinger* (2003),[48] the Supreme Court invalidated quota systems that reserved allotted spaces for racial and ethnic minorities in college and graduate school admissions. However, the Court did allow state universities to consider minority status as an asset when considering admissions. In 2012, the Supreme Court agreed to rehear the issue of granting preferences in the case of *Fisher v. University of Texas*. The Texas university system guarantees admission to its public universities for high school students who graduate in the top 10 percent of their class, which helps bolster minority enrollment because many schools are overwhelmingly Black or Latino. The remaining students are then considered based on other factors, which can include race. When Abigail Fisher, a White student, was not admitted to the University of Texas under this system, she sued, arguing that the state policy discriminated against her on account of race. However, in 2013 the U.S. Supreme Court declined to issue a substantive decision on affirmative action; instead, it sent the case back to the lower court for further analysis.[49] In 2016 the Supreme Court upheld the University of Texas' policy of considering race as one of many factors in its admissions decisions.[50]

Recent Changes in Voting Laws. Another civil rights controversy concerns newly enacted voting laws that are racially neutral on their face but disproportionally harm Blacks (and Latinos). As we mentioned in Chapter 3, voter ID laws require voters to show a government-issued picture identification, such as a driver's license or passport, to cast a vote. Since 2011, some states with Republican-controlled governments have passed voter ID laws arguing that this policy will prevent people from fraudulently impersonating others when voting. Opponents claim that the instances of voter fraud by one person impersonating another are so rare that these laws are not necessary. In addition, opponents argue that these laws will disproportionally harm poor, urban, and elderly voters, many of whom are Black or Latino, because they are unlikely to drive or possess the means to travel abroad and thus have passports.[51]

In 2013, North Carolina passed an extremely restrictive voter ID law that forbade many forms of identification popular with racial and ethnic minorities, including photo IDs for college students, government employees, and welfare recipients. The North Carolina law also shortened the number of early voting days, which are popular with racial and ethnic minorities. Civil rights groups and the Obama administration challenged the law as discrimination in violation of the Voting Rights Act. In 2016 a federal judge upheld the law, but later that year, an appeals court overturned the law, ruling that the North Carolina law blatantly discriminated against African American voters. In 2017 the U.S. Supreme Court refused to hear an appeal from the appeals court decision; therefore, the law is currently not in effect. Although Republican legislators articulated a desire to pass additional restrictive laws, they are not likely to succeed because in 2016 Democrat Roy Cooper defeated Republican incumbent Governor Pat McCrory. Cooper opposes the voter ID law.[52]

Criminal Justice. Disproportionate treatment in the criminal justice system is another civil rights issue that harms African Americans. As we discussed in the previous chapter, racial profiling often leads to police targeting African American suspects, but these criminal justice issues also present civil rights concerns because they affect African Americans as a group. Since 2014 there have been several highly publicized police killings of African Americans, including Eric Garner in New York, Michael Brown in Missouri, Tamir Rice (who was just 12 years old) in Ohio, Eric Harris in Oklahoma, Freddie Gray in Maryland, Walter Scott in South Carolina, Alton Sterling in Louisiana, and Philando Castile in Minnesota. In addition to these high-profile cases, statistics demonstrate that in 2016 African Americans were twice as likely as Whites to be killed by the police, and Black males between the ages of 15 and 34 were nine times more likely than any other group to be killed by law enforcement.[53] In Chapter 16 we discuss the disproportionate rates of Black incarceration, especially as a result of antidrug policies. Since 2013 the group Black Lives Matter has fought against entrenched racism and has been especially active in fighting against the mistreatment of African Americans in the criminal justice system.[54]

Latinos

Like African Americans, Latinos have experienced discrimination and segregation. Since 2003, Latinos have been the largest minority group in the United States,[55] but this statistic is deceiving because there are a variety of subgroups classified as Latino. The term **Latino** refers to those of Spanish or Portuguese colonial ancestry, including Mexican Americans (also called Chicanos), Puerto Ricans, Cuban Americans, and Central and South American immigrants. Recall from the Prologue our preference for the term *Latino* over the term *Hispanic*.

Latino An ethnic category describing people of Spanish or Portuguese colonial ancestry from the Caribbean, North America, Central America, and South America.

Mexican Americans. As a result of the American conquest of Mexico during the Mexican American War (1846–1848) and the Treaty of Guadalupe Hidalgo, which was signed at its conclusion in 1848, Mexico ceded its northern portion to the United States (the area encompassing the present states [or portions thereof] of California, Nevada, Utah, Arizona, New Mexico, Texas, Oklahoma, Kansas, Colorado, and Wyoming). The treaty gave Mexicans living in the ceded land the choice of returning to Mexico or living in American territory, where they could become American citizens. However, despite being citizens, the Mexican Americans who elected to stay in the United States and their descendants experienced the same kinds of discrimination, segregation, and violent intimidation that African Americans faced. As more Mexicans immigrated to the United States during the nineteenth century, they, too, were subjected to unequal treatment and segregation.[56]

The Mexican American Civil Rights Movement did not begin until the late nineteenth century. Disparate organizations throughout the Southwest concentrated on providing Mexican Americans with economic opportunities, organizing voter registration drives, and fighting against discrimination. In 1929, several Latino groups in Texas, loosely following the model of the NAACP, united to form the League of United Latin American Citizens (LULAC). During the 1940s and 1950s, LULAC, like the NAACP, sponsored federal and state litigation that ended segregation of Mexican American schoolchildren and allowed Mexican Americans to be included on juries. Notably, in the late 1940s, before the landmark *Brown v. Board of Education* decision, LULAC sponsored a case that resulted in a lower federal court halting the practice of Orange County, California, segregating White and Mexican American schoolchildren. LULAC has also focused on improving the lives of Latinos by registering them to vote, establishing Mexican American education programs, teaching English, and assisting in economic development.[57]

By the 1960s, Mexican Americans, like Blacks, had secured legal protections for civil rights, although inequality of outcome remained. The Civil Rights Act of 1964 and Voting Rights Act of 1965 applied to Mexican Americans, but during the late 1960s and early 1970s Mexican American civil rights activists organized protests and boycotts to address social and economic issues specific to Chicanos. In 1968, Mexican American high school students in Los Angeles staged a walkout to protest the racist portrayal of Mexican Americans in their classes. During the 1960s and 1970s, César Chávez, a labor leader who founded the United Farm Workers Union, fought for better wages for Chicano agricultural workers by organizing strikes and boycotts of the agricultural products of growers who exploited Mexican farmworkers. In the late 1960s, Chávez convinced consumers to boycott California grapes because of the poor working conditions the mainly Chicano farmworkers endured. The boycott was successful when grape growers agreed to bargain with farmworkers and provide better pay and working conditions.[58]

Mexican Americans achieved a major victory in 1975 when Congress expanded the Voting Rights Act to cover "language minorities." This new policy stipulated that if at least 5 percent of a county did not speak English and less than 50 percent of eligible citizens registered to vote in the previous election did not, then the county was required to print bilingual ballots. A large number of Mexican Americans who spoke only Spanish no longer faced linguistic barriers to voting.[59]

Puerto Ricans. Puerto Ricans are another sizable Latino population in the United States. Puerto Rico was originally a Spanish colony, but the United States assumed control over it after the Spanish-American War in 1899. Puerto Rico then became a territory of the United States, but the Jones Act of 1917 allowed Puerto Ricans to move freely to the mainland United States and conferred American citizenship on all Puerto Ricans who chose to move here. Since 1952, the island of Puerto Rico has been an American commonwealth, which means that its inhabitants do not enjoy the full extent of rights that U.S. citizens enjoy. Puerto Ricans living on the island were eligible for the draft before the shift to an all-volunteer army in 1973, and they do not pay federal income taxes. Puerto Rico falls under the jurisdiction of federal courts (see Chapter 9), but inhabitants on the island are not represented in American government.[60] Puerto Rico sends a resident commissioner to the House, and this person can serve and vote on committees, but he or she is not eligible to vote on legislation. Puerto Rico has no representative to the U.S. Senate, and Puerto Ricans do not vote in the presidential election.[61]

In 2012, residents of Puerto Rico voted on their status in a two-part ballot question. The first question asked if residents of the island wanted to change Puerto Rico's current status, and 54 percent voted to reject commonwealth status. The second part then asked voters to choose among three options: becoming a state, becoming an independent nation, or becoming more independent but still linked to the United States. On this question, 61 percent voted for statehood. This vote marked the first time Puerto Ricans expressed support for statehood, although many voters left these questions blank. Of course, the process of Puerto Rican statehood is not complete because Congress must decide whether to admit Puerto Rico as the fifty-first state, and Congress has not made any progress on making Puerto Rico a state over the past six years.[62]

Puerto Rican statehood emerged as an issue after Hurricane Maria struck the island in September 2017 with 155 mph winds—less than two weeks after Hurricane Irma devastated the island. Virtually the entire island lost power, and even as late as May 2018, more than 100,000 Puerto Ricans still lack electricity. The Federal Emergency Management Agency, which is responsible for helping people recover from natural disasters, devoted more resources to Texas and Florida after they suffered from similar storms (Harvey and Irma, respectively) that same summer (we discuss this issue in more detail in Chapter 8).[63] Despite the initial official death toll of 64 people, a recent Harvard study estimated that more than 4,600 Puerto Ricans died as a result of Maria.[64] Additionally, President Donald Trump was clearly less engaged with Puerto Rico after Hurricane Maria than he was with the mainland after Hurricanes Harvey and Irma. Unlike in Texas and Florida, where President Trump visited immediately after the storm and praised the state and local officials, President Trump fought with Puerto Rican officials, most notably San Juan mayor Carmen Yulín Cruz; made fewer public statements about the situation in Puerto Rico compared to Texas and Florida; and waited almost two weeks to visit the Island. When he visited Puerto Rico, President Trump alienated the population because he focused on how well he handled the recovery and at one point casually threw paper towel rolls to a crowd like he was shooting a basketball.[65] As a result of the response to Hurricane Maria, Puerto Ricans, including its conservative Republican Resident Commissioner Jennifer González Colón, have advocated for Puerto Rican statehood in the hopes that the federal government would treat the island better if it had the political power of a state.[66]

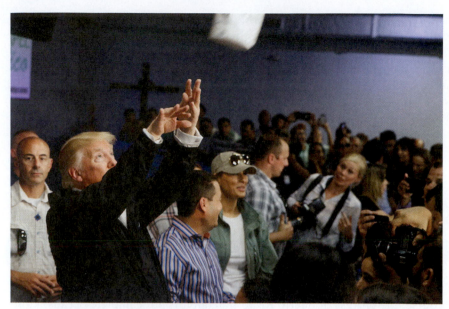

During his visit to Puerto Rico after Hurricane Maria, President Donald Trump appears not to appreciate the seriousness of the situation as he cavalierly throws paper towel rolls to a crowd, as if he is shooting a basketball.

Learn about
Hispanic and other
civil rights groups.

Although Puerto Ricans living on the mainland United States are full American citizens, like Mexican Americans and Blacks they have faced discrimination and segregation. However, they attained legal protection against discrimination through the Civil Rights Act of 1964 and the Voting Rights Act of 1965. As a result, Puerto Rican Americans have legal recourse if they are subjected to political and economic discrimination. Nevertheless, as with other racial or ethnic minorities, Puerto Ricans still suffer from inequality of outcome and de facto segregation.[67]

Cuban Americans. As a result of American foreign policy concerns, the Cuban American civil rights experience has been unique compared to that of other Latino groups. After Fidel Castro instituted a communist takeover of Cuba in 1959, professional and elite Cubans, who stood to lose their wealth under Castro's redistributive policies and faced political persecution, defected to the nearby United States. The United States, which ideologically opposed Castro's rule, readily accepted these immigrants. As a result, Cuban Americans have not always shared the civil rights concerns of the other Latino groups, although Cuban Americans have been victims of discrimination. Like other racial and ethnic minorities, Cuban Americans benefited from civil rights legislation such as the Civil Rights Act of 1964 and the Voting Rights Act of 1965. Cuban Americans can now sue if they are not hired or promoted because of their ethnicity.

In 1980, Cuban president Fidel Castro expelled thousands of political and criminal prisoners to the United States. Keeping with the practice of welcoming

Cuban immigrants, President Jimmy Carter allowed them to enter the United States. These immigrants, known as the *Marielitos*, were poorer and tended to have darker skin color compared to earlier Cuban immigrants. Moreover, not all of the *Marielitos* were political prisoners; some were common criminals. As a result, the U.S. government abandoned its policy of open immigration for Cuban immigrants and detained the *Marielitos* for months before allowing them to enter American society. Since the early 1980s, *Marielitos* and their offspring have become American citizens.[68]

Immigration. Despite the differences among Latino groups, the issue of immigration affects all Latino subgroups, except Puerto Ricans, who are already American citizens. As discussed earlier, many Chicanos' ancestors became Americans after the United States conquered a considerable amount of land from Mexico, and subsequently many Latino people legally immigrated to the United States. However, as the opening story shows, undocumented immigration is an extremely controversial issue, especially since the candidacy and presidency of Donald Trump. On the day he announced his candidacy, Trump stated, "When Mexico sends its people, they're not sending their best . . . They're bringing drugs. They're bringing crime. They're rapists. And some, I assume, are good people."[69] Throughout the campaign, Trump articulated hardline immigration policies, such as preventing undocumented immigrants from becoming citizens; deploying more border patrol forces; major deportations of undocumented immigrants; and, most notably, building a wall on the entire border between the United States and Mexico for which Mexico will pay.[70]

As the opening story about Fernando Espino Casas demonstrates, the Trump presidency has exerted significant influence on immigration policy. Recall that President Trump reversed President Obama's DACA policy that allowed undocumented immigrants like Casas to work and live freely in the United States. Additionally, because Mexico refused to pay for a border wall, President Trump wants Congress to appropriate money for it. In early 2018, Senators Lindsey Graham (R-SC) and Richard Durbin (D-IL) developed a bipartisan compromise bill that would have allowed DACA immigrants to remain in the nation and even become citizens, provided money for border enforcement including building a wall, and limited some legal immigration. Despite initially seeming inclined to support a compromise, President Trump rejected the Graham-Durbin proposal, and during a meeting with the senators, Trump commented that he did not want more immigrants from "shithole countries," referring to Latin American, Caribbean, and African nations.[71]

Additionally, the Trump administration changed immigration policy in 2018, when it initiated a so-called "zero tolerance" policy of separating families of undocumented immigrants and asylum seekers when they reached the border. Specifically, the administration placed thousands of children in separate detention facilities from their parents. Administration officials argue that this policy will deter illegal immigration in general and people from bringing their children across the border in particular. As press coverage focused on the

Watch President
Trump talking about
a border wall.

hardship these families are experiencing, President Donald Trump first falsely blamed the policy on Democrats, but in June of 2018 the administration officially ended the policy. However, as of October 2018, many children are still not reunited with their families, and President Trump as articulated strong support of the policy.[72]

Assess current debates on immigration.

Regardless of the substantive arguments over immigration policies, many advocates for minorities are concerned about the anti-Latino rhetoric that pervades the debate. In some cases, the anti-immigration rhetoric has focused on all immigrants, regardless of legal status, and at times this rhetoric has employed prejudiced stereotypes of Latinos. For example, U.S. Representative Steve King (R-IA) compared immigrants to dogs when he addressed constituents on the issue of immigration and remarked, "You want a good birddog? You want the one that is going to be aggressive? Pick the one that's the friskiest, not the one that's over there sleeping in the corner."[73] The notion of an immigrant "sleeping in the corner" references a long-held stereotype of Latinos—Mexican Americans in particular—as being lazy. More recently, President Trump's Chief of Staff John Kelly stated in early 2018 that undocumented immigrants do not apply for the protections that exist because they are "too lazy to get off their asses,"[74] which again reinforced the stereotype of Mexican Americans being lazy. The Anti-Defamation League (ADL), an organization that monitors hate groups, notes that odious immigration rhetoric was once confined to hate groups, such as the Ku Klux Klan and Neo-Nazis. However, the ADL discovered that now this rhetoric comes from mainstream politicians and media outlets. The ADL report even shows that some groups claiming to be pro-environment proffer discredited claims that legal and illegal immigration harm the environment.[75] The next Evaluating Equality box discusses in more detail how terminology affects public opinion on immigration issues.

Asian Americans

From the founding of the republic through the early twentieth century, federal laws discriminated against Asian immigrants, a racial minority group with origins in southern and eastern Asia, including Korea, China, Japan, Southeast Asia, and the Indian subcontinent. Recall from Chapter 1 that based on the tradition of exclusion, the Naturalization Act of 1790 only allowed free White immigrants to become citizens; therefore, Asian immigrants were not eligible to become citizens. During the 1800s, many Chinese immigrants came to the United States to provide cheap labor to build railroads, and subsequently other Asian immigrants moved to the West Coast of the United States to seek economic opportunities.

As Asian immigration continued, individual states and the national government responded to growing anti-Asian prejudice by passing legislation that discriminated against Asian Americans. For example, based on the premise that the influx of Chinese immigrants "endangers the good order of certain localities," the federal government passed the Chinese Exclusion Act in 1882, which virtually eliminated Chinese immigration and severely discriminated against Chinese immigrants already living in the United States.[76]

evaluating equality

Terminology and Support for Immigration Reform

The debate over immigration has been central to civil rights politics since the 1960s. The U.S. government liberalized immigration during the 1960s by ending stringent ethnic quotas and giving high priority to keeping families together. But it was still difficult for low-skilled Latinos, especially Mexican Americans, to immigrate to the United States. Spurred by poverty in their home country and a demand for cheap labor in the United States, millions of people immigrated illegally from across the Mexican border. In 1986, Congress passed the Immigration Reform and Control Act (IRCA), which increased scrutiny on employers who hire undocumented immigrants. The IRCA did, however, give undocumented immigrants living in the United States for at least five years the opportunity to become American citizens. Despite the act's efforts, the IRCA did not lessen the controversy over immigration, and during the early part of the twenty-first century the debate over immigration has become an extremely contentious issue. In 2007, Congress and President George W. Bush again sought a comprehensive immigration law that would have increased border enforcement and provided a way for existing undocumented immigrants to become legal residents and even citizens. However, the bill never passed. Since then there has been no significant progress on the passage of a meaningful immigration bill.

Americans are split over the issue of immigration reform, particularly the opportunity for undocumented immigrants to become U.S. citizens. To create the impression that this provision would reward people who broke American laws, opponents of the

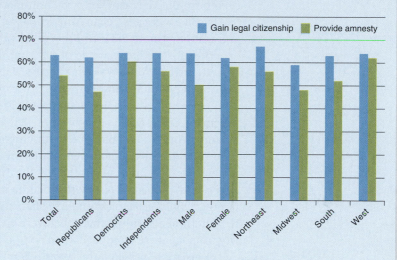

Figure 5.5 Percentage Supporting "Gain Legal Citizenship" for Illegal Immigrants Versus "Provide Amnesty" for Illegal Immigrants

bill couched it in terms of "amnesty," which connotes rewarding lawbreakers. However, supporters of the bill argued that this provision did not grant amnesty; instead, they said it created a path to citizenship for illegal immigrants who had lived and worked in the United States for a long time.

Throughout much of this chapter, we have covered how immigration politics influences civil rights, but here we are specifically interested in how the wording used in the debate affects people's perceptions of it. A 2007 survey conducted by the respected Pew Research Center illustrates how wording can influence public attitudes toward immigration. One question asked whether the respondent agreed with an immigration policy that would "provide a way to gain legal citizenship if they [illegal immigrants] meet certain conditions," and another question asked whether the respondent agreed with a policy that would "provide amnesty

if they meet certain conditions." For each question, Figure 5.5 shows the percentage of different groups that claimed they favored the proposal.

Try an experiment with your friends, family, or coworkers by asking them about their views on whether the government should provide a way for undocumented workers to become legal residents or citizens. However, use the different wordings from the survey with different people. Do you notice different responses? Even when debating the issue among classmates, try to determine if supporters of immigration reform are likely to use different language than opponents do.

Source: Data adapted from Kohut, A. (2007, June 7). *Democratic leaders face growing opposition on Iraq, mixed views on immigration bill.* Pew Research Center for the People and the Press. Retrieved June 16, 2018, from http://www.people-press.org/files/legacy-pdf/335.pdf.

Likewise, the 1913 California Alien Land Act expressly prohibited aliens, mainly Asian immigrants, from owning land or leasing it for more than three years. These laws applied only to the immigrants themselves, not to their children born on American soil, who automatically received citizenship. Similar to African Americans, Asian Americans were also subjected to state-sponsored segregation prior to *Brown v. Board of Education*.[77]

The most severe example of discrimination against Asian Americans occurred during World War II. After the Japanese government bombed Pearl Harbor, the military and many Americans feared Japanese American disloyalty. Consequently, in February 1942, President Franklin Roosevelt issued Executive Order 9066, which empowered the U.S. military to relocate all Japanese Americans, many of them citizens, residing on the West Coast to internment camps, which were stark, inhospitable prison camps located in the desert. The order also allowed the U.S. government to seize Japanese Americans' property. Despite this blatant and cruel discrimination, in the infamous 1944 *Korematsu v. United States* case, the U.S. Supreme Court upheld the internments, ruling that the government's need to protect national security from Japanese espionage was a compelling enough justification.[78]

Legislation passed after World War II extended civil rights to Asian Americans. The 1952 McCarran–Walter Immigration Act increased immigration quotas for Asian immigrants, and it allowed the immigrants to become naturalized citizens. The Civil Rights Act of 1964 and the Voting Rights Act of 1965 (and its extension to language minorities in 1975) applied to Asian Americans as it did to other minority groups. These laws protected Asian Americans' civil rights and guaranteed their right to vote.[79]

Unlike Black and Latino civil rights activism, Asian American activism has not been sustained. There have been limited protest movements, and much of the interest-group activity has focused on a single ethnic background. For example, the Japanese American Citizens League (JACL) was founded in 1930 to fight for civil rights for Japanese Americans. The JACL's most significant accomplishment was successfully lobbying for the Civil Liberties Act of 1988, which provided an apology and $20,000 in compensation to each surviving Japanese American who had been interned during World War II.[80] Similar to LULAC, the Chinese American Citizens Alliance focuses on registering Chinese Americans to vote and teaching the English language to recent immigrants.[81] The group Chinese for Affirmative Action has advocated in support of immigrants' rights and access to bilingual education.[82]

American Indians

American Indian is the term used to describe the racial category of the indigenous people who lived in the geographic area of the United States before European settlers arrived. Recall that the term *American Indian* is preferable to the term *Native American*, which could apply to any person born in the United States. The relationship between Indian tribes and the federal government is unique compared to that of other groups because the U.S. government has treated Indian tribes as separate nations within the United States, even negotiating through treaties. Throughout American history, American Indians have experienced genocide, harsh treatment, discrimination, and segregation at the hands of the U.S. government, but they have gradually gained civil rights.

To create room for White settlers on Indian-occupied land, the federal government forcibly and harshly removed Indian peoples and segregated them on **reservations** in the Western territories during the early nineteenth century. Among the Cherokee Tribe alone, 17,000 people were removed from Georgia to the Oklahoma Territory during the late 1830s and 1840s, and almost 4,000 people did not survive the brutal journey, known as the Trail of Tears.[83]

Reservations Portions of land set aside for American Indians removed from their ancestral lands by the federal government.

During the late nineteenth century, discrimination against American Indians took the form of forced assimilation in which the federal government sought to bring Indian peoples off the reservations and into White society. The Dawes Act, passed in 1887, granted a 160-acre homestead and citizenship to any indigenous person who renounced his or her tribal holdings and heritage.[84] Touted as a way to promote integration of Indian peoples into White society, the law instead undermined tribal culture. Tribal governments lost their authority, and Indians often received nonarable land in the desert.[85]

In the twentieth century, the federal government extended civil rights protections to American Indians, although these advances occurred gradually and suffered setbacks. The Indian Citizenship Act of 1924 conferred American citizenship, including the right to vote, on all Indian peoples regardless of where they lived. In 1934, Congress overturned the Dawes Act with the passage of the Indian Reorganization Act, which, despite some setbacks, eventually restored sovereignty to tribal governments.[86] The Civil Rights Act of 1964 and Voting Rights Act of 1965 increased political and economic equality for American Indians.

Despite this civil rights progress, inequality of opportunity and outcome still existed for American Indians. As a result, American Indian protest movements intensified during the late 1960s and early 1970s. The most significant American Indian civil rights organization is the American Indian Movement (AIM), which was founded in 1968. Initially, AIM focused on offering legal assistance to Indians and fighting police brutality, but in the early 1970s, the organization shifted its focus to protests and marches to demand civil rights. In 1973, members of AIM organized an armed occupation of Wounded Knee in South Dakota (the historic site of an 1890 massacre of Indians), and they claimed the land as the property of the Lakota people. AIM members argued that they were reclaiming historic land, but the FBI and federal marshals confronted the activists, resulting in a standoff that lasted more than two months.[87]

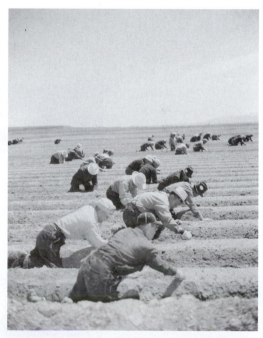

Japanese Americans working in agricultural fields at the Tule Lake internment camp in northeastern California. Despite the Constitution's prohibition against racial discrimination, during World War II the U.S. government mistrusted the loyalty of Japanese Americans and confined many of them, including native-born citizens, in harsh internment camps like this one.

Omaha boys at the Carlisle Indian Industrial School in Carlisle, Pennsylvania, circa 1880. This boarding school was one of many throughout the United States that sought to assimilate American Indians into White culture. In addition to receiving education and training, students were forced to cut their hair and were punished for speaking their native language.

Because American Indian tribes enjoy considerable sovereignty, they are able to own gambling casinos, like the one pictured here, even if the state in which the tribe is located bans or heavily regulates gambling. These casinos have generated significant revenue for Native American tribes, but many critics argue that the profits are not fairly distributed among all tribal members.

In the late twentieth century, the federal government established the policy of **sovereignty**, giving each tribe freedom to regulate its own people and allowing tribes to operate according to their own customs. Most notably, sovereignty has benefited Indian tribes economically by permitting them to operate gambling casinos on their lands, which we discussed in Chapter 3. Although these profitable casinos on reservation lands have allowed these tribes to amass considerable wealth, many Indian activists, including leaders of AIM, have criticized tribal leaders for not equitably distributing gambling profits among all Indians, especially those who do not reside on tribal lands.[88]

Nonracial and Ethnic Struggles for Civil Rights

The Fourteenth Amendment protects racial and ethnic minorities, but it does not specify protections for discrimination on the basis of gender and sexual orientation. Nevertheless, women, members of the LGBTQ community, older adults, and people with disabilities have experienced discrimination. Over the course of the twentieth century, each group has engaged in political activism and gradually achieved civil rights, although inequality still exists.

Women

Discrimination against women has been rampant throughout most of the history of the United States. During the early nineteenth century, most states prevented married women from signing contracts, abused wives from leaving their husbands, and widows from inheriting property. Other laws prevented all adult women, regardless of marital status, from pursuing prestigious occupations. By the early 1800s, every state denied women the right to vote. Because of this discrimination, female civil rights activists initiated their struggle for equal rights during the nineteenth century. In 1848, about three hundred women and men attended a conference in Seneca Falls, New York, to discuss discrimination against women. The conference produced the Seneca Falls Declaration of Sentiments and Resolutions, which called for equal treatment and voting rights for women. Interestingly, the organizers of the conference initially met in other social movements, particularly the abolitionist movement, where they recognized that women were also victims of discrimination despite being highly capable.[89]

During the late nineteenth century, the **suffrage movement**, led by activists such as Susan B. Anthony and Elizabeth Cady Stanton, sought to secure the right to vote for women. Members of this movement objected strenuously when the Fifteenth Amendment prohibited denial of suffrage on the basis of race, color, or previous servitude, but not on the basis of sex. As a result of continued activism, some states eventually granted women the right to vote, although by 1918 most had not. The suffrage movement finally achieved its goal in 1920 with the ratification of the **Nineteenth Amendment** to the Constitution, which gave women the right to vote by prohibiting states from discriminating on account of sex when determining voter eligibility.

Sovereignty A government policy toward American Indians that allows each tribe to regulate its own people and operate according to its own customs.

Suffrage Movement Large-scale efforts of organizations and activists during the late nineteenth and early twentieth centuries to secure the right to vote for women.

Nineteenth Amendment An amendment to the Constitution that prevents states from denying women the right to vote because of their sex.

Despite the adoption of the Nineteenth Amendment, state and federal laws continued to treat women unequally. New Deal programs, which created numerous federal jobs during the Great Depression, were not available to women. Although women had worked factory jobs because of labor shortages during World War II, after the war women were subjected to severe employment discrimination. During the 1960s, the federal government passed modest civil rights laws for women, and the Civil Rights Act of 1964 applied to gender discrimination as well as to discrimination based on race, color, and national origin. But the federal government did not enforce laws against gender discrimination as stringently as it did for race. During the 1970s, the U.S. Supreme Court applied the Fourteenth Amendment to women, but only partially, and not with the same force as it does for racial and ethnic minorities.[90]

Dissatisfied with the weak and poorly enforced federal laws, women's civil rights groups mobilized for stronger protections. The National Organization for Women (NOW), which was founded in 1967 to ensure legal equality for women and abortion rights, led an effort to lobby both houses of Congress to propose an **equal rights amendment** to the U.S. Constitution. Although activists, such as Alice Paul, had been seeking such an amendment since the 1920s, NOW and its allies achieved an initial victory in 1972 when both houses of Congress proposed an amendment that read, "Equality of rights under the law shall not be denied or abridged by the United States or any state on account of sex."[91]

Equal Rights Amendment
A proposed, but unratified, constitutional amendment that would have prevented gender discrimination to the same extent that the Fourteenth Amendment prevents racial and ethnic discrimination.

If ratified, this amendment would have required the Supreme Court to view gender discrimination cases exactly as it viewed racial discrimination and to strike down virtually all state laws discriminating against women unless the government could show a compelling justification. During the ratification process, however, conservative groups organized to oppose the Equal Rights Amendment, arguing that it would undermine women's roles as wives and mothers and would ultimately erode the traditional family. By the time the deadline for ratification had passed in 1982, the amendment fell short of the requisite three-fourths of the states needed for ratification, even though survey evidence indicated that a majority of Americans supported the amendment.[92] Subsequent Congresses have reintroduced the amendment, but it has not been passed. In 2015, Representative Jackie Speier (D-CA) introduced a bill that would end the time limit on the Equal Rights Amendment so that more states would be able to ratify it. Although her bill had 163 cosponsors, it did not pass.[93]

Women also suffer from inequality of outcome because they are paid less than men. Until the twentieth century, women were relegated to performing housework and raising children, and they were not paid for those efforts. During World War II, high demand for munitions and a labor shortage brought women into the workforce for the first time. Nevertheless, women were paid less than their male counterparts, and after the war ended women were dismissed from their jobs. In 1963, Congress passed the Equal Pay Act, which required that women be paid the same as men for the same work.[94] Businesses can circumvent the law by giving men and women different job classifications,

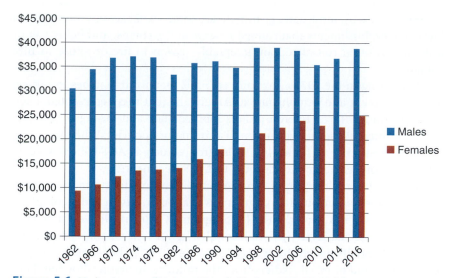

Figure 5.6 Median Income of Male and Female Workers, 1962–2016 (All figures in 2016 dollars)

Source: Adapted from United States Census. (n.d.). Historical Income Tables: People: Table P-2. Race and Hispanic Origin by Median Income and Sex, 1947–2016: All Races. Retrieved June 17, 2018, from https://www.census.gov/data/tables/time-series/demo/income-poverty/historical-income-people.html.

despite performing the same tasks. Since the 1970s, the federal government has strengthened equal pay requirements, but inequities still exist. As Figure 5.6 shows, there is still an income gap between men and women, although that gap has narrowed over the past fifty years.

During the late 1980s and 1990s, **sexual harassment** emerged as an important gender equality issue. Sexual harassment refers to any unwelcome sexual comments or treatment in the workplace or in an education institution. It can include outright sexual assault, a supervisor's offer to a subordinate to exchange favorable treatment for sex, an employer's failure to prevent a sexually hostile work environment, or a professor's offer to a student to exchange good grades for sex.

Even though both men and women can be victims of sexual harassment, this form of discrimination affects women disproportionately. Sexual harassment recently became more salient after well-publicized instances of powerful males harassing and assaulting women, including Donald Trump, movie producer Harvey Weinstein, and journalist Charlie Rose. Actor Alyssa Milano encouraged victims of sexual assault to come forward with the hashtag "#MeToo," and since then, the #MeToo movement has sought to publicize and punish people who used their power to engage in sexual assault and sexual harassment of women.[95]

Sexual Harassment
Unwelcome sexual comments or treatment in the workplace or in an educational institution.

Lesbian, Gay, Bisexual, Transgender, and Queer or Questioning People

LGBTQ people have been subjected to discrimination and violent attacks, and although there has been some civil rights progress, they still face exclusion.

Prior to the 1970s, most states criminalized homosexual activity, police often harassed establishments that catered to gays and lesbians, and being gay or lesbian was often considered an acceptable reason to fire or refuse to hire someone.

Beginning in the 1970s, gays and lesbians organized marches to protest unfair treatment and demonstrate to Americans that they represented a significant political force. Interest groups lobbied state and local governments and sponsored litigation to overturn discriminatory policies. When the AIDS epidemic first broke in the early 1980s, groups such as ACT-UP emerged to lobby for more federal money devoted to AIDS treatment.[96]

In recent years, there has been progress in ending discrimination based on sexual orientation, but this progress has been intermittent and incomplete. As we discussed in Chapter 3, the U.S. Supreme Court invalidated state laws banning homosexual activity.[97] Additionally, in 2011 the Obama Defense Department officially ended the "Don't Ask, Don't Tell" policy that discharged lesbian, gay, and bisexual soldiers from the military, therefore allowing them to continue serving without hiding their sexuality.[98]

Another LGBTQ issue concerns government recognition of same-sex marriage. For many years, LGBTQ rights organizations have argued that the failure to recognize same-sex marriages denied those couples civil rights because they were not able to enjoy the benefits that opposite-sex couples enjoy,

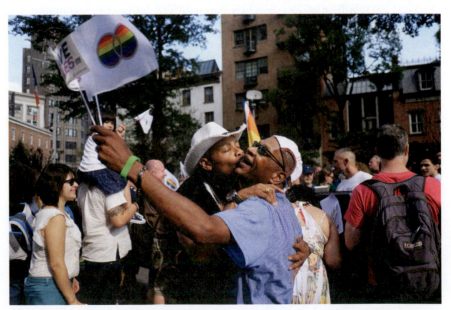

At the turn of the twenty-first century, no states allowed same-sex marriage, but since then states gradually allowed it. In 2015, the U.S Supreme Court ruled that laws banning same-sex marriage were unconstitutional, which legalized it throughout the United States. However, some local judges and government officials have steadfastly refused to sanction same-sex marriages, citing religious objections.

such as inheritance and hospital visitation. Initially, some states adopted **civil unions**, which afforded same-sex couples the same legal rights as opposite-sex married couples without sanctioning the marriage. However, beginning in the late 2000s, states legalized same-sex marriage on their own, although most states still banned it. In 2015 the U.S Supreme Court issued its landmark decision in *Obergefell v. Hodges*, which ruled that laws banning same-sex marriage violated the Fourteenth Amendment Due Process Clause; therefore, the Court legalized same-sex marriage throughout the nation.[99] However, opponents of LGBTQ rights are resisting same-sex marriage. For example, in 2015 Indiana passed the Religious Freedom Restoration Act (RFRA), which exempted people from following certain laws on religious grounds. Therefore, business, such as bakers and florists, could refuse to deal with same-sex couples because of religious grounds. After companies, such as Angie's List and Walmart, and nonprofits, such as the NCAA, threatened to boycott Indiana, the state revised the law to protect against discrimination based on sexual orientation, but LGBTQ supporters still argue that the RFRA allows for discrimination.[100] Additionally, in 2018, the U.S. Supreme Court held in favor of a baker who refused to make a cake for a same-sex wedding after the Colorado Civil Rights Commission ruled that his actions were discriminatory in violation of Colorado law, although the Supreme Court based its decision on narrow procedural grounds. Despite this opposition, a growing majority of Americans support same-sex marriage (see Figure 5.7).

Notwithstanding these advances, there are minimal federal protections for sexual orientation, and as a result many places throughout the United States permit employment, economic, and housing discrimination based on sexual

Civil Unions Government policies that provided official legal recognition of same-sex couples without sanctioning marriage.

Figure 5.7 Public Opinion on Whether Same-Sex Marriage Should Be Valid (Percentage Saying It Should Be Valid Versus Percentage Saying It Should Not Be Valid), 1996–2018. Results were averaged over the year when the poll was taken more than once in a calendar year

Source: Adapted from Gallup. (n.d.). In Depth: Topics A to Z: Marriage. Retrieved June 18, 2018, from https://news. gallup.com/poll/117328/marriage.aspx.

orientation. Additionally, violent crimes based on the victim's LGBTQ status are on the rise. Recent evidence demonstrates that on a per capita basis (i.e., the number of people in the protected class), LBGTQ people are more likely than members of racial or religious minorities to experience hate crimes.[101] States are mixed on their protections for the LGBTQ community against hate crimes. As of June 2018, 31 states (including Washington, DC) prohibit hate crimes based on sexual orientation, and only 18 of those states (including DC) specifically protect gender identity.[102]

Even more recently the issue of transgender discrimination has emerged as a civil rights issue. Some states and localities have laws protecting transgender people from discrimination in areas such as housing and employment, but many places do not. Recently, there has been a controversy over whether transgender people should be able to use public restrooms that correspond to the gender with which they identify. For example, the city of Charlotte, North Carolina, passed an ordinance allowing transgender people to use the public restroom that corresponds to their gender identity. In response, the state of North Carolina passed a 2016 law that required everyone to use the bathroom that corresponds to the sex on their birth certificate, regardless of their gender identity. In response to this discriminatory law, corporations, such as PayPal and the National Basketball Association, and nonprofits, such as the NCAA, threatened to boycott the state. Additionally, activists filed a suit in federal court challenging North Carolina's so-called "bathroom bill." Because of this backlash, the North Carolina legislature voted in 2017 to repeal this controversial bill, which the newly elected Democratic Governor Roy Cooper signed into law. Although this reversal was sufficient to end the boycotts, controversies over transgender rights are still salient in North Carolina and throughout the United States.[103]

Older Adults and People with Disabilities

A number of other groups have experienced discrimination and civil rights progress, including older adults and those with a disability. To combat workplace discrimination based on age, the Age Discrimination in Employment Act (ADEA), passed in 1967, prohibits employers from discriminating in hiring, promoting, compensating, or laying off employees because of age. The American Association for Retired Persons, an organization that represents people over the age of fifty, devotes efforts to litigating against age discrimination in employment.[104]

Likewise, the Americans with Disabilities Act (ADA), passed in 1990, prohibits employers from discriminating against employees because of physical disability. In fact, the ADA requires employers to provide reasonable accommodations, such as sign language interpreters for the hearing impaired and Braille facilities for visually impaired employees or job applicants. The ADA also requires all public accommodations, places where the public should reasonably be able to access, to provide facilities for people with disabilities. Therefore, buildings were required to build wheelchair ramps, install electric doors, and add Braille for the elevators. The ADA has been especially prevalent in colleges

Sharice Davids gives her victory speech after winning the state's 3rd congressional district race on Tuesday, Nov. 6, 2018, at her watch party in Olathe, Kan. Davids is not only one of the two first American Indian women elected to Congress, but she is also the first member of the LGBTQ community elected to represent Kansas in the US House of Representatives.

and universities, which are now required to provide the aforementioned facilities for people with physical disabilities. Additionally, colleges and universities must offer services that assist students with learning disabilities. Similar to other civil rights organizations, the Disability Rights Education & Defense Fund advocates on behalf of disabled Americans.[105]

Conclusion

This entire book focuses on the politics of race and ethnicity, but this chapter concentrated specifically on the history of discrimination and civil rights progress for a select few groups. First, we explained the precise meaning of key terms relevant to civil rights politics. We then focused on different groups' civil rights histories. We devoted a significant portion of this chapter to the Black civil rights struggle because it has been the most active and is the most well known. However, Blacks are not the only racial or ethnic group with a vibrant civil rights history. Accordingly, this chapter addressed the civil rights struggles of Latinos, Asian Americans, and American Indians. Because civil rights politics is not exclusive to racial and ethnic minorities, we also traced the history of civil rights concerning gender, sexual orientation, age, and disability.

Although there are obvious differences among the groups we covered, all the civil rights stories share important similarities. Each group experienced severe forms of unequal treatment, segregation, or both, but each group also engaged in various forms of political activism, such as lobbying legislatures, sponsoring litigation, and protesting. This activism yielded significant civil rights victories for each group, but this progress has not been complete, and important civil rights issues remain.

In addition to discussing the civil rights histories of each group, this chapter addressed political controversies affecting civil rights in general. For example, one controversial issue concerns the policies intended to redress past discrimination. Affirmative-action policies are designed to give minorities assistance in hiring, promotion, and admission to education institutions, but critics point out that these policies violate principles against racial discrimination by favoring racial and ethnic minorities over Whites. Busing promotes more integration of schools, but it places hardships on the children who are bused, as well as their parents. New voter ID laws and shorter early voting periods could hinder minority turnout, but several state governments assert that these measures are necessary to administer elections. **Hate crime legislation** seeks to prevent violent crimes committed out of prejudice, but opponents of these laws believe that violent actions should be punished equally, regardless of the motive.

Immigration is one of the most interesting and controversial civil rights issues. From the founding of the nation, the U.S. government has crafted immigration policies as a means of excluding certain races and ethnicities from coming to the United States. Since the twentieth century, however, immigration law has been overtly used as a means of racial and ethnic exclusion. Today, the controversy centers on undocumented immigration. Debate has centered on federal government immigration policies, such as separating parents and children among people detained at the border. Moreover, as the story of Fernando Espino Casas demonstrates, policies concerning undocumented immigrants significantly affect the lives of millions of people. This chapter illustrated in depth the arguments on all sides of the immigration debate, as well as how issues of wording can affect public perception over the debate. In short, the vexing controversies over illegal immigration illustrate the complex and dynamic nature of civil rights policy.

Hate Crime Legislation Laws that enhance criminal penalties for crimes committed out of prejudice toward certain groups.

REVIEW QUESTIONS

Check your understanding of Chapter 5.

1. Why is President Trump's DACA reversal so controversial?

2. What are the similarities and differences among the civil rights stories for different racial and ethnic groups?

3. How has the policy of sovereignty influenced equality of outcome for American Indian peoples?

4. What civil rights gains did women make during the twentieth century, and where does inequality still exist?

5. What are some of the key current controversies over civil rights concerning sexual orientation?

KEY TERMS

Flashcard review.

Abolitionists p. 135

Affirmative Action p. 144

Black Codes p. 136

Brown v. Board of Education
p. 140

Civil Rights p. 129

Civil Rights Act of 1964 p. 141

Civil Unions p. 161

De Facto Segregation p. 133

readings

ADDITIONAL READINGS

Need to review key ideas in greater depth? Click here.

Abrajano, M., & Hajnal, Z. L. (2015). *White backlash: Immigration, race, and American politics.* Princeton, NJ: Princeton University Press.

> This book uses extensive data analysis to demonstrate how debates over immigration have moved Whites toward the Republican Party while racial and ethnic minorities have moved toward the Democrats.

Kryder, D. (2000). *Divided arsenal: Race and the American state during World War II.* New York: Cambridge University Press.

> This book shows how the government's need for economic production during World War II led to policies that advanced civil rights for African Americans.

Lebron, C. J. (2017). *The making of Black Lives Matter: A brief history of an idea.* New York: Oxford University Press, 2017.

> This book places the equality message of the Black Lives Matter movement within the intellectual history of Black civil rights extending back to the nineteenth century.

McClain, P. D., & Carew, J. D. J. (2018). *"Can we all get along?": Racial and ethnic minorities in American politics* (7th ed.). Boulder, CO: Westview Press.

> This book analyzes the politics surrounding the most prominent racial and ethnic minorities in the United States—Blacks, Latinos, Asian Americans, and American Indian peoples—from historical, legal, institutional, behavioral, and policy perspectives.

McGlen, N. E., O'Connor, K., Van Assendelft, L., & Gunther-Canada, W. (2010). *Women, politics, and American society* (5th ed.). New York: Longman.

> This book explicates the theoretical, historical, and contemporary aspects of the issue of women's rights, including a global perspective on those rights.

Taylor, J. K., & Haider-Markel, D. T. (Eds.). (2014). *Transgender rights and politics: Groups, issue framing, and policy adoption.* Ann Arbor: University of Michigan Press.

> This edited volume examines the role of political messaging and interest groups in shaping transgender rights policies in the United States and in other nations.

Congress: Representation and Lawmaking

Representative Will Hurd (R-TX) at a committee hearing. Representative Hurd is an anomaly in Congress because he is an African American Republican who represents a majority-Latino district. Hurd was first elected in 2014 and was reelected narrowly in 2016 and 2018 despite Donald Trump's anti-Latino rhetoric.

The 23rd Congressional District of Texas is a sprawling district that stretches along the Mexican border from the outskirts of San Antonio all the way to the outskirts of El Paso, with numerous small towns contained within. It is the largest district in the state of Texas, according to landmass; in fact, it is one of the largest in the United States. Given its location, the 23rd District is largely Latino–68.3 percent according to latest estimates—and has only a small African American population—3.9 percent according to the latest estimate.[1] Given its large Latino population, this region has been represented by a Latino member of the House since the 1980s after the Voting Rights Act (see Chapters 3 and 5) was amended to ensure more minority representation in the U.S. House and state legislatures. Moreover, given its vast landscape, the district has actually been fairly competitive between Republicans and Democrats, with Latino representatives from both parties, which is why the election result in 2014 was so unique. Because 2014 was an unfavorable year for Democrats, it was not surprising that Democratic Representative Pete Gallego, who is Latino, narrowly lost his seat to a Republican. However, it was surprising that he was defeated by Republican Will Hurd, who is African American.

In many respects Representative Hurd's background is typical of a member of Congress. He graduated with a degree in computer science from Texas A&M University, where he served as student body president. He then went on to serve as an intelligence officer in the Middle East, and after leaving the CIA, he worked at a cybersecurity firm.[2] Nevertheless, African American Republicans in Congress are rare. In the 116th Congress (2019–2021), he is the only Black Republican House member, and there is only one African American Republican Senator—Tim Scott from South Carolina. Because of the Democratic Party's progressive views on economic and social issues, African American elected officials tend to be Democrats, but Representative Hurd is one of the few exceptions. Additionally, Hurd's victory is surprising because he is a non-Latino who represents an overwhelmingly Latino district. Since the 1980s states have created *majority-minority districts,* which are legislative districts that contain more than

Majority-Minority Districts
Legislative districts that contain a population made up of more than 50 percent of a racial or ethnic minority group.

50 percent of a minority group. Although creating a majority-minority district does not guarantee a minority representative, most majority-minority districts are represented by a racial or ethnic minority. It is even rarer for a representative of a majority-minority district to belong to a different racial or ethnic minority group than the majority race or ethnicity in the district. In short, Representative Hurd's presence in Congress is exceptional.

Given President Donald Trump's controversial presidency and anti-Latino statements, one would expect that Representative Hurd would often oppose President Trump. In fact, in the 2016 election Hurd's district supported Clinton over Trump by 3.4 percent.[3] During his first two terms in Congress, Representative Hurd has occasionally acted in accordance with his competitive and heavily Latino district. For example, in 2018, he forcefully spoke out against the Trump administration's "zero tolerance" policy on undocumented immigration and asylum seekers that separated immigrant children from their parents.[4] However, despite the competitiveness of Hurd's district, he has voted with Trump's preferences 96.3 percent of the time. In 2018 Hurd ran against Latina Democrat Gina Ortiz Jones. Although the Democrats picked up almost 40 seats and assumed control of the House of Representatives after the 2018 midterm elections, Hurd still narrowly won reelection by 0.5 percent.[5]

intro

Will Hurd's story demonstrates several aspects of how Congress works that we address in this chapter. First, the electoral history of the 23rd District represents the importance of elections in determining the functioning of Congress. As we discuss later in the chapter, most U.S House districts are not very competitive between Republicans and Democrats, but Hurd's district is an exception. When there are significant partisan shifts in these competitive districts the party control of the House can change, which has happened three times in the past fifteen years—Democrats gained control in 2006, Republicans regained control in 2010, and Democrats regained control in 2018. As we will show, the party that controls the House of Representatives significantly influences the type of legislation that is passed or not passed.

Finally, Representative Hurd exemplifies the important role that race plays in congressional politics. Most Black legislators represent districts that are majority Black, but Hurd is an exception because his district contains only a small fraction of African Americans. In fact, the 23rd District of Texas is actually a majority-Latino district that has been represented by a Mexican American for the past thirty years. Additionally, most African American representatives are liberal and Democratic, but Representative Hurd is a conservative Republican. In short, he is the exception to the rule that African American representatives tend to be liberal Democrats. Finally, many observers expected that Donald Trump's racially charged rhetoric against Latinos would *significantly affect Congressional races. The outcome demonstrated that Trump's effect was minor in Hurd's case, but Turmp's behavior cost Republicans many other seats.*

Article 1, Section 1, of the U.S. Constitution vests "all legislative power . . . in a -Congress of the United States." As such, Congress is the primary policymaking institution in American government. Article 1, Section 1, also divides Congress into two houses: the Senate and the House of Representatives. The House was designed to closely represent the people. It is apportioned by state population, and all 435 members are up for reelection every two years. The Senate, which was designed to be somewhat removed from the public, contains one hundred senators, with each state represented by two senators who serve six-year, staggered terms.

But the Constitution does not, and cannot, specify congressional politics, which is a complex undertaking. This chapter introduces these complexities by analyzing the nature of congressional representation, the importance of congressional organization and leadership, the lawmaking process, and the competing influences on members' decision making. Throughout the chapter, we pay close attention to the role of race and ethnicity in congressional politics.

To track your House and Senate members' votes, go to Congress.gov and enter their names.

The Nature of Congressional Representation

Congressional representation has two components: the constituents and their representatives. The **representative** is the person chosen to make laws on behalf of a defined group of people, and the **constituency** comprises the people who choose the representative to act on their behalf. For the most part, constituencies are determined by geographic region, and each region possesses a particular character in terms of the constituents' dominant political views, economic interests, cultural values, and racial and ethnic breakdown. These regional socioeconomic and ideological characteristics are reflected in the type of person who serves as a representative. Here we address the complex relationship between geography and representation by focusing on unrepresented areas, the process of drawing legislative districts, and the characteristics of American members of Congress. We pay special attention to the representation of racial and ethnic minorities.

Representative A person chosen to make policy decisions on behalf of a defined group of people.

Constituency The people who choose a representative to act on their behalf.

The Unrepresented

Even though the United States is a representative democracy, a significant portion of people living under American control are denied any representation in Congress. The Commonwealth of Puerto Rico[6] and the territories of American Samoa, Guam, Northern Mariana Islands, and Virgin Islands are subject to American laws, but the over four million people living there, most of whom are American citizens, do not send voting members to the U.S. House or Senate. Instead, each region sends a nonvoting delegate to the House, but not to the Senate. These delegates are able to speak on the floor, offer bills, and participate fully in committees (even as committee leaders), but they lack the most essential power—voting for or against proposed legislation. Additionally, the population of these territories are overwhelmingly non-White.[7]

Gerrymandering often results in bizarrely shaped districts that connect disparate parts of states. The top map shows Pennsylvania's congressional districts that the Republican legislature drew in 2011, and the bottom map shows the congressional districts that the state supreme court drew in 2018 after it invalidated the gerrymandered map. Notice how the district boundaries in the second map are far less convoluted than the boundaries in the first map, and notice how the second map divides far fewer counties compared to the first map.

Washington, DC, which, unlike a commonwealth or territory, is fully a part of the United States, also sends only a nonvoting delegate to the House. This arrangement is especially controversial because full-fledged American citizens reside in Washington, DC, which has more than 690,000 residents, 47.7 percent of whom are Black and 10.9 percent or Latino.[8] Yet, DC residents are still denied any representation in Congress. For many years, the current

our voices

Nonvoting Delegate Eleanor Holmes Norton and Representation for Washington, DC

When introducing legislation, members of Congress usually provide opening remarks to specify the purpose of their bill and thus set the terms for debate on the bill. Following is an excerpt of Delegate Eleanor Holmes Norton's speech to the House floor on January 9, 2007, announcing that she would introduce HR 328, which would grant Washington, DC, a vote in the House of Representatives. These words eloquently express the frustration of Americans denied representation in their government and demonstrate how Washington, DC's lack of a voting representative in Congress amounts to racial discrimination.

Ms. Norton: Mr. Speaker, I come to the House to inform the House that I have today filed a bill to give full voting rights in this House to the people of the District of Columbia, who are second per capita in the Federal income tax they pay to support this government, this House and this Senate, and who have fought and died in every war since the creation

of a Republic, including the outrageous war where we now serve.

I come in gratitude that the House is now governed by my own party, which for decades has supported not only what my bill today would afford, a vote in the House, but a vote in both Houses, and I come to thank my own caucus for that support. But I also come in some frustration and with some impatience. I come in frustration that I am still a second-class citizen in my own House. . . .

I had hoped to be able to vote on the bills we all ran on that are now before the House. I came to speak today, but once again, when the vote came, I could not vote. I couldn't vote because I was not even allowed the vote in the Committee of the Whole that I won when the Democrats were last in power.

. . . I have tried everything, I have tried statehood, I have tried Committee of the Whole. It is time to try

Delegate Eleanor Holmes Norton (D-DC) holds a news conference in late 2012. Because Washington, DC, does not have representation in the House, Delegate Norton is not able to vote on legislation, but she can fully serve on committees. Delegate Norton has pushed to provide Washington, DC, with voting representation.

(Continued)

our voices *(Continued)*

the real thing, Mr. Speaker, when there are 650,000 people who pay their taxes and have met every obligation, and are not recognized as citizens in their own House and send somebody to the House that is not even recognized to vote on this House, not even in the Committee of the Whole.

I come to express their frustration, to say I am leaving all that behind. I have introduced the bill they want. . . . We want our votes. We want it in the 110th Congress, and we want it now. I speak for them as a woman who knows what it means to be a second-class citizen, and who, once she left the District and went to law school, said, "I shall never again be a second-class citizen." Yes, I grew up in segregated schools in this town, in segregated Washington. That is what it meant to be a second-class citizen. Now to

be a second-class civics citizen, after 200 years, has become too much to bear.

So I have introduced a bill to make it absolutely clear, as my people have said I must do today, that there is boiling determination among the people of the District of Columbia to get this vote. . . .

This is the 110th, Mr. Speaker. This is the moment of truth. This is the moment when the Democrats have not only the opportunity, but the obligation to give a vote in the 110th Congress to the people of the District of Columbia.

Source: Adapted from *Congressional Record*, 110th Congress, H231–H232, January 9, 2007. Retrieved June 20, 2018, from https://www.gpo.gov/fdsys/pkg/CREC-2007-01-09/pdf/CREC-2007-01-09-pt1-PgH231-2.pdf.

View an example of a congressional bill, its description, supporters, and status.

nonvoting delegate, Eleanor Holmes Norton (D-DC), has actively advocated the allocation of a voting representative for Washington, DC, which we discuss in the next Our Voices box.

When the Democrats took control of Congress in 2007, there was some progress toward giving Washington, DC, a voting representative. In 2007, the House passed a measure that would add a vote in the House for DC and an at-large seat for Utah (until the next census),[9] thus bringing the total number of House members to 437. However, this bill did not pass in the Senate for reasons we discuss later in this chapter. After Democrats expanded their House and Senate majorities in the 2008 elections, the chances of giving DC a voting representative seemingly increased. In early 2009, the Senate passed the same bill it had rejected in 2007, but the bill stalled in the House.[10] When the Republicans regained control of the House in 2011 the prospects of a voting representative for the District ended, and, in fact, the House further limited the power of nonvoting delegates.[11]

Districts

Reapportionment The process of assigning states a number of representatives to the House of Representatives after each decennial census.

Because members of Congress represent people living within specifically defined boundaries, Congress is a geographically based institution. Senators represent people living in states, and House members represent people living in parts of states or, in a few cases, the entire state. **Reapportionment** is the process of allotting states a number of representatives based on population figures determined after each official decennial census. Because every state regardless of size has two senators, reapportionment is not necessary for the Senate.

As the U.S. population increased and more states were added to the union during the nineteenth century, the House increased its number of members until 1930, when the size of the House was capped at 435.[12] Since then, states that gain the most people after the previous census increase their representation in the House, whereas states that lose population or do not grow as much as other states decrease their representation in the House. As a result, in the past two decades many states in the South and the West have added representatives, whereas states in the Northeast and Midwest have lost representatives.

Once a state receives its allotment of representatives, the state legislature then draws geographical boundaries delineating the area that each member will represent. This process is known as **redistricting**, and it determines the geography of districts for the U.S. House. For example, if a state receives ten representatives to the House, then the legislature divides the state into ten geographical regions, each one represented by a single member.

Because of political motivations, state legislatures do not necessarily redistrict to reflect distinct communities within the state. Instead, **gerrymandering**, which is a group's use of redistricting to maximize its chances of winning seats in a legislative body, is prevalent during the redistricting process. Usually, the political party that controls the state legislature gerrymanders to maximize its chances of winning seats to the U.S. House. Although gerrymandering does not guarantee that one party will represent a particular seat, it does maximize the odds that the majority party in the state legislature will enhance its representation in the House. Although some state courts—for example, Pennsylvania[13]—have ended gerrymandering, the U.S. Supreme Court has thus far refused to interfere in states' use of partisan gerrymandering.[14]

State legislatures enjoy considerable discretion in redistricting, but there are some significant restrictions. First, the district must be contiguous. That is, its geographical shape must be a complete entity; a district cannot be divided into two separate parts of a state. Additionally, the U.S. Supreme Court requires that all House districts within a state be equal in population.[15] In fact, the Supreme Court has overturned redistricting plans with population deviations as small as 0.7 percent.[16]

State legislatures are also required to pay close attention to race and ethnicity when drawing legislative districts. To prevent state legislatures from gerrymandering to fragment areas of minority concentration and, in turn, decrease the numbers of minorities in the House, Congress amended the Voting Rights Act in 1982, and since then state legislatures have created majority-minority districts (districts in which a racial or ethnic minority composes a majority of the population) wherever possible.

As a direct result of majority-minority districts, the number of Black and Latino House members increased significantly after the 1992 election. But in the mid-1990s, the Supreme Court invalidated some majority-minority districts, ruling that state legislatures could use race as one factor in drawing legislative district but that the Constitution prevents them from using race as the predominant factor.[17] As a result, even after the 2010 census many majority-minority

Redistricting The process by which a state is divided into geographical regions, with each region electing a member of the House of Representatives.

Gerrymandering The practice in which a group, usually a political party, uses redistricting to maximize its chances of winning elections.

Assess current debates on redistricting.

Redistricting in Texachusetts.

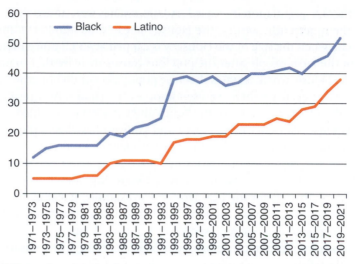

Figure 6.1 Number of Black and Latino Representatives Serving in the U.S. House of Representatives, 1971–1973 through 2019–2021

districts still favored Blacks and Latinos, although the number is lower than it was during the 1990s. Nevertheless, as Figure 6.1 demonstrates, the number of Blacks elected to the U.S. House has generally gradually increased since 1992 and the number of Latinos has increased more sharply.

Members of Congress

Ultimately, the composition of a district helps to determine the type of representative elected. The Constitution imposes only age, citizenship, and residency requirements for serving in the House and Senate (see Chapter 2). There are no requirements concerning occupation or education. Nevertheless, most members are college educated and are socioeconomically well off.

For most of the nation's history, racial minorities were extremely underrepresented in the House and Senate, but in recent years they have closed the gap. In the 116th Congress (2019–2021), African Americans constitute 12.0 percent of the voting members of the House of Representatives, Latinos are 8.7 percent, Asian Americans are 3.0 percent, and American Indians are 0.9 percent. As a result of the creation of majority-minority districts, in 1992 the Southern states of Virginia, North Carolina, South Carolina, Florida, Mississippi, and Alabama elected African Americans to the U.S. House for the first time since Reconstruction. Table 6.1 lists the racial and ethnic minority voting members of the 116th Congress.

Although the drawing of majority-minority districts has undoubtedly increased the number of minority representatives, opponents contend that increased minority representation does not necessarily result in better policies for minority constituents. This debate centers on the tension among

TABLE 6.1 Racial and Ethnic Minority Voting Members of the 116th Congress (2019–2021)

African Americans in the House of Representatives

Alma Adams (D-NC)	Dwight Evans (D-PA)	Donald McEachin (D-VA)
Colin Allred (D-TX)	Marcia L. Fudge (D-OH)	Gregory Meeks (D-NY)
Karen Bass (D-CA)	Al Green (D-TX)	Gwen Moore (D-WI)
Joyce Beatty (D-OH)	Alcee Hastings (D-FL)	Ilhan Omar (D-MN)
Sanford Bishop (D-GA)	Jahana Hayes (D-CT)	Joe Neguse (D-CO)
Anthony Brown (D-MD)	Steven Horsford (D-NV)	Donald Payne, Jr. (D-NJ)
G. K. Butterfield (D-NC)	Will Hurd (R-TX)	Ayanna Pressley (D-MA)
Andre Carson (D-IN)	Sheila Jackson-Lee (D-TX)	Cedric Richmond (D-LA)
Yvette Clarke (D-NY)	Hakeem Jeffries (D-NY)	Lisa Blunt Rochester (D-DE)
William Lacy Clay III (D-MO)	Eddie Bernice Johnson (D-TX)	Bobby Rush (D-IL)
Emmanuel Cleaver (D-MO)	Hank Johnson (D-GA)	David Scott (D-GA)
James Clyburn (D-SC)	Robin Kelly (D-IL)	Robert Scott (D-VA)*
Elijah Cummings (D-MD)	Al Lawson (D-FL)	Teri Sewell (D-AL)
Danny Davis (D-IL)	Brenda Lawrence (D-MI)	Bennie Thompson (D-MI)
Antonio Delgado (D-NY)*	Barbara Lee (D-CA)	Lauren Underwood (D-IL)
Val Demmings (D-FL)	John Lewis (D-GA)	Marc Veasey (D-TX)
	Lucy McBath (D-GA)	Maxine Waters (D-CA)
		Bonnie Watson-Coleman (D-NJ)
		Frederica Wilson (D-FL)

African Americans in the Senate

Cory Booker (D-NJ)
Kamala Harris (D-CA)*
Tim Scott (R-SC)

Latinos in the House of Representatives

Pete Aguilar (D-CA)	Ruben Gallego (D-AZ)	Alexandria Ocasio-Cortez (D-NY)
Nanette Barragan (D-CA)	Chuy Garcia (D-IL)	Lucille Roybal-Allard (D-CA)
Salud Carbajal (D-CA)	Sylvia Garcia (D-TX)	Raul Ruiz (D-CA)
Tony Cárdenas (D-CA)	Jimmy Gomez (D-CA)	Linda Sánchez (D-CA)
Joaquín Castro (D-TX)	Anthony Gonzalez (R-OH)	José Serrano (D-NY)
Gil Cisneros (D-CA)	Vincente Gonzalez (D-TX)	Alberto Sires (D-NJ)
Lou Correa (D-CA)	Raúl Grijalva (D-AZ)	Darren Soto (D-FL)
Henry Cuellar (D-TX)	Jaime Herrera-Beutler (R-WA)	Norma Torres (D-CA)
Antonio Delgado (D-NY)*	Ben Ray Luján (D-NM)	Xochitl Torres Small (D-NM)
Mario Diaz-Balart (R-FL)	Brian Mast (R-FL)	Juan Vargas (D-CA)
Veronica Escobar (D-TX)	Alex Mooney (R-WV)	Filemon Vela (D-TX)
Adriano Espaillat (D-NY)	Debbie Mucarsel-Powell (D-FL)	Nydia Velázquez (D-NY)
Bill Flores (R-TX)	Grace Napolitano (D-CA)	

Latinos in the Senate

Ted Cruz (R-TX)	Catherine Cortez Masto (D-NV)	Marco Rubio (R-FL)
	Robert Menendez (D-NJ)	

Asian Americans in the House of Representatives

Ami Bera (D-CA)	Raja Krishnamoorthi (D-IL)	Grace Meng (D-NY)
Judy Chu (D-CA)	Pramila Jayapal (D-WA)	Stephanie Murphy (D-FL)
Tulsi Gabbard (D-HI)	Ted Lieu (D-CA)	Robert Scott (D-VA)*
Ro Khanna (D-CA)	Doris Matsui (D-CA)	Mark Takano (D-CA)
Andy Kim (D-NJ)		

Asian Americans in the Senate

Tammy Duckworth (D-IL)
Kamala Harris (D-CA)*
Mazie Hirono (D-HI)

American Indians in the House of Representatives

Tom Cole (R-OK)	Markwayne Mullin (R-OK)
Sharice Davids (D-KS)	
Debra Haaland (D-NM)	

*Indicates more than one racial minority category.

Sources: Data compiled from the U.S. House website (www.house.gov) and the U.S. Senate website (www.senate.gov), retrieved May 8, 2014. The authors updated this with 2018 election results.

evaluating equality

Should the Race or Ethnicity of a Representative Matter?

As this section has discussed, political leaders pay considerable attention to the race and ethnicity of elected representatives, especially in the United States House of Representatives. Consequently, civil rights leaders have focused on the creation of majority-minority districts, which since the 1990s have increased the number of Black and Latino representatives. However, many critics argue that focusing on the race or ethnicity of the elected representative is inappropriate and that White representatives can advocate for their minority constituents equally as well as minority representatives can. For example, Steve Cohen (D-TN), who is White, represents the 9th District of Tennessee (Memphis and the surrounding area), which according to the U.S.

Census is 66.1 percent Black. Yet, Representative Cohen receives the highest marks from civil rights organizations on issues of importance to African Americans (as well as Latinos), and he is consistently reelected. Moreover, as this chapter's opening vignette shows, Representative Will Hurd (R-TX) is African American but represents a majority-Latino district, and he will continue to do so for the 116th Congress.

Students should debate the question over whether it is necessary for a minority representative to represent a majority-minority district. When framing this debate, focus on the differences among descriptive, symbolic, and substantive representation. Does the amount of overall minority representation in the U.S.

House affect the kinds of legislation the institution will pass, or not pass? If, as the research we cited in the chapter demonstrates, the creation of majority-minority districts has increased overall Republican representation, then has the increase of minority representatives been a benefit for Blacks and Latinos? Research the careers of Representatives Cohen and Hurd. What do they add to this debate?

Sources: United States Census. (n.d.). *My congressional district: 115th Congress, Tennessee 9th.* Retrieved June 21, 2018, from https://www.census.gov/mycd/?st=47&cd=09; Cohen, S. (n.d.). *Congressman Cohen's vote ratings.* Retrieved June 12, 2016, from https://cohen.house.gov/about/vote -ratings.

Descriptive Representation
The extent to which the characteristics of a representative correspond with the general characteristics of his or her constituency.

Symbolic Representation
The extent to which constituents trust and accept their representative and the legislative institution as a whole.

Substantive Representation
The extent to which representatives advocate policies that benefit their constituents.

competing views concerning the nature of representation. We can divide these views into three types. **Descriptive representation** concentrates on whether the characteristics of representatives match the characteristics of their constituents. **Symbolic representation** emphasizes the feelings of confidence and acceptance that the constituents have for their representative and the legislative institution as a whole. **Substantive representation** concerns whether representatives advocate policies that benefit their constituents.[18]

Majority-minority districts usually elect a minority representative, which satisfies descriptive representation concerns. A minority representative can help to increase the trust that racial and ethnic minorities place in their representative, Congress, and the American government as a whole. As a result, majority-minority districts can enhance symbolic representation.

But in terms of substantive representation, minority-majority districts can be problematic. The creation of these districts often renders the surrounding districts devoid of minority voters, and those districts are not likely to elect a representative who would advocate on behalf of policy issues important to racial or ethnic minorities. In other words, a majority-minority district creates one minority representative and one (or more) representative(s) in surrounding districts who would not be concerned with the plight of racial and ethnic minorities. If the residents of the majority-minority district were to be divided in half and put into larger White districts, then no minority representative would be elected, but there would be two White representatives who would need to advocate on behalf of the policy preferences of the substantial minority populations in their districts because those minority populations could still determine the outcome of an election. These White representatives would provide substantive representation to their racial and ethnic minority constituents.[19]

Because senators represent entire states, it is more difficult for racial and ethnic minorities to win Senate seats. However, there have been some successes, especially in states with larger minority populations. There are nine minority senators at the start of the 116th Congress, which is the same as the start of the 115th Congress. Mazie Hirono (D-HI) and Tammy Duckworth (D-IL) are the two Asian American senators. Catherine Cortez Masto (D-NV), Robert Menendez (D-NJ), Marco Rubio (R-FL), and Ted Cruz (R-TX) are four Latino senators. Tim Scott (R-SC) and Corey Booker (D-NJ) are two African American senators. Kamala Harris (D-CA) is both African American and of South Asian descent. The history of minorities who have served in the Senate is given in Table 6.2.

Overall, the Congress also became more diverse in other ways. Tammy Baldwin (D-WI) became the first openly gay senator; Kyrsten Sinema (D-AZ) became the first openly bisexual member elected to the House and the Senate; and Mark Takano (D-CA) became the first openly gay minority elected to Congress. The 116th Congress has the most minority senators in history (nine), and the House has three Indian Americans, including the first female Indian American (Pramila Jayapal [D-WA]). For the first time, four American Indians serve in the House (Tom Cole [R-OK], Sharice Davids [D-KS], Debra Haaland [D-NM], and Markwayne Mullin [R-OK].

House Minority Leader Nancy Pelosi (D-CA), center, with Democratic women of the House for a group photo on the first day of the 113th Congress in Washington, January 3, 2013. Although the 2012 election resulted in an increase in women in the House and Senate, the 2018 election generated more female members of Congress than at any other time in American history.

TABLE 6.2 Minorities Who Have Served in the United States Senate

Name	State	Party	Race	Dates of Service
Daniel Akaka	Hawaii	Democrat	Asian American	1990–2013
Edward W. Brooke	Massachusetts	Republican	African American	1967–1979
Corey Booker	New Jersey	Democrat	African American	2013–present
Blanche K. Bruce	Mississippi	Republican	African American	1875–1881
Roland Burris	Illinois	Democrat	African American	2009–2010
Ben Nighthorse Campbell	Colorado	Republican	American Indian	1993–2005
Dennis Chavez	New Mexico	Democrat	Latino	1935–1962
Ted Cruz	Texas	Republican	Latino	2013–present
William Cowan	Massachusetts	Democrat	African American	2013
Charles Curtis	Kansas	Republican	American Indian	1907–1913, 1915–1929
Tammy Duckworth	Illinois	Democrat	Asian American	2017–present
Hiram K. Fong	Hawaii	Republican	Asian American	1959–1977
Kamala Harris	California	Democrat	African American and Asian American	2017–present
Samuel I. Hayakawa	California	Republican	Asian American	1977–1983
Mazie Hirono	Hawaii	Democrat	Asian American	2013–present
Daniel Inouye	Hawaii	Democrat	Asian American	1963–2012
Octaviano Larrazolo	New Mexico	Republican	Latino	1928–1929
Melquiades R. Martinez	Florida	Republican	Latino	2005–2009
Catherine Cotez Masto	Nevada	Democrat	Latino	2017–present
Spark M. Matsunaga	Hawaii	Democrat	Asian American	1977–1990
Robert Menendez	New Jersey	Democrat	Latino	2006–present
Joseph M. Montoya	New Mexico	Democrat	Latino	1964–1977
Carol Moseley-Braun	Illinois	Democrat	African American	1993–1999
Barack Obama	Illinois	Democrat	African American	2005–2008
Robert Owen	Oklahoma	Democrat	American Indian	1907–1925
Hiram R. Revels	Mississippi	Republican	African American	1870–1871
Marco Rubio	Florida	Republican	Latino	2011–present
Ken L. Salazar	Colorado	Democrat	Latino	2005–2009
Tim Scott	South Carolina	Republican	African American	2012–present

Source: United States Senate. (n.d.). Ethnic diversity in the Senate. Retrieved June 22, 2018, from https://www.senate.gov/senators/EthnicDiversityintheSenate.htm.

Congressional Organization and Leadership

Every two years, American voters elect the entire House of Representatives and one-third of the Senate, and a new Congress is seated the following January. To conduct legislative business effectively, the two houses must organize themselves, and the most important organizing principle is **political party** (see Chapter 14 for more details on political parties). In each chamber, either the Democratic or Republican Party wins a majority of the seats. If the partisan split in the Senate is 50–50, then the vice president of the United States, who casts deciding votes in the Senate, will cast the vote in favor of his or her party. This situation occurred during the first half of 2001 when Vice President Richard Cheney gave his support to the Republicans. In June 2001, however, former Republican senator Jim Jeffords (VT) left the Republican Party, thus giving Democrats outright control of the Senate.[20]

Political Party Mass organizations that seek to elect candidates to public office and influence policymaking.

The party with more seats is known as the **majority party**, and the party with fewer seats is the **minority party**. In the House and Senate, the majority party controls the organizational structure and occupies the most important leadership positions. Although the House and Senate are similarly organized, there are key differences between the two bodies, and in both chambers, congressional organization is interwoven with the politics of race and ethnicity.

Majority Party The political party in the House or the Senate that has more than half of the seats and therefore controls the leadership, rules, and outcome of legislation.

Leadership in the House

Because the House of Representatives contains 435 members, it must be tightly organized to function. Accordingly, the majority party selects the important House leaders, who exert significant control over the procedures and outcomes of legislation. Most notably, in the House of Representatives, the majority party controls the agenda throughout the legislative process. As a result, majority party leaders are able to ensure the passage of legislation that they favor and prevent the passage of legislation that they oppose.[21]

Minority Party The political party in the House or the Senate that has fewer than half of the seats and therefore does not control the leadership, rules, or outcome of legislation.

The most important position in the House of Representatives is the **Speaker of the House**. Before each Congress commences in the January following the election, the majority party selects its candidate for Speaker, and at the beginning of the congressional term the entire House chooses its Speaker. All members of the majority party are expected to support their party's choice for Speaker; thus, the majority party's Speaker candidate is guaranteed to be elected.

Speaker of the House The most powerful position in the House of Representatives; the leader of the majority party; the person who articulates the House's legislative priorities and ensures their passage.

The Speaker of the House is the leader of the entire House of Representatives, but the primary function of the Speaker is to be the leader of the majority party. Thus, the Speaker will articulate the majority party's legislative priorities and work to ensure that the House passes them. Likewise, Speakers use their authority to prevent the minority party's legislative priorities from being passed into law. Speakers of the House oversee legislative business, refer bills to committees, control debates, act as House spokespeople, and apply rules of parliamentary procedure—in short, they control the fate of the bills that are introduced.

Speakers are also extremely influential in determining the membership and leaders of committees. Consequently, they tremendously influence the power and prestige of the majority party members. Although personal

Run a campaign for
a House race.

House Majority Leader The
second most powerful leader in
the House of Representatives;
the person who assists the
Speaker in passing the majority
party's legislative priorities.

Whip A legislative leader who
assists the party by counting
votes and persuading members
to vote according to the party
leaders' wishes.

House Minority Leader The
leader of the minority party in
the House of Representatives;
the person who articulates
the legislative priorities of the
minority party and opposes the
majority party's priorities but
exerts minimal control over the
outcome of legislation.

leadership styles vary, the Speakers all use their authority over majority party members to ensure that there is enough support for the bills they want passed. No racial or ethnic minorities have been Speaker, and Nancy Pelosi (D-CA) is the only woman to serve in this powerful position.

Administering the House is far too extensive a responsibility to handle alone; Speakers use deputies to help accomplish their goals. The **House majority leader** is the second most powerful position in the House of Representatives, and his or her function is to assist in articulating, planning, and implementing the Speaker's legislative agenda and strategy. Following the Speaker and majority leader in the party hierarchy is the majority **whip**, who is the vote-counter for the majority party. The majority whip surveys the majority party members to determine their views on pending legislation and then persuades them to vote according to the party leadership's wishes.

The majority party alone chooses its majority leader and whip through a secret ballot, although the Speaker, who is selected first, can influence party members' subsequent choices. Like the Speaker, the majority leader and the majority whip occupy extremely powerful positions in the House, and they often use that power on behalf of their constituents. Therefore, racial and ethnic minorities can benefit when they serve in one of these powerful positions, but their influence depends on partisan control of the House. After Democrats took control of the House in 2007, Black Representative James Clyburn (D-SC) became the majority whip. When Republicans took control of the House, Clyburn had to settle for the less powerful and less prestigious position of assistant Democratic (minority) leader, with the primary function of communicating between the House Democrats and President Obama (until the end of Obama's term). Moreover, when he was majority whip, Clyburn had twenty staff members and a $2 million budget, but his staff was reduced to six and his budget decreased sharply after he lost that position.[22] Clyburn will return to the House majority leadership after the Democrats regained control of the House in 2019.

The minority party has leaders as well, but they are typically unable to significantly affect the legislative outcomes of the House. The **House minority leader** is in charge of the minority party, and like the Speaker, she or he articulates the minority party's legislative priorities and keeps the minority party unified behind those priorities. The minority leader helps determine minority party committee assignments and acts as a national spokesperson for the minority party. The minority whip is the second in command for the minority party, serves as a

U.S. Representative James E. Clyburn (D-SC) speaks on stage during the final day of the Democratic National Convention on September 6, 2012, in Charlotte, NC. When Democrats were the majority party in the House from 2007–2011, Representative Clyburn held the powerful position of majority whip. However, after Democrats lost the majority, Clyburn was relegated to the less powerful position of assistant democratic leader. He will return to power because the Democrats won control of the House in the 2018 midterm elections.

party spokesperson, and is responsible for counting votes and persuading members of the minority party to vote as their leadership wishes.

The minority leaders, despite their leadership roles, are unable to push their party's legislative program through the House. Instead, they offer opposition to the majority's legislative agenda in the hopes that their party will capture a majority of the seats in the next election. For example, in January 2011, the newly empowered House Republican majority voted to repeal the controversial Affordable Care Act, a health care reform law passed in 2010. Although Democratic minority leaders opposed repealing the law, they were powerless to stop the majority Republicans, or even slow the passage of the bill and force some concessions from the Republican majority. At best, the Democratic leaders were able to secure virtually universal opposition to the Republican bill. Since Republicans took control in 2011, the House has passed more than fifty bills designed to repeal or significantly alter the Affordable Care Act, but these bills did not pass the Senate until 2016, after Republicans took control of the Senate. Nevertheless, President Obama successfully vetoed the repeal.[23] It is worth noting that in 2017 after Republicans retained complete control of Congress and had Republican President Donald Trump, Congress still failed to repeal the Affordable Care Act.[24]

Assess current debates on healthcare.

Leadership in the Senate

Compared to House leaders, leaders in the Senate exert less influence over their members. The vice president of the United States is the president of the Senate, but this designation is largely formal. The vice president votes only to break a tie and presides over the Senate only on special occasions, such as the State of the Union address or an address to the Senate by a foreign dignitary. The president pro tempore is the presiding officer of the Senate when the vice president declines to serve in that role, which is usually the case. Nevertheless, this position is largely honorary, going to the longest serving member of the majority party. Usually, the president pro tempore does not even preside over Senate meetings, instead appointing junior members of the majority party to perform that duty.

The most important leader of the Senate is the **Senate majority leader**, who is elected by the majority party in the Senate. The majority leader's position is roughly analogous to that of the Speaker of the House, except that it wields far less power. Senate majority leaders articulate the majority party's legislative priorities; determine the legislative calendar; influence majority party members' committee assignments; and schedule debates and votes. Similar to the Speaker of the House, the majority leader uses his or her power to secure majority party support for the party's legislative agenda. The **Senate majority whip**, also known as the assistant majority leader, counts votes and persuades members to vote according to the leadership's wishes. Similar to the House of Representatives, the minority party in the Senate has leaders, but unlike their counterparts in the House, the Senate minority leaders consult with the majority leaders when scheduling debates and votes. The leader of the minority party in the Senate is known as the **Senate minority leader**.

Senate Majority Leader
The most powerful position in the Senate; the person who articulates the majority party's legislative priorities and works to pass them.

Senate Majority Whip (also called the assistant majority leader) A majority party leader in the Senate who counts votes, persuades members to vote according to the leadership's wishes, and assists the majority leader in passing the majority party's legislation.

Senate Minority Leader
The leader of the minority party of the Senate; the person who articulates the legislative priorities of the minority party and opposes the majority party's priorities but exerts limited control over the outcome of legislation.

Committees

Like any other large institution that performs a variety of functions, Congress divides its labor into specialized units known as committees. Most committees are further split into subcommittees, which work on bills in an even more specialized fashion. Once a bill is introduced in either house, the Speaker or the Senate majority leader refers it to the appropriate committees, and then those committees conduct hearings at which experts testify on the bill's merits. In the Senate, committees also conduct hearings when the Senate is deciding whether to ratify treaties and approve presidential nominees to the executive branch and the federal judiciary.

After conducting hearings and collecting other information, the committee amends the original bill at a markup session. Some of these changes can be minor, such as a slight adjustment in spending, but other amendments completely change the bill's nature. Because the majority party enjoys a majority of members on the committee, it controls which amendments are passed. The final product to emerge from the markup session rarely resembles the original bill.

Finally, the committee recommends passage or rejection of the bill. Generally, bills (and nominations in the Senate) that are not reported favorably from committees will not be scheduled for a vote and thus do not pass. The majority party leadership and the majority members on the committees dominate the decisions that the committees make. Table 6.3 lists the standing

The House Armed Services Committee holds a 15-hour markup session on the defense-spending bill!

Learn about your representatives and the committees they serve on.

TABLE 6.3 Standing Committees of the House and Senate, 115th Congress (2017–2019)

HOUSE		
Committee	Size (Party)	Percent of Committee That Is a Racial or Ethnic Minority*
Agriculture	46 (26R/20D)	21.7
Appropriations	52 (30R/22D)	19.2
Armed Services	61 (33R/28D)	14.8
Budget	37 (23R/14D)	24.3
Education and the Workforce	40 (23R/17D)	25.0
Energy and Commerce	55 (31R/24D)	16.4
Ethics	10 (5R/5D)	20.0
Financial Services	60 (34R/26D)	23.3
Foreign Affairs	47 (26R/21D)	23.4
Homeland Security	30 (18R/12D)	33.3
House Administration	9 (6R/3D)	0.0
Intelligence	22 (13R/9D)	22.7
Judiciary	40 (23R/17D)	25.0

HOUSE Committee	Size (Party)	Percent of Committee That Is a Racial or Ethnic Minority[*]
Natural Resources	43 (25R/18D)[a]	34.9
Oversight and Government Reform	41 (23R/18D)	24.4
Rules	13 (9R/4D)	23.1
Science, Space, and Technology	38 (21R/17D)	13.2
Small Business	23 (14R/9D)	43.4
Transportation and Infrastructure	61 (34R/27D)	19.7
Veterans' Affairs	23 (13/10D)	21.7
Ways and Means	40 (24R/16D)	15.0
SENATE		
Agriculture, Nutrition, and Forestry	21 (11R/10D)	0.0
Appropriations	31 (16R/15D)	3.2
Armed Services	27 (14R/13D)	9.7
Banking, Housing, and Urban Affairs	25 (13R/12D)	12.0
Budget	23 (12R/11D)	4.3
Commerce, Science, and Transportation	27 (14R/13D)	11.1
Energy and Natural Resources	23 (12R/11D)	13.0
Environment and Public Works	21 (11R/10D)	9.5
Ethics	6 (3R/3D)	0.0
Finance	27 (14R/13D)	7.4
Foreign Relations	21 (11R/10D)	14..3
Health, Education, Labor, and Pensions	23 (12R/11D)	4.5
Homeland Security and Govt. Affairs	15 (8R/7D)	6.7
Indian Affairs	15 (8R/7D)	6.7
Intelligence	15 (8R/7D)	13.3
Judiciary	21 (11R/10D)	19.0
Rules and Administration	19 (10R/9D)	10.5
Small Business and Entrepreneurship	19 (10R/9D)	26.3
Veterans' Affairs	15 (8R/7D)	6.7

Note: Although Angus King (I-ME) and Bernard Sanders (I-VT) are technically Independents, they both support the Democratic leadership and are organizationally part of the Democratic Party in the Senate.

[*]Because nonvoting delegates can vote in committee, they are included in both the size counts and the percentage of the committee that is a racial or ethnic minority.

Sources: Data compiled from the U.S. House website (https://www.house.gov/committees) and U.S. Senate website (https://www.senate.gov/committees/committees_home.htm), retrieved June 23, 2018.

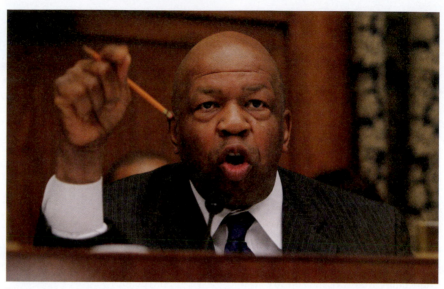

Representative Elijah Cummings (D-MD) became the chair of the House Oversight and Government Reform Committee after Democrats officially regained control of the House of Representatives in 2019. Democratic takeover of the House increased the number of powerful racial and ethnic minority committee chairs. As chair of this committee, Cummings will lead investigations into unethical behavior in the Trump administration.

Explore why incumbents are reelected despite Congress' unpopularity.

committees, their partisan composition, and the percentage of racial and ethnic minorities that serve on them in the 115th Congress.

Committee and subcommittee chairs, who are members of the majority party, possess the authority to call meetings, set agendas for meetings, decide which witnesses testify at hearings, and preside over meetings and markup sessions. By refusing to schedule a bill for committee action, the chair can defeat a bill unilaterally because it cannot proceed to the House or Senate floor for a vote. During the 1950s, conservative White Southern committee chairs used this power to prevent the passage of civil rights bills.[25] A majority (218) of the House can sign a discharge petition to dislodge a bill from a committee's jurisdiction, but a successful discharge petition requires the signature of members of the majority party, who are wary of opposing powerful committee chairs or party leadership. Successful discharge petitions are therefore a rare occurrence.

Long-term service on a committee, known as seniority, is a requirement for becoming a committee chair, but the leadership has the final say on naming committee chairs. After the Democrats won control of Congress in 2006, many Black, Latino, and Asian American Democratic representatives and senators were senior enough to chair powerful committees, but when Republicans regained control of the House in 2010 the number of minority committee chairs sharply decreased. In the 116th Congress, several racial and ethnic minorities chair committees in the House of Representatives because Democrats assumed control of that chamber after the 2018 elections. There are no minority committee chairs in the Republican controlled Senate.

Informal Organizations

In addition to parties, leaders, and committees, members of Congress organize themselves informally into special **caucuses**, which focus on common geographical, economic, or cultural issues or concerns. Some examples include the Congressional Wine Caucus[26] and the Congressional Sportsmen Caucus.[27]

Three caucuses advocate on behalf of racial and ethnic minorities. Since 1971, the **Congressional Black Caucus** (CBC) has promoted African American members for leadership positions and has pushed for legislation beneficial to African Americans. For example, the CBC has recently worked to change criminal justice policies that unfairly discriminate against African Americans.[28] In the 115th Congress, all of the African American Democratic members of Congress were members of the CBC, but former Representative Mia Love (R-UT) was the only African American Republican member—Senator Tim Scott (R-SC) and Representative Will Hurd (R-TX) were not.[29] Likewise, the Congressional Hispanic Caucus (CHC) advocates on behalf of issues of importance to Latinos, such as opposing President Trump's immigration policies.[30] The CHC consists of Democratic members of Congress who are Latino, in addition to Representative Jim Costa, who is of Portuguese descent but does not meet the definition of Latino that we use in this book. Additionally, nonvoting delegate Gregorio Sablan (D-Northern Mariana Islands), who is Chamorro, is another non-Latino member of the

Caucuses Informal organizations within Congress.

Congressional Black Caucus An informal organization consisting of African Americans elected to the United States Congress.

Access an interactive map of African Americans in the House and Senate throughout U.S. history.

Members of the Congressional Black Caucus—G. K. Butterfield, Andre Carson, William Lacy Clay, Shelia Jackson Lee, and Karen Bass—seated at the Wellspring Methodist Church in Ferguson, Missouri. After a Ferguson police officer killed African American teenager Michael Brown in 2014, the city has become a focal point for the question of how law enforcement officers treat minorities. As the primary organization in Congress that advocates on behalf of African Americans, the Congressional Black Caucus highlights issues of importance for African Americans.

CHC. None of the Latino Republican House and Senate members has joined the CHC.[31] The Congressional Asian Pacific American Caucus advocates on behalf of issues relevant to Asian Americans,[32] and it consists of Asian American members of Congress, as well as members who do not have an Asian background.[33]

The Lawmaking Process

The lawmaking process in Congress is extremely complex, and there are major differences between the House and Senate. The different rules in each chamber influence policymaking in that chamber. The majority party in the House dominates the lawmaking process without consulting with the minority, whereas the majority party in the Senate exerts far less control over the process of lawmaking. It is also true that Congress has nonlegislative functions, and these functions influence minority-group politics.

Activity on the House Floor

After the applicable committee in the House of Representatives approves a bill, the House Rules Committee decides how the bill will be considered by the full House. The Rules Committee develops a rule that specifies the additional amendments that can be considered, the amount of time for debate, and the schedule for voting on final passage of the bill. The chair of the Rules Committee works closely with majority party leaders to craft a rule that gives the majority party a legislative advantage. In fact, until the early twentieth century, the Speaker actually chaired the Rules Committee.[34]

When the majority party leadership wants to see a bill passed quickly, the chair of the Rules Committee will not allow the minority party to offer amendments that could change the nature of a bill or delay its passage. The Rules Committee will schedule little time for debate and call for a quick vote to prevent opponents from building opposition to the bill. Rules Committee chairs can prevent the passage of bills they oppose by refusing to schedule those bills for debate and vote. For example, during the 1950s the segregationist chair of the Rules Committee, Howard W. Smith (D-VA), used his authority to prevent civil rights bills from moving to the House floor for a vote.[35]

Once the Rules Committee schedules a rule (i.e., a date and time for voting, time allotted for debate, and amendments that can be considered), the bill proceeds to the House floor; that is, it is put before consideration of all 435 members of the institution. The House first votes on the Rules Committee's rule, which is virtually guaranteed to pass. Once the House approves the rule, it then considers the amendments that the Rules Committee allowed, and amendments that receive a majority vote become part of the bill.

The Rules Committee's allotted time for debate is then divided evenly between the majority and minority parties, and each side designates a floor manager to control the debate. Usually, the floor manager for the majority party is the committee or subcommittee chair and the floor manager for the minority party is the ranking minority member who was most active in developing (or usually opposing) the bill. Each floor manager then organizes the speakers for his or her side. For the most part, there is little actual debate; instead, each representative reads a prepared statement and then is able to enter a longer statement with attachments into the official proceedings of Congress, known as the ***Congressional Record***. House members vote at the time and date that the rule provides. In short, the majority party in the U.S. House of Representatives dominates the content of legislation and the speed at which it passes. The minority party has very little influence over either.

Congressional Record The published record of the official proceedings of Congress.

Action on the Senate Floor

Although the procedures in the Senate generally mirror those in the House, there are crucial differences. Because the Senate has far fewer members than the House, the rules are far less formal. The rules in the Senate allow for more individual freedom and for minority party input. As in the House, Senate bills must pass through committees, although the committees, subcommittees, and the chairs exert far less authority over the outcome of legislation. However, unlike the House Rules Committee, the Senate Committee on Rules and Administration lacks the power to schedule bills on the Senate floor. Instead, the majority and minority leaders try to negotiate a unanimous consent agreement in which every member agrees to which amendments can be considered, the allotment of debate time, and the vote schedule. However, if one senator objects, then he or she can derail the proceedings. Consequently, Senate leaders usually accommodate individual senators' requests to introduce amendments or speak on a bill.

See two filibuster versions: Senator Smith's noble moment, in the movie *Mr. Smith Goes to Washington*, and a real-life example from then-Senator Rand Paul.

The Senate majority leader must also take into account the minority party's concerns when drafting legislation and unanimous consent agreements. Senators who oppose a bill are free to speak as long they want, employing a tactic known as a **filibuster**. Because a vote cannot occur as long as a senator holds the floor, filibusters are a strategy for the minority party to block further consideration of a bill. Senators can end debate only through a **cloture vote**, which requires the support of three-fifths of the Senate (sixty senators). If the minority party has the support of at least forty-one senators (the minimum number to block a cloture vote), then it can prevent the majority party from passing its desired legislation. As we discuss in Chapter 9, filibusters were especially controversial in judicial nominations.

Filibuster A parliamentary technique in the Senate that allows senators to delay or block votes by talking endlessly.

Cloture vote A procedure in the Senate to stop a filibuster that usually requires three-fifths of the senators (sixty) agreeing to end debate.

Unlike the minority party in the House, the minority party in the Senate can use the filibuster to force the majority party to allow the minority party's amendments to be considered, add more time to the debate, and postpone final considerations of a bill. The minority party can also force the majority party to compromise on the substance of a bill or prevent a bill from being passed. In 2018 President Donald Trump encouraged Republican Senators to end the filibuster, which he cites as the primary reason Congress had not enacted most of his policy goals. However, recognizing that Republicans could return to minority status in the future, Majority Leader Mitch McConnell refused to change the rules.[36]

The filibuster has also affected civil rights policy. For example, as we mentioned earlier, the House passed by a significant margin a bill to give Washington, DC (and its large African American population) a voting member of the House. But when the bill arrived in the Senate, Minority Leader McConnell staged a filibuster because he claimed Congress lacked the constitutional authority to give Washington, DC, a voting member in the House. The cloture vote was 57–42,[37] which was not sufficient to end the filibuster. Consequently, even though a considerable majority of the House and Senate supported the bill, the rules of the Senate prevented it from becoming law.

Reconciling Differences Between House and Senate Bills

The Constitution requires that bills emerging from the House and Senate must be identical to become law. But as we have already made clear, bills undergo many changes in both houses, and in the Senate, but not in the House, the majority party compromises with the minority party. As a result, major legislation passed in the House is rarely identical to the same legislation passed in the Senate.

Conference Committee
A committee composed of members of the House and the Senate that reconciles different versions of the same bill.

Congress reconciles different bills through the use of a **conference committee**, whose members are selected by the majority and minority leaders in both houses. As with other committees, the majority party enjoys a majority on conference committees. When naming members to the conference committee, party leaders usually defer to the committee chairs and ranking minority members who worked on the bill. Conference committee members attempt to reconcile the different versions of the bill through compromise. A majority of all the conferees must agree to the compromise for it to take effect. Then the compromise must be approved by a majority of both houses. In short, lawmaking procedures are extremely complex. To clarify this complexity, Figure 6.2 diagrams the process of lawmaking.

Nonlawmaking Functions of Congress

A significant portion of the work that Congress does is not legislative, and these nonlawmaking functions are important for American government, including the politics of race and ethnicity. One nonlegislative congressional function is the Senate's role in confirming presidential appointments. Although most presidential nominees are confirmed, the Senate and the president have occasionally clashed over appointments.

For example, in 1999 President Bill Clinton nominated Ronnie White to be a federal district court judge for the Eastern District of Missouri. Justice White was the first African American to serve on the Missouri State Supreme Court, and most people expected the Senate to confirm him easily. However, Republican Senator John Ashcroft (R-MO) pressured his colleagues to oppose the nomination because he argued that Justice White had reversed too many criminal convictions and death sentences. Senator Ashcroft convinced his Republican colleagues to oppose the nomination, and because the Republicans were then

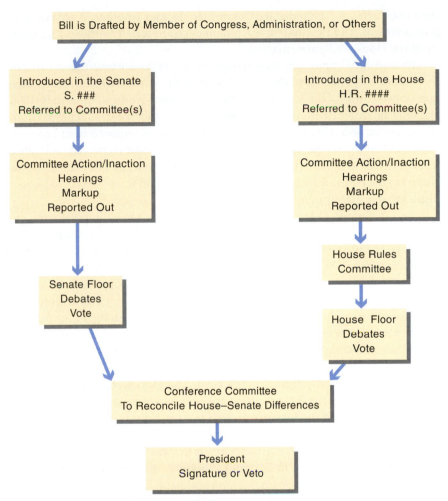

Figure 6.2 How a Bill Becomes a Law.

the majority party, White's nomination failed. Democratic Senators, Democratic politicians in Missouri, and civil rights leaders maintained that Justice White's record on criminal matters was the same as that of other justices in Missouri. Despite Republican denials, White's supporters charged that racism was the real reason for the opposition to White, and this controversy affected Senator Ashcroft's 2000 reelection bid,[38] which he eventually lost. We discuss judicial nominations in more detail in Chapter 9.

Another nonlawmaking function of Congress is the impeachment and removal power. **Impeachment** refers to the power to charge the president, vice president, or a federal judge with "treason, bribery, or other high crimes and misdemeanors." The Constitution gives the impeachment power to the House of Representatives. When a member of the House introduces impeachment charges, the Judiciary Committee conducts hearings featuring testimony from constitutional experts, those making the charges, and those defending

Impeachment The process by which the House of Representatives charges a president, vice president, or federal judge with a high crime or misdemeanor; the Senate can then decide to remove that official from office with a two-thirds vote.

the public official. The Judiciary Committee decides whether to recommend impeachment, and the final impeachment decision is determined by a majority of the House of Representatives.

If someone is impeached, then a committee in the Senate investigates whether there is enough evidence to convict and remove the official, which requires support of two-thirds of the Senate. Only two presidents—Andrew Johnson in 1868 and Bill Clinton in 1998—have been impeached, but they were not removed from office. Several federal judges have been impeached and removed from office. In 1989, Black federal judge Alcee Hastings was impeached and removed from office for accusations of bribery (he was actually acquitted in a trial), but in 1992 he was elected to the House from a district in south Florida, and he still serves today in a district that is slightly more than 50 percent African American.[39]

Because impeachments are rarely used, Congress generally polices the executive branch and the bureaucracy through its oversight power, which allows Congress to investigate apparent problems in an executive (see Chapter 7) or bureaucratic (see Chapter 8) agency that it created. Inherent in the lawmaking power of Congress is the authority to make sure that its laws are enforced according to its intentions and to prevent waste, fraud, or abuse in government. Generally, committees and subcommittees handle oversight, usually in the form of hearings, which not only provide evidence, but also generate publicity for a cause.

Unified Government A period in which both houses of Congress are controlled by the same party as the president.

Divided Government A period in which the president is of one political party and the majority of one or both houses of Congress is of the other party.

Although oversight often features interbranch disputes, it is largely a partisan process. Committee chairs have tremendous discretion in determining whether to conduct oversight investigations. As a result, Congress is less likely to exercise its oversight power in periods of **unified government**, when the president's party is the same as that in the majority of both houses, than in periods of **divided government**, when one or both houses of Congress are controlled by the party opposite the president's. This partisanship was evident when the Republicans assumed control of the House in 2011 and announced that they would sharply increase investigations of the Obama administration on issues such as its perceived failure to enforce immigration laws. House Democrats argued that Republicans were motivated by a partisan desire to embarrass President Obama.[40] The partisanship on oversight continued during the Trump administration. For example, the House Intelligence Committee investigated Russia's interference in the 2016 election and the extent that the Trump campaign conspired with the Russians. The Republican majority on the committee exonerated the Trump campaign and criticized the intelligence officers investigating the issue, whereas the Democratic minority castigated the Republican majority for using its power to protect the president.[41] The new Democratic majority in the House will significantly increase oversight over Russian interference in the 2016 election.

Influences on Congressional Decision Making

There are various influences on legislators' voting behavior, including constituents, party leaders, colleagues, interest groups, and staff. These competing influences are further shaped by minority-group politics.

Constituents

A fundamental basis of representative government is that representatives act on behalf of their constituents. Partisan gerrymandering creates numerous districts that are overwhelmingly Democratic or Republican, and representatives of those districts are easily able to vote according to the preferences of a large majority of their constituents. Likewise, racial and ethnic minority members of the House who represent majority-minority districts are usually able to vote in accordance with their constituents' preferences, especially on civil rights issues. However, states, and even many House districts, have heterogeneous populations, and the political views and policy preferences of these constituents are less clear to their representatives in Congress.

The relationship between members of Congress and their constituents is complex and has been the subject of political science research. David Mayhew's classic study *Congress: The Electoral Connection* is based on the fundamental assumption that members of Congress are primarily motivated by reelection. Consequently, much of their behavior aims more to enhance their prestige than to craft meaningful public policy. For example, members of Congress devote considerable effort to "advertising," in which they generate a favorable image by sending information to constituents and working with the local media. Furthermore, when communicating with their constituents, members of Congress "credit claim," whereby they create the impression that their actions have influenced the government in a positive direction.[42] Additionally, Richard Fenno spent time with a small number of selected members of the House of Representatives both in Washington, DC, and in their districts. He found that representatives adopt a "home style" in how they relate to their different types of constituencies—the entire geographic region they represent, the people they expect to vote for them, the politically engaged supporters who will work on their behalf, and their close political associates.[43]

Building off the work of Mayhew, political scientist Morris Fiorina emphasizes how members of Congress also act on behalf of constituents and secure a reelection advantage through "constituency service" or **casework**.[44] Casework entails members of Congress advocating on behalf of constituents who need assistance in dealing with the federal government, such as finding a lost Social Security check, settling conflicts with the Internal Revenue Service, or appointing students to a military academy. Because members of Congress have influence over government employees, casework requires minimal staff time; in return, members win grateful constituents. A recent study demonstrates that Black representatives have been extremely instrumental in providing casework and funding to their African American constituents.[45]

Casework Favors and other forms of assistance that members of Congress provide to their constituents.

To represent constituents adequately and enhance reelection chances, members of Congress must communicate frequently with their constituents. Senators and representatives who live close to Washington, DC, live in their districts and commute to the Capitol. Others frequently travel back to their districts on the weekends and during recesses. Members of Congress also advertise to their constituents through the mail. The **franking privilege** allows

Franking Privilege The ability of members of Congress to send noncampaign material to their constituents free of charge.

senators and representatives to send newsletters and surveys to their constituents without paying postage fees. Although franked mail cannot be used for campaign material (which must come from the congressperson's campaign account) and cannot be used within 90 days of an election,[46] members of Congress are able to use the franking privilege to promote their accomplishments, which can help them to get reelected.

All members maintain websites that contain text, audio, and visual information about the member, the district, committee work, votes, and casework. Senators and representatives who are concerned about their Latino constituents provide Spanish-language versions of their websites. Some representatives who have a large number of Latino and Asian American constituents even offer multilingual versions of their websites.

Party Leaders

It should be quite evident by now that political party is extremely important in determining members' votes, particularly in the House of Representatives. The party leadership strongly influences committee assignments, allocation of campaign resources, and power within the legislative institution. But at times members go against their party leaders because their constituents' interests clash with those leaders' goals. For example, when the Republicans controlled

U.S Representative Judy Chu speaks during the 100th anniversary celebration of the Colorado Street Bridge at the Pasadena Museum of History on June 22, 2013, in Pasadena, California. Reflecting the fact that her district contains a large number of Latinos and Asian Americans, Representative Chu's official U.S. House of Representatives website (*https://chu.house.gov*) is available in English, Spanish, and Chinese.

the House in 2013, former Republican Representative Ileana Ros-Lehtinen (R-FL), who usually votes with her party, supported Democratic Party legislation that would have provided undocumented immigrants an opportunity to become American citizens because the large Latino population in her district supported that policy.[47] "Measuring Equality: The Influence of Race and Political Party on Congressional Voting" explores in more detail the tension between race and ethnicity and party in congressional voting.

Colleagues

Because Congress is a collegial institution (unlike the executive), senators and representatives often influence each other's behavior. Many legislators develop friendships with colleagues, and these friendships can affect votes. However, **logrolling**, or the trading of votes, is the most common means by which colleagues influence one another. In other words, legislators vote a certain way because another member agreed to support them in a particular vote. Logrolling is common with **pork barrel spending**, in which members propose government funding that affects only their state or district.[48] Because pork barrel projects are crucial to reelection, members are loath to vote against their colleagues' pork barrel spending out of fear of losing those colleagues' votes. The classic example of pork barrel spending is the case of the so-called "Bridge to Nowhere," in which Congress voted in 2005 to appropriate $223 million to build a massive bridge from Ketchikan, Alaska (with a population of about 8,000 people) to Gravina Island (with a population of 50 people).[49]

Logrolling The practice by members of Congress of trading votes or other favors to enhance members' mutual interests.

Pork Barrel Spending Federal money spent on projects that benefit only a specific member's district or state.

Interest Groups

Interest groups, organized collections of individuals who come together to influence public policy (see Chapter 13), are also important influences on members of Congress. Interest groups provide information to members of Congress who tend to support the positions of these groups. Those legislators can use that information when debating with colleagues or when justifying votes to constituents. These groups try to convince as many members of Congress as possible to support their desired legislation. Interest groups also influence legislators' votes by mobilizing constituents to contact members of Congress about public policy issues.

Groups advocating on behalf of racial and ethnic minorities have actively lobbied Congress in support of congressional legislation. The Japanese American Citizens League lobbied individual members of Congress to pass the Civil Liberties Act of 1988, which apologized to and provided reparations for Japanese Americans who had been interned during World War II.[50] The League of United Latin American Citizens, an interest group that advocates on behalf of Latinos, organized a campaign for supporters to contact their representatives and senators about including children of legal immigrants in government-funded children's health insurance.[51]

Staff

Legislators require staff to assist them with their daily responsibilities. Staffers conduct research, correspond with constituents, summarize bills, and write

measuring equality

The Influence of Race and Political Party on Congressional Voting

Students of Congress investigate the competing influences on members' voting behavior, and one key debate concerns the influence of race and ethnicity versus that of political party. Throughout this chapter, we have demonstrated the importance of both party and racial and ethnic background, and here we quantitatively test the influence of both factors by using congressional voting scorecards.

Many interest groups rate members of Congress according to how they voted on a selection of bills that the group identifies as high priority. In this example, we focus on the National Hispanic Leadership Agenda (NHLA), which has rated members of the House of Representatives of the 113th Congress (2013–2015, the most recent data available). The NHLA cares about economic, social, and political issues that affect all racial and ethnic minorities, but its main focus is on Latino concerns. The NHLA scores each House member with a percentage between 0 and 100 for support of its priority bills. To simplify the presentation, we classify House members who support at least two-thirds of the NHLA's bills as "high supporters," those who support between one-third and two-thirds as "moderate supporters," and

those who support less than one-third of the NHLA's priorities as "low supporters." We are specifically interested in comparing the extent to which race and political party influence the likelihood that a House member will be classified as a high supporter, moderate supporter, or low supporter.

Figure 6.3 displays the results for the percent of House members in each racial and ethnic group (White, Black, and Latino) that rank high, moderate, or low on the NHLA scores. The figure shows that all African American House members were in the high category (keep in mind that these data predate the addition of African American Republicans in the U.S. House); therefore, being an African American is clearly related to a House member's support for the NHLA's priorities. Interestingly, support for the NHLA is lower among Latinos than it is for Blacks, with 75.0 percent of Latinos in the high category, 14.3 percent in the moderate, and 10.7 percent in the low category. Figure 6.3 also shows that support for the NHLA among White representatives is the lowest, with 34.6 percent in the high category, 10.7 percent in the moderate category, and 63.7 percent in the low category. There were not

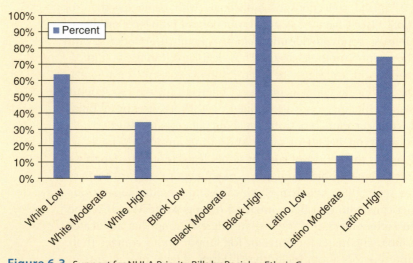

Figure 6.3 Support for NHLA Priority Bills by Racial or Ethnic Group

Source: Data adapted from National Hispanic Leadership Agenda. (2014, August). Congressional Scorecard, 113th Congress. *Retrieved June 25, 2018, from https://nationalhispanicleadership.org/ images/Scorecards/NHLA_2014scorecard_090915_forweb_2.pdf.*

measuring equality *(Continued)*

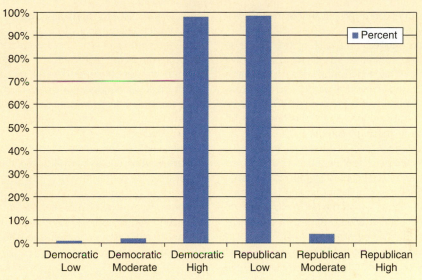

Figure 6.4 Support for NHLA Priority Bills by Political Party

Source: Data adapted from National Hispanic Leadership Agenda. (2014, August). Congressional Scorecard, 113th Congress. *Retrieved June 25, 2018, from https://nationalhispanicleadership.org/images/Scorecards/ NHLA_2014scorecard_090915_forweb_2.pdf.*

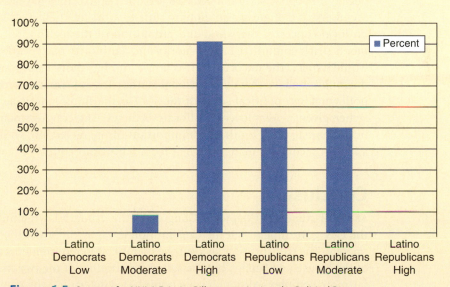

Figure 6.5 Support for NHLA Priority Bills among Latinos by Political Party

Source: Data adapted from National Hispanic Leadership Agenda. (2014, August). Congressional Scorecard, 113th Congress. *Retrieved June 25, 2018, from https://nationalhispanicleadership.org/images/Scorecards/ NHLA_2014scorecard_090915_forweb_2.pdf.*

(continued)

measuring equality *(Continued)*

enough Asian American or American Indian representatives to analyze separately.

These results suggest that race matters because Black and Latino representatives are far more supportive of the NHLA than White representatives are. However, a similar analysis based on political party yields significant information as well. Figure 6.4 shows that 97.0 percent of House Democrats are in the high category, but no Republicans are in the high category. No Democrats are in the low category, but 97.4 percent of Republicans are. Additionally, 2.6 percent of Republicans are moderate supporters, and 2.0 percent of Democrats are rated as moderate. The most significant finding here is that Democrats of any race support the NHLA more than do Whites and even Latinos, which suggests that political party matters more than ethnicity.

Finally, Latino support of the NHLA could be lower than the Black or Democratic support because there were conservative Republican Latinos in the 113th Congress. We test this hypothesis by comparing the scores of Latino Republicans to those of Latino Democrats (see Figure 6.5). Whereas 91.3 percent of Latino Democrats are in the high category (8.7 percent are in the moderate category and there are no Latino Democrats in the low category), none of the Latino Republicans are, as can be seen in Figure 6.5. Instead, 50 percent of Latino Republicans are rated as moderate and 50 percent are rated as low.

Latino Republicans are more supportive of the NHLA than are Republicans as a whole, and they are more supportive than Whites; therefore, their ethnicity does matter. However, Latino Democrats and even Democrats of any race are much more supportive of the NHLA than Latino Republicans are. Moreover, Latino Democrats are closely matched with Democrats of any race. In short, party seems to matter more than ethnicity in supporting the NHLA's priorities.

speeches. At times, staff members will actually write a bill that a member introduces. Although legislators are in charge of their offices, they rely heavily on staff. Members of Congress also employ staff to work in their districts or states on local concerns, casework, and promotion of the legislator's accomplishments. Each committee has a majority and a minority party staff, and, as one would expect, the majority staff is larger and has more resources. Although one might believe that congressional staffers focus primarily on assisting in policymaking, political scientist Morris Fiorina finds otherwise. He writes, "when given . . . employees to allocate as they see fit, congressmen . . . put the lion's share to work on the most important thing, reelection, while reserving a few for secondary matters such as formulating our country's laws."[52]

Conclusion

As we discussed in Chapter 2, Congress is the primary lawmaking branch of the U.S. government, but the Constitution is vague on how Congress should operate. The Constitution lays out the membership requirements and powers of the House and Senate, but the actual functioning of the two institutions is far more complex. Although state boundaries determine the composition of the Senate, creating districts for House seats is more complicated.

The Constitution does not consider political parties in its design for Congress, but political party dominates. Party leaders exert tremendous influence over the outcome of legislation. The committee system divides labor into smaller units, and the committee chairs, who are members of the majority party, use their power to control the work of the committees.

The procedures in the House and Senate differ. The House Rules Committee allows the majority party to determine the fate of legislation that the House considers. Conversely, the Senate filibuster gives the minority party much more influence over the speed at which legislation passes and the content of the legislation.

Finally, there are a variety of influences on the behavior of members of Congress. Some of these influences, such as party leaders, colleagues, and staff, are internal to the institution of Congress. Other influences, such as constituents and interest groups, exist outside Congress.

This chapter emphasized the importance of race and ethnicity in congressional politics. People who live in Washington, DC, Puerto Rico, and the American territories, many of whom are members of a racial or ethnic minority group, currently lack any representation in Congress. The creation of majority-minority districts has increased the number of Black and Latino members of the House. Informal congressional caucuses have been useful for minorities to improve their clout in Congress. Historically, the leadership structure and committee system, especially the power of the chair, were used to subjugate racial and ethnic minorities. But now Black, Latino, and Asian American members of Congress have amassed enough seniority to be able to assume positions of power in the House and Senate, although racial and ethnic minority legislators are more powerful when Democrats control the House or Senate than when Republicans are in charge. The filibuster in the Senate has prevented the passage of progressive civil rights legislation, but it has also prevented the passage of legislation detrimental to civil rights.

Representative Will Hurd's (R-TX) story clearly reveals the intersection between race and congressional politics. Most Black and Latino representatives represent districts that contain a majority of their race or ethnicity and are liberal Democrats, but Representative Hurd is Black and comes from a majority-Latino district. Although he has focused on more nonpartisan issues concerning homeland security, he is still a conservative, and thus far, he has not joined the Congressional Black Caucus. In short, Congress is a complex governing institution that has offered racial minority groups both disappointment and promise.

review
REVIEW QUESTIONS

1. How do majority-minority districts increase minority representation in the House?

2. How do issues of descriptive representation, symbolic representation, and substantive representation affect the impact of racial and ethnic minorities in Congress?

3. How can congressional leaders, committee chairs, and informal organizations influence racial and ethnic politics?

4. What are the nonlawmaking functions of Congress, and how can they influence the politics of race and ethnicity?

5. What are the important influences on the voting behavior of racial and ethnic minority members of Congress?

Check your
understanding of
Chapter 6.

Need to review key ideas in greater depth? Click here.

KEY TERMS

Casework p. 191

Caucuses p. 185

Cloture Vote p. 187

Conference Committee p. 188

Congressional Black Caucus p. 185

Congressional Record p. 187

Constituency p. 169

Descriptive Representation p. 176

Divided Government p. 190

Filibuster p. 187

Franking Privilege p. 191

Gerrymandering p. 173

House Majority Leader p. 180

House Minority Leader p. 180

Impeachment p. 189

Logrolling p. 193

Majority-Minority Districts p. 167

Majority Party p. 179

Minority Party p. 179

Political Party p. 179

Pork Barrel Spending p. 193

Reapportionment p. 172

Redistricting p. 173

Representative p. 169

Senate Majority Leader p. 181

Senate Majority Whip p. 181

Senate Minority Leader p. 181

Speaker of the House p. 179

Substantive Representation p. 176

Symbolic Representation p. 176

Unified Government p. 190

Whip p. 180

Flashcard review.

ADDITIONAL READINGS

Fenno, R. F. (2003). *Going home: Black representatives and their constituents.* Chicago: University of Chicago Press.

> This book updates Fenno's classic work by analyzing the representation styles of four African American members of the House— Louis Stokes (D-OH), Barbara Jordan (D-TX), Chaka Fattah (D-PA), and Stephanie Tubbs Jones (D-OH)—and paying close attention to the issue of race.

Grose, C. R. (2011). *Congress in Black and White: Race and representation in Congress and at home.* New York: Cambridge University Press.

> This book uses a variety of sophisticated methodologies to examine the debate between descriptive and substantive representation for Black members of Congress. The author finds that although Black representatives are not influential on legislative outputs, they are extremely important for constituent services, such as casework and bringing money to Black communities.

Middleton, S. (Ed.). (2002). *Black congressmen during Reconstruction: A documentary sourcebook.* Westport, CT: Greenwood Press.

> This book examines the contribution of each of the twenty-two African American representatives and senators who served from 1870 to 1901.

Singh, R. (1998). *The Black Congressional Caucus: Racial politics in the U.S. Congress.* Thousand Oaks, CA: Sage.

> A European political scientist offers a comprehensive, systematic, and balanced analysis of the impact of the Congressional Black Caucus.

Tate, K. (2003). *Black faces in the mirror: African Americans and their representatives in the U.S. Congress.* Princeton, NJ: Princeton University Press.

> This is a comprehensive, rigorous, empirical study of the extent to which Black representatives work on behalf of their Black constituents and of Black constituents' perceptions of their representatives.

CHAPTER 7

The Presidency: Conventional Wisdom Redefined

White House Chief of Staff John Kelly answers questions at a press conference. In October 2017, Kelly claimed that African American Representative Frederica Wilson (D-FL) had promoted herself during an event that named a federal building after two slain FBI agents. After video evidence clearly contradicted Kelly's account, he repeated his false claims and refused to apologize to Representative Wilson.

John Kelly grew up in the 1950s and 1960s in Boston as part of a working-class Irish Catholic family. Like many teenagers of his time, Kelly was rebellious, even hitchhiking and riding rail cars across the country when he was 16. In 1970, Kelly enlisted in the Marines and fought in Vietnam until 1972. He graduated from the University of Massachusetts, Boston, in 1976 and then embarked on a long and successful career in the Marine Corps, ultimately serving as the Commander of the United States Southern Command during the Obama administration. General Kelly retired from the Marines in 2016, and in 2017, President Donald Trump named him as the Secretary of Homeland Security, which means that he oversaw immigration, security at airports, and responses to natural disasters.[1] About six months into his administration, President Trump named Kelly to be his Chief of Staff because Trump was so dissatisfied with his initial Chief of Staff Reince Priebus. Many observers believed Kelly would be effective in this position because he had capably supported the president's priorities as Homeland Security Secretary and his experience as a military leader would bring order to a chaotic administration.[2] The Chief of Staff position is crucial for a president because it coordinates executive branch employees and serves as a link between other presidential advisors and the president; therefore, General Kelly would be a significant member of the Trump administration.

However, Kelly created controversy within a few months of his tenure. In October 2017, U.S. Representative Frederica Wilson (D-FL), an African American woman, was part of a phone call between President Trump and the family of Sergeant La David Johnson, a soldier who was recently killed while on duty in Niger. Representative Wilson, who is a longtime friend of Johnson's family, publicly stated that President Trump was callous during the phone call because he did not know the fallen soldier's name and said, "I guess he knew what he was signing up for but it still hurts."[3] After Representative Wilson publicized Trump's remarks, General Kelly, whose son was killed in combat, delivered a press conference to defend the president's conduct. Instead of defending the president, Kelly chose to attack Wilson by claiming that he previously attended a ceremony in which a federal building was named after two FBI agents

killed in the line of duty. Kelly claimed that during the ceremony Representative Wilson claimed credit for securing the funds for the building rather than honoring the slain officers. He referred to Wilson as an "empty barrel" and called her "all hat but no cattle" (Wilson is known for wearing colorful hats). Soon after Kelly's speech, a video of Representative Wilson's speech at the ceremony demonstrated incontrovertibly that Kelley's account was a complete fabrication. Wilson did not claim credit; in fact, she credited others and spoke extensively about the heroism of the slain FBI agents. When confronted with evidence that his account was false, Kelly refused to apologize for lying about Representative Wilson.[4]

intro

The story of John Kelly's behavior highlights key elements of the American presidency. American presidents are obvious leaders in American politics, holding what most regard as the most powerful position in the world. Therefore, the person who serves as president exerts tremendous influence on the politics and policy of the nation. When Democrat Barack Obama was president (2009–2017), he promoted liberal policies, such as expanding health insurance, regulating the environment, appointing liberal judges, and working with international organizations. However, since Donald Trump became president, he reversed Obama's policies on health care, the environment, judges, and international relations. Additionally, presidents have different personalities. Whereas President Obama was known as being personable and thoughtful, President Trump has developed a more confrontational and less empathetic approach, as evidenced by the phone call he made to the slain soldier's widow. Additionally, this story demonstrates the importance of the president's staff. Presidents alone cannot manage the executive branch; consequently, they require an extensive array of advisors. Often, as in the case of John Kelly, the actions of the staff can influence the president's success. Finally, this story shows that race (and gender) are central to the politics of the American presidency. Representative Wilson argued that Kelly's use of the term empty barrel *had racist and sexist undertones because African American females have been stereotyped as nonsubstantive loudmouths.[5] The female members of the Congressional Black Caucus (see Chapter 6) insisted that Kelly apologize for his remarks.[6] Kelly has also made other racist statements as a member of the Trump administration, including accusing undocumented immigrants of being "too lazy to get off their asses."[7] As we discussed in Chapter 5, sloth is an enduring, deleterious stereotype of Mexican Americans.*

In this chapter, we discuss the politics of the presidency. We first explain the presidential selection process, and we then discuss the president's formal powers. The latter half of the chapter examines the vast structure of the executive branch, the relationship between the president and Congress, and the importance of the president as a public figure. Throughout this chapter, we demonstrate how the presidency intersects with racial and ethnic politics.

Learn about
presidential
achievements.

Becoming President

Article 2, Section 1, of the U.S. Constitution requires that the president of the United States be at least thirty-five years old, a natural-born citizen of the United States, and a resident of the United States for at least fourteen years. All presidents have been over forty at the time of their inauguration, with most over the age of fifty. Barack Obama was forty-seven when he was inaugurated, which makes him one of the youngest presidents, and Bill Clinton was even younger at forty-six. Donald Trump was seventy at his inauguration, making him the oldest president in American history at the time of his inauguration. Despite the antiquated origins of the citizenship and residency provisions, they are still in effect. These lax requirements notwithstanding, becoming president is extremely difficult and complex.

Diversity

Before explaining the presidential selection process itself, we examine the diversity among those who compete for the presidency. Put simply, American presidents have not been diverse. Until 2009, all presidents were White, male, and Christian. In fact, except for John F. Kennedy, who was Catholic, all other presidents have been Protestant. Some females and non-Whites ran for president prior to 2008. In 1872, Victoria Woodhull became the first woman to run for president. She ran with former slave Frederick Douglass as her vice presidential candidate. In 1972, Shirley Chisholm, who in 1968 had been the first African American female elected to the House of Representatives, sought the Democratic Party nomination for president. Although unsuccessful, she was the first African American to seek the presidency on a major party ticket. In 1984, civil rights activist Jesse Jackson finished third in the battle for the Democratic Party nomination for president. In 1988, Jackson won more votes and delegates than he had won in 1984, and he finished second.[8]

Of course, the 2008 presidential election was historic because for the first time Americans elected a non-White candidate to be president. Notwithstanding President Obama's election, the 2008 presidential election featured a highly diverse group of candidates. Former first lady and then-senator Hillary Rodham Clinton (D-NY) was the first female candidate to launch a significant campaign. In fact, she was the early favorite to win the Democratic nomination and narrowly lost it to Barack Obama. New Mexico governor Bill Richardson (D-NM) became the first major Latino candidate. President Obama ended up winning handily in 2008, earning 52.9 percent of the popular vote and 67.8 percent of the Electoral College vote.[9] See "Our Voices: Barack Obama's First Inaugural Address" on page 000 for excerpts from his 2009 inauguration speech.

The 2016 campaign has also featured a diverse set of candidates. Two Cuban Americans—Senator Ted Cruz (R-TX) and Senator Marco Rubio (R-FL)—ran competitive races for the Republican nomination, but they both lost to the eventual nominee Donald Trump. Additionally, Republican candidates also included an African American, retired neurosurgeon Dr. Ben Carson, and a female candidate, former business executive Carly Fiorina. However, both of those candidates dropped out of the race in early 2016. The Democratic field was initially less diverse, but Democrats made history in 2016 because they nominated Hillary Clinton as the first female nominee of either major party. Clinton picked Senator Tim Kaine (D-VA), who is a White male, as her running mate. However, they lost the election, despite winning the popular vote.[10] As of the summer of 2018, possible Democratic Party contenders for the presidency include minorities such as New Jersey Senator Cory Booker (African American male) and California Senator Kamala Harris (African American and South Asian female).[11]

The Presidential Selection Process

Despite Obama's success, the process a potential nominee must follow to become president has contributed to the lack of diversity among presidents. The presidential selection process is divided into two stages, both of which eliminate many candidates. In the first stage, candidates vie for the Democratic or Republican Party nomination by competing for delegates in each state and the several territories. The candidate who receives a majority of the party's delegates is selected as the party's nominee. Then, in the second stage, the two nominees face each other in the general election.

The Nomination Battle. There are a variety of ways that states select their delegates for each party's presidential nomination contest. Some states award delegates through **caucuses**, in which party activists attend local meetings to pick delegates who are attached to certain candidates. Most states hold primaries, in which voters decide how the state will award its delegates. In closed primaries, only registered members of the party can vote in their party's **primary**, and in open primaries, any registered voter, regardless of party registration, can receive one of the two major party ballots when she or he shows up at the polls. We discuss these processes in more detail in Chapters 14 and 15.

Caucus A method for political parties to select their candidates for office whereby party members convene at local meetings.

Primary A method for political parties to select their candidates for office whereby people vote in an election.

Traditionally, Iowa holds the first caucus and New Hampshire holds the first primary. Candidates generally need to do well in these states to emerge as a serious contender for the nomination. Yet, neither state is diverse—as of 2017, New Hampshire is 93.6 percent White[12] and Iowa is 91.1 percent White.[13] It can be difficult, then, for racial minority candidates to attract voters in these key states and thus start their campaigns in a strong position. However, minority candidates have recently fared well in the Iowa caucus, with President Obama winning in 2008[14] and Senator Ted Cruz winning in 2016.[15]

The General Election. The winners of the Democratic and Republican nominations then face each other in the general election. This election determines the president through the **Electoral College**, in which each state receives a number of electoral votes equal to the number of representatives it sends to the House of Representatives plus two. The presidential election is thus

Electoral College The entity that selects the president and vice president, consisting of 538 electors chosen from the states and the District of Columbia.

our voices

Barack Obama's First Inaugural Address, January 20, 2009

The inauguration of a president is a momentous occasion in American political life. In addition to the formal swearing-in of a president and the official start of a presidential term, presidents deliver speeches that outline their plans for the following four years. President Obama's inauguration in 2009 was especially historic because it marked the first time that a non-White became president. At the same time, President Obama was entering office at a time of national crisis. The nation was engaged in two wars (Iraq and Afghanistan), and the economy was in serious trouble, with hundreds of thousands of jobs being lost each month, a collapsing financial system and stock market, a record number of foreclosures, and plummeting home values. There was also severe political division. President Obama did not have the luxury of focusing on the historic nature of his election; instead, his address focused on the troubles facing the United States. Nevertheless, when discussing the divisions that plague American politics and international affairs, President Obama struck a hopeful tone, promoting cultural, racial, and religious diversity.

> My fellow citizens: I stand here today humbled by the task before us, grateful for the trust you have bestowed, mindful of the sacrifices borne by our ancestors. . . .
>
> Forty-four Americans have now taken the presidential oath. The words have been spoken during rising tides of prosperity and the still waters of peace. Yet, every so often, the oath is taken amidst gathering clouds and raging storms. . . .
>
> That we are in the midst of crisis is now well understood. Our nation is at war against a far-reaching network of violence and hatred. Our economy is badly weakened, a consequence of greed and irresponsibility on the part of some, but also our collective failure to make hard choices and prepare the nation for a new age. Homes have been lost, jobs shed, businesses shuttered. Our health care is too costly, our

> schools fail too many. And each day brings further evidence that the ways we use energy strengthen our adversaries and threaten our planet. . . .
>
> On this day we gather because we have chosen hope over fear, unity of purpose over conflict and discord. On this day we come to proclaim an end to the petty grievances and false promises, the recriminations and worn-out dogmas that for far too long have strangled our politics. . . .
>
> For we know that our patchwork heritage is a strength, not a weakness. We are a nation of Christians and Muslims, Jews and Hindus, and nonbelievers. We are shaped by every language and culture, drawn from every end of this Earth. And because we have tasted the bitter swill of civil war and segregation and emerged from that dark chapter stronger and more united, we cannot help but believe that the old hatreds shall someday pass; that the lines of tribe shall soon dissolve; that as the world grows smaller, our common humanity shall reveal itself, and that America must play its role in ushering in a new era of peace. . . .
>
> This is the price and the promise of citizenship. This is the source of our confidence, the knowledge that God calls on us to shape an uncertain destiny. This is the meaning of our liberty and our creed; why men and women and children of every race and faith can join in celebration across this magnificent Mall, and why a man whose father less than sixty years ago might not have been served at a local restaurant can now stand before you to take a most sacred oath. . . .
>
> Thank you. God bless you, and God bless the United States.

Source: Adapted from Obama, B. (2009, January 20). Inaugural address. In & J. Woolley & G. Peters, *The American Presidency Project.* Santa Barbara: University of California at Santa Barbara. Retrieved June 28, 2018. from http://www.presidency.ucsb.edu/ws/index .php?pid=44.

decided by separate elections in each of the fifty states, plus the District of Columbia, which receives three electoral votes.

In fact, it is possible for a candidate to win more overall votes than his or her opponent but lose in the Electoral College and not become president because a candidate could narrowly win in enough key states but lose by large margins in other states. In the disputed election of 1876 (see Chapter 5) Democrat Samuel Tilden won the popular vote but received fewer electoral votes than Republican Rutherford B. Hayes,[16] and in 1888 the incumbent Democratic president won the popular vote but received fewer electoral votes than Republican Benjamin Harrison.[17]

More recently, this problem occurred in the presidential election of 2000. The results from the state of Florida were disputed because of problems with ballots, as well as widespread reports of difficulties that minorities had faced when voting. The Florida Supreme Court required a hand recount of votes in counties with disputed ballots, but the U.S. Supreme Court then halted that recount, arguing that the Equal Protection Clause of the Fourteenth Amendment requires that the recount rules be uniform for all counties throughout the state.[18] This decision ultimately gave the electors of the state of Florida, and the presidency, to Republican George W. Bush. Regardless of the disputed outcome in Florida, Al Gore received more overall votes nationally than Bush (48.4 percent of the popular vote went for Gore, and 47.9 percent of the popular vote went for Bush). Because Bush was declared the narrow winner in such pivotal states as Florida and Ohio, he was able to eke out the Electoral College victory even though Gore's popular vote totals stemmed from wide victories in large, populous states including California, New York, and Massachusetts.[19]

During the 2008 and 2012 presidential elections, the Electoral College might have worked to Obama's disadvantage because a Black candidate could have experienced difficulty winning states that were overwhelmingly White. Because Obama's appeal cut across racial and ethnic boundaries, he was able to win predominantly White states, such as Iowa, Vermont, New Hampshire, Maine, and Minnesota.[20] In 2016, Hillary Clinton actually did worse in largely White states, losing Iowa and one electoral vote from northern Maine. "Measuring Equality: Scatterplots of Obama and Trump Vote and Minority Populations" shows in more detail how racial and ethnic characteristics of the states correlate to Obama's success in 2012, while comparing how race and ethnicity factored into the 2016 election, which featured two White candidates. Moreover, in 2016, Hillary Clinton won the popular vote by over 2 percentage points (almost three million votes) but lost the Electoral College because she narrowly lost in key states, such as Florida, Pennsylvania, Michigan, and Wisconsin.[21] On several occasions, President Trump claimed that the only reason that Hillary Clinton won the popular vote is that three million undocumented immigrants voted illegally. However, Trump's claim is undoubtedly false. Not only did he fail to provide any evidence to support his assertion, but also every expert has shown that it is impossible for that many people to vote illegally.[22]

Financing Presidential Campaigns

The process of running for president, including both the nomination process and the general election, is extremely expensive. Once a candidate announces a bid for the presidency, he or she is first required to raise considerable sums of money to pay for the extensive costs of travel, polling, advisers, and

measuring equality

Scatterplots of Obama and Trump Vote and Minority Populations

Because presidents are elected by the Electoral College, candidates need to focus their campaigns on winning key states. As a result, the Electoral College has traditionally been viewed as detrimental to minority candidates because most states are majority White. Barack Obama's 2012 and Donald Trump's 2016 general election victories, however, provide evidence rejecting the hypothesis that the Electoral College disadvantages minority candidates. We demonstrate this with the two sets of three graphs in Figures 7.1, 7.2, and 7.3 depicting the relationship of the percentage of the state that is Black, Latino, and White with the percentage of the vote that Obama received in the state. Social scientists refer to these graphs as scatterplots. For each scatterplot, the x-axis reports the percentage of the state that is Black, Latino, or White and the y-axis shows the percentage of the vote Obama received in the 2012 general election. Each data point on the scatterplot represents each state (and one represents the District of Columbia, which has three electoral votes). As a basis of comparison, we

provide the same information in Figures 7.4, 7.5, and 7.6 for Donald Trump, a White candidate.

If the data points in the scatterplot appear to coalesce around a line that trends upward, then there is evidence that the greater the proportion of the group living in a state, the higher the percentage of the vote Obama or Trump received. That is, there is a positive relationship between the presence of the group in a state's population and support for Obama or Trump. If there is a clear pattern of a line trending downward, then the greater the proportion of the group living in a state, the lower the percentage of the vote Obama or Trump received. That is, there is a negative relationship between the presence of the group in a state's population and support for Obama or Trump. If there is no line that discernibly trends upward or downward, then there is no relationship between the percentage of the group living in a state and the vote Obama or Trump received.

In the three scatterplots for Obama, there does not appear to be any obvious pattern. In other words,

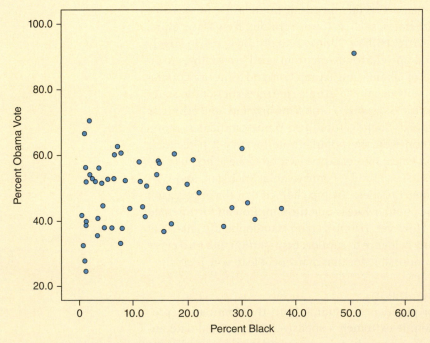

Figure 7.1 Scatterplot of Black Population and Obama 2012 Vote

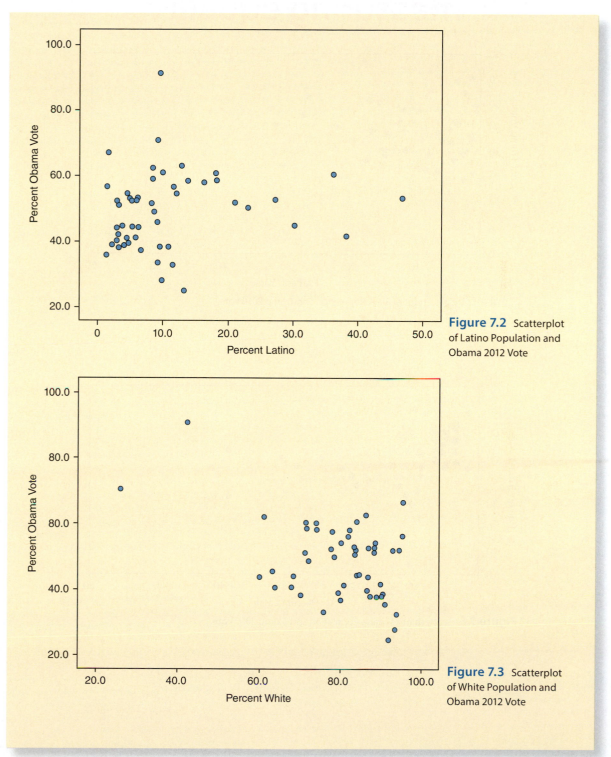

Figure 7.2 Scatterplot of Latino Population and Obama 2012 Vote

Figure 7.3 Scatterplot of White Population and Obama 2012 Vote

(Continued)

measuring equality _(Continued)

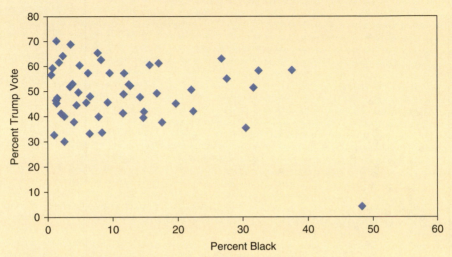

Figure 7.4 Scatterplot of Black Population and Trump 2016 Vote

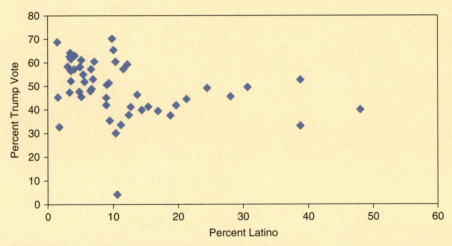

Figure 7.5 Scatterplot of Latino Population and Trump 2016 Vote.

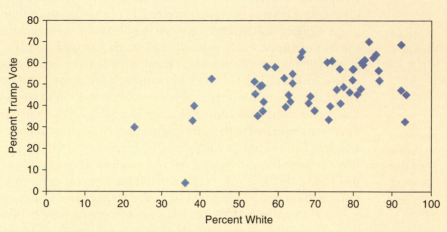

Figure 7.6 Scatterplot of White Population and Trump 2016 Vote

Obama did just as well in states with high Black, Latino, and White populations as he did in states with low populations of each group. Although Obama did better among Blacks and Latinos than he did among Whites, his appeal clearly crossed racial boundaries. He was quite successful in such largely White states as Iowa, Maine, Vermont, and New Hampshire. This appeal among White voters meant that the Electoral College did not present a barrier to the minority candidate. The patterns are generally similar for Donald Trump. Despite the fact that Blacks and Latinos overwhelmingly voted for Clinton, there does not appear to be a relationship between the percent of Blacks and Latinos living in a state and Trump's electoral success. However, there does appear to be a slight relationship between a state's White composition and its support for Trump—he tended to do better in states with a higher concentration of Whites.

Sources: Vote result data from Election of 2012. Adapted from J. Woolley & G. Peters, *The American Presidency Project.* Santa Barbara: University of California at Santa Barbara. Retrieved January 18, 2013, from http://www.presidency.ucsb.edu/showelection.php?year=2012. Population data from U.S. Census. *State and County QuickFacts.* Retrieved January 18, 2013, from http://quick-facts.census.gov/qfd/index.html; CNN. Presidential results. Retrieved November 13, 2016, from http://www.cnn.com/election/results/president; U.S. Census Bureau. *QuickFacts.* Retrieved November 13, 2016, from https://www.census.gov/quickfacts/table/SEX255215/00, both.

advertising. Previous minority candidates had been disadvantaged in raising money, but in his 2008 campaign, President Obama significantly outraised all of his rivals in both the primary and general elections.[23] In 2012, President Obama still outraised his Republican opponents, including his general election rival Mitt Romney, but the margin was closer.[24] A significant reason for Obama's successful fundraising was his campaign's ability to use high-tech data-mining techniques that target individual contributors according to each person's online activity, social media use, and purchases. The Obama campaign also used these techniques to target people to encourage them to vote.[25]

In 2016, Hillary Clinton and her allies raised far more money than Donald Trump and his allies did—$973.2 million to $564.3 million.[26] Nonetheless, Clinton's monetary advantage was not enough to secure victory. In fact, she was not as successful as Obama in generating turnout because overall voter turnout in 2016 was the lowest in terms of percentage since 1996.[27]

A significant difference between the 2008 and subsequent elections was the rise of **Super PACs**. Super PACs, which emerged in 2010, are political action committees allowed to raise an unlimited amount of money from any source, including individuals, corporations, labor unions, and interest groups. They can spend this money in support of or opposition to any political candidate, including people running for president, as long as their activities are not directly coordinated with a campaign. Super PACs are extremely influential in elections because unlike campaigns, which are restricted in how much money they can raise from individuals or corporations, they are able to raise unlimited funds. Furthermore, because individuals or corporations can donate an unlimited amount of money to Super PACs, they can dominate political campaigns.[28] A total of 2,392 Super PACs raised more than $1.79 billion and spent over $1.06 billion in the 2016 election.[29] As Figures 7.7 and 7.8 show, in 2016 Hillary Clinton got more support than Donald Trump did from Super PACs and outside groups, but Super PACs spent more money overall advocating for conservatives than they did advocating for liberals. Figure 7.7 shows the amount of money that outside groups spent on major presidential candidates in 2016. Figure 7.8 shows the general amount of money that the top 20 Super PACs spent on liberal and conservative candidates and messages in 2016.

Super PACs Political action committees allowed to raise an unlimited amount of money from any source, including individuals, corporations, labor unions, and interest groups. These committees are then allowed to spend this money in support of or opposition to any political candidate, including people running for president, so long as their activities are not directly coordinated with a campaign.

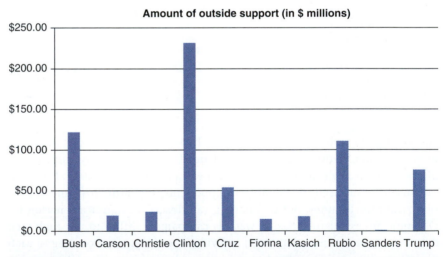

Figure 7.7 Amount of Outside Support (In $ Millions) Each Major Democratic and Republican Presidential Candidate Received in 2016

Source: Data Adapted from Center for Responsive Politics, "2016 Presidential Race: Campaign Funding by Candidate," Open Secrets, Retrieved June 29, 2018 from https://www.opensecrets.org/pres16; Center for Responsive Politics, "Also-Rans 2016 Presidential Race," Open Secrets, Retrieved June 29, 1018 from https://www.opensecrets.org/pres16/also-rans.

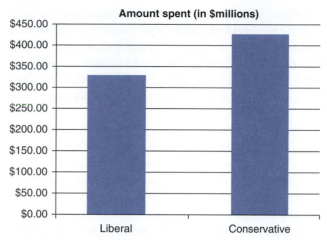

Figure 7.8 Amount in Millions of Dollars that the Top 20 Super PACs (in Terms of Money Raised) Spent in Support of Liberal and Conservative Candidates and Messages
Source: Data Adapted from Center for Responsive Politics, "Super PACs: 2016 Cycle," Open Secrets, Retrieved June 29, 2018 from http://www.opensecrets.org/pacs/superpacs.php?cycle=2016.

Presidential Power

Although the Framers of the Constitution recognized the necessity of a national executive branch, they were wary of executive power. As a result, the U.S. Constitution provides for only limited presidential powers. The Framers designed the presidency primarily to exert minimal influence on policymaking; instead, the president should focus on protecting the nation and administering policies enacted by Congress. As Alexander Hamilton wrote in *Federalist No. 70*, "Energy in the executive is a leading character in the definition of good government. It is essential to the protection of the community against foreign attacks . . . to the steady administration of the laws . . . to the security of liberty against the enterprises and assaults of ambition, of faction, and of anarchy."[30] Nineteenth- and early-twentieth-century presidents kept to this limited role. Clearly, there were exceptions, such as Abraham Lincoln, who increased his authority to fight the Civil War, but for the most part early presidents followed the lead of Congress.

That focus changed with Franklin Roosevelt in 1933. His presidency was the beginning of the **modern presidency**, in which the president shares policymaking power with Congress and attempts to lead Congress.[31] Consequently, presidents can use this power to shape civil rights policymaking. Many scholars see a mixed record on presidents' use of their power to advance civil rights, depending on the president. For example, they consider President Lyndon Johnson a strong advocate of civil rights policies, whereas Ronald Reagan sought policies that minority groups generally opposed. However, scholar Russell Riley shows that both premodern and modern presidents, including Johnson, avoided taking the lead on civil rights action unless public opinion (see Chapter 10) and social movements (see Chapter 12) sufficiently pressured them to do so.[32]

Settle a military crisis from the White House.

Modern Presidency Since Franklin Roosevelt in 1933, the conception of the presidency, which is characterized by a powerful president who seeks to lead Congress, connects with the American public, and presides over an enormous executive branch.

In this section, we analyze presidential power by looking at the administrative, foreign, and domestic powers of the modern president. We explain how presidential power is broad and yet has limitations. In doing so, we address how presidential power affects racial and ethnic minorities. In subsequent sections, we then focus on executive branch organization in the modern presidency and the presidents' success and failure in leading Congress in policymaking.

Administrative Powers of the President

The administrative power of the president refers to the president's authority to enforce laws and ensure that policies take effect. Although administrative power entails presidents carrying out the will of Congress, it often provides presidents with the ability to shape public policy because they enjoy wide discretion when enforcing laws. For example, the Obama administration emphasized enforcement of civil rights laws in an effort to limit racial profiling and stop housing discrimination and hate crimes against racial and ethnic minorities, religious minorities, women, and members of the LGBTQ community, but the Trump administration has not as vigorously enforced civil rights laws for those groups.[33]

Signing Statements
Presidential declarations issued along with legislative bill signings that express reservations about parts of a bill or announce an unwillingness to enforce aspects of a bill.

Presidents have also exercised discretion in enforcing laws using **signing statements**, in which presidents submit a proclamation concerning their interpretation of a bill when they sign it into law. Many signing statements merely comment on the benefits of the law, but they can be more controversial when the president expresses reservations about aspects of a bill. At times, a signing statement can even indicate areas that the president intends not to enforce. Presidents have used signing statements since the administration of James Monroe, but their use has increased tremendously since the 1980s.[34]

Under President George W. Bush, the use of signing statements became more controversial because he used them to ignore aspects of laws requiring better treatment of detainees captured in Iraq and Afghanistan. At the end of 2007 and in early 2008, President Bush angered many civil rights leaders, as well as members of Congress, when he issued a signing statement indicating that he could ignore some of the sanctions that Congress had imposed on the government of Sudan for egregious human-rights violations it was committing in Darfur.[35] As a candidate, Barack Obama criticized President Bush's use of signing statements, but as president, he issued 41. Although this figure seems large, it pales in comparison to the 160 signing statements that George W. Bush issued during his presidency.[36] Despite serving less than two years in office and enjoying majorities in both Houses of Congress during his first two years, President Trump has issued several signing statements. One controversial statement expressed his disagreement with a bill that sanctioned Iran, North Korea, and Russia. Although Trump signed the bill, he called it "significantly flawed."[37]

Executive Orders Directives that the president issues to subordinates in the executive branch and that have the force of law.

Presidents also exert administrative power by issuing **executive orders**, which are directives to executive branch employees to carry out specific actions. Executive orders are administrative in nature because they entail the president's commanding a subordinate. Some executive orders also affect public policy, especially in the area of racial and ethnic discrimination. For example, in 1943,

President Franklin Roosevelt signed Executive Order 9066, which forcibly relocated more than 100,000 Japanese Americans from the West Coast to internment camps in the desert. However, in 1941, Roosevelt advanced racial and ethnic equality by issuing Executive Order 8802, which banned racial, ethnic, and religious discrimination in the federal government and in defense companies under contract with the federal government.[38] In 1965, President Lyndon Johnson issued Executive Order 11246, which required that businesses contracting with the federal government "take affirmative action to ensure that applicants are employed and that employees are treated during employment, without regard to their race, color, religion, sex, or national origin."[39] This executive order was significant in establishing affirmative action and accelerating the economic and social progress of racial and ethnic minorities. Executive orders also affect foreign policy. Figure 7.9 shows the number of executive orders modern presidents have issued on an annual basis.

As we discussed in Chapter 5, executive actions can significantly influence immigration policy, especially concerning undocumented immigrants, many of whom are Latino. Recall that in 2012, President Obama announced the Deferred Action for Childhood Arrivals (DACA) policy, which prevented deporting people whose parents brought them illegally to the United States when they were children.[40] In September 2017, the Trump Administration—Trump had campaigned against DACA—announced that he would end the program

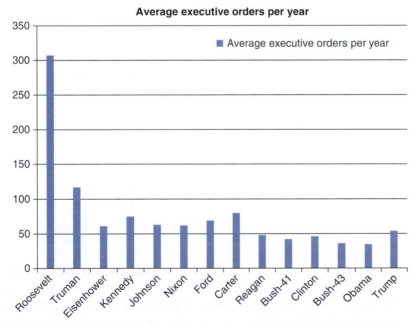

Figure 7.9 Average Number of Executive Orders Issued Per Year, Roosevelt Through Trump
Source: G. Peters and J. T. Woolley, "Executive Orders." The American Presidency Project. Santa Barbara: University of California at Santa Barbara. Retrieved June 29, 2018 from http://www.presidency.ucsb.edu/data/ orders.php.

in March, unless Congress passed a comprehensive immigration bill that included funding for a wall along the border between the United States and Mexico. After President Trump publically opposed a compromise developed in the Senate, Congress was unable to reach an agreement; therefore, President Trump's executive action would remain in effect.[41] However, in April 2018, a federal judge ruled that President Trump's DACA reversal was unconstitutional because his administration provided no legal basis for its decision. The Trump administration still has an opportunity to provide a sufficient legal basis; therefore, the status of this policy is still undetermined.[42]

Article 2 of the Constitution grants presidents the power to nominate executive branch officials (we discuss executive branch personnel in the next section), ambassadors, and federal judges (we discuss judicial appointments in Chapter 9). In the private sector, the hiring of personnel is a key administrative task; similarly, the president's appointment power is an essential part of the presidential administrative function. There is, however, a check on the presidential appointment power because most appointments are subject to Senate confirmation. For the most part, the Senate approves presidents' executive branch nominations, but it has occasionally rejected nominees for character-related reasons, such as dishonest financial dealings or display of inappropriate behavior. In fact, the last time a cabinet member was rejected was in 1989 when the Senate rejected President George H. W. Bush's choice of former Texas Senator John Tower to be secretary of defense because of Tower's reputation for overuse of alcohol and mistreatment of women, as well as his financial dealings with defense contractors.[43] President Trump's nomination of Betsy DeVos to be the Secretary of Education resulted in a tie vote that Vice President Mike Pence had to break. Every Democrat and two Republicans voted against DeVos because of her lack of experience in public education, favoritism of private schools over public schools, and weak performance in her confirmation hearings. This vote was the first time that the Vice President needed to break a tie to confirm a cabinet secretary.[44] Occasionally, presidents will withdraw cabinet nominees who generate controversy and are unlikely to be confirmed. For example, in 2017 President Trump's nomination for Secretary of Labor Andrew Pudzer withdrew after reports emerged that his ex-wife accused him of domestic violence.[45]

Finally, Article 2 grants presidents the power to pardon and grant reprieves to convicted federal criminals. A reprieve alleviates a sentence but the conviction remains, whereas a pardon completely erases the conviction. Normally pardons and reprieves are not contentious, but in 2017, President Donald Trump's pardon of former Maricopa County, Arizona Sheriff Joe Arpaio was extremely controversial. Arpaio was convicted of criminal contempt because he continued to racially profile Latinos as part of his crackdown on illegal immigration, despite a court order to cease his discriminatory actions. Arpaio was facing possible jail time when Trump pardoned him, and civil rights organizations were extremely upset because President Trump rewarded someone who broke the law while targeting Latinos.[46]

Foreign Powers of the President

The Constitution gives the president three basic foreign policymaking powers: (1) receiving ambassadors from other nations, (2) negotiating treaties, and (3) serving as commander-in-chief of the armed forces. Modern presidents have tremendously expanded their power over foreign policy. In fact, in 1936 the U.S. Supreme Court recognized the president as the "sole organ" in foreign affairs.[47] As we will soon see, even when Congress has constitutional authority over foreign affairs in areas such as treaty ratification (for the Senate) and declaration of war, the office of the president has usurped Congress's foreign policy powers.

Article 2 of the Constitution gives the president the authority to negotiate treaties, but it requires that two-thirds of the Senate ratify a treaty for it to take effect. Occasionally, the Senate has rejected treaties that presidents negotiated, but the Senate approves the vast majority of treaties. Most notably, it rejected the Treaty of Versailles at the end of World War I because too many senators opposed the requirement that the United States commit military troops to European conflicts.[48] Despite the ratification requirement, presidents possess the authority to withdraw from treaties without seeking the Senate's consent. For instance, in 2002 President George W. Bush unilaterally withdrew the United States from the Anti-Ballistic Missile Treaty with Russia to pursue a space-based missile defense system.[49]

As an alternative to treaties, presidents have enhanced their foreign-policy authority by negotiating with foreign nations through **executive agreements**, which are pacts between presidents and foreign nations that do not require the Senate's approval. The U.S. Supreme Court has upheld the legitimacy of executive agreements and has ruled that they enjoy the same legal status as treaties.[50] As a result, modern presidents have increasingly relied on executive agreements as a way to avoid the Senate's check on their authority to negotiate with other nations. During the first fifty years of the American Republic (1789–1839), presidents negotiated twice as many treaties as executive agreements. However, since 1990 presidents have used executive agreements nine times more often than treaties.[51]

Executive Agreements
Agreements between the president and foreign nations that, because they are not treaties, do not need the approval of the Senate.

The president's commander-in-chief power gives him considerable influence over foreign policy. The Framers of the Constitution intended for Congress to declare war—granting what are called **Congressional War Powers**— and then, in the role of commander-in-chief, the president assumes the responsibility for fighting the war. This arrangement is consistent with the Constitution's basic design that the president carries out the policies that Congress makes.

Prior to the 1950s, either Congress declared war or presidents only sent troops into limited engagements without congressional authorization. In 1950, however, President Harry Truman dispatched U.S. forces into the Korean conflict without any congressional authorization Congress declaring war. The Korean War, as it came to be called, was different from previously undeclared hostilities in that it required U.S. citizens to be drafted, which meant that ordinary citizens were forced into military service, and it resulted in heavy

Congressional War Powers
The power granted by the Constitution (in Article 1, Section 8) to Congress to decide when the United States goes to war.

See President George W. Bush's dramatic bullhorn speech at Ground Zero.

Enemy Combatants The status given to individuals captured in battle who do not belong to any national military force.

American casualties. Subsequently, presidents dispatched troops into major conflicts including Vietnam, the first Persian Gulf War, the Iraq war, the war in Afghanistan, and combat operations against ISIS without a congressional declaration of war, although Congress did authorize funding for those wars.

From the time of the attacks of September 11, 2001, when terrorists led by Osama bin Laden killed almost three thousand Americans by hijacking airliners and crashing them into buildings, President George W. Bush expanded the president's commander-in-chief power. In the immediate response to the attacks, Bush sent U.S. troops to Afghanistan to search for members of al Qaida—the terrorist group responsible for the attacks—and to topple the Taliban government in Afghanistan because it supported and harbored al Qaida terrorists. President Bush ordered that many of the people captured in this operation be sent to Guantánamo Bay, a naval facility in Cuba that the United States operates.

Because these detainees were not part of any national military force, President Bush classified them as **enemy combatants** instead of prisoners of war, who must be afforded internationally recognized humanitarian protections guaranteed under the Geneva Conventions—a set of treaties and international agreements that control the treatment of civilians and prisoners of war during armed conflict. As a result, the Bush administration claimed

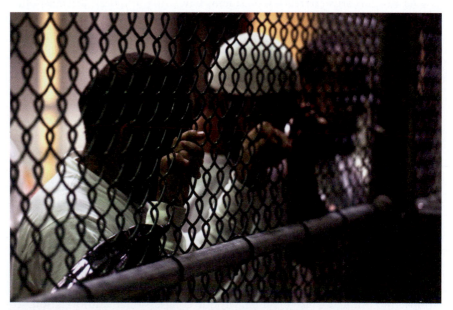

In this photo, Guantánamo detainees are pictured inside a common area at Camp 6 high-security detention facility at Guantánamo Bay U.S. Naval Base, Cuba, March 30, 2010. The vast majority of the detainees are people from the Middle East and South Asia, who were captured in the War on Terror launched after the attacks of September 11, 2011. Upon entering office in 2009, President Obama signed an executive order closing Guantánamo, but as of 2016 it still remains open.

it could bypass the Geneva Conventions in its treatment of these detainees. Furthermore, President Bush argued that these enemy combatants would be processed outside the normal U.S. criminal justice system and be held indefinitely without trial. Congress passed the Detainee Treatment Act and Military Commissions Act, which essentially codified into law President Bush's policy. However, the Supreme Court ruled that the Geneva Conventions do apply to the detainees and that the U.S. government cannot deny the detainees their habeas corpus rights.[52]

President Bush took other extraordinary powers in the name of fighting terrorism after 2001. He allowed "enhanced interrogation techniques" to be used on people captured in Afghanistan and in the subsequent war in Iraq. He claimed that these techniques were legal, but critics charged that they amounted to torture, which is illegal. The most controversial of these techniques was "waterboarding," an ancient method of eliciting information in which an interrogator ties down the victim, puts a cloth in his mouth, and pours water on him. This technique simulates drowning and instills in the victim an intense sense of panic. President Obama announced early in his presidency that the United States would no longer use enhanced interrogation techniques, including waterboarding.[53] However, President Trump has endorsed the use of torture, and he appointed Gina Haspel as the Director of the Central Intelligence Agency. During the Bush Administration, Haspel was a high ranking CIA officer who was people accused of being "intimately imbedded in the torture regime."[54]

President Bush also authorized the use of unmanned drones to attack suspected terrorists, despite the fact that these drones often killed civilians. However, unlike the case with torture, President Obama did not end the use of drones—in fact, he significantly expanded the drone program. According to a recent estimate, Obama ordered ten times more drone strikes than Bush did. He also authorized the killing of ten times more suspected terrorists and about twice as many civilians as President Bush did.[55]

Thus far, President Trump's foreign policy has diverged from President Obama's foreign policy. Trump ended two major executive agreements that Obama negotiated: a deal with Iran to stop their nuclear weapons production in exchange for ending sanctions on Iran[56] and a multinational agreement to curb greenhouse gas emissions in an effort to ameliorate climate change.[57] President Trump has also pursued an agreement with North Korea to end its production of nuclear weapons.[58]

Domestic Powers of the President

Although the Framers did not intend for the president to participate actively in making domestic policy, much of the modern president's activities are geared toward influencing domestic policy. Presidents influence the making of domestic policy through their constitutional power (in Article 1, Section 7) to **veto** bills passed by Congress. The Framers gave the president the veto power to prevent Congress from passing ill-considered laws, but they prevented the

Veto The president's ability to cancel legislation passed by Congress.

Pocket Veto A way for the president to overturn a bill passed by Congress when the president does not act on a bill within ten days of passage (excluding Sundays) and Congress adjourns in the meantime.

State of the Union Address An annual occasion in which the president speaks before Congress to suggest laws that Congress should pass.

president from using the veto in a tyrannical fashion by stipulating that Congress can override a veto by a two-thirds vote in each chamber. If the president neither signs nor vetoes a law after a ten-day period has passed (excluding Sundays), then the bill automatically becomes law. The president can defeat a bill through a **pocket veto**, which occurs if the president does not sign or veto a bill and Congress adjourns before the requisite ten days have elapsed. Pocket vetoes have become increasingly rare, but they can have important policy implications, even in the area of civil rights. For example, in 1990 President George H. W. Bush pocket-vetoed the Indian Preference Act, which would have provided advantages for American Indian–owned companies bidding for federal contracts.[59]

Modern presidents influence domestic policy mainly by suggesting to Congress which laws to pass. Although presidents lack the constitutional authority to introduce bills in Congress, they can suggest legislation, which a member of the House or the Senate then formally introduces. The U.S. Constitution gives the president an opportunity to recommend policy in Article 2, Section 3, which states that the president "shall from time to time give to the Congress Information on the State of the Union, and recommend to their Consideration such Measures as he shall judge necessary and expedient." The advent of television has allowed presidents to use the **State of the Union address** as an opportunity to build public support for their policy objectives. In 1947, President Harry Truman delivered the first televised State of the Union address during the daytime,[60] and in 1965 President Lyndon Johnson moved the State of the Union address to the evening to draw a larger audience.[61] President Johnson took advantage of his audience to promote his policy goals, including civil rights. He specifically promised to improve opportunities for African Americans "through the enforcement of the civil rights laws and elimination of barriers to the right to vote."[62]

However, modern presidents do not restrict themselves to the State of the Union address; they constantly urge Congress to pass their legislative priorities. Specifically, presidents propose an annual budget, which determines how much money the government spends in various sectors (e.g., defense, infrastructure, welfare, education, scientific research, and the arts). Presidents suggest other important economic and social policies that they want Congress to enact.

The types of programs that presidents advocate depend on their ideology and political party. Generally, Republican presidents, such as George W. Bush and Donald Trump, propose cutting domestic spending on social welfare programs (although overall domestic spending did increase under their administrations), restricting abortion rights, lessening business regulations, and decreasing taxes. Conversely, Democratic presidents, such as Bill Clinton and Barack Obama, seek increases in federal domestic spending on education, expansion of health insurance coverage, and preservation of the environment. In President Trump's first year, his legislative success rate was mixed. He successfully convinced Congress to pass tax cuts, but Congress

President Obama delivers his final State of the Union Address to Congress on January 12, 2016. The Constitution requires that the president report on the state of the union, but modern presidents have used this opportunity to set Congress's legislative agenda and take advantage of free media attention. President Obama used this opportunity to highlight what he believed were the achievements of his presidency in the areas of job creation, deficit reduction, environmental protection, health care, and foreign policy.

did not enact other key policy goals, such as repealing the Affordable Care Act (i.e., Obamacare), building a wall on the U.S.–Mexico border, reforming welfare, and investing in infrastructure.[63] Later in this chapter, we address in more detail the resources and strategies presidents use to accomplish their goals in Congress.

Executive Branch Organization

Because the tasks of administering the federal government are too extensive for the president to handle alone, a vast executive branch is necessary. Article 2 of the Constitution creates the office of the vice president and alludes to "public ministers and consuls" but does not specify how presidents should organize their administrations. During the eighteenth and nineteenth centuries, executive branch organization was fairly simple, but as the modern president's powers and responsibilities expanded during the twentieth century, executive branch organization became exceedingly more complex.

In fact, a large, complex executive branch is a defining characteristic of the modern presidency. There are many divisions within the executive branch. The closest circle comprises the vice president and the president's spouse. The circle then extends out to include the cabinet, the Executive Office of the

Vice President Charles Curtis (1929–1933) throws out a baseball before a game. Although he exerted little influence over policy while serving as vice president, Curtis is important because he is the only minority thus far to be vice president.

President, and the White House staff. In this section, we cover the various aspects of the executive branch, and we raise issues concerning racial and ethnic diversity throughout the executive branch.

The Vice President

The Framers intended for the vice president to assume the presidency in case of a vacancy and break tie votes in the Senate. Initially, Article 2, Section 1, of the U.S. Constitution stipulated that the person who received the second highest number of electoral votes would serve as vice president, but the Twelfth Amendment and the development of political parties allowed voters to select the president and vice president as a team. In Chapter 12, we discuss in more detail how the problems of the election of 1800 led to the Twelfth Amendment, as well as the amendment's impact on the development of political parties.

Until the middle of the twentieth century, vice presidents performed mainly ceremonial and official functions, and they had minimal impact on policymaking, except for the rare opportunities to break tie votes in the Senate. In the late twentieth century, vice presidents became more active policy advisers. Vice President Mike Pence has been active in working with Congress to pass the administration's legislative agenda (Pence formerly served in the U.S. House), representing the administration abroad, working with social conservatives to enact their policy preferences (e.g., religious exemptions to LGBTQ protection and limiting abortion), and defending the administration in the media, especially concerning President Trump's scandals.[64]

As with presidents, there has been little diversity among vice presidents. All vice presidents have been male, Christian, and, with one exception, White. President Herbert Hoover's (1929–1933) vice president, Charles Curtis, was a member of the Kaw tribe and thus was the only non-White vice president.[65] There have been major party vice presidential candidates who were neither male nor Christian. In 1984, Democratic presidential nominee Walter Mondale chose Geraldine Ferraro as the first female running mate on a major party ticket, but they lost the election to the all-male Republican ticket of Ronald Reagan and George H. W. Bush. In 2000, Democratic presidential candidate Al Gore chose Senator Joseph Lieberman (D-CT), who is Jewish, as his running mate, but that ticket lost to Republicans George Bush and Dick Cheney, both Protestants. In 2008, Republican candidate John McCain selected Alaska Governor Sarah Palin as his running mate, but they lost to the all-male Democratic ticket of Barack Obama and Joe Biden.

The President's Spouse

Because all presidents thus far have been male, the president's spouse is called the "first lady," and most first ladies have not publicly influenced their husbands' decisions. Until the middle of the twentieth century, cultural norms frowned on women participating in civic life outside the home, so first ladies could be active only behind the scenes. Eleanor Roosevelt (wife of President Franklin Delano Roosevelt) greatly expanded the role of first lady. She was deeply interested in politics and often publicly urged her husband to take positions favoring racial and ethnic minorities, women, and laborers. As social mores regarding the role of women evolved during the 1960s and 1970s, expectations of the first lady changed as well. As the first presidential spouse born after World War II, Hillary Clinton revolutionized the position of first lady. With a law degree and an impressive career in public service and private practice, she was as qualified to serve in a formal capacity as other members of the executive branch were. None of her predecessors, even Eleanor Roosevelt, could have made that claim.[66] As a result, President Clinton relied extensively on her advice, and he was the first president to appoint his wife to an official position besides that of first lady when in 1993 he named her as co-chair of the Health Care Task Force.[67] Since serving as first lady, Hillary Clinton became a successful politician in her own right, serving as a U.S. senator from New York, Secretary of State, and Democratic Party candidate for president in 2016.

In 2009, Michelle Obama became the first African American first lady. Like Hillary Clinton, Obama is an Ivy League–educated lawyer who had earned a six-figure income. She has publicly expressed support for her husband's policy proposals, but, unlike Hillary Clinton, Michelle Obama did not take an active policy role. Instead, she emphasized more family-oriented issues, such as childhood obesity and assisting spouses and children of active military personnel, and she was active in working on "grassroots" efforts on behalf of her husband's political campaigns.[68] First lady Melania Trump has thus far kept a much lower profile than her predecessors did. During the first five months of the Trump presidency, she lived separately from her husband in New York City so that their eleven-year-old son Baron could remain at his school. She has adopted causes, such as addressing the opioid crisis and cyberbullying, but she has generally eschewed media attention.[69] In the summer of 2018, Ms. Trump stirred controversy because she visited a facility that housed migrant children who were separated from their parents (see Chapter 5),

Eleanor Roosevelt (left) and Autherine Lucy smile as they appear together on the speaker's stand during a civil rights rally held in Madison Square Garden. Ms. Roosevelt's predecessors as first ladies, and even most of her successors, focused predominantly on ceremonial duties, but Ms. Roosevelt was deeply engaged in policy, particularly in the area of civil rights.

What did Melania
Trump mean?

Cabinet The key presidential
aides, each of whom heads an
executive branch department,
as well as others that the
president designates.

wearing a jacket emblazoned with words "I Really Don't Care Do U?" Although
observers disagreed over the meaning of the jacket, numerous commentators
contended that it was highly inappropriate for that situation.[70]

The Cabinet

A significant part of the executive branch is the **cabinet**, which consists of
the heads of each executive department and other officials presidents deem
worthy of cabinet-level status. The executive branch is divided into various
departments that specialize in a particular policy area. Table 7.1 lists the current executive departments and information on each department's cabinet secretary (as of November 2018). Cabinet officials are responsible for managing
their departments and advising the president, especially in their specific policy
areas. Although not directly members of the cabinet, deputy secretaries, undersecretaries, and assistant secretaries assist cabinet members in the performance of their duties, and all are important executive branch figures as well.

Although the cabinet members are part of the executive branch, Congress actually creates executive departments. In 1789, Congress created four
cabinet positions—Secretary of State, Secretary of the Treasury, Secretary
of War, and Attorney General—and these are currently considered the most

TABLE 7.1 The Cabinet, 2018

Department	Name	Race	Gender
State	Mike Pompeo	White	Male
Treasury	Steven T. Mnuchin	White	Male
Defense	James Mattis	White	Male
Justice	vacant	N/A	N/A
Interior	Ryan Zinke	White	Male
Agriculture	Sonny Perdue	White	Male
Commerce	Wilbur J. Ross, Jr.	White	Male
Labor	Alexander Acosta	Latino	Male
Health and Human Services	Alex Azar	White	Male
Housing and Urban Development	Benjamin S. Carson, Sr.	Black	Male
Transportation	Elaine L. Chao	Asian	Female
Energy	James Richard Perry	White	Male
Education	Elisabeth Prince DeVos	White	Female
Veterans Affairs	Robert Wilkie	White	Male
Homeland Security	Kirstjen Nielsen	White	Female

*Source: Adapted from White House. (n.d.). The Cabinet. Retrieved November 12, 2018, from https://www.
whitehouse.gov/the-trump-administration/the-cabinet/.*

important cabinet positions, often referred to as the "inner cabinet." Starting in the nineteenth century, as the federal government assumed more responsibilities, Congress added relevant executive departments. The first such department was the Department of the Interior, which Congress established in 1849 to manage expanding American land, as well as to control the native peoples who inhabited that land. Initially, the Interior Department was largely responsible for discriminating against American Indians, but since the late twentieth century, it has provided them with increased civil rights by promoting economic development, education, and health care for Indian tribes.[71]

Although the cabinet was designed to advise the president on policy matters, modern presidents have deemphasized the cabinet's advisory function. Presidents rarely convene meetings of their entire cabinet to consult on policy issues, and those meetings do not involve substantive policy discussions. One member of President Clinton's cabinet described the meetings this way: "Clinton cabinet meetings are informational, not deliberative. They occur when all the members need to be briefed on a particular initiative and told how much and how they will support it."[72] President Obama, especially during his second term, had ignored his cabinet even more than his predecessors. As presidential staff scholar Kathryn Dunn Tenpas notes, "While President Obama is not the first to keep his cabinet members at arm's length, the degree to which this administration has marginalized the critical role of the executive branch is stunning."[73] President Donald Trump has given his cabinet officers wide discretion to mold policy in their agencies. For example, the Department of Homeland Security has withdrawn protections for Salvadoran and Haitian immigrants who came to the United States after natural disasters in their home nations.[74]

Additionally, although each cabinet member deals with a specialized area, presidents rarely consult with their cabinet when seeking advice on a specific policy. Usually, each president calls on a select few cabinet members for advice on substantive issues. For example, when prosecuting the wars in Afghanistan and Iraq, George W. Bush relied more extensively on the advice of Secretary of Defense Donald Rumsfeld than on the advice of Secretary of State Colin Powell.[75] Although President Obama did not rely on many of his cabinet members, he did solicit advice from his secretaries of defense and of state in national security matters. When planning the mission to kill Osama bin Laden in 2011, President Obama relied heavily on his then secretaries of defense and state Robert Gates and Hillary Clinton, respectively.[76]

Instead of relying on the cabinet for policy advice, presidents usually use cabinet officials to build political and public support for policies. For example, President Obama's Labor Secretary, Tom Perez, publically defended President Obama's executive actions on immigration reform, most notably allowing undocumented immigrants with American-citizen children to work legally in the United States. In addition to being Latino, Perez's position as labor secretary meant that his job entailed persuading Americans to support President Obama's policies that relate to workplace issues, such as his immigration actions.[77] In June 2018, President Trump's Secretary of Homeland

Security Kristjen Nielsen publicly defended the administration's "zero tolerance" policy for undocumented Latino immigrants and asylum seekers from Mexico and Central America, even when the administration's enforcement of that policy separated children from their parents.[78]

For most of American history, cabinets consisted solely of White males, but starting in the twentieth century, diversity in the cabinet became more salient. Over a decade after women won the right to vote, Franklin Delano Roosevelt chose the first woman cabinet secretary (Frances Perkins, Secretary of Labor, 1933–1945). Women did not lead one of the four major executive departments (Treasury, State, Defense, and Justice) until the Clinton administration, when women served as attorney general (Janet Reno, 1993–2001) and secretary of state (Madeleine Albright, 1997–2001). Racial and ethnic diversity on the cabinet did not become an issue until the 1960s. In addition to the symbolic importance of a diverse executive branch, bringing the experience of minorities into the cabinet gives those groups a voice in executive branch politics. With pivotal appointments, several modern presidents advanced the diversity of the cabinet. Lyndon B. Johnson chose the first African

Homeland Security Secretary Kristjen Nielsen speaks to the media during the daily briefing, June 18, 2018. Nielsen repeated the Administration's false claims that federal law required them to separate immigrant children from their families, and she insisted that government officials were treating the children well. Because of intense public backlash over the policy, President Trump announced a couple of days later that the administration will no longer separate children from parents, essentially contradicting Nielsen's claims that the president lacked the power to reverse the policy.

American (Robert C. Weaver, Secretary of Housing and Urban Development, 1966–1968); Ronald Reagan chose the first Latino (Lauro Cavazos, Secretary of Education, 1988–1990);[79] and Bill Clinton chose the first Asian American (Norman Mineta, Secretary of Commerce, 2000–2001).[80]

Since the 1990s, presidential cabinets have become even more diverse. During the 1992 campaign, Clinton promised to appoint "an administration that looks like America,"[81] and his cabinet was considerably more diverse than that of any of his predecessors. President George W. Bush's cabinet was diverse as well. He was also the first president to appoint minorities to key cabinet positions. Colin Powell and Condoleezza Rice, both African Americans, served as Secretary of State from 2001 to 2005 and 2005 to 2009, respectively, and Alberto Gonzalez, a Latino, served as Attorney General from 2005 to 2007. Condoleezza Rice was the first Black woman to serve in a major cabinet position. In 2009, President Obama appointed the first African American Attorney General, Eric Holder, and he replaced Holder with Loretta Lynch, the first African American female to serve as Attorney General. However, in President Obama's second term, his cabinet became less diverse than it was in his first term. Critics especially chided the president for replacing female cabinet secretaries with males, particularly because he replaced Secretary of State Hillary Clinton with John Kerry.[82] Despite this trend toward more diverse cabinets, President Trump's cabinet is noticeably less diverse than his predecessors' cabinets, including recent Republican presidents. All of his inner cabinet (State, Treasury, Attorney General, and Defense) have been White males. The few minority and female cabinet members in his administration hold the least important positions. In fact, a recent analysis reveals that President Trump's cabinet is the least diverse since President Reagan's first cabinet in 1981.[83] Table 7.1 lists the members of President Trump's cabinet, as well as their race/ethnicity and gender.

The Executive Office of the President

Because modern presidents do not rely heavily on their cabinet for advice, they use the **Executive Office of the President (EOP)** for expert, reliable counsel. The EOP is divided into different departments (see Table 7.2), each of which provides the president with expert advice. Unlike cabinet officers, who are selected for political reasons, EOP officials are selected for their expertise, which is why presidents prefer to consult with the EOP instead of the cabinet. However, cabinet officers do serve in EOP departments (e.g., the Secretaries of State, Defense, and Treasury are part of the National Security Council).[84] Many EOP members also serve political roles, such as defending the president's proposals; therefore, presidents want to ensure that members of the EOP share their views on relevant public policy issues. For example, the Director of the Office of Management and Budget (OMB) not only prepares the budget but also makes statements and issues press releases in support of the president's fiscal policies. Recently, President Trump's OMB Director Mick Mulvaney argued publicly that President Trump's economic policies,

Executive Office of the President (EOP) A part of the executive branch that is divided into specific offices and contains key advisers who assist the president in managing the executive branch and developing policies.

Early in President Barack Obama's second term, he named a number of new key administration officials, most of whom were White males. This photo emerged after public criticism of the president for his lack of diverse appointments. The photo depicts the president in a staff meeting without any women present; however, Senior Advisor Valerie Jarrett was in the room, although she was not visible in the photo.

including tax cuts, will generate so much economic growth that they will not increase the deficit.[85]

Racial, ethnic, and gender diversity in the EOP is important because it influences public policies that affect the lives of racial minorities, but there has been little diversity in the top echelons of the EOP. One notable exception was Franklin Raines, the first African American to serve as Director of the Office of Management and Budget under President Clinton from 1996 to 1998.[86] In his first term, President Obama appointed minorities to serve in key positions in the EOP, including U.S. Trade Representative Ron Kirk, who is Black. Kirk was the first African American trade representative, and before that, he was the first Black mayor of Dallas, Texas.[87] As of June 2018, none of President Trump's appointments to significant EOP positions is a racial or ethnic minority.

The White House Staff

White House Staff The president's personal advisers, who do not need senatorial approval when appointed and provide critical political and policy advice to the president.

The **White House staff** includes the president's personally selected advisers, in whom he places considerable trust when seeking counsel. Whereas Congress creates executive departments and offices in the Executive Office of the President, and the Senate approves presidential nominees to those positions, the president solely determines the positions that exist on his White House staff, and White House staff members do not require the Senate's approval. Because

TABLE 7.2 Executive Office of the President

Department	Year Established
Council of Economic Advisers	1946
Council on Environmental Quality	1969
Domestic Policy Council	1993
Homeland Security Council	2001
National Economic Council	1993
National Security Council	1947
Office of Administration	1977
Office of Faith-Based and Community Initiatives	2001
Office of Management and Budget	1970
Office of National AIDS Policy	2001
Office of National Drug Control Policy	1988
Office of Science and Technology Policy	1976
Office of the First Lady	Traditional
President's Foreign Intelligence Advisory Board	1956
Privacy and Civil Liberties Board	2004
United States Trade Representative	1963
USA Freedom Corps	2002
White House Fellows Office	1964
White House Military Office	Traditional

Source: *Adapted from White House (n.d.).* Executive Office of the President. *Retrieved July 22, 2008, from http://www.whitehouse.gov /government/eop.html.*

the president is not required to consult with Congress concerning the White House staff, he can trust that those individuals have only his interests in mind.

The White House staff contains key advisers on domestic policy, foreign policy, legal counsel, and communication with the public. A fundamental White House staff position is the **Press Secretary**, who communicates directly with the members of the press who cover the White House. The Press Secretary conducts daily briefings with the media to answer questions and explain the actions of the president. As the opening story demonstrates, presidents also employ a **Chief of Staff**, who oversees executive branch personnel and filters all information from executive branch employees to the president. The Chief of Staff often determines which executive branch individuals meet with the president and for how long.

Racial and ethnic diversity is a key issue with the White House staff. As we discussed earlier, minority representation is important for symbolic reasons as

Press Secretary A member of the president's staff who conducts daily briefings with members of the media.

Chief of Staff A key assistant to the president who coordinates executive branch employees and serves as a link between other presidential advisers and the president.

well as for bringing a racial minority perspective into policymaking (see "Evaluating Equality: Racial and Ethnic Representation in the Executive Branch" for more on this issue). In 1955, President Eisenhower appointed E. Frederic Morrow as White House Administrative Officer for special projects; he was the first African American to have a key position on the White House staff.[88] Even so, racial and ethnic minorities have continued to be underrepresented in important White House staff positions. All Press Secretaries and Chiefs of Staff have been White. Condoleezza Rice (2001–2005) and Susan Rice (2013–2019) are the only minorities (and minority females) who served as the National Security Advisor.

Presidents and Congress

A key aspect of presidential politics concerns the relationship between the executive branch and Congress. In our system of checks and balances (see Chapter 2), the president does not act alone—he must be concerned with Congress. Presidents seek to set Congress's agenda, but they are not necessarily guaranteed success. Accordingly, an important element of the president's policymaking role entails persuading Congress to enact his legislative proposals. Renowned presidency scholar Richard Neustadt explains that presidents are forced to persuade members of Congress by bargaining with congressional leaders.[89] Conversely, leading political scientist Samuel Kernell demonstrates that since the 1970s, bargaining has not been a viable strategy for presidents and they, instead, take their case directly to the public.[90] This section addresses both how presidents negotiate with members of Congress and how presidents try to mobilize public support. In addition, this section covers how executive–congressional relations often influence minority-group politics.

Negotiating with Congress

When dealing with Congress, presidents employ a variety of strategies to impel Congress to agree to support their policies, including the threat of a veto. Presidents must exercise caution when threatening a veto because Congress could put the president in the undesirable position of having to choose between vetoing popular legislation and surrendering to Congress. For example, the Civil Rights Act of 1990 was designed to make it easier for minority employees to sue employers for discrimination. President George H. W. Bush threatened to veto the bill because he believed that technical legal language in the bill would lead to racial quotas, and he tried to convince Congress to change the law so that employers would have a better chance of defending their practices. When Congress refused, the president vetoed the act, despite public support for it and the fact that it had passed by a vote of 273–154 in the House and 62–34 in the Senate.[91] The following year, however, the president negotiated with congressional leaders to fashion the Civil Rights Act of 1991, which included language that made it clear that racial quotas were not required.[92] President Bush signed this bill.

evaluating equality

Racial and Ethnic Representation in the Executive Branch

The modern executive branch is vast and tremendously important to the success of the presidency. It consists of the cabinet, subcabinet, Executive Office of the President, and White House staff. Moreover, race and ethnicity are central to American politics and to the presidency in particular. Therefore, racial and ethnic representation in the executive branch is a key debate in American politics.

Supporters of diversity in the executive branch argue that a diverse cabinet is important for symbolic reasons. Diverse cabinets represent the progress the United States has made in its treatment of racial minorities. Furthermore, presidents who can show the public that their cabinets reflect the background of the nation are able to claim more legitimacy for their actions, especially when those actions affect racial and ethnic minorities. Recall candidate Bill Clinton's 1992 pledge to appoint a cabinet that "looks like America." Additionally, racial and ethnic minorities in the executive branch can bring their unique experiences and perspectives into presidential decision making. Accordingly, there are substantive reasons to insist that presidents have diverse executive branches.

Critics argue, however, that race and ethnicity should not factor into presidential decisions to appoint executive branch officials. Presidents should be concerned solely with nominating individuals based on their qualifications, regardless of race or ethnicity. Moreover, many observers argue that a White executive branch official is just as capable as a minority official to represent, or even promote, minority interests. Recall that President Trump's cabinet is the least diverse in almost 40 years.

- Does the need for diversity vary among the different executive branch divisions—the cabinet versus the Executive Office of the President or the White House staff?
- Does the fact that former President Obama is Black influence the need for diversity?

Because presidents are the highest-ranking elected officials within their political party, they are leaders of their political party, and they use that position to win support in Congress. The importance of party leadership depends on whether the president governs in times of divided government or unified government. **Divided government** occurs when the president is of one party and one or both houses of Congress is controlled by the other party. Presidents face difficulty persuading Congress to adopt their proposals during periods of divided government. **Unified government** occurs when the president and the majority of both houses of Congress are of the same political party; the president's chances of legislative success improve during periods of unified government.

Obama enjoyed unified government during the first two years of his presidency (2009–2011); therefore, he was able to accomplish much of his legislative agenda, including passing laws to stimulate the economy and regulate the banking and financial services industry, as well enacting the Affordable Care Act, which expanded health insurance for millions of Americans. However, President Obama soon faced a divided government, with Republicans controlling the House of Representatives after the 2010 election and the Senate after the 2014 election. After 2011, House Republicans voted numerous times to repeal the Affordable Care Act, but the Democratic Senate refused to pass

Divided Government A period in which the president is of one political party and the majority of one or both houses of Congress is of the other party.

Unified Government A period in which both houses of Congress are controlled by the same party as the president.

a similar bill. However, in 2016, when Republicans controlled both houses, Congress voted to repeal Obama's health care bill, but the president's veto of the repeal legislation kept the Affordable Care Act intact.[93]

Even in periods of unified government, however, presidents cannot always rely on support from other party members in Congress, as constituent pressures could lead members of Congress to oppose the president's proposals. Recall that despite enjoying Republican control of Congress, President Trump has been unable to repeal the Affordable Care Act or pass his immigration policies. After the Democrats assumed control of the House in 2019, it is more unlikely that Trump will be able to enact his agenda. Consequently, presidents must negotiate with individual members of Congress to secure favorable outcomes. In exchange for congressional support, presidents offer political rewards, such as an invitation to dine at the White House, campaign appearances on behalf of a member of Congress, or federal appointments to a senator's or representative's friends and political supporters. Even personal visits and phone calls to individual members of Congress help presidents persuade members of Congress. President Lyndon Johnson was exceptionally skilled at these kinds of negotiations. Johnson convinced Southern senators and representatives to stop obstructing civil rights bills, and he ultimately succeeded in securing the passage of the landmark Civil Rights Act of 1964 and Voting Rights Act of 1965 (see Chapter 5). Johnson's predecessor John F. Kennedy lacked Johnson's negotiation skills; he could not convince Congress to pass these civil rights bills.[94]

President Trump speaks about guns and school safety as Senate Majority Whip John Cornyn (R-TX) and Senator Dianne Feinstein (D-CA) listen. Presidents and congressional leaders often try to work together to accomplish important policy goals, such as gun safety. Despite this meeting, Congress has yet to enact any meaningful policy on gun safety.

Presidents and the Public

Noted political science scholar Samuel Kernell maintains that bargaining directly with congressional leaders is unlikely to yield success; therefore, presidents "go public," which means that they take their case directly to the American people, hoping that increased support for their policies will force Congress to pass them. Presidents deliver these messages to the American people through the media.[95]

Presidents often use their popular support when trying to persuade Congress to pass their policy agenda. Because members of Congress want to please their constituents, they do not want to oppose a popular president. Some presidents have been able to claim a **mandate**, in which they argue that a solid election victory should translate into support for their policy priorities. For example, Lyndon Johnson used his landslide victory in 1964 to push for passage of civil rights laws and his War on Poverty programs.[96] Recent presidential elections have been closer; therefore, presidents have been less able to claim mandate, and, in fact, there is scholarly debate over whether presidential mandates really exist.[97] Nevertheless, public approval is a crucial tool that presidents use to convince Congress to pass their desired legislation.

> **Mandate** A president's claim to Congress that his election victory signifies the public's support for his policy preferences.

Public approval of a president varies by president and during different periods of his presidency. Most presidents' public support peaks early in their presidency, and then as presidents serve into their second term (if they have one), their popularity declines. Shortly after the attacks of September 11, 2001, President Bush enjoyed approval ratings in the upper 80 percent range, and during the early months of the Iraq war, his approval rating was in the 70 percent range. After his close reelection in 2004, President Bush's approval continuously dropped because of rising opposition to the Iraq war, ethical scandals in the administration, and the administration's failure to respond to the devastating effects of Hurricane Katrina. By summer 2008, his approval rating was in the upper 20 percent range. President Obama started in the mid-60 percent range, but opposition to his health care bill and an initially sluggish economic recovery caused his approval to decrease to the mid-40 percent range by early 2012. As President Obama commenced his reelection campaign in 2012, his approval rose to about 50 percent, and by Election Day his approval was over 50 percent. However, after the botched implementation of the health care bill in late 2013, President Obama's approval ratings fell throughout 2014. Nevertheless, by the time he left office, President Obama's approval rating was about 55 percent. Unlike his predecessors, President Trump's approval was low at the start of his presidency—about 45 percent. Because of scandals and his controversial statements, Trump's approval declined to the mid-30 percent range during the first year of his term. By the fall of 2018, Trump's approval rebounded to the low-forties.[98]

How do we know what "the people" think?

Race and ethnicity often influence how members of the public perceive the president. As a Black candidate, Barack Obama strongly appealed to African Americans, Latinos, and Asian Americans, and his approval had consistently been higher among Blacks and Latinos than it had been with Whites.

Additionally, President Clinton also enjoyed significantly higher support among Blacks than he did among whites. Figure 7.10 demonstrates that Republican Presidents Bush and Trump have greater support among Whites than among Blacks, whereas Democratic presidents Clinton and Obama had higher support among African Americans than among Whites. Still, white support for Clinton was higher than White support for Obama, Bush, and Trump.

Congressional Investigations of the Executive Branch

Because the Framers feared executive tyranny, they wanted to ensure that Congress could prevent the executive branch from becoming too powerful. As a result, congressional committees investigate corruption or incompetence within the executive branch. Congressional investigations can even lead to **impeachment** of the president. Impeachment occurs when the U.S. House officially charges the president, vice president, or a federal judge with a serious violation. Once an official is impeached, the Senate decides whether to remove that person from office, which requires a two-thirds vote. Thus far, the House of Representatives has impeached only Andrew Johnson and Bill Clinton. President Johnson was impeached in 1868 because he dismissed Secretary of War Edwin Stanton in violation of the Tenure of Office Act. President

Impeachment The process by which the House of Representatives charges a president, vice president, or federal judge with a high crime or misdemeanor; the Senate can then decide to remove that official from office with a two-thirds vote.

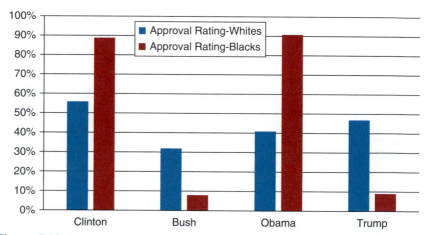

Figure 7.10 Approval Rating Among Whites and Blacks for Presidents Clinton, Bush, and Obama at the End of Their Second Terms and President Trump After One Year

Sources: Clinton: Newport, F. (2010, August 3). Blacks and Whites continue to differ sharply on Obama—Graph: President Clinton's job approval averages by race. Gallup. Retrieved July 3, 2018, from https://news.gallup.com/poll/141725/blacks%20whites-continue-differ-sharply-obama.aspx.
Bush: Bush job approval rating: Little difference among Whites, Hispanics. (2007, June 29). Gallup. Retrieved July 3, 2018, from https://news.gallup.com/poll/28009/bush-job-approval-rating-little-difference-among-whites-hispanics.aspx.
Obama: Obama weekly job approval by demographic groups (averaged). (2016, March). Gallup. Retrieved July 3, 2018, from https://news.gallup.com/poll/121199/obama-weekly-job-approval-demographic-groups.aspx.
Trump: Party ideology, and race play key roles in Trump approval. (2018, January 22). Gallup. Retrieved July 3, 2018, from https://news.gallup.com/poll/226091/party-ideology-race-play-key-roles-trump-approval.aspx.

Clinton was impeached in late 1998, charged with perjury and obstruction of justice because he lied to investigators about an extramarital affair. The Senate declined to convict Johnson and Clinton, and each president remained in office until the end of his term.[99] Even if congressional investigations do not lead to impeachment, they can reveal embarrassing or incriminating information and inflict political damage on presidents.

Although Congress can compel executive branch officials to testify, presidents can in response invoke **executive privilege**, in which they shield confidential communications among executive branch officials to preserve national security or to ensure the integrity of the executive branch. In 1974, President Richard Nixon declared executive privilege to prevent a special prosecutor investigating Watergate from listening to audiotapes of his conversations with executive branch officials. In the case *United States v. Nixon* (1974), the Supreme Court officially recognized the existence of executive privilege but also limited its scope. The Court ruled that presidents can use executive privilege to protect information related to the official functioning of the executive branch, but they cannot use it to shield themselves from investigation of wrongdoing.[100]

Executive privilege was especially controversial during the Bush administration. Private organizations even sued the vice president for information concerning a task force that proposed energy policies, but the Supreme Court ruled that the vice president did not need to submit those documents.[101] President Obama first invoked executive privilege in June 2012 over a congressional investigation into "Fast and Furious," a botched federal sting operation that allowed illegal guns to enter Mexico. Mexican gangs then used these weapons to kill a federal agent. Although the Obama administration answered many questions and submitted thousands of pages of documents to congressional investigators, President Obama cited executive privilege and directed his Attorney General Eric Holder to withhold some information. The Republican-controlled House found Holder in contempt of Congress and sought to challenge the use of executive privilege in federal court. Democrats boycotted that vote, arguing that Republicans were motivated by partisanship. The Democratic-controlled Senate did not vote to find Holder in contempt or challenge the use of executive privilege.[102] Once Holder resigned in 2015, this issue was no longer salient.

As we discussed in Chapter 6, the extent of congressional investigations into the executive branch varies according to whether there is divided or unified government. For example, after a 2012 incident in Benghazi, Libya, in which terrorists killed four Americans (including an ambassador), House Republicans investigated the actions of the Democratic Obama administration, including then Secretary of State Hillary Clinton. This investigation lasted two years, cost $7 million, and resulted in 11 hours of testimony from Hillary Clinton. Democrats complained at the time that Republicans used this investigation only to damage Clinton's presidential campaign. However, in Republican Donald Trump's first two years of his presidency. House Republicans barely

Executive Privilege
Presidential authority to keep some of the communications among executive branch personnel private and free from Congress, the courts, and the public.

Learn about executive privilege and other presidential powers.

investigated charges that the Trump campaign conspired with Russia and that President Trump obstructed justice to cover up the conspiracy. House Republicans finished their investigation of the matter in less than a year, and their report criticized the FBI, which conducted the initial investigation, more than it criticized the Trump campaign. Moreover, House Republicans have attacked the independent investigation into Trump's action, despite the fact that as of July 2018, this independent investigation has secured multiple indictments and three guilty pleas from Trump campaign officials.[103] After Democrats won control of the House of Representatives in 2018, it is extremely likely that they will significantly increase investigations Donald Trump, his family, and his administration.

Conclusion

The presidency is undoubtedly a crucial position in U.S. government, and in this chapter, we discussed key aspects of presidential politics and power. The presidential selection process puts serious demands on anyone who wants to become president. As the chief law enforcer, the president enjoys considerable discretion in how policies affect people's everyday lives, and since the 1930s, the president has even been a leader in shaping foreign and domestic policies. Presidents preside over an expansive executive branch, and they possess considerable resources when dealing with Congress, including mobilizing public support. However, their influence can be limited. In short, the president is the single most important figure in American politics.

Given its political importance, the presidency features prominently in the politics of race and ethnicity. The president's discretion in enforcing laws greatly influences the extent to which civil rights laws actually limit discrimination, and there have been significant variations among different presidents in their willingness to enforce civil rights laws. Moreover, the president's ability to shape the diversity of the executive branch has been instrumental in the symbolic and substantive politics of race and ethnicity. As the opening story demonstrates, presidential staff can significantly affect a president's administration.

Barack Obama's election and presidency are obviously momentous in terms of minority group politics because he is the first non-White president. Although other minorities—such as Shirley Chisholm, Jesse Jackson, Al Sharpton, Bill Richardson, and Herman Cain—have vied for a major party nomination, Obama is the only minority to win a major party nomination and two general elections.

Despite the significance of Obama's election and reelection for minority-group politics, it is important to understand that race was not the only relevant factor. White presidents have affected the lives of racial and ethnic minorities. President Lyndon Johnson, for example, boldly used his powers to ensure that civil rights laws were vigorously enforced, skillfully worked with Congress to ensure the passage of landmark civil rights bills, and appointed more racial and ethnic minorities to key positions than any of his predecessors. Additionally, Americans of all races voted for Obama because of his opposition to the war in Iraq, his foreign policy views, his plans to improve the U.S. economy, and his stances on other issues such as health care, the environment, and gun control—none of which pertain to race and ethnicity. In fact, during his first term, President Obama devoted the bulk of his time and effort to foreign and domestic issues that transcend race. Nevertheless, Obama's replacement Donald Trump has extensively influenced the politics of race and ethnicity, given his racially charged rhetoric and actions, especially in the area of immigration. Moreover, as the opening story shows, even other key executive branch officials, such as chief-of-staff John Kelly, have influenced the politics of race and ethnicity.

review
REVIEW QUESTIONS

1. How can presidential powers influence civil rights?

2. Is diversity in the executive branch important? Why or why not?

3. How has the presidential selection process disadvantaged racial minority candidates, and why was Barack Obama able to overcome these disadvantages in 2008 and 2012?

4. Does Barack Obama's success mean that those disadvantages are no longer present? Why or why not?

5. What do President Trump's failure to secure immigration reform and his subsequent executive actions on immigration reveal about the presidency?

Check your understanding of Chapter 7.

terms
KEY TERMS

Cabinet p. 222
Caucus p. 203
Chief of Staff p. 227
Congressional War Powers p. 215
Divided Government p. 229
Electoral College p. 203
Enemy Combatants p. 216
Executive Agreements p. 215

Executive Office of the President (EOP) p. 225
Executive Orders p. 212
Executive Privilege p. 233
Impeachment p. 232
Mandate p. 231
Modern Presidency p. 211
Pocket Veto p. 218
Press Secretary p. 227

Primary p. 203
Signing Statements p. 212
State of the Union Address p. 218
Super PACs p. 210
Unified Government p. 229
Veto p. 217
White House Staff p. 226

Need to review key ideas in greater depth? Click here.

readings
ADDITIONAL READINGS

Jackson, J., Clemente, F., & Watkins, F. (1989). *Keep hope alive: Jesse Jackson's 1988 presidential campaign.* Boston: South End Press.

This book, a collection of primary source documents related to Jesse Jackson's 1988 run for the presidency, focuses specifically on Jackson's ideal of "hope," his views on economic policy, his national security ideas, and his call for justice for racial and ethnic minorities, women, gays and lesbians, older adults, people with disabilities, and the poor.

Laham, N. (1998). *The Reagan presidency and the politics of race: In pursuit of colorblind justice and limited government.* Westport, CT: Praeger.

This book chronicles President Ronald Reagan's attempts to reverse civil rights

Flashcard review.

policies enacted during the 1960s and 1970s and focuses specifically on Reagan's goals of ending affirmative action and willingness to allow private institutions receiving any federal funding, even indirectly, to discriminate on account of race, gender, age, or health.

Morrow, E. F. (1963). *Black man in the White House: A diary of the Eisenhower years by the Administrative Officer for Special Projects, the White House, 1955–1961*. New York: Coward-McCann.

The first African American to serve in the White House staff recounts his experiences, provides an honest assessment of Eisenhower's civil rights record, and describes the daily life of White House staffers and the critical role they play in serving their presidents.

Riley, R L. (1999). *The presidency and the politics of racial inequality: Nation keeping from 1831 to 1965*. New York: Columbia University Press, 1999.

This book historically analyzes presidents' impact on civil rights policies, from Andrew Jackson through Lyndon Johnson. Riley argues that presidents are so concerned with "nation keeping" that they do not pursue policies of racial equality, unless there is sufficient public will or social-movement pressure.

Thurber, J. A. (Ed.). (2011). *Obama in office*. Boulder, CO: Paradigm.

This is an edited volume in which leading political scientists contribute scholarly chapters that analyze different elements of President Obama's first two years in office.

Wolffe, R. (2009). *Renegade: The making of a president*. New York: Crown.

This book reveals some of the highs and lows of Obama's personal and political life prior to his national political career as well as providing a glimpse into the daily life of a presidential campaign.

The Bureaucracy: Career Government Employees, Accountability, and Race

An aerial photograph shows the devastation in Puerto Rico after Hurricane Maria in September 2017. Similar storms struck Texas and Florida, but many observers contend that the federal government's, particularly the Federal Emergency Management Agency, response was far more effective in Texas and Florida than it was in Puerto Rico.

Every year in late summer and early autumn, the Caribbean islands, the Atlantic Coast of the United States, and the coast of the Gulf of Mexico brace for hurricanes that can devastate communities with high winds and flooding, and 2017 was an especially bad year for Atlantic storms. Three catastrophic category 4 (winds speeds between 130 mph and 156 mph)[1] storms hit Americans within a period of one month: Harvey in Southeastern Texas, Irma in Florida (after wreaking havoc in the Caribbean), and Maria in Puerto Rico. These storms caused considerable damage, such as massive floods, demolished homes, extensive power losses, and numerous injuries and even deaths. The combined cost of the three hurricanes was $265 billion.[2]

Although the president, congress, and state and local officials address natural disasters, such as these hurricanes, the primary organization that responds to natural disasters is the Federal Emergency Management Agency (FEMA). In 1979, President Jimmy Carter created FEMA as an independent agency to coordinate the federal response to major disasters in order to ameliorate damage and aid in recovery efforts. In 2003, the federal government moved FEMA to the Department of Homeland Security, an executive branch department (see Chapter 7).[3] Consequently, FEMA was the entity that was primarily responsible for responding to the three major hurricanes in 2017.

FEMA's response to these storms was undoubtedly mixed because it provided much more assistance to Texas and Florida than it did for Puerto Rico, which actually sustained the heaviest amount of destruction. Not only was Maria the strongest of the three storms, but Hurricane Irma also damaged Puerto Rico before it hit Florida. More specifically, nine days after Maria, FEMA delivered only 5,000 tarps to Puerto Rico, which had almost 500,000 homes damaged. FEMA delivered 98,000 tarps to Florida and 20,000 tarps to Texas nine days after Harvey. FEMA provided Florida more than ten times the number of meals it provided Puerto Rico, and it provided Florida more than twice the water it provided Puerto Rico. Although the gaps were smaller, FEMA gave Texans more food and water than it gave Puerto Ricans. The extent of

FEMA's response diverged as well because FEMA devoted 30,000 federal workers after Harvey and 22,000 workers after Irma, but it spared only 10,000 workers to assist after Maria.[4] In an attempt to compensate for its tepid response in Puerto Rico, FEMA contracted with private companies, paying them millions of taxpayer dollars to provide meals and tarps to Puerto Ricans. However, FEMA did not carefully vet whether those companies were capable of succeeding, despite obvious evidence that they were incapable of filling their orders.[5] As of the summer of 2018—almost one year after Maria struck Puerto Rico—more than 4,600 Puerto Ricans died as a result of the storm[6] and more than 100,000 Puerto Ricans still lack electricity.[7] Finally, because so many Puerto Ricans were homeless as a result of Maria, FEMA provided displaced persons with temporary housing in the mainland United States (mainly in Florida, Massachusetts, and New York). However, in the summer of 2018, FEMA sought to end the housing assistance, and although a federal judge extended the timeframe, the evacuees were forced to leave by mid-September.[8] Democrats in Congress, which has oversight power (see Chapter 5) over FEMA, want to create an independent commission to investigate the failures in Puerto Rico, especially because the federal government severely underestimated the amount of deaths incurred as a result of Maria.[9]

intro *The story of FEMA's response to Hurricane Maria demonstrates the importance of the **bureaucracy** in American government. A bureaucracy is a large, complex organization in which people work within specified levels of rank and authority to carry out the policies of that organization. Bureaucracies exist in corporations, universities, and governments. Bureaucracies exist at all levels of government—local, state, and national—and all levels are relevant when dealing with natural disasters, such as hurricanes. Nevertheless, in this chapter, we are interested in the federal government bureaucracy, which, like FEMA, carries out federal policies and provides services to the American public.*

The response to Hurricane Maria illustrates key aspects of bureaucratic politics. First, the effectiveness of a bureaucracy depends on the actions of its leaders and employees. For example, Brock Long, the head of FEMA, publicly defended FEMA's action by stating erroneously that responding to Hurricane Maria was the "most logistically challenging event" the United States ever faced. Long's excuse angered many Puerto Rican leaders.[10] Second, the fact that the members of the U.S. House of Representatives want to investigate FEMA's response to Maria reveals the issue of oversight of the bureaucracy. Although, as we show in this chapter, the bureaucracy is supposed to be free from politics, elected officials supervise the bureaucracy's functioning in

Bureaucracy A large, complex organization in which employees work within specific levels of rank and authority to carry out the policies of that organization.

American government. Third, a bureaucracy influences racial and ethnic minorities. As we discussed in Chapter 5, Puerto Rico is a commonwealth of the United States, and the overwhelmingly Latino population are American citizens. However, Puerto Rico lacks representation in Congress and it does not participate in the Electoral College that selects the president.

We begin this chapter by examining the organizational structure of the federal bureaucracy and then discuss the bureaucrats, who are the employees of the bureaucracy. In the latter part of the chapter we explore bureaucratic power. We discuss what bureaucracies do, the sources of bureaucratic power, and ways to limit the federal bureaucracy. Throughout the chapter, we emphasize how the bureaucracy affects racial and ethnic minorities.

Bureaucratic Organization

A key aspect of the federal bureaucracy is its organization. The federal bureaucracy is divided into four separate categories: (1) cabinet departments, (2) independent regulatory commissions, (3) independent executive agencies, and (4) government corporations. Each of these sections is further divided and subdivided into units responsible for more specialized functions.

Determining bureaucratic structure is often politically controversial. The president and Congress establish and eliminate parts of the bureaucracy based on the importance that they place on those parts' functions. As we discuss in this section, the organization of the bureaucracy influences the ability of agencies to perform their functions, which, in turn, affects racial and ethnic minorities.

Cabinet Departments

Cabinet departments are major divisions of the executive branch and perform a wide range of executive functions (see Table 8.1). Each executive department contains several divisions, which are then subdivided into specialized functions. In Chapter 7, we discussed the role the cabinet plays in executive politics, but in this chapter we focus more on the cabinet departments as bureaucratic agencies. In other words, we are less concerned now with the cabinet secretaries and undersecretaries, the positions at the top of the departments. Rather, we are interested in the middle- and lower-level positions that carry out the daily, detailed activities necessary for governing.

Many of these specialized units within cabinet departments focus on racial and ethnic political issues. For example, the Department of Justice is in charge of enforcing federal laws, including civil rights laws. Specifically, the Civil Rights Division of the Department of Justice enforces laws that protect against racial and ethnic discrimination, as well as unequal treatment of people with disabilities, older adults, and members of nontraditional religions. The division was created in 1957,[11] and it is divided into various sections (see Table 8.2), each of which specializes in different aspects of civil rights enforcement. An assistant attorney general, who is appointed by the

Hear about bureaucratic pathologies and processes.

Cabinet Departments The major divisions within the executive branch, with each performing a specific function.

TABLE 8.1 Federal Cabinet Departments

Department	Year Established	Number of Full-Time Civilian Employees (Fiscal Year 2017)
State	1789	10,166
Treasury	1789	78,734
Defense	1789/1947[a]	90,054[b]
Justice	1789/1870[c]	111,778
Interior	1849	49,721
Agriculture	1889	73,231
Commerce	1903/1913[d]	35,757
Labor	1903/1913[d]	14,424
Health and Human Services	1953/1980[e]	65,866
Education	1953/1980[e]	3,842
Housing and Urban Development	1965	7,697
Transportation	1967	53,568
Energy	1977	14,249
Veterans' Affairs	1989	342,111
Homeland Security	2003	173,326

[a] *The Defense Department was renamed from the War Department, created in 1789.*

[b] *This figure does not include employees in the Department of the Army or Department of the Navy.*

[c] *The attorney general position has existed since 1789, but the Justice Department was created in 1870.*

[d] *The Commerce Department and Labor Department were originally merged together as the Department of Com-merce and Labor, which was created in 1903.*

Sources: Adapted from White House. (n.d.). President's Cabinet (with links to each department). Retrieved February 17, 2012, from http://www .whitehouse.gov/administration/cabinet/; United States Office of Personnel Management. (n.d.). Table 3: NSFTP Federal Executive Branch Employment by Cabinet Level Agency. Sizing Up the Executive Branch, Fiscal Year 2017. Retrieved July 6, 2018, from https://www.opm.gov/policy-data-oversight/data-analysis-documentation/federal-employment-reports/reports-publications/sizing-up-the-executive-branch-2016.pdf.

president and confirmed by the Senate, runs the Civil Rights Division, but the majority of the attorneys and nonattorneys who carry out the everyday tasks necessary for enforcing civil rights laws are not political appointees. Instead, they are hired based on their qualifications.

Although the cabinet bureaucracies are staffed by career employees who focus mainly on performing their jobs and not serving the president, the president still exercises control over the cabinet bureaucracy. The case of FEMA illustrates how placing an agency in the cabinet bureaucracy affects its performance. FEMA was first created in 1979 to coordinate the government's responses to natural disasters, such as floods, earthquakes, and hurricanes.[12] It was initially established as an independent agency, which, as we discuss

TABLE 8.2 **Sections of the Civil Rights Division of the Department of Justice**

Section	Function(s)
Appellate	Manages appeals for civil rights cases the U.S. government litigates in the U.S. Courts of Appeals and U.S. Supreme Court
Criminal	Investigates and prosecutes parties charged with criminal violations of federal civil rights laws
Disability Rights	Enforces Americans with Disabilities Act (ADA) and assists federal agencies with ADA compliance
Educational Opportunities	Enforces antidiscrimination laws pertaining to education; represents Department of Education in federal court
Employment Litigation	Enforces antidiscrimination laws pertaining to employment
Federal Coordination and Compliance	Enforces antidiscrimination policies for any entity that receives federal and compliance funds
Housing and Civil Enforcement	Enforces laws preventing discrimination in housing, credit, and public accommodations on account of citizenship or immigrant status
Immigrant and Employee Rights	Enforces laws banning employment discrimination on account of citizenship or status; offers educational outreach for employers
Policy and Strategy	Coordinates with other federal agencies to analyze and propose policies and regulations pertaining to civil rights
Special Litigation	Enforces civil rights laws protecting "institutionalized persons, conduct of law enforcement agencies, access to reproductive health clinics and places of religious worship, and religious exercise of institutionalized persons"
Voting	Enforces the Voting Rights Act of 1965 and other laws protecting against voting discrimination

Source: Adapted from U.S. Department of Justice, Civil Rights Division, (n.d.). About the Division. Retrieved July 6, 2018, https://www.justice.gov/crt/about-division.

below, operates independently of the president. By most accounts FEMA was successful when it was an independent agency, especially during the 1990s.[13]

However, after the attacks of September 11, 2001, the federal government reorganized its disaster-response apparatus, and in 2003 FEMA was placed under the jurisdiction of the newly created Department of Homeland Security. This change in FEMA's status diminished the federal government's ability to respond to natural disasters. FEMA's funding decreased under this new arrangement. The Bush administration reduced FEMA's independence and reoriented FEMA's mission toward responding to terror attacks and away from responding to natural disasters. Furthermore, unlike his predecessors who appointed emergency management professionals to lead FEMA, President George W. Bush appointed a political supporter named Michael Brown, who had no experience with emergency management. Consequently, when Hurricane Katrina struck southeastern Louisiana in August 2005 and subsequently flooded the city of New Orleans, FEMA was completely unprepared to deal with the disaster. Essentially the poor residents of

New Orleans, most of whom were African Americans, were unable to evacuate the city, and they were stranded for days without food and water. Many of these evacuees died. Most observers cite FEMA's lack of independence and Michael Brown's incompetence as the source of this failure.[14] Moreover, this bureaucratic failure disproportionately affected African Americans, who were twice as likely as Whites to lack the means to evacuate.[15] As the opening story demonstrates, FEMA response to Hurricane Maria in Puerto Rico generated a similar controversy.

Independent Regulatory Commissions

Independent regulatory commissions are established by Congress to regulate a specific economic or social interest. When Congress deems that legislation alone cannot adequately address an important regulatory need, it creates an independent regulatory commission to perform that function. Independent regulatory commissions make rules, enforce them by conducting investigations of violations, and then adjudicate disputes arising from the enforcement of those rules (although those decisions can be appealed to the federal judiciary). In short, they act as legislature, executive, and judiciary, albeit in a narrowly defined policy area.

Independent regulatory commissions affect public policies, including issues of racial and ethnic discrimination. For example, in late 2017 the Federal Communications Commission (FCC), which regulates broadcast media, cable media, and the Internet,[16] repealed net neutrality rules that prevented

Independent Regulatory Commissions Government bodies that issue and enforce regulations on specified economic and social interests.

Explore major agencies within the bureaucracy.

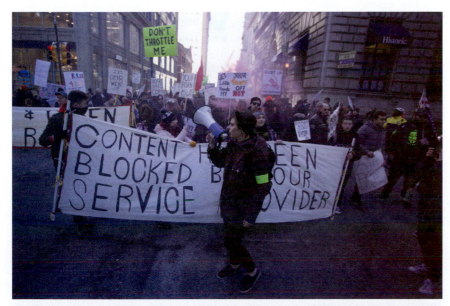

People protesting the Federal Communication Commission's repeal of net neutrality. Opponents of the decision argue that without net neutrality, wealthy large Internet companies will be able to transmit their material faster than small businesses and individuals. Civil rights groups fear that the repeal of net neutrality will disadvantage smaller racial justice organizations.

Internet service providers from charging different rates and providing differential treatment to websites. FCC Chair Ajit Pai argues that repealing net neutrality will not affect people's access to the Internet, but critics of the repeal contend that Internet service providers will be able to charge more money for higher-speed access. Therefore, large media companies will be able to afford to transmit their material at high speeds, whereas individual and small businesses will have to settle for transmitting their Internet material at lower speeds.[17] Moreover, groups that advocate for racial justice, such as the Greenlining Institute[18] and the National Hispanic Media Coalition,[19] argue that repealing net neutrality will decrease the ability of civil rights groups, especially smaller ones, to use the Internet to promote their ideas.

Generally, the president appoints, subject to the Senate's confirmation, each commissioner on independent regulatory commissions, and each commission relies on career staff people, who are hired instead of appointed. Unlike other presidential appointees, the commissioners serve for fixed terms, and the president cannot remove them if he disagrees with their decisions.[20] The statutes that create regulatory commissions require that there be a close balance of Democratic and Republican commissioners. This means that a Republican president could at times be forced to appoint a Democrat, and vice versa. Nevertheless, presidents have opportunities to shape the effect of regulatory commissions through appointments, with Republican presidents generally preferring commissioners who favor less regulation and Democratic presidents generally preferring commissioners who favor more regulation.

For example, although commissioners on the Equal Employment Opportunity Commission (EEOC), which enforces employment antidiscrimination laws,[21] serve fixed terms, presidents can still influence the vigor with which the commission pursues discrimination claims (assuming the Senate confirms their nominees). In 1982 President Ronald Reagan appointed Clarence Thomas (who now serves on the U.S. Supreme Court) as the chair of the EEOC. Reagan sought to limit the number of civil rights suits that the EEOC initiated and, according to a congressional study, under Thomas's leadership the EEOC was less effective in enforcing civil rights laws than it had been prior to his leadership.[22] Conversely, in 2012, President Barack Obama designated Jenny Yang, an Asian American woman, as chair of the EEOC, and under her leadership, the EEOC focused on pay inequity for minority and female employees, especially by requiring better data from employers on how much they pay their employees.[23] After Yang's term ended in 2017, President Trump appointed Victoria Lipnic as the acting chair, and Lipnic has generally opposed the EEOC's past efforts to improve data collection on employee pay.[24]

Independent Executive Agencies Parts of the federal bureaucracy with specified functions that are independent from cabinet departments, do not regulate, and do not charge fees for their services.

Independent Executive Agencies

Independent executive agencies are bureaucratic agencies that focus on narrow areas, but they are independent from cabinet departments, do not regulate, and do not earn revenue. Some of the more well-known independent agencies are the Central Intelligence Agency, which was created in 1947 to gather information necessary for national security,[25] and the National Aeronautics and Space Administration, which was created in 1958 to conduct scientific research on Earth's atmosphere and explore outer space.[26]

The U.S. Commission on Civil Rights is a key independent agency involved in racial and ethnic politics. Unlike the EEOC, the U.S. Commission on Civil Rights does not actually enforce civil rights laws. Instead, it gathers qualitative and quantitative evidence and holds hearings to determine the extent to which discrimination exists. It also evaluates the effectiveness of civil rights laws and writes reports on its findings. The commission consists of eight commissioners, each of whom serves a six-year term. The president appoints four commissioners, who are not subject to Senate confirmation, and Congress appoints the other four commissioners. Staff people conduct the everyday, detailed work of the commission.[27]

Similar to the EEOC, the ability of the U.S. Commission on Civil Rights to affect civil rights policy depends on the ideology of its commissioners, especially the chair. One of the most notable chairs of the commission was Dr. Mary Frances Berry, a historian and academic leader by training. During the 1970s, President Jimmy Carter appointed her to the com-

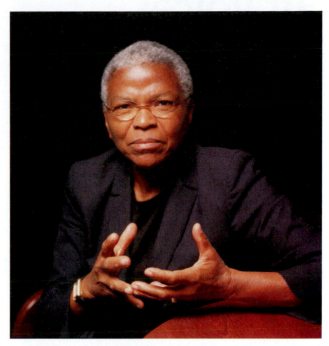

Dr. Mary Frances Berry was a former chair of the U.S. Commission on Civil Rights. As an independent executive agency, the U.S. Committee on Civil Rights does not exert direct authority over policymaking, but Dr. Berry used her position to emphasize issues important to racial and ethnic minorities, such as voting irregularities in Florida during the 2000 election. After she left the commission in 2004, Dr. Berry concentrated her efforts in academia. She is professor of history at the University of Pennsylvania, and she frequently comments on civil rights issues pertaining to minorities and women.

mission, and in 1993 President Bill Clinton promoted her to chair. During her tenure as chair, she aggressively investigated systematic police brutality against minorities and the conditions on Indian reservations.[28] She is best known for her extensive investigation of whether racial discrimination occurred in Florida during the 2000 presidential election. In fact, over the objection of two conservative commissioners, she issued a strongly worded statement arguing that Florida had committed numerous violations of the Voting Rights Act.[29] "Our Voices: The U.S. Commission on Civil Rights and the Controversy over Florida and the 2000 Election" has more detail on her actions.

President George W. Bush replaced Dr. Berry with Gerald Reynolds, who is also African American, but he is a conservative Republican who pursued a more conservative course. For example, in 2007 Reynolds launched an investigation of affirmative action in law schools with the purpose of exposing problems with affirmative-action programs.[30] President Obama's second appointment to Chair the Commission on Civil Rights was Catherine E. Lhamon, who previously served as a law professor and civil rights lawyer.[31] Since the

our voices

The U.S. Commission on Civil Rights and the Controversy over Florida and the 2000 Election

The delayed reporting of the results of the 2000 presidential election outcome in Florida was undoubtedly notorious, but racial discrimination in the state's conduct of the election was especially controversial. Critics charged that (1) Florida's method of purging invalid voters unfairly targeted Blacks, (2) there was an inordinate police presence at polling places in areas with high Black populations, (3) polling places in areas with high Black populations mysteriously changed locations, and (4) the systematic unequal distribution of voting resources unfairly affected minority voters.

As a result of these problems, the U.S. Commission on Civil Rights conducted a thorough investigation of irregularities in Florida's 2000 vote. Here we provide excerpts from a letter that the chair, Dr. Mary Frances Berry, wrote to Florida governor Jeb Bush (R). The letter highlights the problems the commission uncovered. It also reveals how this crucial bureaucratic agency operates and specifically demonstrates the commission's investigative and subpoena powers.

Dear Governor Bush:

I am writing to express my deep disappointment with your statement of priorities that was presented during the opening of the Florida legislative session, in which you did not address the most serious problems. . . . As you know, the Commission has undertaken a formal investigation into allegations by Floridians of voting irregularities arising out of the November 7, 2000, Presidential election. The Commission has held two fact-finding hearings in Florida to examine whether eligible voters faced avoidable barriers that undermined their ability to cast ballots and have their ballots counted in a closely contested election. . . .

. . . Over 100 witnesses testified under oath before the commission, including approximately 65 scheduled witnesses who were scheduled for the two hearings due to their knowledge of and/or expertise with the issues under investigation. The Commission heard testimony from top elected and appointed state officials, including your own testimony, that of the Secretary of State, the Attorney General, the Director of the Florida Division of Elections, and other Florida state and county officials. A representative of . . . a firm involved in the controversial, state-sponsored removal of felons from the voter registration rolls also testified.

We also heard the sworn testimony of registered voters and experts on election reform issues, election laws and procedures, and voting rights. Also, the Chair and Executive Director of the Select Task Force on Election Reforms that you established testified before the Commission. Testimony was received from the supervisors of elections for several counties, county commission officials, law enforcement personnel, and a state's attorney. In addition to the scheduled witnesses, the Commission extended an opportunity for concerned persons, including Members of Congress and members of the Florida State Legislature, to submit testimony under oath that was germane to the issues under investigation. Significantly, the Commission subpoenaed scores of relevant documents to assist with the investigation.

. . . These problems cry out for solutions, for example, a process for ensuring equitable allocation of resources to ensure that poor and/or people-of-color areas are not disproportionally affected. They also include a better process for identifying felons who are ineligible to vote, ensuring coordination between the DMV and election boards to make sure registrations are actually filed and on a timely basis, funds for better training of poll workers, improved and -updated communication systems, funds for voter education, and clarifications in the law to permit provisional ballots to be cast, when appropriate. . . .

Because I believe the need to address these problems is serious, I have determined that the commission should hold additional hearings in Florida . . . to assess what changes have been legislated or enacted at the state and local level and to report to the public what progress has been made. . . .

Respectfully,

Mary Frances Berry

ChairpersonL

Source: Adapted from U.S. Commission on Civil Rights. (2001, March 1). Letter to Governor Bush from Chairperson Berry. Retrieved July 6, 2018, from https://www.usccr.gov/pubs/vote2000/Berry.htm.

inauguration of President Trump, Lhamon has spoken out against the Education Department's weak enforcement of antidiscrimination laws. In fact, under her leadership, the Commission voted to investigate civil rights enforcement in the Trump administration.[32]

Government Corporations

Government corporations perform tasks similar to those in the private sector, charge for those services, and keep the revenue they generate, but unlike private-sector corporations, government corporations are run by the federal government and receive a significant portion of their operating funds from government expenditures. The oldest government corporation is the U.S. Post Office, which Article 1, Section 8, of the U.S. Constitution specifically authorizes Congress to establish. These corporations often assume such responsibilities because disadvantaged citizens cannot afford those services without government involvement and funding.

The National Railroad Passenger Corporation, better known as Amtrak, provides passenger rail service to more than five hundred U.S. cities,[33] and it has been a particularly controversial government corporation. Many citizens use Amtrak because they cannot afford airline or personal automobile travel, which means that Amtrak cannot charge expensive rates. As a result, it relies on federal funding, and there are usually disagreements between Republicans and Democrats over the amount of Amtrak funding. For example, House Republicans slashed President Obama's Amtrak budget request by almost half, and Democrats blamed these budget cuts on safety problems that led to deadly train accidents.[34]

Government Corporations
Parts of the federal bureaucracy that charge fees for the services that they provide to the American public.

The Bureaucrats

In addition to bureaucratic organization, **bureaucrats**—the employees who work in the federal bureaucracy—are an important part of American government. After all, people administer laws on a daily basis; organizational charts do not. The size of the federal bureaucracy has grown immensely since 1940 when there were fewer than one million executive branch civilian employees (excluding the post office) through 2014 when there were over two million executive branch civilian employees.[35] Given the enormous number of employees, it is important to examine who these bureaucrats are and how and why they are hired. The opening vignette exposed the problems with FEMA's response to Hurricane Maria in Puerto Rico, and the story of FEMA's response to Hurricane Katrina demonstrates the difference between a political appointee managing FEMA and an experienced professional managing FEMA. We also discuss issues of racial and ethnic diversity among the bureaucrats.

Bureaucrats The employees who work in a bureaucracy.

Politics versus Merit

During the early years of the American Republic, when the bureaucracy was small, government leaders were not overly concerned with the competence and

Patronage A system of hiring bureaucrats because they supported the winning political candidate, not because they had the skill, training, and experience for their jobs.

Pendleton Act A federal law passed in 1883 that required bureaucrats to be hired and retained according to their demonstrated skill, not their political affiliation.

Civil Servants Federal bureaucrats who are not political appointees, but instead are hired according to their education and performance on an examination.

This Thomas Nast cartoon depicts President-elect Grover Cleveland as the Hercules of civil service reform, opposing the Tammany tiger of patronage. Patronage was a system that gave federal jobs to people based on their support of a winning candidate, and not on merit. Because patronage led to corruption and incompetence, reformers sought to replace the patronage system with a merit system.

skill of federal bureaucrats. Initially, federal bureaucrats were exclusively from the upper classes of American society, but Andrew Jackson's presidential victory in 1828 drastically changed the process of hiring bureaucrats. Jackson expanded the **patronage** system, also known as the "spoils system," in which government bureaucrats were hired based on political and partisan support of the winning candidate, not based on their training, education, experience, or demonstrated ability. Jackson believed that the federal bureaucracy could function only if bureaucrats supported his principles. He also used patronage to give commoners a greater stake in the federal bureaucracy, which he regarded as elitist. As the two-party system emerged in the 1840s and 1850s, patronage became more entrenched. Those who supported the political party of the winning candidate were hired to fill federal bureaucratic positions. The incumbent party then demanded continued support from federal employees, and if they refused, they could be fired. If the incumbent party lost, then existing employees were fired and replaced with the supporters of the winning party.[36] Although the patronage system bred corruption and incompetence in the bureaucracy, it did provide immigrants, and even ethnic minorities, with bureaucratic jobs when the private sector would not hire them. Nevertheless, there is considerable debate over the extent to which patronage actually helped immigrants and ethnic minorities.[37]

After the Civil War, many high-level bureaucrats in the Grant administration were involved in corruption scandals, which engendered calls for reform of the patronage system. With the government expanding its authority over social and economic policy, reformers argued that the patronage system was too corrupt and inefficient to meet the needs of the changing federal government. In 1881, newly inaugurated president James Garfield adhered to these reformist views and refused to staff federal bureaucratic positions based on patronage. Charles Guiteau, who unsuccessfully sought a position from Garfield, assassinated the president so that Vice President Chester Arthur, who opposed reform, could become president. But Garfield's assassination martyred the cause for reforming the federal bureaucracy, and in 1883 Congress passed the Civil Service Reform Act of 1883, better known as the **Pendleton Act**, which transformed the federal bureaucracy from a patronage system into a merit system. It required career bureaucrats, known as **civil servants**, to be hired based on their performance on a competitive examination. It also guaranteed job security to those employees hired through the examination process, and it banned supervisors from compelling political support from their employees. The Pendleton Act created the Civil Service Commission, now known as the Office of Personnel Management, to ensure fair treatment of civil servants.[38]

Politicization of the bureaucracy reemerged during the New Deal, and in response Congress passed the **Hatch Act** in 1939 to forbid federal employees from engaging in virtually all political activities. For example, federal government employees could not run for any political office, even local nonpartisan ones, or work for a political party, or manage an election campaign. By removing employees from political participation, this law clearly depoliticized the federal bureaucracy, but it also limited the freedom of federal employees. In 1993, at the urging of President Bill Clinton, Congress passed the Hatch Act Amendments of 1993, which liberalized the Hatch Act to allow federal employees to participate in campaigns on behalf of other candidates. Federal bureaucrats are still forbidden, however, from displaying blatant partisanship, soliciting campaign contributions, or working on political campaigns while on the job. Under the new regulations, civil servants still cannot run for partisan offices, but they can run for local, nonpartisan offices.[39]

Hatch Act A federal law passed in 1939 and amended in 1993 that restricts federal employees' partisan political activities.

Diversity

Similar to private-sector companies, government bureaucracies have historically discriminated against women and minorities in hiring and promotion. The Civil Rights Act prohibits federal, state, and local governments from discriminatory hiring practices. However, there has been considerable controversy over how to determine the existence of discrimination. Clearly, if plaintiffs (the parties bringing the discrimination complaint) can show that a government agency intentionally discriminated against them, then courts would find a violation and order equitable hiring practices.

Determining that discrimination exists becomes more contentious when government agencies do not intentionally discriminate, but their hiring or promotion procedures wind up disproportionately hurting minorities. For example, racial minorities traditionally score lower on hiring examinations compared to Whites; consequently, some government agencies hire Whites at a greater rate than Blacks or Latinos. In one case, African Americans sued the city of Washington, DC, because their lower scores on an examination to become police officers resulted in lower hiring rates. In 1976, the U.S. Supreme Court ruled that disparate performance on an examination does not by itself constitute a violation of antidiscrimination law.[40] Because of this decision, civil rights plaintiffs experience greater difficulty challenging government hiring practices that are not intentionally discriminatory but that disproportionately harm racial and ethnic minorities.

The federal government has actively tried to increase women and minority employment through affirmative action (see Chapter 5). As early as 1971, the Civil Service Commission (now called the Office of Personnel Management) required federal government agencies to set numerical goals, but not binding quotas, to ensure that women and minorities were represented fairly in the federal workforce. To compensate for past discrimination and achieve a representative workforce, most agencies accorded preferential treatment to minority and female applicants.[41] Disgruntled White male employees argued

evaluating equality

Diversity in the Bureaucracy: The Case of the Bureau of Indian Affairs

As we have seen throughout this chapter, bureaucratic performance greatly affects racial and ethnic minorities; therefore, minority representation in the bureaucracy is a significant issue. As we show, particularly in the Measuring Equality box, racial and ethnic minorities are not well represented in the federal bureaucracy, especially at the higher levels. Given how the work of the bureaucracy affects racial and ethnic minorities (e.g., FEMA and the U.S. Customs and Border Protection), how important is racial and ethnic diversity in the bureaucracy?

One particularly interesting aspect of diversity in federal bureaucracy concerns the Bureau of Indian Affairs (BIA), which was created in 1824 and is the oldest federal bureaucratic department to handle Indian affairs. Because the American government then sought to subjugate Indians through military force, the BIA was initially part of the Department of War. Over the next two decades, the federal government removed Indians from their tribal lands and placed them on reservations in the interior regions of the United States. When the Department of the Interior was established

Command post of the Bureau of Indian Affairs Police after wildfires burned 60,000 acres and dozens of homes on August 6, 2012, in Creek County, Oklahoma. The Bureau of Indian Affairs Police is a bureaucratic agency in the Department of the Interior that provides law enforcement assistance to reservations that lack their own tribal police forces and partially oversees tribal police forces.

in 1849, the BIA was moved from the War Department to the Interior Department.[a]

To get a sense of how this bureaucratic organization shapes the daily lives of American Indians, explore in detail the Bureau of Indian Affairs website, which can be linked from the Department of the Interior

site or accessed directly at *http://www.bia.gov*. Then, debate among your classmates over the importance of diversity in the BIA workforce, particularly for American Indians.

[a] Bureau of Indian Affairs. "About Us." Retrieved October 19, 2018, from https://www.bia.gov/about-us

that this form of affirmative action discriminated against them. However, in 1987 the U.S. Supreme Court ruled that the Civil Rights Act did not prevent governments, even those without a history of discrimination, from employing affirmative action to eliminate gender employment disparities.[42]

There is mixed evidence that antidiscrimination laws and affirmative-action programs have significantly increased the proportion of racial and ethnic minorities serving in the federal bureaucracy. Although women and minorities are represented in the federal bureaucracy in a proportion equal to their proportion of the population, both groups tend to occupy lower-level positions. Minorities are not as well represented in the upper echelons of the federal bureaucracy. "Measuring Equality: Minority Representation in the Federal Civilian Workforce" on page 253 explores in more detail the racial and ethnic composition of the federal bureaucracy.

Bureaucratic Policymaking and Power

Despite being unelected and unaccountable, bureaucrats are important policymakers. In addition to executing orders and statutes, bureaucracies actually make rules and regulations for implementing those decrees. Implementation includes rulemaking and administrative adjudication. These activities provide bureaucracies with considerable power, which they seek to maintain through internal and external means, and bureaucratic power exerts a clear impact on racial and ethnic minorities.

Implementation

Bureaucracies are charged with the function of **implementation**; that is, bureaucracies conduct the daily activities that put into effect the laws passed by legislatures and orders issued by executives. There are several aspects of implementation that we discuss in this section: enforcement, rulemaking, and administrative adjudication.

Implementation The day-to-day process by which bureaucrats enforce laws and carry out policies.

Enforcement. By enforcement of the policies made in the popularly accountable branches of government, bureaucracies influence the lives of racial and ethnic minorities. For example, two bureaucratic agencies enforce immigration laws. U.S. Customs and Border Protection (CBP) is part of the Department of Homeland Security, and it patrols the borders and ports to prevent illegal contraband and undocumented persons from entering the United States.[43] U.S. Immigration and Customs Enforcement (ICE) investigates undocumented immigrants who are already in the United States and then seeks to deport them. It also participates in antiterrorism activities.[44] Given the importance of immigration for Latinos and other racial and ethnic minorities, CBP and ICE play key roles in racial and ethnic politics, not because they shape relevant policies, but because they carry them out on a daily basis. For example, CPB employees have been responsible for implementing the controversial Trump administration policy of separating parents and children of undocumented immigrants and asylum seekers.[45] To demonstrate a full picture of CPB's overall work, Table 8.3 provides a glimpse into the daily activities of the CBP.

Push a program through the bureaucracy.

The way in which laws should be enforced is defined by the policymaking institutions of government, but the bureaucrats carrying out the daily enforcement functions enjoy considerable discretion. Even though Congress writes the policies and expresses its intent on how laws should be enforced, executive branch leaders set clear guidelines on how enforcement should proceed, and bureaucrats receive considerable training and guidance on how to carry out

TABLE 8.3 A Typical Day in U.S. Customs and Border Protection (Based on Fiscal Year 2017 Data)

Processed	
1,088,300 passengers and pedestrians	78,137 truck, rail, and sea containers
Conducted	
21 arrests of wanted criminals at ports of entry	592 refusals of inadmissible persons at U.S. ports of entry
Seized	
5,863 pounds of narcotics	$265,205 undeclared or illegal currency
Deployed	
1,501 canine teams	375 horse patrols
Employed	
59,178 total employees	2,423 agricultural specialists
23,079 CPB officers	610 air interdiction agents (pilots)
19,437 border patrol agents	
Conducted Operations	
328 ports of entry	135 border patrol stations and 35 permanent checkpoints

Source: Adapted from Department of Homeland Security, U.S. Customs and Border Protection,. (n.d.). On a typical day in fiscal year 2017, CPB ... Retrieved July 6, 2018, from https://www.cbp.gov/newsroom/stats/typical-day-fy2017.

enforcement duties. In short, the daily decisions that bureaucrats make when implementing policies greatly influence how a policy is carried out.

For example, federal prosecutors—the bureaucrats who argue criminal cases in federal court on behalf of the U.S. government—are not able to prosecute every crime they encounter. Therefore, these bureaucrats enjoy "prosecutorial discretion" that allows them to decide which cases to prosecute and what sentences to seek. To guide its prosecutors, the U.S. Justice Department issues a statement of "prosecutorial discretion" principles that "assure regularity without regimentation."[46] Despite the government's attempt to be fair, there is evidence that federal prosecutors' discretion can lead to sentencing patterns that disadvantage racial and ethnic minorities.[47]

Rulemaking. Bureaucracies implement laws by **rulemaking**, which is more complex than simply enforcing laws. Rulemaking occurs when bureaucratic agencies issue regulations that apply to other government agencies or to private citizens, and these regulations have the force of law. Starting during the New Deal, Congress delegated much of its complex economic and social regulatory authority to bureaucratic agencies because it did not have the time and staff necessary to write the necessary rules. As a result, unelected, unaccountable bureaucrats have come to influence policy, sometimes greatly.

The Administrative Procedure Act of 1946 requires that bureaucratic rules first be publicly proposed in the *Federal Register*, which is the official collection

View a video about the history and operation of the Federal Register.

Rulemaking The process by which bureaucrats issue regulations that have the force of law.

measuring equality

Minority Representation in the Federal Civilian Workforce

As we have discussed throughout this book, minority representation in government is a crucial issue in racial and ethnic politics, and, as this chapter shows, minority representation in the bureaucracy is a key issue as well. In the text, we provide basic information about minority underrepresentation, but here we explore this question in more detail by examining minority representation at different levels of the federal bureaucracy.

In previous editions of this book, we analyzed minority employment according to the General Schedule (GS), which are the job and salary rankings of the federal workforce. However, the federal government has ceased reporting minority employment according to GS level; consequently, we now use the job category as our basis of comparison. Government jobs are blue collar, which focuses on manual labor, and white collar, which takes place in an office. The government has several rankings of white-collar jobs. Professional jobs entail a highly specialized skill, and administrative jobs focus on managing the daily work within an agency. Professional and administrative jobs usually require a college degree, often a postgraduate degree, and people who occupy those positions are most likely to be promoted to the highest-ranking and best-paying positions. At the next level are technical jobs, which are also specialized but do not require an advanced degree. Clerical jobs entail office work. Bureaucrats who work in clerical and technical jobs are not likely to be promoted to

senior-management positions. Finally, there are "other white collar" positions that capture jobs that do not fit into one of the other four categories.

Not only do these categories indicate rank and prestige, but they are also tied to employees' salaries. In 2017, the average salary for each category was as follows: professional, $109,063; administrative, $96,086; technical, $52,082; clerical, $41,907; other white collar, $65,450; blue collar, $56,366.

To determine the extent of minority representation in the federal civilian workforce, we present graphical data concerning minority representation for Blacks, Latinos, Asian Americans, and American Indians (including

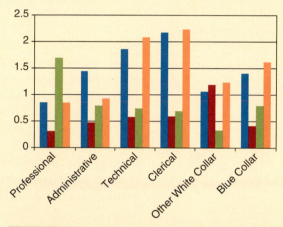

Black **Latino** **Asian American** **American Indian**

Figure 8.2 Minority Representation by Job Category Compared with Minority Representation in the Population

Sources: Bureaucracy statistics are adapted from Office of Personnel Management. (n.d.). Federal Equal Opportunity Recruitment Program Report to Congress, Fiscal Year 2016. *Retrieved July 7, 2018, from https://www.opm.gov/policy-data-oversight/diversity-and-inclusion/reports/feorp-2016.pdf. Job category salary data are from Office of Personnel Management. (n.d.).* Table 6: Federal Executive Branch Salary by Occupational Category, Salary Information for the Executive Branch, Fiscal Year 2017. *Retrieved July 7, 2018, from https://www.opm.gov/policy-data-oversight/data-analysis-documentation/federal-employment-reports/reports-publications/salary-information-for-the-executive-branch.pdf. Year 2017 population data are from U.S. Census. (n.d.).* QuickFacts: United States 2017. *Retrieved July 7, 2018, from https://www.census.gov/quickfacts/fact/table/US/VET605216#viewtop.*

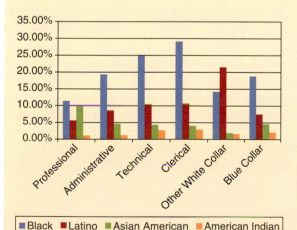

Black **Latino** **Asian American** **American Indian**

Figure 8.1 Minority Representation by Job Category

(Continued)

measuring equality *(Continued)*

Alaskan Natives) in each job category. Figure 8.1 shows the percentage of each minority group employed in each category. Blacks are clearly the best represented minority group for administrative, clerical, technical, and blue-collar positions, and they are about equal to Asian Americans in Professional jobs. Latinos are the best represented in other white-collar jobs. Note that Black, Latino, and Indian representation decreases with higher-ranking job categories, but Asian American representation improves in the highest-ranking positions, professional and administrative.

Figure 8.2 factors the extent to which each group is represented in the population. We divided the percentage of each group in the different job categories by the percentage of that group in the United States population (according to 2017 census figures). A score above 1 signifies that the group is overrepresented, and a score below 1 signifies that the group is underrepresented. As a percentage of the population, Asian Americans are the only group that is overrepresented at the professional level, and African Americans are the only group that is overrepresented at the administrative level. Blacks and American Indians are overrepresented at the lowest-ranking categories—technical, clerical, and blue collar—whereas Asian Americans and Latinos are underrepresented in those categories. Latinos are underrepresented in every category, except for other white collar.

of U.S. government documents published on a daily basis. The public can comment on each proposed rule for a period of at least thirty days, and then the rule is officially promulgated. In some cases, an agency is even required to hold public hearings on certain proposed rules. Agencies can modify rules in response to feedback from the public.[48]

The impact of bureaucratic rules varies. Some rules, such as the Federal Aviation Administration's (part of the Department of Transportation) regulations governing passenger behavior on commercial airliners, have a narrow focus.[49] Other rules, such as the Environmental Protection Agency's (EPA) regulations governing auto emissions or wetlands preservation, enjoy a wide scope.[50]

Bureaucratic rules might not be as significant as congressional statutes or major presidential actions, but they can affect the daily lives of racial and ethnic minorities. For example, in 2010 the Federal Housing Finance Agency (FHFA), which supports and regulates the mortgage industry, issued a final rule that clarified procedures for ensuring fair treatment of women and minorities. This rule was designed to implement the Housing and Economic Recovery Act of 2008, which was designed to address the mortgage crisis brought about by malfeasance in the banking and finance industries. The rule was specifically concerned with preventing these industries from preying on women and minorities. After the initial rule was proposed, the FHFA revised aspects of the rule in response to public comments.[51]

Administrative Adjudication

The quasi-judicial process by which a bureaucratic agency resolves a dispute between the agency and a private citizen.

Administrative Adjudication. Bureaucracies also implement policies through **administrative adjudication**, in which a bureaucratic agency resolves a dispute between a private party and a governmental entity through a quasi-judicial process. Administrative law judges, who work for the various bureaucratic agencies, hear the disputes and offer solutions. Administrative adjudication decisions can be appealed to the federal judiciary, usually to the DC Circuit Court of Appeals and ultimately to the U.S. Supreme Court.

Some bureaucratic agencies try to avoid administrative adjudication by providing for alternative dispute resolution, or mediation. For example, after an employee brings a discrimination complaint to the EEOC, the EEOC provides for a neutral third party to hear both sides of the dispute. This mediation is purely voluntary, and the mediator's goal is to encourage both sides to reach a solution that eliminates the need for further government action.[52]

Sources of Bureaucratic Power

Understanding bureaucratic power requires knowing more than how bureaucracies enforce laws, make rules, or adjudicate disputes; it also requires knowing how bureaucracies gain and keep power. Much bureaucratic power emanates from sources internal to the bureaucracies themselves. One internal source of power is expertise. Generally, bureaucrats know their substantive area better than members of Congress and even political appointees in the executive branch do. For example, the Division of Civil Rights in the Department of Justice can be a powerful force in civil rights policy because it is staffed with attorneys who are experts in civil rights and antidiscrimination law. However, as we saw with the opening story on FEMA's response to Hurricane Maria (especially compared to its response after Harvey and Irma) as well as its failures after Hurricane Katrina, bureaucrats do not always successfully perform their functions, and their failures affect people's everyday lives, including racial and ethnic minorities.

Because bureaucratic agencies do not make policy in isolation, they derive power by relying on alliances with other parts of the federal government. Many people view these alliances as an **iron triangle** consisting of a bureaucratic agency, corresponding congressional committees (and subcommittees), and corresponding client interest groups (see Figure 8.3).[53] According to the iron triangle metaphor, these three sides control policymaking over their substantive issue area, and it is difficult for outside forces to penetrate this triangle. Bureaucrats foster good relations with congressional committees and subcommittees to ensure that their agencies are well funded and laws are crafted in a way that is advantageous for the agency. Bureaucrats use interest groups to enhance public support for their actions. In turn, both congressional committee members and interest groups benefit from their relationship with bureaucrats because they can influence how the agencies carry out their functions. A classic example of an iron triangle is in defense policy, which tends to be dominated by the defense contractors

Iron Triangle A conception of bureaucratic policymaking that is dominated by congressional committees, interest groups, and bureaucratic agencies.

Executive Branch Agencies

Congressional Committees and Subcommittees

Interest Groups

Figure 8.3 The Iron Triangle

Issue Networks A conception of policymaking as dynamic and not controlled by any particular set of groups or institutions.

Explore the concepts of monetary and fiscal policy.

(corporate interests), members of the House and Senate Armed Service Committees, and officials in the U.S. Department of Defense.

Another view of bureaucratic policymaking uses an **issue networks** metaphor, which perceives the relationships among bureaucracies and other actors more informally. In addition to the three components of the iron triangle, issue networks contain the following: a variety of opposing interest groups, law firms, think tanks, academics, the media, public relations experts, political consultants, courts, and legislative staff. Moreover, unlike the stable iron triangles, issue networks are dynamic and constantly evolving as the nature of an issue changes.[54]

For example, immigration policy is not dominated by a monolithic coalition of bureaucratic agencies, congressional committees, and a dominant client interest group. Instead, many bureaucratic agencies and congressional committees (and subcommittees) are involved in immigration policy. Some interest groups (e.g., Latino civil rights groups) support expanded immigration and amnesty for illegal immigrants, whereas other citizen groups hold opposite views. The media, think tanks, academics, the agriculture industry, the high-tech industry, immigration attorneys, and courts all participate in making immigration policy.

Controlling Bureaucracies

Thus far, we have shown that bureaucracies exert tremendous influence on the daily lives of American citizens. Because in the age of the merit system most bureaucrats are hired, not elected or even appointed by elected officials, bureaucracies are not directly accountable to the people whose lives they influence. This system can be problematic in a representative democracy. To check bureaucracies, the three branches of government have attempted to limit bureaucratic power.

Executive Control over Bureaucracies

Just because the president is the chief of the bureaucracy does not mean that presidents and key administration officials, such as the chief of staff, are always able to manage the federal bureaucracy without worrying about dissent. The same situation holds true for bureaucratic supervisors and their subordinates. In some bureaucracies, such as the armed forces, the president and military supervisors control their subordinates with minimal difficulty. In other bureaucratic arenas, conflicts exist between career bureaucrats and higher-level political appointees, including the president.

For example, the Department of Justice criminally prosecuted two Latinos border patrol agents—Jose Compean and Ignacio Ramos—for firing on an unarmed drug suspect and concealing evidence in 2005. After the two men were convicted and sentenced each to more than a decade in prison, the 13,000 career border patrol agents unanimously and publicly expressed their lack of confidence in border patrol chief David Aguilar, whom President

George W. Bush had appointed. On his last day in office, President Bush commuted Compean's and Ramos's sentences, which allowed them to leave prison and be placed on three years of probation.[55] Likewise, in 2012, the union representing border patrol agents protested the two-year prison sentence given to Latino Border Patrol agent Jesus Diaz for violating the constitutional rights of a fifteen-year-old suspected of marijuana smuggling.[56]

Presidents can control such embarrassing bureaucratic conflicts by reorganizing bureaucracies to suit their ideology and personal management styles. In this way, presidents can ensure that bureaucrats act in accordance with their wishes. As we discussed earlier in this chapter, after the attack of September 11, 2001, President Bush put FEMA under the control of the Department of Homeland Security because he thought states should bear more of the emergency response duties and FEMA should concentrate on

Border patrol agents escort an undocumented immigrant to a holding area prior to deportation. As federal bureaucrats, border patrol agents carry out the daily tasks necessary to enforce immigration policies made by Congress and the president.

responding to terrorist attacks. However, it bears mentioning that presidents have found that their authority to reorganize the bureaucracy is limited by the requirement that Congress must actually pass the reorganization as a bill.

During the late 1970s, President Jimmy Carter was especially concerned about controlling the bureaucracy. As a result, he persuaded Congress to pass the Civil Service Reform Act of 1978, which imposed modern management principles on the federal bureaucracy. This law created the **Senior Executive Service**, consisting of trained administrators the president could place in any agency to ensure compliance with his orders.[57] Although the Senior Executive Service helps presidents control bureaucracies, it has also fomented racial and gender discrimination in the federal bureaucracy. A 2016 report from the federal government demonstrates that women, Blacks, Latinos, Asian Americans, and American Indians are underrepresented in the Senior Executive Service.[58]

Presidents can control the bureaucracy through **central clearance**, which requires that all budget requests and legislative proposals coming from a federal agency be approved by the Office of Management and Budget (OMB) before the president submits them to Congress.[59] Presidents fear that agencies' budget requests and legislative proposals are based more on the selfish interests of the agencies and client groups than on concern for the administration or the American public. Because the OMB is under presidential control, central clearance allows presidents to ensure that the budget requests they submit to Congress serve solely their interests.

At times, bureaucrats sidestep central clearance and go directly to members of Congress to achieve objectives. Recall the iron triangle metaphor,

Senior Executive Service High-level bureaucrats the president places in different agencies to ensure compliance with his directives.

Central Clearance A requirement that all agency budget requests receive approval from the Office of Management and Budget before the president submits them to Congress.

which maintains that bureaucrats and their client groups can try to curry favor with specific members of congressional committees who might be receptive to their proposals. In other words, bureaucrats rely on their alliances with groups and other institutions as a way to limit presidential control over their jobs.

Whistleblowers Bureaucrats who publicly expose waste, fraud, or abuse in their agency.

Whistleblowers are another concern of presidents, administration officials, and even senior-level bureaucrats. A **whistleblower** is a bureaucrat who publicly exposes incompetence, mismanagement, or corruption within his or her agency. Whistleblowers are considered vital to the national interest because by exposing problems in the federal bureaucracy, they make the government more responsive and accountable to its citizens. But whistleblowers often face reprisals from their supervisors, and at times they have even been fired. The Civil Service Reform Act of 1978 and the Whistleblower Protection Act of 1989 prevent bureaucratic supervisors from retaliating against whistleblowers by firing them or subjecting them to adverse consequences.[60] One of the most famous recent whistleblowers is Edward Snowden—a former contractor for the Central Intelligence Agency who leaked information about American surveillance programs throughout the world. In order to escape prosecution, Snowden moved to Russia, which granted him asylum.[61]

Whistleblowers have occasionally exposed racial and ethnic discrimination in the federal bureaucracy. For example, during the 1990s, Marsha Coleman-Adebayo, an African American female, worked for the U.S. Environmental Protection Agency focusing on South Africa. She discovered that a multinational company's mining of vanadium, which is a dangerous chemical, had caused numerous deaths in South Africa. However, the EPA refused to do anything about it; therefore, Coleman-Adebayo publicized what was happening. EPA officials retaliated against her in ways that she describes as sexist and racist. For example, they referred to her as "uppity," which is a term that has usually been used against women and African Americans who do not accept unequal treatment. They also referred to her as an "honorary White person" and sarcastically called her "Rosa Parks." Several years later Coleman-Adebayo won a discrimination suit against the EPA.[62]

Legislative Control over Bureaucracies

Despite the close connection between Congress and the federal bureaucracy, the two institutions conflict when Congress tries to control the bureaucracy. Congress creates, alters, or eliminates bureaucratic agencies and positions, and it can use that power to exert control over bureaucrats. Congress also controls bureaucracies through budgeting. Because bureaucrats desire optimal funding for their agencies, they often adhere to the wishes of congressional leaders, particularly those serving on committees relevant to the bureaucrats' work. Congress can reduce budgets for bureaucratic agencies that refuse to submit to its control, although often the mere threat of a budget reduction is sufficient to influence bureaucratic behavior.

Furthermore, as we discussed in the opening vignette, Congress can supervise the bureaucracy through its oversight power (see Chapters 6 and 7), in which relevant committees conduct investigations and hearings to maintain control over the executive branch and the federal bureaucracy. Congress uses these investigations to determine whether bureaucracies execute laws according to congressional intent and to evaluate the effectiveness of a law or policy. Congress also conducts investigations into bureaucratic fraud and wasteful practices. In March 2018 the Subcommittee on National Security of the House Oversight and Government Reform Committee conducted a hearing on how federal agencies responded to Hurricane Maria.[63] However, Democrats, particularly members of the Congressional Hispanic Caucus, still demand that Congress create an independent commission to investigate why the federal government severely underestimated the number of people killed in Hurricane Maria. [64]

Congressional oversight of the bureaucracy was critical after Hurricane Katrina. In addition to investigating FEMA's failure in planning to deal with intense flooding in New Orleans, Congress probed problems with the long-term aftermath of the storm. For example, FEMA was responsible for providing displaced persons, including a large number of African Americans, with trailers to be used as temporary residences. After residents complained that the trailers contained noxious fumes, FEMA field workers recommended testing all the trailers for poisonous gas, but FEMA leaders refused to accept responsibility and would not conduct the tests. Some residents were sickened, and one even died from formaldehyde exposure. In 2007, the House Oversight and Government Reform Committee, which was then controlled by Democrats after they won the House in the 2006 elections, investigated the incident. After uncovering FEMA's attempt to cover up its failure to address the problem, the committee held a public hearing at which then FEMA director R. David Paulison apologized and promised to monitor more closely the safety of the trailers.[65]

Congress also conducts oversight through the **Government Accountability Office (GAO)**. The GAO is an independent, nonpartisan part of the legislative branch that audits the executive branch's expenditures and supervises how bureaucracies actually spend money appropriated by Congress. The head of the GAO, known as the **comptroller general**, is appointed to a fixed fifteen-year term by the president from a list of names provided by a bipartisan panel of congressional leaders.[66] In 2018 the GAO initiated an investigation into how the federal government awarded contracts to clean up after the 2017 hurricanes.[67]

Until the 1980s, Congress used a legislative veto to control the bureaucracy. The **legislative veto** was a provision in a law that allowed one or both houses to overturn bureaucratic actions. However, the U.S. Supreme Court overturned the legislative veto in the 1983 case of *Immigration and Naturalization Service v. Chadha*, a ruling that also affected racial and ethnic minority politics.

Jagdish Chadha was a Kenyan of Indian descent who held a British passport; he was admitted to the United States on a student visa, as are numerous international students who study today at U.S. colleges and universities.

Government Accountability Office (GAO) The part of the legislative branch that is responsible for auditing how bureaucratic agencies spend money appropriated by Congress.

Comptroller General The head of the Government Accountability Office.

Legislative Veto An act of one or both houses of Congress that overturns an administrative action. The Supreme Court invalidated such acts in 1983.

Jagdish Rai Chadha sits with his wife Terry Lorentz and daughter Sashi. Bowling Green State University student Chadha, born of Indian parents in Kenya, won a U.S. Supreme Court battle that prevented his deportation when his visa expired and the Kenyan and British governments refused to acknowledge his citizenship. The Supreme Court ruled that the legislative veto, which was the process used to deport Chadha, violated the Constitution. Chadha eventually became an American citizen.

Because neither Kenya nor India would allow him to return, Chadha and his family continued to stay in the United States past the expiration date of his visa. The Immigration and Naturalization Service (INS) began the process of deporting Chadha, but after the attorney general intervened because of Chadha's hardship case, the INS suspended the deportation. Because the INS was subject to a legislative veto, the House of Representatives overturned the INS suspension and ordered Chadha to be deported. The Supreme Court then ruled that the legislative veto amounted to congressional interference with the executive branch and therefore violated the Constitution.[68] As a result, Chadha was not deported, and he is currently a U.S. citizen.

Judicial Control over Bureaucracies

Courts also possess authority to control bureaucracies by ruling that bureaucratic actions violate the U.S. Constitution or a federal statute. Because much of the Constitution deals with race and ethnicity, judicial control over the bureaucracy can affect the lives of racial and ethnic minorities. For example, prior to the mid-1970s, border patrol agents would stop automobiles near, but not at, the Mexican border merely because the occupants appeared to be of Latino descent. The Supreme Court ruled in 1975 that this bureaucratic practice violated the Fourth Amendment guarantee against unreasonable search and seizures.[69]

Despite the occasions when the judiciary overturns bureaucratic practices, its effectiveness as a control is limited. Whereas executives and legislators are free to act of their own accord to control bureaucracies, courts can act only when an aggrieved party initiates a case challenging a bureaucratic decision or action. Judicial rules require that an aggrieved party be able to demonstrate that the bureaucratic agency directly caused injury, and if the judiciary enforces these rules strictly, then it can restrict access to the courts. As we discuss in Chapter 9, the political composition of the Supreme Court determines whether the federal judiciary will employ open or restrictive rules of access. The more conservative Court since the 1990s has limited the ability of groups to challenge bureaucratic procedures.

The high cost of litigation designed to contest bureaucratic decisions also limits courts' ability to control bureaucracies. Because of the complex and expensive nature of administrative litigation, specialized attorneys require extensive legal fees. The Equal Access to Justice Act, passed in 1981, authorizes federal courts to award attorneys' fees to successful plaintiffs litigating in the public interest.[70] Although attorneys' fees presumably offset some of the costs of litigation, judges still enjoy tremendous discretion in awarding fees, which means that challenging bureaucracies in the courts is still a difficult task. As a result, many racial and ethnic minority activists have established public interest groups that litigate, often against bureaucracies, to achieve the desired political results. For example, the Mexican American Legal Defense and Education Fund litigates on behalf of immigrants who face adverse actions at the hands of federal bureaucrats.[71]

Conclusion

Although often out of the limelight, the federal bureaucracy is undoubtedly an important part of the federal government. The bureaucracy and the bureaucrats who work for it perform the detailed work of governing by providing services and implementing policies, the latter of which entails enforcing laws, making rules, and adjudicating disputes. Bureaucracies perform a wide variety of essential tasks, such as regulating the economy, preserving the environment, exploring outer space, and delivering the mail. This chapter covered the basics of bureaucratic politics by explaining the structure of the federal bureaucracy, the bureaucrats who work for it, the activities of the bureaucracy, sources of bureaucratic power, and attempts to limit bureaucracies.

Most important, this chapter emphasized how the federal bureaucracy affects racial and ethnic politics. For example, moving FEMA from an independent agency to a cabinet department hurt its ability to respond to Hurricane Katrina, which adversely affected African Americans. Additionally, the daily activities of border patrol agents and employees who work for the Bureau of Indian Affairs greatly affect the lives of Latinos and American Indians, respectively. Furthermore, as with other aspects of American government, minority representation is a significant issue in the bureaucracy. Government policies to ensure more minority representation have certainly improved diversity, but racial and ethnic minorities are not well represented at the upper echelons. We also showed that bureaucratic organization and bureaucratic power (as well as attempts to limit it) are crucial in the everyday lives of racial and ethnic minorities. Throughout this chapter, we demonstrated that the federal bureaucracy influences specific issues in racial and ethnic politics such as immigration and enforcement of civil rights laws.

A recent glaring bureaucratic concern for racial and ethnic politics is the comparatively inadequate job that FEMA did responding to Hurricane Maria, especially compared to its response after Hurricanes Harvey and Irma. Similar to FEMA's failures before, during, and after Hurricane Katrina, different aspects of bureaucratic politics led to FEMA's substandard effort. Observers credited FEMA's rapid and effective response in Texas and Florida, but these same people have noted that FEMA did not devote the same amount of resources in Puerto Rico. The overwhelmingly Latino population in Puerto Rico suffered through the destruction of their homes and businesses, months without electricity, and thousands of deaths. We also saw how legislative oversight of the bureaucracy can be a key aspect of investigations into the wrongdoing surrounding FEMA's response to Hurricane Maria. Although the Republican-controlled Congress conducted some investigations into the disaster response, Democrats claim that their efforts have been insufficient, and they are calling for an independent commission to conduct the investigation. These investigations are likely to increase after the Democrats formally assume control of the House of Representatives in 2019. The fact Puerto Rico is overwhelmingly Latino, coupled with its status as a commonwealth and not a state, surely demonstrates how the bureaucracy greatly affects racial and ethnic minorities.

review
REVIEW QUESTIONS

Check your understanding of Chapter 8.

1. How does the professionalism of bureaucratic employees affect their ability to function effectively?

2. What are some examples of federal cabinet departments (and subunits), independent regulatory commissions, independent executive agencies, and government corporations that are important for racial and ethnic minorities?

3. What are some of the measures that the federal government has used to increase diversity in the federal bureaucracy? To what extent have those measures been successful?

4. How can implementation, especially rulemaking and administrative adjudication, affect the daily lives of racial and ethnic minorities?

5. How effective is the judiciary in preventing bureaucrats from discriminating on account of race or ethnicity?

terms
KEY TERMS

Need to review key ideas in greater depth? Click here.

Administrative Adjudication p. 254
Bureaucracy p. 239
Bureaucrats p. 247
Cabinet Departments p. 240
Central Clearance p. 257
Civil Servants p. 248
Comptroller General p. 259
Government Accountability Office (GAO) p. 259

Government Corporations p. 247
Hatch Act p. 249
Implementation p. 251
Independent Executive Agencies p. 244
Independent Regulatory Commissions p. 243
Iron Triangle p. 255
Issue Networks p. 256

Legislative Veto p. 259
Patronage p. 248
Pendleton Act p. 248
Rulemaking p. 252
Senior Executive Service p. 257
Whistleblowers p. 258

readings
ADDITIONAL READINGS

Flashcard review.

Coleman-Adebayo, M. (2011). *No fear: A whistleblower's triumph over corruption and retaliation at the EPA*. Chicago: Chicago Review Press.

    The author recounts her experience as a whistleblower while working at the Environmental Protection Agency. The book discusses the deleterious effects of the mining operation that caused numerous deaths in South Africa; the EPA's initial refusal to act; her public exposure of the problem; the sexist and racist retaliation she endured; her successful court victory; and her establishment of an organization dedicated to protecting whistleblowers.

Cooper, C., & Block, R. (2006). *Disaster: Hurricane Katrina and the failure of Homeland Security.* New York: Times Books.

> In this book, two reporters for the *Wall Street Journal* closely examine the bureaucratic reasons for FEMA's failure to respond adequately to Hurricane Katrina.

Erie, S. P. (1988). *Rainbow's end: Irish Americans and the dilemmas of urban machine politics, 1840–1985.* Berkeley and Los Angeles: University of California Press.

> This book contends that Asian Americans, Blacks, Latinos, and even many Irish Americans did not benefit from patronage as much as others have claimed.

Hernández, K. L. (2010). *Migra! A history of the U.S. Border Patrol.* Berkeley: University of California Press.

> This book carefully chronicles the history of border patrol and immigration enforcement in the United States, concentrating specifically on how the border patrol came to exclusively focus on Mexican immigrants.

Landsberg, B. K. (1997). *Enforcing civil rights: Race discrimination and the Department of Justice.* Lawrence: University Press of Kansas.

> The author, a former career attorney for the Civil Rights Division of the Department of Justice, provides an insider's account of how this key bureaucratic division has enforced civil rights laws.

Maril, R. L. (2004). *Patrolling chaos: The U.S. Border Patrol in Deep South Texas.* Lubbock: Texas Tech University Press.

> This work examines the daily activities of border patrol agents from the perspective of the agent on the front lines.

The Judiciary: Blending Law and Politics

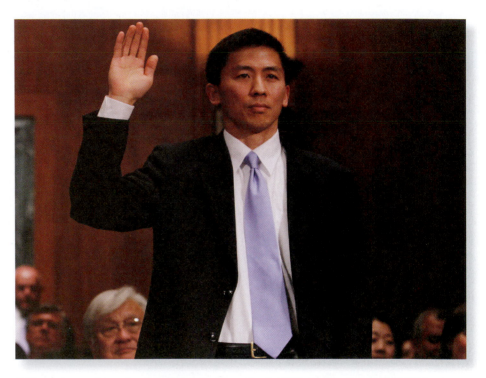

California law professor Goodwin Liu is sworn in on Capitol Hill in Washington, April 16, 2010, prior to testifying before the Senate Judiciary Committee hearing on his nomination to be U.S. Circuit Judge for the Ninth Circuit. Liu was never confirmed because Senate Republicans filibustered his nomination, arguing that he was too liberal. He now serves on the Supreme Court of California.

Goodwin Liu was born in 1970 in Georgia to parents who immigrated to America from Taiwan. As a child, Liu moved to Sacramento, California, where he was an extremely successful student. Liu graduated from Stanford University, earned a Rhodes Scholarship, helped found the AmeriCorps national service organization, and then graduated from Yale Law School in 1998. After law school, Liu clerked for U.S. Supreme Court Justice Ruth Bader Ginsburg and subsequently worked in the private sector. He soon joined the faculty of Boalt Law School at the University of California–Berkeley, one of the top American law schools. He quickly developed a reputation as a prolific and groundbreaking scholar, and he was promoted to associate dean.[1]

In early 2010, President Barack Obama nominated Liu to be a judge on the Ninth Circuit Court of Appeals. This court is extremely important in the U.S. judicial system because it handles appeals in federal cases originating in Alaska, Hawaii, Washington, Oregon, California, Arizona, Nevada, Idaho, Montana, and Pacific territories. Liu's nomination was especially important because Asian Americans have been underrepresented in the federal judiciary, and President Obama sought to rectify that problem by nominating more Asian American judges than any of his predecessors. Additionally, Liu was a well-known liberal legal scholar, who had written books and articles advocating that the Constitution be interpreted by contemporary standards, instead of in accordance with the intention of its authors. Consequently, Democratic senators and many in the legal community praised Liu's nomination, but archconservatives and Republican senators immediately complained that Liu would be an activist judge who would not rule according to legal precepts. Liu's Republican critics pointed to his vast legal writings and the fact that in 2005 Liu testified before the Senate Judiciary Committee against the confirmation of Supreme Court Justice Samuel Alito. Senate Democrats, the Obama administration, and legal scholars (including some conservatives) countered that Liu's nontraditional roots and scholarly achievements merited his confirmation. Moreover, they noted that the Senate had previously confirmed conservative judges with controversial publications. In May 2010, the Senate Judiciary Committee approved Liu's nomination by a 12–7 vote, with all Democrats voting in favor of him and all Republicans opposing him.[2]

After a year-long delay, Liu finally came to the full Senate for a vote, but Republicans launched a filibuster (see Chapter 6) against the nomination. The final cloture vote was 52 to 43; therefore, even though a majority of the Senate supported Liu's nomination, there were not a sufficient number of votes to end the filibuster. Consequently, he was not seated on the bench. Senate Democrats and the Obama administration were outraged. Senator Dianne Feinstein (D-CA) said, "To prevent an up-or-down vote for Professor Liu is to keep us from fulfilling our responsibility as senators."[3] However, we should note that in 2003, when the Republicans controlled the Senate, Democrats successfully filibustered Republican President George W. Bush's appeals court nomination of conservative Latino Miguel Estrada. Many of the same Democratic senators who criticized the Republican filibuster of Liu, including Senator Feinstein, voted to filibuster Estrada.[4] Although Liu would not serve on the federal bench, in September 2011, California Governor Jerry Brown named Liu to be a justice on the California Supreme Court.[5] Moreover, in 2013, the Democratic-controlled Senate changed the rules to prevent filibusters from obstructing lower-court nominees who enjoy the support of the majority of the Senate,[6] and in 2017, the Republican-controlled Senate ended the filibuster for Supreme Court nominees.[7]

intro

Justice Liu's story reveals important aspects of the federal judiciary, particularly the significance of the lower courts, such as the Ninth Circuit Court of Appeals. Although the U.S. Supreme Court is the most important and most well-known court in the federal judiciary, there are a vast number of federal courts and federal judges that significantly influence American politics. Liu's story also demonstrates the political nature of the appointment of federal judges, despite many people's notion that law and judging are above politics. As we discuss later in this chapter, the political fight over President Donald Trump's Supreme Court nominations of Neil Gorsuch and Brett Kavanaugh have been extremely controversial, but it is important to recognize that the same political forces influence nomination battles in the lower courts as well. Finally, although Liu's race did not directly affect his rejection, this story emphasizes the importance of racial and ethnic representation on the federal bench.

This chapter discusses the politics of the federal judiciary. It examines the complexity of judicial politics by first defining law and explaining how the federal judiciary *is organized. Then we examine the powers and limitations of the federal judiciary, especially concerning issues of civil rights. The chapter proceeds to a detailed discussion of the judicial selection process, which as the story of Goodwin Liu demonstrates, evidences the highly political nature of the federal courts. We then explain judicial decision making. Throughout this chapter, we emphasize the importance of race and ethnicity in judicial politics.*

Law and Courts

The primary task of the judicial branch is to interpret the law, but the concept of "law" is multifaceted and complex. Because the law cannot administer itself, courts are the political institutions that interpret the law and apply it to everyday situations. American courts exist under a dual system of authority, with state courts responsible for interpreting state law and federal courts responsible for interpreting federal law. Both systems operate simultaneously, but because we focus on the national government in this chapter, here we concentrate primarily on the structure of the federal court system. We addressed state courts in Chapter 3.

Dimensions of Law

Many Americans intuitively understand the meaning of the word *law*, but furnishing a workable definition is more difficult. Henry Abraham, an esteemed political scientist, defines law as "the rules of conduct that pertain to a given political order in society, rules that are backed by the organized force of the community."[8] Although generally helpful, this definition does not cover the many types of law that are relevant to American government. Most of this chapter deals with **public law**, which refers to legal matters that concern the government, at least as one of the parties to a legal dispute. Conversely, **private law** generally concerns disputes that arise between individuals—the government acts only as a referee. There are a variety of types of public law, including constitutional law, statutory law, and administrative law. **Constitutional law** refers to the rules for our government expressed in the Constitution. This kind of law is relevant for questions concerning separation of powers, federalism, civil rights, and civil liberties. **Statutory law** concerns laws that are made by the U.S. Congress and by state legislatures. **Administrative law** encompasses the rules and regulations made by bureaucrats and administrative agencies (see Chapter 8), which are not directly accountable to the public. The federal judiciary's power to interpret law gives it tremendous authority in shaping constitutional, statutory, and administrative politics.[9]

American law also divides into criminal law and civil law. **Criminal law** is law that pertains to violations of a code of behavior specified by local, state, or federal statutes; therefore, it falls under the category of public law. Serious crimes, such as homicide, rape, and armed robbery, are classified as felonies, and they often receive stiff sentences, including the death penalty for some homicides. The less serious crimes are known as misdemeanors, which are punishable

How do judges interpret the Constitution?

Public Law A type of law in which the government is a party to the case.

Private Law A type of law that concerns disputes between individuals.

Constitutional Law A type of law pertaining to the rules for our government expressed in the Constitution.

Statutory Law A type of law pertaining to rules made by legislatures, especially Congress.

Administrative Law A type of law pertaining to the rules made by bureaucrats and administrative agencies.

Criminal Law A type of law that pertains to violations of a code of behavior specified in local, state, and federal statutes.

by short jail terms, a modest fine, or both; in some cases, there is no penalty. Criminal cases involve a government prosecutor, who argues that a defendant is guilty of a crime, and a defense attorney, who argues that the evidence against the defendant is insufficient to prove guilt beyond a reasonable doubt.[10]

Civil Law A type of law that pertains to a dispute between two parties, at least one of which is a nongovernmental private party.

Civil law refers to disputes between private parties; therefore, legal experts consider it private law. Most civil cases involve disputes over a monetary value, such as alimony in a divorce case, compensation for negligent actions, and contract disputes. Some civil actions involve nonmonetary issues, such as custody battles in divorce cases. Regardless of whether monetary damages are sought, civil cases do not result in prison time or fines. Civil law cases feature a plaintiff (the party litigating the claim) and a defendant (the party against whom the claim is brought). Unlike criminal cases, civil cases do not always involve the government, although a government agency can be a plaintiff or a defendant in a civil case.[11]

Organization of the Federal Judiciary

The American judiciary consists of two simultaneously operating tracks—state courts and federal courts. The bulk of cases take place at the state court level, and the federal judiciary does not rule on a case unless it falls under federal jurisdiction. In criminal law, federal jurisdiction involves accusations of breaking federal statutes (e.g., abetting international terrorists, engaging in counterfeiting, kidnapping across state lines, and committing crimes on federal property). Civil law cases become federal only when the plaintiff and defendant are from different states and the value of the suit exceeds $75,000. The federal judiciary also exercises jurisdiction over controversies arising from the U.S. Constitution.[12]

Article 3 of the U.S. Constitution creates "one Supreme Court and . . . such inferior courts as Congress may from time to time ordain and establish." In 1789, Congress fulfilled this obligation by passing the Judiciary Act, which created the federal judiciary's three-tiered structure. It consists of U.S. District Courts, U.S. Circuit Courts of Appeals, and the U.S. Supreme Court.[13] Each level of the federal judiciary performs a distinct task (see Figure 9.1).

The U.S. District Courts serve primarily as the federal trial courts for both criminal and civil cases. Congress establishes each district, which is determined by geography. During the 2017 fiscal year, the ninety-four districts in the United States contained 677 authorized judgeships and 344,787 cases were filed, for an average of 509.3 cases per judge.[14] In federal criminal trials and civil suits, the district courts serve as the fact-finding institution, with judges presiding over trials and juries usually deciding if defendants are guilty (in criminal cases) or negligent (in civil cases). District courts also rule on constitutional cases. When people challenge government actions as unconstitutional, the case is often first heard in a district court, but the judge renders the decision without a jury.

Each district court is responsible for applying Supreme Court decisions to its specific geographic area. After the Supreme Court ruled in the second

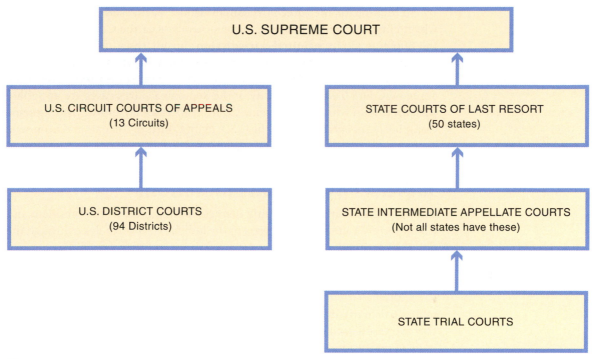

Figure 9.1 Ladder of Authority of American Courts

Brown v. Board of Education decision in 1955 that Southern states had to desegregate their schools with "all deliberate speed,"[15] federal district court judges in the South were responsible for deciding exactly how much time schools in their districts would be given to integrate. The geographic concentration of the federal district courts put these judges in a difficult position because they lived in their districts and faced intense pressure from their neighbors, friends, and associates to delay integration. Some of these judges were even victims of harassment.[16]

The federal judiciary also contains an intermediate level of appeals, known as the U.S. Circuit Courts of Appeals. An appeal reviews legal questions arising from a district court trial or a district court ruling on a specific legal matter. During fiscal year 2017, there were 167 authorized circuit court judgeships and 50,506 appeals were filed—an average of 302.4 cases per judge. However, appeals courts hear cases through a panel of judges, and in 2017 there were an average of approximately 907 cases filed per panel.[17]

A panel of three judges decides most appeals, and the side that earns the vote of at least two of the judges prevails. The nation is divided into eleven geographical circuits, each of which consists of a combination of neighboring states. The U.S. Court of Appeals for the Federal Circuit handles customs and patent cases, and the Circuit Court of Appeals for the District of Columbia hears appeals from cases involving federal government agencies and many administrative law cases.

Discover how to pursue a case through the court system.

Original Jurisdiction A defined set of cases that avoids a lower court and goes directly to the Supreme Court.

Appellate Jurisdiction The types of cases in which the Supreme Court reviews legal issues decided by a lower court.

At the top of the judicial hierarchy ladder is the U.S. Supreme Court, which currently consists of nine justices. Article 3 of the Constitution grants the Supreme Court **original jurisdiction** "in all cases affecting ambassadors, other public ministers and consuls, and those in which a state shall be a party." In those rare instances, a case avoids the lower courts and starts at the Supreme Court. The vast majority of the Supreme Court's cases are **appellate jurisdiction** in which the Supreme Court hears cases on appeal. The Supreme Court hears appeals from both the U.S. Circuit Courts of Appeals and from state supreme courts if the case concerns a federal constitutional or statutory issue.

Judicial Powers and Limitations

Judicial Review The power of a court to overturn a law or official government action because it is deemed unconstitutional.

Although the Constitution clearly defines the functions of the president and Congress, it is vague on the powers of the judiciary. Nevertheless, through the power of **judicial review**, whereby a court can nullify a law, policy, or government action by deeming it unconstitutional, the federal judiciary plays a critical role in shaping policy. Because it is not mentioned in the Constitution, the Supreme Court took the power of judicial review. This power is important, particularly in advancing civil rights. Legal scholars and political scientists propose a variety of philosophies on how judges should use the power of judicial review and on the limits of judicial review. These different views also interact with minority-group politics.

The Origins and Development of Judicial Review

A major facet of the federal judiciary is that the Framers designed it to be independent from popular control; that is, it was designed to go against the will of the majority. Article III of the U.S. Constitution states that once confirmed, federal judges serve a term of "good behavior"—that is, they can be removed from office only through the impeachment process. Impeachment of federal judges has generally been reserved for judges who commit ethical violations, not for judges who make unpopular decisions. Thus, Americans and their elected representatives lack recourse to remove federal judges who issue unpopular decisions, which allows federal judges to follow the law instead of public opinion.

Although the Constitution does not specifically mention judicial review, there is evidence that many Framers wanted the federal judiciary to possess this power. That the judiciary was designed to be independent from public opinion indicates that the Framers intended for the judiciary to check the popularly accountable branches of government, which is the basis of judicial review. After the Revolution, many state courts invalidated statutes that violated state constitutions.[18] Nevertheless, the early Supreme Court did not use the power of judicial review until the 1803 case of *Marbury v. Madison*.[19]

The controversy that led to judicial review began after the presidential election of 1800, in which Thomas Jefferson defeated incumbent John Adams. At the end of his presidency, Adams nominated and the Senate approved a number of new federal judges, including William Marbury, who was named the Justice of the Peace for the District of Columbia. Although duly appointed and confirmed by the end of Adams's term, Marbury did not receive his official paperwork by the time of Jefferson's inauguration. Incoming Secretary of State James Madison was required to deliver Marbury's paperwork, but, because of residual bitterness from the 1800 election and resentment over Adams's late appointments, Jefferson ordered Madison not to deliver Marbury's paperwork, thus denying him the judicial position. Marbury sued Madison and argued that a provision in the Judiciary Act of 1789 required the Court to order Madison to deliver the paperwork through original jurisdiction.

In 1803, Chief Justice John Marshall decided this seemingly insignificant case. Since assuming the position of chief justice in 1801, Marshall had sought to establish judicial review to increase the power of the federal judiciary and the national government. However, Marshall knew that Jefferson and congressional leaders opposed judicial review. He therefore needed to act carefully. Marshall shrewdly saw the *Marbury v. Madison* case as his perfect opportunity. He ruled that the portion of the Judiciary Act on which Marbury staked his claim was unconstitutional; thus, he could not order Madison to deliver the paperwork. Although the outcome of the decision favored Madison (and Jefferson), Marshall was the real winner. Because Jefferson and Madison won the case, they felt vindicated and did not vigorously challenge Marshall's use of judicial review. The Supreme Court has retained the power of judicial review since the *Marbury v. Madison* ruling.[20]

Judicial Review and Constitutional Interpretation

By striking down many important laws, judicial review plays a critical role in policymaking. Since 1803, the U.S. Supreme Court has used judicial review to overturn laws and official actions at the national, state, and local levels. Given its extraordinary power, the way in which justices approach judicial review and interpret the Constitution becomes extremely important.

There are different views on the extent to which judges should use judicial review to interfere with the elected branches of government. The **judicial restraint** view argues that the courts should defer to the will of the elected branches of government unless there is a blatant violation of the Constitution. Advocates of judicial restraint believe that because federal judges are unelected and unaccountable to the public, they should rarely be involved in policymaking. That task belongs to the popularly accountable branches of government—executives and legislatures. Conversely, the doctrine of **judicial activism** holds that the courts should vigorously check the other branches of government, even if the Constitution has not been explicitly violated. Advocates of judicial activism believe that the role of the judiciary is to correct injustices, especially for groups and individuals who are disadvantaged in the popularly elected branches of government.[21]

A related issue concerns the proper way to interpret the Constitution. Because judicial review entails judges' deciding whether laws or actions violate the Constitution, the way in which judges interpret the Constitution shapes

Judicial Restraint A conception of judicial review that believes courts should not overturn laws or government actions unless there is a clear directive in the Constitution.

Judicial Activism A conception of judicial review that believes courts should overturn laws or government actions even if there is no clear constitutional directive.

Original Intent A belief that the Constitution should be interpreted only according to the intent of its authors.

Living Constitution A belief that the Constitution should be interpreted to reflect contemporary times.

how they perform the task of judicial review. The doctrine of **original intent** argues that the Constitution should be interpreted strictly according to the intention of the people who wrote it, mainly the delegates to the Constitutional Convention, the Congresses that proposed the amendments, and the state legislatures that ratified the amendments. Advocates of original intent believe that unelected and unaccountable judges should not substitute their personal views of the Constitution for the views of the Framers.

In contrast, the doctrine of a **Living Constitution** argues that judges should update the meaning of the Constitution to fit contemporary controversies and social mores. Advocates of the Living Constitution believe that the meaning of the Constitution and its amendments should not be frozen in past eras that are no longer relevant.[22]

Judicial Review and Civil Rights

Judicial review has been especially important in advancing civil rights. In the 1950s, many state legislatures and governors—predominantly but not exclusively in the South—were insensitive or even hostile to the claims of African Americans seeking equal treatment and an end to segregation. Because Blacks were disenfranchised (see Chapter 5), these elected institutions were not responsive to their concerns. In fact, most politicians were responsive to the prejudice that existed among Whites. The U.S. Congress was also unresponsive to issues of racial and ethnic discrimination, and although Presidents Truman and Eisenhower contributed to the expansion of civil rights, they did not consistently support minority groups' efforts against discrimination.

The Supreme Court's use of judicial review was the only recourse at the time for racial and ethnic minority groups combating inequality and segregation. In the landmark 1954 case *Brown v. Board of Education*,[23] the U.S. Supreme Court employed judicial review to declare state segregation laws to be a violation of the Fourteenth Amendment to the Constitution, thereby invalidating those segregation laws. This use of judicial review resulted in a shifting policy in relation to federalism. Prior to the *Brown* decision, states believed that it was their "right" to discriminate because of race, but the Supreme Court's use of judicial review made the issue of racial discrimination a national one. There are other ways (discussed in this chapter) in which the federal judiciary's use of judicial review (or refusal to overturn laws or actions) has affected civil rights.

The debates between judicial activism and judicial restraint and between original intent and the Living Constitution have therefore affected civil rights. Because most of the people involved in drafting the Fourteenth Amendment did not intend for it to prohibit segregation, and the same Congress that proposed the Fourteenth Amendment also voted to segregate schools in the District of Columbia, a strict original-intent approach to interpreting the Fourteenth Amendment would rule that the amendment does not prevent segregation. Consequently, civil rights advocates have preferred judicial activism and a Living Constitution interpretation. The justices deciding *Brown v. Board of Education* updated the meaning of the Fourteenth Amendment—taking a

evaluating equality

Judicial Review, Legal Interpretation, and Civil Rights

Although it is an accepted aspect of our political system, judicial review is still controversial. Because federal judges are unelected and unaccountable, judicial review gives them the authority to thwart the will of the majority, which is undemocratic. In his classic book, *The Least Dangerous Branch: The Supreme Court and the Bar of Politics,** legal scholar Alexander Bickel created the term "counter-majoritarian difficulty" to describe how judicial review conflicts with democratic government and majority rule. However, most legal scholars support judicial review, even if they disagree with specific decisions, because it

prevents the majority from violating the rights of the minority. Judicial review preserves the Constitution as the supreme law of the land.

Judicial review is also important for civil rights. As we discussed previously, it was responsible for landmark civil rights cases, such as *Brown v. Board of Education*. However, it was also responsible for cases that infringed on civil rights, such as *Dred Scott v. Sandford* (see Chapter 5). Moreover, as we discussed in Chapter 5, judicial review has limited affirmative action. In addition to judicial review itself, the way in which courts interpret the Constitution can affect civil rights. Recall that an

original-intent method of constitutional interpretation usually results in limiting civil rights.

Debate among your classmates the merit of judicial review in general and how it could influence civil rights outcomes in particular. Then debate the relative virtues of original intent versus the living Constitution and the virtues of judicial activism and judicial restraint. Again, focus the debate on how each method of interpretation can influence civil rights outcomes.

* Bickel, A. M. (1962). *The least dangerous branch: The Supreme Court at the bar of politics*. Indianapolis and New York: Bobbs-Merrill.

Living Constitution approach—by using recently published social science data demonstrating that segregation greatly harmed Black schoolchildren.[24] The Evaluating Equality box explores in more detail how judicial review and legal interpretation influence civil rights.

◁))

Listen to oral arguments on the United States v. Texas immigration case.

Limitations on the Courts

Because judicial review provides the federal judiciary with considerable power, limitations on judicial authority are important. One limitation is that courts cannot enforce their own rulings; to implement these rulings, judges must rely on other branches. This limitation was evident when President Andrew Jackson refused to enforce a Supreme Court decision that protected the sovereignty of the Cherokee Nation and supremacy of the national government against the state of Georgia.[25] Conversely, Presidents Dwight Eisenhower and John Kennedy deployed the military to enforce federal court orders to integrate public schools in the South.[26]

The constitutional amendment process can also check Supreme Court decisions. If enough members of Congress and states disagree with the way that the Supreme Court interprets the Constitution, then a constitutional amendment can change the Constitution according to the preferences of that majority. One reason that Congress proposed the Fourteenth Amendment (1868), which confers full citizenship on all citizens regardless of race, was to reverse the holding of the infamous 1857 *Dred Scott v. Sandford* decision.

In that case, the Court ruled that Blacks, whether free or slave, were not citizens under the Constitution, and it invoked judicial review to invalidate the Missouri Compromise, in which Congress demarcated where slavery would be allowed. The Court held that Congress lacked the authority to decide the free or slave status of the states and territories.[27] The Thirteenth Amendment's ban on slavery throughout the nation effectively overturned that aspect of the *Dred Scott* decision.

Congress can also constrain the Court's power to interpret statutes by clarifying or rewriting a law in response to a Court decision. For example, in the 1989 case *Wards Cove Packing, Inc. v. Atonio*, the Supreme Court ruled that the Civil Rights Act of 1964 required plaintiffs claiming discrimination to prove that the employer practices in question intended to discriminate,[28] which made it more difficult for racial and ethnic minorities to win employment discrimination cases. In response to these decisions, Congress passed the Civil Rights Act of 1991, which explicitly placed the burden of proof on the employer to show that hiring practices were related to nondiscriminatory business necessities.[29] In short, Congress explicitly changed the language of the statute to reverse the Court's interpretation of the Civil Rights Act.

Justiciable The requirement that there must be an actual case or controversy between two parties for the federal judiciary to decide a case.

The federal judiciary also places internal restraints on itself by requiring that cases be **justiciable**. That is, the Court will only hear cases that feature two real parties requesting review to resolve an existing dispute. One key aspect of justiciability is **standing**. It requires litigants to demonstrate that they have actually been injured; one party may not sue on another party's behalf. Determining whether the litigants bringing suit have actually been injured can be extremely ambiguous, and the outcome of standing cases often reflects the prevailing ideology on the Court. For example, in the early 1970s the Supreme Court granted standing to environmentalists by ruling that environmental or aesthetic damage constituted sufficient injury to a person challenging a government policy that causes environmental damage.[30] The more conservative Supreme Court during the 1990s limited environmental suits by restricting standing for environmentalists.[31]

Standing An aspect of justiciability that requires the party bringing the case to show that the policy in question has caused it an injury.

Mootness An aspect of justiciability that requires that the conflict causing the case must still be germane; it could not have resolved itself on its own.

Another aspect of justiciability is **mootness**, which requires that a case still be germane; it cannot have resolved itself. Sometimes, the Supreme Court is able to postpone deciding a particularly controversial issue if it deems a case moot. For instance, in 1974, the Supreme Court would not entertain a White student's claim that the University of Washington Law School's use of affirmative action unconstitutionally discriminated against him because he was denied admission, whereas minorities with lower grades and LSAT scores were admitted. The district court ordered that the student be admitted, and the state appealed. By the time the case reached the Supreme Court in 1974, the student was about to graduate. Thus, the case was deemed moot,[32] and the Court was able to postpone ruling on the controversial issue of affirmative action.

Precedent A principle articulated in a previous case that judges use to decide current cases.

Precedent is a legal concept that checks judicial power. Precedent means that when ruling on a case, judges should use the principles established in similar cases that were previously decided. The American legal tradition expects judges to adhere to precedent because it makes the law stable and predictable. Nevertheless, strict adherence to precedent can stifle progressive legal change, especially with cases concerning racial and ethnic discrimination. For example, in 1896 the U.S. Supreme Court issued its first interpretation of the extent to which the Fourteenth Amendment equal protection clause banned segregation. In the *Plessy v. Ferguson* decision, the Supreme Court allowed states to segregate facilities by race through its now discredited principle of "separate but equal."[33]

A strict adherence to precedent would have required future courts to use that principle when deciding segregation cases. However, *Brown v. Board of Education* overturned the "separate but equal" precedent, with Chief Justice Earl Warren writing: "In approaching this problem, we cannot turn the clock back . . . to 1896 when *Plessy v. Ferguson* was written. We must consider public education in light of its full development."[34] By recognizing that the *Plessy* precedent was no longer relevant, the Court advanced civil rights.

Precedents are occasionally overturned because of personnel changes on the Court. The issue of affirmative action (see Chapter 5) illustrates this point. In 1990, the U.S. Supreme Court upheld by a 5–4 vote a federal policy that gave racial minorities a preference when seeking broadcasting licenses, ruling that the government need to ensure diversity in broadcasting outweighed possible discrimination suffered by nonminorities.[35] In 1991, Justice Clarence Thomas, who opposes affirmative action, replaced Justice Thurgood Marshall, who supported it. Consequently, in 1995 the Supreme Court reversed the 1990 precedent and overruled government policies that favored minorities.[36] After President Trump's appointment of Brett Kavanaugh to replace Justice Anthony Kennedy on the U.S. Supreme Court, observers are speculating whether the Court will uphold the precedent in *Roe v. Wade*,[37] which establishes a constitutional right to an abortion. Justice Kennedy had voted several times to uphold *Roe v. Wade*, and based on Kavanaugh's past, civil rights groups are concerned that he could provide a crucial fifth vote to overturn the precedent. During his Supreme Court confirmation process Kavanaugh told Senator Susan Collins (R-ME) that *Roe v. Wade* is "settled law," but Democratic Senators were not convinced that he will preserve this precedent.[38]

Thurgood Marshall—the first non-White Supreme Court Justice—was appointed in 1967. When he retired in 1991, he was replaced by Clarence Thomas who, like Marshall, is African American, but Thomas holds different views than Marshall. In 2009, for the first time in American history, the Supreme Court included two non-Whites: Clarence Thomas and Sonia Sotomayor, the first Latina justice.

Judicial Selection

Given the federal judiciary's power and the fact that once confirmed, judges serve a term of "good behavior," we want to focus on the characteristics of federal judges and the process by which they are selected. This selection process is the only time the elected branches of government (and the people) have any influence over the composition of the federal judiciary. The process in turn influences the racial and ethnic composition of the federal bench.

Nominating Judges

When selecting federal judges, presidents, with the help of staff, look for qualified candidates, but not necessarily for the top legal minds. Technically, there is no requirement that a federal judge have a formal legal education, and until 1957, at least one justice without a formal law degree served on the Supreme Court.[39] There is now an expectation that federal judges not only have a law degree, but also have experience in the federal legal system; many believe that Supreme Court justices should have appellate judicial experience. In fact, Elena Kagan is the only current justice who never previously served as a judge, but she was the Dean of Harvard Law School and U.S. Solicitor General.[40]

Even though merit is important, presidents are more concerned about satisfying political considerations when filling judicial vacancies. For lower court appointments, presidents rely on **senatorial courtesy**, by which they consult with senators in their party who represent the states where the vacancy occurs. Those senators often select qualified individuals, but they are generally more concerned with rewarding political supporters. Nevertheless, scholars have shown that presidents do not always adhere to senatorial courtesy.[41]

Senatorial Courtesy The practice whereby a president consults with senators in his party to find potential lower court vacancies that occur in the senators' states.

There is evidence that political service is relevant for Supreme Court nominations. For example, when nominating Earl Warren to be chief justice of the Supreme Court in 1953, Republican president Dwight Eisenhower strongly considered Warren's past service to the Republican Party, including running as the Republican nominee for vice president in 1948.[42]

Presidents are primarily concerned that their judicial appointees share their ideology. Republican presidents tend to support advocates of judicial restraint and original intent in controversial civil rights and civil liberties cases; Democratic presidents tend to back judicial activists and supporters of a living Constitution.

The U.S. Supreme Court Justices in their robes. Front row, left to right: Ruth Bader Ginsburg, Anthony Kennedy (who has since retired), Chief Justice John G. Roberts, Clarence Thomas, and Stephen G. Breyer. Back row, left to right: Elena Kagan, Samuel A. Alioto, Jr., Sonia Sotomayor, and Neil M. Gorsuch.

As a result, most judicial nominees come from the same party as the nominating president. Since 1977, at least 79 percent of district and appeals court appointments have been of the same party as the appointing president.[43]

Supreme Court appointments are extremely important and receive considerable attention. (See Table 9.1 for a list of current justices and see the photo on the previous page.) It follows, then, that presidents are especially concerned about ideological compatibility. Candidates for president even campaign on the kinds of justices they would appoint to the Supreme Court if elected. Although presidents usually have succeeded in appointing ideologically compatible justices, sometimes they are disappointed. President George H. W. Bush appointed Justice David Souter from New Hampshire based on the advice of his White House Chief of Staff John Sununu, who had been governor of New Hampshire. Bush wrongly expected Souter to be conservative and restrained on civil rights and civil liberties issues, but Justice Souter emerged as more liberal than expected (see Table 9.2).[44]

TABLE 9.1 Justices of the U.S. Supreme Court, 2018*

Name	Race	Born	Year Appt.	Appt. Pres.	Party
John Roberts, Chief Justice	White	1955	2005	G. W. Bush	R
Clarence Thomas	Black	1948	1991	G. H. W. Bush	R
Ruth Bader Ginsburg	White	1933	1993	Clinton	D
Stephen Breyer	White	1938	1994	Clinton	D
Samuel Alito	White	1955	2006	G. W. Bush	R
Sonia Sotomayor	Latina	1954	2009	Obama	D
Elena Kagan	White	1960	2010	Obama	D
Neil M. Gorsuch	White	1967	2017	Trump	R
Brett M. Kavanaugh	White	1965	2018	Trump	R

Source: Adapted from U.S. Supreme Court. (n.d.). Biographies of current justices of the Supreme Court. Retrieved October 20, 2018, from https://www.supremecourt.gov/about/biographies.aspx.

TABLE 9.2 Average Ideology Score of U.S. Supreme Court Justices Appointed since 1937 (Arranged from Most Liberal to Most Conservative)

Justice	Appointing President and Party	Average Ideology
William Douglas	Franklin Roosevelt, Democrat	−4.680
Thurgood Marshall	Lyndon Johnson, Democrat	−2.813
Sonia Sotomayor[a]	Barack Obama, Democrat	−2.151
William Brennan	Dwight Eisenhower, Republican	−1.931
John Paul Stevens	Gerald Ford, Republican	−1.820
Hugo Black	Franklin Roosevelt, Democrat	−1.756

(Continued)

TABLE 9.2 *(Continued)*

Justice	Appointing President and Party	Average Ideology
Ruth Bader Ginsburg[a]	William Clinton, Democrat	−1.598
Frank Murphy	Franklin Roosevelt, Democrat	−1.587
Elena Kagan[a]	Barack Obama, Democrat	−1.529
Abraham Fortas	Lyndon Johnson, Democrat	−1.430
Wiley Rutledge	Franklin Roosevelt, Democrat	−1.412
Earl Warren	Dwight Eisenhower, Republican	−1.258
Stephen Breyer[a]	William Clinton, Democrat	−1.133
Arthur Goldberg	John F. Kennedy, Democrat	−1.054
David Souter	George H.W. Bush, Republican	−0.784
James Byrnes	Franklin Roosevelt, Democrat	−0.190
Harry Blackmun	Richard Nixon, Republican	−0.030
Stanley Reed	Franklin Roosevelt, Democrat	0.381
Byron White	John F. Kennedy, Democrat	0.423
Potter Stewart	Dwight Eisenhower, Republican	0.438
Felix Frankfurter	Franklin Roosevelt, Democrat	0.501
Tom Clark	Harry Truman, Democrat	0.504
Anthony Kennedy[a]	Ronald Reagan, Republican	0.665
Robert Jackson	Franklin Roosevelt, Democrat	0.700
Lewis Powell	Richard Nixon, Republican	0.942
John Roberts[a]	George W. Bush, Republican	0.954
Sandra Day O'Connor	Ronald Reagan, Republican	0.981
Harold Burton	Harry Truman, Democrat	1.045
Fred Vinson	Harry Truman, Democrat	1.046
Sherman Minton	Harry Truman, Democrat	1.124
Charles Whitaker	Dwight Eisenhower, Republican	1.239
Neil Gorsuch[a]	Donald Trump, Republican	1.503
John Harlan II	Dwight Eisenhower, Republican	1.624
Samuel Alito[a]	George W. Bush, Republican	1.677
Warren Burger	Richard Nixon, Republican	1.858
Antonin Scalia	Ronald Reagan, Republican	2.478
William Rehnquist	Richard Nixon, Republican	2.948
Clarence Thomas[a]	George H. W. Bush, Republican	3.578

[a] *Data available up through the 2017–2018 term.*

Source: Data adapted from Martin, A. D., & Quinn, K. M. (n.d.). Martin-Quinn scores: Measures. Retrieved July 9, 2018, from http://mqscores.lsa.umich.edu/measures.php. For each justice, the authors averaged the mean scores for each year provided by Martin and Quinn.

Confirming Judges

The appointment process does not end with the president's nomination because ultimately the Senate decides whether to confirm the nominee. The Judiciary Committee conducts hearings at which the nominee and any other interested parties testify. Then the committee issues a recommendation, and the entire Senate votes on the nomination. More recently, the Judiciary Committee hearings last for days, often involving extensive questioning of nominees themselves in addition to hours of testimony from individuals supporting and opposing the nominee.

The majority of judicial nominations are approved with little opposition, even in periods of divided government (see Chapters 6 and 7), but there have been some exceptions. The Senate might reject lower court nominations if a president fails to abide by senatorial courtesy. If a senator in that president's party who represents the state where the vacancy occurs opposes the nomination, then the Senate Judiciary Committee will most likely refuse to act on the nomination, thus preventing that person from being confirmed.

The Senate has also rejected Supreme Court nominees because of accusations of character flaws. For example, in 1969 the Senate rejected appeals court judge Clement Haynsworth when President Richard Nixon nominated him to the U.S. Supreme Court because Haynsworth had ruled in cases where he had a financial conflict of interest.[45] Clarence Thomas was almost rejected in 1991 because he was accused of sexually harassing a female employee. Law professor Anita Hill claimed that while she worked for Clarence Thomas at the Department of Education and Equal Employment Opportunity Commission, Thomas had frequently made sexually suggestive comments to her. Although this allegation was initially part of a confidential FBI background investigation, it was publically disclosed, and the Senate Judiciary Committee subsequently required Hill to testify. Hill's testimony provided graphic detail about the sexual harassment, and because the proceedings were televised, millions of Americans viewed Hill's testimony. When Clarence Thomas testified before the Senate Judiciary Committee, he commented that the hearing was "a high-tech lynching for uppity Blacks who deign to think for themselves." Thomas was contending that he was being persecuted for being a Black conservative. The Senate conformed Thomas by a narrow 52–48 margin, and his confirmation generated a long-lasting impact by putting the issue of sexual harassment on the national stage and prompted many women to run for political office in 1992.[46]

The Senate has also rejected Supreme Court nominees who are perceived to be ideologically extreme. This means that a nominee who advocates extreme restraint is less likely to be confirmed in a Democratic-controlled Senate and a nominee who advocates extreme activism is less likely to be confirmed in a Republican-controlled Senate. In 1987, the Democratic Senate rejected Ronald Reagan's nomination of Robert Bork because Bork had cultivated a reputation as a proponent of extreme restraint and original intent views, such as the unwillingness to recognize a constitutional right to privacy (see Chapter 4) or to extend Fourteenth Amendment protections to women (see Chapter 5).

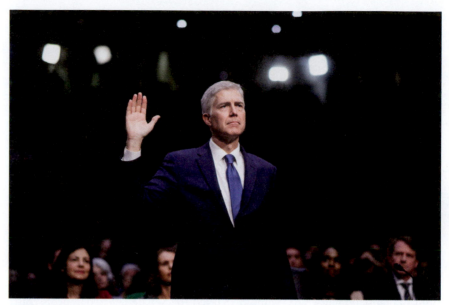

Judge Neil Gorsuch is sworn in to testify at his Senate Judiciary Committee hearing on Capitol Hill in Washington, DC, on March 20, 2017. Senate Republicans invoked the so-called nuclear option to confirm Gorsuch, which lowers the number of votes required to confirm Supreme Court nominees to 51 from 60. Although Gorsuch's predecessor on the Court, Antonin Scalia, died in February 2016, the Republican-controlled Senate refused to act on President Obama's nominee Merrick Garland. Therefore, President Trump was able to nominate Gorsuch and secure his confirmation.

Moreover, Bork's rejection changed the nomination process because the Senate, the media, and the public have paid closer attention to the nomination process, particularly the ideology of the nominee.[47] Nevertheless, to date there have not been any Senate votes that have resulted in a rejection.

When Justice Antonin Scalia unexpectedly died in February 2016, President Obama had an opportunity to appoint his third Supreme Court justice. However, immediately upon Justice Scalia's passing—before President Obama nominated anybody—Senate Majority Leader Mitch McConnell announced that the Senate would not even vote on a nomination, arguing that because President Obama's presidency was almost concluded, the next president should name the replacement. Regardless, President Obama nominated DC Appeals Court Judge Merrick Garland as Scalia's replacement. Garland is generally regarded as a centrist who was overwhelmingly approved for the appeals court and earned praise from many Republicans.[48] However, Republicans never acted on Garland's nomination, and he was never appointed to the Supreme Court. Instead, President Trump nominated conservative judge Neil Gorsuch, who was confirmed by a 54–45 vote.[49]

President Trump's nomination of Brett Kavanaugh in 2018 highlighted issues of both ideology and character issues. Initially most Democrats opposed Kavanaugh because of his views, especially his likely opposition to abortion rights and belief in strong executive authority.[50] However, similar to the Clarence Thomas nomination, a report surfaced that when Kavanaugh was in high school he sexually assaulted a female student. Subsequently, another woman indicated that Kavanaugh assaulted her while he was a freshman at Yale University. Kavanaugh and one of the alleged victims, Dr. Christine Blasey-Ford, appeared before the Senate Judiciary Committee to testify about the sexual assault allegation. Many observers found Dr. Ford's testimony to be very compelling, but Kavanaugh's interaction with the Democratic Senators on the committee was extremely combative. The debate over Kavanaugh's nomination was extremely controversial, especially in the context of the #MeToo movement that seeks to combat sexual assault and sexual harassment. Ultimately, the Senate confirmed Kavanaugh, but the two-vote margin was the slimmest that any Supreme Court Justice has received since 1881.[51]

Recently, lower court nominees have not been confirmed because of procedural maneuvering in the Senate. Beginning in the 1990s, the Republican-controlled Senate thwarted some of President Bill Clinton's nominees because the Judiciary Committee Chair, Orrin Hatch (R-UT), refused to act on lower court nominees deemed too activist. The Senate would have most likely confirmed those nominees if there had been a vote, but Senator Hatch used his power as chair to prevent that vote from occurring. When the Democrats controlled the Senate (2001–2002 and 2007–2008), the Judiciary Committee chair, Patrick Leahy (D-VT), held up President Bush's nominees who advocated extreme restraint. Furthermore, when the Republicans controlled the Senate from 2003 through 2006, Senate Democrats filibustered some of President Bush's more extreme restraint nominees, such as Miguel Estrada, and, as the opening vignette shows, Republicans were willing to filibuster President Obama's nominees when Democrats controlled the Senate in 2011. Despite these more controversial procedural rejections, a significant majority of judicial nominees have been confirmed.[52] Moreover, as we mentioned earlier, Senate Republicans in 2017 ended the ability to use the filibuster for Supreme Court nominations, which secured the confirmations of Neil Gorsuch and Brett Kavanaugh.[53]

Race and Ethnicity and Judicial Nominations

For much of American history, many aspects of representativeness have influenced federal court appointments. Because Supreme Court decisions affect particular regions, presidents have used region as a key criterion for selecting nominees. Presidents have also been concerned with religious representativeness, particularly ensuring that Catholic and Jewish justices serve on the Supreme Court. Currently, three justices on the Court are Jewish—Ginsburg, Breyer, and Kagan. Thus far, no other non-Christians (e.g., Muslims or Buddhists) have served on the Supreme Court.

Gender is a concern as well. In 1981, President Reagan appointed Sandra Day O'Connor as the first female justice, and in 1994, President Clinton appointed Ruth Bader Ginsburg as the second female justice. Justice O'Connor's retirement in 2005 left only one woman serving on the Supreme Court, but both of President Obama's Supreme Court appointments (Sonia Sotomayor and Elena Kagan) were female; consequently, since 2010 there have been three women on the Supreme Court—the most ever. As of 2016 about 27.1 percent of all judges (federal or state) are female.[54]

Race and ethnicity have also emerged as a significant factor in lower court appointments. Presidents John Kennedy, Lyndon Johnson, and Richard Nixon appointed a few members of racial and ethnic minority groups, primarily to the district courts, but it was not until the Carter administration that presidents became more concerned with representing minorities. The Measuring Equality box discusses in more detail presidents' records on appointing minorities to the federal district and appeals courts, and it demonstrates how President Obama significantly outpaced other presidents in terms of nominating minorities to the federal judiciary, especially Asian Americans, which we discussed in the opening vignette.

Unlike nominations to the lower courts, however, race and ethnicity have not been a crucial factor with Supreme Court nominations. In 1967, President Johnson appointed Thurgood Marshall as the first African American to serve on the Court, and this was undoubtedly a historic appointment. When Justice Marshall retired in 1991, President George H. W. Bush faced the prospect of an all-White Supreme Court; therefore, he placed a high priority on appointing another racial minority member. At the same time, President Bush

U.S. Supreme Court judge Sonia Sotomayor arrives in San Juan, December 16, 2009. Sotomayor was visiting Puerto Rico for the first time since becoming the U.S. Supreme Court's first Latina justice, on the invitation of local and U.S. federal judges for a few private engagements and to spend time with relatives.

measuring equality

Presidents' Records of Minority Judicial Appointments to the Lower Federal Courts

This chapter has shown that the federal district courts and courts of appeals are important institutions in American government. These lower courts shape policies that affect racial and ethnic minorities. The extent to which racial and ethnic minorities are represented on these courts often translates into the legal protections those groups receive.

Presidential nomination is crucial to minority representation on the federal judiciary, but, as we discuss in this chapter, presidents did not pay attention to race or ethnicity when nominating federal judges until the 1960s. Only presidents Lyndon Johnson and George H. W. Bush appointed African Americans to the U.S. Supreme Court, and Barack Obama appointed the only Latina to the Supreme Court. To date, no Asian American or American Indian has ever served on the Supreme Court. There are considerably more opportunities, however, to appoint racial and ethnic minorities to the lower courts. President Jimmy Carter (1977–1981) was the first president to emphasize expanding racial minority representation on the federal bench. When it comes to appointing minorities in general and Blacks and Asian Americans in particular, President Barack Obama has far surpassed his predecessors.

Figure 9.2 examines the minority appointment records of Presidents Jimmy Carter, Ronald Reagan, George H. W. Bush, Bill Clinton, George W. Bush, Barack Obama, and Donald Trump (nominees in his first year). We display the data in the form of a bar chart, or histogram, which visually shows for each president the proportion of nominees according to race (White,

Black, Latino, Asian American, and American Indian). We have combined the data for the two courts.

- As you examine the data, try to ascertain whether presidents over time have been more likely to nominate minorities. Have there been any retrenchments?
- To what extent does a president's political party (Carter, Clinton, and Obama are the three Democratic presidents here) influence this minority appointment record?
- Are there variations among the different minority groups?

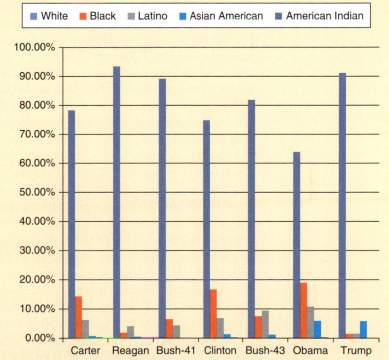

Figure 9.2 Race/Ethnicity of Judges in the Lower Federal Courts Selected during the Carter, Reagan, G. H. W. Bush, Clinton, G. W. Bush, and Obama (through the end of 2014) presidencies

Sources: Data adapted from McMillion, B. J. (2018, May 2). U.S. Circuit and District Court nominations during President Trump's first year in office. Congressional Research Service. Retrieved October 8, 2018, from https://fas.org/sgp/crs/misc/R45189.pdf; Slotnick, E., Schiavoni, S., & Goldman, S. (2017). Obama's judicial legacy: The final chapter. Journal of Law and Courts, 3, 363–422; Diascro, J. S., & Solberg, R. S. (2009). George W. Bush's legacy on the federal bench: Policy in the face of diversity. Judicature, 92(6), 294–295.

was also determined to appoint a supporter of judicial restraint and original intent, so he picked conservative African American appeals court judge Clarence Thomas. As we discussed above, Justice Thomas's confirmation was extremely controversial.

President Obama nominated Judge Sotomayor not only as a female, but also as the first Latina representative to serve on the Supreme Court. Judge Sotomayor is Puerto Rican, and she became the first Supreme Court justice who is both a member of an ethnic minority group and a woman. As of yet, there have been no American Indians or Asian Americans on the Supreme Court, although we should expect such nominations in the future. Nevertheless, both of President Trump's Supreme Court nominations (Neil Gorsuch and Brett Kavanaugh) have been White males.

Race and ethnicity can also play a role in the Senate confirmation of judicial nominees. In Chapter 6, we discussed the Senate's rejection of President Clinton's district court nomination of African American Ronnie White. Furthermore, as the opening vignette demonstrated, Republican senators successfully filibustered President Obama's nomination of Goodwin Liu. Goodwin Liu was not the only Asian American judicial nominee who faced a Republican filibuster. In 2009, President Obama nominated Edward Chen to the U.S. District Court for the Northern District of California, and Republicans delayed his confirmation, also claiming that he was too liberal. Judge Chen was eventually confirmed, but the process took more than 600 days, and only four Republican senators supported him.[55] As the opening vignette indicated, in 2013 the Senate amended its rules to prevent filibusters for lower-court nominees.

The confirmation battle over President Obama's nomination of Sonia Sotomayor to the Supreme Court also centered on race and ethnicity. As the first Latina nominated to the Supreme Court, she had tremendous support from Latinos and Latino groups. Latino activists were not only pleased about the possibility of the first Latina representative on the Supreme Court, but they also emphasized her personal story of growing up poor and being raised by a single mother. Similar to other successful Latinos, she worked hard and earned scholarships to prestigious schools (Princeton and Yale Law School in her case) and distinguished herself with a successful career. She serves as an inspiration to Puerto Ricans and other Latinos throughout the United States.[56] Even Florida senator Mel Martinez, then the lone Latino Republican senator, who took conservative positions on legal matters, was happy with Judge Sotomayor. Senator Martinez commented that he was "very impressed with her, not only her personal qualities, but her understanding of the role of the judiciary and the role of the judge."[57]

Vocal opponents of Sotomayor's confirmation, mainly Republicans and conservative activists, also focused on aspects of race and ethnicity. Some critics attacked her ruling in the case of *Ricci v. DeStefano*, which she decided as a judge on the U.S. Second Circuit Court of Appeals. This case concerned the affirmative-action policy of the city of New Haven, Connecticut, which promoted African American firefighters over Whites who scored higher on an examination. Judge Sotomayor sided with the city in this case. Before her confirmation vote, the U.S. Supreme Court sided with the White firefighters by a 5–4 vote, which provided more fodder for Sotomayor's critics.[58]

Additionally, critics attacked a previous statement that Judge Sotomayor had made. Specifically, she was quoted as saying, "A wise Latina woman with the richness of her experience would, more often than not, reach a better conclusion than a White male who hasn't lived that life." Even though her decision in *Ricci v. DeStefano* was consistent with the rulings of White justices and her statement was clearly meant to emphasize the importance of diversity in the federal judiciary, critics attacked her views on race. Most notably, former Republican Speaker of the House of Representatives Newt Gingrich and talk radio host Rush Limbaugh referred to her as "racist" or a "reverse racist." Although other Republican leaders refused to use the word *racist*, they still criticized her views on race and the law.[59] Despite these controversies, the Senate overwhelmingly confirmed Sonia Sotomayor by a 68–31 vote, with nine Republicans and all Democrats voting in her favor.[60]

Decision Making on the Supreme Court

Because the Supreme Court is a critical policymaking institution, we now look at how the justices arrive at decisions. There are procedures by which the Supreme Court arrives at decisions, as well as influences on that decision making. The decision-making process in turn affects minority-group politics.

Decision-Making Procedures

When a party loses in the U.S. court of appeals or a state supreme court, then that party can appeal its case to the U.S. Supreme Court. For more than a century, the Supreme Court automatically heard the appeals that came before it, but by the early twentieth century, its caseload had become too burdensome. In response, Congress passed the Judiciary Act of 1925, which gave the Supreme Court the authority to decide whether to hear a case.[61]

Now virtually all litigants seeking to appeal a case to the U.S. Supreme Court must file a **writ of *certiorari***, which asks the Court to hear the case. *Certiorari* is a Latin word meaning "to be informed of, or to be made certain in regard to." The so-called "Rule of Four" requires that four of the nine justices must agree to grant certiorari for the Court to hear the case, but the Court annually rejects approximately 99 percent of the certiorari petitions it receives.[62] When the Supreme Court denies a certiorari petition, the lower court opinion stands. Thus, the circuit courts of appeals and state supreme courts are extremely important in our judicial system.

Writ of *Certiorari* A formal legal document filed by the losing party in a lower court case that asks the Supreme Court to hear an appeal.

For the few cases in which the Court grants certiorari, the justices solicit briefs (i.e., the written legal arguments) from the attorneys for the two parties involved in the case. These briefs must follow a specified legal format and argue the legal merits of their clients' position. Justices read these briefs and often use them as a guide in reaching a decision and writing an opinion. Additionally,

***Amicus Curiae* (Friend of the Court)** Briefs filed by parties that have an interest in the outcome of a case but are not directly involved in it.

the justices read ***amicus curiae***—Latin for "friend of the court"—**briefs**, which are filed by parties who are not direct litigants in the case but have a stake in the outcome. Just like regular briefs, amicus curiae briefs can influence how the justices decide both certiorari decisions and case outcomes.[63]

The justices also listen to the litigants' oral arguments. Usually, the Court grants an hour total of oral argument for each case—each side is allotted one-half hour. In rare exceptions, the Court grants each side an hour. During the oral argument, justices are free to interrupt the litigants with questions, which are charged to the lawyers' time. Justices intend for questions to point out flaws in litigants' arguments or to help them make their case.[64]

After oral argument, the justices then confer privately in conference to discuss each case. The chief justice establishes rules for and presides over the conference discussion. The conference also includes a vote on the issue, with the side garnering at least five votes constituting the majority. If the chief justice is in the majority, then he assigns one of the justices (or himself) to write the opinion for the majority, known as the **majority opinion**. If the chief justice is not in the majority, then the most senior justice in the majority assigns the opinion. The justice assigned to write the majority opinion circulates a rough draft to the other justices, who can opt to endorse it or write their own opinions. A **concurring opinion** agrees with the outcome of the case but for reasons different from those expressed in the majority opinion. If a justice does not agree with the outcome of a case, then he or she writes a **dissenting opinion** arguing why the majority opinion was incorrect.[65]

Majority Opinion The opinion reflecting the winning outcome of a Supreme Court case that is signed by at least a plurality of the justices.

Concurring Opinion An opinion that agrees with the outcome of a Supreme Court case but for reasons different from those expressed in the majority opinion.

Dissenting Opinion An opinion that disagrees with the winning side of a Supreme Court case and explains why.

Because dissenting opinions represent the "losing" viewpoint, they have no legal validity, but they might ultimately prove useful. When the Supreme Court allowed racial segregation in *Plessy v. Ferguson* (1896), Justice John Marshall Harlan dissented, arguing that the Constitution prevents racial segregation.[66] Although Justice Harlan was the lone dissenter, the Supreme Court essentially adopted his opinion more than fifty years later when it declared segregation unconstitutional in *Brown v. Board of Education* (1954).[67] "Our Voices: Opinions of African American Supreme Court Justices" on page 289 examines in more detail the importance of dissenting opinions in civil rights cases.

Investigate the background of the justices.

The Influence of a Judge's Background on Judicial Decision Making

Since the middle of the twentieth century, political scientists have recognized that judges' backgrounds influence how they decide cases. We discussed above the importance of race and gender in the selection process. In addition to the issue of representation in an important branch of government, the race and gender of judges could also influence how they decide cases. However, the empirical research on the influence of race on judicial decision making for federal and state judges is mixed. Many studies demonstrate that race exerts no effect on judges' decisions in criminal and civil rights cases.[68] Nevertheless, others have argued that minority judges bring the perspective of their community to their work as judges,[69] and there is some evidence that minority judges are more "even-handed" than White judges are when sentencing Black and White defendants.[70] There is also considerable debate over the extent that gender directly affects judicial decision making in civil rights cases. Some studies have shown that gender exerts no impact on judicial decision making,[71] whereas other studies have found that women judges tend to rule in a more liberal fashion compared to male judges.[72] The bulk of empirical research has uncovered mixed evidence that gender influences judicial decision making.[73]

Despite the lack of clarity on the influence of race and gender on judges' decision making, there is overwhelming evidence that judges' personal beliefs also influence judicial decision making. As we discussed above, there are different philosophies of legal interpretation—judicial activism versus judicial restraint and original intent versus the living Constitution—and judges' personal beliefs shape which philosophy they embrace. Political scientists Jeffrey Segal and Harold Spaeth wrote a groundbreaking book titled *The Supreme Court and the Attitudinal Model*,[74] which argues that in deciding key cases Supreme Court justices are in fact policymakers—similar to members of Congress and the executive branch. Moreover, the justices make decisions based on their policy preferences, with liberal justices desiring liberal rulings on civil rights, civil liberties, and economic regulation cases, whereas conservative justices desire conservative outputs in those cases. Segal and Spaeth's book is especially interesting because they do not merely advocate for the importance of judicial ideology as a factor in judicial decision making; they argue that ideology is by far the best explanation of judicial decision making. Table 9.2 reports the ideology of recent Supreme Court justices, using scores developed by legal scholars Andrew Martin and Kevin Quinn, which are based on how the justices actually vote, with negative numbers indicating a more liberal justice and positive numbers indicating a more conservative justice. Notice the pattern whereby Democratic presidents appoint justices who are more liberal and Republican presidents appoint justices who are more conservative. However, there are notable exceptions.

Attorney Influence on Court Decision Making

Judges do not constitute the entirety of the American judicial system. Different types of attorneys also influence judicial decision making. The **solicitor general** is an executive branch attorney who argues the U.S. government's position, particularly the views of the president, before the U.S. Supreme Court. The Supreme Court allows the solicitor general to file amicus curiae briefs in any case he or she chooses. Because the solicitor general appears so frequently before the Court, he or she not only gains litigation experience, he or she also develops a close relationship with the justices. This helps to increase the solicitor general's chances of success in the federal judiciary, and empirical evidence demonstrates that the solicitor general is more likely than other parties to succeed in the Supreme Court at both the certiorari and merit stages.[75]

Law clerks, who are recent law school graduates, assist federal judges, and in doing so, they also influence judicial decision making. Law clerks research cases and write drafts of opinions, and Supreme Court clerks issue

Solicitor General A high-ranking lawyer in the Justice Department who argues cases before the Supreme Court on behalf of the U.S. government.

recommendations on certiorari petitions. Law clerks at the federal level start in the lower courts, usually right out of law school. After one year of experience at the lower court level, a select few clerks then move on to the Supreme Court. Law clerks generally serve for a period of one year and then often use their clerkships to obtain teaching positions at prestigious law schools or lucrative work in private practice.

Many Supreme Court justices once served as law clerks. Of the current justices, Chief Justice John Roberts clerked for Justice William Rehnquist, Justice Stephen Breyer clerked for Justice Arthur Goldberg, Justice Elena Kagan clerked for Justice Thurgood Marshall, Justice Neil Gorsuch clerked for Justices Byron White and Anthony Kennedy, and Justice Kavanaugh clerked for Justice Anthony Kennedy.[76] Law clerks generally hail from elite law schools and tend to be White and male. Since the early 1980s, approximately 5 percent of law clerks have been Asian American; approximately 2 percent have been African American; and approximately 1 percent have been Latino.[77]

Interest-Group Litigation
The practice of interest groups arguing cases before the judiciary as a means of influencing public policy.

Many attorneys who litigate before the Supreme Court work for interest groups (see Chapter 13) that use litigation as a means to affect public policy. **Interest-group litigation** refers to litigation by organized groups on behalf of clients to influence public policy, and such litigation has been especially useful for racial and ethnic minority interest groups. Because prior to the 1970s the elected branches of government were usually not receptive to the claims of racial and ethnic minority groups, the politically independent federal courts, where success depends on skillful legal argument and not on political support, became an attractive option.

The most significant example of an interest group that litigates is the National Association for the Advancement of Colored People and its offshoot, the NAACP Legal Defense and Education Fund (LDF). The NAACP won landmark Supreme Court cases that ended racial discrimination in housing and voting.[78] The LDF carefully planned the litigation campaign for the extremely crucial case of *Brown v. Board of Education*.[79] In the process, the group has contributed immensely to ending racial discrimination. The LDF still uses litigation to advance civil rights in issues related to voting, criminal law, education, and economic equality.[80]

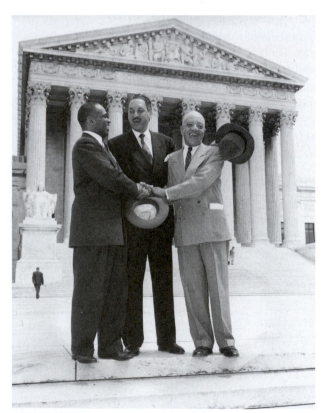

NAACP Legal Defense Fund attorneys George E. C. Hayes, left, Thurgood Marshall, center, and James Nabrit, right, outside of the U.S. Supreme Court building after their historic victory in *Brown v. Board of Education*. This victory underscores the importance of interest groups in the judicial process because these attorneys carefully planned a strategy that revolutionized education for racial and ethnic minorities. However, the NAACP Legal Defense Fund and other civil rights interest groups argue that education has been resegregating in recent years.

our voices

Opinions of African American Supreme Court Justices

Opinions are an essential part of the judicial process. In addition to merely rendering a decision, judges write lengthy opinions that explain the reasons for their rulings, and these opinions are responsible for the development of American law. Opinions generally contain legal analysis that discusses the key precedents that led the author to his or her decision. Occasionally, opinions reveal the personal values and experiences of the authors.

The values and experiences reflected in opinions written by racial minority judges sometimes emphasize the relevance of race in American law in a way that few other government words or actions can. Following we excerpt opinions from the two African American Supreme Court justices—Thurgood Marshall and Clarence Thomas. Justice Marshall's opinion is from his dissent in *University of California v. Bakke*, in which a majority of the Court required that the University of California–Davis Medical School admit a White applicant. Marshall argued that the Court should not interfere with a state university's use of a quota system that favors minority candidates as a way to compensate for past discrimination. Justice Thomas's opinion is from *Virginia v. Black*, which concerned the constitutionality of Virginia's ban on cross burning. Black argued that cross burning should be protected under the First Amendment's freedom of speech. The Supreme Court upheld the ban, but it ruled that the First Amendment does offer some protection to cross burning. Justice Thomas disagreed with that view, declaring that cross burning is different from mere speech because of its close ties to Ku Klux Klan terrorism. Notice how both justices use race in their dissenting opinions even though one is identified as a liberal judge and the other as a conservative.

Marshall Dissent: . . . For it must be remembered that, during most of the past 200 years, the Constitution as interpreted by this Court did not prohibit the most ingenious and pervasive forms of discrimination against the Negro. Now when a state acts to remedy the effects of that legacy of discrimination, I cannot believe that the same Constitution stands as a barrier. . . . The position of the Negro today in America is the tragic, but inevitable, consequence of centuries of unequal treatment. Measured by any benchmark of comfort or achievement, meaningful equality remains a distant dream for the Negro. . . . At every point from birth to death the impact of the past is reflected in the still disfavored position of the Negro. In light of the sorry history of discrimination and its devastating impact on the lives of Negroes, bringing the Negro into the mainstream of American life, should be state interest of the highest order. To fail to do so will ensure that America will forever remain a divided society.

Thomas Dissent: I believe that the majority errs in imputing an expressive component to the activity in question [cross burning]. . . . In my view, whatever expressive value cross burning has, the legislature simply wrote it out by banning only intimidating conduct undertaken by a particular means. A conclusion that the statute prohibiting cross burning with an intent to discriminate sweeps beyond a prohibition on certain conduct into the zone of expression overlooks not only the words of the statute but also reality. . . . Indeed, the connection between cross burning and violence is well-ingrained. . . . To me, the majority's brief history of the Ku Klux Klan only reinforces the common understanding of the Klan as a terrorist organization, which, in its endeavor to intimidate, or even eliminate those it dislikes, uses the most brutal of methods. . . . In our culture, cross burning has almost invariably meant lawlessness and understandably instills in its victims well-grounded fear of physical violence.

Sources: Regents of the University of California v. Bakke, 438 U.S. 235 (1978), 387, 395–396; *Virginia v. Black*, 538 U.S. 343 (2003), 388–391.

Based on the LDF's success, other interest groups advocating on behalf of racial and ethnic minorities have employed a litigation strategy to improve the civil rights of the people they represent. The Mexican American Legal Defense and Education Fund (MALDEF) argues cases on behalf of Latinos to influence policies concerning education and employment discrimination, immigration, and voting rights.[81] The Native American Rights Fund (NARF) litigates civil rights issues for American Indians, such as protecting tribal identity and resources, ending discrimination against Indians, and negotiating with the federal and state governments on behalf of tribes and individuals.[82] Asian Americans Advancing Justice (AAAJ) argues cases for Asian Americans concerning discrimination, voting rights, anti-Asian violence, language barriers, and immigration.[83] Recently MALDEF and AAAJ collaborated to sue the Trump administration because it plans to ask people if they are citizens of the United Sates as part of the 2020 United States Census.[84]

Conclusion

Despite the political independence of the federal judiciary, there is no doubt that it is a highly political institution. Congress creates the organization of the federal judiciary, and because the certiorari process prevents the Supreme Court from hearing most appeals, lower courts serve a vital function in the federal judiciary. Moreover, debates over the extent to which federal judges should use judicial review manifest themselves along political lines, especially during the process of appointing judges. When selecting judicial nominees, presidents generally employ political and ideological criteria, and the Senate considers political ramifications when it decides whether to confirm those nominees. Finally, interest groups and executive branch officials play an important role in the judicial process.

Throughout this chapter, we have demonstrated the important connection between the judiciary and the politics of race and ethnicity. The federal judiciary interprets constitutional, statutory, and administrative law, all of which pertain to civil rights. Because federal judges are not accountable to the public, they are able to act on behalf of racial and ethnic minority groups, which often lack political support for their goals. Additionally, the organization of the federal judiciary and the judiciary's decision-making procedures, especially on the Supreme Court, greatly affect the extent of legal protections for racial and ethnic minorities.

Debates over the power of judicial review also affect racial and ethnic minorities. Most groups advocating on behalf of civil rights rely on judicial activism and the notion of a living Constitution more than on judicial restraint and original intent. The president's willingness to enforce judicial decisions and Congress's reaction to key rulings can also affect the advancement of civil rights. Constraints on the judiciary, such as justiciability and strict adherence to precedent, can stifle civil rights progress.

The story of President Obama's appointment of Goodwin Liu emphasizes the relevance of race and ethnicity in judicial politics. Although 109 of the 114 individuals who have served on the U.S. Supreme Court have been White, recent presidents, especially President Obama, have sought to increase the presence of African Americans, Latinos, and Asian Americans on the lower courts. In other words, minority representation is a key issue in the judicial system as a whole.

Goodwin Liu's story and the confirmation battle over Justice Sotomayor also reveal that the issue of the presence of racial and ethnic minorities on the federal bench extends beyond descriptive and symbolic representation. Minority representation affects the substance of the decisions reached. Because most racial and ethnic minority judges have experienced firsthand the harmful effects of discrimination, they embrace judicial activism on civil rights and civil liberties cases. Of course, there are exceptions, such as Supreme Court Justice Clarence Thomas and President Bush's appeals court appointment of conservative Black female Judge Janice Rogers Brown.[85] In sum, there is no doubt that the nomination and confirmation of racial and ethnic minorities to the federal judiciary are crucial issues in minority group politics.

review REVIEW QUESTIONS

1. What was the role of federal district court judges in enforcing desegregation laws?

2. How do debates about judicial activism versus judicial restraint and about a Living Constitution versus original intent relate to minority-group politics?

3. How does the judicial nomination and confirmation process influence racial and ethnic minority representation on the federal bench?

4. What proportion of lower court judges are Black, Latino, Asian American, and American Indian, and what impact do these proportions have on civil rights decisions?

5. How has interest-group activity led to judicial decisions that have advanced civil rights?

Check your understanding of Chapter 9.

terms KEY TERMS

Administrative Law p. 267

Amicus Curiae (Friend of the Court) p. 286

Appellate Jurisdiction p. 270

Civil Law p. 268

Concurring Opinion p. 286

Constitutional Law p. 267

Criminal Law p. 267

Dissenting Opinion p. 286

Interest-Group Litigation p. 288

Judicial Activism p. 271

Judicial Restraint p. 271

Judicial Review p. 270

Justiciable p. 274

Living Constitution p. 272

Majority Opinion p. 286

Mootness p. 274

Original Intent p. 272

Original Jurisdiction p. 270

Precedent p. 274

Private Law, p. 267

Public Law, p. 267

Senatorial Courtesy p. 276

Solicitor General p. 287

Standing p. 274

Statutory Law p. 267

Writ of *Certiorari* p. 285

Need to review key ideas in greater depth? Click here.

Flashcard review.

readings

ADDITIONAL READINGS

Foskett, K. (2004). *Judging Thomas: The life and times of Clarence Thomas.* New York: Morrow.

> This book offers an objective and personal account of Justice Thomas's life and career.

Law, A. O. (2010). *The immigration battle in American courts.*
New York: Cambridge University Press.

> This book examines the historic role of the federal judiciary in shaping immigration law. The author's careful analysis demonstrates that immigrants fare better in the U.S. Circuit Courts of Appeals than in the U.S. Supreme Court.

Rowan, C. T. (2002). *Dream makers, dream breakers: The world of Justice Thurgood Marshall* (New York: Welcome Rain, 2002).

> This is a rerelease of the distinguished journalist Carl T. Rowan's classic biography of the nation's first non-White U.S. Supreme Court justice.

Soltero, C. R. (2006). *Latinos and the American law: Landmark Supreme Court cases.* Austin: University of Texas Press.

> This book provides a chronological account of key U.S. Supreme Court cases that have affected Latino civil rights since the nineteenth century.

Tsesis, A. (2008). *We shall overcome: A history of civil rights and the law.* New Haven, CT: Yale University Press.

> This book carefully traces the history of the extent to which law and courts have affected discrimination, particularly against African Americans, in the United States.

10

Public Opinion: Divided By Race?

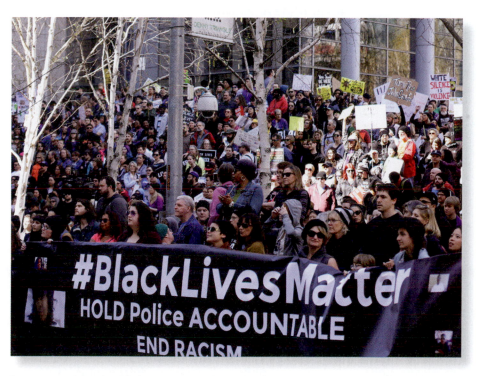

Protesters took part in a Black Lives Matter rally in Seattle, April 15, 2017.

R ace relations have deteriorated considerably in the United States since Donald Trump's election in November 2016. As one political commentator poignantly stated, President Trump has chosen "to draw political sustenance from the poisoned well of racial resentment."[1] Moreover, Trump has wholeheartedly embraced the two elements of the politics of racism, namely by attacking individuals and groups solely on the basis of their race, and by purposefully appealing to White voters in order to win their support by focusing on issues that may heighten hate, fear, and racial resentment among White Americans.[2]

Americans' perceptions of President Trump and assessments of his job performance are largely influenced by demographic factors and attitudinal traits that typically shape presidential approval ratings—party affiliation, political ideology, and racial/ethnic identification.[3] According to a Pew Research Center poll, 60 percent of Americans believe that Donald Trump's election has worsened the state of race relations in this country.[4] The results of the poll reveal a growing bipartisan sentiment that the Trump administration has created a political environment that symbolizes a regressive step in race relations in the United States.[5] A 2018 poll by the Associated Press–NORC Center for Public Affairs Research revealed that 57 percent of Americans think Trump's policies have been bad for Muslims, and 56 percent think that his policies have been bad for Hispanics. Forty-seven percent, including three-quarters of African Americans, believe that Trump's policies have been detrimental for African Americans.[6] The results of the poll show deep pessimism among Blacks about the state of politics and race relations in the United States.[7]

More than half of Americans, including a large percentage of Blacks and Hispanics, believe that President Donald Trump is a racist. Fifty-seven percent of all adults polled, including more than 8 in 10 African Americans, three-quarters of Hispanics, and nearly half of Whites, believe that Trump is racist.[8] Views about President Trump being a racist diverge based on political ideology. An overwhelming majority—85 percent of Democrats—consider Trump racist, whereas only 21 percent of Republicans feel the same way.[9]

intro

These events highlight the delicate nature of race and racial issues in the country and how different populations view events with racial overtones. This also highlights the complexity of public opinion and how demographic differences affect how individuals perceive and see them. In this instance, Blacks, Latinos, and Whites see these events through starkly different lenses. So race and what it represents in the United States has an influence on the attitudes people have on events and issues. Attitudes are also affected by gender, partisan, economic, and regional differences, among others. What people think about political events, how they behave, and the opinions they hold are influenced by these as well as other factors. What individuals think about government policies and the politicians who formulate them, how individuals vote, and how they view the political system are all influenced by public opinion. Yet the formation of public opinion arises out of a complex set of factors that affect individuals differently. Whereas some factors might be universal, other factors are related to the complex inequalities in the American political system. These are questions that arise when we talk about Americans' attitudes toward social and political issues.

Explore polls to discover how different factors influence opinion.

Public Opinion Overview

Public opinion is the collective opinion of large segments of the population on an issue, candidate, or public policy on which the public might be much divided and lack a consensus. Concern about public opinion is as old as the nation. As the Framers drafted the Constitution, they realized that acceptance of the document would require convincing the American public of the importance of ratification. To this end, Alexander Hamilton, James Madison, and John Jay wrote a series of newspaper columns now called the *Federalist Papers* to convince the American public that the new Constitution should be ratified. Through these columns, Hamilton, Madison, and Jay were trying to influence public opinion because they recognized that the support of the majority of the people for this new document was essential if the document was to be considered legitimate.

Likewise, during the Civil War, Abraham Lincoln was keenly aware of the importance of cultivating public opinion and maintaining public support for the Union's war effort and for the Union's efforts to secure help from foreign countries. Lincoln sent a commission to Europe for the purpose of influencing "the two great governments [England and France] by bringing the press and the clergy, and then the people, to an understanding of the causes and purposes of the Civil War."[10] President Lincoln himself did as much as he could through speeches and open letters published in the newspapers to influence public opinion. Perhaps the best testament to his concern with public opinion is exemplified in this statement: "In this age, in this country, public sentiment is everything. With it, nothing can fail; against it, nothing can succeed. Whoever moulds public sentiment, goes deeper than he who enacts statutes or pronounces judicial decisions."[11]

A century later, President John F. Kennedy found himself in the midst of a public opinion imbroglio. On September 10, 1962, the Supreme Court ruled

Public Opinion The collective opinions of large segments of the population on an issue, candidate, or public policy on which the public might be much divided and lack a consensus.

that the University of Mississippi had to admit James Meredith, a Black Mississippi resident, to the University of Mississippi. Mississippi Governor Ross Barnett refused to obey the Supreme Court's decision, setting up an inevitable conflict with President Kennedy and the federal government.

Kennedy had paid little attention to civil rights up to this point in his presidency and had not followed through on his promise to issue an executive order banning housing discrimination in federally funded agencies. His explanation for this lack of follow-through, given in an interview, was that the order would be issued "in a way which will maintain a consensus [national public opinion]," and he expressed concern about not getting too far ahead of public opinion.[12] The situation in Mississippi, however, required action that would put Kennedy ahead of public opinion on integration in general and school integration in particular.

After negotiations with Governor Barnett failed, and Barnett reneged on a proposed solution, Attorney General Robert F. Kennedy told the governor that President Kennedy was going to give an address to the nation (see "Our Voices: Transcript of Conversation between Attorney General Robert F. Kennedy and Governor Ross Barnett of Mississippi"). If Barnett did not agree to a plan to register Meredith, President Kennedy would reveal to the nation, and to Barnett's supporters in Mississippi, that Barnett had struck a deal to allow Meredith to register and then had reneged. Barnett finally agreed to a plan, and on Sunday, September 30, James Meredith was moved onto the campus of the University of Mississippi under the protection of federal marshals, and President Kennedy addressed the nation to say that the Supreme Court decision was being enforced.

At the same time that President Kennedy was speaking, however, thousands of White students and other individuals were rioting in Oxford, Mississippi, over the admission of James Meredith.[13] As a result of the violence, public opinion actually started to reflect a belief that President Kennedy was moving too fast on civil rights.[14] Nevertheless, Kennedy became more committed to civil rights after the University of Mississippi crisis, and he realized that civil rights was an issue about which government would have to take action and public opinion would simply have to catch up.

A few years later, during the Vietnam War, the U.S. military, under the command of General William Westmoreland, tried to mislead the American public about U.S. success in the war so as to maintain support for the war. General Westmoreland and the officers under his command began to release daily body counts of the North Viet Cong killed by U.S. and South Vietnamese forces in an effort to portray the United States and its South Vietnamese allies as winning the war. Later investigations revealed that these figures had been false and had been doctored to portray the United States as winning a war that it had actually been losing.

In the fall of 1967, the Johnson administration began a public relations campaign to sell the increasingly unpopular war to the American people and the press. In so doing, General Westmoreland went on tour to declare to the

our voices

Transcript of Conversation between Attorney General Robert F. Kennedy and Governor Ross Barnett of Mississippi (Sunday, September 20, 1962)

RFK: I don't think that will be very pleasant, Governor. I think you are making a mistake handling it in that fashion. I suppose that if you feel it is helpful to you politically. It is not helping the people of Mississippi or the people of the United States. But I gather that is secondary in your judgment. I think it is silly going through this whole facade of your standing there; our people drawing guns; your stepping aside; to me it is dangerous and I think this has gone beyond the stage of politics, and you have a responsibility to the people of that state and to the people of the United States. This is a real disservice. . . .

RB: I'm not interested in politics personally. I have said so many times—we couldn't have integration and I have got to do something. I can't just walk back. . . .

RFK: The President is going on TV tonight. He is going through the statement [he] had with you last night. He will have to say why he called up the National Guard; that you had an agreement to permit Meredith to go to Jackson to register, and your lawyer, Mr. Watkins, said this was satisfactory; and you would let him fly in by helicopter.

RB: That won't do at all.

RFK: You broke your word to him.

RB: You don't mean the President is going to say that tonight?

RFK: Of course he is; you broke your word; now you suggest we send in troops, fighting their way through a barricade. You gave your word. Mr. Watkins gave him his word. You didn't keep it.

RB: Where didn't I keep it, in what particular?

RFK: When you said you would make an agreement and that Meredith would come into Jackson; send everybody to Oxford.

RB: Don't say that. Please don't mention it.

RFK: The President has to say that. You said we would fly him into Jackson and register him while you had everyone at Oxford. Then you would say he has been registered and you would permit him to come to Oxford by helicopter on Tuesday and go to school. Mr. Watkins pledged his word to the President; we

have it all down. You talk to Mr. Watkins and reach an agreement between the two of you, and how you are going to handle this.

Mississippi Governor Ross Barnett, left, enjoys a laugh with former Mississippi Governor Hugh White (back to camera) prior to the Ole Miss–Kentucky football game on September 29, 1962, in Jackson, Mississippi. Barnett was obviously unaware the president ordered troops assembled in Memphis to use in Ole Miss integration, if necessary. Students waved Rebel flags as Barnett arrived.

James Meredith (right), the first Black student to enroll in the University of Mississippi, visits Attorney General Robert F. Kennedy at the Justice Department. The meeting was arranged by Kennedy after Meredith appeared on a nationwide TV show. Meredith urged the attorney general to press for stronger civil rights.

public that American armed forces were wearing down the communist enemy and winning the war of attrition. Westmoreland, among others, was very concerned with the public's perception of the war. Public support for the war had been deteriorating at a steady rate throughout the conflict, and as the war dragged on, that support declined even further.[15]

Thirty-four years later, after the devastating terrorist attacks on the World Trade Center in New York and on the Pentagon in Washington, DC, the United States began an air attack on Afghanistan and later initiated ground operations. Afghanistan was the country from which attackers, led by Osama bin Laden, planned the September 11, 2001, attack on the United States, although all of the attackers but one were Saudi Arabian. Despite overwhelming public support for retaliatory action, President George W. Bush and his advisers knew that to sustain a "war" effort against terrorism, they would have to continue molding public opinion to this cause. So the Bush administration hired a former Madison Avenue advertising executive to develop strategies to get its message across to the country's allies and to the American people in an effort to maintain support for the war effort.[16]

The administration, however, decided to use the September 11 attacks as a pretext for invading Iraq and removing from power Saddam Hussein, its leader at the time. Members of the administration used a variety of mechanisms to convince the domestic and international communities that Hussein had weapons of mass destruction. For example, Secretary of State Colin Powell made a presentation to the United Nations, putting his reputation on the line, in which he stated that Iraq did indeed have weapons of mass destruction. U.S. forces invaded Iraq on March 20, 2003. As time wore on and more information was revealed, it became clear that the Bush administration had misled the American public on the reasons for the invasion of Iraq. Over the years, the administration was unable to maintain public support for a war that most Americans came to view as unwarranted.

Political Culture and Public Opinion

How are opinions formed? What makes some people fervently support a particular policy position or candidate whereas others oppose the position or candidate with equal passion? Public opinion is not formed in a vacuum. Life experiences, environment, family background, education, race, gender, and the intersection of the two and the political culture of the United States all contribute to the formation of public opinion. Here we want to explore these factors to identify how they contribute to the formation of public opinion.

Political culture is the attitudes, beliefs, and values that undergird or are at the foundation of a political system.[17] America's political culture is grounded in the founding principles of the country—freedom, equality, representative government, and the conflicting tradition of exclusion of segments

Political Culture The attitudes, beliefs, and values that undergird or are at the foundation of a political system.

of American citizens, among others—and encompasses how people view government and its role. As Chapter 1 demonstrated, the theoretical foundations on which the country was built were varied; thus, people can have different opinions on what government should and should not do. Despite differences of opinion on the role of government, however, most Americans view the American system of government as legitimate and support the country's political process. There are many aspects of political culture that influence how people think and why they think the way they do.

Public opinion provides indications of the current thinking and direction of American culture.[18] Public opinion on certain issues provides the lens through which to view current trends in American life (see "Measuring Equality: Donald Trump, Barack Obama, and the "Birthers" on page 317). For example, growing public support for the belief that people should be more self-sufficient could mean declining tolerance or sympathy for welfare recipients. This changing belief could signal public support for overhaul and reform of the welfare system.

Political Socialization

One major influence on public opinion is **political socialization**, the process through which a person gains political understanding and forms a set of political beliefs. The early influences in political socialization are the family and the school. Conversations about politics at the dinner table, overheard by children when parents, older siblings, or relatives are talking, play a major role in the development of political opinions and attitudes. Children often adopt the political positions and support for particular candidates of their parents. As children form new friendships, however, and expand their sphere of activities, their political views and attitudes might change to reflect these new experiences.

Schools are essential to political socialization because governments, including that of the United States, use schools to develop students' civic values. If a political system is to continue to exist and thrive, it must have citizens who believe in its ideals and support its political institutions. Children say the Pledge of Allegiance and learn that the United States is the principal democracy in the world. They learn democracy through election for class officers, express their preferences in mock presidential elections, and, as they enter higher grades, study civics, social studies, and history.

Political socialization continues throughout a person's life as political understanding deepens and political beliefs and values shift over time. Later influences include work experience and changing family circumstances. The views that a person holds as a young adult might be very different from the views he or she holds after marriage and children and could be different still when the person retires and sees the political system from the view of someone on a fixed income who is concerned about whether the Social Security system is financially sound.

Political Socialization The process through which a person gains political understanding and forms a set of political beliefs.

Expressions of Public Opinion

People express their opinions about government, politics, and politicians in several ways. Clearly, election results reflect public opinion. Citizens express their opinions by voting for candidates who share some of their political and policy preferences. Winning candidates invariably interpret their victories as mandates for their policy preferences. Even though such interpretations offer a very simplistic view of voters' preferences, most politicians assume that a vote cast for a candidate means the voter supports the candidate's positions.

Writing letters or sending emails to elected officials and newspapers is another expression of public opinion. Elected officials pay attention to these communications and assume, rightly or wrongly, that they represent public opinion on a particular subject. Newspapers use letters to the editor as a measure of public support or discontent with an official policy, issue, or program. Television news programs often use "person-on-the-street" interviews to represent public opinion on an issue.

Participation in demonstrations is another form of public opinion. Large events can attract considerable attention and might influence decision-makers to take some action. On March 25, 2006, an estimated 500,000 people gathered in downtown Los Angeles to protest proposed legislation in Congress

Hundreds of immigrant rights advocates and others participate in a rally and demonstration at the Federal Building in lower Manhattan against the Trump administration's policy that enables federal agents to take migrant children away from their parents at the border on June 1, 2018, in New York. In coordinated marches across the country, people are gathering outside U.S. Immigration and Customs Enforcement field offices, U.S. attorneys' offices, and the Department of Justice headquarters in Washington, DC, to put increasing pressure on the Trump administration's family separation policy at the border.

that would have placed restrictions on immigrants in the United States and would have addressed aspects of illegal immigration into the country. As a result of the Los Angeles demonstration, in April of that year rallies for immigrant rights were held in numerous cities across the country and drew millions of people in support of immigrant rights.[19]

The increasing uses of the Internet and email have made it easier for individuals to express their opinions to network and cable news organizations, talk shows, national public affairs programs, and elected officials. It is commonplace for these entities to invite people to log on and "vote" for a particular policy option or to express their favorable or unfavorable view of a politician who has become controversial. Organizations conducting electronic polls will always preface their comments about the results with the phrase "in our non-scientific poll" because the technique by which the data were gathered is not representative of the American public. The opinions are representative only of those individuals who choose to log on and respond to the survey. Illustrative of this point is the notice that ABCNews.com posts explaining the nonrepresentative nature of its online polls:

> ABCNews.com posts online ballots as a way of encouraging users to express their views and participate in our community. These ballots, however, are not polls. They are not based on scientific, representative samples and their results are vulnerable to manipulation by individuals or groups with an interest in the outcome. They are for entertainment only. To avoid confusion and discourage manipulation, we do not offer percentaged results of online ballots—only vote totals. We do not refer to them as "polls" or "surveys," words that indicate the use of a representative sample. These ballots do not constitute a reliable sounding of public opinion.[20]

Each of these responses is an expression of public opinion, but not one of them measures the opinion of the entire American public. They represent the views—sometimes very effectively—of only those who vote, write letters, send email messages, participate in mass demonstrations, or complete online surveys. Individuals who participate in demonstrations, write letters, and send email messages are those who are the most active and committed to a particular issue. If none of these activities reflects the views of the entire American public, is there any way to discover the opinion of the entire U.S. population on some issue or on a candidate for the presidency? The answer to this question is survey research.

James Surowiecki discusses the power—and danger—of crowds, including online 'mobs.'

Measuring Public Opinion

Survey research, the administration of questionnaires to a sample of respondents selected from some population, is particularly useful for making descriptive and explanatory studies of large populations. Survey research takes a number of forms. One form of survey research is the questionnaire we complete after purchasing a computer or appliance or the customer satisfaction survey we are given after we have used a service or filed a complaint. The most

Survey Research
Administration of questionnaires to a sample of respondents selected from a particular population, useful for making descriptive and explanatory studies of large populations.

common form of survey research is public opinion polling. Public opinion polls assess the attitudes, opinions, and behaviors of a population, for example, U.S. voters' views of policy issues and electoral candidates.

Survey research and public opinion polling as it now exists were developed almost exclusively in the United States by academics and commercial polling organizations. Businesses use public opinion polling to determine their markets or assess the quality of their service. Today public opinion polls are conducted by universities, commercial polling organizations, and news organizations. The American National Election Study (ANES) is conducted by the University of Michigan, and now in partnership with Stanford University, during presidential election years in an effort to understand why people voted the way they did and what factors influenced their votes.[21] The General Social Survey, collected by the National Opinion Research Center at the University of Chicago, gathers data on social aspects of the U.S. population.

The most prominent commercial polling organizations are the Gallup Organization, Harris Polls, and Roper Center for Public Opinion Research. These organizations conduct surveys on a variety of topics ranging from attitudes toward the economy to whether people watched a particular sporting event to how people feel about a particular political event or a political candidate. Unlike university surveys done once a year or every election cycle, commercial polling organizations might conduct a survey each week. Many of the major newspapers, such as the *New York Times*, the *Washington Post*, and the *Los Angeles Times*, have polling directors and staff.

Newspapers are interested in how people feel about issues and candidates nationally as well as locally. For national polls, many news organizations have formed partnerships with commercial polling organizations or with other news organizations to conduct national polls. Some of the pairings are CNN/*Time*/Opinion Research Corporation, ABC News/*Washington Post*, *New York Times*/CBS News, and NBC News/*Wall Street Journal*.

Craft and interpret surveys to advise Congress.

The Mechanics of Polling

The mechanics of conducting a poll determine how much confidence we should have in the survey's results. The mechanics include how the **sample**, a small set of people gathered from a larger population, is drawn; how the questions are worded; in what order they appear; when (time) the data are gathered; and how the data are gathered. When the mechanics are done incorrectly or sloppily, the results could be suspect or completely wrong.

Sample A small set of people carefully drawn from a larger population to reflect its overall characteristics.

How the Sample Is Drawn

The *Literary Digest*, published between 1890 and 1938, was a respected news magazine that had predicted correctly the elections of 1924, 1928, and 1932. In 1936, it predicted that Alf Landon would defeat Franklin D. Roosevelt in a landslide. Culling names from telephone books and auto registration lists across the country, the *Literary Digest* sent out 10 million ballots asking people to check their preferences for president.[22] More than 2 million ballots were returned, and the results predicted Republican Alf Landon would win with a stunning 57 percent to 43 percent landslide over the incumbent Democratic president, Franklin Roosevelt.[23] In actuality, Roosevelt beat Landon in a landslide with 61 percent of the vote.[24] Although the process by which the *Literary Digest* sampled public opinion had worked in the past, it failed miserably in the midst of the Depression, when only the wealthy had telephones and automobiles. Thus, the sample was not representative of the extraordinarily large proportion of the population that was poor and turned out in large numbers at the polls.

George Gallup predicted that Roosevelt would win by a substantial margin. In conducting his poll, Gallup used a method called **quota sampling**, a procedure in which interviewers choose people to be interviewed based on their proportion or quota in the general population being polled. In a quota sample, the number of women polled, for example, would be proportionate to the number of women in the general population. Gallup's sample, then, was more representative of the population of the United States than was the *Literary Digest* sample, which was biased toward wealthy and Republican voters.

Although Gallup correctly predicted the outcome of the 1936 presidential election, in the presidential election of 1948, all of the pollsters, including

Quota Sampling A type of sample in which individuals to be interviewed are selected based on their proportion or quota in the general population being polled.

Listen to excerpts from Roosevelt's fiery 1936 campaign speech, helping him overcome opposition among wealthier voters.

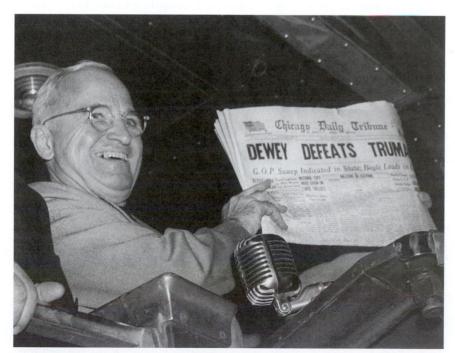

In this November 4, 1948, file photo, U.S. President Harry S. Truman holds up an Election Day edition of the *Chicago Daily Tribune*, which, based on early results, mistakenly announced "Dewey Defeats Truman."

Gallup, predicted that Republican candidate Thomas Dewey would beat Democratic president Harry Truman. But Truman beat Dewey 49.5 percent to 45.1 percent. This election showed that, even though quota sampling had been accurate in the past, new ways of drawing samples were necessary. At the time, a number of academic statisticians, particularly Leslie Kish of the University of Michigan, were experimenting with **probability sampling** methods, ways of drawing a sample that use probability theory to ensure that every person in the population has an equal chance of being selected for the sample. A basic principle of probability sampling is that a sample will be representative of the population from which it is drawn if all members of the population have an equal chance of being selected in the sample.[25]

Statistically drawn samples tend to have respondents who are representative of the target population. Such a sample will approximate the gender, racial, and regional distribution of the population under study. Additionally, the development of probability sampling took the decision of whom to interview out of the hands of the interviewer, which had led to bias in the results because interviewers tended to select people like themselves. Using probability sampling techniques, Kish and his associates had correctly predicted that Truman would prevail in the election. Yet even samples drawn using probability methods cannot be assumed to reflect the opinions and behaviors of the entire U.S. population with absolute accuracy. Probability sampling deals with this uncertainty by calculating a **sampling error**, the degree of expected error in the results that comes from estimating the responses of the population from a sample. Sampling error is expressed as plus or minus a certain percentage rate, depending on the size of the sample for the results of the survey. Often survey results will note a sampling error of "plus or minus three percentage points" (+/–3). For example, for the results indicating that 48 percent of the people support Candidate A and 44 percent of the people support Candidate B, the actual range for Candidate A is 51 percent (+3) to 45 percent (–3), and the range for Candidate B is 47 percent (+3) to 41 percent (–3). When political races are described as being a statistical dead heat, which this example is, even though it looks like one candidate is leading, it means that the results fall within the sampling error, thereby making the differences not significant.

Probability Sampling A general term for a sample selected in accordance with probability theory, which ensures that every person in the population has an equal chance of being selected for the sample.

Sampling Error The degree of expected error in sampling results that comes from estimating the responses of the population from a sample.

How a Question Is Worded

Sampling is the most important mechanic in assuring a poll's accuracy, but other factors have been shown to have significant effects in certain circumstances. As we saw in the chapter opening vignette, the way in which a question is worded can make a difference.

Table 10.1 shows the difference in responses people gave to questions on support for affirmative action. When the question was worded using the phrase "affirmative action programs for racial minorities," a majority of the respondents (58 percent) favored affirmative action programs. When the question was phrased to "programs which make special efforts to help blacks and

TABLE 10.1 Different Wording for Questions Measuring Support for Affirmative Action Programs

Do you generally favor or oppose affirmative action programs for racial minorities? (June–July 2015 Gallup Poll)	
Favor	37%
Oppose	37%
In order to make up for past discrimination, do you favor or oppose programs which make special efforts to help blacks and other minorities get ahead? (May 2013 PRRI Poll)	
Favor	68%
Oppose	24%
We should make every possible effort to improve the position of blacks and other minorities even if it means giving them preferential treatment. (2012 Pew Poll)	
Completely/Mostly agree	33%
Completely/Mostly disagree	62%

Note: Responses are in percentages.

Source: Riffkin, R. (2015). Gallup. https://news.gallup.com/poll/184772/higher-support-gender-affirmative-action-race.aspx; Cox, D., Navarro-Rivera, J., & Jones, R. P. (2013, May). Public Religion Research Institute Religion & Politics Tracking Survey. https://www.prri.org/research/may-2013-religion-politics-tracking-survey/; Pew Research Center. (2012, June 4). Values about immigration and race. http://www.people-press.org/2012/06/04/section-8-values-about-immigration-and-race/

other minorities get ahead," more than three-fourths (68 percent) supported affirmative action programs. But when the phrasing was "We should make every possible effort to improve the position of Blacks and other minorities, even if it means giving them preferential treatment," support dropped significantly (to 33 percent). The questions were trying to get at the same thing, but clearly the use of "preferential treatment" triggered negative responses to affirmative action.

When a Question Is Asked within the Survey

The order in which questions are asked can also affect responses. The response to a question at the beginning of a survey can affect the answers to later questions, for instance.[26] For example, in 1980 a poll conducted by the Harris organization asked respondents at the beginning of the survey if they intended to vote for President Jimmy Carter or Senator Edward Kennedy (D-MA), who was challenging Carter in the Democratic primaries. This question was followed by a series of questions about domestic and foreign policy. Toward the end of the survey, the respondents were asked again for whom they would vote. By the end of the survey, support for Carter had declined sharply, as the domestic and foreign policy questions related to President Carter's performance in office. Clearly, putting these questions in between the questions about candidate preference primed negative feelings about President Carter as respondents moved through the questionnaire.

With the popularity of online surveys, researchers have begun to explore whether question ordering makes a difference. If all the questions are on the same page and respondents can see all the questions and pick the order in which they answer questions, then the order of the questions does not change how people respond. But if questions are put on separate pages and respondents cannot move forward without providing a response and cannot go back to a previous page to change an answer, then question ordering does make a difference.[27]

When Data Are Gathered

The time at which a poll is taken can also dramatically affect the accuracy of the poll results. Polls taken very early in a political race are usually poor predictors of the eventual outcome. Nowhere is this more evident than in presidential races. The presidential election cycle usually begins about eighteen to twenty-four months before the actual election, but except for the news media, few Americans are focused on the election until after Labor Day of the election year. For that reason, public opinion polls taken far in advance of the election tell us little about who is going to win the election.

In the 2008 presidential primaries, early polls in 2007 indicated that Senator Hillary Rodham Clinton was going to be the presidential nominee for the Democrats and former New York City mayor Rudy Giuliani was going to be the nominee for the Republicans. By January 2008, pollsters were collecting data on a head-to-head matchup between Clinton and Giuliani in the November presidential general election, so convinced were they of the accuracy of their early polling data. Not only did the pollsters believe the data, but both Giuliani and Clinton also believed the poll numbers and made strategy decisions based on those early numbers.

But Giuliani's campaign failed to gain traction, and he dropped out, and Senator Clinton battled Senator Barack Obama for the nomination until summer 2008. The inevitability of Clinton's nomination, based on early polling, fell short, and she was not able to gain the Democratic presidential nomination.

During the 2016 presidential primaries, in early 2015, even before former governor Jeb Bush entered the race, pollsters were predicting that he would be the Republican nominee and were polling on the eventual matchup between Bush and Hillary Clinton, the presumed Democratic nominee. Unlike 2008, Clinton did not assume the mantle of inevitability in 2016 and this time did not believe the polling and ran a successful campaign to become the Democratic nominee. Jeb Bush, on the other hand, did not gain traction after he announced his candidacy in June 2015 and dropped out on February 20, 2016. Assuming that polls taken a year before or even months before a presidential election are meaningful misses the shifting nature of public opinion.

How Data Are Gathered

The way in which data are gathered also makes a difference in poll results. Most of the public opinion polls conducted by news organizations, commercial pollsters, politicians, and political campaigns are telephone interviews.

One complicating factor for telephone surveys is the growing prevalence of cell phones as the primary phone for many Americans. Survey researchers have begun to develop techniques that will sample cell phone numbers to see if the attitudes of cell phone users are different from those of landline users. A recent report found that these two populations do not differ substantively in their attitudes on key political measures such as presidential approval, Iraq policy, presidential primary voter preference, and party affiliation, but that the cost of interviewing a cell phone user is about three times more than the cost of interviewing a landline user.[28] Another challenge to telephone interviewing is the increasing use of caller ID and respondents' resistance to being interviewed.

Since the 2000 presidential election, online Internet polling has become much more prevalent. As previously discussed, Internet polls are not scientifically grounded and cannot be trusted to yield accurate results. There are many reasons for this, including the fact that only a portion of the total electorate has access to the Internet (even though these numbers have been growing) and Internet poll respondents tend to be self-selected rather than scientifically constructed according to good sampling techniques.

The unreliability of Internet polling and daily tracking polls is part of the reason that the 2012 presidential nomination and election processes were difficult to follow with any accuracy. The differences in results were directly related to how the samples were drawn, the size of the sample, how the poll was conducted, and how the questions were worded, all the factors we have been exploring. Table 10.2 shows the final Gallup Tracking Poll for the 2012 presidential election. Gallup's Daily Tracking Polls favored Mitt Romney and were considered an outlier from the other tracking polls. Gallup had Romney up by as much as seven points during the final week of the election. The poll

TABLE 10.2 2012 Pre-Election Presidential Ballot

Gallup Final 2012 Pre-Election Presidential Ballot, November 1–4, 2012

	Mitt Romney/ Paul Ryan %	Barack Obama/ Joe Biden %	Other (vol.) %	No Opinion %
Likely voters	49	48	1	3
Final allocated estimate*	50	49	1	—
Registered voters	46	49	1	4

*The allocated estimate represents the vote choice of likely voters with undecided voters removed from the sample. Undecided votes were allocated proportionally; due to rounding this resulted in one-percentage-point increases in the final result for each candidate.

(vol.), volunteered response.

Source: Gallup Daily tracking, GALLUP.

Gallup released the day before the election gave Romney a one-point lead over President Obama. Analysis suggests that Gallup's sampling frame was biased toward Republican voters, overestimated the size of the White portion of the electorate, and that its formula for the likely-voter screen not only overestimated White voters, but underestimated younger voters.[29] President Obama won the election 51 to 47 percent. As you can see from Table 10.2 the registered voter sample was closer to the final vote total than was the likely voter sample. Virtually all of the 2016 pre-election polls predicted that Hillary Clinton would win the presidency. As in 2012, the polls were off. Donald Trump won the Electoral College vote, but lost the popular vote.

The Association of Public Opinion Research (APOR) put together a committee to try to figure out what went wrong in 2016. The report, which came out in May 2017, indicated several potential reasons for why the various polls appeared to predict a Clinton victory. First, the national polls were generally accurate in estimating the popular vote. In fact, the report says that the national estimates were the most accurate since 1936. The national polls indicated that Clinton had a three percentage point lead, and she won the popular vote by two percentage points.[30]

Second, the state-level polls showed a competitive race, but slightly overestimated Clinton's narrow lead and underestimated Trump's support in the Upper Midwest. The explanations why the state polls were problematic were varied. One explanation was they found that about 13 percent of voters in Wisconsin, Florida, and Pennsylvania decided on their presidential vote choice in the final week. The data show that Trump was the choice of these voters by near 30 points in Wisconsin and by 17 points in Florida and Pennsylvania. Another explanation was that many state polls had an overrepresentation of college educated voters and did not adjust to match the educational levels of those in the state.[31]

Third, the problem of the predictions from polling data were not the problem of the polls themselves, but a problem of those that aggregated and averaged the various polls. A poll aggregator is an individual or organization that brings together many poll results from a number of different sources.[32] Many of the predictions of Clinton having a 90 percent chance of being elected were predictions from the poll aggregators and not from the pollsters.[33] As the report says—"However well-intentioned these predictions may have been, they helped crystalize the belief that Clinton was a shoo-in for president, with unknown consequences for turnout."[34] Most of the public, along with many in the media, focused on the poll aggregator predictions and not on the actual polls themselves.

Finally, the report highlighted the difference between election polls and survey research in general. The committee was concerned that the errors associated with the 2016 election polls not tarnish survey research in general and makes the case for why people should continue to have confidence in survey research, while acknowledging the errors of election polling in 2016.

Race, Gender, and Public Opinion

The U.S. population is a multiracial one, and increasingly so, yet many generalizations about American public opinion were developed from survey data coming largely from White respondents. Race influences public opinion because the historically disparate treatment of racial minorities in American society has an effect on public opinion. The effects of race on public opinion, in particular, take on added significance as the demographics of the U.S. population continue to change. These demographic shifts are likely to influence changes in public opinion that will, in turn, lead to changes in the U.S. political system.

For example, the 2017 census population update indicated that Latinos were 18.1 percent of the population, up from 12.5 percent in 2000, and non-Latino Whites were 60.7 percent of the population, down from 69.1 percent in 2000. Estimates based on the 2010 census predict that by 2060, Latinos will constitute 28.6 percent of the U.S. population, African Americans will be 14.3 percent of the population, Asian Americans will make up 9.3 percent of the population, and non-Latino Whites will be only 43.6 percent of the population.[35] California was a majority-minority state, with Blacks, Latinos, and Asians making up the majority.[36]

Gender differences in public opinion have also been identified, but they are much less dramatic than racial differences. Nevertheless, the changing nature of the role of women in American society has resulted in some public opinion differences. The intersection of race and gender for Black women and other women of color adds an additional dynamic and complexity to the examination of public opinion. For these reasons, the effects of race and gender on the formation of public opinion merit special attention.

Race

From its inception, the United States has had tremendous difficulties in dealing with issues of race. Black Americans were officially enslaved beginning about 1641, the date that slavery was incorporated into colonial law by the colony of Massachusetts, until after the Civil War.[37] Notwithstanding emancipation, Blacks endured continued segregation, discrimination, and denial of political freedoms and constitutional guarantees until the Civil Rights Movement of the 1950s and 1960s began to break down those barriers.

Despite tremendous advancements in diminishing inequalities between Blacks and Whites, many realities of life suggest that Black Americans live in a different world and have different life chances from those of White Americans. A study published in 2001 by economist and law professor Ian Ayers found that there were continued inequalities between Blacks and Whites but that these were often more subtle. For instance, car dealers regularly charged Blacks more for cars than White men. Blacks had more difficulty than Whites getting kidney transplants, and Black defendants were frequently required to post higher bail bonds than their White counterparts.[38]

The history of racism and discrimination and the continuing inequalities between the races are the context in which public opinion held by Blacks and other racial minorities is formed. Political scientist Paul Abramson suggests that Blacks and Whites experience different political realities, the extent to which each group can participate in the political system results in differences in political attitudes and in different beliefs about how much influence each group has on the system. He argues that many of the attitudes of Black Americans reflect an accurate response to the realities of Black political life in the United States.[39]

This difference in political realities is reflected in the opinions and attitudes held by different racial groups in the United States. For example, in a June 15 to July 10, 2015, Gallup Poll, 72 percent of Whites believed that Blacks had as good a chance as Whites to get any kind of job for which they were qualified; a majority (63 percent) of Blacks disagreed. Given that Blacks believe they do not have an equal chance to get any kind of job, 69 percent of Blacks felt that new civil rights laws were needed to reduce discrimination, whereas only 31 percent of Whites believed new laws were needed. Additionally, 58 percent of Whites believed that a solution to relations between Blacks and Whites would eventually be worked out, whereas 59 percent of Blacks felt that relations between Blacks and Whites will always be a problem.[40]

These differences in opinion are rooted in the reality that Blacks have experienced numerous forms of discrimination, particularly racial profiling (being targeted by police on the basis of race alone and not behavior), from the police.[41] Whites by and large have not experienced discriminatory treatment. As a result, they have a different perspective on equality of opportunity and on treatment by the police than do Blacks, who have experienced and continue to experience discrimination (see "Evaluating Equality: Differences in Perception of Racism against Black Americans").[42]

During every election cycle, the news media conflate Black support for the Democratic Party with the belief that this means that Blacks are politically liberal. But those who study Black and Latino political attitudes argue that it is inappropriate to use the standard political ideology labels of "liberal," "moderate," and "conservative"—which were developed through national studies that contained few non-Whites—and apply them to the Black and Latino populations. Describing all racial minorities in general as liberal overlooks the complexity and variability of attitudes within the various racial communities. Moreover, the application of such labels implies that there is an agreed-on definition of their meaning and that individuals who identify themselves by these labels are able to define what they mean.[43]

Beliefs that the federal government should take an active role in reducing unemployment, providing services for the poor, and improving the socioeconomic position of Blacks or other racial minorities are generally regarded as representing liberal attitudes. Support for prayer in public schools is considered a conservative attitude. Yet these two positions—support for an active role for government and for prayer in schools—are found within African

evaluating equality

Differences in Perception of Racism against Black Americans

Blacks and Whites experience life differently, and that difference results in differences in perceptions of issues. Figure 10.1 shows differences in perception about whether racism against Black Americans is or is not widespread.

Figure 10.1 Race Relations: Perceptions of Discrimination Against Blacks
Source: Gallup Poll, June 7–July 1, 2016.

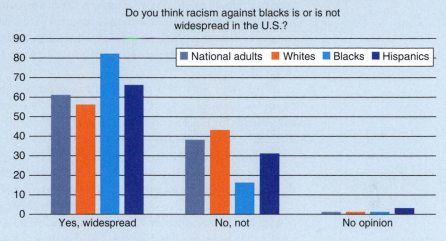

Do you think racism against blacks is or is not widespread in the U.S.?

■ National adults ■ Whites ■ Blacks ■ Hispanics

American public opinion, which raises doubts about the assignment of such labels as liberal and conservative. According to all of the available data, Blacks identify themselves across the ideological spectrum, with just as many Blacks self-identifying as some variant of liberal as identifying as some variant of conservative.[44] Regardless of self-identified ideological labels, Blacks' policy preferences are generally liberal across a variety of issues, such as increased government spending on food stamps, Medicare, crime, and employment and jobs. But with the exception of capital punishment, Blacks are relatively conservative on a range of social policy issues, such as abortion, school prayer, and same-sex marriage.[45]

The designations of liberal and conservative do not accurately reflect the attitudes of various Latino groups.[46] The 2006 Latino National Survey reported that Mexican Americans are more likely to describe themselves as some variant of conservative than as liberal. But more identify themselves as moderate than as conservative or liberal. Puerto Ricans and Cubans, however, are more likely to self-describe as some degree of conservative than as liberal or moderate. Regardless of self-identified ideological labels, large majorities of all three groups support what could be characterized as liberal domestic policy issues, such as increased spending for public education, child care services, the environment, and public assistance and welfare.[47]

On the surface and according to the standard political science explanations, there appears to be a conflict between the varied ideological orientations among these groups and their support for a policy agenda that calls for active federal government in solving problems (a liberal position). If, however, we take into account the social and political realities of these groups, it is not difficult to understand how Blacks and Latinos can call themselves conservatives but still feel strongly that the government has a role to play in creating an equal playing field, expanding opportunities, and enforcing antidiscrimination laws. Historical context has a forceful explanatory power, and we must recognize that it is the lens through which the public opinion held by racial minorities is formed that differs substantively from the historical perspective of Whites.

Table 10.3 illustrates racial differences on two important policy issues—the death penalty and gun regulation—that are connected to different political realities for Blacks and Whites. As Table 10.3 illustrates, there is a dramatic difference in support for the death penalty among Blacks and Whites, with about one-half (50.75 percent) of Blacks supporting the death penalty compared to more than three-fourths (71.56 percent) of Whites; Latinos anchor the middle of the continuum (59.56 percent in favor).

These differences in opinion are rooted in the reality that Blacks have less confidence in the equal application of the law and are more critical of police tactics.[48] Whites are less likely to believe that the criminal justice system is biased, and their interactions with police, for the most part, have been cordial.[49]

TABLE 10.3 Racial Differences on Social Policy Issues

Do you favor or oppose the death penalty for persons convicted of murder?

	Percent		
	Blacks	**Latinos**	**Whites**
Favor	50.75	59.56	71.56
Oppose	47.49	38.22	26.43
	n = 398	*n* = 450	*n* = 3,038

Nearly half of Black Americans are opposed to the death penalty, while nearly three-fourths of Whites are in favor.

Do you think the federal government should make it more difficult for people to buy a gun than it is now, make it easier for people to buy a gun, or keep these rules about the same as they are now?

	Percent		
	Blacks	**Latinos**	**Whites**
More difficult	73.12	60.44	48.95
Easier	6.53	8.00	6.35
The same	20.10	30.44	44.27
	n = 398	*n* = 450	*n* = 3,038

Source: 2016 American National Election Study.

As we demonstrated in Chapter 5, the presence of racial and ethnic minorities on death row is disproportionate to their numbers in the population and contributes to differences in such perceptions.

Racial differences are also present on the issue of gun regulation. Almost three-quarters (73.12 percent) of Blacks, compared to more than two-fifths (48.95 percent) of Whites, think the federal government should make it more difficult for people to purchase a gun. Blacks are more likely to be victims of violent crimes than are Whites and to live in neighborhoods with higher levels of crime.[50] For example, 2013 data collected by the United Nations on homicide across the world showed that a Black American is eight times more likely to be a homicide victim than a White American is.[51] Thus, Blacks exhibit a heightened fear of crime and concern about crime compared with Whites. As such, Blacks are more likely to be supportive of gun regulation than are Whites. Latino support for more difficulty in purchasing guns (60.44 percent) is between the views of Blacks and Whites.

Gender

The effect of gender on the formation of public opinion was not recognized as an important factor until the 1980s.[52] Before then, public opinion studies focused on other factors that influenced public opinion formation, such as race, religion, and social class.[53] The belief at the time was that women's public opinion was identical to men's.[54]

In discussing **gender**, political science literature makes a distinction between sex, which refers to biological characteristics, and gender, which refers to social relations between the sexes and attitudes about how the sexes interact and the roles that society assumes they will play. The use of the term *gender* in public opinion refers to how the social roles assigned to women and the nature of their interaction with men affect how they perceive issues. This is different from the ascriptive category of sex—male and female.

Gender Social relations between the sexes and attitudes about how the sexes interact and the roles that society assumes they will play.

In politics, differences between men and women on partisan identification and voting are referred to as the **gender gap**.[55] The date of the emergence of the gender gap is debated by scholars. The common date given is the 1980 presidential election, when women were less likely than men to support Ronald Reagan. Female support for Reagan was 6 to 9 percent less than male support.[56] Yet others suggest that the earliest emergence of the contemporary gender gap was in the 1964 election of Lyndon Johnson, when women were more aligned with the Democratic Party than men were.[57]

Gender Gap The difference between men and women on such crucial issues as partisan identification and voting for certain candidates.

The 1990s saw an increase in the gender gap. The 1992 and 1996 presidential elections showed a new increase in the gender gap at levels above those during the Reagan era.[58] Bill Clinton received 8 percent more votes from women in 1992 than did George H. W. Bush and a whopping 16 percent more votes from women in 1996. In the 2000 election, Al Gore's margin with female voters was 11 percentage points higher than George W. Bush's, but the gap narrowed considerably in 2004, when John Kerry's margin with women was only 3 percentage points over George W. Bush's.[59]

The gap widened again in 2008. Despite the presence of Alaska governor Sarah Palin as the vice presidential nominee on the Republican ticket, women voted for Senator Barack Obama by 7 percentage points over Senator John McCain. What is interesting about the 2008 presidential contest is that the gender gap appears to be the result of support for Obama among Black women (96 percent for Obama), Latina women (68 percent), and women of other races (64 percent). The majority of White women (53 percent) voted for McCain, as did the majority of White men (57 percent).[60]

The gender gap was still present in the 2012 elections. Exit polling showed that President Obama took the majority of the female vote (55 percent), but only 46 percent of the White female vote. His margin of victory among women came from the votes of Black women (96 percent), Latina women (68 percent), and Asian and other non-White women (64 percent). These groups voted in similar proportions for President Obama in 2008. It is therefore important, where possible, to break out various groups of women to get a better sense of which women contribute to the gender gap.

As in 2012, the gender gap was present in the 2016 elections.[61] Exit poll data showed that Hillary Clinton received 54 percent of the female vote compared to Donald Trump, who received 42 percent. But the majority of White women (53 percent) voted for Trump, so Clinton's margin among female voters once again came from women of color—94 percent of Black women voted for Clinton as did 68 percent of Latinas.

Political science research has found that as more women went to work, they came to view themselves as being limited by their gender in the labor market. The research has also shown that women became more gender conscious between 1972 and 1983.[62] The view that their gender limited their employment opportunities, coupled with increasing gender consciousness, began to move women's public opinion preferences in a direction opposite that of men's. Notably, the gender gap was generally attributed to women's liberal preferences on policy issues such as abortion and equal rights, social welfare, women's rights, and the environment.[63] The largest gender differences appeared on policies related to aid to the unemployed and war and peace issues.[64] The most enduring differences surrounded the latter, with women consistently less approving of policies that involve the use of violence, either domestically or internationally, than are men.[65]

Yet the gender gap is not the result of women's changing attitudes alone. Another contributor to the gender gap is attitudinal changes in male party identification and voting. From 1952 to 1996, men were more conservative than women were on social welfare questions. Also, men were more conservative across social spending issues.[66] From 1952 to 2004, the percentage of women identifying with the Republican Party declined by 5 percentage points, from 58 to 53 percent. Yet during this same period, the percentage of men identifying with the Democratic Party dropped 16 percent, from 59 to 43 percent.[67] Thus, men's political behavior was a major contributor to the gender gap.

The social and political context in which women have existed in American society contributes to the formation of public opinion. Although all women are not influenced in the same way, for many the recognition of gender limitations contributes to the development of attitudes that differ from those of men. Table 10.4 shows gender differences on the same two social policy issues—the death penalty and gun regulation. As Table 10.4 demonstrates, women favor the death penalty in smaller proportions than do men, and women are far more likely to favor making it more difficult to buy a gun than are men.

Even with both racial and gender differences present, we want to look within those categories to see if the intersection of race and gender makes even more of a difference on these policy preferences. As Table 10.5 indicates, there are differences among White men and women, Black men and women, and Latino/a men and women in these two policy areas. Of all of the race and gender groups, Black women are the least supportive of the death penalty (47.68 percent) and White women, surprisingly, are the most supportive (79.33 percent). White men are closer to White women on support for the

TABLE 10.4 Gender Differences on Social Policy Issues

Do you favor or oppose the death penalty for persons convicted of murder?

	Percent	
	Men	**Women**
Favor	70.81 (1,407)	65.14 (1,454)
Oppose	27.78 (552) $n = 1,987$	32.12 (717) $n = 2,232$

Do you think the federal government should make it more difficult for people to buy a gun than it is now, make it easier for people to buy a gun, or keep these rules about the same as they are now?

	Percent	
	Men	**Women**
More difficult	46.75 (929)	58.74 (1,311)
Easier	7.85 (156)	5.24 (117)
The same	45.04 (895) $n = 1,987$	35.30 (788) $n = 2,232$

A majority of women feel that it should be more difficult to buy a gun, while less than half of men think the same way. Nearly half of men think that the rules should be kept about the same.

Source: 2016 American National Election Study.

TABLE 10.5 Support for the Death Penalty and Gun Control by Race and Gender

Do you favor or oppose the death penalty for persons convicted of murder?

Race and Gender	Death Penalty	
	Favor	Oppose
White men	74.45	24.42
White women	79.33	27.84
Black men	55.70	43.04
Black women	47.68	50.21
Latino men	62.28	35.96
Latina women	56.94	40.28
Other men	68.82	28.82
Other women	62.07	35.63

Do you think the federal government should make it more difficult for people to buy a gun than it is now, make it easier for people to buy a gun, or keep these rules about the same as they are now?

Race and Gender	Gun Control		
	More Difficult	Easier	The Same
White men	42.15	8.23	49.40
White women	54.93	4.71	39.72
Black men	66.46	6.96	26.58
Black women	77.22	6.33	16.03
Latino men	55.70	8.33	35.53
Latina women	65.28	7.87	25.00
Other men	55.88	5.29	37.65
Other women	57.47	5.75	36.21

Note: Column numbers are percentage of total number of people responding in the category.

Source: 2016 American National Election Study.

death penalty. A higher percentage of Latino men favor the death penalty than do Latina women (62.28 percent to 56.94 percent).

On the issue of gun control, Black women again are the most supportive of the federal government, making it more difficult to purchase a gun (70.31 percent), with Latino women close behind (66.60 percent). Majorities or half of White women, Black men, and Latino men also favor making it more difficult to purchase a gun, but there is a 15 to 20 percentage point difference in their support from that of Black women. The difference between these groups'

measuring equality

Donald Trump, Barack Obama, and the "Birthers"

In 2011, Donald Trump, the 2016 Republican presidential nominee, talked incessantly about his questions of whether President Obama was actually born in Hawaii. He even said that he had sent private investigators to Hawaii to see what they could find, and that no one seemed to remember him in school or any other place. President Obama then released his Hawaiian long-form birth certificate proving that he was, indeed, born in Hawaii and is a natural-born United States citizen. But Trump's "Birther" campaign did become a talking point in the 2012 election because of Trump's support for Mitt Romney, the 2012 Republican nominee. In the 2016 Republican primaries, one of the presidential contenders Senator Ted Cruz *was* born in Alberta, Canada, to a United States citizen mother and a Cuban-born father. Yet, an August 28–30, 2015, survey by Public Policy Poll of Republican voters found that, despite the evidence to the contrary, only 29 percent of Republicans believed that President Obama was born in the United States, while 40 percent believed Senator Cruz was born in the United States.

What factors might explain this difference?

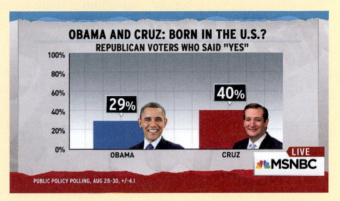

Figure 10.2 Obama and Cruz: Born in the United States? Republican voters who said "yes"

Protesters gather outside the Capitol during the Democrat sit-in, June 22, 2016. The Democratic members of the House of Representatives, led by Congressman John Lewis, staged a sit-in to protest the House's failure to hold a vote on gun control legislation after the mass murder of forty-nine people at a gay bar in Orlando, Florida.

support and that of Latino women ranges from 11 to 15 percentage points. What these figures suggest is that race, gender, and the intersection between the two have significant influences on public opinion.

Demographic Factors

Educational level affects a person's opinions and attitudes, as do income, region, and urban, suburban, or rural location. Political science research has found that persons with higher incomes, education levels, professional occupations, and suburban residence are more inclined to identify with the Republican Party, whereas those with lower incomes, lower education levels, labor and blue-collar jobs, and urban residence are more inclined to identify with the Democratic Party.[68]

Regional location and urban versus rural environments also influence public opinion. People living in different parts of the country often have different political views. For example, people in the Northeast are generally more liberal on social issues than are people in the South. Even within the same section of the country, however, the views of people living in rural areas might be markedly different from those of people living in urban areas. Those living in suburban areas might hold views different from those living in rural or urban areas. The social and political environments of rural, urban, and suburban locales differ, and consequently, the issues that are significant to residents of each type of area also vary.[69]

Table 10.6 shows the differences in attitudes toward the federal government, making it more difficult to obtain a gun, by selected demographic characteristics. People who live in the Northeast (64.71 percent) are significantly

TABLE 10.6 Differences in Support for Gun Control by Selected Characteristics—Region, Income, and Religion

Do you think the federal government should make it more difficult for people to buy a gun than it is now, make it easier for people to buy a gun, or keep these rules about the same as they are?
Gun Control

	More Difficult	Easier	The Same
Region			
Northeast	64.71	6.00	28.71
n = 700	n = 453	n = 42	n = 201
Midwest	52.65	5.39	41.56
n = 1,001	n = 527	n = 54	n = 416
South	47.85	6.63	44.97
n = 1,630	n = 780	n = 108	n = 733
West	53.47	7.55	38.27
n = 980	n = 524	n = 74	n = 375

Income			
<$19,999	49.15	9.80	40.20
n = 704	*n* = 346	*n* = 69	*n* = 283
$20,000–39,999	52.52	6.73	39.84
n = 773	*n* = 406	*n* = 52	*n* = 308
$40,000–59,999	48.79	6.44	44.61
n = 621	*n* = 303	*n* = 40	*n* = 277
$60,000–74,999	53.33	6.22	40.00
n = 450	*n* = 240	*n* = 28	*n* = 180
$75,000–89,999	50.14	6.16	43.42
n = 357	*n* = 179	*n* = 22	*n* = 155
$90,000–99,999	56.25	5.11	38.64
n = 176	*n* = 99	*n* = 9	*n* = 68
$100,000–124,999	57.10	5.36	37.27
n = 373	*n* = 213	*n* = 20	*n* = 139
$125,000–149,999	50.00	6.02	43.98
n = 166	*n* = 83	*n* = 10	*n* = 73
$150,000+	64.59	4.68	30.73
n = 449	*n* = 290	*n* = 21	*n* = 138
Religion			
Protestant	43.09	5.44	50.60
n = 919	*n* = 396	*n* = 50	*n* = 465
Catholic	57.70	6.84	35.30
n = 643	*n* = 371	*n* = 44	*n* = 227
Jewish	67.39	10.87	21.74
n = 46	*n* = 31	*n* = 5	*n* = 10
Other	52.71	7.79	39.16
n = 886	*n* = 467	*n* = 69	*n* = 347

Note: Column numbers are percentage of total number of people responding in the category.

Source: 2016 American National Election Study.

more supportive of making it more difficult to obtain a gun than are those who live in the South (47.85 percent). In general, those at the upper end of the income scale are more supportive of making it more difficult to purchase a gun than are those in some of the middle income ranges. Based on broad religious categories, although the sample size is small, Jewish individuals are far more likely to support efforts to make it more difficult to purchase a gun than are Protestants.

Partisan Identification

Partisan Identification The political party an individual most identifies with.

Another influence is **partisan identification**, or which political party an individual most identifies with. A person who identifies with the Democratic Party is more likely to favor Democratic policy positions and candidates. A person who identifies with the Republican Party will favor Republican positions and candidates. There is also a relationship between ideology and partisan identification. If a person feels that government should be used to resolve societal problems, then she might be drawn to the Democratic Party. If a person feels that government should have a limited role in society, then he might be attracted to the Republican Party.

Research further suggests that positions on racial policies are also a defining difference between Republicans and Democrats. On issues of race, the current Republican Party is viewed by Blacks and other individuals as hostile to Blacks and other non-White groups, and the party has had a tortured history with race throughout most of the twentieth century. Republican presidents and presidential candidates from Herbert Hoover forward have employed a Southern strategy—using issues of race to bring former Southern White Democrats into the Republican Party—to move the party away from its image as the party of Lincoln (read as the party of Blacks) and to win elections.[70] Political scientist Tasha Philpot argues that modern Republican presidents from Ronald Reagan onward extended the Southern strategy past the Mason-Dixon line to exploit racial divisions among working- and middle-class White Democrats, pulling them into the Republican Party.[71]

The Democratic Party, in contrast, is perceived by Blacks and others as being more welcoming to and supportive of Blacks, although it has been criticized for taking Black voters for granted in past elections. The nomination and election of Barack Obama have reinforced the view of the Democrats as being more amenable and open to Blacks. President Lyndon Johnson's push for civil rights legislation during the 1960s resulted in another kind of "push": of White Democrats into the Republican Party. Even though not every Republican or Democrat fits these particular characterizations, the overall perception exists. Moreover, the perceptions were reinforced by the tenor and tone of the 2016 presidential election and the visual pictures presented by the national conventions of both parties. The Republican Party sent fewer Black delegates to the convention in 2016 than it had "at any point in the past century."[72] Less than 1 percent of delegates at the RNC were African American (only 18 out of 2,472).[73] Hispanic delegates made up a slightly higher percentage of delegates than African Americans.[74] There were at least 133 Hispanic delegates at the RNC.[75] In direct contrast to the 2016 Republican National Convention, half of the delegates at the Democratic National Convention were non-White. Twenty-five percent of delegates were Black, 16 percent Latino, and 9 percent Asian American or Native American. According to the Clinton campaign, 1,182 delegates were Black, 747 were Latino, 292 were Asian American, and 147 were Native American.[76]

To recap, children initially adopt the political party identification and political views of their parents, and many will stick with those initial identifications. As people grow older, they might be attracted to the party opposite their parents' for a number of reasons. Political science research reports that some people will gravitate toward one party or another based on such factors as income, education, occupation, and place of residence. The factors mentioned earlier concerning which people are more likely to be Democrats and which are more likely to be Republicans are generalizations based on political science research. Clearly, there are individuals from high socioeconomic categories who are Democrats and from lower socioeconomic categories who are Republicans, but political science research has identified broad generalizations of which individuals are more likely to be attracted to one party or the other.[77]

The Media

The media strongly influence public opinion. Television, in particular, has become increasingly important in transmitting information. A Gallup poll taken in April 1937 reported that 91 percent of Americans said they read a newspaper daily. When questioned in April 1981 about their major source of news, 70 percent of respondents reported getting their news from daily newspapers. By July 1998, the percentage of Americans reporting that they got their news from daily newspapers had dropped to 50 percent.[78] A January 1999 survey by the Media Studies Center reported that 65 percent of those in the sample received most of their news from television and only 21 percent received their news from newspapers.[79] A 2012 survey of news consumption by the Pew Research Center found that 55 percent of their sample received their news from television and 50 percent indicated that they also got their news from online and digital sources, whereas only 29 percent read a newspaper for their news.[80] A 2013 Gallup survey also found that television was the main place Americans turned to for news about current events (55 percent), significantly ahead of the Internet at 18 percent. Television was the primary source of news for all age groups, although those age 18 to 29 and 30 to 49 had lower percentages (50 percent) than those age 50 to 64 (58 percent) and 65 and older (68 percent).[81]

Even though most people report getting their news from television, they do not always mean television news programs. Many indicate that they receive their news from entertainment shows such as *Saturday Night Live, Entertainment Tonight,* and *Inside Hollywood.*[82] It has also been suggested that young voters, eighteen to twenty-four years old, get their news from the late-night

Consider how this negative ad influences you.

television talk shows such as *The Tonight Show Starring Jimmy Fallon*, *The Late Show with Stephen Colbert*, *Last Week Tonight with John Oliver*, and *Politically Incorrect with Bill Maher*. A 2014 study from the University of Delaware found that on the issue of net neutrality, those who watched *The Daily Show*, *Colbert*, and *Last Week Tonight* were more informed about the issue than those that watched cable news, read news online, or read newspapers.[83] In a 2014 Public Religion Research Institute and Brookings Institution survey, Jon Stewart was viewed as a more trusted source of news than MSNBC.[84]

A 2016 survey by the Pew Research Center: Journalism and Media found that only 2 and 3 percent of respondents regularly learned something about the 2016 candidates and campaign from national or local daily newspapers, respectively, and 11 percent received their campaign news from the radio. Although more people received their news about the campaign from cable news programs (24 percent) than from nightly network news programs (10 percent), the percentage of people getting their campaign news from either cable or network news programs had dropped significantly since 2000, when 48 percent of Americans got their campaign news from the local news programs and 45 percent got it from the networks. The number of people (27 percent) getting their campaign news from the Internet (combined social media and news website/app) in 2016 increased significantly from the 9 percent who had indicated the Internet was their main source of campaign news in 2000. Republicans are twice as likely as Democrats to say cable news is the most helpful with 2016 campaign news, while Democrats are slightly more likely to identify local news as their source. Late-night comedy shows also have a partisan bent—three in ten Democrats indicate that these shows are one source of their political knowledge, but only 16 percent of Republicans and 25 percent of Independents identified them as such. About a third, 34 percent, of those age 18 to 29 learned about the candidates and campaigns from late-night comedy shows, the highest percentage of any group.[85]

What is interesting, however, especially in light of the emphasis placed on young voters during the 2008, 2012, and 2016 presidential elections, is that six in ten, 61 percent, of millennials (individuals born between 1981 to 1996) report getting political news on Facebook in a given week, a much larger percentage than mentioned any other news source. This is a major shift from the 2012 election, when only 29 percent of people under age thirty were going online to get campaign news. This also stands in stark contrast to baby boomers (individuals born between 1946 and 1964) for whom local TV news, 60 percent, tops the list of sources for political news. Generation X, individuals born between 1965 and 1980, bridge the gap between millennials and baby boomers, with about half (51 percent) indicating that they get political and government news on Facebook in a given week and a little less than half (46 percent) saying they do so from local TV.[86] Figure 10.3 shows data from the Pew Research Center indicating where people said they got their campaign news. We explore the role of media in political attitudes and effects much more in the following chapter.

The Bradley Effect

Throughout the 2008 presidential election, many journalists and even more political pundits began to speculate about whether the poll numbers for Senator Obama were an accurate reflection of how people felt or whether the **Bradley effect**—the difference between how Black candidates poll and how they perform at the ballot box—was in play. The term stems from the 1982 run of Los Angeles mayor Tom Bradley for governor of California. The polls indicated that Bradley was significantly ahead of his opponent heading into the election, and even exit polling indicated that Bradley was going to win. Yet Bradley lost by a narrow margin, which raised the question of a subtle anti-Black bias among White voters who were unwilling to tell pollsters that they would not vote for a Black man.

The Bradley effect, sometimes also called the Wilder effect, was present in the 1989 gubernatorial race in Virginia, in which L. Douglas Wilder, a Black candidate, was 15 percentage points ahead two weeks before the election, but won by just 6,582 votes out of the 1.7 million cast.[87] Once again, the explanation for Wilder's underperformance in actual ballots versus people who said they were going to vote for him was the anti-Black bias of some White voters and their unwillingness to admit it to pollsters.

The influence of racial attitudes on White voting patterns is one that political scientists grapple with and the question that news media hyped during the 2008 election. Were the poll numbers for Barack Obama real? Or were they an artifact of some White voters not wanting to say that they would not vote for a Black candidate? Political scientist Daniel J. Hopkins explored the question of the Bradley/Wilder effect on elections with Black candidates running against White candidates to see if it was still present in electoral races. His results suggested that the Bradley/Wilder effect was present in a number of political contests throughout the 1980s and 1990s, but that since then it appears to be dissipating in some instances or disappearing altogether in others.[88]

Until more research is conducted, we will not know if the Bradley/Wilder effect is truly gone, as race is still a potent factor in American politics. In the

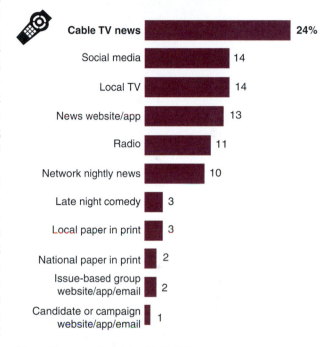

Vast majority of Americans learning about 2016 presidential election; cable news seen as most helpful source type

91% of U.S. adults learned about the 2016 presidential election in the past week

*Among those who learned about the election, % who name each source type as **most helpful***

Source	%
Cable TV news	24%
Social media	14
Local TV	14
News website/app	13
Radio	11
Network nightly news	10
Late night comedy	3
Local paper in print	3
National paper in print	2
Issue-based group website/app/email	2
Candidate or campaign website/app/email	1

Source: Survey conducted Jan 12–27, 2016

PEW RESEARCH CENTER

Figure 10.3 Where People Get Their Campaign News
Source: Pew Research Center. (2016, February 4). The 2016 presidential campaign—a news event that's hard to miss. Retrieved October 8, 2018, from http://www.journalism.org/2016/02/04/ the-2016-presidential-campaign-a-news-event-thats-hard-to-miss/

Bradley Effect The difference between how Black candidates poll and how they perform at the ballot box (also called the Wilder effect).

case of President Obama, evidence suggests that the Bradley/Wilder effect was not in play. The final average of all of the tracking polls reported by RealClear Politics had Senator Obama at 52.1 percent to Senator McCain's 44.5 percent. The final results of the presidential election were Senator Obama at 52.9 percent and Senator McCain at 45.6 percent. In this instance, Obama's vote total tracked very close to his standing in the polls on the day of the election.

The 2012 exit polls did show a racial dimension in voting. Romney took the majority of the White vote (59 percent), Obama took 93 percent of the Black vote, 71 percent of the Latino vote, and 73 percent of the Asian vote. These numbers coupled with the smaller portion of the White vote (39 percent) secured Obama's clear and substantive victory over Romney. Obama had a higher proportion of the White vote in 2008 (43 percent) than he did in 2012 (39 percent).

Public Opinion and Politics

Public opinion is a central element of politics in the American political system and serves many purposes. First, it reflects the degree of public support for government actions. Public officials recognize that some government actions need the support of the public to succeed. Moreover, the loss of public support for a government action might signal declining political fortunes for elected officials. For example, as a result of negative public opinion, President Ronald Reagan's administration had to back off of a proposal to classify catsup as a vegetable so that it could cut funding for the federal school lunch program in 1981. In 2008, President George W. Bush's administration backed away from its decision to allow increased levels of arsenic in drinking water.[89]

Second, public opinion serves as an effective check on political leadership because it can often keep politicians from gathering too much political power or from making decisions or policies that are contrary to the public will.[90] Public opinion can influence politicians who show poor judgment or who are incompetent or corrupt to resign their offices.[91] For example, Richard Nixon's presidential approval ratings declined steadily from his highest rating of 67 percent in the last week of January 1973 to a low of 24 percent in the second week of August 1974 when he resigned.[92] Although public opinion was not the only influential factor in Nixon's decision to resign, it played a key role because it indicated that Nixon could not survive the Watergate scandal and his involvement in covering it up.

Although not necessarily leading to resignation, falling approval ratings can severely curtail a president's political influence. Such was the case with President George W. Bush. President Bush's approval ratings were in the high 80s right after the terrorist attack on September 11, 2001. They declined somewhat in early 2003, but spiked again with the invasion of Iraq. Unfortunately, as the Iraq war dragged on and more information was revealed about the administration's manipulation of the American public with false claims of Iraqi stockpiles of weapons of mass destruction, President Bush's approval rating sank to almost 25 percent. As his term ended, his approval ratings dipped below that of President Nixon twenty-seven years earlier.

Third, during elections candidates and political parties do extensive polling to find out which candidates are running ahead and which policy positions taken by the candidates resonate with voters. Few politicians today will embark on major public policy initiatives without first knowing how the public might react to them. Critics often charge that "governing by polls" reduces innovativeness in public policy and diminishes a political leader's willingness to make difficult and unpopular decisions.[93] In response, those in public office say that knowing how the public will react to a decision, particularly an unpopular one, provides them with advance warning and allows them to prepare the public for an unfavorable decision.

Candidates for political office, especially for president, rely heavily on polling to fine-tune or retool their campaign message and strategies. In the 2008 presidential race, Senator McCain changed campaign strategies and messages in the face of polling data indicating that Americans wanted change and therefore that he would have to appeal to that sentiment if he were going to be successful.

But sometimes polls can be misleading. Late in the campaign, McCain, in an October 26, 2008, appearance on *Meet the Press,* confidently indicated that his campaign was doing fine and that he was going to win. This statement resulted from internal campaign polling that indicated he was only 4 percentage points behind Senator Obama in the presidential campaign.[94] Public opinion polling is now a staple of political campaigns and has fluctuated from year to year in its accuracy and predictive capacity.

Finally, in a representative democracy like the United States, public opinion provides a gauge of how people feel about their government and their institutions. Public opinion might reflect support for the actions of government or a distrust of government and those who run it. Public opinion is also a way for the American public to influence the issues and the behaviors of elected officials.[95]

Conclusion

Public opinion is an essential part of the U.S. political process. On the one side, it is used by politicians to gauge public support for or disapproval of particular policies and to gauge their own standing with the public. It also serves as a barometer of how well candidates' campaigns are faring. On the other side, individuals see public opinion polls as a measure of how well their politicians are doing or as a mechanism for the collective public to let politicians know how the electorate feels about policy issues. Yet the factors that help form public opinion are complex and varied. The opening vignette highlighted racial differences on the question of affirmative action.

This chapter has explored the importance of public opinion to democracy and how concern about public opinion has been a part of the U.S. political system since the beginning of the nation. The measuring of public opinion is a precise and scientific process, and much of what are called public opinion surveys are really only the opinions of individuals who are willing to participate in online ballots. The material presented in this chapter has given a broad overview of public opinion and the process of gathering data and identifying attitudes and behaviors of the American public.

As the opening vignette illustrated, racial dimensions and divisions exist on important issues within the American electorate. Race, gender, and the intersection of the two produce differences in public opinion that are often not identified in general discussions and presentations of public opinion. Yet race, gender, and other factors play a major role in the formation of what people think and why they feel the way they do. Taking those differences into account presents a broader picture of the variety of public opinion in the American political system and how those varied factors affect what people think about issues.

Check your understanding of Chapter 10.

REVIEW QUESTIONS

1. Why is public opinion important to a representative democracy?
2. What factors influence the formation of public opinion?
3. How do race and gender affect the formation of public opinion, and why do different groups have such different opinions on key issues?
4. What is survey research?
5. What is the Bradley effect?

Need to review key ideas in greater depth? Click here.

KEY TERMS

Bradley Effect p. 323
Gender p. 313
Gender Gap p. 313
Partisan Identification p. 320

Political Culture p. 298
Political Socialization p. 299
Probability Sampling p. 304
Public Opinion p. 295

Quota Sampling p. 303
Sample p. 302
Sampling Error p. 304
Survey Research p. 301

Flashcard review.

ADDITIONAL READINGS

Asher, H. (2007). *Polling and the public: What every citizen should know* (7th ed.). Washington, DC: Congressional Quarterly Press.

> This book is an introduction to the philosophy, mechanics, and interpretation of public opinion polling and polls.

Glynn, C. J., Herbst, S., O'Keefe, G. J., Shapiro, R. Y., & Lindeman, M. (2004). *Public opinion* (2nd ed.). Boulder, CO: Westview Press.

> This book is a comprehensive and interdisciplinary examination of public opinion formation and change. It analyzes the nature of political and social attitudes in the United States.

Harris-Lacewell, M. (2004). *Barbershops, bibles, and BET: Everyday talk and Black political thought.* Princeton, NJ: Princeton University Press.

> This book examines the multiple venues and influences that shape African American political and social opinions.

Sapiro, V., & Shames, S. L. (2009). The gender basis of public opinion. In B. Norrander & C. Wilcox (Eds.), *Understanding public opinion* (3rd ed.). Washington, DC: Congressional Quarterly Press.

> This chapter provides an excellent overview of the role of gender in public opinion formation, the gender gap, and how gender roles, gender identities, and gender stereotyping affect public opinion.

Schumann, H., Steeh, C., Bobo, L., & Krysan, M. (1997). *Racial attitudes in America: Trends and interpretations.* Cambridge, MA: Harvard University Press.

> This book examines the trends in Black and White public opinion from the 1940s through the late 1990s.

The Media: Reinforcing Racial Stereotypes?

This Facebook ad, created on October 14, 2016, targeted people who already liked the fake "Being Patriotic" page. It received more than 3,000 impressions and 760 clicks. Russia propagated these ads to appeal to people with anti-Black prejudice to create dissension among American voters and potentially influence the outcome of the 2016 election.

O ver the past decade, social media sites, such as Facebook, Twitter, and Instagram, have become integral to people's lives, including their political lives. Campaigns use social media platforms to connect with campaign workers and volunteers, as well as potential voters. Americans also use social media to connect with like-minded people to discuss politics and encourage each other to engage in political activism. However, the 2016 election demonstrated how foreign powers, especially those hostile to the United States, can influence the behavior of American voters. Specifically, a Russian business called Internet Research Company, which has connections to Russian President Vladimir Putin, created a number of phony social media accounts with seemingly legitimate origins and used those accounts to spread fabricated stories about American politics. These fake accounts tried to sow divisions among Americans by distributing inflammatory political messages, such as encouraging African Americans to vote for a third party instead of Hillary Clinton or encouraging people to attend anti-Muslim rallies. Overall, this Russian attempt to influence American political behavior reached 126 million Facebook accounts and almost 700,000 Twitter users. The Internet Research Agency also used automated accounts (or "bots") to retweet campaign messages, but this operation retweeted ten times more pro-Trump messages than pro-Clinton messages. The Internet Research Agency's deceptive attempt to divide America along political lines was so severe that in February 2018, Robert Mueller, the Special Counsel investigating Russian influence in the 2016 election, indicted the Internet Research Agency and several Russian individuals for illegally interfering in the American election.[1]

Social media users are accustomed to seeing ads on their sites, and based on sophisticated algorithms, these ads tend to reinforce the individual user's attitudes. The Internet Research Agency created approximately 3,500 ads intended to arouse strong feelings based on people's political and social attitudes. Although these fake ads addressed a variety of political issues, more than half of their messages focused on issues of race. Some of these phony ads targeted racial and ethnic minorities by raising issues of police brutality against minorities. However,

**even more ads stoked anti-Black, anti-Muslim, and anti-Latino preju-
dices. One especially inflammatory fake ad showed a police officer's
funeral with the caption reading "Another Gruesome Attack on Police
by a BLM [Black Lives Matter] Movement Activist." The text of the fake
post describes the case of Ed Figueroa, who exchanged gunshots with
Boston police officers. The picture and caption implies that Figueroa
was a member of Black Lives Matter who killed law enforcement officers.
Although Figueroa did shoot at police, no police officers died in the incident; in fact, Figueroa was the only person who died. More importantly,
Figueroa was someone with a violent, troubled past, but he was in no
way associated with Black Lives Matter, as this Russian ad claimed.[2]**

intro

*This controversy over Russia's use of social media to interfere in the 2016 election
demonstrates the importance of the mass media in American politics. The **mass
media** are those sources of information, including print, radio, television, and the
Internet, that reach a significant number of people. Although the scope of the media
includes nonpolitical news, entertainment, and sports, it also focuses on politics. The
mass media's coverage of politics influences how the public perceives political events,
which, in turn can influence how political leaders view those events.*

*Moreover, this story reveals the significance of newer media. Traditionally, news-
papers covered politics, and during the twentieth century, broadcast radio and television emerged as important. However, by the turn of the twenty-first century, politically
biased cable news stations, such as Fox, which advocates a conservative view, and
MSNBC, which advocates a liberal view, as well as entertainment shows became
major sources from which people receive political information. By the 2016 election,
the Internet in general and social media in particular has largely supplanted traditional media—newspapers, television, and radio. In fact, many people who consume
traditional media sources do so through the Internet and social media.*

*Finally, this story also reveals the key role that race and ethnicity plays in the
mass media. The 2016 presidential election sought to replace America's first Black
president, Barack Obama. Although much of Obama's presidency eschewed issues of
race, many of his opponents focused on his race when criticizing him. In fact, during
much of Obama's presidency, Donald Trump used the media to propagate a false,
racist conspiracy that President Obama was born in Kenya and thus ineligible to be
president.[3]*

*This chapter covers mass media and politics. We begin by tracing the history of
the media's coverage of politics, focusing on the different types of media that have
emerged. Then we address the media industry, examining the owners of media
outlets and the profession of journalism. The chapter concludes with a discussion
of the media's coverage of elections, government officials, and political institutions.
Throughout this chapter, we examine how the politics of race and ethnicity intersects
with the politics of the mass media.*

Mass Media Sources of
information, including print,
radio, television, and the
Internet, that reach a large
number of people.

Fact-check the
media.

A History of Media and Politics

The relationship between government and the media has continually changed throughout American history, especially as technological advancements have altered the way in which the media transmit information to the public. Here we look at the evolution of print media from the early years of the Republic through the twenty-first century, and we discuss the impact that newspapers, radio, broadcast television, cable television, the Internet, and social media have exerted on politics.

We also investigate the key role the media play in **agenda setting**. That is, the media are powerful because when the press chooses to focus on particular issues, the public tends to think those issues are important. We also address the media's role in **framing**, that is, its ability to shape how viewers interpret political events and issues. [4] Throughout American history, the media's power of agenda setting and framing have significantly affected minority-group politics.

Print Media

During the early years of the American Republic, newspapers were highly biased and opinionated; they made no pretense of reporting the news and political issues in an objective fashion. As a result, newspapers were instrumental in shaping public opinion during the American Revolution and during debates over ratification of the Constitution. As political parties developed during the early nineteenth century (see Chapter 14), each political party controlled at least one newspaper that exclusively contained favorable coverage of its own politicians and unfavorable coverage of the opposition. [5] Moreover, interest groups and religious organizations of that era published newspapers to expound their political and social views. In contrast, another kind of newspaper, known as the **penny press**, covered human-interest stories, rather than political issues, in an attempt to attract readers. [6]

The early nineteenth-century media covered issues of race and ethnicity. Penny presses were especially interested in the Mexican-American War, and much of their coverage perpetuated negative stereotypes of Mexicans. The penny press and popular novels of the late 1840s depicted Mexicans as inferior to Whites and in need of Whites to civilize them, a portrayal that increased public support for the Mexican-American War and fomented anti-Mexican prejudice. [7]

During this era, abolitionists relied heavily on the use of the media to advocate an end to slavery. In 1821, Quaker abolitionist Benjamin Lundy founded a newspaper called *The Genius of Universal Emancipation*, which recounted the horrors of slavery and the slave trade. The paper advocated for gradual abolition and recolonization of the slaves. William Lloyd Garrison, another abolitionist, joined Lundy's paper, but Garrison assumed the more radical position of immediate abolition and integration of the former slaves into American society. Garrison later formed his own newspaper, *The Liberator*,

Explore the role of agenda setting in the media.

Agenda Setting The media's power to influence the importance that the public places on issues.

Framing The media's ability to shape how viewers interpret political events and issues.

Penny Press Nineteenth-century newspapers that eschewed coverage of politics and instead focused on human-interest stories.

which was the most influential abolitionist periodical. *The Liberator* published accounts of the horrors of slavery, as well as morally persuasive pieces that convinced many Americans to join the abolitionist cause (see "Our Voices: *The Liberator* and Abolitionism" on page 333). When emancipating the slaves, President Abraham Lincoln cited the influence of Garrison.[8]

Garrison's paper also inspired former slave and antislavery advocate Frederick Douglass to start his own abolitionist newspaper, called the *North Star*, out of Rochester, New York. Like *The Liberator*, the *North Star* advocated abolition, but it took more radical positions for the time, such as suggesting that Blacks arm themselves and supporting women's rights. The *North Star* was especially important because it was the first major U.S. newspaper operated by an African American. In fact, not only did free Blacks in the North read Douglass's paper, but also many Whites read it. Douglass's success set a crucial example that Blacks were capable of significant intellectual achievement.[9]

By the late nineteenth century, many newspapers were engaging in **yellow journalism**, which consisted of sensationalist reports intended to titillate the masses to sell papers and advertising space. Yellow journalism papers focused on crime and vice stories, perpetuated scientific hoaxes, and offered bogus "miracle cures." They often distorted facts to make stories more enticing, especially when perpetuating stereotypes and influencing public opinion about issues of race and ethnicity. For example, William Randolph Hearst's *San Francisco Examiner*, an early yellow journalism paper, often referred to Chinese and Japanese immigrants in highly unflattering terms. Hearst suggested that Asian immigrants stole jobs from hard-working, honest White laborers. The paper also falsely claimed that Chinese and Japanese immigrants caused crime, gambling, prostitution, and opium addiction.[10]

Yellow Journalism A form of journalism popular during the late eighteenth and early nineteenth centuries that sensationalized stories and distorted facts to sell more papers.

Other newspapers such as the *New York Times* pursued a different type of journalism by focusing primarily on disseminating accurate information. This more objective press relegated opinion to the editorial pages and eschewed crass gossip or human-interest stories. Yet even these so-called objective newspapers still perpetuated stereotypes of racial and ethnic minorities. For example, *the New York Times* referred to Indian tribes that tried to assimilate into White culture as "semi-civilized" and tribes that did not assimilate as "wild and predatory."[11]

By the turn of the twentieth century, journalism had become a major industry, with the print media expanding tremendously throughout the United States. Every city, every town, and even many rural areas had their own daily newspaper, and many cities had two major daily newspapers. Technological advances such as the telephone and photography enhanced newspapers' ability to report events and the quality of their presentation. Moreover, during this print media explosion, weekly news magazines such as *Time* and *Newsweek* emerged. These periodicals summarized the events of the week and offered editorial opinions through syndicated columnists.[12]

Parallel Press Newspapers and other forms of media geared toward specific racial and ethnic minority groups.

Part of the twentieth-century print media explosion consisted of the growth of the **parallel press**, or newspapers that advocated on behalf of

ILLUSTRATED NEWSPAPER.   [APRIL 3, 1880.

SAN-FRAN TO KEARNEY SIX MONTHS JAIL

ELATION OF THE "HEATHEN CHINER" OVER A RECENT EVENT IN
SAN FRANCISCO.

FISHERMEN!
TWINES AND NETTING!
MANUFACTURED BY
WM. E. HOOPER & SONS, Baltimore, Md.
Send for Price-List, naming your County and State.

N.Y. Central & Hudson River R.R.
THE BEST ROUTE EAST OR WEST.
Through Cars between New York or Boston and Chicago
or St. Louis.

THE
Union Mutual Life Ins. Co.
JOHN E. DE WITT, President.
HOME OFFICE, Augusta, Maine.
DIRECTORS' OFFICE—150 Tremont St., Boston, Mass
Commenced Business in 1849.

Nineteenth-century newspapers were instrumental in perpetuating racial and ethnic stereotypes. This picture, from an 1880 edition of *Frank Leslie's Illustrated*, depicts a Chinese "heathen" laughing at another person's misfortune. These types of images created the unfair stereotype of Chinese immigrants as alien and untrustworthy.

specific racial or ethnic minority groups. Minorities who published parallel press newspapers sought to counteract the stereotypical portrayal of minorities in the White press. The parallel press traced its roots to the nineteenth century, but these publications proliferated during the twentieth century. Many White newspapers and journalists dismissed the parallel press as inferior to the White newspapers, but during the twentieth century the parallel press was instrumental in inspiring activism on behalf of Blacks, Latinos, Asian Americans, and American Indians.

There are too many examples of the parallel press to recount all of them here, but some leading publications stand out. Ida Wells-Barnett published the *Memphis Free Speech*, which spoke out against the lynching of African Americans and pushed for antilynching legislation. The *Chicago Defender*, established by Robert Abbott in 1905, became a leading force in journalism. Whereas other Black newspapers included human-interest stories, Abbott sought to raise the intellectual level of his newspaper, and he wanted it to be an instrument for improving the lives of Blacks. Most notably, the *Chicago Defender*'s circulation reached the South, and Abbott explicitly encouraged Black Southerners to migrate to Northern cities, where they would face less discrimination and enjoy more economic opportunity. To this day, the *Chicago Defender* is still a leading African American newspaper in the United States.[13]

Latino newspapers during the nineteenth century focused on issues pertaining to Latino immigrants. The earliest Spanish-language newspapers were founded in San Francisco in the 1850s after many Mexicans immigrated to northern California in search of gold and the United States had conquered what is now the southwestern portion of the United States (see Chapter 5). These papers, such as *Sud Americano*, reported the news from the immigrants' home countries. Other Spanish-language papers were concerned with issues facing immigrants in the United States. In the Los Angeles area, *El Heraldo de México* focused on the rights of immigrant laborers, whereas *El Espectador* argued that immigrants should assimilate into White society. Asian American parallel press publications concentrated mainly on news relevant to the immigrants' country of origin, but during the twentieth century they also examined issues pertaining to life in the United States.[14]

Tribal newspapers report on the news relating to each tribe. Tribal governments sponsored most of these newspapers, but more recent independent papers criticized tribal governments and institutions, as well as the U.S.

our voices

The Liberator and Abolitionism

William Lloyd Garrison is one of the most well-known abolitionists, and he spread his views by publishing *The Liberator*. Like many of the partisan presses of the early nineteenth century, Garrison's *The Liberator* convinced people to support the immediate abolition of slavery. Garrison's publication often took radical stances on abolition, chastising both the slave trade and moderate abolitionists.

The excerpt here comes from the first edition of *The Liberator*, published on January 1, 1831. Garrison was fined for libel because of an earlier depiction of the slave trade, and the court would have waived the penalty if Garrison had apologized to the ship's owner, Francis Todd. However, Garrison refused to apologize. Instead, he devoted his first edition of *The Liberator* to justifying his actions by reprinting his depiction of the slave trade. Although Garrison started his newspaper without a guaranteed audience, the power of this account garnered 450 subscribers. The writing style is different from that of contemporary media, but the tone of this piece is similar to that of many opinionated blogs of the contemporary era.

> The ship . . . sailed a few weeks since from this port with a cargo of slaves for the New Orleans market. . . . I am determined to cover with thick infamy all who are concerned in this nefarious business. I have stated that the ship *Francis* hails from my native place, Newburyport (Massachusetts), is commanded by a Yankee captain, and owned by a townsman named Francis Todd. . . . It is no worse to fit out practical cruisers, or to engage in the foreign slave trade, than to pursue a similar trade along our coast; and the men who have the wickedness to participate therein, for the purpose of heaping up wealth, should be sentenced to solitary confinement for life; they are the enemies of our own species—highway robbers and murderers; and their final doom will be, unless they speedily repent, to occupy the lowest depths of perdition. I know that the man who is allowed to freight his vessel with slaves at home, for a distant market, would be thought worthy of death if he should take a similar freight on the coast or Africa; but I know, too, that this distinction is absurd, and at war with the common sense of mankind, and that God and good men regard it with abhorrence. I recollect that it was always a mystery in Newburyport how Mr. Todd contrived to make profitable voyages to New Orleans and other places, when other merchants, with as fair an opportunity to make money, and sending at the same ports at the same time, invariably made fewer speculations. The mystery seems to be unraveled. Any man can gather up riches, if he does not care by what means they are obtained. The *Francis* carried off seventy-five slaves, chained in a narrow place between decks. Captain Brown originally intended to take one hundred and fifty of these unfortunate creatures; but another hard-hearted ship-master underbid him in the piece of passage for the remaining moiety. Captain B., we believe, is a mason. Where was his charity or brotherly kindness? I respectfully request the editor of the *Newburyport Herald* to copy this article, or publish a statement of the facts contained herein—not for the purpose of giving information to Mr. Todd, for I shall send him a copy of this number, but in order to enlighten the public mind in that quarter.

Source: Adapted from Nelson, T. (Ed.). (1966). *Documents of upheaval: Selections from William Lloyd Garrison's* The Liberator, *1831–1865*. New York: Hill & Wang, pp. 1–3.

government. Pan-Indian newspapers dealt with issues affecting American Indians throughout the United States. Some Indian parallel press publications advocated assimilation with Whites, whereas others more stridently called for preserving tribal identity.[15]

Broadcast Radio and Television

The invention of broadcast technology greatly changed the influence of the media. Although first invented at the beginning of the twentieth century, radio

A stack of Diario Las Américas newspapers as they are prepared for delivery in Miami, Florida. Diario Las Américas is one of multiple examples of the media explosion of the parallel press.

Hear Reagan's "Operation Coffee Cup" recording.

Go online to see the Harry and Louise ad.

broadcasting did not flourish until the 1920s, when the economy boomed and the price of radios dropped significantly. Impressed by radio's ability to transmit voices across the nation in seconds, political leaders used the medium to communicate with the American public.[16] President Franklin Delano Roosevelt shrewdly recognized the importance of radio for building public support. During the Great Depression, Roosevelt's radio addresses, known as fireside chats, calmed a nervous population.[17]

Although television began as an entertainment medium, by the late 1940s it began to broadcast the news. Not only could Americans hear the news while it occurred; they also could see it. However, initial news broadcasts would be unrecognizable today because they used still sets, interspersed with film footage, and they only lasted for 15 minutes each day. Later, television stations expanded news broadcasts to 30 minutes.[18]

Additionally, by the early 1950s political candidates used television to promote their messages. The 1952 election, in particular, demonstrated television's importance in politics. Presidential candidate Dwight D. Eisenhower aired catchy advertisements on television stations,[19] and television stations covered the campaign and election results.

Television's ability to bring moving pictures into people's living rooms influenced Americans' attitudes on major political issues during the 1960s, such as the Vietnam War, cultural changes, and, most notably, civil rights for racial and ethnic minorities. Many White Americans were not familiar with the extent of the oppression that minorities, especially Southern Blacks, endured. Television coverage of key civil rights events, such as sit-ins and integration of schools, introduced Whites to the salience of the issue.

Two televised events in particular were instrumental in shaping public opinion about the Civil Rights Movement. Television stations widely covered the 1963 March on Washington. Millions of Americans witnessed the widespread support for civil rights among Blacks and Whites, as well as Dr. Martin Luther King, Jr.'s historic "I Have a Dream" speech. Furthermore, televised coverage of the police brutality inflicted on civil rights protesters in Alabama alerted previously uninformed Americans to the severe injustices that Blacks suffered. Civil rights activist and current member of the U.S. House of Representatives John Lewis (D-GA), who was beaten by police and Klansmen numerous times during the early 1960s, credits televised coverage of that police brutality with increasing public support for the Voting Rights Act of 1965.[20]

There are, however, systematic studies that dispute the notion that the media helped the cause of civil rights. The Kerner Commission, which investigated the causes of racially oriented civil unrest during the late 1960s, blamed the media for their failure to report on the problems of discrimination against Blacks and for their reinforcement of negative stereotypes. Scholarly research further shows that in some non-Southern cities, such as Los Angeles, the coverage of civil rights actually declined during the 1960s—at the height of the Civil Rights Movement. Other research has found that when Northern newspapers and television stations did cover civil rights, the tone of the reporting was not positive toward the movement. Newspapers often referred to the

See the controversial "Daisy" ad from the 1964 Johnson campaign.

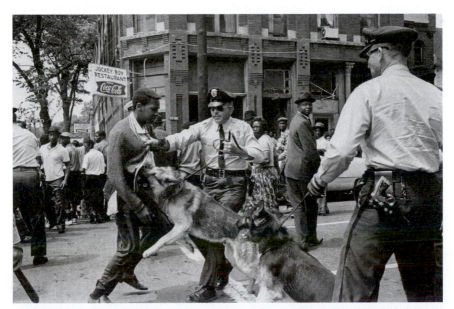

This 1963 picture of police attacking a peaceful civil rights protestor made the front page of major national newspapers, such as the *New York Times*. As a result, the American public, as well as President Kennedy, recognized the brutal treatment of African Americans in the South, thus demonstrating the media's agenda-setting power.

protesters as "outside agitators" or "communists," and some media coverage even reinforced stereotypes of Blacks as angry and uncivilized.[21]

Similar to the parallel press in the print media, there are minority-owned radio and television stations that can influence the coverage of minority-group politics. Black Entertainment Television (BET) is primarily an entertainment-oriented television network that since 1980 has emphasized cultural issues, but it also covers news events that are important to Blacks. However, in 2000, BET was sold to media corporation Viacom.[22] Likewise, Univision is a Spanish-language television network that appeals to Latinos, and it provides its own Spanish-language news program, *Noticiero Univision*.[23]

Cable and Satellite

Technological advances during the late twentieth century generated an expansion of media outlets. The use of satellites has greatly expanded the number of television stations that American households are able to receive. Some households have their own satellite receivers, and others subscribe to cable companies that transmit through cable hookups. Cable and satellite television can provide a wide variety of channels, including news channels, to the American public along with expanded news coverage. Conversely, broadcast media have limited space for news stations.

Cable and satellite television have tremendously altered the way in which the media cover politics. Launched in 1980, CNN provides nonstop news coverage and public affairs programming. Whereas network news stations usually wait until the evening to report the day's events, CNN broadcasts stories as they happen and provides continual coverage. Other cable and satellite news stations, such as MSNBC and Fox, followed CNN's lead, thus expanding the number of cable news channels. Recent evidence demonstrates that people who view cable news spend twice as much time watching the news as do people who view broadcast news stations.[24]

Another important cable and satellite station is C-SPAN, which provides live coverage of the U.S. House and U.S. Senate. Three C-SPAN stations carry floor debates, committee hearings, markup sessions, and press conferences, and the network also airs public affairs programming beyond the activities of Congress. C-SPAN is most significant because Americans have an opportunity to follow the activities of their elected representatives, and it lets representatives communicate directly with their constituents.[25]

Since the late twentieth century, cable and satellite television have been instrumental in the framing of issues relevant to minority-group politics. Because there are a large number of cable news outlets, each channel (even each program) has specific ideological slants and political focuses. Accordingly, there is ample space for programming that deals with issues pertaining to minority-group politics.

For example, former CNN and current Fox Business News television host Lou Dobbs focuses on immigration. According to the Fox Business News website, the host of the program is an award-winning journalist who is supported by a wide variety of groups across the political spectrum.[26] However, according to the Southern Poverty Law Center (SPLC), an organization that tracks the activities of racists and hate groups, a number of Lou Dobbs's guests on his CNN show made overtly prejudiced claims about Latinos, as well as about Blacks and other minorities. The SPLC reports that some of Dobbs's guests are connected to White supremacist groups, such as the Council of Conservative Citizens. Dobbs never divulged these guests' racist views and treated these individuals as heroes of the working class.[27]

More remarkably, cable and satellite television entertainment shows have provided some of the most serious news coverage. Although he was not the first host of Comedy Central's *The Daily Show*, comedian Jon Stewart advanced the idea of mixing late-night comedy entertainment with news. Stewart offered a humorous take on the news that has provided some of the most significant analysis of key events in the 2000s and 2010s, such as the war in Iraq, the economic collapse of 2008, and the Obama presidency. In 2015 Stewart left the show and was replaced with Trevor Noah, a South African comedian who is half Black and half White.[28] At the same time, Comedy Central also aired *The Colbert Report*, featuring comedian and actor Stephen Colbert's ironic portrayal of an obnoxious right-wing pundit, which was a vehicle to discuss key news events. Colbert ended *The Colbert Report* in 2015 to become the host of *The Late Show* on the broadcast network CBS, replacing the venerable David Letterman. Colbert continues to provide humorous accounts of key news events, particularly the 2016 election, Trump presidency, but he no longer plays the conservative media pundit character.[29] Other late-night cable television comedy shows that address politics include TBS's *Full Frontal with Samantha Bee* (an alumnus of *The Daily Show*),[30] Last HBO's *Last Week Tonight with John Oliver* (another *Daily Show* alumnus),[31] and HBO's *Real Time with Bill Maher*.[32] A humorist offering insightful commentary on politics is not a new phenomenon in American culture, and scholars regard these late-night comedians as contemporary versions of Benjamin Franklin and Mark Twain.[33]

These late-night comedy shows have addressed issues of race and ethnicity, often more honestly than traditional news. For example, in 2016 comedian John Oliver devoted a significant portion of his show *Last Week Tonight* to explain that public schools are becoming more segregated (we discussed this issue in Chapter 5). Oliver even noted that schools in Northern urban areas,

Robert Johnson, the founder of Black Entertainment Television (BET). Johnson started BET in 1980 as the first Black-owned and Black-themed television station. Over the next two decades, Johnson oversaw BET's tremendous growth, as the station expanded beyond entertainment to cover matters of political and social importance to African Americans and other minority groups. Johnson served as a rare exception to the White dominance of the media industry. In 2000, Johnson sold BET to media conglomerate Viacom, and as a result, he became the first African American billionaire. Since then, he has branched into other ventures, such as hotel management and temporarily co-owning the Charlotte Bobcats of the National Basketball Association.

such as New York City, are actually more segregated than schools in the South. Although Oliver's presentation was extremely humorous, he addressed a topic that very few traditional news outlets have reported. In fact, these traditional sources subsequently covered Oliver's story.[34] More recently, Samantha Bee aired an hour-long episode that explored the problems still facing Puerto Rico after Hurricane Maria.[35]

The Internet and Social Media

Because an increasing number of Americans, especially younger ones, rely on the Internet, it has become a significant medium for transmitting news. Internet news sites such as Politico.com[36] are now competitive with major cable and broadcast television news stations for reporting and analyzing political news. In fact, even traditional media outlets, such as magazines, newspapers, broadcast television networks, and cable channels, have their own websites. Since 2000 the Internet has evolved and produced innovative ways to influence politics. For example, YouTube allows people to upload videos, and then any user can access those videos. When Barack Obama was elected president, he had delivered a weekly radio address through YouTube, and currently the White House has its own YouTube channel.[37]

The importance of YouTube for minority-group politics became evident during the 2006 Virginia Senate election, which featured Republican incumbent George Allen against Democratic challenger Jim Webb. Allen was heavily favored for reelection, and he was even touted as a leading candidate for the

Trevor Noah as host of *The Daily Show*. Noah, who is multiracial, replaced Jon Stewart as host of this late night comedy show. Noah provides a humorous take on news events, especially those concerning race and ethnicity, such as police shootings of unarmed African Americans and Republican presidential candidate Donald Trump's bigoted statements against Latinos and Muslims.

2008 Republican presidential nomination. However, in summer 2006 Allen confronted a Webb volunteer named S. R. Siddarth who was video recording one of Allen's rallies. Siddarth was a college student born in the United States, but Allen emphasized Siddarth's South Asian heritage during their confrontation. Allen referred to Siddarth as "macaca," which is an archaic pejorative applied to people of South Asian descent, and Allen "welcomed" the native-born Siddarth to America. Siddarth recorded Allen's offensive, prejudiced tirade, and the Webb campaign downloaded the video to YouTube. After the video of Allen spread throughout the Internet, the mainstream news channels reported the story, and as a result of the negative publicity, Allen narrowly lost the election and never launched a campaign for the presidency.[38]

Podcasts are another form of new media that influences politics. Specifically, a podcast is a file that users can download on their computers or phones. These podcasts feature discussions and interviews that are serialized into multiple episodes. Podcasts usually support themselves financially through advertisements or charging subscription fees to users. Podcast topics often focus on culture and entertainment, but many of them address political issues, especially pertaining to race and ethnicity. For example the podcast *Our National Conversation About Conversations About Race* feature a number of hosts who lead discussion about racial politics issues, such as drug laws, NFL players protesting police brutality, and the Black Lives Matter movement.[39] The *Native Opinion Podcast: An American Indian Perspective* features stories that pertain to indigenous peoples.[40] The podcast *They Call Us Bruce* focuses on cultural and political issues concerning Asian Americans.[41]

The parallel press also uses the Internet to communicate with the public. For example, the *Chicago Defender*, a venerated parallel press newspaper, now has a website that covers local (Chicago), state (Illinois), national, and international news important to African Americans. Unlike the newspaper version, the *Chicago Defender* website is updated frequently, and readers are able to provide their opinions on key news events.[42] Additionally, *La Gaceta* has been a parallel press publication in Tampa, Florida, since 1922 that appeals to Latinos, particularly Cuban Americans, and it is also a significant publication that focuses on cultural and political issues throughout Central Florida. It started as a print publication, but it is also online. Both the print and online formats appear in three languages—English, Spanish, and Italian.[43]

Not all Internet news comes from professional media outlets. Much of the Internet is not professionally supervised, and any person possesses the ability to broadcast his or her often uninformed opinion as news. Unlike the more professional media sources (e.g., newspapers, broadcast, and cable), websites, blogs, and even purveyors of email rumors do not necessarily check the accuracy of their stories. Many unsubstantiated Internet stories have affected politics, especially on matters of race and ethnicity. Racially motivated, baseless Internet rumors concerning former President Obama have been prevalent since he commenced his first presidential campaign. These rumors claim, for example, that he is a secret Muslim; that he is not a legitimate president because he was

Podcast A file that users can download off the Internet and that often features discussions about cultural and political issues.

born in Kenya; and that he even appeared in the 1993 video for the hip-hop hit, "Whoomp! (There It Is)."[44]

As the opening story demonstrates, social media sites, such as Facebook, Twitter, and Instagram, are extremely relevant in American politics. These sites allow people with similar interests or even groups of friends to share information, ideas, photographs, games, and videos with one another. Moreover, politicians and even mainstream media outlets use social media extensively to communicate with the American public. Social media has also served as an instrumental communication tool among the youth activists throughout the world, including the Arab Spring, grassroots revolts against longtime dictators in Arab nations (e.g., Egypt, Libya, Syria, and Tunisia).[45]

By the 2010s the Internet and social media have emerged as a significant source of news for Americans. According to a 2017 survey, approximately two-thirds of Americans receive some news from social media, and about 20 percent of Americans receive most of their news from social media. As one would expect, there is an age gap in social media news consumption, but this gap is narrowing. About 80 percent of people age 18 to 49 use social media for their news, whereas 55 percent of people over age 50 use social media for their news. However, even as recently as 2016, this gap was 78 percent to 45 percent.[46] Overall, online news consumption has also grown tremendously in recent years. Although people over age 50 tend to get more of their news from television than from online sources, the opposite is true for people under age 50. Online news consumption among all Americans is close to television news consumption—50 percent from television and 43 percent online. Americans rely far less on radio and print sources—25 percent and 18 percent, respectively.[47]

President Donald Trump often uses Twitter to communicate his views, especially about race. In this tweet from when he was only a candidate, Trump accuses federal judge Gonzalo Curiel, presiding over a fraud claim against him, of exhibiting bias because the judge ruled against him. Specifically, Trump complained that the judge was biased against him because he is a "Mexican," despite the fact that Judge Curiel was born and raised in the United States. Republicans and Democrats rebuked Trump for exhibiting racial bias against Latinos.

The impact of social media on civil rights is mixed. Civil rights groups can use social media to promote their ideas and organize events. For example, Black Lives Matter uses social media to share their ideas and plan protests.[48] However, as we discussed in the opening vignette, foreign governments have been able to use social media to divide Americans. Moreover, even without foreign intervention, social media allows people to advance racist and other hateful ideas. In fact, a recent study shows that 1 percent of all Twitter messages in Louisiana contained hateful expression toward racial and ethnic minorities, women, or the LGBT community.[49] Republican presidential candidate Donald Trump has used Twitter extensively to promote his campaign, and many of his "tweets" have expressed inflammatory messages about racial and ethnic minorities. For example, in late 2015 Trump claimed on Twitter that 81 percent of Whites who are murdered are killed by African Americans, despite the fact that the real number is closer to 15 percent. The fact-checking organization PolitiFact rated his claim "Pants on Fire," which is the lowest rating on its "Truth-O-Meter."[50] As president, Donald Trump has continued disseminating racist posts on social media. For example, in November 2017 Trump retweeted a video that claims a Muslim immigrant in the Netherlands assaulted a White teenager. Dutch authorities confirmed that the assailant was native born and there was no clear evidence that he was Muslim. Even more disturbing, the original tweet came from Britain First, a White nationalist group that espouses hatred toward racial minorities and non-Christians. The White House officially deemphasized the source of the videos and the fact that the videos were misleading, arguing that the "threat" from immigration is a genuine problem.[51]

The Media Industry

The news media are a major industry and for that reason deserve close attention. The media industry has become increasingly more concentrated, and there is a lack of diversity in professional journalism.

The Media Business

Until the middle of the twentieth century, newspapers, radio stations, and network affiliates were separately owned enterprises that thrived economically. Beginning in the 1990s, however, many newspapers began to lose their profitability, and by 2000 the newspaper business was in severe decline. Newspapers found it increasingly difficult to compete with cable television and Internet-based media, especially among young people. Many newspapers completely folded or switched to an Internet-only delivery system. For example, in March 2009 the *Seattle Post-Intelligencer*, a venerated newspaper in existence since 1863, announced that it was ceasing its print newspaper production and providing only Internet content. The *Post-Intelligencer* had lost about half of its readership during the previous few years, and in 2008 it lost $14 million. By 2009, there was no money to support the newspaper. Although the *Post-Intelligencer*

Members of the New England Patriots of the National Football League protest racial injustice by "taking a knee" during the playing of the National Anthem before the start of their game. President Donald Trump criticized these protests for being "unpatriotic." Although this debate occurs in stadiums and on television, much of the controversy rages on social media. The Twitter hashtag #TakeAKnee encourages tweets supporting the protests and the hashtag #BoycottNFL opposes the protests.

retained its Internet site, the vast majority of the newspaper's employees lost their jobs.[52] Additionally, many cities once supported two newspapers, but over the past decade, one of those two papers closed in almost every city. For instance, in 2016 the *Tampa Bay Times*, operated by the Poynter Institute, purchased its competitor the *Tampa Tribune*, which had published every day since 1895. Shortly after the purchase, the *Times* stopped publishing the *Tribune*.[53]

The radio and television industries have recently experienced similar difficulties. To help radio and television stations survive, larger companies, such as iHeartMedia,[54] have bought local radio stations. Broadcast networks and cable stations are also owned by major corporations. For example, Comcast Cable owns NBC Universal (including cable stations CNBC and MSNBC),[55] and Disney owns ABC.[56] In fact, six large corporations (Comcast, News Corp, Disney, Viacom, Time Warner, and CBS) own a substantial majority of American media outlets.[57] This degree of corporate involvement in the media can undermine the objectivity and credibility of the news, especially because these large corporations are often embroiled in financial, labor, and environmental controversies. For example, Sinclair Broadcast Group owns 193 local broadcast stations, and it requires their local news stations to air conservative messages that support the Trump administration.[58]

Media Personnel

The people who work for the media, especially professional journalists and editors, are among the elites in American society. Most journalists regard their field as a profession, similar to a doctor, lawyer, or engineer.[59] After all, many journalists have college degrees (often postgraduate degrees) in journalism. However, the expansion of the media to include the Internet and social media has undoubtedly allowed people without journalism training to become members of the media.[60] As we discussed earlier, late-night comedians provide as much coverage of important issues as professional journalists provide. Moreover, many journalists and columnists move back and forth between working for the press and pursuing political careers. For example, Joe Scarborough, who is the cohost of MSNBC's morning news program *Morning Joe*, was a member of the U.S. House of Representatives (a Republican from Florida) from 1995 through 2001.[61]

Even if journalists intend to report political events objectively, they are human beings whose personal experiences undoubtedly influence their reporting. Political leaders and the American public often accuse journalists of exhibiting a liberal bias. Indeed, surveys of members of the media reveal that journalists lean more toward the Democratic Party than the American public does.[62] Still, the increasingly more corporate character of media organizations and reliance on advertisements suggest a conservative bias in the media. As we mentioned previously, Sinclair Broadcast Group requires its local news program to air conservative views.

Furthermore, this emphasis on liberal and conservative biases in the news media disregards a more significant form of media bias. All members of the media—journalists and publishers—share the goal of increasing newspaper circulation, ratings, website hits, or social media followers. This commonly shared goal results in a bias toward negative coverage of virtually all political leaders, regardless of their ideology. Specifically, the press exhibits a bias toward reporting scandals, which is a lucrative endeavor.[63]

Given that media professionals are at least somewhat biased, diversity of the profession is a critical issue. If the news media are dominated by White men, then issues pertaining to women and minority groups might not get the attention they would if the media were more diverse.

Prior to the women's liberation movement of the 1960s (see Chapter 5), Americans considered journalism to be one of the few acceptable occupations for women. But this has not translated into gender equity in the newsroom. In 2017, women accounted for 39.1 percent of all newspaper (print and online) employees, and only 38.9 percent of "newsroom leaders" are women.[64]

Racial and ethnic minorities are also underrepresented in the media. Figure 11.5 demonstrates that racial and ethnic minorities are not well represented as newspaper employees. The graph demonstrates that minority representation has grown since the late 1970s, most likely as a result of greater attention paid to diversity, but this growth leveled from 2000 until 2015. In the past couple of years minority representation has increased slightly. Overall, representation of racial and ethnic minorities in newspapers has remained extremely low. The Measuring Equality box addresses in more detail minority-group presence in broadcast radio and television.

measuring equality

Racial and Ethnic Minority Representation in the Media

The extent to which racial and ethnic minorities are represented in the media undoubtedly can influence the way in which the media frame issues of race and ethnicity. Just as the presence of minorities in political institutions affects the way in which those institutions treat minorities, the presence of minorities in the media should influence how the media cover racial and ethnic minority politics. As we discussed in previous chapters, minority representation in government institutions has improved since the 1980s. Therefore, we would expect that minority representation in media would have increased as well. Likewise, the number of minorities in supervisory positions, the ones that exert the most control over coverage, should also increase.

Here, we measure White, Black, Latino, Asian American, and American Indian representation in broadcast radio and television news jobs, and we compare those results from 2000 to 2017. Given the emphasis on minority representation during this time frame, we would expect that minority representation has grown since 2000. We therefore must test this hypothesis.

However, raw percentages of minority-group representation alone will not provide a complete picture because racial and ethnic populations have changed since 2000. To elaborate further, we use ratios to compare groups' representation between 2000 and 2017.

Specifically, the ratios measure the percentage of the group in a media position divided by the percentage of the group in the population. A ratio of 1 means that the group is as well represented in the position as it is in the population. A ratio above 1 indicates overrepresentation, and a ratio below 1 indicates underrepresentation. Each figure examines White, Black, Latino, Asian American, and American Indian representation on four levels: total workforce in broadcast television news (Figure 11.1), total workforce in broadcast radio news (Figure 11.2), news directors in broadcast television (Figure 11.3), and news directors in broadcast radio (Figure 11.4).

To begin, it is important to note that currently Whites are the only group that are overrepresented in almost every category—Whites are slightly below 1.0 in broadcast radio news employment. Although American Indians were overrepresented in every category in 2000, they are currently underrepresented in every category—in most cases severely underrepresented. Blacks, Latinos, and Asian Americans are underrepresented, often severely, in every category—both in 2000 and in 2017. These results are also interesting because, despite increased attention to minority recruitment, minority representation has decreased in almost every category since 2000. The only exceptions are a slight increase in Black representation as broadcast television

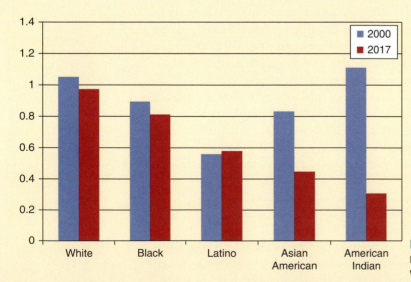

Figure 11.1 Minority Group Presence in Broadcast Television Workforce 2000 and 2017

measuring equality *(Continued)*

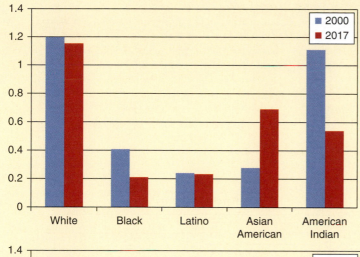

Figure 11.2 Minority Group Presence in Broadcast Radio Workforce 2000 and 2017

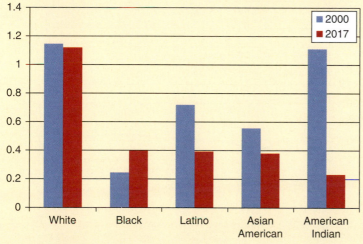

Figure 11.3 Minority Group Presence as Broadcast Television News Directors 2000 and 2017

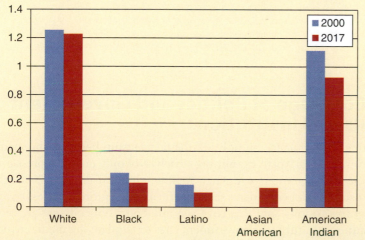

Figure 11.4 Minority Group Presence as Broadcast Radio News Directors 2000 and 2017

(Continued)

measuring equality *(Continued)*

news directors, Asian American representation in broadcast radio news employment, and Asian American representation as broadcast radio news directors. American Indian representation has dropped precipitously in all categories, except for the slight drop in representation as broadcast radio news directors.

Sources: Data adapted from Papper, B. (2017, July 3). *RTNDA research: Women and minorities in newsrooms.* Washington, DC:

Radio Television Digital News Association. Retrieved July 14, 2018, from https://rtdna.org/article/rtdna_research_women_and_minorities_in_newsrooms_2017; United States Census Bureau. (n.d.). *Table 1: Population by Hispanic or Latino Origin and by Race for the United States. Overview of Race and Hispanic Origin: 2000.* Retrieved July 14, 2018, from https://www.census.gov/prod/2001pubs/c2kbr01-1.pdf; United States Census Bureau. (n.d.). *QuickFacts: United States.* Retrieved July 14, 2018, from https://www.census.gov/quickfacts/fact/table/US#viewtop.

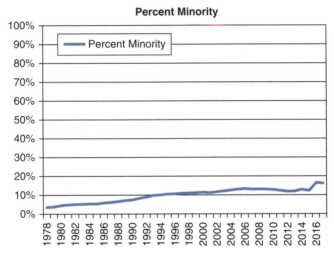

Figure 11.5 Percentage of Minorities Employed in Daily Newspapers, 1978–2014

Sources: Data for 1978 through 2015 adapted from American Society for Newspaper Editors. (n.d.).
Table A – Minority Employment in Daily Newspapers. Diversity Newsroom Diversity Survey. *Retrieved July 14, 2018, from https://www.asne.org/content.asp?contentid=129; data for 2016 and 2017 adapted from American Society for Newspaper Editors. (n.d.).* Table A. Percentage of Minorities in the Overall Workforce of Daily Print and Online Only Organizations. Diversity Newsroom Diversity Survey. *Retrieved July 14, 2018, from https://www.asne.org//Files/census/2017%20ASNE%20diversity%20survey%20tables.pdf.*

Press Coverage of Politics and Government Officials and Institutions

Given the media's influence on politics, the relationship between the media and the government is worth examining closely. Not only does the press provide information that voters use when making electoral decisions, but the media are also a tool for candidates seeking office. In addition, the press covers government institutions, and this coverage influences how citizens perceive these institutions. In turn, the government tries to regulate the media, which is a significant aspect of media politics. Media coverage of minority candidates and government officials is especially important in minority-group politics.

Reporting of Elections

Major political campaigns have a symbiotic relationship with the media. The press reports elections because of the public's interest, and the campaigns need the media to communicate their message and appeal to voters. Elections often entail vigorous and complex debates over competing visions of public policies, yet media outlets tend to focus their coverage on the aspects of elections that attract more readers and viewers. During elections, the press covers key campaign events on a daily basis, and it devotes considerable prime-time coverage to major events, such as national party conventions and televised debates.

Media coverage often extends beyond mere reporting of the events. Most newspaper, radio, television, and Internet sources also feature commentators who offer analyses on the races they cover. Most media stations, except for rare exceptions such as C-SPAN and PBS, often focus on the personalities of the candidates and the poll numbers of the race, instead of on the relevant issues.

The media affect political campaigns through the power of **priming**, in which the press's evaluation of a candidate influences how the public perceives the candidate.[65] For example, during the 2016 presidential election campaign the media generally primed Donald Trump as undisciplined, erratic, and boorish and Hillary Clinton as untrustworthy and insincere. Of course, conservative news outlets, especially Fox News, prime Donald Trump more positively and Hillary Clinton negatively, whereas liberal news outlets, especially MSNBC, prime Hillary Clinton positively and Donald Trump negatively.

Priming The media's ability to influence how the public perceives politicians and candidates.

There is considerable debate about media coverage of minority candidates, especially about whether minority candidates receive less coverage than White candidates and whether minority candidates receive less favorable coverage than White candidates. Although the parallel press provides considerable positive coverage of minority candidates, empirical studies of the mainstream press have shown that there is mixed evidence as to whether minority candidates receive more coverage than their White opponents and whether coverage of minority candidates is favorable, unfavorable, or neutral. Anecdotally, minority candidates claim that their coverage is unfavorable, White opponents claim that the coverage of minority candidates is favorable, and the media claim that the coverage is neutral. When different racial and ethnic minority candidates run against each other, particularly Blacks against Latinos, then the coverage of the race increases compared to when a minority candidate runs against a White opponent.[66]

The issue of media coverage of Black candidates became more salient during Barack Obama's historic candidacy in 2008. Both of Obama's main opponents (Democrat Hillary Rodham Clinton during the primary and Republican John McCain in the general election) claimed that the media were far more favorable to Obama than to them. Neither campaign claimed that the media were acting out of racial favoritism, but their charges were quite evident. The McCain campaign website even sponsored a contest titled "The Media is in LOVE with Barack Obama" and asked supporters to select a song that best characterized the media's favoritism toward Obama. Although the media devoted more coverage to Obama than to his opponents, media coverage is always more extensive for the newer candidates.[67] It bears noting that the media did emphasize negative aspects of Obama's campaign, such as his association with Reverend Jeremiah Wright, who was recorded making incendiary comments suggesting that the United States deserved some blame for the attacks of September 11, 2001.[68]

Questions of media bias and race were particularly relevant during the 2012 campaign. After Black Republican presidential candidate Herman Cain emerged as a leading candidate, media coverage of his background naturally intensified. When the media reported that Cain had engaged in extramarital affairs and sexual harassment, Cain's conservative and Tea Party supporters claimed that the media was against Cain because he is a Black conservative who attacked a liberal Black president.[69] After Cain faded from public view, issues of racial bias in the media still persisted, largely because of President Obama's presence in the race. For example, less than two weeks before the election, former Republican vice presidential candidate and Fox News contributor Sarah Palin criticized President Obama's response to a terrorist attack on the U.S. Embassy in Libya that resulted in the deaths of four Americans, including Ambassador Chris Stevens. Believing that the president was covering up his culpability, she employed the term "shuck and jive," which is a racist term dating back to the slavery era that depicts African Americans as disingenuous. Palin denied that her use of the term was racist, stating that others, including liberals, had used the term before.[70]

There were minority candidates during the 2016 Republican presidential nominating process—including Latinos Marco Rubio and Ted Cruz and African American Ben Carson. Interestingly, the coverage focusing on Ben Carson's race has also included President Obama because had Carson won the presidency, then he would have followed as the second Black president. In October 2015, News Corporation (which owns Fox News) CEO Rupert Murdoch said that Ben Carson would be the first Black president, implying that President Obama is not really Black.[71]

Coverage of Government Officials and Institutions

Media coverage of politicians once they are elected is important because elected politicians require the media to communicate their message, especially if they plan to run for reelection, and the media need to cover elected politicians to satisfy the public's interest. Because the president is the single most powerful person in American government, press coverage of the president is even more important. This coverage is carried out by the **White House press corps**, which include the print, radio, television, and Internet reporters who cover presidents and their administrations. With varying degrees of success,

White House Press Corps
Those elite journalists responsible for covering the president and key executive branch officials.

presidents cultivate friendly relations with the White House press corps to elicit better coverage and, ultimately, a positive public image.

President Trump's relationship with the press has been conflictual. He often states that news stories about him are "fake news," which refers to completely fabricated stories that people claim are actual news. Often President Trump uses the phrase "fake news" to refer to stories that he dislikes or believes do not portray him in a glowing light. The fact-checking organization Factcheck.org, which the University of Pennsylvania's Annenberg Public Policy Center maintains, has uncovered numerous instances in which President Trump has accused stories of being "fake news" when, in reality, the news stories' claims were easily verified.[72]

The **press secretary** is a member of the White House staff who handles the bulk of the president's press relations. He or she holds daily briefings with the members of the White House press corps, who then use the information they gather to report on the presidency. Some cable channels, such as C-SPAN, air the full briefings. Press secretaries shape significantly how the press and ultimately the public view the president's performance. Presidents also communicate with the media through **press conferences**, which are formal question-and-answer sessions that the press secretary, and occasionally the president himself, holds with members of the White House press corps.[73]

The White House press corps and the position of press secretary have been dominated by White men. To date, there have been no minority press secretaries, and only three press secretaries have been female (Dee Dee Meyers for Bill Clinton, Dana Perino for George W. Bush, and Sarah Huckabee Sanders for Donald Trump). Even Barack Obama's press secretaries, Robert Gibbs, Jay Carney, and Josh Earnest, were all White men. The vast majority of the White House press corps is also White, but there are some leading minorities who cover or have covered the White House. April Ryan is an African American who works for American Urban Radio Network[74] and Kristen Welker is an African American who works at *NBC News*.[75]

Media coverage is also crucial for members of the U.S. Congress because they must continually communicate with their constituents. House and Senate party leaders schedule weekly press briefings when Congress is in session, and many individual members appear on national television broadcasts. Members of Congress also use C-SPAN to generate exposure to their constituents.

Just as the White House press corps specializes in covering the president, journalists for major national news organizations specialize in covering Congress. This coverage tends to be negative, emphasizing partisan gridlock and scandals plaguing individual members. Because the national media coverage is negative and scandal-driven, members of Congress prefer to communicate with their constituents through their hometown media. Local television and print journalists benefit from interviews with members of Congress and tend to provide more favorable coverage.

There is mixed evidence as to whether coverage of minority members of Congress differs from coverage of White members. Systematic comparisons

Press Secretary A member of the president's staff who conducts daily briefings with members of the media.

Press Conferences Formal question-and-answer sessions that the president or the press secretary holds with the White House press corps.

of coverage have been conducted for Black and White members of Congress. These studies have shown that Black representatives are portrayed as more compassionate but less honest than their White counterparts. Another study has found that, although the majority of coverage of both races is neutral, there have been instances in which White members of Congress are shown in a better light than Black members are.[76]

Government Regulation

The relationship between the media and government is also characterized by government attempts to regulate the press. The First Amendment to the Constitution stipulates that "Congress shall make no law . . . abridging the freedom . . . of the press." This amendment has provided newspapers, radio broadcasts, television, cable, and the Internet with a significant amount of protection from government regulation.

Prior Restraint A usually impermissible governmental regulation that prevents the publication of written material.

One type of government attempt to regulate the press is known as **prior restraint**, in which the government prevents publication of material it deems objectionable. Since the early twentieth century, the Supreme Court has clearly prevented most forms of prior restraint. In 1931, the Supreme Court overturned a Minnesota law that empowered judges to enjoin the publication of malicious, scandalous, and defamatory newspapers. The state used this law to stop the publication of the *Saturday Press*, which was a highly racist and anti-Jewish newspaper. The U.S. Supreme Court ruled that Minnesota's form of prior restraint violated the First Amendment.[77] The military is able to prevent the publication of certain materials that could jeopardize national security, but even in those cases the government must present clear evidence that a genuine national security issue is at stake, or the Court will protect the press against prior restraint. In the 1971 case *New York Times v. United States*, the executive branch sought to prevent the *New York Times* from publishing the Pentagon Papers, which were leaked government documents that revealed the U.S. government's serious mistakes during the Vietnam War, which was still being waged at the time. The Supreme Court ruled that the government lacked a sufficient national security justification to engage in prior restraint, even though publication of the Pentagon Papers would undermine public support for the Vietnam War.[78]

The U.S. Supreme Court has also prevented state and local governments from censoring the media even if the government possessed noble intentions. For example, to protect the privacy of rape victims, Georgia prevented the publication or broadcast of their names, but in 1975 the U.S. Supreme Court overturned that law, ruling that any legal obstacle to publishing public information violated the First Amendment.[79] The Supreme Court has even overturned state laws preventing the publication of names of juveniles involved in crimes as either offenders or victims.[80] The Supreme Court has ruled in favor of freedom of the press when it conflicts with other constitutional liberties. The Court overturned a Nebraska trial court judge who stopped press coverage of a trial based on a fear that the publicity would endanger the defendant's Sixth Amendment right to a fair trial.[81]

There are some exceptions to the Court's absolutist stance. For example, the Court has ruled that trial judges can hold journalists in contempt and even jail them for refusing to reveal their sources. In other words, journalists do not have a First Amendment right to withhold their sources.[82] Another exception to the Court's absolutist stance on freedom of the press concerns broadcast radio and television. Because the airwaves are a publicly owned scarce resource, the federal government, primarily through the **Federal Communications Commission (FCC)**, has assumed authority to regulate the content of these broadcasts. The Supreme Court has allowed the FCC to prohibit sexually explicit content on broadcast radio or television, even if that material would have been protected if it appeared in print, on cable, or on the Internet. The Supreme Court justifies this distinction because the broadcast media are more intrusive on unwitting consumers, especially children.[83] However, it is important to recognize that the FCC only regulates the "decency" content on broadcast television and radio; it does not regulate sexually explicit content on cable or satellite television and radio or the Internet.[84]

Federal Communications Commission (FCC) An independent regulatory commission that licenses and regulates the content of broadcast radio and television.

Conclusion

There is no question that the media play an extremely important role in American politics, and this chapter covered the significant aspects of media and politics. The media can set the political agenda, and through the power of framing and priming, they can influence how the public interprets events and political actors. During the nineteenth century, the press took the form of partisan and interest-group propaganda newspapers, penny presses, and yellow journalism newspapers, all of which appealed to the masses. During the twentieth century, a more professional press boomed, and new technologies, such as radio, television, cable television, the Internet, and social media changed the way in which Americans received their political news. Currently, the media are a form of big business, and journalism is a respected profession. The press influences not only the coverage of political campaigns, but also the institutions of government.

The press has affected many aspects of American government, including minority-group politics. Throughout American history, most forms of the media perpetuated stereotypes against racial and ethnic minorities, and because the media influence public opinion, this biased coverage shaped Americans' attitudes toward minorities (see the Evaluating Equality" box).

There is no doubt that the media bear responsibility for mistreatment of Blacks, Latinos, Asian Americans, and American Indians. Nevertheless, the media have also helped minorities overcome discrimination. The parallel press helped to mobilize minorities to fight for civil rights, and there is even some evidence that the mainstream media's coverage of the 1960s Civil Rights

Learn about organizations that monitor the media.

evaluating equality

Racial Bias in the Press Coverage of Hurricane Katrina?

On August 29, 2005, Hurricane Katrina made landfall in southeastern Louisiana and triggered considerable flooding throughout New Orleans and other Gulf Coast communities. Low-income residents of New Orleans who lacked the means to evacuate were forced to remain in their homes during the storm and the ensuing flooding. While they were stranded, they had no access to electricity, money, or food. Moreover, there was a shortage of public safety officials, which increased the possibility of civil disorder. Because people were enduring such hardships, journalists, photographers, and television cameras descended on New Orleans and the surrounding areas.

A considerable amount of media attention focused on the racial aspects of Hurricane Katrina. On the one hand, media coverage alerted many Americans to the horrendous living conditions that the low-income, and largely Black, residents of New Orleans endured. On the other hand, most of the journalists and photographers covering the hurricane and its aftermath were White, and at times the coverage was racially prejudiced. The media exaggerated reports of looting and lawlessness among the mainly Black residents. David Wellman, a leading American sociologist, suspected that the media's depiction of Blacks as criminals reinforced society's belief that Blacks are predisposed to criminal behavior, which could have "delayed relief" to the victims.

The racial bias was most notable when Yahoo! News, an Internet news website, showed two photographs of people carrying groceries after the storm. One photograph showed a young Black male wading through water and carrying a case of soda and a bag, and the caption read that the man was "looting." A second photograph depicted a White couple, who were also wading through water carrying food, but this caption said that the couple was "finding" groceries.

Racial and ethnic minorities, as well as many Whites, regarded this double standard as evidence of racial bias in the media, and because news on the Internet travels quickly, many Americans were aware of it within one day. Despite this controversy, a survey showed that about three-quarters of both Blacks and Whites regarded media coverage of Katrina as "responsible."

Closely examine both photographs and captions shown here.

- Debate among your classmates over the extent that racial bias influenced the juxtaposition of these photographs and captions.
- Based on everything you have learned in this chapter, debate the extent of racial bias in the media overall. Has coverage of racial and ethnic minorities improved over the years?
- Pay close attention to how arguments in this debate vary according to one's race and ethnicity.

Sources: Dahlberg, C. P. (2005, September 3). Images of disaster bring race issue to the fore. *Sacramento Bee,* p. A1; CNN/USA Today/Gallup Poll cited in McDaniel, M. (2005, September 19). Katrina's aftermath: Racial bias comes to the forefront; terms, pictures used by the media prompt debate. *Houston Chronicle,* p. 1; Rulli, T. (2005, September 5). Who's a looter?: In storm's aftermath, pictures kick up a different kind of tempest. *New York Times,* p. C1.

Actual photo caption: "Residents wade through chest-deep water after finding bread and soda from a local grocery store after Hurricane Katrina came through the area on August 29, 2005, in New Orleans."

Actual photo caption: "A young man walks through chest-deep flood water after looting a grocery store in New Orleans on August 30, 2005."

Movement increased Americans' support for civil rights legislation. Despite clear improvements, it is still the case that racial and ethnic minorities are underrepresented in employment in the media.

Finally, the story about the Russian government's use of social media to influence American political behavior illustrates the significance of the media in American politics. Powerful entities have used the media to influence Americans since the colonial era, but social media is especially susceptible to manipulation, particularly on issues pertaining to racial and ethnic minorities. As we showed in this chapter, civil rights groups are able to employ social media to promote equality; however, the story of Russian involvement in the 2016 election shows that a foreign government was able to manipulate social media to sow racial divisions. Even without foreign intervention, social media and traditional media provide a forum for people to espouse racial and ethnic bigotry. In short, the issue of the media and minority politics is complex and dynamic.

REVIEW QUESTIONS

1. What were abolitionist newspapers, and how did they influence the controversies over slavery?

2. What is the parallel press, and what are key examples of it in print, radio, television, and the Internet?

3. How much did television influence the success of the Civil Rights Movement?

4. How has social media influenced the coverage of issues of race and ethnicity?

5. How well is each minority group (Blacks, Latinos, Asian Americans, and American Indians) represented in the media, and to what extent is each group represented in the top echelons of the media?

Check your understanding of Chapter 11.

KEY TERMS

Agenda Setting p. 330
Federal Communications
    Commission (FCC) p. 351
Framing p. 330
Mass Media p. 329

Parallel Press p. 331
Penny Press p. 330
Podcast p. 339
Press Conferences p. 349
Press Secretary p. 349

Priming p. 347
Prior Restraint p. 350
White House Press
    Corps p. 348
Yellow Journalism p. 331

Flashcard review.

ADDITIONAL READINGS

Gibbons, A. (1993). *Race, politics, and the white media: The Jesse Jackson campaigns*. Lanham, MD: University Press of America.

    This book looks at Jesse Jackson's campaigns for president in 1984 and 1988 and the function of race in press treatments of those campaigns.

Larson, S. G. (2006). *Media and minorities: The politics of race in news and entertainment*. Lanham, MD: Rowman & Littlefield.

    This book demonstrates how the media's portrayal of racial and ethnic minorities in news and entertainment has perpetuated stereotypes, which, in turn, has hindered civil rights progress.

Need to review key ideas in greater depth? Click here.

Nelson, T. (Ed.). (1966). *Documents of upheaval: Selections from William Lloyd Garrison's* The Liberator, *1831–1865*. New York: Hill & Wang.

> This volume, containing key excerpts from *The Liberator*, provides primary source evidence of the media's influence on public opinion.

Roberts, G., & Klibanoff, H. (2006). *The race beat: The press, the civil rights struggle, and the awakening of a nation*. New York: Knopf.

> This meticulously researched book examines the history of the media's coverage of racial discrimination in the South and the civil rights struggle that followed.

Washburn, P. S. (2006). *The African American newspaper: Voice of freedom*. Evanston, IL: Northwestern University Press.

> This book traces the history of Black newspapers from their founding as abolitionist tracts during the early 1800s, through their growth after the Civil War, to their height in the first half of the twentieth century, as well as to their decline (along with all newspapers) during the early twenty-first century.

Social Movements: Civil Rights as a Movement Model

Group portrait of some of the more than 100 students named in the legal case *Dorothy Davis, et al. v. County School Board of Prince Edward County, Virginia*, a lawsuit filed to seek, initially, repairs for Robert Morton High School, a segregated school in Farmville, Virginia, March 1953. The case was later, on appeal, attached to the landmark *Brown v. Board of Education* case. Among those pictured is Dorothy E. Davis (center, with glasses), for whom the suit was named.

On April 23, 1951, M. Boyd Jones, the Black principal of the segregated Robert R. Moton High School in Farmville, Virginia, received an anonymous call saying that two of his students were about to encounter trouble with police at the Greyhound bus station. After Jones left the building, notes, supposedly from Jones, were delivered to each classroom calling an emergency assembly. When students and teachers arrived, instead of Jones, they saw Barbara Rose Johns, a sixteen-year-old junior, standing at the lectern.

Johns demanded that the teachers leave and pounded her shoe on the lectern for effect. The teachers left. Barbara then gave an impassioned speech about the numerous problems at the school: tar-paper additions that served as overflow classrooms, used and outdated textbooks, no science labs, and broken-down buses, among other complaints. She implored her classmates to go on strike until the county's White supervisors met student demands for a new school. The students marched out of the school to the county courthouse and confronted the school superintendent with their demands.

The students then contacted a National Association for the Advancement of Colored People lawyer in Richmond, Oliver W. Hill, who expressed an interest in taking the students' case. But he had one crucial stipulation: The students would have to agree to challenge segregation outright and not just ask for a new segregated school. The strike continued to the end of the school year.

White officials responded by firing Jones, but at the same time they did appropriate $875,000 to build a new high school for Blacks. On May 23, 1951, after hundreds of Black parents signed a petition of support, Hill and his associates filed suit in federal court in Richmond on behalf of the 117 Moton students, demanding that the Virginia law enforcing segregated schools be voided. This case was combined with three others from Kansas, South Carolina, and Delaware on appeal to the Supreme Court, which issued its unanimous decision on May 17, 1954, in the famous *Brown v. Board of Education of Topeka* ruling. The Court affirmed that "in the field of public education the doctrine of 'separate but equal' has no place."[1]

intro

The 1951 strike by Black high school students in Virginia is just one example of numerous protest activities by Black Americans in many communities around the nation. According to historian John Hope Franklin, beginning shortly after the end of Reconstruction in the late 1870s and then gathering speed and intensity in the 1880s, many states and localities passed laws segregating Black Americans in almost every aspect of their daily lives. In addition, many states rewrote their state constitutions to remove as many Blacks as possible from the voting rolls and make it almost impossible for them to register to vote.[2]

Over time, these local protests aimed at local governments and local segregation ordinances grew into a national movement for Black civil rights aimed at the federal government. From early local protests in the 1950s, the Civil Rights Movement (CRM) gained momentum and supporters. It presented to the nation and the world the determination of Black Americans to dismantle the separate system of laws under which Blacks were forced to live. Despite fierce violence, murders, and reprisals from those who wanted to maintain segregation, the CRM's goals of the removal of the legal structures of racial inequality and political rights would become realities. The CRM is among the most prominent and successful social movements to have occurred in the United States. The promise of political inclusion that resulted in the election to the presidency of Barack Obama is directly related to the CRM and all of those Americans who risked life and limb to force the United States to live up to its ideals.

Social movements play an important role in democracies. They are one mechanism through which changes are brought about. In representative democracies such as the United States, change can come through legislation passed by city councils, state legislatures, and the national Congress. It also can occur through decisions by the courts at all levels of government. All of these methods of change, however, are achieved through individuals working within government structures.

What mechanisms are available to those outside of government to influence change? A first mechanism is individuals expressing their opinion to elected officials to push those officials, where possible, to make changes in the system. A second mechanism is electing individuals who are sympathetic to making those changes. A third mechanism is mounting a social movement.

A Social Movement Defined

A **social movement** is a sustained challenge to those in power put forth by individuals, acting in concert with others, who have been excluded from the political process or who consider themselves political outsiders. Social movements provide a way for those without a voice in the political system to make their concerns known to decision-makers. Those inside government or with access through interest groups, political action committees, wealth, or position have no need for social movements as they already have the ability to get the attention of decision-makers. Those involved in social movements are usually a minority of the population, but over time their activities might change

Social Movement A sustained challenge to those in power put forth by individuals, acting in concert with others, who have been excluded from the political process or who consider themselves political outsiders.

the attitudes of the majority and garner their support. Social movements can pressure decision-makers to make changes.[3]

In the United States, a number of successful social movements, such as the Civil Rights Movement, the women's suffrage movement, and later the women's rights movement, the labor movement, and the gay rights movement, have brought about significant changes.

There have also been social movements that failed to maintain their momentum and achieve their goals, such as the poor people's campaign, a campaign to push for economic opportunities for Blacks that was begun shortly after the assassination of Dr. Martin Luther King, Jr. in 1968. Other campaigns were repressed by federal, state, or, in a few instances, private authority, such as the Bisbee miners' strike.[4] The Bisbee, Arizona, Mexican and Mexican American miners' strike in July 1917, which was part of a larger movement by Mexican and Mexican American miners demanding wage equity and the ability to organize into unions, was ended when private police for Phelps-Dodge Mining Company rounded up striking miners, put them in railroad boxcars, and sent them to New Mexico, where the miners were imprisoned for two months in an army stockade.[5]

Participation in social movements can be dangerous, as often those who disagree with the movement's demands might retaliate against the participants and threaten them with violence or loss of employment. Many participants in the Civil Rights Movement, for example, were beaten, and some were even murdered.

Conditions That Give Rise to Social Movements

Scholars have identified several conditions necessary for the rise of social movements. First, these movements arise from **shared grievances**, complaints against the political system (national, state, or local) by a group of people who agree generally on the causes of the complaints and the possible means of resolving them. This discontent is produced by some combination of structural conditions; for example, government laws and governmental action, coupled with a shared belief by those affected that something should be done, cause people to come together in collective action to push the system to resolve the grievances.[6] The aggrieved provide the necessary resources and labor to support the movement. In the United States, the Civil Rights Movement arose from shared grievances and drew support from existing social organizations with experienced leaders, potential followers, communication networks, money, and labor.

Second, the formation of social movements requires a **supportive environment**. This is an environment that is receptive to the ideals and demands of the social movement, even though the entire political system might not be willing to listen to its concerns. Events in the larger society might provide an opportunity for a social movement to evolve, enlarge its base of support, or make significant headway in its goals. Society as a whole might have become more tolerant of or receptive to the concerns espoused by the movement.

Shared Grievances
Complaints against the political system (national, state, or local) by a group of people who agree generally on the causes of the complaints.

Supportive Environment An environment receptive to the ideals and demands of a social movement.

For example, during the Vietnam War, as the U.S. public grew increasingly concerned about the large number of casualties, and despite government assertions that the United States and its South Vietnamese allies were winning the war, more and more people came to believe the war was being lost and thus began to support the antiwar movement. Recently, public opinion data show that Americans are becoming more supportive of gay and lesbian rights and more comfortable with same-sex marriage. Polls suggest that the public is evolving on the question of rights and protections for gay and lesbian citizens. In the 2012 elections, voters in Maine and Maryland legalized same-sex marriage, and in Minnesota voters rejected a ban on same-sex marriage.

Third, a **catalyst**, an event that pushes an issue to the forefront and galvanizes people to action, will spark a social movement. On Friday, June 27, 1969, New York City police raided a Greenwich Village gay bar called the Stonewall Inn.[7] Police raids on gay bars in New York were not unusual; police routinely raided these bars, ostensibly looking for liquor law and other violations. What was unusual about this night was the reaction of the patrons to the raid. They confronted the police "first with jeers, then a hail of coins, paving stones, and parking meters."[8] This spontaneous resistance continued throughout the weekend. Out of the Stonewall "uprising," the modern phase of the gay liberation movement arose. In the wake of Stonewall, demonstrations in response to the events there were held in New York as well as many other cities across the country. Gay liberation groups organized in the summer of 1969 in cities as diverse as New York, San Francisco, and Minneapolis.[9] Within two years of what was now referred to as the Stonewall rebellion, gay liberation groups operated in every major city and on almost every campus in the United States, Canada, Australia, and Western Europe.[10]

Fourth, sometimes **catalytic leadership**, social activists who create or recognize opportunities to protest a group's concerns, can be a trigger. Catalytic leadership can help create a social movement when the leaders highlight and draw on deep-rooted feelings of injustice.[11] César Chávez of the National Farm Workers Association, later the United Farm Workers Union, is an example. Chávez was executive director of the Community Service Organization, a civil rights organization of urban Mexican Americans. Beginning in 1962, Chávez, along with Dolores Huerta, founder of the Agricultural Workers Association, began organizing Mexican grape workers in Delano, California. He created a program of services for the workers that included a credit union, a consumer co-op, welfare and citizenship counseling, and programs that addressed community issues such as racism in the local schools and rental price gouging.[12] His National Farm Workers Association grew from three hundred members in 1962 to more than one thousand by 1964.

A strike by Filipino grape workers in 1965 reluctantly forced Chávez's organization to participate in the strike because the Mexicans and Filipinos worked side by side in the same fields. The strike was broken within a week, and Chávez knew that he had to mobilize outside support for his efforts.

Catalyst An event that energizes and coalesces a social movement.

Catalytic Leadership Social activists who create or recognize opportunities to galvanize people to organized action.

Dolores Huerta, a labor leader and civil rights activist, co-founded the United Farm Workers Union with César Chávez.

He toured the country speaking at universities, church gatherings, and union meetings. The response was overwhelming. He not only raised money for his union, but also recruited volunteers to come to California to help organize the farm workers.[13]

A hallmark of social movement activity is the use of unconventional methods, like mass demonstrations, sit-ins, and marches, to push the agenda and draw attention to the cause. A single demonstration, however, does not constitute a social movement. For example, the Million Man March on October 16, 1995, in Washington, DC, was a political demonstration to promote African American unity and family values. The National Park Service estimated the crowd at somewhere between 400,000 and 600,000, but that estimate was disputed, as Washington, DC, officials estimated the crowd at more than 1 million.[14] The hope was that it would spark a social movement, but it turned out to be a demonstration with little lasting effect.

Another more recent example is the October 16, 2011, Right2Know March for Genetically Modified Foods, a coalition of organizations, businesses, and individuals concerned about labeling of genetically engineered foods in the United States. The march began in New York City, continued 313 miles to Washington, DC, and then demonstrated in front of the White House. The number of marchers is estimated to have been around five hundred. Social movements are sustained activities that occur over long periods of time, and the Right2Know March does not qualify.

In the final sections of the chapter, we discuss the broader reasons why some social movements flounder or actually fail, and why other social efforts do not become formal movements.

Social Movements and Democracy

The United States has seen a number of successful social movements that have enriched its democracy by bringing previously excluded groups into the political process or by highlighting conditions that called for government intervention. Social movements play a valuable role in American democracy. Many of the changes that have occurred in the American political system would not have happened without a social movement.[15]

Despite the democratic foundation of the United States, throughout the nation's history many groups—Blacks, Mexican Americans, American Indians, and women—have been excluded from the political process. The political system treated these citizens differently and inequitably. They were designated as "second-class" citizens based solely on their physical characteristics. These excluded groups used social movements as one of the mechanisms to bring about their inclusion in the political process and to achieve legal and political rights. These social movements forced the United States to ensure that the rights and guarantees expressed in the Constitution were extended to all Americans.

Social movements, which are most often organized by a minority of the populace, may, by changing public opinion, sway a majority of the public to accept and embrace the movement's cause. Changing public opinion is a powerful force in moving decision-makers to grapple with the concerns of a movement. The environmental movement has produced fundamental changes in Americans' attitudes toward nature and the environment. In 1965, when questions about the environment first appeared on public opinion surveys, only about one in ten Americans considered the issue to be very serious. By 1970, however, approximately seven in ten Americans believed that air pollution and water pollution were very or somewhat serious problems.[16] By 2012, Americans were concerned with environmental issues beyond air and water. When questioned about how much individuals worried about specific environmental issues, majorities indicated that they worried a great deal or a fair amount about global warming, the loss of tropical rain forests, and contamination of soil and water from toxic wastes.[17]

Changing public policy is a principal objective of a social movement. Once a social movement has brought its concerns to the attention of decision-makers, changes in public policy are possible. The modern women's rights movement produced profound changes in public law, social policy, basic economic relationships, and social and cultural attitudes toward women.[18]

Social movements can bring about increased participation in the political process on the part of those who are directly affected by an issue and those who have sympathy with the affected. Increases in voter registration and voter turnout might result from increased attention to issues of concern to a social movement.

Social movements can bring about changes in the structures of political institutions. Many participants in social movements might choose careers in government—national, state, and local—to ensure that the issues of concern to them continue to receive attention from multiple levels of government.[19] As "outsiders" become "insiders" in government, they can change the way governments operate. Research on the effect of minority mayors shows that the appointment of minorities in leadership positions, such as police chief or department heads, changes the demographic character of the personnel in those departments and how those departments operate.[20]

Not all social movements have had a positive effect on American democracy—for example, the various phases of what sociologists Betty Dobratz and Stephanie Shanks-Meile call the White supremacy/separatist movement.[21] The founding of the Ku Klux Klan in 1865 by former Confederate soldiers upset with the South's loss and the abolition of slavery was the beginning of a movement whose basis for organization was hatred of Blacks and loss of a slave-based economic system. Over time, the movement spawned multiple hate groups, such as the White Aryan Resistance, the National Socialist White

James Alex Fields, who killed Heather Hyer, at the Charlottesville, Virginia, protest "Unite the Right" by running his car into a group of people protesting the presence of the alt-right protestors.

People's Party, and the National Alliance, which hate not only Blacks, but also Catholics, Jews, gays, and lesbians. Many of the activities of these groups are aimed at denying individuals their rights to participate in the political process and, in some extreme instances, their right to live.

Another element of the White supremacy/separatist movement is a hatred of the U.S. government.[22] The groups whose dominant theme is antigovernment hatred are referred to as "patriot" or militia groups. They include the John Birch Society, the Sons of Liberty, the Police against the New World Order (Idaho), and the Constitution Party. Militia groups, such as the Illinois State Militia, also exist in many states.[23]

These groups define themselves as opposed to the "New World Order," what they see as the emergence of a unified worldwide global government. They claim that the federal government is illegitimate because its policies—gun control, affirmative action, legalization of abortion for White women, tolerance of illegal immigration—have declared war on the White race.[24] According to these groups, the federal government should be destroyed. Timothy McVeigh, who bombed the Alfred P. Murrah Federal Building in Oklahoma City on April 19, 1995, killing 168 people, was a part of this movement, which sees the federal government as the enemy. Until his execution, McVeigh maintained that his action was justified.

The Southern Poverty Law Center (SPLC) of Montgomery, Alabama, estimates that there were approximately 954 organized hate groups in 2018, a 22 percent increase since 2017, with the most active being the Ku Klux Klan, neo-Nazis, and racist skinhead groups.[25] Although not an overwhelming force, the White supremacy/separatist movement has many active members. These groups were particularly active in cyberspace in attacking candidate Barack Obama during the 2008 presidential election and predicting doom for the United States if a Black man was elected president. Although not all threats to President Obama came from hate groups, news reports have indicated that the Secret Service investigated about ten threats per day against him, which was a reduction from the fifty per day just after his election in 2008.[26] With the election of President Trump, these groups have become more active, not only in cyberspace, but in protests and marches as well. The most infamous of these was the march "Unite the Right" that took place in Charlottesville, Virginia, on the evening of August 11 and 12, 2017. Nationalist and supremacist groups marched through town with torches chanting the Nazi slogan "blood and soil," "Jews will not replace us," and "White Lives Matter." Many had not seen anything like the torch light rally since the 1960s Ku Klux Klan rallies or the Nuremberg rallies during the 1930s in Nazi Germany. The images were frightening! A car driven by James Alex Fields, a White nationalist, crashed into a crowd of counter-protestors, killing one woman, Heather Heyer, and injuring many. Fields has been charged with 30 charges including hate crime charges. On December 7, 2018, Fields was convicted of first degree murder and nine other charges. He still faces the federal hate crime charges.

On the one year anniversary of the Charlottesville "Unite the Right" march and tragic events, the original organizer, Jason Kessler, received a permit for a march in Lafayette Park across from the White House, for "Unite the Right 2." The permit he requested indicated that he anticipated that 400 people would attend. In actuality, there were more antiracist protestors, several thousand, to the two dozen or so White nationalists, White supremacists, and neo-Nazis that showed up. A *New York Times* article indicated that the pressure on the various racist groups had been so intense that many of those that attended the first rally and were exposed and lost their jobs did not attend. Yet, the article indicated that people should not take the small group as an indication that the hate groups have gone away. They are still very active, primarily online, and growing, but the groups that came together for the Charlottesville rally have fractured on tactics and leadership.[27]

Successful American Social Movements

Some of the most successful social movements in the United States have been the Civil Rights Movement, the women's suffrage movement, and later the women's rights movement, the labor movement, the environmental movement, and the anti–Vietnam War movement. Most recently the LGBTQ movement is having success at both the national and state levels. The objective of social movements is change, and change, in many instances, does not come about quickly. Many social movements therefore persist for a long time, and some social movements take a long time to mature.[28]

The Civil Rights Movement

The Civil Rights Movement was not one overall movement led from the top; rather, it was a collection of local movements that, when added together, constituted a national social movement and produced massive social change. Although the movement was most active in the 1950s and 1960s, its roots extend back to the nineteenth century. As discussed in Chapter 5, in the 1896 *Plessy v. Ferguson* decision, the U.S. Supreme Court upheld as constitutional "separate but equal" facilities for Blacks and Whites.[29] The ruling, which gave the stamp of constitutionality to racial segregation, allowed the states, especially in the South, to continue the system of social segregation that became known as **Jim Crow laws**. The *Plessy* decision also provided the constitutional cover for Southern states to change their state constitutions or pass laws that removed the vote from Blacks.

Jim Crow Laws The Southern practice of racially segregating all public facilities such as transportation, schools, libraries, hotels, hospitals, theaters, parks, and cemeteries.

Start of the Movement: 1900–1920. The Court decision in *Plessy* and the removal of the franchise sparked an immediate response from Black Americans. In at least twenty-five Southern cities between 1900 and 1906, Blacks organized boycotts to protest new laws enforcing segregation in streetcars. At the same time, violence and terrorism against Blacks increased as Whites sought to reinforce the legal structures that ensured their dominance.[30]

The struggle against Jim Crow continued into the twentieth century. The National Association for the Advancement of Colored People (NAACP) was formed in 1909, and in later years its legal arm, the NAACP Legal Defense and Education Fund, began to go to court to challenge segregation in, initially, higher education and other aspects of daily life. Blacks returning from military service in World War I, the war that had promised "to make the world safe for democracy," argued that the democracy they had fought for in Europe should be extended to Blacks at home. Black Americans became more vocal in their opposition to racial discrimination and segregation through demonstrations, newspaper articles, and meetings and discussions held at activist Black churches, barber shops, beauty salons, and other venues.[31] Whites responded to this increased activity with anti-Black campaigns, increased **lynchings**, and more than twenty-five riots in the summer of 1919. Little change occurred in the legal and political life of Blacks during the 1920s.

Lynching The practice of killing people by mob action outside of the formal judicial process. In the United States, lynching was used as an intimidation tactic against Black Americans.

Movement Spurred by New Deal and World War II: 1930–1950.

President Franklin Delano Roosevelt's New Deal included a number of programs intended to provide relief and recovery during the Great Depression of the 1930s. Although the New Deal programs were not aimed specifically at Blacks, a number of Black leaders, such as Ralph Bunche, Mary McLeod Bethune, Robert Weaver, and William Hastie, became informal advisers to Roosevelt and pushed for the creation of commissions, executive orders, government programs, and changes in policy intended to break down legal and social barriers for Blacks. In 1939, the Supreme Court ruled in *Missouri ex rel Gaines v. Canada* that Lloyd L. Gaines, a Black who had been denied admission to the University of Missouri Law School because of his race, had to be admitted.[32] The Gaines decision marked the first major break in the wall of segregation that had been established after *Plessy*.[33]

More than one million Black men and women served in the armed forces in World War II. Black civil rights activity increased significantly during the war years as many Black leaders linked the fight against fascism in Europe with the fight against racial discrimination and segregation in the United States.[34] By the end of the war, returning veterans and Blacks at home were determined to eliminate the Jim Crow laws governing life for Black Americans in the United States. It was out of this increased commitment and the changes wrought by World War II that the modern phase of the Civil Rights Movement emerged.

Modern Phase Begins: 1950–1960.

A bus boycott in Baton Rouge, Louisiana, began on June 19, 1953. The boycott sought to have the city enforce an ordinance that allowed Black riders to be seated in city buses on a first-come, first-served basis. The city refused to discipline drivers who failed to enforce the ordinance, and Blacks staged a mass boycott of the bus system. Within days, the White political and business leaders of Baton Rouge offered a compromise that would make most of the seats on the bus open on a first-come, first-served basis. At a mass meeting of more than 8,000 Black Americans, the compromise was approved and the boycott called off.[35]

In December 1955, Rosa Parks, a seamstress and NAACP activist, refused to give her seat on a bus in Montgomery, Alabama, to a White man. A local segregation ordinance required Blacks to sit in the back, but if all of the White seats in the front were filled, Blacks were supposed to give up their seats to Whites and stand. Parks was arrested for violating the segregation ordinance, and her arrest energized the Black citizens of Montgomery to mobilize and boycott the bus system. The Montgomery bus boycott—initially organized by the Women's Political Council, a group of women who were faculty members at Alabama State College or teachers in the Montgomery school system, founded by Mary Fair Burks in 1946 and headed at that time by Jo Ann Gibson Robinson—enlisted the young Reverend Martin Luther King, Jr. to lead the protest. It lasted 381 days. The Montgomery Improvement Association, the group formed to guide the bus boycott, filed suit in February 1956 in U.S. district court challenging the constitutionality of bus segregation. The boycott ended when the Supreme Court declared Alabama's state and local laws requiring segregation on buses unconstitutional in December 1956.[36]

The success of the Montgomery Improvement Association launched a national movement for Black civil rights by motivating other communities to engage in local protests against local and state governments. Although the Baton Rouge boycott had occurred earlier, it did not launch a national movement for several reasons. It lasted only a couple of days because concessions were offered relatively quickly. In contrast, the extended length of the Montgomery boycott required dynamic leadership and extensive organization and generated local and national publicity. The Baton Rouge boycott did not lead to a court case, whereas the Montgomery boycott took its petition all the way to the Supreme Court, whose ruling affected all Alabama state and local bus segregation ordinances.

In 1957, King, along with civil rights activists Bayard Rustin and Ella Baker, formed the **Southern Christian Leadership Conference (SCLC)**, which was designed to be the umbrella organization that would link church-based affiliates throughout the South in the nonviolent struggle for racial justice. King was elected SCLC's president, and Ella Baker was its first executive director.[37]

While Blacks were coming together to protest for their rights, White Southerners were organizing in opposition to the growing Civil Rights Movement. In 1956, Alabama passed a law that banned the NAACP from operating in the state, as did several other states. In Mississippi, the **White Citizens' Council**, formed in 1954, used economic reprisals and legal repression to intimidate and repress civil rights activists and supporters.[38]

Nonviolent Civil Disobedience Increases: 1960–1965. The Civil Rights Movement in the 1960s focused on two primary objectives—eliminating segregation and discrimination and removing barriers to Black voter registration and participation. To achieve these goals, movement participants engaged

Southern Christian Leadership Conference (SCLC) Group designed to be the umbrella organization that would link church-based affiliates throughout the South in the nonviolent struggle for racial justice.

White Citizens' Council Formed in 1954 in Mississippi to prevent the implementation of *Brown v. Board of Education*, the White Citizens' Council's membership consisted of plantation owners, bankers, doctors, legislators, and others opposed to Black civil rights and determined to maintain segregation.

in actions of nonviolent civil disobedience. A primary tactic was the sit-in. On February 1, 1960, in Greensboro, North Carolina, four freshmen from North Carolina A&T University sat down at a Whites-only lunch counter in Woolworth's. They were refused service, but remained all day at the counter. The next day, twenty students occupied the lunch counter. Some White students from a local women's college joined the sit-in on the third day, and the number of students at the lunch counter swelled to eighty-five.[39] By the end of the week, sit-ins had spread to other cities in North Carolina, and by the end of the month sit-ins were happening in other towns and cities in the South. In April 1960, college students, with Ella Baker in attendance, formed the **Student Non-Violent Coordinating Committee (SNCC)** to continue directing the campaign started by the North Carolina A&T students.

In spring 1961, the Congress of Racial Equality (CORE) decided to test the enforcement of the Supreme Court's decision outlawing segregation in interstate transportation by having interracial groups ride buses from Washington, DC, to various Southern cities. One bus was firebombed outside of Birmingham, another ran into a vicious mob assault at the bus station in Montgomery, and bus riders were arrested in Jackson, Mississippi. CORE and SNCC continued to send individuals to replace those arrested until Attorney General Robert F. Kennedy finally directed the Interstate Commerce Commission to enforce regulations barring segregation in interstate terminals.[40]

Martin Luther King, Jr. emerged as the national leader of this growing protest movement. King was an eloquent and powerful speaker able to articulate the ideals of the movement and the power of the principles of nonviolent protest. In 1963, at the invitation of local Blacks who were organizing against segregation and demanding the right to vote, King and some members of SCLC went to Birmingham, Alabama. SCLC, in concert with local groups, organized a boycott of downtown businesses during the height of the Easter season to protest the stores' refusal to hire Black sales clerks. Demonstrators marched to city hall to protest the city's segregation laws.

Many people were arrested, including King. While in jail, King wrote to the White clergy of Birmingham who condemned the demonstrations, explaining to them in his famous "Letter from Birmingham Jail" why the protests and demonstrations were occurring in Birmingham (see the Our Voices box on page 000). Eight White Alabama clergy had issued a statement critical of King and the demonstrations, saying that protests and demonstrations were not the right approach to addressing grievances. King chastised these clergymen for criticizing the demonstrations but not the conditions that had led to them.[41]

Birmingham police commissioner Eugene "Bull" Connor was determined to stop the civil rights demonstrators. As the protesters, including a great many Black schoolchildren and teenagers, marched, sang, and prayed, Connor and his forces turned on them with nightsticks, snarling attack dogs, and high-pressure water hoses. Millions of television viewers watched in horror at the images of the young demonstrators being blown off their feet by water hoses and attacked by dogs.[42]

Student Non-Violent Coordinating Committee (SNCC) Organization of college students dedicated to continuing the campaign for social justice started by the North Carolina A&T students.

With the assistance of negotiators sent by the Kennedy administration, the city's businesses began to negotiate with the demonstrators. After three days of meetings, the two sides reached an agreement to desegregate downtown stores and employ Black clerks. Whites responded to the compromise agreement with numerous bombings, which ignited further rioting. Finally, under pressure from the federal government, the mayor ratified the agreement and repealed the city's segregation laws.[43] The Birmingham demonstrations touched off similar demonstrations throughout the South and pushed Black civil rights to the forefront of national policy.[44]

On June 11, 1963, President John Kennedy addressed the nation in the wake of Governor George Wallace's unsuccessful attempt to block the admission of two Black students to the University of Alabama. Wallace stood in the door of the Registrar's Office in an attempt to keep the students from registering. A representative of Attorney General Robert Kennedy announced that he had a proclamation from President Kennedy ordering Wallace "to cease his illegal resistance to the federal court order on integration."[45] In the address, Kennedy pledged that he would urge Congress to act on legislation that he would be sending forward, and on June 19 he submitted his civil rights bill.[46]

On August 28, 1963, between 200,000 and 500,000 people (estimates varied depending on who was doing the counting) marched on Washington, DC, to lobby for the civil rights bill. The March on Washington for Jobs and Freedom was organized by a coalition of civil rights organizations—the NAACP, SCLC, CORE, SNCC, and the National Urban League—and a Black union active in civil rights, the Brotherhood of Sleeping Car Porters and Maids. The principal organizer, however, was Bayard Rustin, an important behind-the-scenes organizer and civil rights activist and a confidant of A. Philip Randolph, the organizer and founder of the Brotherhood of Sleeping Car Porters and Maids. (Both Rustin and Randolph had called for a march on Washington in 1941 to protest discrimination in the defense industry, but they called it off after President Franklin Roosevelt issued Executive Order 8802 [Fair Employment Act], which banned discrimination in the defense industry and in federal bureaus. Rustin was also gay and became an advocate for gay and lesbian issues toward the end of his life.)

It was the largest political demonstration the United States had ever seen. Hundreds of thousands of participants gathered at the Washington Monument and at noon began marching toward the Lincoln Memorial. Once at the memorial, many people spoke on the steps of the monument, but the most memorable was Martin Luther King, who delivered what became known as his "I Have a Dream" speech.[47] His words rang out over

Firefighters turn their hoses full force on civil rights demonstrators, July 15, 1963, in Birmingham, Alabama, one of the focal points of the desegregation movement.

our voices

Excerpt from Martin Luther King Jr.'s Letter from Birmingham Jail

April 16, 1963

MY DEAR FELLOW CLERGYMEN,

While confined here in the Birmingham city jail, I came across your recent statement calling my present activities "unwise and untimely." Seldom do I pause to answer criticism of my work and ideas. If I sought to answer all the criticisms that cross my desk, my secretaries would have little time for anything other than such correspondence in the course of the day, and I would have no time for constructive work. But since I feel that you are men of genuine good will and that your criticisms are sincerely set forth, I want to try to answer your statements in what I hope will be patient and reasonable terms....

You deplore the demonstrations taking place in Birmingham. But your statement, I am sorry to say, fails to express a similar concern for the conditions that brought about the demonstrations. I am sure that none of you would want to rest content with the superficial kind of social analysis that deals merely with effects and does not grapple with underlying causes. It is unfortunate that demonstrations are taking place in Birmingham, but it is even more unfortunate that the city's white power structure left the Negro community with no alternative....

I must make two honest confessions to you, my Christian and Jewish brothers. First, I must confess that over the past few years I have been gravely disappointed with the white moderate. I have almost reached the regrettable conclusion that the Negro's great stumbling block in his stride toward freedom is not the White Citizen's Counciler or the Ku Klux Klanner, but the white moderate, who is more devoted to "order" than to justice; who prefers a negative peace which is the absence of tension to a positive peace which is the presence of justice; who constantly says: "I agree with you in the goal you seek, but I cannot agree with your methods of direct action"; who paternalistically believes he can set the timetable for another man's freedom; who lives by a mythical concept of time and who constantly advises the Negro to wait for a "more convenient season." Shallow understanding from people of good will is more frustrating than absolute misunderstanding from people of ill will. Lukewarm acceptance is much more bewildering than outright rejection.

I had also hoped that the white moderate would reject the myth concerning time in relation to the struggle for freedom. I have just received a letter from a white brother in Texas. He writes: "All Christians know that the colored people will receive equal rights eventually, but it is possible that you are in too great a religious hurry. It has taken Christianity almost two thousand years to accomplish what it has. The teachings of Christ take time to come to earth." Such an attitude stems from a tragic misconception of time, from the strangely rational notion that there is something in the very flow of time that will inevitably cure all ills. Actually, time itself is neutral; it can be used either destructively or constructively. More and more I feel that the people of ill will have used time much more effectively than have the people of good will. We will have to repent in this generation not merely for the hateful words and actions of the bad people but for the appalling silence of the good people. Human progress never rolls in on wheels of inevitability; it comes through the tireless efforts of men willing to be co-workers with God, and without this hard work, time itself becomes an ally of the forces of social stagnation. We must use time creatively, in the knowledge that the time is always ripe to do right. Now is the time to make real the promise of democracy and transform our pending national elegy into a creative psalm of brotherhood. Now is the time to lift our national policy from the quicksand of racial injustice to the solid rock of human dignity....

I hope this letter finds you strong in the faith. I also hope that circumstances will soon make it possible for me to meet each of you, not as an integrationist or a civil rights leader but as a fellow clergyman and a Christian brother. Let us all hope that the dark clouds of racial prejudice will soon pass away and the deep fog of misunderstanding will be lifted from our fear-drenched communities, and in some not too distant tomorrow the radiant stars of love and brotherhood will shine over our great nation with all their scintillating beauty.

Yours for the cause of Peace and Brotherhood,

MARTIN LUTHER KING JR.

Source: Reprinted by arrangement with the Heirs to the Estate of Martin Luther King, Jr., c/o Writers House as agent for the proprietor New York, NY.

the crowd and were carried live on national television: "I say to you today, my friends, so even though we face the difficulties of today and tomorrow, I still have a dream. It is a dream deeply rooted in the American dream. I have a dream that one day this nation will rise up and live out the true meaning of its creed: 'We hold these truths to be self-evident that all men are created equal.'"[48]

Increasing organized protest activity in the South fueled the Civil Rights Movement in 1964 and 1965, as did the commitment of President Lyndon B. Johnson to see strong civil rights legislation enacted. Despite opposition from Southern legislators, Johnson was able to persuade Congress to pass the Civil Rights Act of 1964, which banned discrimination in public facilities and employment. The next year, Johnson convinced Congress to pass the Voting Rights Act of 1965, which provided federal supervision of voter registration practices and elections. The act effectively opened the polls to Black Americans for the first time since the end of Reconstruction.[49]

The Women's Suffrage and Women's Rights Movements

Many White women were involved in the abolitionist movement that sought to end slavery. As these women became skilled at organizing, and became aware not only of the inequities of slavery, but also of the inequities in women's status, they began to voice their own grievances.[50] Thus, the impetus for the early origins of the movement sprang from two main sources—women's growing awareness of their common conditions and grievances and the growth of the antislavery movement.[51]

The First Wave of the Women's Rights Movement. The first wave of the women's rights movement developed in the twelve years preceding the Civil War. In July 1848, antislavery activists Elizabeth Cady Stanton and Lucretia Mott organized a convention to be held in Seneca Falls, New York, which would call for the extension of political, legal, and social rights to women. The convention aimed to improve the nation by making it guarantee equal rights to all its citizens.

One of the few men present at Seneca Falls was former slave and prominent abolitionist Frederick Douglass. Of the convention and women's rights, he wrote in an editorial in his newspaper the *North Star* on July 28, 1848, "We

Frederick Douglass (1818–1895) was one of the few men at the Seneca Falls Convention and remained committed to women's rights throughout his life.

hold woman to be justly entitled to all we claim for man. We go farther, and express our conviction that all political rights which it is expedient for man to exercise, it is equally so for woman."[52]

Using the Declaration of Independence as a framework, Stanton wrote a "declaration of sentiments" in which she connected the emerging women's rights movement to the principles in the declaration.[53] Convention delegates unanimously approved the Declaration of Sentiments and most of the resolutions proposed to address women's grievances. The only resolution that did not pass unanimously was the call for women's suffrage, but opposition dissipated after the convention.[54] As a result of the Seneca Falls convention, women's rights conventions were held regularly from 1850 until the start of the Civil War.

Sojourner Truth was among a small group of free, Black, feminist abolitionists in the North in the early nineteenth century. This group also included Maria Stewart (1803–1879), born a free Black but later became an indentured servant until she was sixteen and then an abolitionist and lecturer, and Frances E. Watkins Harper (1825–1911), a free Black abolitionist, suffragist, author, and poet.[55] Sojourner Truth, born Isabella Baumfree, as a slave in Ulster County, New York is recognized as the individual who was most responsible for connecting the abolition of slavery and women's rights during the nineteenth century. At a time when most people thought of slaves as male and women as White, Sojourner Truth was particularly concerned with highlighting the complexities of Black women's race and gender identities.[56] In fact, some scholars suggest that Truth was the first to identify what we now call the intersection of race and gender in the lives of Black and other women of color. Sojourner Truth attended her first women's right's convention in Worcester, Massachusetts, in 1850, where Frederick Douglass was also present. The two had first met in 1842 in Northampton, Massachusetts, at the Northampton Association. Beyond their race, Frederick Douglass and Sojourner Truth had little in common. Douglass "saw himself as a statesman-in-the-making and modeled his comportment on the well-educated antislavery leaders with whom he worked."[57] Douglass had a condescending attitude toward Truth and viewed her as a "genuine specimen of the uncultured Negro."[58]

In 1851, Sojourner Truth (1797–1883) addressed the audience at the Women's Rights Convention in Akron, Ohio, and emphasized the important difference between White women and Black women in terms of their relationships to White men.[59] Truth's legendary "Ain't I a Woman" speech was recorded by presiding officer Frances D. Gage and was published in *Truth's Narrative* (1875) and *History of Woman Suffrage* (vol. I, 115–117).[60]

One problem that developed for the women's movement after the Civil War was that because it had been closely tied to the antislavery movement, it also continued to be closely tied to the debate and ratification of the Thirteenth, Fourteenth, and Fifteenth Amendments. Some of those who had been members of the abolitionist movement

Sojourner Truth (1797–1883), born a slave in Ulster County, New York, and escaped with her child in later years, was among a small group of free, Black, feminist-abolitionists active in both the abolitionist and early wave of the Women's Rights Movement.

focused their efforts solely on Black male suffrage, but others who had been involved in the abolitionist movement felt that Black men should not get the vote before White women did.

In 1866, Frederick Douglass and Charles Remond (1810–1873), a free Black abolitionist activists and lecturer, were among the vice presidents chosen to helm the leadership of the newly established Equal Rights Association (ERA) in 1866 after the American Anti-Slavery Association disbanded. Douglass was concerned that the ERA would become an organization that focused solely on women's rights.[61] Sojourner Truth played an active role in the ERA, along with Francis Watkins Harper. While both women were nationally renowned orators, they did not hold positions of power within the ERA.[62] By comparison, Black women's involvement in the ERA was as limited as Black men's involvement had been in the prewar Anti-Slavery Society. Over the course of the ERA's three-year history, the organization had over fifty national officers and speakers participate at its conventions, but of that number, there were only five Black women and five Black men.[63]

In debates over Black and women's suffrage that were directly connected to the ratification of the Fourteenth Amendment that added "male" to the discussion of denying the right to vote and connecting that to representation, Truth opposed Frederick Douglass and other Black abolitionists, including Frances Harper, who were against removing "male" from the amendment. Instead, she sided with White feminists on the issue. In a speech delivered at the annual meeting of the American Equal Rights Association, in New York in 1867, Truth talked about her fear that Black men would ignore the plight of Black women once they got the vote.[64]

As a result, the women's movement splintered into two groups over the Fifteenth Amendment, which explicitly prohibited denial of the franchise because of race, color, or previous condition of servitude. Stanton and Susan B. Anthony formed the National Woman Suffrage Association (NWSA), which focused on all-inclusive suffrage at the national level. Lucy Stone and her daughter, Alice Stone Blackwell, formed the American Woman Suffrage Association (AWSA), which supported the Fifteenth Amendment even though it excluded women. They argued that women's suffrage would best be achieved at the state level.[65]

At this point, Frederick Douglass publicly broke with Stanton and Anthony over their increasing opposition to the Fifteenth Amendment and Stanton's increasingly racist rhetoric.[66] While Sojourner Truth was actively involved in the issue of women's suffrage, she also split from Susan B. Anthony and Elizabeth Cady Stanton due to conflicting positions on the Fifteenth Amendment to the U.S. Constitution after Stanton had stated that she would not support the Black vote over women's suffrage.

After the Fifteenth Amendment was ratified, Black women began organizing for the right to vote even though they had been largely excluded by White women from their push for the franchise for women.[67] The emergence of the Black women's club movement in the late 1890s was the result of Black women forming organizations to contribute to the "uplift" of Black America and to address problems facing Black communities, such as health, education, and women's suffrage. Douglass's and Truth's break with the early founders of the women's suffrage movement and the exclusion of Black women from the agenda of White women in later years created a tension between Black and White women that has remained in the contemporary women's rights movement.

In 1890, NWSA and AWSA were reunited in the National American Woman Suffrage Association (NAWSA), with Elizabeth Cady Stanton as its president.[68] NAWSA began to petition and lobby states where women could vote, such as Kansas, Wyoming, and North Dakota, for passage of an amendment to the U.S. Constitution. Women, both White and Black, demonstrated, lobbied, and protested for women's suffrage, with one of the largest marches of women and their supporters, five thousand strong, taking place in Washington, DC, on March 3, 1913. The National Woman's Party also formed during this time.

In 1920, the Nineteenth Amendment, which granted women the right to vote, was finally ratified. After ratification, Black women who tried to vote were met with resistance from the National Woman's Party and were excluded from its efforts.[69] In 1923, Alice Paul, the leader of the National Woman's Party, drafted an equal rights amendment for the Constitution. The text of the amendment was simple: "Men and women have equal rights throughout the United States."[70] Paul's amendment was introduced into both the Senate and the House of Representatives, but it was not passed by either body at the time.

Pauli Murray (1910–1985), civil rights and feminist activist, lawyer, university professor and college president, and one of the first females to be ordained an Episcopal priest, was a co-founder of the National Organization of Women (NOW) in 1966.

The Second Wave of the Women's Rights Movement. From the 1920s through the late 1950s, no national women's movement existed that was devoted to the issue of women's rights. Two events in the 1960s triggered the second wave of the women's rights movement. President Kennedy appointed Esther Peterson, a labor and consumer activist, head of the Department of Labor's Women's Bureau, and she convinced Kennedy to appoint a presidential commission on the status of women. Its 1963 report documented discrimination against women in virtually every area of American life, which ultimately resulted in the Equal Pay Act of 1963.[71] This, in turn, set the stage to extend Title 7 of the Civil Rights Act of 1964, the amendment that outlaws discrimination in employment, to include sex.[72]

The second event was the publication in 1963 of *The Feminine Mystique* by journalist Betty Friedan, which documented the emotional and intellectual oppression that White middle-class educated women were experiencing because of limited life options.[73] In 1966, the National Organization for Women was founded. Its goal was to bring women into full participation in the mainstream of American society immediately in true equal partnership with men.[74]

Each of these events sparked a large increase in protests, demonstrations, and lobbying and renewed interest in an equal rights amendment. Like Alice Paul's earlier proposal, the new Equal Rights Amendment was simple and direct: "Equality of rights under the law shall not be denied or abridged by the United States or by any state on account of sex." Congress approved the amendment on March 22, 1972, and sent it to the states for ratification. The campaign for ratification drew millions of women of all races to pressure their state legislatures to ratify the amendment. By the end of the year, twenty-two of the required thirty-eight states had ratified the amendment. Women's rights activists thought that ratification was a foregone conclusion.[75]

Not all women supported the Equal Rights Amendment, however. A STOP ERA campaign led by the late Phyllis Schlafly was particularly effective in mounting opposition to the amendment. Schlafly and her group argued that the Equal Rights Amendment would decriminalize rape, legitimize homosexuality, integrate public restrooms, guarantee abortion rights, lead men to abandon their families, and subject women to the military draft.[76] For a discussion of the arguments on both sides of the Equal Rights Amendment, see the Evaluating Equality box.

The STOP ERA forces persuaded some male legislators in several states to reject ratification. As the 1982 deadline for ratification approached, the Equal Rights Amendment was just three states short of the thirty-eight states needed for ratification. Seventy-five percent of female legislators in the three states that were still considering the measure—Virginia, Illinois, and Arkansas—supported the Equal Rights Amendment (which meant that some female legislators voted against the measure), but only 46 percent of male legislators voted to ratify.[77] In the end, the three states failed to ratify and the amendment went down to defeat. Despite the loss of the Equal Rights Amendment, the second wave of the women's rights movement accomplished a number of goals: It pushed through the passage of numerous pieces of legislation to protect women in the workplace and equalize funding for women's sports, it opened up doors for women in almost all professional fields, and it raised the consciousness of millions of American women.

Third Wave of the Women's Rights Movement. Some argue that a third wave of the women's rights movement began in the early 1990s. Women's issues are still central to political debates, as we saw in the 2012 and 2016 elections, although scholars might debate whether the women's rights movement is still as prominent and as active as it once was. Nevertheless, the first piece of legislation signed by President Obama after he took office was the Lilly Ledbetter Fair Pay Act of 2009. The Ledbetter Act, amending the Civil Rights Act of 1964, states that the 180-day statute of limitations for filing an equal pay lawsuit resets with each paycheck that continues to result in unequal pay.

Ledbetter had worked as a supervisor for Goodyear Tire and Rubber Company for twenty years. Shortly before she retired she found that she was being paid significantly less per month than the three male supervisors doing the same job. She sued, but the U.S. Supreme Court ruled that she had not filed within the 180-day requirement. The Ledbetter Act remedied this, as it is unlikely that many women will know within 180 days that they are being paid less than their male counterparts for the same work. Some activists have argued that the attack on women's rights over contraception and the funding of Planned Parenthood, especially present in the 2012 and 2016 elections, calls for a renewed women's rights movement.[78] The question of whether the women's rights movement is in a fourth wave or a continuation of the third is an open question that scholars will have to address.

Yet one could argue that the election of President Trump has brought the fourth wave of the movement into sharp relief. The Women's March was a coordinated protest held worldwide on January 21, 2017, following the presidential inauguration of Donald J. Trump. The protest brought together an estimated five million people on every continent to advocate legislation and policies addressing human rights issues, immigration reform, healthcare reform, racial equality, freedom of religion, and worker's rights.[79] The women-led movement mobilized diverse groups of people of all races, ages, genders, political affiliations, and religious backgrounds, with the hope of affirming shared humanity and declaring a mission of "resistance and self-determination."[80] The protests were largely in response to offensive, misogynistic statements made by Trump during his presidential campaign and his policy positions on women's issues, which have widely been regarded as "antiwomen." There was also concern about Congress cutting funding for Planned Parenthood, after U.S. House Speaker vowed to take action to roll back the group's funding as part of the repeal of the Affordable Healthcare Act, and apprehension about President Trump's ability to appoint Supreme Court justices who could eventually try to overturn *Roe v. Wade*, the landmark 1973 decision that established a woman's right to abortion.[81]

Protesters took to the streets again in January 2018, in cities around the globe, including Miami, Las Vegas, Milwaukee, Melbourne, and Munich.[82] As they marched in support of women's rights, the protesters also denounced the Trump administration's policies on abortion, immigration, and LGBTQ rights. While the 2017 marches were primarily a movement of solidarity for those who were against Trump's leadership, the protests in 2018 focused more on politics and gender issues that had become salient since the 2017 marches. Organizers explained that the protests were galvanized by the #MeToo movement,[83] which has become an international phenomenon that seeks to directly confront the widespread prevalence of sexual harassment and assault. More than 250 anniversary marches and events took place around the world on January 20, 2018.[84] The passion behind the women's march has not subsided and we will see if it does truly represent the fourth wave of the women's rights movement.

evaluating equality

What Arguments Did Supporters and Opponents of the Equal Rights Amendment Put Forth?

On March 22, 1971, the U.S. Senate passed the Equal Rights Amendment by a vote of 84–8 and sent it to the states to be ratified.* The entire amendment consisted of three sections:

Section 1. Equality of Rights under the law shall not be denied or abridged by the United States or any state on account of sex.

Section 2. The Congress shall have the power to enforce, by appropriate legislation, the provisions of this article.

Section 3. This amendment shall take effect two years after the date of ratification.

In Support of the Equal Rights Amendment

The pro–Equal Rights Amendment forces contended that the amendment would accomplish the following:

- Invalidate pay schemes called dual pay schedules for men and women being paid differently when they performed the same job.
- Eliminate state statutes that automatically exempted women from serving on a jury.
- Abolish restrictions on the legal capacity of married women, such as their right to establish a domicile, hold a driver's license in their own names, or go into business

for themselves; on provisions in family law giving greater responsibility to a husband and presuming dependence in a wife; and on the presumptions in divorce that a wife should care for any children and receive alimony.

- Eliminate gender differences in state and federal pension and Social Security benefits.
- Eliminate laws establishing different sentences for the same crime (in some states, Georgia, for example, men convicted of a crime would be given fixed sentences, whereas women convicted of the same crime would be given indeterminate sentences).
- Abolish restrictions on women entering and advancing in the armed forces.**

In Opposition to the Equal Rights Amendment

The anti–Equal Rights Amendment forces argued that the amendment would result in the following:

- Hurt homemakers and the family because it would abolish a husband's duty to support his wife.
- Mean that women had to be admitted to West Point in numbers equal to those of men.
- Subject women to the draft.
- Make girls eligible for the same athletic teams as boys in public schools and state universities.

- Render separate athletic competitions for men and women illegal.
- Reduce certain Social Security retirement benefits for women to the same level as those available to similarly situated men.
- Abolish freedom of choice among boys' schools, girls' schools, and coed schools (individuals would no longer be able to choose the type of educational setting they wanted for their children).
- Eliminate separate physical education classes for girls and boys in public schools.
- Abolish separate prison cells for men and women.
- Make separate public bathrooms for men and women illegal.***

Read the text of the amendment and then examine the claims of the pro– and anti–Equal Rights Amendment forces.

- What effect do you think the proposed amendment would have actually had on the legal and social aspects of women's lives?
- What is your assessment of the validity of the claims of both sides?

*Berry, M. F. (1986). *Why the ERA failed: Politics, women's rights, and the amending process of the Constitution*. Bloomington: Indiana University Press, p. 64.

**Mansbridge, J. J. 91986). *Why we lost the ERA*. Chicago: University of Chicago Press, pp. 56–59.

***Ibid., pp. 90–117.

The Labor Movement

In the years following the Civil War, the United States experienced phenomenal industrial expansion and tremendous economic changes. Manufacturing became increasingly mechanized, and corporations with nationwide scope controlled many industries, including mining, transportation, and steel. At the same time, massive immigration provided a large labor supply for the new factories and mines. Conditions in these new factories, mines, and steel plants were often unhealthy and frequently dangerous. Wages were low, and in many instances entire families, including children as young as six, worked twelve to sixteen hours a day just to earn enough money to subsist.[85]

Craft-based unions for skilled workers such as bricklayers, carpenters, and shoemakers had existed for some time in the United States, but these unions were usually local in character and concerned primarily with maintaining the standards of a particular craft. The nationalization of American business convinced labor leaders that labor had to organize on a nationwide basis to meet the challenge of industry.[86] One early attempt at national union organization occurred in 1866 with the creation of the National Labor Union (NLU). One of the NLU's objectives was the establishment of an eight-hour workday. The NLU's emphasis on this goal bore fruit in 1868 when Congress established an eight-hour day for federal workers, but the union dissolved in 1872.

In 1869, the Noble and Holy Order of the Knights of Labor was started in Philadelphia. On January 1, 1878, the Knights of Labor held a national convention and adopted a national structure and platform. By 1883, the union had grown from 9,000 to nearly 60,000 members.[87] The Knights of Labor's first strike against the telegraph companies in 1883 failed, but a year later its strike against the railroad companies succeeded in forcing them to rescind their attempt to reduce workers' wages. This was the first major victory of a union against a monopolistic giant, and workers flocked to join.[88]

In 1881, the Federation of Organized Trades and Labor Unions (FOTLU) was established to unite independent trade unions of skilled workers into a single federation. By 1886, FOTLU had evolved into the American Federation of Labor (AFL), whose aim was to protect skilled labor, such as carpenters, cigar makers, printers, iron and steelworkers, and iron molders. The AFL convinced these skilled workers that craft organizations could represent their interests better than could an organization that included millions of unskilled workers.[89]

The power of unions and the labor movement itself waxed and waned during the late 1800s and early 1900s, making gains on some fronts and losing ground in others. A horrific tragedy on March 25, 1911, pushed the issue of worker safety to the forefront. The Triangle Shirtwaist Company in New York City, a sweatshop that employed primarily immigrant women, caught fire. The exits had been locked by the company to prevent theft and the workers had no way out. Many of the women scrambled onto a fire escape that collapsed because of the excess weight. The fire department's ladders only reached to the sixth floor of the building, but the fire was on the top two floors. Many women jumped to their death trying to escape the flames, and others perished in the fire. All told, 146 people died in the fire. This tragic event pushed various levels of government to begin to do something about the health and safety of workers, including instituting fire codes and child labor laws.

In 1925, the first labor union organized by Blacks, the Brotherhood of Sleeping Car Porters and Maids, came into existence. The union was headed by A. Philip Randolph and organized by Black porters and maids who worked for the Pullman Company. Blacks were excluded from certain jobs, such as conductor, worked many hours without pay, and were charged for items stolen by their White passengers.[90] The Pullman Company fought the union and even cultivated many members of the Black press, particularly the Chicago *Defender* and its publisher, Robert Abbott, who joined with the company in denouncing the union.[91] It won a charter from the AFL in 1935, and the Pullman Company finally recognized the union in 1937. The union negotiated a landmark contract with the Pullman Company, winning $2 million in pay increases, a shorter work week, and overtime pay.

At the time, more than 20,000 Blacks worked for the railroads, the largest category of Black labor in the United States and Canada.[92] Many of the members of the Brotherhood of Sleeping Car Porters and Maids became major players in the later phases of the Civil Rights Movement. They included A. Philip Randolph, one of the organizers of the 1963 March on Washington; E. D. Nixon, who played a key role in the Montgomery bus boycott; Thurgood Marshall, the lead attorney on *Brown v. Board of Education of Topeka* in 1954 and the first Black Supreme Court justice; and Malcolm X, a civil rights activist whose approach was at odds with that of Martin Luther King and other mainstream civil rights leaders.[93]

Despite opposition to and repression of various aspects of the labor movement, it achieved a number of benefits for workers, including the standards of an eight-hour workday (1916) and a forty-hour workweek. Labor movement activities led to other accomplishments as well, such as prohibitions against child labor (1916, 1938), creation of the Department of Labor (1913), workplace safety rules and regulations (1938), a minimum wage (1938), and collective bargaining (1933, 1935).

Scholars view the 1930s and 1940s as the "glory" years for organized labor,[94] as it had a friendly national government in the administration of Franklin Roosevelt. One major piece of labor legislation that passed early in Roosevelt's administration was the Wagner Act (1935), more

On March 25, 1911, 146 immigrant garment workers were killed after they were trapped on the upper floors of the Asch Building after the Triangle Shirtwaist Factory caught fire. The owners of the factory had chained shut the exit doors, and the workers, who were mostly young women, perished in the fire or died after jumping from the ten-story building. This photo shows the gutted remains of the tenth floor, with only the floors and walls intact.

commonly known as the National Labor Relations Act. The act allowed the right to strike and the right to choose a union and imposed a number of prohibitions on the behavior of management.[95]

At the conclusion of World War II in 1945, organized labor had a membership of more than 14 million workers, but labor had lost an ally in the White House with Franklin Roosevelt's death, and coalitions to fight labor reemerged. In 1947, Congress passed the Taft-Hartley Bill, which amended the Wagner Act by defining a set of unfair labor practices for labor in response to the Wagner Act's setting of unfair acts by management.[96]

In 1955, the Congress of Industrial Organizations (CIO), headed by Walter Reuther, and the AFL, headed by George Meany, merged to form a new union, the AFL-CIO. At the time, the new union covered one-third of all non-agricultural workers in the United States. Traditionally, the day-to-day practices of unions across the country discriminated heavily against Black and female workers, but once these two organizations became one, George Meany, the new head of the AFL-CIO, pushed the labor movement to actively support the Civil Rights Movement and was influential in helping to pass the Civil Rights Act of 1964, the Voting Rights Act of 1965, and the 1972 amendments to the Voting Rights Act.[97] Scholars suggest that Meany's interest was increasing membership in the AFL-CIO, and Black workers were a ready source of new members. Yet the merger did not remove the discrimination Black workers and female workers of all races experienced from the unions.

In the late 1970s, the first signs of union decline became apparent when President Jimmy Carter could not win congressional approval, in a Democrat-controlled Congress, to reform the National Labor Relations Act. President Ronald Reagan actively pursued aggressive antiunion policies, and in 1981 he broke a strike by the Professional Air Traffic Controllers Organization by firing all 11,000-plus members when they refused an order to return to work.[98] The union was decertified by the Federal Labor Relations Board in 1981. This strike is seen as pivotal in undermining the ability of unions, both private and public, to bargain and to use strikes as leverage.

If we look at union membership, we see that the labor movement does not have the strength and influence that it once had. Union membership fell from a high of 20.1 percent of the workforce in 1983 to just above the all-time low at 10.7 percent in 2017 (see the Measuring Equality box). Much of the growth in the U.S. economy over the last several decades has been in the service industry or in manufacturing jobs in nonunion businesses.

Yet other indicators suggest that labor still plays a major role in the U.S. economy. Although membership is down, belonging to a labor union is still beneficial to workers. In 2017, members of unions made approximately 23 percent more in wages per week than nonunion members did (as shown in "Measuring Equality"). Evidence also suggests that unions are beneficial to the wage structure for Blacks and female workers of all colors. Black workers are more likely to belong to a union than White workers are, and the gap between women and men on this same dimension has narrowed considerably in

measuring equality

Unions and Wages

Unions grew out of the labor movement and have had a significant effect on the wages and working conditions of its members. Union membership is on the decline, but workers who are members of unions still earn higher wages than workers who are not members of unions. Figures 12.1 and 12.2 display the percentage of union members in the workforce and the higher wages earned by that decreasing share of the workforce.

Sources: U.S. Bureau of Labor Statistics. (n.d.). *Union membership, 1983–2012.* Table 1, Union Affiliation of Employed Wage and Salary Workers by Selected Characteristics (calculated from data), and Table 2, Median Weekly Earnings of Full-Time Wage and Salary Workers by Union Affiliation and Selected Characteristics

http://www.bls.gov/webapps/legacy/cpslutab1.htm.; Bureau of Labor Statistics, U.S. Department of Labor. (n.d.). *The Editor's Desk,* Union Membership Declines in 2012. Retrieved February 14, 2013, from http://www.bls.gov/opub/ted/2013/ted_20130124.htm. Union affiliation data from Current Population Survey available at: http://www.bls.gov/cps/cpslutabs.htm. U.S. Bureau of Labor Statistics. (2018, January 19). *Union members — 2017.* News release. Retrieved July 16, 2018 from https://www.bls.gov/news.release/pdf/union2.pdf. U.S. Bureau of Labor Statistics. (2018). Economic News Release: Table 2. Median Weekly Earnings of Full-Time Wage and Salary Workers by Union Affiliation and Selected Characteristics. Retrieved from https://www.bls.gov/news.release/union2.t02.htm.

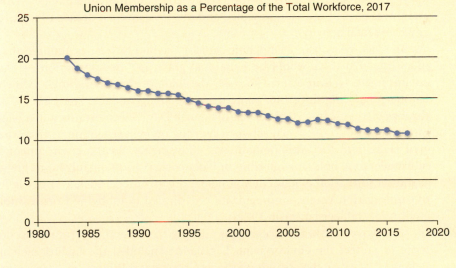

Figure 12.1 Union Membership as a Percentage of the Total Workforce, 2017

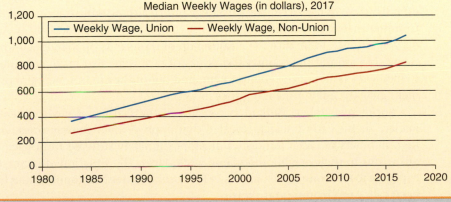

Figure 12.2 Median Weekly Wages (in dollars), 2017

the last thirty years. So even though the argument that the labor movement is dead is a popular one, working in jobs backed by a union still carries benefits for workers that are not matched in nonunion jobs.

The Environmental Movement

Assess current debates on climate change.

In 1962, biologist Rachel Carson published *Silent Spring*, which identified and highlighted the negative effects of pesticides on the environment and on human health. Carson's book spawned the modern environmental movement. Public attention shifted from land preservation and resource management, the predominant concerns of the conservation movement, to the effects of pollution and the environment on public health and quality of life.[99] Americans began to view their environment through the lenses of technology and its side effects—smog and petrochemicals such as plastics, solvents, pesticides, abrasives, and fuel additives—along with increases in environmentally triggered diseases. The public became cognizant of the toxins in waterways that killed fish, polychlorinated biphenyl in the Hudson River, high mercury levels in fish, and oil spills off the various coasts of the United States. This awareness pushed individuals to act, and the 1970s were a decade of intense environmental activity.

In 1969, Wisconsin Democratic Senator Gaylord Nelson announced that in spring 1970 there would be a national grassroots demonstration on the environment. Nelson wanted to push the issue of the environment, which had been building since 1962, onto the national agenda. On April 22, 1970, throngs of Americans celebrated the first Earth Day. The environmental movement tapped into the social activism swirling on college campuses from the civil rights and the anti–Vietnam War movements. As the environmental movement took hold, membership in older conservation organizations grew, as did the formation of new environmental organizations, such as the League of Conservation Voters, an organization dedicated to lobbying Congress for environmental legislation, in 1970.

The movement was successful in pushing the federal government to do more to protect the environment. Legislation included the Environmental Policy Act of 1970, the creation of the Environmental Protection Agency, the establishment of the Occupational Safety and Health Administration, and the Comprehensive Environmental Response, Compensation, and Liability Act, or "Superfund," to finance the cleaning-up of thousands of abandoned toxic waste sites around the country. Yet issues of race were also intimately intertwined with issues of the environment, and out of the environmental movement grew the environmental justice movement.

Environmental Racism

Intentional or unintentional racial discrimination in the enforcement of environmental laws and regulations and in the targeting of racial minority communities for the siting of pollution-producing industries or hazardous waste sites and other related environmentally hazardous entities.

Sociologist Robert Bullard is considered the "father of environmental justice," as his early research revealed that impoverished communities with high numbers of racial minorities disproportionately suffered from hazardous toxins in their neighborhood and workplaces. The situation of increased exposure to environmental hazards in Black rural and urban communities has been called **environmental racism**.

Bullard began his work in this area in the late 1970s, right after he had finished graduate school, when he was asked by his wife to collect data for a lawsuit filed against the city of Houston over its plans to locate a landfill in the middle of a predominantly Black, middle-class suburban neighborhood where 85 percent of the people owned their homes. Through his research, Bullard discovered that 100 percent of all the city-owned landfills in Houston were in Black neighborhoods, although Blacks were only 25 percent of the city's population.[100] His book *Dumping in Dixie: Race, Class, and Environmental Quality* (first published in 1990) grew out of his initial work in Houston.[101] Bullard was one of the organizers of the first National People of Color Environmental Leadership Summit in 1991, which developed the organizing principles for the environmental justice movement.

Despite early successes, the broader environmental movement suffered setbacks during the administrations of Ronald Reagan and George W. Bush. Industries and conservatives pushed back on environmental regulations, pushed to open federal lands to logging, and lobbied successfully to have national parks opened to snowmobiles. Funds were cut for enforcement of environmental laws and regulations, and questions were raised about the existence of global warming. Each of these decisions was aimed at retarding the federal government's efforts to protect or clean up the environment and, in some instances, allowed people, businesses, and industries to continue behaving in ways that contributed to the destruction of the environment. President Obama's administration has tried to roll back some of these Bush-era regulations, but he has run into resistance from Republican members of Congress. Congress continued to resist his environmental policies throughout the remainder of his term.

The Anti–Vietnam War Movement

The Vietnam War (1959–1975) was a nationalist struggle between forces in North Vietnam that wanted to unify the country under a communist regime and forces in South Vietnam, who, along with the United States, did not want that unification to occur. Vietnam had been a French colony for more than sixty years and tensions between the Vietnamese and French existed as a result. In 1945, the Viet Minh, the group that lead the struggle for independence from French colonialism, established a new government, calling it the Democratic Republic of Vietnam. The French, with military aid from the United States, fought against what amounted to independence for the French colony. The French were defeated at the battle of Dien Bien Phu in spring 1954 and pulled out of Vietnam.[102]

A convention in Geneva that same year partitioned the country into two governments—the Democratic Republic of Vietnam in the north (communist) and the Republic of Vietnam (anticommunist) in the south. The United States was concerned about a communist takeover of the entire country, so President Eisenhower sent in military advisors to assist the South Vietnamese in 1959, with President Kennedy increasing the number of advisors in 1961 and 1962 to 11,300 U.S. troops. Kennedy had planned to begin to withdraw the advisors, but his assassination brought Lyndon Johnson into the presidency and he, based on more optimistic military advice about a U.S. victory, increased the number of U.S. advisors to 21,000. Combat troops were committed in early 1965, rising from 3,500 to 184,000 by the end of 1965 and to 429,000 by the end of 1966.[103]

The first glimpse of opposition to U.S. involvement in Vietnam occurred in 1963 on a small number of college campuses in reaction to what was perceived as religious intolerance in Vietnam when Buddhist monks set themselves on fire in protest of the treatment of Buddhists by the South Vietnamese. Shortly after Johnson's inauguration in early 1965, the United States began bombing and moving troops into North Vietnam, and in response the antiwar movement began to take form. College students were concerned about increased draft call-ups as the number of ground troops in Vietnam increased and the differential draft deferments given to those seeking them. The first antiwar organization was the National Committee to End the War in Vietnam.[104] At first, this movement sought to change policy by educating the nation and its leaders in Washington. The first "teach-in" discussion about the merits of the war began in March, and a priority was put on explaining to the public and members of Congress the folly of beginning military engagement.[105]

On April 17, 1965, the recently formed student activist movement called Students for a Democratic Society, along with the SNCC, organized what was then the largest antiwar demonstration march in Washington, with 25,000 people attending. As the year progressed, more demonstrations occurred, with some attracting hundreds of thousands, even millions, of protesters.[106] Early protesters also expressed their discontent through the burning of draft cards. The practice caught on in the summer of 1965 and became such a popular form of protest that Congress passed, and President Johnson signed, a law making it a federal crime to willfully destroy one's card.[107]

As the antiwar movement grew in visibility and popularity, some celebrities took public antiwar stances and suffered severe consequences. In 1967, heavyweight champion Muhammad Ali, declaring himself a conscientious objector, refused three times to step forward when his name was called to be inducted into the military. He was arrested and later that year convicted. The public response to Ali's actions was largely negative, and he was stripped of his license to box in every state in the United States as well as his World Boxing Association title. These actions prevented him from fighting for more than three years until the Supreme Court unanimously overturned his conviction in 1971. At that time, the backlash against Blacks and other members of racial groups who opposed the war was swift and ferocious.[108]

One of the most well-known demonstrations occurred at the 1968 Democratic National Convention. When President Johnson decided not to run for reelection, his vice president, Hubert Humphrey, became the de facto front-runner. Senator Eugene McCarthy of Minnesota entered the race first on an antiwar platform, with Senator Robert F. Kennedy of New York entering later, also with an antiwar stance. Kennedy eclipsed McCarthy and was considered the most likely challenger to Humphrey for the nomination. Tragically, Kennedy was assassinated, and the nomination campaign culminated at the Democratic National Convention in Chicago, pitting Humphrey, again the front-runner, against McCarthy and Senator George McGovern of South Dakota, another opponent of the war.[109]

Meanwhile, several thousand members of the antiwar movement had converged on the city to protest the convention. Chicago Mayor Richard Daley had promised that law and order would be maintained. Demonstrators gathered in parks and in the streets to engage in various protest activities. The police used tear gas in an attempt to disband the crowds, and a major rally in Grant Park turned ugly when police resorted to violence and protesters responded in kind.[110] Several other confrontations between protesters and the Chicago police and Illinois National Guard occurred, with one conflict escalating into a massive brawl on Michigan Avenue that received extensive local and national coverage.[111] Humphrey gave his acceptance speech to an amphitheater full of Daley's patronage workers and loyalists, who chanted, "We want Daley; we want Daley," as the melee stormed outside.[112]

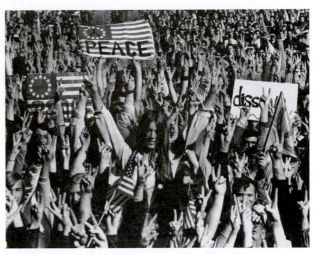

The biggest demonstration in Boston's history happened on Vietnam Moratorium Day as an estimated 100,000 persons shouted in cadence on Boston Common that they wanted the Vietnam War ended "Now!" The Moratorium to End the War in Vietnam was a peace rally held on the Boston Common, October 15, 1969.

For much of this period, the civil rights and antiwar movements were happening concurrently, but not in concert. At first, the issues appeared separate and the interests involved not necessarily aligned. As the movements matured, however, activists in both groups recognized that there was at least some degree of overlap between the goals of each group and that forging a common cause could be mutually beneficial.

Dr. Martin Luther King, Jr., the most visible leader of the Civil Rights Movement, was initially hesitant to speak in opposition to the war, for fear of alienating President Johnson. As the war developed, however, King began to express increasingly strong opposition. He first spoke out in a speech at Howard University in March 1965, claiming that the war was "accomplishing nothing" and calling for a negotiated settlement. Other mainstream civil rights groups followed suit shortly thereafter. The Mississippi Freedom Democratic Party, a political party organized primarily by Black Mississippians that challenged the seating of the all-White Mississippi delegation to the 1964 Democratic National Convention in Atlantic City, argued against Black participation in the war, citing as absurd the request for Blacks to risk their lives and to kill so that White Americans could get richer. SNCC adopted an antiwar stance, claiming that the government had been deceptive in the war effort, just as it had been in its concern for the freedom of minorities, both at home and abroad.[113]

Another argument for opposition to the war was that Black youths were disproportionately likely to be drafted and disproportionately likely to see combat. Deferment options allowed by the Selective Service favored middle- and upper-class men and male college students, who were generally more likely to be White.[114] As such, Blacks were carrying an overlarge share of the burden of the war on behalf of a country that would not fully recognize their rights.

In 1967, at New York's Riverside Church, Dr. King gave one of his most stirring speeches, arguing passionately against the war. King enumerated his reasons for advocating an end to U.S. involvement in Vietnam. He was dismayed at how the expense of the war drew funds away from the antipoverty programs started only a few years before, and he noted that such conflicts were a drain on the lives, productivity, and finances of the country. King made explicit the connection between the civil rights and peace movements.

Reaction to this speech was largely negative. The *New York Times* published an editorial claiming that the two problems of the war and of equality were separate and distinct, and that by addressing the war, King was diffusing the efforts of his movement, as well as undermining the appeal of the Civil Rights Movement to those not opposed to the war. Despite the backlash, King continued to participate in the antiwar movement until his assassination in 1968.

Compare liberties and poverty levels among nations.

Lesbian, Gay, Bisexual, Transgender, and Queer Movement

Social movements by lesbian, gay, bisexual, transgender, and queer (LGBTQ) people share the goal of social acceptance of homosexuality, bisexuality, and transgenderism. The communities have collaborated and worked separately to organize for gay liberation, lesbian feminism, the queer movement, and transgender activism. LGBTQ activists work through political and cultural avenues—organizing lobbying and street marches, support groups, community events, magazines, film, literature, academic research and writing, and business activity, for example—to challenge the dominance of heterosexual norms and constructions of femininity and masculinity and to combat homophobia. Political goals include extending civil and legal rights and protections.[115]

The LGBTQ movement dates back to the eighteenth and nineteenth centuries. In 1924, the Society for Human Rights was established in Chicago. This was the first recorded gay rights organization in the United States. The organization was founded by Henry Gerber, a World War I veteran, who had experienced relative freedom as a gay male in Europe. The organization disbanded soon after its founding because of a police raid of Gerber's home and the arrest of the small group of members of the organization. Although all charges were dropped, the raid doomed the organization. The modern movement was launched immediately following World War II with the word *homophile*, which emphasized love instead of sex.[116]

In 1950, The Mattachine Society, the first national gay rights organization, was formed in Los Angeles by Harry Ray and a group of his male friends. The Mattachine Society was an activist organization whose primary goal was to protect and improve the rights of homosexuals. The Daughters of Bilitis, a lesbian organization, was formed in San Francisco in 1956. The first lesbian civil rights and political rights organization in the United States, it was conceived as an alternative to lesbian bars, which were subjected to frequent raids and police harassment. In 1962, Illinois became the first U.S. state to decriminalize homosexual acts between consenting adults done in private. On July 4, 1965, picketers at Independence Hall in Philadelphia staged the first Reminder Day to call public attention to the lack of civil rights for LGBTQ people. The gatherings continued annually for five years.[117]

In 1966, gay bars were technically legal in New York, but the State Liquor Society had a regulation against serving LGBTQ people in bars because they were assumed to be disruptive. This refusal to serve gay people had no basis in law. As such, agents used their internal regulation to raid gay bars and other bars refused to serve gay individuals. On April 21, 1966, the Mattachine Society, drawing from the civil rights sit-ins, decided to stage a "sip-in"— several men would go into a bar, identify themselves as gay, then wait to be served or denied service and then file suit if denied service. On that day, three young men set out to test whether they would be served. The first set of bars they tried to enter had been tipped off and closed to avoid the protesters. At the next couple of restaurants, the group handed the waitress a note that said, "We are homosexuals. We believe that a place of public accommodation has

In April 1966, these men walked into Julius's, a local bar, and announced that they were gay; the bartender put his hand over the glass and refused to serve them.

an obligation to serve an orderly person, and that we are entitled to service as long as we are orderly." At both of these restaurants, they were served drinks. They then went to a bar called Julius', knowing that they would be denied service. They walked in, the bartender put glasses down, they announced that they were gay, and the bartender put his hand over the glass. The picture was captured by a photographer from *The Village Voice*. (In April 2016, Julius' marked the Sip-In's fiftieth anniversary.)[118]

Out of the gay liberation movement of the 1970s arose the gay rights movement, a reformist movement that sees gays and lesbians as a minority group demanding civil rights. On June 28, 1970, the first gay pride march was held a year after the Stonewall riots. The riots spurred this group into activism, and served, as mentioned earlier, as a catalyst for the modern phase of the movement. The marchers traveled up a single lane of traffic on New York's Sixth Avenue.

Lesbian feminism also arose in the 1970s to emphasize the male dominance of the LGBTQ movement. In the 1970s and 1980s, gay rights organizations proliferated throughout the United States. Prominent among them were the National Gay and Lesbian Task Force, the Human Rights Campaign, and ACT UP (AIDS Coalition to Unleash Power). The 1980s, in particular, launched a new era with the emergence of AIDS and the decimation of leaders. Gay activists were able to garner significant support from the Democratic Party, when the party added a nondiscrimination clause on sexual orientation to its platform in 1980. Additionally, campaigns urging gay men and women to "come out of the closet" (e.g., National Coming Out Day) were critical factors that enabled openly gay individuals to run for public office and work to promote gay rights.[119]

More militant groups focusing on direct action also emerged such as ACT UP (1987), Queer Nation (1990), and Lesbian Avengers (1992). "Queer" became the referential term for younger activists who saw "gay and lesbian" as too normatively and politically conservative; conversely, the acronym *LGBTQ* has also become a commonplace descriptor in an effort to unify the various communities.

Slowly, some members of mainstream civil rights groups began to see solidarity with the goals of the LGBTQ movement, albeit slowly. In 1998, Coretta Scott King, the widow of Martin Luther King, Jr., called on the civil rights community to join the struggle against homophobia. She received criticism from members of the Black Civil Rights Movement for comparing civil rights to gay rights. But in 2012 the NAACP came out in support of same-sex marriage, much to the consternation of some Black ministers.

Also in 1998, Matthew Shepard, a student at the University of Wyoming, was attacked and tortured near Laramie. He was lured from a bar by Aaron McKinney and Russell Henderson, taken to a remote site, beaten, and killed. Shepard was murdered because he was gay, and his death ignited demonstrations across the United States and highlighted hate crimes against LGBTQ individuals. Henderson pleaded guilty to murdering Shepard and is serving life in prison. McKinney was convicted of second-degree murder and felony robbery and kidnapping, which made him eligible for the death penalty.[120] McKinney was spared the death penalty when Shepard's parents asked the court to show mercy on McKinney, saying, "This is the time to begin the healing process, to show mercy to someone who refused to show any mercy." McKinney was sentenced to two consecutive life sentences.

In 2009, President Obama signed the Matthew Shepard and James Byrd Jr. Hate Crimes Prevention Act, named for Shepard and James Byrd, Jr., a Black man who was chained to a pickup truck in Jasper, Texas, and dragged to his death, also in 1998. It took more than a decade to get this legislation through Congress, but it was finally accomplished with support from more than three hundred national law enforcement, professional, education, civil rights, religious, and civic organizations and more than twenty-six state attorneys general. Among the organizations were the Gay and Lesbian Alliance Against Defamation, the Human Rights Campaign, the NAACP, the National Association of Latino Elected and Appointed Officials, the Sikh American Legal Defense and Education Fund, and the National Organization of Women, among others.[121] The champion within the U.S. Senate was the late Senator Edward M. Kennedy (D-MA) and among those pushing the legislation were the Gay and Lesbian Alliance Against Defamation and the Human Rights Campaign.

Support of civil unions and same-sex marriage began to gain strength in 2000, when Vermont became the first state to recognize civil unions between gay and lesbian couples and the Massachusetts Supreme Court ruled that only full marriage rights are consistent with the state constitution.[122]

Same-sex marriages became legal in Massachusetts in 2004. Nineteen states and the District of Columbia followed suit, making same-sex marriages legal. As this book goes to press, same-sex marriage is legal in thirty-two states and the District of Columbia. But court battles continue in those states with legislative and state constitutional prohibitions and in those states where the courts struck down restrictive legislation.

Successes for the movement continued to come with President Obama pushing Congress to repeal the "Don't Ask, Don't Tell" policy banning gay and lesbian soldiers from serving openly in the military in 2011. The policy came into being in 1993, when President Clinton tried to lift the ban. The compromise was that they could serve as long as they did not tell anyone or openly declare their sexual orientation. The lifting of the ban, a tremendous accomplishment, was followed in 2012 when President Obama declared his support for same-sex marriage. He had previously supported civil unions, but this was the first time he expressed his support for same-sex marriage. In his January 21, 2013, inaugural address, President Obama mentioned the gay rights movement and the Stonewall uprising, placing the rights of LGBTQ citizens in the forefront of the struggle for civil rights.

The public attitude toward issues related to LGBTQ issues is also changing, suggesting a more supportive environment for the goals of the LGBTQ movement. According to a 2014 report by the Williams Institute at the University

People in Asheville, North Carolina, protest the state's Public Facilities Privacy & Security Act, or HB2, that restricts the rights of those who are transgender.

of California Los Angeles, the shift in support is something that is not only due to younger generation's support, but they find that a "broader cultural shift affects people of all ages."[123] A 2018 Gallup poll showed that 67 percent of Americans, two-thirds or two out of three, now support same-sex marriage. What is interesting from their finding is that this is the highest level of support found by Gallup polls since they first asked the question in 1996.[124] In 1996, only 27 percent asked were in support, so the marked change within the last two decades is an important implication to consider.

In addition to a shifting tide in public opinion, the LGBTQ movement has had very important successes and challenges occur in recent years that has pushed the conversation forward in public discourse. The movement to gain legal recognition of same-sex marriages has become one of the most recent areas where LGBTQ rights is being pushed forward. In 2015, thirty-seven states had made same-sex marriage legal. This shifted to becoming legal nationally with the landmark case of *Obergefell v. Hodges*. June 26, 2015, served to be a historic day of victory for advocates and supporters of the LGBTQ movement. The court voted 5–4 in in the case of *Obergefell v. Hodges*.

In a 5–4 majority, led by Justice Anthony Kennedy, the Supreme Court ruled that the U.S. Constitution provided the right for same-sex couples to marry within the United States. In the Supreme Court's opinion, Justice Anthony M. Kennedy wrote for the majority. Justice Kennedy said, "No longer may this liberty be denied. . . . No union is more profound than marriage, for it embodies the highest ideals of love, fidelity, devotion, sacrifice and family. In forming a marital union, two people become something greater than once they were." Justice Kennedy argued that the plaintiffs in the case were seeking for "equal dignity in the eyes of the law."[125]

The decision came upon the second anniversary of the *United States v. Windsor* ruling, whereby the U.S. Supreme Court had struck down Section 3 of the Defense of Marriage Act (DOMA). This ruling, which had occurred in 2013, had previously denied federal recognition to same-sex marriages, and the striking-down of the law provided federal benefits to same-sex couples, in the same manner afforded heterosexual couples.[126]

While the 2015 ruling has served to be an important historic moment that has gained public support, as the 2018 public opinion polls highlight, challenges still persist. In the state of Alabama, for example, eleven counties refused to comply with the law at the time of the court decision.[127]

Beyond the recognition of same-sex marriage, additional challenges still remain for LGBTQ communities and advocates to address. In 2016, the state of North Carolina passed into law "House Bill 2." Better known as HB 2, it was passed into law by the Republican-dominated General Assembly in a special one-day session in March 2016. This law requires transgender people to utilize restrooms that correspond to the sex on their birth certificate.[128] Moreover, the legislation prevents cities from passing their own ordinances that would be more accommodating to the transgender people's accommodations and preferences.[129]

The passage of the law caused national uproar and calls for boycotts. Major musicians, including Bruce Springsteen, Demi Lovato, and the bands Pearl Jam and Maroon 5, canceled concerts in the state. Moreover, companies such as PayPal and Deutsche Bank USA announced they are canceling plans to expand within the state of North Carolina.[130] The NBA has also expressed serious concern and has been outspoken against the law. The 2017 All-Star Games were scheduled to occur in Charlotte, but since the passage of the law, the NBA moved the games to New Orleans.[131] The Atlantic Coast Conference (ACC) and the NCCA moved play-off and championship games out of North Carolina.

The Obama U.S. Department of Justice filed a lawsuit against the state, as have civil rights organizations including the ACLU and Equality North Carolina, among others. Then Attorney General Loretta Lynch said this has put the state of North Carolina in "direct opposition to federal laws prohibiting discrimination on the basis of sex and gender identity. More to the point, they created state-sponsored discrimination against transgender individuals who simply seek to engage in the most private of functions in a place of safety and security, a right taken for granted by most of us."[132]

According to a 2016 poll of North Carolina registered voters conducted by Elon University, 39 percent were in support of the state lawmakers allowing cities to pass transgender-friendly rules, and 49 percent of the population were in opposition to the HB 2 proposal.[133] The poll highlights how this issue had become divisive among registered voters in the state of North Carolina. In March 2017, the North Carolina legislature passed a compromise bill that repealed the portion of the legislation that dictated that individuals use restrooms based on their gender identification on their birth certificates, a win for the civil rights of transgender citizens of North Carolina. But, they left in place the provision that prohibited localities from passing antidiscrimination ordinances protecting LGBTQ individuals. Neither side was pleased with the compromise, but it allowed those organizations that had boycotted North Carolina, such as the NCAA and the NBA, to consider North Carolina as a site for sporting events.[134]

North Carolina is not the only state that has tried to push forward legislation that has disparate effect on LGBT communities. In the state of Mississippi, HB 1523 was signed into law, allowing court clerks the right to refuse wedding licenses to same-sex couples.[135] On July 1, 2016, Judge Carlton W. Reeves struck down that part of the law, reinforcing the Supreme Court ruling on same-sex marriage. Interestingly, Reeves is an African American judge, and tied the potential discrimination this law has back to the racist past of the state. Reeves also noted, "In physics, every action has its equal and opposite reaction. In politics, every action has its predictable overreaction. . . . The Supreme Court's same-sex marriage decision, *Obergefell v. Hodges*, has led to HB 1523. The next chapter of this back-and-forth has begun."[136]

Other Important U.S. Social Movements

The Chicano Civil Rights Movement

The Chicano civil rights movement, otherwise known as *"El Movimiento,"* extended the Mexican American civil rights movement, which began in the 1940s, to counteract negative stereotypes of Mexicans in mass media and culture; assert economic and political rights around the restoration of land grants, farm workers' rights, and voting; address discrimination; and cultivate an awareness of collective history. "Chicano" was originally a derogatory reference to migrants' children, who were seen by the culture at large as neither "American" nor "Mexican." Mexican Americans adopted the term in the 1960s as a symbol of ethnic pride and self-determination. Despite the emergence of national groups such as the American G. I. Forum and the Mexican American Legal Defense and Educational Fund (1968), the movement remained limited in scope and was focused on the Southwest region, and did not become pan-Hispanic.

The movement was influenced by the Black Civil Rights Movement both in the general activism the latter inspired and in the involvement of Chicano student leaders. Student organizers, concerned about the conservatism of the earlier Civil Rights Movement, created mass walkouts and sit-ins to call awareness to the movement. The 1964 "Crystal City Revolt," in which the Political Association of Spanish-Speaking Organizations was formed and collaborated with the predominantly Mexican American local chapter of the Teamsters Union, elected Mexican Americans over White candidates for the city council. In 1968, mass walkouts of high school students were organized in Denver and East Los Angeles. The Chicano movement's focus on local economic and political control generated solidarity and established Chicano institutions.[137]

Farm workers' rights became an important issue in the second half of the twentieth century, with one of the most prominent leaders being César E. Chávez, a notable Chicano national leader in the Civil Rights Movement. With Dolores Huerta, he cofounded the United Farm Workers Movement, which galvanized a lot of attention around farm workers' rights, with activism occurring as early as 1957 well into the 1980s. The movement helped generate the creation of such present-day Latino organizations as the National Council of La Raza (NCLR) and the Mexican American Legal Defense and Educational Fund (MALDEF).

American Indian Movement

American Indians, after a seventy-year hiatus following the Wounded Knee massacre of 1890, started agitating for greater political, cultural, and economic rights in the 1960s and 1970s.[138] American Indians did not receive U.S. citizenship until 1924 and did not gain suffrage until the Voting Rights Act of 1965. The American Indian Religious Freedom Act (1978) was vital in securing religious rights, and American Indians continued to press for other rights, including those concerning tribal sovereignty, hunting and fishing, travel, and land.

Dennis Banks, George Mitchell, Herb Powless, Clyde Bellecourt, Eddie Benton-Banai, and others founded the American Indian Movement (AIM), an activist organization modeled on Black protest groups, in 1968. AIM organized several mass demonstrations in the 1970s to call attention to the American Indian plight, including the takeover of the Bureau of Indian Affairs (1972), the occupation of Wounded Knee on the Pine Ridge reservation (1973), and the Longest Walk (1978) from San Francisco to Washington, DC.

AIM and other groups continue to advocate for American Indian interests, renew their diverse heritages, assist in urban and rural employment programs, and monitor police activity. They are also involved in fighting symbolic degradation or marginalization of American Indians by protesting national holidays such as Thanksgiving or Columbus Day. In 2007, a delegation of Lakota Sioux declared secession from the United States, citing broken treaties and loss of territory. The group declared its intention to the State Department to form a separate nation, the Republic of Lakotah.

Asian American Movement

The Black Civil Rights Movement inspired student leadership and activism on several fronts, and Asian Americans were one such minority group that walked this path. Although each ethnic group had litigated, organized, and participated politically when able and necessary, a national panethnic coalition had not transpired. The Civil Rights Movement intensified awareness about racism and discrimination. Like the Black Civil Rights Movement, the Asian American movement developed from local actions. In 1968, Chinese Americans in San Francisco organized to get the city government to pay attention to the problems in Chinatown. They eventually organized a protest march down Grant Avenue, the main street that runs through Chinatown.

In 1968 and 1969, Asian American college students at San Francisco State and the University of California–Berkeley expressed their displeasure with their treatment at the institutions. The anti–Vietnam War movement, particularly prevalent on college campuses, placed middle-class Asian Americans in a unique position to consider the cultural, political, and military implications of being "Asian" and the racial implications of U.S. military policy.[139]

A number of organizations grew out of this movement, such as the Asian American Legal Defense Fund and Asian Americans Advancing Justice (AAJC). These groups represent Asian American interests at the national level. At present, Asian American groups are tackling issues such as equitable wages for immigrant workers, language access programs for voting rights, and post-9/11 civil liberties.

The Antinuclear Movement

Opponents of nuclear technology and power have been active since the 1960s in organizing against nuclear technology, the use of depleted uranium in warfare, and the practice of food irradiation or radiation. The environmental movement's emergence and the use of atomic weapons in Japan during World War II coalesced with a cultural suspicion of technology and radioactivity.

At one point, there were fifty loosely affiliated grassroots antinuclear organizations in the United States. These organizations and individual activists engage in public education via the Internet, demonstrations, and concerts; in nonviolent direct action such as demonstrations, picketing, or blockages; or in violent confrontation through sabotage or demonstrations. Campaigns involving the Calvert Cliffs Nuclear Power Plant, Seabrook Station Nuclear Power Plant, Diablo Canyon Power Plant, Shoreham Nuclear Power Plant, and Three Mile Island captured public attention in the 1970s. The movement has also been successful in delaying construction or stopping commitments to build new nuclear plants. Concerned with nuclear accidents and waste, activists advocate nuclear-free energy alternatives such as biomass, wind and solar power, and geothermal power.[140]

The movement includes not only grassroots organization but also scientists, including Nobel laureates such as Linus Pauling and Hermann Joseph Muller. The Committee for Nuclear Responsibility, the Federation of American Scientists, and the Union of Concerned Scientists are notable national organizations that have been very influential in advocating for this issue.

Religious Fundamentalist Movement

In the United States, Christian fundamentalism is rooted in the Niagara Bible Conference (1878–1897), which sought to define the fundamentals of belief. The movement quickly moved beyond the conservative Presbyterian academics and theologians who originated the movement to other denominations such as the Baptists. The original meaning of fundamentalism has changed over time, and it is now associated with a particular segment of evangelical Protestantism that looks to separate and distance itself from modernity and modern culture. Yet, there are variants of fundamentalism that see one way of distancing themselves from modernity and modern culture is to participate in politics to assert their views and influence government in their direction.[141]

Rob Grant and Jerry Falwell are among the fundamentalist clergy who advocated Christian intervention in U.S. politics in the 1970s. Now known as the Christian Right, religious fundamentalists have been instrumental in shaping policy and determining elections through organizations such as the Christian Coalition and the Family Research Council. By the mid-1990s, the Republican Party had gained control of the White House, Congress, and some seats on the Supreme Court, through the activism of the Christian Right.

Recently, the Religious Right has focused on preventing the passage of same-sex marriage legislation as part of their agenda. In February 2014, they pushed forward a bill in Arizona to give restaurants the right to refuse service to gay couples; the legislation passed with a 33–27 vote. Jan Brewer, the governor of Arizona, vetoed the bill.

Why Some Social Movements Decline and Some Fail

Social movements are not permanent entities. They arise out of specific conditions and even successful movements find it difficult to sustain themselves over time. Moreover, some movements that have a major presence in society might fail in their efforts to bring about change. A number of factors account for both outcomes.

Factors That Contribute to Social Movement Decline

Social movements do not go on forever and the reasons for their decline are varied. Some social movements decline because members have difficulty maintaining a commitment to the movement over long periods of time. Activists who have worked hard for a long time may grow weary and believe that it is time for others to take the lead. Sometimes a new generation of leaders is not available or their view of the goals of the movement might be different from those of the previous generation.

Another factor that contributes to the decline of social movements is **factionalism**, divisions that develop within the movement. Participants in social movements might disagree about goals and strategies for achieving those goals. During the early years of the Civil Rights Movement, participants generally adhered to tactics of nonviolent civil disobedience and recognized that progress might be slow. By the late 1960s, however, some participants, especially college students, felt progress was too slow and that nonviolent methods were no longer effective. More militant groups emerged, such as the SNCC and the Black Panthers, as part of the Black Power movement, to press for faster action and more radical tactics. Black Power advocates argued for separation from Whites rather than integration, which was the goal of older civil rights organizations. The gulf between the newer and older groups was

Factionalism Divisions that develop within a movement that may weaken it or cause its demise.

too great to be repaired and the factionalism severely affected the ability of the CRM to remain unified.

Changes in public opinion can also contribute to the decline of social movements. A supportive environment is important not only for the development of a social movement, but for the maintenance of a movement as well. The public might begin to feel that the movement's grievances have all been addressed or solved and thus is no longer receptive to the continued or further demands. This change in public opinion might signal that issues related to the movement's goals no longer have the support of the majority of the public. When a social movement begins to lose favorable public opinion, the movement can begin to decline. The ability of the CRM to continue pushing for Black advancement was affected by the shift in public opinion on the importance of civil rights as the most important issue facing the country. In January 1965, 52 percent of Americans saw race relations as the most important issue, but by January 1967 close to 55 percent saw the war in Vietnam as the most important issue.[142]

Sometimes social movements generate counter-movements that organize in opposition to the goals and objectives of the social movement. Counter-movements can be very effective in working against the ideals of the social movement. A good example is the organization of the major tobacco companies—Philip Morris, R. J. Reynolds, Brown and Williamson, American Tobacco, and Lorillard—to unsuccessfully fight the antismoking movement's success in banning smoking in workplaces in California.[143]

Success itself may contribute to the decline of a social movement. Once a social movement has achieved its objectives, some participants might feel that there is nothing left to do. For example, once the war in Vietnam ended, the antiwar movement dissolved. The main issue around which the movement arose no longer existed.

Factors That Contribute to Social Movement Failure

Not all social movements succeed. First, a social movement might fail if its goals are too broad or unrealistic. Social movements with limited objectives have a higher probability of success than those whose goals are very broad and not well defined, such as the early 1900s goal of the International Workers of the World (the Wobblies) to restructure the entire U.S. government. That objective was clearly impossible to achieve.

Second, the inability to organize effectively is another contributor to failure. Groups seeking policy changes within existing political structures must organize to negotiate with the political system.[144] Failure to organize doomed the poor people's campaign in 1968.

Third, suppression, the use of physical, legal, and violent force against a social movement, might lead to failure. For example, in the late nineteenth century large corporations fought labor unions' efforts to unionize employees, and in many instances the struggles between the unions and corporations involved considerable violence. One example is the violent struggle between the

Amalgamated Association of Iron and Steel Workers, an AFL affiliate, and the steel industry, especially steel baron Andrew Carnegie, in 1892.[145] Carnegie hired a private army from the Pinkerton Company that, with the help of 6,000 federal and state troops, violently put down the strike and left ten dead.[146]

Historically, more social movements probably fail than succeed. Yet failure to achieve social movement goals does not mean that participants did not take away valuable lessons from the experience. Movement participants can learn from their mistakes and bring increased knowledge and experience to other social movements. Failed social movements can also raise issues that American society will focus on in the future.

The populist movement and its resultant Populist Party of the 1890s were not successful in changing public policy at the time, but later, during the Progressive Era (1900–1916), many of their goals were achieved. These achievements included the adoption of the Australia ballot (or secret ballot) system, enforcement of the eight-hour workday, introduction of initiative and referendum techniques (forms of legislative input from the electorate), and direct election of U.S. senators.

As a more recent example, in 1968 the SCLC had planned to erect a tent city, Resurrection City, on the mall in Washington, DC, to house Black, White, American Indian, and Latino poor. Residents of Resurrection City were to demonstrate daily to focus attention on the plight of the poor in the United States. The assassination of Martin Luther King, Jr. in April of that year threw the SCLC and the Civil Rights Movement in general into turmoil. Despite King's death, the SCLC decided to move forward with the poor people's campaign.

Looking west, people fill Pennsylvania Avenue during the "March for Our Lives" rally in support of gun control, on March 24, 2018, in Washington, DC.

Resurrection City was muddy from rain, its inadequate sanitation facilities created an unhealthy environment, and those leading the campaign did not possess the necessary leadership and organization skills. The result was failure of the movement.

Social movements spring from a variety of sources, often from grievances by groups that have been excluded from the political process. Social movements are important to democracy because they push the system to be more responsive to the needs of a portion of its citizens. Social movement activity also enriches democracy because, in some instances, it brings people into the system and expands participation. Social movement activity, however, is not easy, and those who participate can suffer financially and, sometimes, physically. Both successful and failed social movements contribute to and strengthen democracy by changing public policies and opening up the system to individuals previously excluded.

Social Movement or Political Activism?

As you have seen, social movements are difficult to launch and even harder to sustain. Many span decades of activity from multitudes of people, and for some, the loss of life before seeing any glimmer of success. Some people assume that if people organize and hold large rallies or even support candidates, this constitutes a social movement. As you can see from this chapter, social movements are more than rallies and support for candidates. Three recent groups, March for Our Lives, Black Lives Matter, and the Tea Party, are organizations of people who are politically active, but do not constitute social movements as discussed in this chapter. Only time will tell if they grow into new social movements.

March for Our Lives

March for Our Lives is a student-led movement in support of gun legislation reform in the United States, specifically stricter gun laws throughout the country. The main demonstration took place on March 24, 2018, in Washington DC, with more than 700 sister protests nationwide as part of a wave of activism to address the scourge of gun violence.[147] According to a report in the *New York Times*, a team of crowd science researchers led by a professor at Manchester Metropolitan University in England estimated that about 180,000 people attended the March for Our Lives rally in Washington, DC.[148] In total, there were over 800 similar protests around the world in places like Argentina, Chile, Colombia, Costa Rica, Finland, Ghana, India, Japan, and Spain, with hundreds of thousands of demonstrators marching in public protests calling for decisive action against gun violence.[149]

The March for Our Lives movement emerged after the Marjory Stoneman Douglas High School massacre in Parkland, Florida, in which 17 people were fatally shot and 17 others were wounded by a former student on February 14, 2018. The death toll in the Stoneman Douglas shooting surpassed the 1999

Columbine High School massacre, making it the deadliest high school shooting in American history.[150] The 2007 massacre at Virginia Tech in Blacksburg, Virginia, in which 32 people were killed and 17 injured by a student, is the deadliest school shooting overall in U.S. history. In 2012, the mass shooting at the Sandy Hook Elementary School in Newtown, Connecticut, resulted in the deaths of 20 children and six teachers.[151]

Student organizers from Never Again MSD planned March for Our Lives with support from the American nonprofit organization Everytown for Gun Safety, which advocates for gun control and works actively to institute measures that will help to prevent gun violence. Everytown for Gun Safety was founded—and is financially backed—by Michael Bloomberg, an American businessman who was the mayor of New York City from 2002 to 2013. The organization tracks school shootings nationwide.[152] Never Again MSD is a student-led gun control organization that advocates for stricter gun ownership regulations to prevent gun violence. The group was formed by twenty current students of Marjory Stoneman Douglas High School in the aftermath of the deadly shooting at their school. The students started a social media campaign that they labeled with the hashtag #NeverAgain, explaining that their main goal was to influence the 2018 midterm elections.[153] The student organizers also held town hall meetings across the United States on April 7, in an effort to hold Congressional representatives accountable for their individual positions on gun laws.[154]

President Trump and gun rights activists have accused the student organizers of March for Our Lives of having political motives and alleged that the student organizers are trying to repeal the Second Amendment. The student activists have strongly denied this accusation, even releasing a statement to address the claims made against the movement: "March for Our Lives' position is not to repeal the Second Amendment, but to effectively address the gun violence issues that our rampant in our country."[155]

Black Lives Matter

The Black Lives Matter movement began in 2012, after the death of seventeen-year-old Trayvon Martin.[156] The suspect, George Zimmerman, was recorded and verified for having shot Trayvon, but said he had done so under Florida's "Stand Your Ground" law.[157] Extensive discussion occurred about the racial profiling of a young Black teenager. Zimmerman went to trial and was acquitted. Trayvon's death and the release of the suspect created national uproar as individuals perceived that justice was not served in the death of Trayvon.[158]

Patrisse Cullors, Opal Tometi, and Alicia Garza, three community organizers, began discussing whether Black lives matter.[159] Cullors developed the hashtag #BlackLivesMatter, in an effort to assert that there should be accountability when unarmed African Americans are murdered. These three organizers began a national conversation via social media on the disparate effect of violence toward Black Americans, particularly at the hands of law enforcement.[160] As the deaths of unarmed Black Americans continued, the movement began to gain national popularity. The death of Michael Brown in Ferguson, Missouri, on August 9, 2014, became an important moment for the movement.[161] The movement began to include more vocal leaders, including DeRay Mckesson, a public school administrator who became a vocal activist within the movement, providing strong critique of the police response that occurred within Ferguson. Protest demonstrations began increasing, as more deaths at the hands of the police continued with the high-profile case of the death of Freddie Gray in Baltimore and Sandra Bland in Texas. Within the one-year span of August 2014 to 2015, over 950 protest demonstrations occurred nationwide.[162]

The movement's influence has two points that need to be kept in mind. One, the founders of the movement include members of the Black American community that are typically within the margins, providing a strong platform for queer Black women, and members of the African American community from other marginalized communities—such as undocumented people, the working poor, and agnostics and atheists. They emphasize that the struggle is meant to include and uplift traditionally marginalized experiences. In a magazine interview, co-founder Opal Tometi emphasized, "It's not just about Black heterosexual lives. . . . It's about all Black lives."[163]

Second, this is not just a national movement, but has spread internationally, with chapters now in Canada and Ghana. In Canada, activists in Toronto shut down a major highway to protest the death of two Black Canadians at the hands of police.[164] Additional international campaigns included the #Palestine2Ferguson campaign, where protestors in Ferguson began a conversation with Palestinians residing in Gaza, later resulting in an international convening between organizers in Ferguson with activists in Gaza.[165]

In addition to protesting the death of unarmed Black men and women, Black Lives Matter activists have utilized nonviolent protest mechanisms to bring issue to police brutality by protesting Black Friday and organizing protest movements during the 2015–2016 campaign cycle.[166] They brought attention to the 2016 Democratic campaign process, pressuring Bernie Sanders and Hillary Clinton, as the majority of Black American voters vote for the Democratic ticket. They have utilized different tactics at specific campaign rallies as a means to ensure that the Black vote is not taken for granted by the Democratic Party. As a result of these efforts, both Sanders and Clinton have incorporated more conversations around the issues that Black Lives Matter is pointing out. The movement decided not to endorse any presidential candidate for the elections, but sought to continue holding individuals within government accountable through their organizing strategies. Events during the summer of 2016—the police shootings of Alton Sterling in Baton Rouge, Louisiana, and Philando Castile in Minneapolis, Minnesota, and the shooting death of five police officers in Dallas by a lone Black Army veteran shooter after a peaceful march to protest the deaths of Sterling and Castile—have raised the issue of police killing of Black men and support for police officers front and center. We will see if the two sides are able to find common ground moving forward. Killings in 2018, like that of Stephon Clark by the Sacramento Police in the backyard of his grandmother's house, have kept Black Lives Matter in the fore-front of activism against the violence against Blacks, especially Black men. Yet, at this point, Black Lives Matter is an activist group, not a social movement.

Tea Party

The origins of the Tea Party are in dispute. One view is that the Tea Party began in 2009 in protest of the economic stimulus package and bank bail-out that was implemented by President Obama's administration.[167] According to Goldstein, "The Tea Party is a nationalist movement that uses originalist rhetoric to advance a narrow conception of what America is, what ideas are American, and who is truly American."[168] Tea Party supporters believe that the fundamental values on which America was founded—limited government, free market, and libertarian principles of individualism—are embodied in the Constitution. "The Tea Party movement's constitutional rhetoric is built around a narrative of the golden age of the nation's founding, in which the nation's fundamental principles were established fully formed and eternal by the Founders and embodied in the Constitution."[169] In February 2009, Keli Carendar, a blogger, organized a protest in Seattle, Washington. This protest is considered to be the first Tea Party–type protest.[170] That same month, CNBC Business News editor Rick Santelli made mention of the existence of a Tea Party movement in the United States in a rant against President Obama sign-ing the $787 billion stimulus bill into law. Also in February, the Nationwide Tea Party Coalition held a conference call with conservative activists to plan a series of protests, which occurred on February 27 with thousands of demon-strators protesting in fifty-one cities.[171]

Another view is that it is not a grassroots-organized protest activity, but an example of corporate "astroturfing"—defined as a movement that "appears to be grassroots, but is either funded, created, or conceived by a corporation or industry trade association, political interest group or public relations firm."[172] A 2013 study found that national organizations funded by corporations, for example, Americans for Prosperity and FreedomWorks, played pivotal roles in structuring, organizing, and supporting the Tea Party in its early stages. These organizations provided training, communication, and materials for the earli-est Tea Party activities, including the February 27, 2009, demonstrations. The study identifies that Americans for Prosperity and FreedomWorks have their origins in the tobacco industries' organization of smokers' rights groups in the 1980s to fight control of tobacco. Citizens for a Sound Economy, a Koch Industry–funded group organized in 1984, split into Americans for Prosper-ity and FreedomWorks in 2004. Koch Industry and other companies created these third-party groups for decades and Tea Party strategy and leadership came out of these groups.[173] If this second view is accurate, then the origins of the groups would not be in keeping with the theory of how social move-ments arise.

Regardless of which history of the origins of the Tea Party is correct, the fact is that it has been extremely active in the electoral politics arenas. Supporters of the Tea Party had "vowed to purge the Republican Party of officials they [considered to be] not sufficiently conservative and to block the Democratic agenda on the economy, the environment, and health care."[174] Their activities have had a profound effect on the internal politics of the Republican Party, and on the electoral fortunes of the Democratic Party in the 2010 midterm elections. Their influence in the 2012 presidential elections was considerably less than in 2010 and the question has been raised as to whether it is on the decline. There are varying views about the long-term sustainability of the Tea Party, as prominent candidates that ran for office in 2012, from Alaska to Indiana to Delaware, failed to win primaries and elections, and, in 2014, many of the Tea Party candidates lost in Republican primaries. Nevertheless, six Tea Party candidates won open senate seats—Dan Sullivan (Alaska), Tom Cotton (Arkansas), Cory Gardner (Colorado), Joni Ernst (Iowa), Steve Daines (South Dakota), and Ben Sasse (Nebraska)—which was a major accomplishment.

In the 2016 Republican presidential primary, of the seventeen contenders, six—Senators Ted Cruz, Rand Paul and Marco Rubio, former Senator Rick Santorum, and former Governors Rick Perry and Mike Huckabee—were considered Tea Party candidates. Of the six, only Cruz, Paul, and Rubio were considered serious contenders. In the end, only Cruz's campaign survived to the end of the primary season, but lost out to Donald Trump, who became the Republican presidential nominee. Many of the Tea Party candidates that challenged Republican incumbents or vied for open seats lost. For example, in Indiana, the Republican establishment candidate, Todd Young, overwhelmingly bested Tea Party candidate Marlin Stuztman for the Republican nomination for an open Senate seat. Speaker of the House Paul Ryan drew a Tea Party challenger, but easily won his primary contest. By the 2018 midterm elections, almost half of the 87 House of Representatives members elected in 2010 were no longer in Congress. Time will tell if the Tea Party's influence is on the demise, particularly with the unlikely rise of Trump as the GOP 2016 presidential nominee and his election as president, but what is not in dispute is that the Tea Party is not a social movement, but a politically active collective of individuals.

Conclusion

This chapter has explored the important phenomenon of social movements. Social movements spring from a variety of sources, often from grievances by groups that have been excluded from the political process. Social movements are important to democracy because they push the system to be more responsive to the needs of a portion of its citizens. Social-movement activity also enriches democracy because, in some instances, it brings people into the system and expands participation. But social movement activity is not easy, and those who participate often suffer, financially and sometimes physically.

Both successful and failed social movements contribute to and strengthen democracy by raising issues that are then debated in the political arena.

We have explored several successful social movements and the positive effects they have had in bringing previously excluded groups into the political life of the United States. Each of these movements used different tactics to achieve their results, and for many the results were achieved over long periods of time. Yet not all social movement activity makes positive contributions to democratic systems. Those social movements that intend to deprive some citizens of their rights and that use domestic terrorism to push their agenda act contrary to the principles of representative government. Nevertheless, the strength of the American government system is such that these social movements have little effect on its overall structure.

When Barbara Rose Johns stood at the lectern in her segregated high school in Farmville, Virginia, in 1951 and led a boycott against the unequal conditions Blacks experienced under segregation, she and others involved in what became known as the Civil Rights Movement opened the door and laid the path for the election of former Senator Barack Obama to the presidency. Without the CRM pushing open the doors of access to millions of Black Americans and knocking down barriers to political participation for Blacks, as well as other disenfranchised groups, Obama's successful campaign for the highest office in the United States would not have been possible.

In fact, the election of President Obama in 2008 and his reelection in 2012 saw the participation of several historical social movements in his victory—labor, women, and Blacks and Latinos. Even though young voters, particularly Black young voters, were mobilized in support of his candidacy, as is clear from the discussion in this chapter, their mobilization does not fit the definition of a social movement. But their mobilization, combined with the mobilization of several historical social movements, propelled him to victory. In a sense, President Obama is a product of a number of America's successful social movements.

Hillary Clinton's nomination as the first woman presidential candidate for one of the two major political parties is also a product of the waves of the women's movement, as well as other historical social movements. Unfortunately, Hillary Clinton was not successful in being elected the first female President of the United States. Her election, like that of President Obama, would be the product of a number of successful social movements and would have been a major prize for the various waves of the women's movement.

Most of the social movements discussed have waned or are weakened as they have had success and achieved their goals. But the LGBTQ movement is still pushing forward and gaining steam. Its struggle, like those of other social movements, has taken place over decades and it is possible that it still has decades of struggle ahead before it achieves all of its objectives. But, like other movements, time is on its side and the American public is moving in its direction.

Check your understanding of Chapter 12.

review
REVIEW QUESTIONS

1. What is a social movement, and why are social movements important in general? Why are social movements important to democracies?

2. What conditions give rise to social movements?

3. What are the similarities among the successful social movements discussed in this chapter?

4. What role does a supportive environment play in the success or failure of social movements?

5. Why do social movements fail?

Flashcard review.

terms
KEY TERMS

Catalyst p. 359
Catalytic Leadership p. 359
Environmental
    Racism p. 380
Factionalism p. 393
Jim Crow Laws p. 363

Lynching p. 364
Shared Grievances p. 358
Social Movement p. 357
Southern Christian
Leadership
    Conference (SCLC) p. 365

Student Non-Violent
    Coordinating
    Committee (SNCC) p. 366
Supportive
Environment p. 358
White Citizens' Council p. 365

Need to review key ideas in greater depth? Click here.

readings
ADDITIONAL READINGS

Banaszak, L. A. (1996). *Why movements succeed or fail: Opportunity, culture, and the struggle for woman suffrage*. Princeton, NJ: Princeton University Press.

This is a comparison of the movement for women's suffrage in the United States and in Switzerland.

Dulles, F. R., & Dubofsky, M. (2004). *Labor in America: A history* (7th ed.). Arlington Heights, IL: Harlan Davidson.

This history of labor in the United States focuses on organization, leaders, and strikes, but is also a good general history of the labor movement.

Euchner, C. C. (1996). *Extraordinary politics: How protest and dissent are changing American democracy*. Boulder, CO: Westview Press.

This book is a study of the effect of American social movements on the structures of government.

Tarrow, S. (2011). *Power in movement: Social movements and contentious politics* (3rd ed.). Cambridge, UK: Cambridge University Press.

This is a good summary of the resource mobilization and cultural interpretations approaches to the study of social movements.

Weisbrot, R. (1990). *Freedom bound: A history of America's Civil Rights Movement*. New York: Norton.

This book covers the origins of the Civil Rights Movement and highlights the peak years of the struggle for racial equality.

Goodwin, J., & Jasper, J. M. (Eds.). (2009). *The social movements reader: Cases and concepts*. Oxford, UK: Wiley.

This edited book includes essays on various aspects of social movements from their origins, their organization, who participates, why people drop out, and case studies of several social movements.

Interest Groups: Good Outcomes with Few Resources

Attorneys Shereef Akeel (left), Gadeir Abbas (center), and Lena F. Masri (right) stand as Council on American-Islamic Relations (CAIR) national executive director Nihad Awad speaks during a news conference, January 30, 2017, in Washington. The group announced the filing of a federal lawsuit on behalf of more than twenty individuals challenging an executive order signed by President Donald Trump.

Hate crimes against Muslims in the United States have been on the rise in recent years.[1] In March 2017, a Muslim family's restaurant in Wichita, Kansas, was burned down, and the two words painted in bold black letters on the wall of a storage unit behind the restaurant—"Go Back"—led the owners (who are originally from Syria but have lived in the United States for many years) to believe the incident was a hate crime.[2] In June 2017, a Muslim man dressed in traditional clothing was violently attacked outside an electronic store in Bronx, New York.[3]

A November 2017 report from the Southern Poverty Law Center attributed some of the increase in anti-Muslim rhetoric and violence in the United States to President Donald Trump, contending that "President Trump has energized the radical right with his xenophobic rhetoric and has given bigots a license to act on their worst instincts."[4] In 2017, the number of hate crimes targeting Muslim Americans rose again by 15 percent, with a total of total of 300 recorded hate crimes, according to a study released by the Council on American-Islamic Relations (CAIR).[5] CAIR is an Islamic advocacy group that is headquartered in Washington, DC, and also has regional offices throughout the United States. CAIR's mission is "to enhance understanding of Islam, protect civil rights, promote justice, and empower American Muslims."[6]

Along with CAIR, other Muslim advocacy groups in the United States, including the Muslim Public Affairs Council, Muslim Advocates, the Muslim Legal Fund of America (MLFA), Muslims for Progressive Values (MPV), the American-Arab Anti-Discrimination Committee (ADC), and the Islamic Networks Group (ING) have been working to ensure that the civil rights of Muslim-Americans are not violated and fighting against anti-Muslim prejudice and discrimination.[7] While CAIR has partly attributed the increase in hate crimes against Muslim Americans to anti-Islamic rhetoric from President Trump, as well as Trump administration policies that restrict immigration from majority-Muslim nations, the White House denies these claims, stating: "the Trump Administration stands for the rule of law and abhors all forms of lawlessness including hate crimes."[8]

intro *Groups like the CAIR, Muslim Public Affairs Council, Muslim Advocates, the Muslim Legal Fund of America, Muslims for Progressive Values, the American-Arab Anti-Discrimination Committee, and the Islamic Networks Group take on issues and practices that disadvantage and discriminate against Muslim Americans. These groups also provide a counter-narrative of American Muslims to the one presented by Donald Trump and other members of his administration, such as Secretary of State Mike Pompeo when he was in Congress, John Bolton before he was appointed National Security Advisor, and Stephen Miller, Trump's policy advisor and the architect of the Muslim travel ban. The ability of interest groups to initiate action is significant and important. Interest groups are players in American politics and can wield a great deal of influence in policymaking at all levels of government—local, state, and national.*

This chapter explores the role of interest groups in American politics. It examines not only the role of interest groups in general, but also the role of interest groups whose agendas and activities focus on non-White populations or whose membership consists primarily of various non-White groups. We begin by exploring interest groups—what they are, what they do, and the influence they wield. We look at interest groups through the theoretical lens of pluralism because it views the political system as a competition among groups. We then discuss the various types of interest groups, their strategies, and why some interest groups are successful. Moreover, we discuss the significance of interest groups to the politics and policy preferences of Black Americans and other racial and ethnic groups.

Interest Groups and Their Functions

Interest groups (also known as pressure groups) are private (i.e., nongovernment) organizations whose members act together to influence public policy to promote their interests. These groups act as intermediaries, representing the public's and private group's interests and preferences to policymakers at all levels of government—federal, state, and local—with the intent of influencing decisions on public policy.[9] The members of interest groups can be individuals or institutions, such as corporations, nonprofit groups, or associations. What binds members of interest groups together is a common interest, which might be an economic issue, a social issue, or a particular policy issue.

For example, the NAACP is concerned with civil rights issues for African Americans, but it takes up issues related to other non-White groups as well. It was founded in 1909 by sixty Blacks and Whites partly in response to the continued and increasing practice of lynching and the 1908 race riots in Springfield, Illinois. Among those who founded the NAACP were W. E. B. Du Bois, Ida B. Wells-Barnett, Mary Church Terrell, and Oswald Garrison Villard (see "Our Voices: Ida B. Wells-Barnett").[10]

The National Urban League, originally named the Committee on Urban Conditions among Negroes, founded in 1910, grew out of concerns for the

Interest Groups Organizations whose members act together to influence public policy to promote their common interests (also known as pressure groups).

new Black migrants from the South moving into the urban areas of the North in the early 1900s. The organization was spearheaded by a White woman, Ruth Standish Baldwin, a wealthy widow with a strong social conscience, and a Black man, Dr. George Edmund Haynes, a graduate of Fisk University, who became the organization's first executive secretary. In 1911, the National League on the Urban Conditions among Negroes was created through the merger of the committee with the Committee for the Improvement of Industrial Conditions among Negroes in New York (founded in New York in 1906) and the National League for the Protection of Colored Women (founded in 1905). In 1920, the name was shortened to the National Urban League.[11]

Interest groups are not the same as social movements. The latter arise from specific circumstances that galvanize people to action to pressure government to make changes. Many of these movements are short-lived, and no permanent organization emerges. Some successful social movements, however, have led to the formation of interest groups. For example, the American Federation of Labor–Congress of Industrial Organizations, a labor union, evolved into an interest group for labor interests, and the women's rights movement generated the National Organization for Women (NOW).

A Group-Based View of American Politics

James Madison envisioned the United States as a society in which conflict, rather than consensus, would predominate. In *Federalist No. 10*, he warned that the United States would be subject to the development of factions. For Madison, a faction was a number of citizens united by some common impulse or passion that might adversely affect the rights of other citizens or the interests of the larger community.[12] He believed that the most common and durable sources of factions were economic differences among people. Madison explained, "Those who hold and those who are without property have ever formed distinct interests in society. Those who are creditors, and those who are debtors, fall under a like discrimination. A landed interest, a manufacturing interest, a mercantile interest, a moneyed interest, with many lesser interests, grow up of necessity in civilized nations, and divide them into different classes, actuated by different sentiments and views."[13]

Pluralism A theory of politics that contends that power is group based and that, because there are multiple points of access within American government, each group possesses an equality of opportunity when competing with other groups for power and resources (also known as interest-group theory).

Madison saw these factions as potential dangers for democracy if they gained too much political power. But Madison also believed that because individuals would have numerous interests and move in and out of factions, no one faction would dominate and control political outcomes. In political science, this view of American politics as dominated by interest groups is called *pluralism*, or interest-group theory.

Pluralism

Pluralism, or interest-group theory, is a theory of politics that contends that power is group based and that political outcomes are the result of competition among groups. Early in the twentieth century, sociologist Arthur Bentley

our voices

Ida B. Wells-Barnett (1862–1931)

Ida B. Wells-Barnett was one of the first antilynching activists in the early 1890s. She traveled to lynching sites, gathering details and publishing pamphlets about the horrors of mob violence. She was also a suffragist, women's rights advocate, and journalist. She was co-owner of the *Memphis Free Speech and Headlight* in Memphis, Tennessee. It was burned out in 1892 as a result of her articles on lynching and other injustices, and she was forced to leave town. She settled in Chicago and continued her journalism career, was a central figure in the Negro clubwoman movement, and was a founding member of many organizations that she believed would work to eliminate the injustices experienced by African Americans.

Wells-Barnett was acutely aware of the importance of interest groups. We can see that in the following letter she wrote to the *Chicago Defender*, a prominent Black newspaper, on March 19, 1910. In this letter, she discusses the Original Rights Society, a short-lived group in New York committed to the basic civil rights stated in the Declaration of Independence and the Constitution, but not protected for many citizens.

Editor Defender:

In last week's issue you spoke of the sign in the State street car which advertised a certain cemetery that sold lots exclusively to white people. . . . Every one seems indignant and feels that something should be done, but no one seems to know just what may be done to have the objectionable sign removed.

Two things occur to me that might be tried, but both of them require what our people have not—effective organization in the race for civic and racial purposes.

In the disorganized condition in which we stand today, we could not bring pressure enough to bear perhaps to have those objectionable signs removed, but if we could count on the entire race for moral and financial support unitedly, the mayor, the city council, the aldermen of the ward would find a way to have these signs removed. . . .

And right here comes the need of organization that would take in every Negro, man, woman and child, in Chicago, especially the Second ward. If the Negroes would join the Original Rights Society, they would have their organization for themselves, and they would have the moral and active support of others in the movement. For the Original Rights Society is not composed alone of colored people. It is an organization established in New York City, and with growing branches throughout the country, composed largely of white people. They are fighting for the original rights of every American citizen, and that means us, too. . . .

If we should join the Original Rights Society in large numbers here in Chicago, we would not only be organized ourselves to do effective combined work along any line needed for our benefit, but we would have the help of the white members in any fight for our rights. Who knows but it might help us win the aldermanic victory. . . .

Ida B. Wells-Barnett, 3234 Rhodes Ave., Tel. Douglas 2960

Source: Wells-Barnett, I. B. (1910, March 19). The original rights society. *Chicago Defender*.

Ida B. Wells-Barnett (1862–1931), Mary Church Terrell (1863–1954), and Anna Julia Cooper (1858–1964) were important figures in the Black Women's Club Movement, whose purpose was to "uplift" Black America. All three were also active in numerous other Black social and political organizations and women's rights organizations, and all were accomplished authors.

discussed the influence of political interest groups in American politics. In *The Process of Government* (1908), he argued that the "stuff of politics and government were not structures and laws but interest groups and their activity."[14] Bentley contended that Madison's conception of factions formed the basis for a theory of democratic government that views competition among groups as the foundation for policymaking and political outcomes. Bentley stressed the benefit to representative government of the struggle among a "plurality" of interest groups, and he believed that political preferences grew out of group affiliation and identifications. For Bentley, American politics was group politics.[15]

David Truman applied Bentley's interest-group theory to political science in his work *The Governmental Process*.[16] Truman studied interest-group formation and viewed the number and existence of interest groups as a measure of the stability of a democratic system. He assumed that all interest groups would adopt a democratic perspective and produce alliances and coalitions that were in the best interest of the public good. For Truman, the prime objective of interest groups is to influence the making of public policy. Policy outcomes, for Truman, are the result of pressure from interest groups at various points in the political process.[17]

Truman's work influenced other scholars, among them political scientist Robert Dahl, who is considered the founding influence on pluralism and is identified as the most influential of the pluralist scholars. Dahl first stated the fundamentals of pluralism in his 1961 book, *Who Governs? Democracy and Power in an American City*.[18]

Pluralism makes several assumptions about politics and the political system:

1. Politics is group based. The distribution of power and policy formation comes through competition among groups.
2. Although groups might differ in the political resources they hold, the process of competition will balance out these differences.
3. Government will act as a neutral arbiter of the competition, but groups will try to influence government at various points.
4. Many centers of power exist, and different groups have access to a variety of power centers. Thus, if a group is blocked from one center of power, it will always have access to another.
5. Change in a pluralistic system is gradual or incremental, primarily because of the bargaining that occurs among interest groups.
6. Every group has equal access to the political process. Even though not every group will win all of the time, each group will win or lose depending on the issue and on the group's ability to use political resources.

Criticisms of Pluralism

Critics of pluralism contest several of these assumptions. In *The Semisovereign People*, E. E. Schattschneider argued that, despite the positive benefits to the political system that Bentley and Truman saw from interest groups, the majority of Americans do not have any interest-group representation.[19]

Schattschneider saw interest-group representation skewed in the direction of those who have political resources and influence, particularly the wealthy. He stated that "the flaw in the pluralist heaven is that the heavenly chorus sings with a strong upper-class accent."[20]

Theodore J. Lowi, in *The End of Liberalism*,[21] agreed with Schattschneider that most Americans are not represented by interest groups and are shut out of the policymaking process, which has been captured by a wide array of interest groups. These groups influence not only the formation of legislation through pressure on legislators, but also the implementation of legislation through pressure on the executive agencies responsible for policy implementation.

Lowi described this process as the **iron triangle**, the interlocking three-way relationship among a well-financed interest group, a congressional committee or subcommittee that makes the laws, and bureaucratic agencies that administer the law.[22] Lowi coined the phrase "interest-group liberalism" to refer to the perversion of pluralism by the dominance of private interests in the policymaking process. The effect of interest-group liberalism is that Congress, which has the constitutional responsibility to determine broad goals for American society, has abdicated its responsibility to interest groups.[23] Nevertheless, pluralism assumes that what happens in the political system is the result of the contest among groups, and interest groups play an important role in this contestation.

Iron Triangle A conception of bureaucratic policymaking in which it is dominated by congressional committees, interest groups, and bureaucratic agencies.

Interest-Group Formation

Why do interest groups form, and why do people join? The early group theory of politics scholars assumed that interest groups would form automatically once a group of individuals identified their common interests or recognized a threat to their interests. Later research failed to support this assumption. Economist Mancur Olson argues that individuals who have an interest in a particular policy might share that interest with others who will also be affected.[24] Yet they will not necessarily organize to achieve those policies. Individuals do not necessarily act in their common interest, particularly if they feel that their participation in a large group makes little difference to the eventual outcome. It is the proverbial "I am one person, so my participation does not count for much" syndrome. In addition, if people feel that benefits will go to more people than participated in pushing for the policy, that feeling also serves as a deterrent to joining an interest group.[25] Consequently, the incentive for any one individual to become involved in an interest group is very low. This view is known as the **logic of collective action**.

Olson further argues that the rational individual (an individual who is interested in what is best for her- or himself) will seek to become a **free rider**; that is, she or he will benefit from a policy without having contributed to its formulation or paying for the advantages it confers. In other words, if someone else works to provide a collective good that will also benefit me without my having to work for it, then I, as a rational individual, will choose to become a free rider. For example, if I live in a place where it snows and all owners are responsible for clearing the snow from their garages in the alley, the neighbors might band

Logic of Collective Action The view that the costs of large groups collectively organizing are high and the benefits to individual members are relatively low; thus, the appeal to rational members is one of deterrence to organizing collectively.

Free Rider A person who profits from the activities of others without participating in those activities.

Collective Good Any benefit that if available to one member of the community cannot be denied to any other, regardless of whether he or she bore any of the costs of providing it.

together to hire someone to come plow out the alley every time it snows. But my house is at the end of the alley, and I figure that my neighbors in the middle of the block will pay for the service and I will get the snow from my garage removed anyway because a path has to be made for my neighbors to get out. So, I choose not to pay. Olson would say that I am a "rational individual." This cleared alleyway would be considered a **collective good**, which is any benefit that if available to one member of the community cannot be denied to any other, regardless of whether the individual bore any of the costs of providing it.[26]

Scholars have tested Olson's theories and have concluded that in some respects Olson is correct. Many organizations, such as environmental and consumer groups, have few members but provide collective goods that the majority of people "free ride" on. Indeed, the difficulties that political actors have in stimulating voters and policymakers to address key challenges such as global warming and health care reform are examples of the continued relevance of the free rider syndrome.

According to Olson's theory, no one would ever get involved in an interest group, yet lots of people do. James Q. Wilson argues that people join organizations and interest groups in exchange for particular benefits.[27] AARP is an interest group that works on behalf of senior citizens and tries to influence public policies that will benefit them. One factor in the organization's influence is a large membership base and the ability to say that AARP represents 38 million senior citizens.[28] Even though AARP works on behalf of seniors, however, many join not for that reason, but for the tangible benefits the organization offers in the form of reduced insurance rates (auto, health), senior discounts for services and products such as prescription drugs, investment advice, and a host of other programs. Some people join for the benefits even if they disagree with the political work the organization does.

Social organizations, such as sororities, fraternities, and social clubs, might have larger public service goals than the social scene with which they are associated. Yet they know that many people will want to become members because they perceive the organizations as prestigious and believe that becoming a member will add to their own self-esteem or professional résumé.

Other organizations, such as the American Red Cross and the American Cancer Society, do not offer material or other incentives, but they know that many people will want to be involved because they believe in the long-range objectives of the organization. These members might also have had personal experiences that compel them to be involved. These types of organizations push their objectives to the broader public in an effort to attract people who believe in what the organizations are doing.

Types of Interest Groups

A French visitor to the new United States in 1831–1832, Alexis de Tocqueville, commented on the ability of citizens of the new nation to organize into groups to participate in the political system. Tocqueville stated, "As soon as several inhabitants of the United States have taken up an opinion or a feeling which they wish to promote in the world, they look out for mutual assistance; and as soon as they have found each other out, they combine. From that moment they are no longer isolated men, but a power seen from afar, whose actions serve for an example, and whose language is listened to."[29] It is as true now as in the 1830s that the United States is a nation in which people participate in organizations. A recent survey found that there are approximately 24,269 national organizations (see Table 13.1 for a categorization of some of them).

Interest groups are political organizations formed principally for the purpose of representing the groups' interests in government decision making and policy formation. As already noted, there are a great many interest groups, and they cover a wide range of issues. Despite the great numbers of interest groups, it is possible to classify them.

TABLE 13.1 Total Number of National Interest Groups and Associations, 2016

Category	National	%[a]
Athletic and Sports Organizations	903	3.72
Chambers of Commerce and Trade and Tourism Organizations	129	0.53
Cultural Organizations	1,625	6.70
Educational Organizations	1,352	5.57
Engineering, Technological, and Natural and Social Science Organizations	1,545	6.37
Environmental and Agricultural Organizations	1,435	5.91
Fan Clubs	119	0.49
Fraternal, Nationality, and Ethnic Organizations	418	1.72
Greek and Non-Greek Letter Societies, Associations, and Federations	318	1.31
Health and Medical Organizations	4,233	17.44
Hobby and Avocational Organizations	1,305	5.38
Labor Unions, Associations, and Federations	169	0.70
Legal, Governmental, Public Administration, and Military Organizations	897	3.70
Public Affairs Organizations	1,568	6.46
Religious Organizations	981	4.04
Social Welfare Organizations	3,175	13.08
Trade, Business, and Commercial Organizations	3,548	14.62
Veterans', Hereditary, and Patriotic Organizations	557	2.30
Total	**24,269**	

[a] *Percentages might not add to 100 because of rounding.*

Source: Encyclopedia of associations: National organizations of the U.S. *(54th ed.). (2015). Accessed using Gale Directory Library, Duke University Library.*

Note: The information for this table was found using the advanced search function in the Gale Directory Library. I selected "Encyclopedia of Associations – National Organizations of the U.S." under select directories. Then, I used the drop-box in the advanced search field and clicked "section heading(sh)," and typed each interest-group category in the box to the right.

H. R. Mahood has developed a typology that divides interest groups into two broad categories: economic and noneconomic.[30] Mahood places business (Walmart stores), labor (AFL-CIO), professional (American Bar Association), and agriculture (National Cattlemen's Association) interest groups in the economic category. In the noneconomic category, he lists civil rights (National Council of La Raza [NCLR]), government (American Federation of State, County, and Municipal Employees [AFSCME]), ideological (American Conservative Union), public interest (League of Women Voters), and single-issue (National Abortion Rights Action League) groups. Mahood does not mention religious interest groups, but they constitute another subcategory of noneconomic groups (National Council of Churches [NCC]).

Economic Interest Groups

These are interest groups whose primary concern is the economic well-being of their members. We can look at four broad categories of economic interest groups: agriculture, business, labor, and professions.

Agriculture. A wide variety of interest groups represent agriculture, including groups that represent farmers and groups that represent particular crops and commodities.[31] In direct reaction to the increasing influence of business, particularly railroad barons, American farmers were among the first to organize as an interest group to promote and protect their interests. They did this through the Grange, which was organized in Minnesota in 1867. The National Grange, as it is called today, is still a very active interest group that pushes for legislation and policies that benefit agriculture.

Farming has become a more complex sector in the twenty-first century. Most of the family farms that existed in the days of the Grange have been replaced by big agribusinesses. Farming interests are now more diverse, and agriculture does not speak with a united voice. Agriculture also consists of food export businesses, farm equipment dealers, pesticide and fertilizer manufacturers, and a myriad of other interests.[32]

Business. Business interest groups form to protect the ability of businesses to sell their products and services and make a profit with as little government oversight and regulation as possible.[33] Whereas agriculture interests began to organize in the 1860s, business interests began to organize in the early twentieth century. The U.S. Chamber of Commerce, founded in 1912, is the world's largest business federation and represents 3 million businesses of all sizes, sectors, and regions, as well as state and local chambers and industry associations. Its core function, according to its website, "is to fight for free enterprise before Congress, the White House, regulatory agencies, the courts, the court of public opinion, and governments around the world."[34] The Business Roundtable, established in 1972, is an association of chief executive officers of leading U.S. companies.[35] Like the Chamber of Commerce, the Business Roundtable provides an authoritative voice on business to pressure decision makers to make business-friendly public policy.[36]

The economic crisis of 2008 and 2009 saw business groups organize even more intensely to push policies favorable to business. The Obama administration proposed regulations to regulate the derivatives (a generic name for a variety of financial investments) market and sent bills to Congress in 2009. Seven large trade associations, including the Business Roundtable, the National Association of Manufacturers, and the U.S. Chamber of Commerce, recently formed the Coalition of Derivatives End-Users to oppose new regulations.[37] Congress eventually passed the Dodd-Frank Wall Street Reform and Consumer Protection Act in July 2010. The act seeks to regulate financial markets, so that the financial meltdown experienced in 2008 and 2009 will not happen again. It establishes a Consumer Financial Protection Agency that will oversee credit reporting agencies, debit and credit cards, payday and consumer loans, and credit card fees, among other things. It also creates the Financial Stability Oversight Council that will identify risks that might bring about another financial collapse. There is continuing controversy surrounding Dodd-Frank, but it appears to be working.

Watch President Trump criticize Amazon in 2018— helping spur the e-commerce giant to double its lobbying force.

Labor. Labor interest groups represent a wide variety of workers, from miners (United Mine Workers of America), teamsters (Teamsters), and steelworkers (United Steel Workers of America), to teachers (National Education Association), professional football players (National Football League Players Association), and Hollywood screenwriters (Writers Guild of America). Thus, labor interests span a broad segment of the employment arena.

All of these groups represent unionized workers. Like agriculture interests, labor interests are also diverse and do not speak with a united voice. Each labor interest group works to push its specific interests. Labor unions are not as powerful today as in past decades. In 2017, only 10.7 percent of the U.S. workforce was unionized, down from 20.1 percent in 1983.[38]

Even though older unions are losing members, others in new job arenas are growing. As the service industries expand, the Service Employees International Union (SEIU) is growing at a fast pace. SEIU represents workers in three sectors—health care, property services, and public employment. SEIU is also active in lobbying for specific public policies. For example, as of October 16, 2016, the union, its PAC, and its members contributed about $5.7 million to political candidates for the 2016 election.[39] (Table 13.2 provides a list of the various types of labor unions in the United States.)

Professions. Numerous professions have organized into professional associations, many of which also function as interest groups on issues that affect their profession. An example of a well-known professional interest group is the American Medical Association (AMA), an association of medical professionals and medical doctors, founded in 1847. Since its formation, the AMA has worked to advance the art and science of medicine. It is the premier association involved with health care in the United States, and no other health-related organization can match it in terms of political access or influence on decision-makers.

TABLE 13.2 SELECTION OF DIFFERENT TYPES OF LABOR UNIONS

Labor Union	Inception	Website
Actors' Equity Association	1913	http://www.actorsequity.org
AFL-CIO	1955	http://www.aflcio.org
American Federation of Television and Radio Artists (AFTRA)	1937	www.sagaftra.org
Alliance of Canadian Cinema, Television and Radio Artists (ACTRA)	1943	http://www.actra.ca/actra/control/main
American Federation of State, County and Municipal Employees (AFSCME)	1932	http://www.afscme.org
Association of Flight Attendants (AFA)	1930	www.afacwa.org
American Federation of Teachers (AFT)	1916	http://www.aft.org/about
American Postal Workers Union, AFL–CIO (APWU)	1970	http://www.apwu.org
Bakery, Confectionery, Tobacco Workers and Grain Millers International Union	1886	http://www.bctgm.org
Brotherhood of Locomotive Engineers and Trainmen	1863	http://www.ble.org
Brotherhood of Maintenance of Way Employees Division–International Brotherhood of Teamsters (BMWE-IBT)	1887	http://www.bmwe.org
Chicago Federation of Labor, AFL-CIO	1852	http://www.chicagolabor.org
Coalition of Graduate Employee Unions (CGEU)	1992	http://thecgeu.org
Communications Workers of America (CWA)	1938	http://www.cwa-union.org
Directors Guild of America	1936	http://www.dga.org
Electronic and Space Technicians (EAST) Local 1553	1953	http://www.east1553.com
Exotic Dancers Union SEIU Local 790 (San Francisco)	1993	http://www.bayswan.org/eda-sf
Fraternal Order of Police	1915	http://www.fop.net
Glass, Molders, Pottery, Plastics & Allied Workers International Union (GMP)	1842	http://www.gmpiu.org
Graphic Communications International Union (GCIU)	2005	https://teamster.org/divisions/graphic-communications.
Industrial Workers of the World	1905	http://www.iww.org
International Alliance of Theatrical Stage Employees	1893	http://www.iatse-intl.org
International Association of Fire Fighters (IAFF)	1918	http://www.iaff.org
International Association of Machinists and Aerospace Workers (IAMAW)	1888	http://www.goiam.org
International Brotherhood of Electrical Workers (IBEW)	1891	http://www.ibew.org
International Longshoremen's Association, AFL-CIO (ILA)	1892	http://www.ilaunion.org/
International Union of Bricklayers and Allied Craft Workers (BAC)	1865	http://www.bacweb.org

Labor Union	Inception	Website
International Union of Industrial and Independent Workers	1997	http://iuiiw.us/
International Union of Operating Engineers (IUOE)	1896	http://www.iuoe.org
International Union of Painters and Allied Trades	1887	http://www.iupat.org
International Union of Police Associations (IUPA)	1954	http://www.iupa.org
Laborers' International Union of North America (LIUNA)	1903	http://www.liuna.org
Major League Baseball Players Association	1885	http://www.mlbplayers.com
National Air Traffic Controllers Association (NATCA)	1987	http://www.natca.org
National Education Association (NEA)	1857	http://www.nea.org
National Association of Catholic School Teachers (NACST)	1978	http://www.nacst.com
National Association of Letter Carriers (NALC)	1889	http://www.nalc.org
National Football League Players Association	1956	http://www.nflpa.com
National Hockey League Players' Association	1967	http://www.nhlpa.com
Office & Professional Employees International Union (OPEIU)	1936	http://www.opeiu.org
Pride@Work	1905	http://prideatwork.org
Screen Actors Guild (SAG)	1933	http://www.sag.org
Seafarers International Union of North America (SIU)	1938	http://www.seafarers.org
Security, Police and Fire Professionals of America (SPFPA), International Union	1938	http://www.spfpa.org
International Brotherhood of Teamsters	1903	http://www.teamster.org
Newspaper Guild	1933	http://www.newsguild.org
United Electrical, Radio & Machine Workers of America	1936	http://www.ueunion.org
United Association of Journeymen and Apprentices of the Plumbing and Pipe Fitting Industry of the United States and Canada (UA)	1889	http://www.ua.org
United Automobile, Aerospace and Agricultural Implement Workers of America (UAW), International Union	1935	http://www.uaw.org
United Farm Workers of America (UFW), AFL-CIO	1962	http://www.ufw.org

Source: Unions.org, http://www.unions.org/home/.

Despite its prominence, however, in 2012, the latest year for which figures are available, only 234,360 of 926,000 physicians with active licenses in the United States were members of the AMA (see "Evaluating Equality: The AMA Apologizes to Black Physicians").[40]

Another example of a professional interest group is the American Bar Association (ABA), founded in 1878. Its stated mission is "to serve equally our members, our profession and the public by defending liberty and delivering

Explore interest groups in depth.

evaluating equality

The AMA Apologizes to Black Physicians

The American Medical Association is a powerful interest group, but it historically excluded Black physicians from membership. In 1870, the integrated National Medical Society (an organization of primarily Black doctors) delegation was excluded from the AMA annual meeting in Washington, DC. In 1874, the AMA adopted a system of governance that allowed each state medical society to decide which local societies would be recognized by the AMA. In the face of exclusion from the AMA, the National Medical Association (NMA) was founded in 1895 as an association for Black physicians. The NMA still remains the collective voice for more than 25,000 Black physicians in the United States.

In addition to refusing Black physicians membership, the AMA worked to restrict opportunities for the education of Black physicians. In 1910, the AMA undertook a review of Black medical schools and forced all but two, Meharry Medical College and Howard University, to shut their doors. As a result, only two medical schools remained in the entire nation for the training of Black physicians.

In July 2008, the AMA officially apologized for having excluded Black physicians from membership, for listing Black doctors as "colored" in its national physician directories for decades, and for failing to speak against federal funding of segregated hospitals and in favor of civil rights legislation. The apology came as a response to an AMA-sponsored report on the historical racial divide in organized medicine. The AMA report indicated that racism in

Daniel Hale Williams (1856–1931) was a famous cardiologist and surgeon who performed the first successful open heart surgery in the United States. A graduate of Chicago Medical School, he was not allowed to practice in Chicago hospitals because of his race. He founded Provident Hospital and Training School for Nurses, which employed a racially integrated staff. Williams was one of the founders of the National Medical Association (NMA) in 1895 as an alternative to the American Medical Association that did not allow Blacks to join.

medicine created and perpetuated poor health outcomes for America's Black citizens. As a result, the United States continues to face severe health disparities based on race in the twenty-first century.

Sources: AMA apologizes for past inequality against Black doctors. (2008, July 28).

amednews.com. Retrieved July 15, 2009, from http://www.ama-assn.org/amednews/2008/07/28/prsb0728.htm; *History of the National Medical Association.* (n.d.). Retrieved July 15, 2009, from http://www.medpagetoday.com/publichealthpolicy/publichealth/10094.

justice as the national representative of the legal profession."[41] In 2017, the ABA had more than 400,000 members.[42]

Noneconomic Interest Groups

Noneconomic interest groups are concerned about issues of benefit to society as a whole or to large groups of individuals even if they are not members of the group. We can divide these groups into six broad categories: civil rights, government, ideology, public interest, single issue, and religion.

Civil Rights. Civil rights interest groups are concerned with issues such as equal opportunity, voting rights, civil liberties, and race and gender discrimination. Examples of civil rights interest groups are the National Association for the Advancement of Colored People, the National Council of La Raza, and the National Organization for Women.

The NAACP, founded in 1909, is the nation's oldest and largest civil rights organization. The NAACP has over 2,000 branches and chapters and more than 300,000 members. The NAACP is made up of hundreds of thousands of volunteer activists in some 2,200 NAACP Adult, Youth, and College Units across the United States, as well as in the organization's overseas branches in Japan, Germany, and Korea. The NAACP's principle mission "is to ensure the political, educational, social, and economic equality of rights of all persons and to eliminate race-based discrimination." The NAACP is active at the national, state, and local levels addressing problems, lobbying for legislation, and protesting racial injustices. The NAACP also has a significant online and

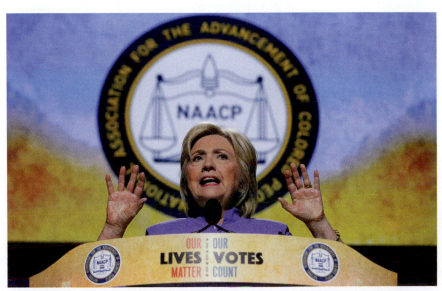

Hillary Clinton speaks at the National Association for the Advancement of Colored People (NAACP) 107th Annual Convention in July 2016.

social media presence. As of July 2016, the organization had 555,893 Facebook fans, 144,300 Twitter followers, and 177,717 followers on NAACPConnect on Google Plus.[43]

The NCLR, founded in 1968, is the largest Latino organization serving all Latino groups—Mexican Americans, Puerto Ricans, Cubans, and South and Central Americans—in all regions of the country. The organization has more than three hundred affiliates in forty-one states, Puerto Rico, and the District of Columbia. Its objective is to work to improve opportunities for Latino Americans. As a nonpartisan organization, NCLR partners with its affiliates across the country "to serve millions of Latinos in the areas of civic engagement, civil rights and immigration, education, workforce and the economy, health and housing."[44] Like the NAACP, NCLR works at all levels of government.

The NOW, established in 1966, is the largest feminist organization in the United States, with over 500,000 contributing members. The organization describes itself as "an intersectional, multi-issue, multi-strategy organization that takes a holistic approach to women's rights." NOW has more than 500 chapters, including local chapters and Campus Action Networks, in all fifty states and the District of Columbia. Through intersectional grassroots activism, NOW works "to promote feminist ideals, lead societal change, eliminate discrimination, and achieve and protect the equal rights of all women and girls in all aspects of social, political, and economic life."[45]

Representative Patricia Roybal Caballero (D-Albuquerque) speaks in Santa Fe at a New Mexico House Business and Employment Committee on January 29, 2015. Caballero has been elected to the board of the nation's oldest Latino civil rights group despite concerns over partisanship and bylaw violations. Caballero became national treasurer for the League of United Latin American Citizens at the group's convention in Salt Lake City.

Government. Most government interest groups are state or local organizations that push their interests with the federal government. The National League of Cities (NLC) is an American advocacy organization that is dedicated to helping city leaders build better communities. The organization, which works in partnership with forty-nine municipal leagues, represents over 19,000 cities, towns, and villages. The mission of the NLC is to strengthen and promote cities as centers of opportunity, leadership, and governance by advocating in Washington, DC, for cities and towns through lobbying efforts and grassroots campaigns. The organization also provides educational programs and training, networking opportunities, and other services to local officials. More than 2,000 municipalities around the country are members of the National League of Cities.[46]

A government interest group that functions like a union for public employees is the American Federation of State, County, and Municipal Employees. AFSCME has more than 1.6 million members, and they include nurses, corrections officers, child care providers, emergency medical technicians, and sanitation workers. Over the years, it has lobbied for collective bargaining for public employees and actively supports political candidates in national, state, and local elections. When Dr. Martin Luther King, Jr. was assassinated in 1968, he was in Memphis to support the Memphis AFSCME sanitation workers.[47]

Ideology. Ideological interest groups are groups that adhere to a particular belief system or ideal about how society and government should be structured and what public policies are most desirable.[48] Ideological interest groups range along the political continuum from the far left to the extreme right and include organizations such as the American Civil Liberties Union (ACLU), the American Conservative Union, the Cato Institute, and People for the American Way (PFAW).

The Cato Institute, for example, is a Washington, DC–based public policy research organization established in 1977. Its name derives from the *Cato Letters*, libertarian pamphlets disseminated in the American colonies prior to the Revolutionary War. A libertarian organization,[49] the institute's mission is to increase the understanding of public policies based on the principles of limited government, free markets,

Photo 13.8: Florynce (Flo) Kennedy, a feminist lawyer and civil rights activist, was a founding member of the National Organization for Women in 1966, but she left in 1971 because of the organization's inability to tackle head-on issues she considered important. She was one of the few Black women involved in a White feminist organization. She went on to found the Feminist Party, which supported Shirley Chisholm's bid for president in 1972.

individual liberty, and peace. Cato's goal is to push public policies that are consistent with the principles of limited government, individual liberty, and peace.[50] The institute's key research foci include education and child policy, law and civil liberties, government and politics, energy and the environment, trade policy, health care and welfare, foreign policy and national security, and social security.

A counter to the Cato Institute is the liberal advocacy group People for the American Way. Founded in 1981 by Hollywood television and movie producer Norman Lear, the original mission of PFAW was to counter the growing clout and divisive message of right-wing televangelists, popular in the 1980s. Its objectives today are to push public policies that embrace America's diversity, respect Americans' rights, and defend liberty, democracy, and the American way.[51]

Public Interest. Public interest groups aim to speak for broad groups of citizens, such as consumers, environmentalists, and political reformers. An example of a public interest group is Public Citizen, founded in 1971 by Ralph Nader. The nonprofit organization views itself as representing "consumer interests in Congress, the executive branch and the courts."[52] Headed most recently by Robert Weissman, Public Citizen has more than 400,000 members and supporters and fights for "openness and democratic accountability in government, for the right of consumers to seek redress in the courts; for clean, safe and sustainable energy sources; for social and economic justice in trade policies; for strong health, safety and environmental protections; and for safe, effective and affordable prescription drugs and health care."[53] Among its accomplishments are: (1) pushing the U.S. Occupational Safety and Health Administration to adopt safety measures that protect workers from exposure to crystalline silica dust; (2) urging Congress to adopt standards that would protect consumers' First Amendment right to post anonymous reviews of products and services online; (3) protecting students from exploitative practices of for-profit colleges and universities; (4) ensuring that airbags are now standard in automobiles; and (5) urging the removal of dangerous drugs and dietary supplements such as Rezulin and ephedra from the market. (Public Citizen also pushed congressional legislation that would have limited damage awards in medical malpractice and product defect cases, but it was defeated.)[54]

Single Issue. Single-issue interest groups focus solely on one specific issue, such as abortion or gun control. The issues usually generate a great deal of emotion, and these groups are able to marshal enormous resources and energy in their quest to achieve their single objective.[55] Mothers Against Drunk Driving (MADD) is an example of a single-issue interest group. Candace Lightner founded MADD in 1980 after her thirteen-year-old daughter was killed by a hit-and-run driver in California. MADD has more than three hundred affiliates with approximately 3 million members.[56] MADD is one of the largest and most influential nonprofit organizations in the United States, working to address issues related to drunk driving. MADD's mission is "to end drunk driving, help fight drugged driving, support the victims of these violent crimes and prevent underage drinking." Since its founding, MADD, according to its own publicity, was instrumental in the passage of the national minimum drinking age (of twenty-one) law in 1984 and has helped pass more than 2,300 anti–drunk driving and underage drinking laws.[57] In 2006,[58] MADD launched the Campaign to Eliminate Drunk Driving. The campaign focuses on high visibility enforcement to catch drunk drivers and discourage individuals from driving drunk, requiring ignition interlock devices (in-car breathalyzers) for anyone who has had a past conviction for drunk driving, and supporting the development of advanced vehicle technology that can determine if a driver is drunk.[59]

Religion. Religious interest groups represent a particular denomination or a coalition of several denominations. Their objective is to push a particular set of policy issues that conform to their religious beliefs or to speak out on issues that they feel reflect those beliefs. An example of a religious interest group is the Christian Coalition of America, commonly referred to as the Christian Coalition, founded by Pat Robertson in 1989 to "give Christians a voice in government."[60] The Coalition is one of the largest conservation grassroots political organizations in the United States and is associated with evangelical and fundamentalist Christians. The Coalition describes its mission as representing the pro-family point of view before local councils, school boards, state legislatures, and Congress; training leaders for effective social and political action; and defending the rights of Christians.

The National Council of Churches (NCC), formed in 1950, is a cooperative agency of thirty-eight Protestant, Evangelical, Orthodox, Anglican, and historic African American denominations. Its activities include working for peace and justice in the United States and addressing issues ranging from poverty and racism to the environment and family ministries. The NCC makes the views of the worldwide Christian community known to government and keeps its constituents informed of legislative and other developments of interest to the churches.[61]

Techniques of Interest Groups

Interest groups participate in the political process in a variety of ways to make sure that their interests are pushed and will benefit favorably from government decisions. To achieve this outcome, interest groups use a number of techniques: lobbying; electioneering, which includes the use of political action committees (PACs); education; litigation; and media campaigns to influence public opinion.

The choice of techniques by an interest group is related to the particular goals of the group and the intended targets of the group's efforts. For example, if the goal is to pass a particular piece of legislation, then an interest group might choose lobbying. If the goal is to elect more public officials sympathetic to the objectives of the group, it might choose some form of electioneering.

Lobbying

Lobbying is the communication of data or opinions to a government decision maker in an effort to influence a specific decision.[62] Lobbying is typically done by an individual working for or representing an interest group. The word originated from the behavior of people who waited in the lobbies of government buildings to talk with legislators. Mythology has it that the word *lobby* originated during the administration of President Ulysses S. Grant, who, it is said, would drink brandy and smoke cigars in the lobby of the Willard Hotel in Washington, DC, and people who wanted something from the government would meet Grant in the lobby. The term, however, most likely originated with the British Parliament, specifically the House of Lords, in the first half of the nineteenth century.[63] Whatever the origins, lobbying and lobbyists are important players in the political process.

Lobbying strategies are either direct or indirect. Direct lobbying consists of personal contact between a lobbyist and a public official. Lobbyists who participate in direct lobbying are often former public officials, former members of Congress, or members of past presidential administrations. Because these individuals have personal relationships with current members of Congress and have contacts in other branches of the government, they can be particularly effective lobbyists. Direct lobbying is also done by law firms in Washington, DC, that work for specific business sectors, such as oil or tobacco industries. Special interest groups also hire public relations firms to engage in lobbying activities.[64]

Lobbying The process by which an individual, a group, or an organization seeks to influence government policymakers.

Discover how to lobby Congress on a specific issue.

Leaders and volunteers from AARP's state and territorial offices converged on Congress on April 25, 2018, pressing lawmakers to protect policies and programs vital to Americans age 50 and older.

Indirect lobbying involves the use of more roundabout techniques to communicate with decision makers. One aspect of indirect lobbying is the orchestrating of what might appear to be a groundswell of support for a particular issue from the constituents of the policymaker. Organized letter-writing campaigns, phone calls, email messages, text messages, and other types of "grassroots" activity are forms of indirect lobbying. AARP has been very successful with indirect lobbying techniques on behalf of its members on issues related to middle-aged and senior citizens.

Electioneering

Another technique of interest groups is **electioneering**, working actively on behalf of a political candidate or political party. There are a number of electioneering activities. One is endorsement, a public declaration of support, of political candidates. Interest groups give their public support to candidates in the expectation that if the candidate is elected, her or his decisions and policies will be favorable to the interest group. Every national, state, and local election finds interest groups supporting different candidates in the hopes of gaining favorable consideration once they are elected.

Electioneering Working actively on behalf of a political candidate or political party with activities that might include publicly endorsing a candidate, making a campaign contribution, or making phone calls.

Another aspect of electioneering is campaign donations. Because many interest groups are prohibited by law from using their own funds to contribute to political candidates, they establish political action committees through which they can funnel contributions to political candidates. Since 1907, Congress has periodically passed legislation aimed at controlling contributions to political campaigns.

In 1971, Congress consolidated its earlier reform efforts into the Federal Campaign Act, which authorized corporations and interest groups to set up political action committees or PACs that could raise and spend money and pool campaign contributions to elect or defeat political candidates. PACs are able to contribute more money to political candidates than individual donors. PACs are nevertheless limited to contributions of $5,000 per candidate each election cycle. Each primary, general, or runoff election is considered a separate election. This $5,000 limit was preserved in the Bipartisan Campaign Reform Act of 2002.

Yet PACs can also give $15,000 per calendar year to a national party committee; $5,000 per year to state, district, and local party committees; and $5,000 per year to any other political committee. PACs are able to spread money around to lots of different political entities during an election year and in the years leading up to an election year.[65]

The limits on individual contributions ($2,700 per candidate per election in 2015–2016) make PACs important sources of campaign money for political candidates.[66] Table 13.3 lists the top twenty PACs (according to the Federal Election Commission) with the largest campaign contributions in 2015–2016. Table 13.4 shows the top ten corporate PACs by contributions to candidates, from January 2015 to June 30, 2015. According to information released by the Federal Election Commission, as of December 31, 2016, there were a total of 8,666 PACs in the United States, with 1,803 of that number having corporate interests.[67]

TABLE 13.3 Top Twenty PAC Contributors to Candidates, 2017–2018

Rank	Contribution	Percent to Democrats	Percent to Republicans
Northrop Grumman	$2,525,240	42%	58%
AT&T	$2,412,700	40%	60%
National Beer Wholesalers Assn.	$2,316,500	44%	55%
National Air Traffic Controllers Assn.	$2,090,500	51%	49%
Lockheed Martin	$2,022,000	38%	62%
Honeywell International	$1,985,710	44%	56%
Credit Union National Assn.	$1,936,499	47%	53%
Boeing	$1,936,499	39%	61%
American Crystal Sugar	$1,893,500	52%	47%
Operating Engineers Union	$1,886,925	76%	23%
Intl. Brotherhood of Electrical Workers	$1,871,973	96%	4%
American Bankers Assn.	$1,869,630	25%	75%
Prosperity Action	$1,860,000	0%	100%
United Parcel Service	$1,844,699	31%	69%
American Assn. for Justice	$1,787,500	94%	6%
Majority Cmte. PAC	$1,765,000	0%	100%
Comcast	$1,725,500	36%	64%
New York Life Insurance	$1,665,575	44%	56%
Carpenters and Joiners Union	$1,656,000	79%	21%
Blue Cross/Blue Shield	$1,645,300	41%	59%

Note: For ease of identification, the names used in this section are those of the organizations connected with the PACs, rather than the official PAC names.

Sources: Based on data released by the FEC on July 23, 2018; Open Secrets.org, https://www.opensecrets.org/pacs/toppacs.php.

What makes a PAC a Super PAC?

In addition to PACs, another set of campaign actors are groups called 527s, independent political groups named for the section of the IRS tax code that regulates the financial activities of all political groups whose purpose is to influence elections.[68] In the 2004 election, both George W. Bush and Senator John Kerry were targeted by 527 groups. The 527 Swift Boat Veterans for Truth went after Senator Kerry by challenging his service in Vietnam and attacking his patriotism.

The activities of the Swift Boat group caused a great deal of controversy and called into question the role of 527s. Although the Bipartisan Campaign Reform Act (commonly known as the McCain-Feingold Act) prohibits political parties and campaigns from accepting unlimited, unregulated donations from corporations, unions, and individuals, the law does not mention 527s. If the 527s do not coordinate their activities with candidates or political parties, they can raise unlimited amounts of money and run political ads as long as they do not explicitly endorse a particular candidate. This latter requirement is easy to get around because the focus in 527 ads makes clear which candidate is favored.[69]

The Bipartisan Campaign Reform Act was challenged in the Supreme Court. In early September 2009, the Supreme Court heard arguments in the case *Citizens United v. Federal Election Committee.* The case involves an anti–Hillary Clinton movie, *Hillary: The Movie* that the commission said was a campaign attack ad regulated under the act. The conservative group that made the film, Citizens United, said the movie was a documentary and not a political advertisement. The central question put before the Court was whether corporations and labor unions have the same protected First Amendment free speech rights as individuals to participate in elections without facing censorship. The questions from the justices suggested that a majority might be inclined to declare that corporations have a First Amendment right to spend their money and express views during elections just as individuals do.[70] On January 21, 2010, the Supreme Court did, indeed, rule that corporations and labor unions have the same protected First Amendment rights as individuals and that they could give unlimited amounts of money to PACs. This decision opened the floodgates for corporate donations to PACs and the creation of Super PACs in the 2012 presidential election. In some instances, the Super PACs were funded by one individual, a practice raising the specter that individuals and corporations are able to "buy" elections.

Education

Almost every interest group feels that it must educate the public on the issues that it wants resolved by government. One way to educate the public is to disseminate information about the issue in the hopes that the "facts" will persuade the public to support the interest group's position.[71] If a group is able to generate public support or sympathy for its position, then the group is able to cite that support when presenting arguments to decision makers.

Most interest groups do not have the resources and staff to do extensive research, so what they do produce might be limited. Nevertheless, every day in Washington and in state capitols around the country, interest groups inundate the public and politicians with the results of studies that support their position. It is essential to the success of their overall objectives that interest groups be viewed as experts in the area in which they have an interest. High-quality research reports go a long way toward establishing that credibility. The Union of Concerned Scientists, an antinuclear public interest group, has been able to establish this credibility and is viewed by news organizations and legislators as a credible source on nuclear energy matters, despite their own views.[72]

Litigation

The goals that interest groups pursue through litigation are varied, but some of the main objectives are establishing principles of constitutional right and challenging the constitutionality or legitimacy of legislative and executive actions.[73] Using the courts as a venue to pursue interest-group aims might seem counterintuitive, but courts are important policymaking institutions that have the power to settle disputes and to make sweeping changes to or initiate new policies.[74]

For interest groups, one direct approach to litigation is to sponsor individuals who want to go to court to challenge an issue. This particular approach can be time-consuming and very expensive, so many interest groups avoid it. But a successful suit can bring big rewards to the interest group and its members.

In 2002, individuals at the Cato Institute filed suit challenging Washington, DC's Firearms Control Regulations Act of 1975, which restricted Washington residents from owning handguns. The district court originally dismissed the suit, but the U.S. Court of Appeals for the DC Circuit overturned the dismissal and struck down some provisions of the law as unconstitutional. On June 26, 2008, the Supreme Court ruled in a 5–4 decision in *District of Columbia et al. v. Heller* that the District of Columbia cannot ban a citizen from keeping a handgun at home. The Court thereby threw out one of the nation's most restrictive gun control laws.[75] The day after the U.S. Supreme Court ruling that affirmed the rights of individuals to own handguns,[76] the NRA filed suit against the city of San Francisco (*Guy Montag Doe v. San Francisco Housing Authority*) to overturn the ban on handguns in public housing.[77] In 2009, the San Francisco Housing Authority reached a settlement with the NRA, allowing residents to legally possess firearms within public housing facilities.

In December 2012, the United States experienced the deadliest mass shooting at a grade school or high school when twenty children and six adults were murdered at Sandy Hook Elementary School in Newtown, Connecticut. Following that shooting, there was a significant push for legislation on gun control and ammunition legislation. In January 2013, the Obama administration introduced a proposal that included twenty-three executive actions designed to curb gun violence. Congress has been unable to pass any gun control legislation, except for renewing a ban against firearms that can pass undetected through metal detectors (Undetectable Firearms Act of 1988) in 2013.[78] In a CNN/ORC poll conducted in December 2015, 48 percent of Americans said they were in favor of stricter gun control laws, while 51 percent said they were opposed to stricter gun control laws.[79] The NRA, which represents the business interests of gun manufacturers and distributors,[80] has vehemently opposed any form of gun and ammunition regulation.

In 2015, the U.S. Supreme Court rejected the NRA's appeal over two San Francisco gun control measures in *Jackson v. City and County of San Francisco*, 14–704. The NRA was challenging a 2007 law that required people who store handguns at home to put them in a lockbox or disable them with a trigger lock.[81]

Another direct approach is to file *amicus curiae* (friend of the court) briefs on cases that will have an effect on the interest group. In the *Heller* case, amicus briefs were filed by the NRA and the Institute for Justice, among forty-seven others, against the handgun ban. Briefs in favor of upholding the ban were filed by the NAACP Legal Defense and Education Fund (LDF), the American Bar Association, and the American Academy of Pediatrics, among twenty others.[82]

Because the courts are highly attuned to the articulation of political interests, interest groups also use indirect, nonlitigation approaches to influence juridical outcomes. Although the techniques and tactics for influencing the courts are more limited, one tactic is to try to influence the judicial selection process so that judges favorable to an interest group's aims are nominated to the bench. At the federal level, all judges are appointed by the president, and interest groups can exercise a great deal of influence on a president who shares their objectives.

Interest groups can also be influential in blocking a nomination to the court. President Ronald Reagan's nomination of Robert Bork in 1987 to the Supreme Court was blocked with the help of strong opposition from interest groups, such as the ACLU, the NAACP, the Gay and Lesbian Alliance, NOW, the Nation Institute (a liberal think tank), and the National Urban League.[83]

Another indirect tactic is to educate judges, lawyers, and other members of the legal community on issues of concern to the interest group to establish that there is growing support for a particular viewpoint. This particular tactic is expressed through law review articles that advocate an approach that the interest groups feel the courts should take. The NAACP has used this tactic in its push to eliminate racial discrimination in all aspects of American society. As part of the organization's efforts to outlaw restrictive covenants in real estate (language in deeds that forbade the property from being sold to Blacks and, in some instances, Jews), between 1946 and 1948 the NAACP coordinated the appearance of more than thirty books and law review articles urging the Supreme Court to reverse itself on restrictive covenants. The Court finally did in 1948 in *Shelly v. Kramer*, a decision that has been attributed to the legal educational work of the NAACP.[84]

Media Campaigns

Interest groups use mass media to influence public opinion, but because media campaigns are very expensive, not all interest groups have the resources to engage in them. As a result, media campaigns are usually undertaken by trade or business interest groups or well-financed groups such as the NRA and health care associations such as the Health Insurance Association of America.[85]

There are three types of media campaigns: goodwill, offensive, and defensive. A goodwill campaign attempts to create a favorable image for the interest group. To create such an image, a group might sponsor cultural programs on public broadcasting or underwrite a public service campaign.[86] For example, the tobacco industry—specifically Lorillard Tobacco Co., Philip Morris USA, and R. J. Reynolds Tobacco Co.—has been the primary force behind the Coalition for Responsible Tobacco Retailing, an organization of retailers, wholesalers, and manufacturers whose objective is "to educate and train retailers on preventing underage tobacco sales."[87] The coalition sponsors a series of "We Card" public service announcements.[88] This program encourages retail stores to display the "We Card" sign, to require identification from individuals wanting to buy cigarettes who appear younger than twenty-seven, and to train salesclerks to comply with state laws on the sale of tobacco to minors. The coalition and its "We Card" program attempt to portray the tobacco industry as trying to do its part to combat teenage smoking.

In an offensive media campaign, an interest group tries to generate public support for a specific positive policy objective. For example, when the Chrysler Corporation almost went bankrupt in 1979 and asked the federal government to bail it out, the company placed full-page ads in leading newspapers under the broad headline "Would America be better off without Chrysler?"[89] The implication was that if Chrysler went under, that would be the end of an American institution and would be bad for the country. The campaign was successful.

The question of the survival of the U.S. auto industry arose again in late 2008 and early 2009. The U.S. government provided billions of dollars in bailout money to General Motors (GM) and Chrysler (Ford did not require bailout money at the time). In an effort to build support for the bailout and change public perceptions of the automakers, GM and Chrysler developed Internet ads and videos aimed at individuals searching the Web for information on the bailout or a specific automaker. GM, for example, created the GM "Facts and Fiction" campaign, which gave GM's perspective and asked people to "Support the U.S. Auto Industry."[90]

In another example, forty-five scientists in 2002 accused the publishers of an academic journal of being influenced by the tobacco industry and of not upholding the normal academic process of peer-reviewed articles. The editor of the journal was paid $30,000 by the Tobacco Institute to write an article for the journal that dismissed the dangers of secondhand smoke.[91]

Defensive media campaigns are designed to rally the public behind an interest group's position to prevent a change or a bill from being enacted.[92] In early 2009, the U.S. Chamber of Commerce was one of the major opponents of the Employee Free Choice Act (EFCA), a bill supported by organized labor that would make it easier for unions to organize workers. EFCA would amend the National Labor Relations Act to require the National Labor Relations Board to certify a union as the employees' bargaining representative without an election if a majority of employees sign cards indicating that they want to be represented by a specific union. These cards, referred to as card checks, are authorizations from the signatories that they want to form a union or be represented by a specific union.

Under current law, workers can select union representation either through an election process or through a majority sign-up card check. The National Labor Relations Board will certify a union as an exclusive representative only if the union is chosen through a secret ballot process or if the employer agrees to accept the card check results. The employer is not required to honor the card checks and can insist on a secret ballot election.[93]

Supporters of EFCA want more control in the hands of the workers, whereas opponents want more control in the hands of employers. As part of the campaign against EFCA, the Chamber of Commerce has run a number of television ads, which have been replayed numerous times on YouTube, characterizing the issue as a voting rights issue. According to the ads, EFCA would strip workers of their secret ballot right. The ads even have a union "boss" named Bill who posts the names and pictures of those who support or oppose the union, underscoring the chamber's argument that workers' voting rights would be removed if EFCA passed. After the Democrats lost control of the House of Representatives in 2010, the bill has stalled in Congress.

Factors That Make Interest Groups Effective

A study asking legislators to identify the factors that make one interest group more effective than another determined that the most influential factors are the following:

1. The size, wealth, and cohesion of the group and the amount of information and services it can provide the legislator.
2. The importance and reliability of the group as perceived by the legislator.
3. The type of interests that the group represents, with legislators more likely to give more credence to business and economic interest groups than to consumer groups.
4. The interest group's position on pending legislation (lobbyists are often more successful at preventing legislation than at pushing a bill through the legislative maze).
5. The strength and cohesion of the political parties within a legislator's state or within Congress on the issue in question.
6. The degree of competition among the interest groups on either side of the issue.[94]

These criteria help explain why some interest groups have more power and access than others. Many business and labor interest groups are large and well financed and can employ full-time lobbyists to provide information to legislators.[95] These groups can also provide legislators with the perks associated with lobbying; these range from minor perks such as social engagements and dinners to major perks such as international trips.

Groups without size, wealth, and full-time lobbyists find it difficult to compete. If, as the saying goes, money talks, how can interest groups with fewer financial resources influence decision-makers? Can these less wealthy groups ever be on an equal footing with wealthier groups?

Political and Financial Inequalities

Pluralism assumes that all groups have equal access to the political system and its decision-makers. Although the theory acknowledges that some interest groups will have more of one type of resource than other groups do, it concludes that resources of one type will counterbalance resources of another type. For example, an interest group with more money will be checked by another that has better organizational skills, or an interest group with large numbers will be checked by another that has more media access. Critics of these assumptions charge that this kind of equilibrium does not exist.

Pluralism has also been criticized for obscuring the role that race has played and continues to play in American society. For example, pluralism assumes that interests will become diversified across economic, social, and political issues; thus, there will be little need for racial and ethnic groups to organize around group-based issues. Race and ethnicity will be eclipsed as these other issues take precedence.

Pluralism also contends that once groups realize their subjective interests, they will become incorporated into the political system. This view would suggest that once the NAACP had legal successes, such as *Brown v. Board of Education of Topeka* in 1954, its focus would have broadened beyond issues related to Black Americans. Indeed, there would have no longer been a need for the NAACP to exist as an interest group.

Also, pluralism's notion that all groups have equal access to the political process assumes that there are no legal or structural barriers that might keep some groups from gaining access. The sustained history of the denial of the vote to Black Americans in the past, and in some instances present, hurdles to registration and voting make it difficult to maintain that interest groups such as the NAACP have had equal access to the political process.

Although in theory the political system might be open to everyone, all groups do not have the same access to decision-makers. In a political world that is more and more dependent on money, groups with more financial resources are going to have an edge. To paraphrase a line from George Orwell's *Animal Farm*, all interest groups are created equal, but some groups are more equal than others. Less well-financed groups must use different tactics to get the attention of decision-makers. These tactics, such as mobilizing the membership, as the environmental movement has done through grassroots lobbying, are more difficult to organize and manage successfully. "Measuring Equality: Selected Racial and Ethnic Interest Groups and Their Resources" lists a number of interest groups that focus on issues of concern to racial and ethnic groups. As Table 13.4 demonstrates, the resources they have available to them are quite modest. For example, in 2016 the NAACP Legal Defense Fund (LDF) had a total revenue of approximately $24.4 million, and in 2016 the Mexican American Legal Defense and Education Fund (MALDEF) had a budget of $8.8 million. In contrast, the well-funded ACLU had more than $144 million in total financial support and revenue in 2017.[96]

All three of these organizations use litigation as their strategy, but the ACLU has far more resources at its disposal to battle in court than do MALDEF and the LDF. Most of the interest groups that represent the concerns of racial and ethnic groups do not have substantial budgets. These groups cannot afford

measuring equality

Selected Racial and Ethnic Interest Groups and Their Resources

Racial and ethnic interest groups compete with other interest groups from a position of constrained resources. This resource deficit suggests that for these groups to bring issues to the fore and to be successful they must rely on their organizational, litigation, and political activity rather than on a foundation of healthy budgets to support their work. The text discusses the difference between the budgets of the NAACP Legal Defense and Educational Fund and the American Civil Liberties Union. Both are successful interest groups, but the LDF has done so from an incredibly smaller resource base, as shown in Table 13.4.

TABLE 13.4 **Selected Racial and Ethnic Interest Groups and Their Resources**

Name of Group	Year of Founding	Revenue*	Current Concerns
African Americans			
Congress of Racial Equality (CORE)	1942	2016: <$1 million **	Self-determination, equality, equal access to information, technology and healthcare
Joint Center for Political and Economic Studies	1970	2016: $1.8 million	Black economic studies and minority economic advancement, Black voter registration and participation, business development, civil rights, education, health policy, welfare and poverty
NAACP Legal Defense and Educational Fund, Inc. (LDF)	1940	2016: $33.9 million	Affirmative action (education and workplace), civil rights, fair employment, housing reform, felon disenfranchisement, voting rights
National Association for the Advancement of Colored People (NAACP)	1909	2016: $24.4 million	Affirmative action, environmental racism, economic opportunities, equal access to education, Supreme Court
National Urban League	1910	2016: $53.1 million	Civic engagement, civil rights, economic self-sufficiency, education and career development, employment and job training, health and quality of life
Latinos			
LatinoJustice PRLDEF	1972	2015: $2.6 million	Immigrant discrimination, rights of Latina immigrant workers, redistricting
League of United Latin American Citizens (LULAC)	1929	2016: <$1 million	Economic conditions, educational attainment, political influence, housing, health and civil rights
Mexican American Legal Defense and Education Fund (MALDEF)	1968	2016: $8.8 million	Education, employment, immigrants' rights, political access, public resource equity
UnidosUS (formerly National Council of La Raza [NCLR])	1968	2015: $36.7 million	Assets/investments, civil rights, immigration, education, employment, economic status, health, census policy

measuring equality _(Continued)_

Name of Group	Year of Founding	Revenue[*]	Current Concerns
Asian Americans			
Asian American Legal Defense and Education Fund	1974	2016: $1.4 million	Immigrant rights, civic participation, voting rights, economic justice for workers, language access, census policy, affirmative action, educational equity, elimination of anti-Asian violence, police misconduct, human trafficking
American Indians			
National Congress of American Indians	1944	2016: $3.5 million	Tribal governance, community development, health and human services, land and natural resources, cultural protection, federal recognition
Native American Rights Fund (NARF)	1970	2016: $30.8 million	Tribal existence/sovereignty, tribal natural resources, religious freedom, voting rights

[*] _The most recent financial data available is provided in this table._

[**] _GuideStar. (2016). GuideStar report generated for Congress of Racial Equality. Retrieved August 4, 2016, http://www.guidestar.org/ViewPdf.aspx?PdfSource= 0&ein=30-0454763._

Sources: http://www.guidestar.org; http://www.charitynavigator.org.

many of the amenities that allow them to gain access to decision-makers on the same footing as other better-financed interest groups do.

There is an additional element of complexity for organizations that represent the interests of what political scientist Dara Z. Strolovitch refers to as "marginalized groups": How well do these interest groups represent the concerns of members within their groups who are further marginalized? Strolovitch suggests that within each of these larger groups are issues that affect the group's population as a whole, issues that affect the majority of the members equally, issues that affect an advantaged subgroup within the group, and issues that are related to an economically, socially, or politically disadvantaged subgroup within the broader membership group. What she finds is that, even though the relevant interest groups provide some representation for their disadvantaged members, they are substantially less active when it comes to issues affecting disadvantaged subgroups than they are when it comes to issues affecting more advantaged subgroups.[97]

For example, Black and Latino interest groups are more likely to highlight majority issues such as racial profiling (Black) and census undercount (Latino) than either is to emphasize welfare (disadvantaged-subgroup issue).

Both interest groups address universal issues, such as Social Security, and advantaged-subgroup issues of affirmative action in government contracting and higher education. In the past, general civil rights organizations address the majority issue of hate crimes, but shy away from disadvantaged-subgroup issues such as discrimination against lesbian, gay, bisexual, transgender, and queer (LGBTQ) individuals. But recently, the NAACP has come out in support of same-sex marriages and support for antidiscrimination laws to protect LGBTQ individuals. What Strolovitch's research reveals is that within the broader system of inequalities among the interest groups representing Blacks and other racial and ethnic groups, there are further inequalities within those groups over which issues and which segments of their constituents are addressed.

Conclusion

This chapter has explored what interest groups are and what role they play in a democratic society. There are many different types of interest groups, with differing objectives, and these groups vary in many substantive ways. The various techniques interest groups use to influence political leaders on issues of importance to them have been discussed, along with some of the constraints that interest groups face in contributing money to politicians they feel will be important to their policy positions.

The common assumptions about interest groups are that "special interests" are code words for forces that operate against the public good and that the only special interests that matter are those funded by big money. In contrast, the story of racial and ethnic interest groups reveals that some special interests are very important for protecting and asserting the rights of groups often pushed to the margins of American society.

Even though the NAACP, the Urban League, and other interest groups that operate on behalf of racial and ethnic minorities are not the best funded, they can be effective. When they are effective, it is because their message or cause catches the attention and spirit of the general public or a significant portion of the public. In this instance, numbers can be as important as dollars. These interest groups are also effective when they employ strategies that do not rely entirely on money or numbers, for example, when they file specifically chosen and carefully researched lawsuits. Interest groups have been pivotal in American politics in the struggle for civil, political, and constitutional protections and rights for racial and ethnic groups. The vignette at the beginning of the chapter demonstrated how various Muslim civil rights groups organized to oppose what they perceive to be attacks on Muslim Americans. This is not the only Muslim civil rights group and they have joined forces to protect the rights of Muslim Americans in many different arenas.

Check your understanding of Chapter 13.

review
REVIEW QUESTIONS

1. What are interest groups, and what do they do?

2. Why do interest groups form, and who belongs to interest groups?

3. What tactics and strategies do interest groups use?

4. How do racial and ethnic interest groups differ from other types of interest groups?

5. What factors contribute to the success of racial and ethnic interest groups?

Flashcard review.

terms
KEY TERMS

Collective Good p. 410
Electioneering p. 423
Free Rider p. 409

Interest Groups p. 405
Iron Triangle p. 409
Lobbying p. 422

Logic of Collective Action p. 409
Pluralism p. 406

Need to review key ideas in greater depth? Click here.

readings
ADDITIONAL READINGS

Lowi, T. J. (1979). *The end of liberalism*. New York: Norton.

> This book contains a classic analysis of the extent to which interest groups have captured various parts of the American political process.

Schattschneider, E. E. (1960). *The semisovereign people*. New York: Random House.

> This critique of pluralism identifies the elitist nature of interest groups and their effect on the political system.

Schlozman, K. L., & Tierney, J. T. (1986). *Organized interests and American democracy*. New York: Harper & Row.

> The authors present a thorough examination of interest groups, their tactics and techniques, and their activities.

Strolovitch, D. (2007). *Affirmative advocacy: Race, class, and gender in interest group politics*. Chicago: University of Chicago Press.

> This book explores how interest groups concerned with racial, ethnic, and gender issues have difficulty addressing the concerns of the most marginalized among their constituencies.

Sullivan, P. (2009). *Lift every voice: The NAACP and the Civil Rights Movement*. New York: New Press.

> This book is the first major history of the NAACP.

14

Political Parties: Linking Voters and Governing Institutions

Democratic National Committee (DNC) Chair Tom Perez (left) and Deputy Chair Keith Ellison (right) joining forces to promote the Democratic Party. Perez and Ellison fought a divisive battle for the Chair position, and progressive and more centrist Democrats, who clashed in the 2016 election, fought over these two candidates as well. Perez secured a close victory over Ellison to become the first Latino DNC Chair. To placate the progressives, he named Ellison Deputy Chair.

Thomas Edward Perez was born in Buffalo, New York, in 1961 to parents who immigrated from the Dominican Republic. Perez's father died from a heart attack when Perez was only 12; despite this, Perez was a high-achieving student. He went to Brown University, where he supported himself through manual labor jobs, such as collecting trash, and after graduating from Brown, Perez earned a law degree and a master's in Public Policy, both from Harvard. Perez began his legal career working in the Office of Civil Rights in the U.S. Department of Justice. He then worked on Senator Edward Kennedy's (D-MA) staff. During President Bill Clinton's administration (1993–2001), Perez was Attorney General Janet Reno's deputy attorney general and then ran the Office for Civil Rights in the Department of Health and Human Services. After Republicans assumed control of the White House in 2001, Perez concentrated his efforts on state and local politics. He was elected as the first Latino to serve on the Montgomery County (Maryland) Council, and Democratic Governor Martin O'Malley appointed him as the head of the Maryland Department of Labor, Licensing, and Regulation. After Democratic President Barack Obama assumed office in 2009, Perez returned to work in the federal government. In Obama's first term, he was the Assistant Attorney General for Civil Rights, and in Obama's second term, he was the Secretary of Labor, a cabinet positon (see Chapters 7 and 8).[1]

As the Obama administration was ending in 2016, Perez considered his future. He was on the shortlist to be Hillary Clinton's running mate; he would have been the first Latino running mate for a major political party. However, Clinton selected Senator Tim Kaine (D-VA) instead of Perez. After the Democrats' poor performance in the 2016 election, especially Clinton's loss to Donald Trump, Perez decided to run for the position of chair of the Democratic National Committee (DNC).[2] The chair of a party's national committee is responsible for fundraising, candidate recruitment, and messaging for the party in its upcoming election. For the party out of power, the DNC chair also leads opposition to the Republican-controlled government, especially President Trump.

The party national committee members each vote to select their chair, and in 2017 Perez's main competition for the chair position was House of Representative member Keith Ellison (D-MN), who is African American and the first Muslim elected to the House. Whereas Ellison represented the progressive wing of the Democratic Party, Perez represented the mainstream or "establishment" wing of the party. Although President Barack Obama was able to reconcile differences between these two wings, their disagreements emerged in the 2016 election primary battle between the Hillary Clinton against the progressive Vermont Senator Bernie Sanders. On the first ballot DNC members chose among Perez, Ellison, and a handful of other candidates. After the first ballot, Perez had one more vote than Ellison did, but no candidate won a majority of the votes; therefore, Perez and Ellison faced each other in a run-off election. Perez's supporters heavily lobbied the committee members who voted for another candidate or abstained on the first ballot, and Perez edged Ellison to become the DNC chair—the first Latino to do so. To reconcile with the party's progressive wing, Perez named Ellison as the deputy chair.[3]

Explore party values
and factions.

intro

This story illustrates the importance of political parties in American politics. **Political parties** are mass organizations that seek to elect candidates to public office and ultimately influence public policy by linking voters with governing institutions. Consequently, the position of a national committee chair, such as the one that Tom Perez holds, plays a key role in American politics. Because political parties seek to win elections and influence public policy, they need to develop political strategies to attract as many voters as possible, especially among America's growing racial and ethnic minority populations. It is important to note that Perez is only the fifth racial or ethnic minority to chair a major political party. The others are Ron Brown, who was African American and chaired the Democratic National Committee in the 1990s; Mel Martinez, who is Latino and chaired the Republican National Committee in the 2000s; Michael Steele, who is African American and chaired the Republican National Committee in the early 2010s; and Donna Brazile, who is African American and was the interim chair of the DNC during the 2016 election.

This chapter focuses on the important aspects of political parties. We begin by tracing the development of the American two-party system. Then we examine how parties are organized at the national, state, and local levels. We also address voters' connections to political parties and group attachments to them. Although the political parties also function in government, we covered this aspect of political

Political Parties Mass organizations that seek to elect candidates to public office and influence policymaking.

parties in Chapters 6, 7, and 9; therefore, in this chapter, we pay less attention to the role of political parties in governing. This chapter emphasizes the relationship between political parties and minority-group politics.

The Development of the Two-Party System

Two-Party System A government system in which only two political parties realistically compete for elected offices.

The United States currently has a **two-party system** in which only the Republican Party and the Democratic Party realistically compete for most elected offices. For that reason, we begin by looking at the development of our two-party system. We first discuss the history of early political parties, specifically focusing on the formation of the Republican Party and the Democratic Party. We then address how the Republican Party and the Democratic Party have changed in terms of balance of power and ideology. We also discuss the important **minor parties**—that is, political parties other than the Democrats and Republicans—that still can influence American politics. We emphasize how political party development has intersected with the politics of race and ethnicity.

Minor Parties Political parties in a two-party system that are not one of the dominant two political parties.

Reforming The Two-Party System in Iowa

The Early Parties

President George Washington, like most of the Framers, vociferously opposed the formation of political parties. In fact, he included within his administration people who held divergent political views. His Secretary of the Treasury, Alexander Hamilton, favored increasing national power, expanding the urban areas, and using the national government to promote economic expansion. Conversely, Washington's Secretary of State, Thomas Jefferson, supported preserving state and local power, limiting the national government, and promoting an agricultural economy.[4]

Democratic-Republicans An early political party that Thomas Jefferson formed to oppose the nationalist policies of John Adams and Alexander Hamilton.

When President Washington declined to run for a third term in 1796, Jefferson and Adams faced each other in the presidential election. The supporters of Jefferson became known as the **Democratic-Republicans** (or Jeffersonian-Republicans) and the supporters of Adams were known as the **Federalist Party**. Despite the similar name, the Federalist Party is not necessarily the same as the Federalists who supported ratification of the Constitution. This development marked the beginning of the American two-party system.[5]

Federalist Party An early political party led by John Adams and Alexander Hamilton that supported nationalizing the economy.

After Adams's narrow Electoral College victory, Jefferson's supporters continued to attack Adams, especially in the press. In response, the Federalists, who controlled Congress, passed the **Sedition Act**, which criminalized harsh criticism of Adams and his policies. Many of Jefferson's supporters were severely punished under this act. In response, Jefferson used his opposition to the Sedition Act to organize against Adams and the Federalists. The election of 1800 featured a rematch between John Adams, the Federalist candidate, and Thomas Jefferson, the Democratic-Republican candidate. In preparation for that election, Jefferson organized Democratic-Republicans throughout the country at the local level. In addition to focusing on his own campaign, Jefferson seeded Democratic-Republican candidates to run for the U.S. House of Representatives and state offices.[6]

Sedition Act A 1798 law that criminalized harsh criticism of President John Adams and his policies.

The Democratic-Republicans won handily in races throughout the nation, and the party won a majority of electoral votes. However, Jefferson and another Democratic-Republican, Aaron Burr, actually received the same number of electoral votes. Ultimately, the House of Representatives selected Jefferson as president. Because of the problems with the election of 1800, the **Twelfth Amendment** to the Constitution was ratified in 1804 to require that the presidential and vice presidential selections take place on separate ballots. This change allowed political parties to flourish because it ensured that a party's presidential and vice presidential candidates could run as a team representing the party.[7]

Twelfth Amendment An amendment to the Constitution that requires the president and vice president to be elected on separate ballots.

The election of 1800 also brought about the demise of the Federalists and in essence created a one-party system in the United States. Throughout the early nineteenth century, Democratic-Republicans dominated national, state, and local governments. Despite the one-party government, political, geographical, and social cleavages persisted. Northerners clashed with Southerners over the issue of slavery, class differences were widening, and the coastal cities conflicted with the interior region over economic development.[8]

By the election of 1824, these factions could no longer coexist in the same political party, and four significant candidates were running for president as Democratic-Republicans. Although Andrew Jackson, who represented commoners and Western settlers, won a plurality of the electoral votes, he did not win a majority. Speaker of the House Henry Clay finished fourth in the election, but he used his power to give the presidency to John Quincy Adams (recall that the House selects the president when no candidate secures a majority of the Electoral College), who represented the Northern elite and finished second to Jackson in the Electoral College and popular votes. Adams then appointed Henry Clay to be secretary of state. Andrew Jackson and his supporters referred to this arrangement as a "corrupt bargain," and they organized at the local level throughout the nation to oppose the Adams administration. This organization became the **Democratic Party**. Unlike previous party organizations, which revolved around political elites, Jackson used common people to organize campaigns. In 1828, Jackson and his Democrats challenged John Quincy Adams, and the Democratic Party's superior organizing ability gave Jackson a solid victory.[9]

Democratic Party One of the two major political parties, established by Andrew Jackson in the 1820s to champion the interests of commoners.

Additionally, Jackson used his authority over federal appointments and federal contracts to reward Democratic Party activists who brought voters to the polls; that is, he instituted the patronage system, which we discussed in detail in Chapter 8. Although patronage had existed previously, Jackson greatly expanded it to cover most federal workers, and he established local patronage organizations, known as machines, to bring in voters at the local level. Undoubtedly, the exchange of votes for jobs and contracts was corrupt. Nevertheless, Jackson argued that patronage was the right of the victor, and it made the bureaucracy more responsive and democratic by giving commoners government jobs. The patronage machines were also inclusive of immigrants who faced ethnic discrimination in the private sector. As long as party activists produced votes, patronage machines would provide them with jobs regardless of their ethnic background. However, there is considerable debate over the extent to which patronage actually helped immigrants and ethnic minorities.[10]

Opposition parties soon developed over disagreement with Jackson's policies and his aggressive use of presidential power. Henry Clay, who in 1832 had failed to unseat Jackson for the presidency, unified a diverse group of Jackson's opponents into a political party known as the **Whigs**. Although there was a diversity of beliefs among the Whigs, all party members shared an antipathy toward Andrew Jackson. By 1840, Whigs had won twenty gubernatorial elections spanning the nation, and Whig candidate William Henry Harrison had won the presidency.[11]

The Whigs and the Democrats competed for national, state, and local positions throughout the 1840s, thus reestablishing a two-party system. However, both parties suffered from internal factional strife, primarily over the issue of slavery in the expanding territories. During the 1850s, internal disagreements over slavery permanently destroyed the Whig Party. In 1854, antislavery

Whigs A political party founded in the 1830s to oppose the politics and policies of President Andrew Jackson.

Immigrants are naturalized in Tammany Hall in New York City. During the nineteenth century, Tammany Hall was the most important political party machine and exerted a significant influence over American politics. Because party organizations were most concerned about winning elections, they were more open to immigrants than were most other segments of American life. Although immigrants are undoubtedly treated better today than they were during the nineteenth century, the issue of immigration is still central to party politics.

Whigs, unaligned abolitionists, and even some antislavery Northern Democrats formed the **Republican Party**. The party opposed expanding slavery, insisted that the Union remain united, and promoted industrialization. In 1860, slavery divided the Democratic Party to the point that it named two presidential candidates, which allowed Republican Abraham Lincoln to win the presidential election.[12]

Republican Party One of the two major political parties, founded in the 1850s by former Whigs who opposed slavery.

Realignment and Republican Party Dominance

Immediately following the Civil War, there was competition between the two parties, but the Republicans tended to be more successful. From the end of the Civil War until 1896, the Republicans controlled the presidency, with only one Democrat—Grover Cleveland—serving as president during that period. However, it is worth noting that Democratic presidential candidates won the popular vote in 1876 (Samuel Tilden) and 1888 (Grover Cleveland), but they lost in the Electoral College.[13] During this period, the parties generally split control of the House of Representatives,[14] but Republicans controlled the Senate for all but three terms (one of which the parties evenly split).[15]

By the election of 1896, groups of voters in the United States had shifted their support to the Republican Party. The upper class, middle class, farmers, Northerners, Midwesterners, Westerners, and even the few African Americans who could vote supported Republicans; Democratic support came only from the South and some parts of Northern urban areas, although most urban areas voted Republican during this time. Moreover, this shift in support in favor of the Republican Party lasted for an extended period; it was not a one-time phenomenon. Between 1897 and 1933, the only Democratic president was Woodrow Wilson (1913–1921). Republicans also controlled the House and Senate for the majority of that period. During this period, the Republican Party was successful in every region of the nation, except for the South, where the Democrats dominated. The election of 1904 best illustrates this regional divide. Although the Democratic candidate, Alton Parker, was from New York, he won only in the eleven former Confederate states plus Kentucky and Maryland. Theodore Roosevelt—the Republican—won in every other state.[16]

Political scientists use the term **realignment** to refer to periods when voter allegiances toward the political parties shift for an extended period of time, resulting in one party's emerging as dominant.[17] (See Table 14.1 for a view of party domination and demise.) There is some disagreement among political scientists concerning which elections initiated a realignment, especially because some of the early examples coincided with the initial development of the two-party system (e.g., 1800, 1828, and 1860). Nevertheless, 1896 is commonly regarded as the beginning of a realignment in favor of the Republican Party. However, David Mayhew, an eminent political scientist, doubts the validity of the realignment concept.[18]

Realignment Periods when voter allegiances toward the political parties shift for an extended period of time, resulting in one party emerging as dominant.

During this period of Republican dominance, there were key policy differences between the Republicans and the Democrats. The Democratic Party generally represented the interests of laborers; it supported breaking up monopolies,

TABLE 14.1 Major Political Parties in the United States

Political Party	Year Founded	Successes
Federalist	1796	Competitive with Democratic-Republicans until 1816 No longer exists
Democratic-Republican	1796	Competitive with Federalists Dominant until 1824 No longer exists
Democratic	Late 1820s	Competitive with Whigs until 1852 Competitive with Republicans until 1896 Weaker party until 1932 Dominant party until 1968 Competitive with Republicans through present
Whigs	Early 1830s	Competitive with Democrats until 1852 No longer exists
Republican	1854	Competitive with Democrats until 1896 Dominant party until 1932 Weaker party until 1968 Competitive with Democrats through present

ensuring legal protections for workers, and lowering tariffs. Republicans represented wealthy and middle-class voters in the North, Midwest, and West; the party favored less government intervention in the economy.

The issue of extending federal protections for Blacks also separated the two parties. Although the Northern urban Democratic machines incorporated ethnic immigrants, they were not concerned about Blacks. The Southern wing of the Democratic Party, which dominated throughout the South, was adamantly opposed to civil rights and sought to preserve segregation. The Republican Party during this period was split on the issue of civil rights. The party was founded on its opposition to slavery, and during Reconstruction, many "Radical Republicans" in Congress used the power of the federal government to secure civil rights for the former slaves. However, in 1877 Republican president Rutherford B. Hayes formally ended Reconstruction and abandoned the Republican Party's commitment to civil rights. Consequently, the Republican Party fractured into two wings: **Black and Tan Republicans** supported federal enforcement of civil rights for African Americans, whereas **Lily White Republicans** did not.[19]

Black and Tan Republicans
A wing of the Republican Party that supported civil rights for African Americans.

Lily White Republicans
A wing of the Republican Party that opposed civil rights for African Americans.

The New Deal Coalition and Democratic Party Dominance

The Republican Party's domination of American politics ended with the 1932 election, which initiated a realignment in favor of the Democrats. In 1932, during the height of the Great Depression, Democratic presidential candidate Franklin Roosevelt promised that, unlike the actions of incumbent Republican president Herbert Hoover, his New Deal would use the federal government to alleviate suffering, stimulate the economy, and prevent similar problems from recurring. This message, coupled with Roosevelt's unique ability to bring optimism to a gloomy electorate, gave him, as well as House and Senate Democrats, a landslide victory that made Democrats the majority party for the first time since the Civil War.[20]

Democratic control persisted throughout the 1930s and 1940s because Roosevelt assembled a **New Deal coalition** consisting of traditional Democratic supporters in the South and in Northern cities, as well as farmers, the middle class, and even African Americans. All of these groups allied with the Democrats because they viewed the New Deal as the best solution to their economic problems.[21] From 1933 through 1968, only one Republican served as president (Dwight Eisenhower, from 1953–1961) and the Democrats controlled Congress almost 90 percent of the time.[22]

Despite the dominance of the Democratic Party during this period, there were conflicts within the party, especially over the issue of civil rights. Traditionally, the Democratic Party had vigorously opposed civil rights legislation, whereas Republicans had been divided over the issue. However, after Roosevelt brought more African Americans into the Democratic Party, many party leaders advocated federal enforcement of civil rights laws. This controversy erupted during the Democratic National Convention in 1948 when presidential nominee Harry Truman insisted that the Democrats support civil rights. Under the leadership of South Carolina governor Strom Thurmond, Southern delegates walked out of the convention and formed the States' Rights Party. The fledgling party nominated Thurmond as their presidential candidate.[23] Despite the fact that Truman was reelected, Thurmond won the states of South Carolina, Louisiana, Alabama, and Mississippi, which had voted Democratic in every other election since Reconstruction.[24]

White Southerners' ties to the Democratic Party weakened again in 1964. Democratic president Lyndon Johnson successfully pushed for key civil rights legislation, but Republican presidential nominee Barry Goldwater vigorously opposed the federal government's involvement in civil rights. Although Johnson won a landslide victory, Goldwater did extremely well in the South.[25]

The End of Party Dominance and the Rise of Party Competition

With the election of 1968, conflicts within the Democratic Party resulted in a loss of its dominance. That is to say, the 1968 election began a period of **dealignment**, a period in which voters abandon their ties to the political parties; consequently, there has been balance between the two parties since 1969.[26] During the period between 1968 and 2016, Republicans won eight presidential elections and Democrats won five, although Democrats Al Gore and Hillary Clinton did win the popular vote in 2000 and 2016, respectively, despite losing the Electoral College and thus the election. Democrats completely controlled Congress slightly more than half the time during that same period, and Republicans completely controlled Congress about one-fifth of the time. There was a split in the control of Congress slightly more than one-fourth of the time.[27] Presidential elections since 2000 have been close in the

New Deal Coalition
The groups that supported President Franklin Roosevelt's policies and as a result made the Democrats the dominant party during the 1930s and 1940s.

Dealignment A period in which voters abandon their ties to the political parties, resulting in a balance of power between Republicans and Democrats.

popular vote, and, although 2000 and 2004 were close in the Electoral College, Democratic President Barack Obama scored sizable Electoral College victories in 2008 and 2012, but in 2016 Republican Donald Trump won the Electoral College while losing the popular vote by almost three million votes.[28]

The Democrats fractured during the late twentieth century because of continued policy disputes among party members. Foreign-policy disagreements contributed to the loss of the party's dominance. In 1968, the Democrats were extremely divided over the Vietnam War, which President Johnson had perpetuated, and during the 1980s, many people who had generally voted Democratic supported Republican presidential candidate Ronald Reagan because of his hardline stance against communism. Social issues such as abortion, gay rights, and prayer in school also splintered the Democratic Party. Socially conservative working-class voters, who had been voting for Democrats because of economic reasons, began supporting the Republican Party because of its conservative positions on social issues. Likewise, many wealthy and suburban voters, who had traditionally voted Republican because of economic issues, switched to the Democratic Party because the Republicans' conservative stance on social issues alienated them.[29]

Race has been a major cause of changes in party balance. By the 1960s, Democratic Party leaders fully embraced civil rights, which earned them the support of most African Americans. In 1968, segregationist Alabama governor George Wallace left the Democratic Party and ran for the presidency on the American Independent Party ticket. Wallace won the states of Arkansas, Louisiana, Mississippi, Alabama, and Georgia. Except for President Johnson's home state of Texas, all other Southern states supported Republican candidate Richard Nixon.[30] Nixon and his strategists, particularly Kevin Phillips, employed the so-called *Southern Strategy*, in which Republicans would espouse conservative positions, especially on race, in order to win in the South and be more competitive nationally with the Democrats.[31]

Since then, the South has tilted Republican, with Whites largely supporting the Republicans and Blacks overwhelmingly supporting the Democrats. Barack Obama did narrowly win in Florida, North Carolina, and Virginia in 2008 and in Florida and Virginia in 2012, which indicates slight improvement from the 2000 and 2004 elections, when Democrats were shut out in the South. Nevertheless, in 2016 Hillary Clinton only won in Virginia,[32] and as of November 2018 there are only three Democratic governors in the former Confederacy (Ralph Northam in Virginia, John Bel Edwards in Louisiana, and Roy Cooper in North Carolina). Republicans control all eleven state legislatures.

Minor Parties

Although American political party development has been characterized by the two major parties, there have been important minor parties throughout American history. Minor parties have focused on specific issues, such as the Prohibition Party, which seeks to ban alcohol, although it also opposes abortion, same-sex marriage, and gambling (including state lotteries).[33] Conversely,

A pin supporting the candidacy of Alabama Governor George Wallace (1919–1998) for president. Originally a Democrat, Wallace ran as an Independent in 1968 because he was dissatisfied with the Democratic Party's support for civil rights policies. Although he lost the election, Wallace performed well for a minor party candidate, winning 9 million votes and 46 electoral votes (all from the South). Moreover, his actions split the Southern states from the Democratic Party and ensured a period of Republican domination in the region. In 1972, Wallace rejoined the Democratic Party and again ran for president, but he was paralyzed in an assassination attempt during the primary. He then returned to Alabama to serve three more terms as governor. Later in life, he sought the forgiveness of Alabama's Black population and their votes were crucial to maintaining him in office.

the United States Marijuana Party pursues exclusively the decriminalization of currently illegal drugs, especially marijuana.[34] Other minor parties represent socioeconomic groups that the two parties have ignored. For example, during the late nineteenth century the People's Party (also known as the Populist Party) promoted the interest of small famers, laborers, and miners, arguing that the Republicans and Democrats ignored their concerns. The People's Party advocated for ending corruption, establishing silver as currency, instituting a progressive income tax, and regulating corporations.[35]

Minor parties can be ideologically based. During the early twentieth century, the Progressive Party was concerned with political and electoral reform, including women's suffrage. It also advocated for minimum wage, labor rights, and preserving the wilderness.[36] In 1912 former Republican president Theodore Roosevelt ran as the Progressive Party candidate. Although Democrat Woodrow Wilson won that race, Roosevelt performed better than incumbent Republican president William Howard Taft did.[37]

Some minor parties have emphasized race and ethnicity (see the Evaluating Equality box). During the late nineteenth century, the Equal Rights Party sought civil rights for Blacks and women's suffrage. In fact, in 1872, it nominated a female presidential candidate, Victoria Woodhull, and an African American vice presidential candidate, Frederick Douglass.[38] Unfortunately, most minor parties dealing with race and ethnicity have been based on maintaining prejudice, not on advancing civil rights. The States' Rights Party and the American Independent Party both supported segregation and decried federal involvement in enforcing civil rights laws,[39] and they were successful in the South in the 1948 and 1968 elections, respectively.[40]

Party Organization

To organize voters, win elections, and influence public policy, political parties require complex organizations to articulate a coherent set of policy goals and run campaigns. Although government leaders, such as members of Congress and of the executive branch, are important to political party organizations, much of the work of political parties is conducted by party activists, who operate away from public view. There are different components of political party organization: the party conventions, the national committees, and state and local organizations. In each component, there is a relationship between minority-group politics and party organization.

National Party Conventions

Distinguish between the groups that make up a party.

The national party conventions are held every four years (during the summer of election years), and they are important features of political party organizations. At these national conventions, delegates nominate their presidential and vice presidential candidates, offer a statement of the party's principles and beliefs, and make rules to govern the party. Each state sends a number of delegates proportional to the size of its population. These delegates are party activists who are usually attached to a specific candidate for the presidential nomination.[41]

The method for selecting delegates to the convention has been extremely controversial. Early in our nation's history, party members in Congress nominated presidential and vice presidential candidates, but in 1832, the Democrats moved to the caucus-convention system in which party members met in local meetings called **caucuses** to select convention delegates. By taking away the nomination decision from elite government leaders and giving it to local party activists, the caucus-convention system increased commoners' political access. However, local party leaders used power that they amassed through patronage to direct the outcome of the caucuses and thus influence presidential and vice presidential nominations.[42]

Caucuses A method for political parties to select their candidates for office whereby party members convene at local meetings.

Primaries A method for political parties to select their candidates for office whereby people vote in an election.

To limit the control of local party leaders, many states switched from caucuses to **primaries**, in which party members select nominees through elections. Registered members of the political party vote for candidates in the

evaluating equality

Minor Parties and Racial and Ethnic Minorities

As we have demonstrated in this chapter, the United States has a two-party system in which the Republican Party and the Democratic Party dominate politics and government. Minor parties, albeit occasionally important, rarely win elections to major federal and state offices.

Our election system is one reason that the two major parties continue to dominate elections, especially in the House of Representatives. All House seats are single-member districts, with winner-take-all elections. Thus, each state is divided into geographical regions, known as districts, and a single representative represents each district. The candidate who gets the most votes in that district wins the election, even if he or she has not received a majority of the votes and has finished only a few votes ahead of the second-place finisher. As a result, it is virtually impossible for a minor party candidate to finish first in any district. Therefore, minor party candidates are unlikely to serve in representative institutions.

An alternative system, known as proportional representation, has multimember districts. In this system, as seen in nations such as Israel, Italy, and Germany, a state is not divided into single-member districts. Instead, the entire state, or a region of the state, selects several representatives, and the top vote-getters are awarded seats. For example, if a region sends five representatives to a legislative chamber, then the region is not divided into five separate districts. Instead, the top five vote-getters are sent to the chamber. Therefore, minor party candidates have a decent chance of finishing in the top five and being elected. In some nations, such as Israel, there are no districts; legislative seats are awarded by party proportional to the outcome of the vote.

There has been considerable debate over whether the United States should adopt a proportional representation system to give minor parties more of a voice, and this debate is especially relevant for minority-group politics. On the one hand, if the United States adopts a proportional representation system, then racial and ethnic minority groups can form political parties specifically geared to their needs, and those parties could win seats in the U.S. House and in state legislatures. Alternatively, minority groups could coalesce to form a political party that focuses on the general needs of racial and ethnic minority groups. Even if minority groups do not form their own political parties, other minor parties could be an attractive alternative for minority voters. For example, in 2016 the Green Party ticket featured Ajamu Baraka, an African American, as its vice presidential candidate.[*]

Conversely, proportional representation could result in the election of overtly prejudiced parties or other people whose views are contrary to the goals of racial and ethnic minorities. In some proportional representation nations, such as Germany, outright racist political parties are banned. However, because the First Amendment guarantees free-speech and free-association rights (see Chapters 2 and 4), it is difficult to ban prejudice-based parties in the United States.

Debate among your classmates the merits of a proportional representation system for the United States, which would give more power to minor political parties. In doing so, investigate the following websites of the minor parties that are currently active in the United States: the Libertarian Party (*https://www.lp.org*), the Green Party (*http://www.gp.org*), the Constitution Party (*http://www.constitutionparty.com*), and the Socialist Party (*http://socialistparty-usa.org/theorganizer/*). Which system is better for American politics overall? Which system is better for racial and ethnic minorities in the United States? For a more in-depth analysis of the effect of the type of voting system, see Amy, D. J. (2000). *Behind the ballot box: A citizen's guide to voting systems*. Westport, CT: Praeger.

[*] Jill2016. (n.d.). Meet Ajamu. Retrieved July 18, 2018, from https://www.jill2016.com/meet_ajamu.

primary, and the state awards delegates based on the outcome of that vote. The Democratic Party generally awards delegates proportionally to the outcome in each state, whereas the Republican Party often gives all or most delegates to the winner of the state primary, regardless of the closeness of the result.[43]

Superdelegates Delegates to the Democratic National Convention who are not selected by primaries or caucuses but instead are established party leaders.

The clash between primaries and caucuses exploded during the Democratic Party Convention in 1968. Despite winning numerous primaries, Minnesota senator Eugene McCarthy did not capture the nomination because Vice President Hubert Humphrey secured the nomination through party leaders and delegates selected in caucuses. After the Democrats lost that presidential election, the party changed its rules to better represent regular party members and encourage states to use primaries or at least caucuses that would be more open to the public.[44]

Since the 1970s, many states have switched from caucuses to primaries. Although these reforms increased public access to the party, the Democrats also established the use of **superdelegates**, or party leaders who are automatically selected as delegates and vote to nominate the candidate they prefer regardless of the results of primaries and caucuses. The Republican Party encouraged its states to use primaries, but it did not adopt all of the Democratic reforms. The use of superdelegates was extremely controversial during the 2016 Democratic Party nomination. Because most superdelegates (as well as a majority of the pledged delegates) supported Hillary Clinton, Bernie Sanders and his supporters complained that the superdelegates give an unfair advantage to candidates who have the support of the party leader but not necessarily the Democratic Party voters. After the 2016 election, Democrats created a Unity Reform Commission to consider superdelegate reforms, such as reducing the number of superdelegates at the Convention and requiring superdelegates to be awarded according to the vote in their states. However, as of the summer of 2018, the party has yet to institute any meaningful superdelegate reforms.[45]

Keynote address by Representative Barbara Jordan, Democratic National Convention, July 12, 1976. In 1972, Jordan became the first African American woman elected to the U.S. House of Representatives from a Southern state. The speech she delivered at this convention is regarded as one of the most rousing convention speeches in American history. In addition to being groundbreaking as a Black female leader, Representative Jordan, who died in 1996, suffered from multiple sclerosis and was confined to a wheelchair for much of her adult life. Moreover, although she never publically announced it, Representative Jordan was a lesbian.

The Democratic reforms of the 1970s also increased the number of racial and ethnic minorities, women, and young people serving as delegates to the national conventions. The Republicans have not adopted these reforms, which is one reason that the delegates to the Democratic National Convention are far more diverse than are the delegates to the Republican National Convention. Figure 14.1 reports Black representation at the Democratic and Republican National

Senator Ted Cruz (R-TX) addresses the Republican National Convention in Cleveland, Ohio, on July 20, 2016, with his image on video in the background. Cruz was the eventual nominee Donald Trump's main opponent during the nominating process. It is common for former opponents to speak during a national convention, but Cruz's speech was extremely controversial because after strongly advocating for conservative principles, Senator Cruz refused to endorse nominee Donald Trump. The crowd reacted with boos. He later stated that during the nominating contests Trump had harshly attacked Cruz's wife Heidi. Trump also suggested that Cruz's father, who was born in Cuba, had been part of the plot to assassinate President John F. Kennedy. There was absolutely no evidence to support this claim, and Cruz did not forgive Trump for these allegations, although he eventually endorsed Trump in the fall.

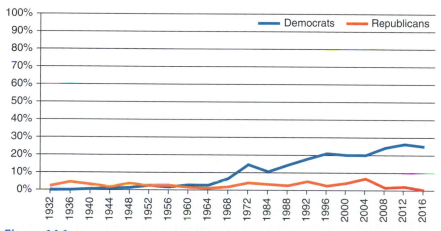

Figure 14.1 Percentage of Convention Delegates Who Are African Americans

Conventions from 1932 through 2016. Black representation at the Democratic National Convention increased after 1968 and especially in 2008 and 2012, when Barack Obama was the nominee. Black representation at the Republican National Convention remained low, especially in 2016.[46]

Party Platform A statement a political party produces at its national convention that summarizes the basic policy principles of the party.

Conventions produce a **party platform**, which delineates the party's basic principles (see "Our Voices: Political Party Platforms and Civil Rights" on page 451). Initially, a committee drafts a platform, which convention delegates must then approve. Because platforms define the party for a particular election, they are important. However, they are nonbinding; in fact, when convenient, candidates oppose parts of their own party's platform. The 2016 Republican Party Platform contains some extremely controversial positions, including allowing states to require transgender people to use the bathroom that corresponds with the sex indicated on their birth certificate; seeking to overturn the U.S. Supreme Court decision that legalized same-sex marriage; claiming that children raised by an opposite-sex married couple are least likely to experience emotional and psychological difficulties (despite the lack of scientific evidence supporting this claim); and declaring pornography to be a public health problem.[47]

National Party Committees

National Committee The organization responsible for making rules and regulations for a party when the conventions are not in session, raising money for the party, and directing the party's electoral strategy.

Because national conventions meet only once every four years, the everyday work of running a national party falls to the national committee—the Republican National Committee (RNC) or the Democratic National Committee (DNC). **National committees** determine the national parties' policy goals, devise electoral strategies, make rules and regulations to govern the party, and raise money for the party and its candidates.[48]

The two parties structure their committees quite differently from one another. Because the Republican Party values state sovereignty, the RNC contains three representatives from each state, the District of Columbia, American Samoa, Guam, Puerto Rico, and the Virgin Islands. At least one of those three representatives must be a woman. The Democratic Party is less concerned with state sovereignty and favors diversity. As a result, state representation on the DNC is proportional to population, and the DNC contains at-large positions designed to increase the representation of minorities and women.[49]

Hard Money The heavily regulated money that is directly raised by political candidates.

Soft Money The less-regulated money that is raised by a political party to support and maintain the party.

In the 1980s and 1990s, the RNC and the DNC increased their power through their control over fundraising. The Federal Election Campaign Act of 1974 limited the amount of donations of **hard money**, through which individuals and groups give money directly to candidates.[50] However, the law had not limited the amount of contributions of **soft money**, unregulated campaign donations that go to support the infrastructure of the party but cannot be used directly on campaigns.[51] By the 1990s, both national committees were using soft money to fund advertisements that did not explicitly suggest voting for a particular candidate, but these ads greatly influenced how people voted. To correct the problems that these advertisements posed, the Bipartisan Campaign Reform Act of 2002 prohibited parties from using soft money for political advertisements; they could use only hard money for that purpose. Political leaders challenged the act as a violation of the First Amendment guarantee of free speech, but the U.S. Supreme Court upheld the constitutionality of the ban.[52] In the next chapter, we discuss campaign financing in more detail.

Explore domestic issues and party platforms.

our voices

Political Party Platforms and Civil Rights

Political party platforms are significant aspects of party politics. They state the party's basic principles, but candidates and elected officials are not bound to them. A committee consisting of party leaders drafts the platforms, a practice that can mean they do not necessarily represent the views of a majority of party members or even party leaders. Nevertheless, because platforms are statements of fundamental party principles, they are a vital way to understand the views of the political parties and predict the type of policies that candidates in that party would seek to enact if elected.

Throughout American history, the issue of race has been crucial in certain party platforms, and here we provide excerpts from different party platforms pertaining to race. Some excerpts represent advancements in civil rights, such as the 1856 Republican Party platform calling for an end to slavery in the territories and the 1948 Democratic Party platform embracing civil rights. Conversely, some excerpts represent a retreat from civil rights, such as the States' Rights Party platform in 1948 and the American Independent Party platform in 1968, both of which emphatically opposed civil rights.

> Republican Party Platform, 1856: As our Republican forefathers, when they abolished Slavery in all our National Territory, ordained that no person shall be deprived of life, liberty, or property without due process of law, it becomes our duty to maintain this provision of the Constitution against all attempts to violate it for the purpose of establishing Slavery in the Territories of the United States . . ., prohibiting its existence or extension therein. . . . We deny the authority of Congress, of a Territorial Legislation, of any individual, or association of individuals, to give legal existence of Slavery in any Territory of the United States. . . . [t]he Constitution confers upon Congress sovereign powers over the Territories of the United States for their government; and that in the exercise of this power, it is both the right and the imperative duty of Congress to prohibit in the Territories those twin relics of barbarism—Polygamy and Slavery.

> Democratic Party Platform, 1948: The Democratic Party commits itself to continuing its efforts to eliminate all racial, religious, and economic discrimination. We again state our belief that racial and religious minorities must have the right to live, the right to work, the right to vote, the full and equal protection of the laws, on a basis of equality with all citizens as guaranteed by the Constitution. We highly commend President Harry S. Truman on his courageous stand on the issue of civil rights. . . . We pledge ourselves to legislation to admit . . . displaced persons found eligible for citizenship without discrimination as to race or religion.

> States' Rights Party, 1948: We stand for the segregation of the races and the integrity of each race. . . . We oppose the elimination of segregation, the repeal of miscegenation statutes, the control of private employment by Federal bureaucrats called for by the misnamed civil rights program. . . . We oppose and condemn the action of the Democratic Convention in sponsoring a civil rights program calling for the elimination of segregation, social equality by Federal fiat, regulations of private employment practices, voting, and local law enforcement.

> American Independent Party, 1968: The Federal Government has adopted so-called "Civil Rights Acts," particularly the one adopted in 1964, which have set race against race and class against class, all of which we condemn. It shall be our purpose to take such steps and pursue such courses as may be necessary and required to restore to the states the power and authority which rightfully belong to state and local governments, so that each state shall govern and control its internal affairs without interference or domination of the Federal Government.

Source: Adapted from Woolley, J., & Peters, G. (1999–2018). Political party platforms. In *American Presidency Project*. Santa Barbara: University of California, Santa Barbara. Retrieved July 18, 2018, from http://www.presidency.ucsb.edu/platforms.php.

National Committee Chair
The head of each party's national committee, who is most responsible for directing the party's electoral strategies.

Because both national committees meet only several times per year, they leave the primary operations of the party to the **national committee chair**. For the party that controls the presidency, the president recommends a committee chair, whom the national committee automatically approves. As the opening vignette shows, the national committee selects the chair on its own for the party that does not control the presidency. The national committee chair and a staff of permanent advisers work behind the scenes to develop the party's political positions, devise electoral strategies, raise money, and coordinate national party goals with those of state and local parties. When a party controls the presidency, its national chair avoids upstaging the president by assuming a less public role than the national committee chair for the party that does not control the presidency.[53]

National committee chairs often influence election outcomes. For example, after the Democratic defeat in the 2004 election, DNC chair Howard Dean instituted the "Fifty State Strategy," in which Democrats would compete in all parts of the country instead of concentrating only on large urban areas and the coastal regions of the United States where Democrats traditionally do well. Dean's strategy was instrumental in the Democrats' success in the 2006 elections when the party won control of the House and Senate, doing exceptionally well in areas where Republicans traditionally win. The Democrats' continued triumphs in 2008, including Barack Obama's comfortable victory, are further evidence of the success of Dean's strategy.[54]

As the opening vignette further indicates, racial and ethnic minorities are not well represented in national party leadership. Ron Brown, who was African American, was the first non-White who chaired the Democratic National Committee. Brown was a key leader of Jesse Jackson's 1988 presidential campaign, and in 1989, the DNC elected him to be chair. Brown's service as DNC chair was crucial to paving the way for Bill Clinton's 1992 presidential victory.[55]

Two minorities have chaired the RNC. In 2006, the RNC named Florida senator Mel Martinez, a Cuban American, as its co-chair, largely to reach out to Latinos. However, Martinez clashed with Republican leaders over his moderate stance on undocumented immigration, and he could not balance his duties as senator and RNC chair; Martinez resigned the RNC position in 2017.[56] In 2009, after President Obama handily defeated Senator John McCain (R-AZ) to become the first Black president, the Republican National Committee elected Michael Steele, an African American and former lieutenant governor of Maryland, as the RNC chair.[57] Although Steele was successful during the 2010 midterm elections, the Republicans returned to a White male national committee chair in 2011 when Reince Priebus defeated Michael Steele. Although Republicans lost the 2012 election, the RNC still reelected Priebus to a second and third term because of his fundraising prowess and success in the 2014 midterm elections.[58] The current chair of the RNC is Ronna McDaniel,[59] who is a White female. The RNC elected her after Reince Priebus left the position to become President Trump's first chief of staff.

There is slightly more minority representation at lower levels of national party leadership. As we have mentioned, the DNC reserves positions for racial and ethnic minorities, and the DNC makes an explicit effort on its website to reach out to Blacks, Latinos, Asian Americans, and American Indians, as well as seniors, LGBTQ communities, and people with disabilities.[60] Also, several DNC officers, in addition to Tom Perez and Keith Ellison, are minorities, including vice chairs Maria Elena Durazo (who is Latina), Michael Blake (who is African American), and Grace Meng (who is Asian American). Additionally, National Finance Committee Chair Henry Muñoz and Treasurer Bill Derrough are Latinos.[61] The RNC currently has no minorities in its leadership,[62] but its website does explicitly reach out to women, Latinos, Blacks, and Asian Americans.[63]

State and Local Organizations

State and local party organizations are important in American politics. The bottom level of local party organization consists of the elected committee members for the smallest political district in the state, usually called a ward or a precinct. Wards or precincts are generally the size of neighborhoods. All interested party members living in the ward select committee members at caucus meetings or through primaries. Each ward committee selects a chairperson. At the next level are the local committees, which cover the geographic region of an urban area, county, or congressional district. Depending on the state, local committee members are chosen at county party conventions or by candidates for office. Local party organizations coordinate election volunteers, telephone local residents, campaign door-to-door, and place campaign signs throughout the area. Additionally, local party committees run candidates in local elections, although many cities and counties are nonpartisan.[64]

The state party central committee is the highest level of state party organization. State central committees perform a variety of important functions, including organizing state conventions, writing state party platforms, raising money, overseeing how the party spends money, selecting the state party's presidential electors, representing the state in national committees, recruiting candidates, and providing candidates with funds, public opinion polling, and media services. Although the state party establishes the rules and regulations for the local parties, the local parties select the members to the state committee; thus, local parties are able to influence the state party's policies.[65]

State and local party organizations used to be extremely powerful, but that power has eroded during the twentieth century. State and local party leaders historically used their positions to control patronage and, as a result, they amassed great wealth and power. One of the most renowned local party leaders was William M. Tweed, known as "Boss Tweed," who ran the Tammany Hall Democratic Party organization in New York City. Beginning in the late nineteenth century, reforms limited their influence. Because precinct bosses could dominate their local area by knowing how many votes each party worker brought, states moved to a secret ballot, which prevented party leaders from knowing who voted for which candidate. Many cities moved to nonpartisan elections, which further limited the power of state and local party leaders.[66]

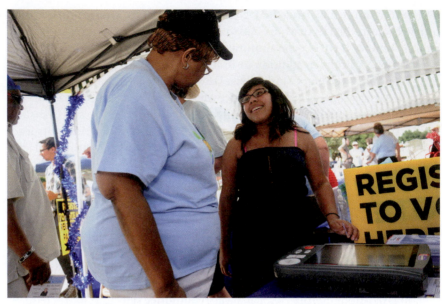

Shelba Richardson (left) explains an electronic voting machine to Brenda Carillo (right). Richardson works for the Montgomery County (Texas) Democratic Party, and she is seeking to ensure that Latinos register and vote in upcoming elections. County party officials, such as Richardson, often interface directly with individuals to increase their party's chance of success in local, state, and national elections.

Find out how political culture shapes government.

White Primary A practice by Southern state Democratic parties in the late nineteenth and early twentieth centuries intended to disenfranchise Blacks by preventing them from voting in the crucial Democratic Party primary elections.

National policies have also limited the power of state and local parties. In 1976[67] and again in 1990,[68] the U.S. Supreme Court overturned patronage practices in state and local governments. Specifically, the Court ruled that hiring government employees based on partisan affiliation punishes applicants from nonfavored political parties, which violates their First Amendment right to freedom of association. Without the ability to promise employment in exchange for party service, state and local parties cannot always easily attract volunteers to work for the party.[69] Despite their decreased influence, state political parties still exert significant authority within their respective states.

The politics of race and ethnicity is relevant in state and local parties. State parties historically perpetrated discrimination by adopting **White Primary** rules, which prevented Blacks from voting in primaries. Southern state Democratic Party organizations claimed that as private groups they were free to prohibit Blacks from voting in primary elections. In the early twentieth century, because the Democrats were the only viable party in the South, primaries effectively determined who would win office. By prohibiting Blacks from voting in the primaries, the state parties effectively disenfranchised all Black voters. In 1944, the U.S. Supreme Court ruled that state party organizations were government institutions, not private organizations, and thus they were constitutionally prohibited from disenfranchising Blacks in primaries.[70]

Since then, racial and ethnic minorities have not only been able to participate in state party primaries, but they have also been better represented in state and local party organizations. Although most state party chairs have been White, there have been some minorities leading state parties. For example, Jennifer Carnahan, the Chair of the Minnesota Republican Party, is Asian American,[71] and the current chair of the Nevada Democratic Party is African American William McCurdy II, who was only 28 years old when he became chair.[72]

Parties and Voters

Ultimately, political parties are concerned with winning elections, which means that understanding how parties function in the electoral process adds to a more complete view of American politics. As we have shown in this chapter, parties recruit and nominate candidates, raise money, and provide election strategies. Because we cover elections in detail in Chapter 15, here we focus more on how the parties function in the minds of the voters: how voters connect with the major political parties and how groups, especially racial and ethnic minorities, attach to those parties.

Party Identification

Voters' psychological attachment to the political parties can be measured through party identification. As we saw in Chapter 10, party identification is ascertained though public opinion surveys. It is usually expressed on a

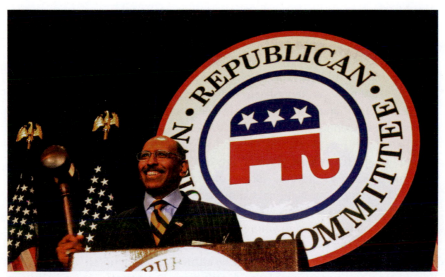

Michael Steele bangs the gavel shortly after being elected as Chair of the Republican National Committee (RNC) in January 2009. Steele was the first African American to serve as the RNC chair, and despite engineering a successful 2010 election campaign for Republicans, the RNC selected Reince Priebus to replace Steele in 2011. Steele is now a commentator on MSNBC.

seven-point scale where a respondent characterizes his or her party identification as Strong Democrat, Weak Democrat, Independent-Leaning Democrat, Independent, Independent-Leaning Republican, Weak Republican, or Strong Republican. Because party identification measures a voter's psychological attachment to the party, it is different from that voter being a registered party member.[73]

It seems intuitively correct that voters' views of the parties' candidates and stances on the issues would influence party identification. This is certainly the case, but political scientists have also shown that individuals establish their party identification because of their upbringing, race and ethnicity, religion, and social class. Therefore, party identification explains how people view the candidates, which in turn affects how they vote. Ultimately, people who identify as Democrats are likely to vote Democratic, and people who identify as Republicans are likely to vote Republican. The Independents and leaners tend to split their votes between the two parties or vote for minor party candidates.[74]

Parties and Group Attachments

Because party identification is so closely tied to social background, it is also tied to geography, a connection we have already discussed. The South used to be solidly Democratic, but it now leans Republican. The Northeast used to be solidly Republican, but now it is much more Democratic. Although region is still important, group attachment to political parties is more complex and includes religious affiliation, income, gender, and race and ethnicity.

There is some relationship between partisanship and age. Recently, younger voters have identified more as Democratic and Independent versus Republican, largely because of their rejection of Republicans' conservative stance on social issues, such as same-sex marriage.[75] A survey from the 2016 election shows that whereas 40 percent of the people born before 1945 identify as Republicans, only 27 percent of Generation X (people born between 1965 and 1980) and 22 percent of millennials (people born between 1981 and 1996) identify as Republican. However, millennials do not necessarily identify as Democrats—they are more likely than older generations to identify as Independents.[76] Exit polls from the 2016 election confirm this age gap. For example, 18- to 29-year-olds voted 55 percent for Clinton and 36 percent for Trump, whereas voters over 65 years old voted for Trump over Clinton by a margin of 52 to 45 percent.[77] Both political parties try to court the younger voters. The Democratic National Committee website devotes a specific section to young voters and students,[78] and the Republican National Committee website also devotes a section to young people.[79]

Because of the two parties' stances on economic issues, such as taxes and welfare spending, one might expect wealthier people tend to identify with Republicans and poorer people to identify with Democrats. However, survey evidence tells a different story. In 2016, party identification for people with annual incomes over $30,000 was roughly equally distributed among Republicans, Democrats, and Independents. Only people with incomes under $30,000 are more likely to identify as Democrats—43 percent Democratic, 17 percent Republican, and 34 percent Independent.[80]

Party identification also corresponds to religious groups. Protestants have traditionally identified with Republicans, and Catholics, many of whom were immigrants and labor union members, tended to be Democrats. However, because Protestantism is so vast, the connection between party and Protestantism is less clear. Adherents to fundamentalist or evangelical Protestant sects are more Republican than are adherents to mainstream or liberal sects of Protestantism. White Protestants identify with the Republicans, whereas Black Protestants overwhelmingly identify with the Democrats. Moreover, some Catholics, particularly religious conservatives, have moved away from the Democratic Party largely because of its liberal stance on social issues, especially abortion and LGBTQ rights.[81] Still, White Catholics tilt Republican, whereas Latino Catholics are more than three times as likely to identify as Democrats than as Republicans. Jewish voters of all age groups have overwhelmingly identified as Democratic.[82]

Soon after women earned the right to vote, there was no relationship between party and gender, but the feminist revolution of the 1960s spawned a gender gap in which women identify with and vote for candidates of the Democratic Party more than men do. In Chapter 10, we discussed the gender gap in terms of differences between male and female opinion on policy issues; here we focus more on the gap's impact on party identification.

Recall that since the 1970s, the Democratic Party has reserved leadership spots for women and adopted positions favoring equal rights. Consequently, women have gravitated toward the Democratic Party. In 2015, there was a 14-point gap between men and women who identified with the Democratic Party (40 percent for women and 26 percent for men).[83] The gender gap in party identification helps explain different voting patterns between men and women. During the 2016 election, Donald Trump won 52 percent of the male vote, whereas Hillary Clinton won 54 percent of the female vote.[84]

Patterns exist for party attachment and racial minority status, which Table 14.2 shows in detail. Because the Republican Party began as an abolitionist party, the few African Americans who could vote in 1856 naturally gravitated toward the Republicans. During Reconstruction, Republican leaders in Congress insisted on federal protections for the civil rights of African Americans. Southern Blacks were active in Republican Party organizations, and all African American politicians were Republicans.[85]

Franklin Roosevelt's presidency caused many African Americans to support the Democratic Party. Not only did African Americans benefit from Roosevelt's economic policies, but also Roosevelt consulted Black intellectuals, such as Robert Weaver, Ralph Bunche, and Mary McLeod Bethune. First Lady Eleanor Roosevelt's outspoken support of civil rights also endeared African Americans to the Democratic Party.[86]

As Blacks migrated to Northern cities, such as Detroit and Chicago, they found a far more welcoming Democratic Party than the segregationist

TABLE 14.2 Partisan Identification by Race and Ethnicity (in Percent)

Group	Democrat	Pure Independent	Republican
African American	88	10	3
Mexican American	56	29	15
Puerto Rican	64	16	20
Cuban American	32	20	48
Dominican	73	17	9
Salvadoran	57	30	13
Other Central American	50	28	22
Other Latino	60	23	17
Japanese American	59	7	34
Chinese American	51	30	18
Korean American	70	3	27
Filipino American	52	13	33
Asian Indian	71	14	13
Vietnamese American	45	25	29
Cambodian	68	6	14
Hmong	76	18	6
American Indian	54	12	34

Note: All numbers are rounded to the nearest percent. Leaners are included with Democrats and Republicans; therefore, Independents are those who would not indicate even a preference for either political party.

Source: Data adapted from McClain, P. D., & Carew, J. D. J. (2018). "Can we all get along?": Racial and ethnic minorities in American politics (7th ed.). Boulder, CO: Westview Press, pp. 95, 98–99, 102–103, 106.

Democratic Party they had known in the South.[87] Lyndon Johnson's strong civil rights record brought most African Americans to the Democratic Party, whereas Republican opposition to the goals of Black civil rights leaders, especially since the 1980s, drove many Blacks away from the Republican Party. Now African Americans overwhelmingly identify as Democrats.

Even though African Americans overwhelmingly identify with Democrats, many observers argue that the Democratic Party takes Blacks for granted. The party actively seeks Black support during elections, but when the election is over, Democrats abandon Blacks by failing to elevate them to leadership positions and ignoring policy issues central to many African Americans. Of course, much of this criticism stems from Black Republicans who seek to draw Blacks to the Republican Party. Even Black leaders who argue that the Democratic Party takes Blacks for granted still promote voting for the Democratic Party. For example, in 2004 Jesse Jackson, who has frequently clashed with White Democratic leaders, quipped, "While some Democrats take Blacks for granted, Republicans take Blacks for fools."[88] In Chapter 15, we discuss in more detail how the Obama presidency may alter the perception that Democrats take Blacks for granted.

Because Latinos are composed of a variety of ethnicities, Latino partisan identification is not uniform. Mexican Americans and Puerto Ricans tend to be Democratic, primarily because of the party's strong commitment to civil rights

measuring equality

Latinos, Religious Preference, and Party Support

As the text, especially Table 14.2, demonstrates, Latino party identification is a complex issue. Mexican Americans and Puerto Ricans are much more likely to identify with Democrats than with Republicans, but Cuban Americans lean toward the Republicans. In other words, Latino political party identification depends on nation of origin. Here we explore another layer of how Latinos view the political parties—religion. We are interested not in national origin, but in the extent to which religious preference influences political party identification among Latinos. We use data from a 2007 survey of Latinos (the most recent figures that are available for these specific issues) in the United States conducted by the Pew Hispanic Center, which is a leading public opinion researcher of Latinos in America.

We compare results among four different religious preferences. First, we examine Catholics, who practice the traditional religion of Latinos because it is the primary religion in Spain. As we discuss in this chapter, Catholics have traditionally identified with the Democrats, but because of issues such as abortion, many Catholics have moved to the Republican Party. Second, we investigate mainline Protestants, the traditional sects of Protestantism (e.g., Baptist, Episcopalian, Lutheran, Methodist, and Presbyterian). Party identification among mainline Protestants generally varies considerably. Third, we look at evangelical Protestants, or born-again Christians. Evangelicals are adherents to newer sects of Protestantism, such as Pentecostals and Assembly of God, and they are extremely religious. They hold conservative views on social issues such as abortion and LGBTQ rights. Consequently, evangelicals in general tend to identify with the Republican Party. Fourth, we examine seculars; that is, Latinos who are not religious. Because nonreligious

people tend to be more liberal than religious people are, seculars in general tend to identify with Democrats.

In addition to looking at Latino party identification among religions, we divide our analysis among different issues. The Pew Hispanic Center asked Latinos to identify which party is better at handling a wide variety of issues, and we selected five issues that are relevant to minority-group politics in general and to Latino politics in particular: (1) the economy, (2) education, (3) immigration, (4) morality, and (5) civil rights. Figure 14.2 reports the results that the Pew Hispanic Center found. Each graph shows the percentage of Latinos in each religious preference category who identify with Democrats and the percentage of Latinos who identify with Republicans. We report only the Democratic and Republican identifiers, not those who answered "independents," "both," or "neither." Consequently, the percentages do not add up to 100 percent.

Although there is some variation in the responses among the different religious groups and across the different issues, there is a clear pattern. On all five issues, Catholic Latinos, mainline Protestant Latinos, and secular Latinos are considerably (two to three times) more likely to identify with Democrats than with Republicans. Conversely, on all five issues, evangelical Latinos split evenly between Democrats and Republicans. These findings indicate that, in addition to national origin, religious preference influences Latino party support.

Source. Data adapted from Suro, R., et al. (2007, April 25). *Changing faiths: Latinos and the transformation of American religion.* Washington, DC: Pew Research Center, pp. 82–83. Retrieved July 19, 2018, from http://www.pewforum.org/2007/04/25/changing-faiths-Latinos-and-the-transformation-of-american-religion-2/.

(Continued)

measuring equality

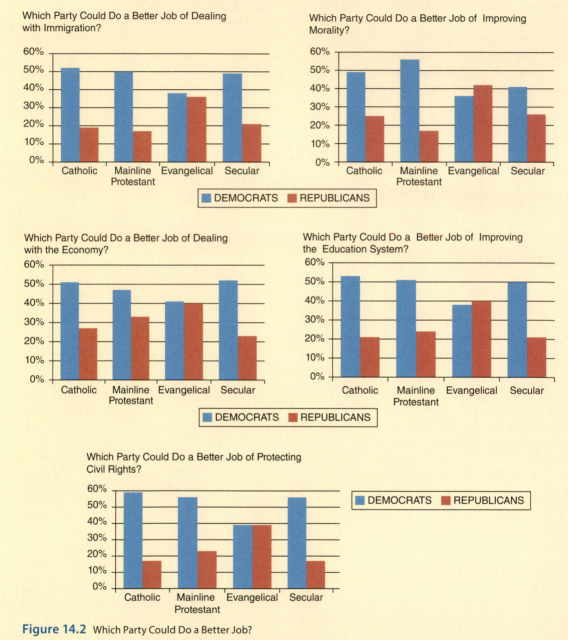

Figure 14.2 Which Party Could Do a Better Job?

and economic policies that benefit the working and middle classes. Cuban Americans, however, are more Republican than Democratic because the Republican Party was strongly opposed to the communist regime of Fidel Castro in Cuba. Moreover, many of the Cuban refugees who came to the United States between 1960 and 1980 were from the upper classes and, as we demonstrated earlier, wealthier people tend to identify with the Republican Party.[89]

There is recent evidence of a slight shift of Cubans toward the Democrats. Many of the post-1980 Cuban immigrants and second- and even third-generation Cuban Americans are less concerned with Fidel (and Raúl) Castro and more concerned with civil rights and economic equality. Moreover, Republican politicians' anti-immigration rhetoric has alienated some Cuban Americans from the Republican Party.[90]

A growing proportion of Latinos come from the Dominican Republic, Central America, and South America. Because they are emerging Latino groups, there is no extensive research on their party identification trends. Nevertheless, Table 14.2, which reflects the most recent analysis of Latino party identification, shows that Central Americans, Dominicans, Salvadorans, and other Latinos are overwhelmingly Democratic. In addition to national origin, Latino party identification differs according to religious intensity. The Measuring Equality box demonstrates that evangelical Latinos are far more likely to identify with Republicans than are other Latino religious groups.

Asian Americans identify with Democrats, most likely because of the Democratic Party's more favorable policies on civil rights and immigration. Nevertheless, for many Asian Americans, particularly Chinese Americans, party affiliation has been fleeting. In the 1970s and 1980s, Chinese Americans and Vietnamese immigrants supported the Republican Party because of its staunch opposition to communism, but more recently, Asian Americans of all ethnicities have favored the Democrats.[91]

There has been scant research conducted on the party affiliation of American Indians. Generally, American Indians identify with the party that exhibits more pro-Indian policies. For example, during the 1970s many Navajos supported Republicans because the Nixon administration conferred more sovereignty to the Navajos over their land. However, by the 1980s American Indians had shifted to Democrats.[92]

Conclusion

Although political parties are not official governing institutions recognized by the U.S. Constitution, they play a crucial role in American politics because they link voters with elected governmental positions. This chapter covered the key aspects of political parties. We examined the complex development of our two-party system, and although the Republicans and the Democrats currently dominate our government, minor parties have occasionally played an important role. We also looked at the organizational structure of political parties, examining the significance of national conventions, national committees, and state and local organizations. The chapter concluded with a discussion of the concept of party identification, as well as group attachments to political parties.

The politics of race and ethnicity has also been quite relevant in political party politics. The issue of slavery divided the Democratic Party, destroyed the Whig Party, and created the Republican Party. After the Civil War, the Democratic Party was staunchly segregationist, whereas the Republicans were split over civil rights. Since the 1940s, the Democratic Party has supported civil rights and attracted African Americans, as well as other racial and ethnic minorities. At the same time, the Democratic Party's support of civil rights has alienated many White southerners, who have drifted to the Republican Party.

Issues of race and ethnicity are also relevant to party organization. The Democratic Party actively sought to increase the representation of racial and ethnic minorities (as well as women and young people) at its national convention and on the DNC. As a result, Democratic Party leadership has more racial and ethnic minorities than Republican Party leadership does. Both parties have had minorities serve as committee chair (Mel Martinez and Michael Steele for the Republicans and Ron Brown, Donna Brazile, and Thomas Perez for the Democrats), but there have been no other racial or ethnic minorities running political parties.

Party identification also has a racial and ethnic component because group attachments to political parties are evident. African Americans, Mexican Americans, Puerto Ricans, Central Americans, Asian Americans, and American Indians tend to identify with the Democratic Party. Cuban Americans tend to identify with the Republican Party. Interestingly, differing religious preference influences party identification for Latinos.

Our opening story about Tom Perez's selection reveals key information about party politics in general and racial and ethnic elements of parties in particular. It illustrates the power and relevance of the national committee chair position.

Perez's selection as DNC chair in 2017 was controversial, especially because the Democrats underperformed in the 2016 election. They were successful with minority voters, but not enough turned out. Additionally, White voters significantly favored Donald Trump, giving him the victory in the Electoral College. However, the Democrats, including Perez, were successful in 2018 because the Democrats won control of the U.S. House of Representatives by a significant margin and flipped several governor seats and state legislatures.

Check your understanding of Chapter 14.

REVIEW QUESTIONS

1. What impact did debates over slavery have on the Whig Party, Democratic Party, and Republican Party?

2. How did issues of race influence the loss of Democratic Party dominance during the late twentieth century?

3. How representative are delegates to the Democratic and the Republican national conventions?

4. What are some examples of racial and ethnic minorities who have led party organizations?

5. What are the party identification breakdowns for Blacks, Mexican Americans, Puerto Ricans, Cuban Americans, Central Americans, Asian Americans, and American Indians? Why does each group tend to identify with a certain party?

KEY TERMS

Flashcard review.

Black and Tan Republicans p. 442
Caucuses p. 446
Dealignment p. 443
Democratic Party p. 439
Democratic-Republicans p. 438
Federalist Party p. 438
Hard Money p. 450

Lily White Republicans p. 442
Minor Parties p. 438
National Committee p. 450
National Committee Chair p. 452
New Deal Coalition p. 443
Party Platform p. 450
Political Parties p. 437
Primaries p. 446

Realignment p. 441
Republican Party p. 441
Sedition Act p. 438
Soft Money p. 450
Superdelegates p. 448
Twelfth Amendment p. 439
Two-Party System p. 438
Whigs p. 440
White Primary p. 454

ADDITIONAL READINGS

Need to review key ideas in greater depth? Click here.

Bruns, R. (2005). *Jesse Jackson: A biography.* Westport, CT: Greenwood Press.

> This book examines Reverend Jesse Jackson's life and career, including his run for the Democratic Party nomination in 1984 and 1988.

Erie, S. P. (1988). *Rainbow's end: Irish-Americans and the dilemmas of urban machine politics, 1840–1985.* Berkeley and Los Angeles: University of California Press.

> In this book, Erie shows that racial and ethnic minorities, immigrants, and even Irish Americans did not benefit from patronage as much as others have claimed.

Goff, K. (2008). *Party crashing: How the hip-hop generation declared political independence.* New York: Perseus Books.

> In this informative and highly readable book, Goff surveys a sample of four hundred African Americans from the post–baby boom generations (those born between 1963 and 1990) and finds that, although these generations of Blacks still have ties to the Democratic Party, these are not as strong as the ties held by their parents and grandparents.

Holmes, S. A. (2000). *Ron Brown: An uncommon life.* New York: Wiley.

> This book chronicles the life and career of Ron Brown, the first Black chair of the Democratic National Committee.

Lublin, R. (2004). *The Republican South: Democratization and partisan change.* Princeton, NJ: Princeton University Press.

> This book examines why the Republican Party has transformed itself from a moribund party in the South into the majority party in that region.

Voting and Elections: The End of the Obama Era

Democratic Senatorial candidate Doug Jones takes a group picture with Sen. Cory Booker (D-NJ) (R) and Rep. Terri Sewell (D-AL) (third from right) and supporters during a campaign event held at Alabama State University on December 9, 2017, in Montgomery, Alabama.

On December 12, 2017, the state of Alabama held a special election to fill the Senate seat that Jeff Sessions had vacated earlier in the year. Sessions had resigned following the Senate's approval of his nomination by President Donald Trump for U.S. Attorney General. About 1.3 million Alabama residents turned out to vote in the December 2017 election, which was more than twice the number of voters who participated in the primary elections.[1] Democrat Doug Jones pulled off a stunning upset in the historic race, defeating Republican nominee Roy Moore in what was a major setback for the Republican Party and a huge blow to President Trump.[2] Jones was the first Democrat in the deeply conservative state of Alabama to win a Senate seat since 1992, and his election represented a monumental victory for the Democratic Party.[3] Jones's victory also signified a rejection by progressive voters of the "divisive brand of politics" that have long been part of the political landscape in Alabama.[4] Jones's win was a major embarrassment for President Trump and other Republican leaders who backed Roy Moore's candidacy, despite a litany of allegations against Moore of past sexual misconduct with teenage girls and bigotry.[5] Jones is a former federal prosecutor who won convictions against two Ku Klux Klan members for the bombing of the 16th Street Baptist Church in Birmingham, Alabama, in 1963, in which four young Black girls were killed. Jones's win also narrowed the Republicans' senate majority,[6] limiting the GOP advantage to 51–49.[7]

African Americans played a decisive role in propelling Jones to victory in the Alabama special election. Local NAACP chapters and other groups engaged in grassroots organizing throughout the state of Alabama. Voting rights groups registered people, participated in voter education efforts and awareness campaigns about voter ID laws, and also focused on specifically addressing issues that would potentially keep Black voters away from the polls.[8] Alabama authorities had imposed stringent voter ID laws in recent years and had also refused to implement and support voter education initiatives. On Election Day, there were some reports of voter suppression and voter intimidation tactics being used against minority voters.[9] Many voters, primarily in majority-Black counties, had difficulty casting their ballots,[10] while some individuals were not allowed to vote at all. Others were given provisional ballots that required them to take further action in order to validate their votes later.[11] Despite concerns of reduced voter turnout and fears that voter suppression tactics would disproportionately affect African Americans, Black voters "made a commanding display of political power."[12] Black turnout surpassed expectations by far, defying the narrative and challenging conventional notions about racial turnout during off-year and special elections.[13] Exit polling data showed that Black voters made up 29 percent of the electorate, and a full 96 percent of that number supported Jones, including 98 percent of African American women.[14] Following Jones's momentous victory, Democratic National Committee chairman Tom Perez posted on Twitter: "Black women led us to victory. Black women are the backbone of the Democratic Party, and we can't take that for granted. Period."[15]

Black voters in Alabama were mobilized to vote in the 2017 special election for a variety of reasons. Some Black voters explained that they were motivated to vote in the special election because they feared that if Roy Moore won the Senate seat, he would work with President Trump to institute policies that would be harmful to the African American community, such as reduced government support for aid initiatives and no criminal justice reform. Many African American voters also expressed dissatisfaction with the general direction the country had been going in, particularly in terms of race relations, since Trump's election in 2016.[16]

intro

Chapter 1 detailed the political philosophies undergirding the U.S. political system. In that discussion, we noted that the representative democracy structure of the United States is based on the principle that individuals elect representatives to present their views and make informed choices on their behalf. This also implies another principle, that individuals have the ability to hold their representatives accountable by voting them out of office if they prove dissatisfactory.

Given these dual principles, and hence dual responsibilities, elections and the electoral process are central to the workings of the Republic. Although elections are at the core of the system, there are many different electoral systems within the United States. By law, every U.S. citizen eighteen years of age and older is eligible to vote. (Exceptions to this include convicted felons in some states, prisoners in correctional facilities in most states, and other people prohibited by state laws.) Yet the rates at which various groups of U.S. citizens register to vote and then actually do vote vary by race, gender, ethnicity, and region of the country. The reasons for the differences are not simply reasons of personal preference. In many cases, historical and structural barriers account for some of the disparity.

Understanding the role of elections and how and why people vote is essential to comprehending the core principles of representative democracy. This chapter explores the electoral process of the United States, and voting is one of the key ingredients of that process. We also look at the 2016 election, the 2017 and 2018 primaries, and the 2018 midterm elections to provide a context for many of the concepts and issues discussed in the chapter.

The Electoral Process: Nominating a Candidate

Elections are the process by which individuals make political choices by voting. In representative democracies such as the United States, elections provide legitimacy to the system by implying that individuals have a say in who runs their government and what policies are initiated.

Elections The process by which individuals make political choices by voting.

The nomination process in the United States is not uniform across offices or levels of government. The nomination procedure depends on the office being sought, and nomination rules vary depending on whether the office is at the national, state, or local level. No matter what the level of the office being sought, however, states and local governments control the election process. The three procedures for nomination are caucuses, primary elections, and party conventions.

Caucuses

As introduced in the previous chapter, a caucus is a private meeting or gathering of individuals or representatives of political parties who choose delegates standing for or pledged to candidates running for particular offices. The early caucuses were composed of private citizens who were prominent and active in politics in their communities. As political parties developed, they assumed control of the caucus process. By the late 1790s, they used caucuses to choose congressional, state, and local candidates.

In addition, caucuses of congressional members of a political party would choose the party's presidential nominees.[17] The election of Andrew Jackson in 1828 and his renomination in the first national political party convention in 1832 signaled the end of the congressional caucus method of selecting parties' presidential nominees.[18] The caucus system is still a part of the presidential selection process, but it functions much differently from the congressional caucuses of the nineteenth century.

During the presidential election season, Americans hear a lot about the Iowa presidential caucuses, the first presidential selection contest in the country for both Democrats and Republicans since 1972,[19] as the news media cover the multitude of visits that presidential hopefuls from both parties make to that state. These caucuses, however, do not directly choose the presidential candidate; they are used to elect delegates committed to a particular candidate at each political party's sequence of conventions from the local to the state to the national level. These delegates are called **pledged delegates**. In 2016, fourteen states, including Alaska, Colorado, Iowa, Maine, Washington, and Hawaii, held Democratic caucuses, and twelve others (including the District of Columbia and Kentucky, which were not caucused by Democrats) held Republican caucuses.[20] Both parties held caucuses in American Samoa, Guam, the Northern Mariana Islands, and the U.S. Virgin Islands.

Pledged Delegates Party members elected or chosen at the state and local levels to support a particular candidate at the party's national convention.

The 2016 presidential party nomination process produced an interesting and unexpected rise of unlikely candidates in both the Democratic and the Republican parties. During the 2016 presidential primary season, Iowa's caucuses for both Democrats and Republicans were held on February 1, 2016. At the beginning of the 2016 Democratic presidential primaries, several individuals seriously considered running for office. These included Rhode Island's former governor, Lincoln Chafee, Maryland's former governor, Martin O'Malley, Harvard law professor Lawrence Lessig, and senators Hillary Clinton and Bernie Sanders.[21] Another name floated was that of Massachusetts senator Elizabeth Warren, who some thought would make a bid for the presidency.[22] Heading into the Iowa caucuses, however, the only two candidates who stepped forward to run for the nomination were Hillary Clinton and Bernie Sanders.

Hillary Clinton was considered the front-runner and the odds-on favorite to become the Democratic nominee.[23] Bernie Sanders was considered a very long shot because he was not a Democrat, but an independent senator from Vermont, who caucused with the Democrats in the Senate but was not a member of the party. He also identified himself as a democratic socialist, a label not usually associated with U.S. politicians. As such, his challenge to

The nine remaining Republican presidential candidates participated in a debate in Las Vegas, Nevada, on Tuesday, December 15, 2015. From left, John Kasich, Carly Fiorina, Marco Rubio, Ben Carson, Donald Trump, Ted Cruz, Jeb Bush, Chris Christie, and Rand Paul.

Clinton was not taken seriously.[24] Clinton won the Iowa caucus; however, she won it by the closest margin within the history of the Iowa caucus. This slim margin of victory generated debate about the popularity of Sanders's bid for the position and Clinton's potential vulnerabilities.

The road to the Republican nominee went through twelve primary debates beginning on August 6, 2015. Republican primary voters tend to be far more conservative than the general voting population and the more or extreme conservative portions of the primary voting populations pushed the primary candidates to the extreme right on many public policy issues, including immigration, contraception, abortion, revenues, and taxes.

The wide range of individuals running for the Republican nomination made the 2016 Republican primary process particularly newsworthy. At the beginning of the process, it remained unclear as to who the favorite was for the Republican Party. When the primary season began, early in 2015, seventeen candidates were considering running for the Republican ticket—reality star and businessman Donald Trump; former Governors Jeb Bush (Florida), Rick Perry (Texas), George Pataki (New York), Jim Gilmore (Virginia), and Mike Huckabee (Arkansas); Senators Rand Paul (Kentucky), Marco Rubio (Florida), Ted Cruz (Texas), and Lindsey Graham (South Carolina); former senator Rick Santorum; Governors John Kasich (Ohio), Scott Walker (Wisconsin), Chris Christie (New Jersey), and Bobby Jindal (Louisiana); Carly Fiorina, the former chief executive officer of Hewlett Packard, the only woman in the field; and retired neurosurgeon Ben Carson, the only Black candidate.[25] The Iowa caucus was the first place where voting began, on February 1, 2016. Ted Cruz won, with Marco Rubio and Donald Trump following narrowly behind. The former governor of Arkansas, Mike Huckabee, dropped out after the Iowa caucus, as did the former senator of Pennsylvania, Rick Santorum. (Santorum had won the Iowa caucus against Mitt Romney in 2012.) Kentucky senator Rand Paul also ended his campaign bid after a poor performance in Iowa.

The next caucus was in Nevada on February 23, 2016, which Donald Trump won. On March 1, Ted Cruz won the Alaska caucus and Marco Rubio won the Minnesota caucus. On March 5, Donald Trump won the Kentucky caucus and Ted Cruz won the Maine and Kansas caucuses. Donald Trump won the Hawaii caucus on March 6 and that in the Northern Mariana Islands on March 15.

In the 2016 election, Sanders's campaign focused heavily on caucus states. Many of the caucus states were states with few electoral votes, such as Hawaii and Alaska, but the hope was that Sanders would be able to overcome Clinton's strength in primary states and allow him to overtake Clinton's pledged delegate lead. Sanders won eleven of the sixteen caucus states. Sanders attempted to take a page out of President Obama's playbook in the 2008 contest against Hillary Clinton, where Obama received 324 pledged delegates from caucus states compared with Clinton's 170 pledged delegates. Some analysts might argue that the story of Obama's success in gaining the nomination is told, in large part, by his victories in these states and his ability to organize large numbers of volunteers, a group crucial to winning in caucus states. (See Table 15.1 in the Measuring Equality box) In the end, this approach did not work for Sanders.

Primary Elections

As previously mentioned, a primary election is an election in which voters choose among several candidates who have declared for an office. Primary elections for state and local offices and for U.S. House and Senate nominations are **direct primaries**, in which voters select the individual to represent the party in the general election by voting directly for the candidates on the ballot. By contrast, in a presidential primary election, voters vote for delegates committed to a candidate. These delegates then cast their votes at the political party's national convention to choose the party's presidential candidate.

A **closed primary** is one in which only those affiliated with a particular political party can vote for the party's candidate in the election. The most rigid form of closed primary is one in which a voter must be registered to vote with a political party affiliation in advance of the primary election. (State law determines the date by which people must be registered to vote to participate in a primary election.)

In 2016, nine states used a completely closed primary system: Delaware, Florida, Kentucky, Maryland, Nevada, New Mexico, New York, Oregon, and Pennsylvania.[26] A voter registered as a member of one political party who wants to vote in the primary election of another party must reregister as a member of the other party.[27] Closed primaries are intended to ensure that only voters who are identified as party members will have input into the selection of the party's candidates and to prevent crossover voting, in which voters registered as members of one political party would have input into the selection of a candidate from another party. Closed primaries also help contribute to strong party organization.[28] The deadline for reregistering is usually substantially in advance of the primary, a ruling that makes it more difficult for an individual to change parties. **Political independents** must declare a party affiliation to vote in such primaries.

Seven states have a closed primary system that is more flexible: Alaska, Connecticut, Idaho, North Carolina, Oklahoma, South Dakota, and Utah.[29] In these states, voters may change their political party affiliation on Election Day or in the weeks close to the election.[30] Under the closed primary system, state law allows political parties the option of choosing whether to allow political independents or voters who are not registered with the party to participate in nomination processes prior to each election cycle.[31]

Other states have a mixed system, where the rules may vary about which voters can participate in which primaries and when and how individuals are able to register to vote in the primary.[32] In 2016, six states used a mixed primary system: California, Oklahoma, Massachusetts, Rhode Island, South Dakota, and West Virginia.[33]

An **open primary** is one in which a registered voter can participate in the primary election of any political party without having to be a registered

---

Direct Primaries Elections in which voters select the individual to represent the party in the general election by voting directly for the candidates on the ballot.

Closed Primary A primary in which only registered members of a particular political party can vote in that party's primary election to choose the party's candidate or delegate.

Political Independents Voters who do not designate a political party affiliation when registering to vote.

Open Primary A primary election in which a voter does not have to declare a political party affiliation but may participate in the primary election of any party.

member of that party. In 2016, primary elections in fifteen states were open primaries.[34] In some of these states, voters must request the primary ballot of one particular party at the polls. In other states, voters do not have to declare a party affiliation and they can vote in the primary election of any party. This system permits individuals to choose in which primary they wish to vote when they get to the polls and to request a ballot for that political party's primary.[35]

Six states have partially open primaries where voters can cross party lines. These states are Illinois, Indiana, Iowa, Ohio, Tennessee, and Wyoming. Under the partially open primary system, either voters are required to publicly declare their ballot choice or their ballot selection may be classified as a form of registration with a party.[36]

Open primaries weaken political parties' influence over the nomination process because they permit individuals who are not registered as members of the party to vote in the party's primary.[37] Supporters of the open primary method argue that voters should be able to participate freely in primaries without having to reveal their political preferences or give up their status as political independents, people who are not aligned with either political party.[38]

Most primaries use a **plurality** system in which the candidate who receives the most votes is the winner. Nine Southern and border Southern states, however, use a **majority** system in which winning requires receiving more than half of the votes cast. If no candidate receives a majority of the vote in the initial primary election, the top two vote-getters face each other in a **run-off primary**.

The latter system was instituted in the South in the early 1900s when the Democratic Party was the dominant party. The run-off primary was viewed by party officials as a means of ensuring party strength and unity behind one candidate and preventing independent challenges to that candidate.[39] Racial motives were also at work, as many of the Southern states that passed bills imposing a primary and run-off provisions stated explicitly that the intent was to ensure that Whites maintained political control by making it difficult, if not impossible, for Blacks to participate in the primary process.[40] In many Southern jurisdictions, the person who won the primary was the guaranteed winner of the office.

After the Iowa caucuses, the first primary was held in New Hampshire on February 9, 2016. New Hampshire has been the first primary state since 1920. Sanders went on to win the New Hampshire primary. The New Hampshire victory pushed Sanders into becoming a serious contender for the party's nomination.

Although Clinton went on to secure important victories in major states such as California and New York, the reality that it was not a landslide victory across primaries came as a surprise to many pundits.[41] There were unpredictable moments, such as Sanders's victory in the Michigan primary that gave people within the Sanders campaign hope that their victory was viable. The Sanders campaign stated they would continue their campaign until the Democratic National Convention, but Bernie Sanders formally endorsed Hillary Clinton

Plurality Winning of an election by the candidate who receives the most votes (also known as "first past the post").

Majority Winning of an election by the candidate who receives at least 51 percent of the vote.

Run-off Primary A second election held in some states if no candidate in the primary election receives a majority of the votes.

measuring equality

Obama's Attention to Caucus States in the 2008 Presidential Election

Caucus votes can be important in presidential primaries, especially in extremely competitive primaries. In the 2008 presidential primaries, then-Senator Barack Obama concentrated on caucus states as a strategy to knit together pledged delegates from states with small numbers of electoral votes, at the same time building a strong volunteer network. His campaign's Fifty-State Strategy provided him with numerous routes to get to 270 electoral votes in the general election, and the early attention to the caucus states was integral to this strategy. Table 15.1 shows the importance of the delegates Obama received from caucus states to his overall pledged delegate lead over Hillary Rodham Clinton. In 2012, President Obama did not have a challenger in the presidential primaries, so he did not have to develop a strategy to gain the nomination. But he kept his 2008 network in place in those caucus states that were so important and that network was important to his 2012 campaign strategy. In very competitive presidential primaries, caucus states can mean the difference between victory and defeat. Senator Bernie Sanders tried to follow this strategy in 2016, but he was not as effective as President Obama was in 2008.

TABLE 15.1 Pledged Delegates from Primaries and Caucuses, 2008 Presidential Election

Final Results	Pledged Delegates	
	Obama	Clinton
Primaries	1,429	1,463
Caucuses	324	170
American Samoa*	1	2
Democrats abroad	4	3
Guam**	2	2
Virgin Islands**	3	0
Total	1,763	1,640

*Deemed "territories" by the Democratic National Committee.

Source: CNN Election Center, http://cnn.com.

on July 12.[42] The sizeable support that Sanders garnered was unexpected and caused concern among Clinton supporters.

In considering the tumultuous road to victory for Clinton, it is important to keep in mind how racial and ethnic minority voters participated in this process. Although Sanders was relatively successful in gaining delegates, Black and Latino voters were not as swayed by him, as were White millennials and many White progressive voters. According to entrance polls, in Iowa, 58 percent of non-White voters voted for Clinton, and only 34 percent voted for Sanders.[43] According to exit polls taken in Ohio, 71 percent of Black voters supported Clinton, whereas only 28 percent voted for Sanders.[44] Clinton captured a key number of delegates and victories in Florida and Texas, where we see similar patterns by minority voters. In Florida, 81 percent of Black voters and 68 percent of Latino voters supported Clinton. In Texas, 83 percent of Black voters supported Clinton, as did 71 percent of Latino voters.[45] Black voters in the Deep South, or the region that is referred to as the Black Belt (Alabama, Georgia, Louisiana, Mississippi, South Carolina), provided Clinton with a major boost. She won 225 delegates, whereas Sanders only captured 70 delegate votes in those six states. Exit poll data suggest that support from racial and ethnic minority voters assisted tremendously in Clinton's victory over Sanders.

New Hampshire, traditionally considered an important primary, pushed Trump into national headlines as he won the overwhelming number of delegates for the state.[46] By the time of the first Republican primary, twelve candidates were serious contenders for the nomination and actively campaigning. Chris Christie, the governor of New Jersey, had focused his campaign resources into New Hampshire. Christie placed sixth in that race and formally withdrew on February 10. Subsequent to the conclusion of Christie's campaign, Carly Fiorina suspended her campaign that day as well, and Jim Gilmore exited the race following New Hampshire.

As the race continued forward, Trump's increasing share of victories continued, and the remaining candidates left the race, one by one. Jeb Bush withdrew after the South Carolina primary on February 20. One of the key moments for the campaign was Super Tuesday (which occurred on March 1, 2016), known for being the day that the greatest number of states hold their primary elections and caucuses. After Super Tuesday, Ben Carson dropped out. Florida senator Marco Rubio left the race on March 15, after losing his home state. Rubio stated, "America's in the middle of a real political storm, a real tsunami," he said. "And we should have seen this coming."[47] Ted Cruz left the race on May 3, and John Kasich left on May 4.

On May 26, Donald Trump secured the requisite number of delegates required to attain the Republican nomination of the party. The Republican National Convention was held July 18–21 in Cleveland, Ohio. The Republican platform, with Trump as the designated nominee, had become staunchly more conservative.[48] This included specific language calling for a wall to be built between Mexico and the United States. The party platform also advocated using religion as a guide for legislation, noting "that man-made law must be consistent with God-given, natural rights."[49]

The number of minority voters in the Republican Party is small. As a result, capturing the trends of Black voters through primary exit polls, for example, is not possible, given the small margin that appear in the sample. Latino voters have a marginally larger presence within the Republican Party. This mattered in Nevada, where Donald Trump claimed he captured the Latino vote.[50] It is important to be mindful of Trump's assertions for several reasons. First, Nevada has a significant Latino population, but a substantial portion are undocumented individuals, who do not participate in the primary process. Second, of Latinos who are citizens and eligible to vote, the vast majority vote as Democrats.[51] Last, the CNN exit poll that Trump utilized to make the claim of getting the majority of the Latino vote is based on a sample of 100 people.[52] Given the small number of individuals captured from very specific precincts, the survey has a large margin of error that is plus or minus 10 percentage points. Given the inconsistency of support from Latinos supporting Trump across states and given this margin of error, it is important to heed caution in accepting the Trump campaign's claims that Republican Latino voters support Trump. Moreover, according to a poll conducted by Latino Decisions of 400 Latino registered voters in Nevada, with a sample that was representative of the state's Latino electorate, the support for Trump looks starkly different than that highlighted by the exit polls.[53] According to this poll, 87 percent of the Latino electorate held unfavorable views of Donald Trump. If we look only at self-identified Republicans, 64 percent of Latino Republicans in the sample held unfavorable views of Donald Trump.[54] In the same sample, 78 percent believed that the Republican either does not care or, more so, may be hostile toward Latinos.[55]

Party Conventions

Party conventions are assemblies held by political parties to nominate candidates, set party rules, and develop a party platform—a statement of the principles and policy positions of the party. Every four years, the Democratic, the Republican, and, in recent years, the Libertarian parties climax the presidential primary season with a convention to nominate their presidential candidate and write the party platform, among other things. These conventions are held in the summer before the November election. Presidential candidates, through either caucus or primary vote, gather pledged delegates who will vote for the candidates at the party's convention.

Both political parties assign each state a specific number of delegates based on population, the number of votes that are cast during the primaries and caucuses, and other factors.[56] In addition to pledged delegates, the Democratic Party has a number of superdelegates who are free to support any candidate, regardless of the popular vote.[57] These superdelegates are Democratic members of Congress, governors, national committee members, and party leaders such as former presidents and vice presidents who are given automatic delegate status.[58] In the 2016 primary, there was a great deal of consternation that Hillary Clinton was able to sew up an overwhelming majority of the superdelegates in her contest with Bernie Sanders for the nomination. As a result of this situation, in August 2018, individuals at the summer meeting of the Democratic National Committee (DNC) stripped superdelegates of much of their power. The new rule says that if the presidential nomination is contested, superdelegates would not be able to vote on the first ballot. This change dramatically reduces the influence of these individuals, about 700 or 15 percent, to influence the choice of the party's nominee. This change makes the primaries and the number of pledged delegates far more important than in the past and will shift how future candidates approach the primary contests.[59] The Republican Party also has a number of unpledged delegates. These individuals are referred to as unbound delegates, not superdelegates. About 150 delegates were unbound, meaning that they are free to support any candidate.[60] The majority of the Republican unpledged delegates are actually elected, just like the pledged delegates, and are often pledged to a particular candidate.[61] A minority of the unpledged delegates automatically become delegates by virtue of their position as a state party chair or as a national party committee member. By party rule, only the 168 members of the Republican National Committee— a state party chairman and two national committee members in each of the fifty states, five territories, and the District of Columbia—get automatic votes, accounting for about 7 percent of the total convention votes.

In 2016, there were 4,763 delegates to the Democratic National Convention. Of the 718 total superdelegates, 602 expressed support for Hillary Clinton and 47 expressed support for Bernie Sanders.[62] A candidate had to win 2,382 delegates at the convention; Hillary Clinton won 2,807. There were 2,472 delegates to the Republican National Convention. A total of 127 unbound delegates supported Donald Trump and 50 unbound delegates supported Ted Cruz.[63] Trump won a total of 1,542 delegates (1,237 delegates were needed to win the party nomination). There were 4,769 delegates and 347 alternates to the Democratic National Convention and approximately 2,470 delegates and 2,302 alternate delegates from all fifty states to the Republican National Convention in 2016.[64]

Republican Convention. The 2016 Republican National Convention, which the media has described as a "Trump-centered" event, was held in Cleveland, Ohio, on July 18–21.[65] Republican presidential nominee Donald Trump won 1,542 of the 2,472 delegates.[66] A simple majority of 1,237 of the total number is needed to win the presidential nomination. The primary focus of the Republican National Convention was job creation, trade, and economic policy.[67] Convention speakers also offered some remarks on immigration.[68] After a rather unpredictable and tumultuous campaign season, some of the party leadership expressed support for Trump's candidacy, but most leading Republicans—including living Republican presidents and recent Republican presidential nominees—refused to appear at the convention.[69]

Republicans have faced scrutiny over the lack of diversity within the party in general and at the Republican National Convention specifically.[70] The statistics on racial diversity have been particularly troubling during the current election cycle.[71] According to *the Washington Post*, the Republican Party sent fewer Black delegates to the convention in 2016 than it had "at any point in the past century."[72] Less than 1 percent of delegates at the Republican National Convention were African American (only 18 of 2,472).[73] Hispanic delegates made up a slightly higher percentage of delegates than African Americans.[74] According to news reports, there were at least 133 Hispanic delegates at the convention.[75]

One journalist described the convention as the "most flagrant display of GOP racism America has seen in years."[76] Some members of the Republican Party have used racist rhetoric and racist policies to garner support from a conservative White base.[77] Representative Steve King (R-Iowa) caused a firestorm when he defended the lack of diversity, arguing that White people had contributed the most to civilization.[78] Donald Trump has been heavily criticized, including by members of his own party, for the many incendiary, racist, and xenophobic statements he has made since launching his presidential campaign. Nonetheless, a small number of people of color took the convention stage in support of the presidential candidate.[79] Donald Trump and Mike

Pence accepted the presidential and vice presidential nominations, respectively, on July 21, 2016.

Democratic Convention. The Democratic National Convention took place in Philadelphia, Pennsylvania, on July 25–28, only a few days after the Republican National Convention. The Democratic conventions in 2008 and 2012 were held in late August and early September, respectively, but the schedule was changed in 2016 to avoid a protracted primary battle and suppress the GOP nominee's momentum following the Republican convention.[80] Hillary Clinton officially accepted the Democratic Party presidential nomination after receiving support from 2,807 of the 4,763 delegates.[81] To win the Democratic nomination, Clinton needed to secure 2,382 delegates and superdelegates.[82] Clinton's nomination was historic because she became the first woman to win the presidential nomination for a major political party.

The Democratic Party had initially struggled to present a unified front during the first couple of days of the convention, following revelations that some party officials were complicit in attempts to undermine Bernie Sanders in his race for the nomination.[83] Tensions subsided after Sanders addressed his supporters and expressed his support for Hillary Clinton. The party platform included raising the minimum wage, supporting public education, implementing a progressive jobs plan, abolishing the death penalty, reviewing trade policy, and working toward Wall Street reform.[84]

In direct contrast to the 2016 Republican National Convention, half of the delegates at the Democratic National Convention were non-White. Twenty-five percent of delegates were Black, 16 percent were Hispanic or Latino, and 9 percent were Asian American or American Indian. According to the Clinton campaign, 1,182 delegates were Black, 747 were Latino 292 were Asian American, and 147 were American Indian.[85]

On the final day of the Democratic National Convention, Khizr Khan, a Muslim American and Gold Star father, gave a speech about his son, U.S. Army captain Humayan Khan, who had been killed in 2004 during the Iraq war. Khan was accompanied by his wife, Ghazala, who stood silently beside him in support. During the speech, Khan criticized Republican presidential nominee Donald Trump for his anti-Muslim rhetoric and proposed ban on Muslim immigration. At the end of what has been described as "one of the finest and most damning addresses of the Democratic National Convention," Khan pulled out a copy of the U.S. Constitution and offered to lend it to Trump.[86]

In the days following Khan's speech, Donald Trump responded to Khan's address in a series of statements, even verbally attacking Ghazala Khan and implying that she was not allowed to speak at the convention because of the Khans' Islamic faith.[87] Many Republican leaders, including Senator John McCain (R-Arizona), denounced Trump for his disparaging statements about the Gold Star family.[88] Hillary Clinton and Tim Kaine officially accepted the Democratic Party nominations for president and vice president, respectively, during the 2016 Democratic National Convention on July 26, 2016.

Khizr Khan and his wife Ghazala, parents of deceased Muslim U.S. soldier Humayun S. M. Khan, holds up a booklet of the U.S. Constitution as he delivers remarks asking Republican nominee Donald Trump if he understands the Constitution at the Democratic National Convention on July 28, 2016, in Philadelphia, Pennsylvania.

The final vote at the convention is anticlimactic in that the nominee has already secured the necessary number of votes prior to the convention. Everyone already knows who the nominee-elect will be. But the convention serves as a rallying point to energize each party's political base for the fall campaign and to introduce the candidates to the nation as a whole.

Although primaries are the predominant method of selecting candidates for national and statewide office, thirteen states either permit or require conventions for the nomination process. Alabama, Georgia, South Carolina, and Virginia permit political parties to use conventions or primaries to nominate their candidates for national and statewide office.[89] In Virginia in 2013, the Republicans held a convention to nominate their candidates for governor, lieutenant governor, and attorney general. In contrast, Virginia Democrats used a primary election to determine their nominees. State political parties decide whether they will nominate candidates in primaries or conventions, but they must follow state election law in carrying out their choice.

Although caucuses and primaries are important tools for established political parties to choose their candidates, they are not advantageous for independents and third-party candidates. These candidates might have to take out **nomination petitions** and collect a specified number of signatures from registered voters to qualify for inclusion on a ballot. Collecting signatures on nominating petitions is time-consuming and can be difficult if the number of signatures required is sufficiently large that the candidate might have to use volunteers or employ people to circulate petitions. In North Carolina, Michael Munger, a political science professor at Duke University and the Libertarian candidate for governor, had to collect 69,736 signatures of registered voters to

Nomination Petitions The number of signatures of registered voters that independent or third-party candidates must collect to qualify for inclusion on a ballot.

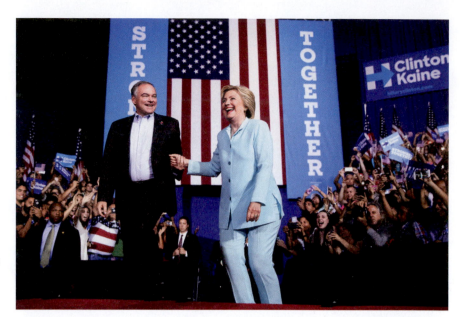

Democratic presidential and vice presidential candidates Hillary Clinton and Senator Tim Kaine (D-VA) take the stage together at a rally in Miami, July 23, 2016.

U.S. President Barack Obama delivers remarks at the Democratic National Convention on July 27, 2016, in Philadelphia, Pennsylvania.

gain a position on the 2008 general election ballot for governor. This number represented 2 percent of the total number of people who had voted in the 2004 gubernatorial election. To reach that number of verified signatures, he collected a total of 107,349 and ended up with 73,472 verified signatures—3,736 more than he needed. Nomination petition requirements in some states are aimed at keeping third-party candidates off the ballot. His success in getting on the ballot and in garnering 2.9 percent of the vote in the 2008 general election meant that the 2012 Libertarian candidate for governor did not have to circulate a petition.

In 2016, the former New Mexico governor Gary Johnson was nominated as the Libertarian Party's presidential candidate at its national convention in Orlando on May 29. The Green Party nominated Dr. Jill Stein as its 2016 presidential nominee at its August 6 presidential nominating convention in Houston.

General Elections

General elections are elections in which the winner is elected to office and takes office after the end of the term of the current officeholder. These elections take place on dates specified by state or federal law. In 1845, Congress passed legislation that established the general election date for presidential elections as the first Tuesday after the first Monday in November. As a result, almost all general elections for federal offices—president, House, and Senate—and for most state offices occur on the same November date.

General Elections Elections in which the winner is elected to office and takes office after the end of the term of the current officeholder.

A presidential election is held once every four years. Elections to the House of Representatives are held every two years, with the elections occurring in even-numbered years. Members of the U.S. Senate are elected to six-year terms, with one-third of the Senate up for election every congressional election cycle. Elections to the Senate are held in conjunction with House elections.

Electing the President: How the Electoral College Works

The Electoral College was created by the Founders for several reasons, the most important being to keep the people from having a direct say in the election of the president. The Founders put in place an indirect election process for the presidency that would keep the masses of voters from directly selecting the president. The Founders were suspicious of direct election of the president because they feared that voters could be manipulated and, as a result, that an unsuitable person could be elected president.

To avoid this possibility, the Founders established a system whereby individuals voted for electors, initially chosen by the state legislators and now by the political parties, who would then cast their votes for president at a later date. The Founders believed that, unlike the public, the electors could not be manipulated; they would ensure that only people acceptable to the leaders of the country were elected president. The public's preferences were not to be considered.

Today, presidential electors are chosen by the political parties, and each party has a slate of electors. When individuals go to the polls, they are actually voting for the electors committed to a presidential candidate and not directly for the candidate. Although the Constitution does not prescribe how states are to select their electors, in 1845 Congress passed legislation that electors be appointed on the Tuesday after the first Monday in November of every fourth year (November 6 in 2018), which is the reason elections of the president, and of all national elected officials as a result, occur on the same day in November. In some states, the names of the electors are listed next to the name of the presidential candidate to whom they are committed, but in other states the names are not listed.

In forty-eight states, the presidential candidate who wins the most votes in the state receives all of that state's electoral votes; this is the **winner-take-all** rule. It does not matter if the candidate wins by 500,000 votes or by 537 votes, as George W. Bush did in Florida in 2000. All of the states' electoral votes go to the winner of the state's popular vote. Only two states, Nebraska and Maine, allocate electoral votes via **proportional representation** instead. In each state, two electors are chosen at large by statewide popular vote and the rest are selected by the popular vote in each congressional district.[90] Table 15.2 shows the distribution of electoral votes in presidential elections from 1968 to 2016.

The electors from each state meet on the first Monday after the second Wednesday in December and cast their votes for president.[91] In the 2016 elections, electors met on December 19. In twenty-one states, electors are under no constitutional or statutory requirement to vote for the person to whom they are pledged, but most do so by custom.

There have been some exceptions to this custom. In the 1976 election, a Washington elector pledged to President Gerald Ford voted for Ronald Reagan. In the 1988 election, a West Virginia elector voted for Senator Lloyd Bentsen as president and for Governor Michael Dukakis as vice president (which was the reverse of their positions on the ticket). In the 2000 presidential election, Al Gore received one less electoral vote than he had won because an elector from Washington, DC, submitted a blank ballot to protest DC's lack of representation in Congress. In 2004, one Minnesota elector voted for former North Carolina Senator John Edwards for both president and vice president. There were no wayward electoral votes in 2008: President-elect Barack Obama and senator John McCain received the electoral votes they had won on election night. In 2012, there were again no renegade electors, with President Obama and Governor Romney receiving the electoral votes they won on election night.

Some states, however, require electors to cast their votes according to the popular vote and provide that so-called faithless electors could be fined or disqualified for casting an invalid vote and be replaced by a substitute elector. Despite a law in Washington, DC, along with twenty-six states, that requires electors to vote for the candidate who won the District's electoral vote, in the 2000 presidential election the elector who submitted a blank protest ballot was not penalized in any way. The Supreme Court has found that the Constitution does not make electors free agents in their voting for president and thus that state laws could be passed to require electors to vote for the presidential candidate who won the state's popular vote and for political parties to extract pledges from electors to vote for the party's nominee.[92]

Over the decades, there have been many calls for the abolition of the Electoral College or an overhaul of the method of distributing electoral votes.

Winner-Take-All An election system in which the candidate who gets the most votes in that district wins the election, even if he or she has not received a majority of the votes and has finished only a few votes ahead of the second-place finisher.

Proportional Representation An election system that uses multimember districts in which seats are awarded by political party roughly in proportion to the results of the election.

TABLE 15.2 Presidential Electoral Votes, 1968–2016

Year	Candidate	Electoral Votes
1968	Richard M. Nixon (R)	301
	Hubert H. Humphrey (D)	191
1972	Richard M. Nixon (R)	520
	George S. McGovern (D)	17
1976	Jimmy Carter (D)	297
	Gerald R. Ford (R)	240
1980	Ronald Reagan (R)	489
	Jimmy Carter (D)	49
1984	Ronald Reagan (R)	525
	Walter F. Mondale (D)	13
1988	George H. W. Bush (R)	426
	Michael S. Dukakis (D)	111
1992	William J. Clinton (D)	370
	George H. W. Bush (R)	168
1996	William J. Clinton (D)	379
	Bob Dole (R)	159
2000	George W. Bush (R)	271
	Albert Gore (D)	266
2004	George W. Bush (R)	286
	John F. Kerry (D)	251
2008	Barack H. Obama (D)	365
	John W. McCain (R)	173
2012	Barack H. Obama (D)	332
	Mitt Romney (R)	206
2016	Donald J. Trump (R)	306
	Hillary R. Clinton (D)	232

Sources: National Archives, Electoral Box Scores, 1789–1996, http://www.archives.gov/federal-register/electoral-college/scores.html; Electoral Box Scores, 2000, 2004, and 2008, http://www.archives.gov/federal-register/electoral-college/scores2.html#2000; 2012 Electoral College Results, http://www.archives.gov/federal-register/electoral-college/2012/election-results.html; 2016 Election Results, http://www.cnn.com/election/results.

The outcome of the 2000 presidential election turned on the outcome of the popular vote in Florida, which would determine whether Vice President Gore or Governor George W. Bush would receive the state's 25 electoral votes and thus give one candidate more than 270 electoral votes. The incredible closeness of the vote—less than 1,700 on election night of 6 million votes cast—triggered an automatic recount under Florida law. At the end of the automatic recount and the counting of absentee ballots, Bush led by 537 votes.

After the 2000 presidential contest, in which the Supreme Court ruled in a 5–4 vote that the Florida recount should be halted and George W. Bush

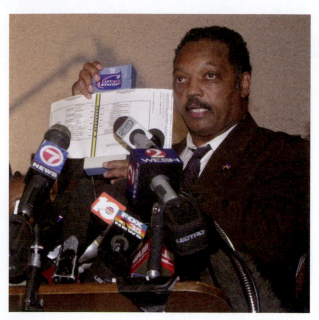

The Reverend Jesse Jackson, who ran for president in 1984 and 1988, holds the ballot that Palm Beach voters used to cast their votes during a rally at the Palm Beach elections office, November 9, 2000, in West Palm Beach, Florida. The elections of 2000 and 2004 were marred by charges of intimidation of Black and other racial group voters, coupled with an inordinately high number of invalid ballots in Black precincts in Florida.

declared the winner, the utility of the Electoral College was once again called into question. One proposal, among many, is to eliminate the Electoral College entirely and move to a direct election of the president. If this system had been in place, Al Gore would have been elected president because he received approximately 540,000 more popular votes than George W. Bush did. Another proposal is to keep the Electoral College, but to apportion electoral votes based on the proportion of a state's vote that a candidate receives. A third proposal is to allocate a state's electoral votes based on which candidate wins the popular vote in each congressional district.[93] Nebraska and Maine already allocate their electoral votes this way.

Because each state makes its own determination as to how its electoral votes will be apportioned, these last two proposals mean that each state would have to decide to switch to a proportional allocation system. Despite the controversial 2000 and 2016 elections, the probability that the Electoral College will be eliminated is remote. The all-or-nothing method of apportioning electors gives an advantage to large states with large numbers of electoral votes, and these factors are enduring and powerful. We say more about the Electoral College later, when discussing the winning of the presidential election.

Campaigning for Elections

The election of individuals to public offices in general elections does not "just happen." Candidates put together campaign staffs, hire consultants, use polling, and map strategies for targeting specific groups of voters. Campaigns must also turn their supporters out to the polls for early voting (many states allow voters to vote before the official Election Day), where available, and on Election Day for those who do not vote early. Candidates must also raise money to pay for everything they will need to win. Thus, to be elected, candidates must be organized.

Developing a Campaign Strategy

After securing the nomination, the major party nominees face each other in the general election. Although political campaigns have been ongoing during the nomination process, at this point the campaigns go into full gear. At the presidential level, candidates develop a strategy that will best secure a majority of electoral votes (270). In essence, presidential selection constitutes fifty-one separate elections (fifty states plus the District of Columbia) to award electoral votes.

Prior to the 2008 presidential elections, presidential candidates typically did not focus their attention on the entire nation, instead concentrating their resources in vote-rich states and tending to avoid those states in which they had little chance of winning. For example, in 1996 Bill Clinton ceded Kansas to Bob Dole, who had represented it in the House and Senate for almost a half-century. Prior to the 2008 presidential election, campaigns used to consider the four states with the most electoral votes the most significant: California (55 votes), New York (31 votes), Texas (34 votes), and Florida (27 votes). In 2008, however, other key states that were highly competitive were considered just as important for their electoral votes: Pennsylvania (21 votes), Illinois (21 votes), Ohio (20 votes), Michigan (17 votes), and New Jersey (15 votes). Together, these nine states constituted 243 of the 270 votes needed to secure a majority of electoral votes in 2008.

In 2008, Senator Barack Obama focused not only on Democratic and Democratic-leaning, or Blue, states, but also on Republican, or Red, states. His strategy was to pursue as many combinations as possible to reach 270 electoral votes. At the time, many political analysts thought Obama's strategy was foolhardy and that there was no way he was going to be able to make inroads into such traditionally Republican, or Red, states as North Carolina, Virginia, and Ohio. But Obama's strategy of focusing on a variety of states, described as the Fifty-State Strategy, resulted in his winning nine states that had gone for the Republican candidate in 2004: North Carolina, Virginia, Nevada, Colorado, New Mexico, Florida, Indiana, Iowa, and Ohio.[94] When combined with the traditionally Blue states, Obama won with 365 electoral votes compared to McCain's 173.

In 2012, President Obama pursued much the same strategy, although one state that he won in 2008, Indiana, did not receive a great deal of attention from his campaign. The assumption was that Romney would take Indiana, which he did, but Obama's campaign did spend resources in all of the other states. Once again, his campaign was trying to knit together as many combinations as possible to get to 270 electoral votes. In the end, he carried seven of the nine states that he won in 2008, losing Indiana and North Carolina, giving him 332 electoral votes to Mitt Romney's 206. It was less than his number in 2008, but a substantial victory nonetheless.

Clinton's 2016 campaign strategy was different from the approach that she used during her 2008 presidential campaign, when she lost the Democratic nomination to Barack Obama. Although Clinton acknowledged that she is not a "natural campaigner," her primary focus was convincing voters to support her, by appealing to the middle class, and highlighting her electability by emphasizing that she has the skills necessary for governing the country.[95] "Clinton had nearly 100 percent name recognition" among voters, as well as support from many working-class women.[96] The former first lady had an enormous amount of political experience, having served as the secretary of state

Use social media to urge people to action.

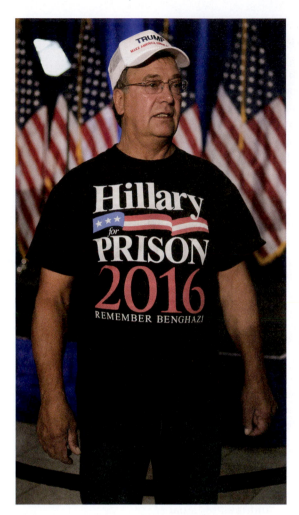

A chant at Trump rallies was to "lock her up," referring to the Democratic presidential nominee Hillary Clinton. An attendee wears a "Hillary for Prison" shirt at a campaign event for Donald Trump in Youngstown, Ohio, August 15, 2016.

and senator of New York. Clinton also had a seasoned campaign organization that incorporated much of Obama's machinery from the 2012 election.[97]

The Clinton campaign undertook significant fundraising efforts, and donors raised millions of dollars for the Democratic candidate. Clinton's biggest super PAC supporter, Priorities USA Action, reserved $158 million for an advertising campaign, pumping money into television ads and digital advertising, including on a number of social media platforms.[98]

During the primary season, Clinton's campaign employed a "hyper-local" strategy, identifying a local issue that was of interest to Democratic voters in each state and then championing that issue.[99] To that end, Clinton campaigned against voter identification (ID) laws in Alabama and Missouri, spoke about high concentrations of lead in the water in Jackson, Mississippi, discussed wind energy in Iowa, and focused on the heroin epidemic in New Hampshire.[100]

Clinton focused her presidential bid on several clearly defined issues. Her platform included expanding civil rights for women, racial minorities, and the LGBTQ community; combating terrorism; instituting a fair tax system; strengthening Social Security and Medicare; fixing America's infrastructure; comprehensive immigration reform that creates a pathway to full and equal citizenship; making America the world's clean energy superpower; and building an economy that works for all Americans.[101]

Trump's campaign slogan was "Make America Great Again!" His platform included health-care reform, immigration reform (policies centered on deporting all undocumented immigrants and building a wall across the U.S.–Mexican border), restructuring the Department of Veterans Affairs, tax reform, and U.S.–China trade reform.[102] In November 2015, following the Paris terror attacks, Trump advocated a temporary ban on Muslim immigrants, including Syrian refugees, to the United States, as well as expanded surveillance of "certain mosques."[103]

In terms of campaign fundraising, Trump's strategy was rather unconventional. Initially, Trump stated that his campaign would be fully self-funded and that he would not accept money from donors because "he is rich and didn't need anyone's money."[104] Although Trump's campaign during the primaries was mostly self-funded, by May 2016, donors had raised $5.4 million—significantly less than the amount raised by his Democratic opponent; Clinton's campaign raised more than $25 million that month.[105] During the primaries Trump raised a total of $17 million from individual contributors.[106] After Trump clinched the Republican Party's nomination, he announced that he would write off the $50 million he had lent to the campaign.[107] In early September 2016, the Trump campaign announced that it had raised $90 million during the month of August.[108]

The general election campaigns can be divided into two parts—the "ground war" and the "air war." The **ground war** consists of candidate public appearances, voter registration drives, mobilization of registered voters to get them to the polls on Election Day, fundraising, and public opinion polling, among other efforts. The **air war** consists of advertisements on television, radio, and print. In recent years, presidential campaigns have been waged on the Internet, Twitter, and Facebook as well, with all major candidates hosting campaign websites and having Twitter feeds.

In 2008, Obama effectively used what has come to be called "new media," including text messaging, Facebook and other social networking sites, emails, campaign ads in video games, YouTube, campaign blogs, and user-generated content, among other things.[109] Obama used the Internet and other technologies in 2008 in a manner that echoed John F. Kennedy's groundbreaking use of television as a campaign tool in 1960. Obama's 2008 campaign changed forever how presidential campaigns will be run. His campaign used the same strategy in 2012 and had a much more new-media-savvy campaign operation than did Mitt Romney's.

Presidential and vice presidential candidates also face each other in a series of televised **debates**. Candidates Richard Nixon and John F. Kennedy faced off in the first televised presidential debate, but televised debates did not occur again until 1976, when the League of Women Voters, a nonpartisan group, agreed to sponsor them. In 1987, the Democratic Party and the Republican Party created the Commission on Presidential Debates to administer the debates. The commission consists of a balance of Democrats and Republicans, but no third-party or independent members.

This format disadvantages minor-party candidates. Only once has the commission agreed to allow an independent candidate to participate in the debates: Ross Perot in 1992.[110] John Anderson was allowed by the League of Women Voters, as opposed to the Commission on Presidential Debates, to participate in a debate in 1980, which Jimmy Carter then refused to attend. The two major parties' domination over presidential debates undoubtedly excludes many Americans from the process. In the 2016 presidential election, secretary Hillary Clinton and Donald Trump had three televised debates; the vice presidential candidates, senator Tim Kaine and governor Mike Pence, had one televised debate.

Financing a Campaign

Money is undoubtedly the most important factor in presidential elections. Jesse Unruh, a Democratic politician from California, once said, "Money is the

Ground War The part of election campaigns conducted using "pavement-pounding" methods, including candidate public appearances, voter registration and mobilization, fundraising, and public opinion polling, among others.

Air War The part of election campaigns conducted through broadcast media including radio, television, and the Internet.

Debates Important public face-offs between candidates discussing issues in a variety of formats (including traditional question-and-answer sessions as well as town hall forums) and through a variety of media, most important television and, more recently, the Internet.

mother's milk of politics."[111] Travel, advertising, support staff, and overhead require a great deal of money. In 1757, George Washington, while seeking a seat in the Virginia House of Burgesses, gave each voter one and a half quarts of rum, wine, or beer.[112] Big business began to play a major role in campaign financing in the election of Ulysses S. Grant and became truly integrated into politics and fundraising with the presidential election of 1896.

William McKinley's campaign manager, "Dollar Mark" Hanna, solicited major business players, such as J. P. Morgan, Standard Oil, and banks, to contribute to McKinley's 1896 campaign, which they did. Hanna raised between $3.5 million and $10 million and established the pattern of major campaign fundraising.[113] McKinley outspent William Jennings Bryant in 1896 and won, a pattern not lost on modern politicians.

As soon as candidates began to solicit funds from big business, legislation was passed to try to keep these funds out of the process or at least limit their influence. As such, a series of campaign finance reform measures was passed during the twentieth century: the Tillman Act of 1907, the Federal Corrupt Practices Act of 1925, the War Labor Disputes Act of 1943, the Taft–Hartley Act of 1947, and the legislation that currently regulates campaign financing, the Federal Election Campaign Act of 1971 (FECA), which was amended in 1974.

In addition to regulating campaign financing, the amended FECA set up the Federal Elections Commission in 1975 to administer and enforce FECA. Congress passed the **Bipartisan Campaign Reform Act (BCRA)** in 2002, also known as the McCain-Feingold Act, which further amended FECA to strengthen the limits, regulations, and reporting of campaign contributions.

BCRA limits individual contributions for 2017–2018 to a candidate for federal office to $2,700 in any given election cycle.[114] This means that individuals can give $2,700 to a candidate during a primary or the same amount to several candidates and then another $2,700 in the general election to one or a similar amount to both. Primary, general, and run-off elections are each considered separate elections. Individuals can contribute up to $33,400[115] to a national party committee per calendar year and a combined limit of $10,000 per calendar year to state, local, or district political parties.[116] Individuals are limited to $5,000 per calendar year in contributions to political action committees (PACs) that support federal candidates.[117] In addition to imposing these individual limits on contributions, the McCain-Feingold Act did the following (among other things):

- The act bans **soft money** (unregulated money that that can be used for anything the political parties deem necessary, from pencils to pamphlets to phone banks) and prohibits candidates from using "leadership PACs," which are created to circumvent spending limits in promoting issues.
- The act bans special interests from collecting unlimited and unregulated amounts of money to fund "issue ads," which are designed to push an issue but in reality are used to support or oppose a particular candidate.[118]

Bipartisan Campaign Reform Act (BCRA) A campaign finance reform law passed in 2002 that amended the Federal Election Campaign Act of 1971 and strengthened the limits, regulations, and reporting of campaign contributions (also known as the McCain-Feingold Act).

Soft Money The less regulated money that is raised by a political party to support and maintain the party.

- The act allows candidates who decide to forgo **public funding** for their campaigns to spend without any limits, although contribution limits still apply.[119]
- Under the BCRA, campaign contribution limits can be increased and indexed for inflation every odd-numbered year.[120]

Presidential campaigns in the 1950s through the early 1970s saw the greatest increase in spending, setting the pace for campaigns in the 1980s and 1990s. In 1956, Dwight Eisenhower and his Democratic opponent, Adlai Stevenson, spent a combined $11.6 million in their presidential campaigns. In 1968, Richard Nixon spent around $30 million and Hubert Humphrey laid out around $10 million. The biggest jump in campaign costs came in 1972 when Richard Nixon and George McGovern spent more than $90 million combined.[121]

Campaign costs in the 1980s hovered around $100 million for combined primary spending. But in 1988, the first year with no incumbent running since Richard Nixon in 1968, campaign costs soared to $213 million for the primary alone.[122] In 1988, both the Republicans and the Democrats had numerous candidates vying for their respective nominations.

In the 1996 presidential campaign, Republican candidate Bob Dole spent $34.5 million and incumbent Democratic president Bill Clinton spent $30.4 million.[123] In the 2000 presidential election, both George W. Bush and Al Gore accepted public funding in the general election and each was given $67.6 million to spend. In 2004, both George W. Bush and John Kerry accepted public funding and were given $74.6 million each to spend during the general election.

The 2008 presidential election was, until recently, the most expensive on record. Initially, Barack Obama indicated that he would participate in the public financing of the general election, but he changed his mind in June 2008. He then revealed that he thought the public financing system was broken and that if he participated in it, he would not be able to compete effectively against Senator John McCain and the Republican Party. Obama therefore decided to forgo public funding, the first time this has happened in a presidential election since public financing was introduced.

Obama was then free to raise and spend as much as he wanted to secure the Democratic nomination during the primary season, as well as during the 2008 general election. It is estimated that Obama raised more than $750 million through traditional fundraising methods and from more than 3 million online donors to his Internet site. McCain accepted public financing and received $83 million in public funds. Obama's financial advantage allowed him to campaign and compete in traditionally Republican states, whereas McCain found it difficult to compete in traditionally Democratic states.

In 2012, Romney enjoyed support from a number of conservative super PACs that either supported his candidacy directly or spent considerable money attacking Obama.[124] The largest pro-Romney super PAC was Restore Our Future, and most of the money it raised came from the financial industry, including private equity executives and hedge fund managers.[125] Restore Our

Public Funding The financing of election campaigns by the American public through tax allocations as distinct from private fundraising by candidates.

Future raised approximately $157 million during the 2012 campaign, the largest amount raised by any group.[126] The U.S. Supreme Court's 2010 decision in *Citizens United v. Federal Election Commission* ruled that corporations and unions have the same political speech rights as individuals under the First Amendment and are thus able to donate directly to political candidates and PACs.

President Obama initially resisted super PACs, but eventually decided to support their creation on his behalf because of the amounts of money that Romney and his supporters were able to raise. Priorities USA was the main super PAC supporting President Obama, which raised $79 million, significantly less than the super PACs supporting Governor Romney.[127] Despite the support of super PACs, Obama's campaign still focused on individual donors and in the end outraised Romney's campaign, $715 million to $446 million.[128] The super PACs supporting Romney were the source of much of his financial support.

In 2016, Hillary Clinton's super PAC, Priorities USA Action, was a "big-money machine."[129] According to information released by the Federal Election Commission, Priorities USA Action raised more than $100 million between January 1, 2015, and August 22, 2016.[130] A large percentage of the money raised by Priorities USA Action came from twenty individual donors.[131] The group has also collected nearly $1 million through a joint fundraising agreement with EMILY's List.[132] EMILY's List is a PAC that works to help elect pro-choice Democratic female candidates to political office. Other pro-Clinton super PACs, namely Blue Answer PAC, Balance of Power PAC, Faith Voters PAC, and America's Teachers, raised a combined total of more than $250,000 during the current election cycle.[133] Priorities USA Action has been devoted to running a multi-million-dollar advertising campaign to boost Hillary Clinton, reserving $158 million for this purpose.[134]

Efforts to fundraise by Donald Trump's supporters fell far short of that of Hillary Clinton's allies, meaning that less money was spent on paid television advertising.[135] During the primaries, Trump criticized major donors and insisted that he did not need the help of super PACs, but by July his campaign announced that it had dropped its opposition to fundraising from super PACs and encouraged donors to provide their financial support.[136] Several competing strategists started collecting money for pro-Trump super PACs in an attempt to try to match Clinton supporters' fundraising efforts.[137] Super PACs supporting Donald Trump raised a combined total of more than $12 million as of August 2016, with Great America PAC bringing in more than half of that amount.[138] Other pro-Trump super PACs included Rebuilding America Now, Make America Great Again PAC, Committee to Restore America's Greatness, Patriots for Trump, and Committee for American Sovereignty. The total cost for both candidates for the 2016 presidential election was approximately $2.6 billion, the most expensive on record.

Running a Campaign

During a campaign, candidates use a number of avenues to get their message across and to gauge how the public is reacting to them and their message.

Campaign commercials and public appearances, coupled with polling and media interviews, are some of the most important mechanisms. As mentioned earlier, Obama also used new forms of technology in the campaign to expand his message beyond traditional election approaches.

Candidates invest incredible amounts of money in campaign advertising, which includes not only posters and buttons, but also professional campaign commercials. Purchasing expensive airtime results in the production of thirty-second advertisements that are short on substance and long on symbolism. It is difficult to determine a candidate's stance from these thirty-second features, but they are designed to strike at some value or chord in a targeted group of voters that will pull them toward one candidate and away from another. Moreover, these spots often "shade" the truth or distort the other candidate's position. It is impossible to present anything but short sound bites.

Few candidates can afford to purchase airtime to make a half-hour speech, and many campaign consultants will say that few Americans would listen. Yet in 2008, Obama purchased thirty minutes of airtime on CBS, NBC, Fox, MSNBC, BET, TV One, and Univision on the evening of October 29, 2008, to talk to the American public. Despite the warnings of campaign consultants that no one would listen, Obama drew 33.5 million viewers, more than watched the conclusion of the World Series also airing that evening. Neither Obama nor Romney did this in 2012.

Another aspect of campaign advertising is the use of negative campaign advertisements. Although the American electorate decries it, this type of advertising is extremely effective in putting opponents on the defensive and eroding their support. Most campaigns, whether national or local, have people who are involved in **opposition research**, finding ethical lapses, past problems, or questionable behavior that can be used to undermine the public's confidence in and support for the opposition. Often, campaigns use this "opposition material" in ways that raise ethical concerns, and in some instances candidates will resort to "playing the race card" by tugging at the fragile racial and ethnic threads that are interwoven throughout the fabric of the U.S. political system.

Opposition Research
Campaign activity devoted to undermining the public's confidence in and support of a candidate, a key component of negative campaigning.

Scholars have identified the 1988 presidential campaign between George H. W. Bush and Michael Dukakis as one in which George Bush played on the racial animus of Whites toward Black Americans to gain an advantage over Dukakis, although racial issues were not at the forefront of the campaign. Bush's campaign determined that Dukakis was vulnerable on the crime issue and that if it played on Whites' fear of being victimized by Blacks, that would bring White votes to Bush. Wanting to avoid a backlash against the official campaign by appealing openly to the racist feelings of Whites, Bush's campaign developed on a two-track system. The official campaign would attack Dukakis's views on crime and his record as governor, while outside groups (taking advantage of a loophole in campaign finance rules) would run an operation that would appeal to the basest instincts of the American public on the subject of race.[139] Thus was born the infamous Willie Horton ad.

Horton was a young Black man convicted of murder and sentenced to life in a Massachusetts prison. He escaped while on furlough and assaulted a White couple in their home, raping the woman. George Bush made Horton a household name by repeatedly mentioning Horton's story and pinning the blame on Michael Dukakis, who was the governor of Massachusetts.[140] Political scientists Donald Kinder and Lynn Sanders later found that the Willie Horton ad had increased the resentment of Whites toward Blacks and moved White voters in Bush's direction.[141]

Bush was not the first presidential candidate to resort to racial appeals. Barry Goldwater's 1964 and Richard Nixon's 1968 campaigns relied implicitly on racial appeals. Ronald Reagan continually used a welfare queen anecdote and other anecdotes on the campaign trail that were code words for race.

Although direct racial appeals were not present in the 2000 election, a racial dynamic was. In 2000, Florida counties with punch-card balloting systems, such as Miami-Dade and Palm Beach, had the highest percentage of uncounted ballots. Palm Beach also had a large number of overvotes, with more than one candidate for president punched; this was, in large part, caused by the format of the ballot, which was a butterfly ballot. Elderly citizens in Palm Beach complained that the ballot layout was so confusing that they found it difficult to find the hole to punch for Al Gore and inadvertently voted for Pat Buchanan instead.[142] The estimate is that more than 19,000 overvotes in Palm Beach County were related to confusion with the ballot that caused people to vote twice in the presidential race.[143]

In 2000, a precinct-by-precinct analysis of Florida counties by the *Washington Post* found that heavily Democratic and African American neighborhoods had lost many more presidential votes than other areas because of outmoded voting machinery and rampant confusion about ballots. In fact, the analysis identified a racial component to Florida's election process: Counties with high proportions of Black voters were more likely to have outmoded voting machinery than were counties with predominantly White populations.[144]

As a result of the 2000 debacle, in the presidential election of 2004 massive mobilization efforts occurred, particularly among racial and ethnic communities for the contest between Massachusetts Senator John Kerry and President George W. Bush. A 2000 Gallup Poll reported that almost 70 percent of Blacks felt "cheated" after the 2000 election, 50 percent felt that Bush had stolen the election, and more than 75 percent said that the U.S. election system is discriminatory.[145] Although non-Whites increased their proportion of all votes, President Bush achieved a decisive reelection victory by increasing his vote margin among White voters, particularly among White women.[146]

Racial appeals were present throughout the 2008 election. For instance, an Inland (California) Republican women's group published an "Obama Bucks" welfare coupon in its October 2008 newsletter. Obama is surrounded by a watermelon, ribs, and a bucket of fried chicken, playing on the worst stereotypes some Americans have of Black Americans. This is but one of many instances of the use of Obama's race as a campaign tactic to push those with negative racial views toward the Republican candidate, Senator John McCain, and to degrade Obama at the same time.

In another instance, in Minnesota, racist fliers were mailed to the predominantly White constituents in representative Betty McCollum's (D) district. The fliers stated that if Obama were elected, property values would decrease because low-income Blacks would be moving into the neighborhood. The fliers further suggested that criminals, including O.J. Simpson, would be among the new neighbors.

The 2012 race saw more of the same. A bumper sticker began to appear that said "Don't Re-Nig in 2012," with a red line through Obama's campaign symbol. Underneath the phrase were the words "Stop repeat offenders. Don't reelect Obama." There were many versions of this particular sticker and a video of cars with several of them was uploaded to YouTube and went viral. At first, many people thought the stickers were photoedited on the cars, but it soon became apparent that they were real.

During the Republican primaries, Newt Gingrich declared that President Obama was "the food stamp" president. Gingrich said that he was talking about the fact that the number of people on food stamps had increased during President Obama's first term, but most took his comments as alluding to the stereotype that most Blacks are on welfare and rely on government assistance, also harkening back to the "Obama Bucks" welfare coupon from the 2008 election.

At the Republican National Convention, two delegates threw nuts at a Black camerawoman for CNN, saying "This is how we feed the animals." To the convention's credit, the two people were removed from the convention.[147]

Black voters cast their ballots during early voting at a polling station at Truman College on October 31, 2016, in Chicago.

Mitt Romney's campaign ran an ad during the general election falsely stating that President Obama had gutted the work requirement in welfare reform. Despite reporters and nonpartisan fact-checker organizations stating that Romney's claim was false, Romney continued to state this as "fact" on the campaign trail. A line in the ad said, "On July 12th, President Obama quietly announced a plan to gut welfare reform by dropping work requirements. Under Obama's plan, you wouldn't have to work and wouldn't have to train for a job. They just send you your welfare check."[148] Again, the allusion was to Blacks not working and a Black president giving them a pass on being responsible. In October 2012, Romney revived this false claim, possibly in the hopes of triggering negative racial attitudes on the part of some White voters.

At a rally for Romney in Lancaster, Ohio, on October 12, a supporter inside the arena was photographed wearing a shirt that said "Put the White back in the White House."[149] When the shirt was called to their attention, the Romney campaign disavowed the supporter. A criticism of Romney is that he never called individuals on these types of actions at the time they happened, only after the fact.

The 2016 Republican primary and presidential general election was rife with race and racism. One of the key undertones to Donald Trump's success in the primaries was his attack of non-Whites. These include explicitly anti-immigrant commentary, policy suggestions meant to profile Muslim Americans, and suggestions of travel bans targeted toward them. As a result of such rhetoric, White nationalists, typically marginalized by the Republican Party, entered the picture and were more vocal in their support of Donald Trump than they had been in past campaigns.[150]

On June 16, 2015, Donald Trump announced his candidacy for the Republican nominee for president.[151] In the one-hour speech, he addressed issues from Chinese oligarchs to ISIS. Most prominent was his discussion on immigration policy and Mexico. Trump stated, "When Mexico sends its people, they're not sending their best—they're not sending you. They're not sending you. They're sending people that have lots of problems and they're bringing those problems with us. They're bringing drugs. They're bringing crime. They're rapists. And some, I assume, are good people."[152] On July 11, Trump held one of his major rallies in Phoenix, Arizona, and incorporated the issue of "illegal immigration" explicitly within this campaign stop.[153] Trump invited Maricopa County Sheriff Joe Arpaio, who is notorious for his racial-profiling tactics targeted toward the Latino community. Most notably, Trump suggested building a wall at the U.S.–Mexico border.[154] This idea began a chant in the rally of "Build the Wall!"

On August 25, at a press conference in Iowa, Trump had anchor Jorge Ramos of Univision forcibly removed from the beginning of the press conference when he tried to ask a question.[155] Ramos was escorted from the room by a member of Trump's private security. In the hallway, a middle-aged White man, his face flushed with anger, accosted Ramos, jabbing a finger at him. "Get out of my country," he said. "Get out." The man had a Trump sticker on his lapel.

Ramos told him that he, too, was a U.S. citizen. Ramos was eventually let back into the room.

Many other instances of racial statements and racial insensitivity occurred during Trump's campaign, including acting as if he did not know who David Duke was, the former grand dragon of the Ku Klux Klan group and neo-Nazi sympathizer who endorsed him. One of the more sensational events that went on for several weeks was Trump's attack in June 2016 on the Mexican American judge Gonzalo Curiel, who was overseeing the fraud case against Trump University in San Diego. Trump began referencing Curiel's Mexican American background and implying that because of it, he could not be fair in his rulings on Trump University because Trump was building a wall and Curiel was a "Mexican."[156]

Racial appeals were also present in state and local races. Rick Tyler, an independent candidate for Congress from the 3rd Congressional District in Tennessee, put up a billboard along a highway that said "Make America White Again." He said he put it up to make a point that "the 'Leave It to Beaver,' 'Ozzie and Harriet,' 'Mayberry' America of old was vastly superior to what we are experiencing today."[157] David Duke, as a result of Donald Trump's hesitancy to denounce him, decided to run for senator in Louisiana. Duke said that Trump's attacks on Muslims and illegal immigration brought Duke's values and the values of White nationalists into the mainstream of American politics.[158] He also says that Trump's voters are his voters, but an August 2, 2016, poll found that 80 percent of Louisiana voters had an unfavorable opinion of Duke.[159]

Although Clinton did not use race in a pejorative sense in her campaign, she was called out by some, including some members of Black Lives Matter, for comments she made in 1996, when she was first lady and was supportive of her husband's crime bill. In 1994, Congress passed the Violent Crime Control and Law Enforcement Act, a bill that expanded the use of the death penalty, created new three-strikes rules, made it harder for people to get parole, and

2016 Independent Congressional candidate Rick Tyler faced a tremendous backlash for a campaign billboard in Tennessee telling voters to "Make America White Again." Tyler took the billboard down 12 hours after it was put up.

provided federal funds for states to build more prisons, among other things. Some suggest that the bill increased the incarceration rate for young Black males.[160] Clinton defended her husband's bill in 1996 and made a statement about young Black children that came back to haunt her in the 2016 election: "They are often the kinds of kids that are called 'super-predators, . . .' No conscience, no empathy, we can talk about why they ended up that way, but first we have to bring them to heel."[161] She was heckled at a private fundraiser in February 2016 in Charleston, South Carolina, by a Black Lives Matter protester, Ashley Williams, for her 1996 comments. Williams called Clinton's statement racist and wanted her to apologize for it. Shortly after the event, Clinton said that she regretted having said what she said and disavowed much of the 1994 bill that she says did lead to mass incarceration.[162]

Winning the Election: How Elections Are Decided

Most elections in the United States are decided by a plurality (or first past the post), the candidate who receives the most votes, or a majority, the candidate who receives more than 50 percent of the votes cast in a given election. In a majority system, if no candidate receives 51 percent of the vote, then a run-off election is held between the top two vote-getters.

Most elections for the U.S. House of Representatives and U.S. Senate are decided by a plurality of the votes. In a plurality, or first past the post, electoral system, a candidate can win with any number of votes as long as it is more votes than anyone else receives. Thus, in an election in which there are more than two candidates, an individual can win with only a small proportion of the vote as long as that is the highest percentage received among all of those running.

The process by which the United States elects its president is a combination of a plurality system and a majority system, which adds complexity to understanding the process of electing the president. Given the Electoral College system, Americans do not elect the president directly. The votes Americans cast in the presidential election on Election Day are actually votes for a slate of electors who are committed to each presidential candidate. All of the states use a plurality system for determining which slate of electors wins the states' electoral votes. Figure 15.1 shows a map of the Electoral College with the distribution of votes across states.

Voting

The right to vote and the exercise of that right are at the core of the nation's representative form of government. Yet the United States has had a history of denying the vote to certain citizens, experiences lower voter turnout rates than many other countries (especially other Western democracies), and exhibits differences in voter registration and turnout rates based on race, gender, socio-economic class, and a number of other dimensions.

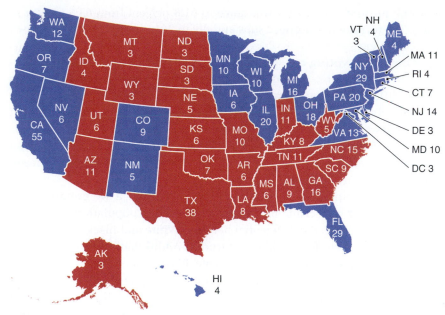

Figure 15.1 2016 Map of Number of Electoral Votes by State

Factors That Affect Voter Participation

Political scientists have learned that people who follow elections in the newspapers or on television, who have a high level of interest in political campaigns, and who overall are interested in politics and public affairs and follow them closely are more likely to feel that voting is an important thing to do than are those who are not interested in politics and public affairs. Also, people who believe that government is responsive to their needs are more likely to think voting is important and to vote than are people who feel the government is not concerned with them and their needs.[163]

The United States is among the premier democracies in the world, yet it has lower voter turnout rates than many countries. An analysis of election turnout by the International Institute for Democracy and Electoral Assistance for all national elections held since 1945 in 172 countries found the United States ranked 139 in average voter turnout (48.3 percent), just ahead of Mexico. Italy was ranked first, with an average voter turnout rate of 92.5 percent. Given the position of the United States as a model democracy that others strive to emulate, why do U.S. citizens vote in such low numbers?

Figure 15.2 shows voter data for the **voting-eligible (citizen) population (VEP)** of the United States in presidential elections from 1960 to 2016. (The voter-eligible, or citizen, population is important because only U.S. citizens are eligible to vote.) As Figure 15.2 demonstrates, voter turnout declined continually from 1960 to 1980, jumped up and down a bit between 1984 and 1996, and then steadily increased from 2000 to 2008, although it dipped slightly in 2008.

Compare voter participation by country and group.

Voting-Eligible Population (VEP) The population of U.S. citizens age eighteen or older.

The VEP turnout rate in 2012 was down to 61.8 percent from 63.6 percent in 2008. The turnout rate dropped substantially in 2016 from that of 2012, down to 55.4 percent.

Voting-Age Population (VAP)

The population of both citizens and noncitizens in the United States age eighteen or older.

Often, the **voting-age population (VAP)**, which includes both citizens and noncitizens, is used to calculate voter turnout rates. This presents a very different picture from voter turnout rates calculated using VEP. For example, Table 15.3 in "Evaluating Equality: Calculating Voting Turnout Rates" shows that VAP in 2012 was approximately 235.2 million, whereas VEP was 215 million. Using VAP for calculating voter turnout in 2012 yields a 56.5 percent rate, whereas using only VEP produces a higher rate, 61.8 percent. Which is the more accurate number?

These differences are particularly illuminating when we examine voter turnout rates for Whites and Blacks. Using the citizen population only shows that, at least in 2012, the differential between White and Black voter turnout was plus 2.1 percent for Black voter turnout. Additionally, when we look at those Americans who were registered to vote, Black Americans had the highest voter turnout rate, 90.5 percent, of all groups of voters displayed in Table 15.3.

Whether VAP or VEP is used as the basis for calculating voter turnout rates for Latinos and Asians yields quite different results. When VAP is used, Latinos and Asians have extremely low voter turnout rates, 31.8 percent and

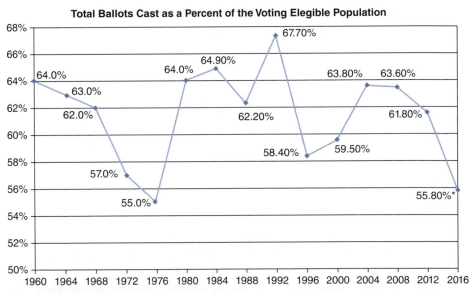

Figure 15.2 Voting Eligible Population.

*Source: Voting-eligible figures for 1976–1980 are taken from calculations made by Dr. Michael McDonald, U.S. Election Project, http://www.electproject.org/national-1789-present; figures for 1980–2012 are taken from Table A-6, Reported Voting and Registration for Total and Citizen Voting-Age Population by Race and Hispanic Origin: Presidential Elections 1980 to 2012, http://www.census.gov/data/tables/time-series/demo/voting-and-registration/voting-historical-time-series.html; *2016 estimates taken from Dr. McDonald's U.S. Election Project data.*

31.3 percent, respectively. Yet turnout rates with VEP, although still lower than those of Blacks and Whites, increase approximately 16.2 percentage points for Latinos and 16 percentage points for Asians.

Why Americans Do Not Vote

The reasons for the low voter turnout rate in the United States vary. A survey by the U.S. Census Bureau after the 2016 presidential elections found that of the approximately 157.6 million American citizens who were registered to vote, 11.9 percent, or 18.9 million people, did not vote. The reasons given for not voting included individuals reporting they were too busy to vote or had scheduling conflicts, did not like the candidates and so did not vote, were simply not interested, or just forgot. For others, some lacked transportation, some were ill or disabled, and some were out of town.[164] What are we to make of these reasons, particularly because voting is the least the U.S. government system expects from its citizens?

In a 1992 study of U.S. voting behavior, Ruy Teixeira, a political scientist whose work focuses on political participation and public opinion, concluded that a combination of structural, social, and psychological factors accounts for low voter turnout.[165] The system of voter registration in the United States is complex and varies from state to state. It has been estimated that the labyrinth of laws and administrative procedures that pertains to voting suppresses voter turnout by 9 percent nationally.[166] Individuals must be motivated to register to vote and to work their way through the process. In many countries, voter registration is automatic and done by the state; individuals do not have to seek to be registered on their own.[167]

In 1993, Congress passed the **National Voter Registration Act**, which provides for mail registration and for registration at motor vehicle departments and other public offices, such as libraries. This registration process is commonly referred to as motor voter. A 2007 report by the U.S. Election Assistance Commission found that making the process of registering to vote easier increased the number of registered voters in 2006 by nearly 12.1 million.[168]

National Voter Registration Act A law passed in 1993 that provides for voter registration by mail and in departments of motor vehicles (also called the "motor voter" act).

Yet problems have arisen from this legislation. Most notably, voters in the 2000 election who showed up to vote in many jurisdictions around the country found that the motor vehicle departments had never submitted the registration forms to the local registrars' offices. This problem has abated somewhat since 2000, but issues remain in some jurisdictions.

Another barrier is the ability to get to the polls on Election Day. In many countries, Election Day is a holiday or elections are held on the weekend, thereby making it more convenient for people to vote. In the United States, only eleven states have made Election Day a state holiday so that it is easier for people to get to the polls. In eleven other states, state employees are given two hours off to cast their ballots, but in twenty-five states private employers do not give time off on Election Day for their employees to vote.[169] In these states, individuals must vote either before or after work. Only sixteen states open their

evaluating equality

Calculating Voting Turnout Rates

Table 15.3 shows the difference in the calculation of turnout rates using VAP and VEP. The turnout rates are higher when only citizens are taken into account, rather than the total population of those eighteen years of age and older.

TABLE 15.3 Differences between Using VAP and VEP for Calculating Voting Turnout Rates

2016	Population in Thousands				
	All	White	Black	Latino	Asian
VAP[a]	245,502	157,395	30,608	38,990	14,881
VEP[b]	224,059	154,450	28,808	26,662	10,283
Registered	157,596	114,151	19,984	15,267	5,785
Voted	137,537	100,849	17,119	12,682	5,043

2016	Population in Percentages				
	All	White	Black	Latino	Asian
Turnout (VAP)	56.0	64.1	55.9	32.5	33.9
Turnout (VEP)	61.4	65.3	59.4	47.6	47.6
Women (% VEP)	63.3	66.8	63.7	50.0	48.4
Men (% VEP)	59.3	63.7	54.2	45.0	49.7
Ages 18–24 (% VEP)	43.0	46.6	42.3	34.4	38.0

Note: Whites include only non-Hispanic Whites. Blacks include only non-Hispanic Blacks. Asians include only non-Hispanic Asians. American Indians and mixed-race groups are not shown.
[a] VAP includes all individuals eighteen years of age and older, regardless of citizenship status in the United States.
[b] VEP includes only U.S. citizens eighteen years of age and older in the United States.
Source: Compiled from Tables 2.1, 2.3, 2.4, 2.5, and 2.6, Voting and Registration in the Election of 2016, Detailed Tables, https://www.census.gov/data/tables/time-series/demo/voting-and-registration/p20-580.html, retrieved November 14, 2017.

$\triangleright$

Why do some countries have higher voter turnout than others?

polls at 6:00 A.M., with most opening at 7:00 A.M., a time at which many Americans are already at or on their way to work. A few states open their polls at 8:00 A.M. Most states close their polls either at 6:00 P.M. or 7:00 P.M., when many people are still commuting home from work. A few states keep their polls open until 8:00 P.M., and New York and Iowa keep their polls open until 9:00 P.M.

In the summer of 2001, a report from the National Commission on Federal Election Reform, formed in the wake of the 2000 election and chaired by former Presidents Jimmy Carter and Gerald Ford, recommended, among other things, that Election Day be made a holiday. The reason is not only to provide greater access for people to come to the polls, but also to have more qualified people available to serve as election workers and to allow more schools, which are more accessible for handicapped people, to be used for polling places. The commission also recommended that every state allow provisional voting, that every state adopt a system of statewide voter registration, and that state governments and the federal government take additional steps to ensure the voting rights of all citizens.[170]

In 2002, Congress passed the **Help America Vote Act**, the purpose of which is to reform aspects of the voting process that failed in 2000 and increase voter education and turnout. The act provides money for states to replace outdated voting machines, reforms voter registration procedures, provides better access to voting for the disabled, and offers better training for poll workers. The act also created a new federal registration form to make it easier for new voters to register. In addition, all states now have provisional ballots for voters who believed they are registered to vote but whose names do not appear on the rolls. The provisions of the act were to be phased in, with all provisions being implemented by 2006.[171]

The deadlines were not met. According to a 2008 report by Election Data Services, despite the 2006 deadline on the replacement of lever and punch-card voting machines with whatever new voting machine the local jurisdiction chose, in 2008 approximately 11.3 million registered voters lived in counties that still used lever machines or punch-card ballots.[172] More than $3 billion was sent to the states to upgrade their voting machinery. By the 2012 elections, most of the punch-card and lever machines had been replaced, and "old" technology appeared to be touchscreen voting machines.[173]

Help America Vote Act
A law passed in 2002 to reform aspects of the voting process that failed in the 2000 presidential election and to increase voter education and turnout.

Voter ID Laws

As a result of the election and then successful reelection of President Obama and the significance of the votes of racial and ethnic minorities in 2008 and 2012, many Republican-controlled state legislatures passed laws that opponents claimed were aimed at suppressing or making it more difficult for those groups to vote. The push for voter ID laws began in 2003 when Alabama, Colorado, Montana, North Dakota, and South Dakota passed new laws. These laws were the result of provisions in the 2002 Help America Vote Act that required that new registrants provide their driver's license number or the last four digits of their Social Security number with their registration application. In addition, states that allowed individuals to register by mail had to obtain identification from first-time voters. These early laws did not require photo identification to vote and allowed for the use of a number of pieces of identification. For example, in Montana voters could use a driver's license, tribal photo identification, a current utility bill, bank statement, paycheck, government check, or any other document that showed the person's name and current address.[174]

Heading into the 2008 and particularly the 2012 elections, states began to pass stringent photo voter ID laws that were criticized as being aimed at reducing and suppressing the votes of racial and ethnic minorities, who tend to vote Democratic. The argument made by the legislature is that these laws would prevent in-person voter fraud, a problem for which a number of studies have found little to no evidence. (Evidence of in-person voter fraud is virtually nonexistent. An extensive examination of voting found that of 1 billion votes cast between 2000 and 2014, only 31 cases of in-person voting fraud were identified.[175]) These charges were particularly aimed at states controlled by Republican legislatures whose voter ID laws required voters to present state- or federal government–issued photo ID cards. A study by the Brennan Center for Justice identified that 11 percent of voting-eligible Americans—or 21 million citizens—do not have driver's licenses and other nondriver's state-issued IDs.[176] Those without photo IDs are disproportionately seniors (18 percent do not have photo IDs), African Americans (25 percent), the poor (15 percent), and students or people with disabilities.

In 2013, North Carolina's Republican-led legislature had put into place voter ID restrictions by passing legislation that has been described as some of the "most far-reaching" in the United States.[177] On July 29, 2016, the U.S. Court of Appeals for the 4th Circuit struck down North Carolina's voter ID law. The court argued that the law suppressed Black voter turnout because of the way in which it specifically targeted African Americans.[178] The court noted that the law violated the Constitution and the Voting Rights Act and was enacted with "racially discriminatory intent."[179] The North Carolina voter ID law required voters to present state-issued photo identification at the polls and was described as discriminatory for targeting African Americans "with almost surgical precision."[180] In addition to tossing out this requirement, the federal appeals court decision restored voters' ability to register on Election Day and cast early ballots and also allowed individuals who would be eighteen years old on Election Day to register before their eighteenth birthday.[181] The legislature has placed an amendment to the North Carolina State Constitution on the 2018 ballot requiring voter identification for in-person voting. The amendment passed with 55.54 percent voting for the amendment to 44.46 against. It is anticipated, however, that this will again be challenged in court.

Earlier in July, the 5th Circuit Court of Appeals ruled that Texas' 2011 photographic voter ID law violated the Voting Rights Act. Commenting on the court's ruling, attorney general Loretta Lynch said, "Texas's highly restrictive voter ID law abridges the right to vote on account of race or color."[182] The law required voters to present only certain government-issued photo IDs when voting and exclude federal or state government IDs and student IDs.[183] Texas was one of nine states that required "strict photo ID," and it only had a few acceptable forms of identification.[184] On April 10, 2017, a federal judge ruled, for the second time, that the law discriminated against minority voters. On June 2, 2017, the state legislature enacted a nonstrict, photo voter ID requirement in Texas. A nonstrict photo ID law means that a voter without the appropriate identification will be able to cast a ballot and it will be counted without the voter having to do anything. For example, the voter might sign an affidavit at the poll attesting to their eligibility to vote or someone else, such as a poll worker, can verify the identity of the voter.

In Wisconsin, U.S. District Judge James Patterson ruled that some sections of the state's 2011 voter ID law were unconstitutional because they discriminated against minority voters.[185] Wisconsin's voter ID law required voters to possess specified forms of photo identification to vote. According to the American Civil Liberties Union, the law disproportionately affected Black and Latino voters, who were unlikely to have the types of photo ID required for voting.[186] Judge Patterson's ruling noted that "[Wisconsin's] preoccupation with mostly phantom election fraud leads to real incident of disenfranchisement which undermine rather than enhance confidence in election."[187]

A Kansas voter ID law had also been overturned in May 2016. The law, which had been championed by Republicans,[188] required people to prove American citizenship to register to vote when applying for a driver's license.[189] U.S. District Judge Julie Robinson ruled that the state's proof-of-citizenship requirements violated a provision in the National Voter Registration Act, which only requires "minimal information" to determine whether an individual is eligible to vote.[190] Critics of the law had argued that it was implemented in an attempt to "depress voter turnout among groups that lean Democratic, including low-income and minority voters."[191] The rulings in North Carolina, Texas, Wisconsin, and Kansas "suggest a growing judicial suspicion of the wave of voting-restriction legislation" that have been passed by Republicans.[192]

Demographics and Voting

Throughout the book, we have talked about the complexities of the American political system and the inequalities that exist within it. Some of the inequalities were intentional, such as racial and gender inequality, and were implemented through a system of exclusion. Even after the system was changed, institutional and structural barriers were erected to prevent excluded groups from obtaining equality within the system. The effects of the myriad racial and gender inequalities in the United States manifest in differences in voter registration and voter turnout. Voting differences exist on other dimensions as well, such as age, marital status, socioeconomic status, and region of the country.

Race

The data in Table 15.4 show that race plays a role in voter registration and turnout. Voting data on the 2016 presidential election are used to illustrate demographic voting patterns in the following section. In the 2016 presidential election, non-Hispanic Whites had higher registration and voting rates than did non-Hispanic Blacks, Asians, and Hispanics. This is a shift from the 2012 presidential election when non-Hispanic Whites had slightly higher registration rates, but non-Hispanic Black voter rates were 2.1 percent higher than the voting rate for non-Hispanic Whites. The gap between non-Hispanic White and non-Hispanic Black political participation disappeared in 2012, with Blacks outvoting Whites for the first time since the Census Bureau began reporting voting statistics by race. But in the 2016 presidential elections the gap reappeared, with Whites registration and voting rates 4.5 percent and 5.9 percent, respectively, higher than non-Hispanic Blacks. In the 1950s, the difference between Whites and Blacks was significant, but a number of factors—a lowering of de jure and de facto barriers to political participation, mobilization by the Civil Rights Movement, and a dramatic increase in the proportion of Black Americans with higher levels of education and higher-status occupations—contributed to a narrowing of the gap.[193] In the 2008 election, the racial gap between non-Hispanic Whites and non-Hispanic Blacks almost disappeared, with only 1.4 percentage points separating the two. Clearly, Barack Obama's candidacy energized Black voters and narrowed the racial gap in voting between Blacks and Whites. The momentum begun in 2008 erased the gap in 2012, with Blacks outvoting Whites.

Yet the gap between non-Hispanic Asians and Whites and Hispanics and Whites in voting remained at 16.3 and 17.7 percent, respectively. The reasons for these continuing lower rates for non-Hispanic Asians and Hispanics can be attributed to a host of factors, among them continued barriers to registration and voting, lower income and education levels, and a higher proportion of younger people not of voting age.

Gender

In 1998, women overall were registered and voted in slightly larger numbers than did men. That year saw the first election in which women outregistered and outvoted men. A number of social changes for women, such as increased participation in the workforce and increased educational attainment (an important contributor to voting), could account for this change. Research in the 1990s found that women were less likely than men to participate in politics.[194]

Yet the 2016 data indicate that increases in women voting occurred among non-Hispanic White, non-Hispanic Black, and Hispanic women. Non-Hispanic Asian women voted in similar numbers to their non-Hispanic Asian male counterparts. Non-Hispanic White, non-Hispanic Black, and Hispanic women were registered and voted in greater numbers than did the men in their respective groups. In fact, Black women's turnout rate was similar to that of White males in 2016, 63.7 percent. The reasons for non-Hispanic White, non-Hispanic Black, and Hispanic women voting in larger numbers than their male counterparts vary, but one explanation is that these women experience the American political system both as women and as members of racial groups and that, as political scientists Jane Mansbridge and Katherine Tate describe it, this "doubly bound" situation is a significant contributor to political participation among these women.[195]

Age

Age makes a difference in voter registration and voting. Traditionally, young people age eighteen to twenty-four are registered in lower numbers and the turnout rate is lower, 43.0 percent, as shown in the 2016 data. Voter registration and voting increase with age, with those sixty-five to seventy-four having

Learn about the role of the younger Americans in the 2012 election.

TABLE 15.4 Demographic and Geographic Voting Patterns for Citizen Population in the 2016 National Elections

	Citizen VEP Population	
	Reported Registered to Vote (%)	**Reported Voting (%)**
Total citizen VEP[a]	70.3	61.4
Gender		
Male	68.6	59.3
Female	72.0	63.3
Race		
Non-Hispanic White	73.9	65.3
Male	72.5	63.7
Female	75.2	66.8
Non-Hispanic Black	69.4	59.4
Male	65.0	54.2
Female	72.9	63.7
Non-Hispanic Asian	56.3	49.0
Male	56.8	49.7
Female	55.8	48.4
Hispanic	57.3	47.6
Male	54.6	45.0
Female	59.8	50.0
Age		
18–24 years	55.4	43.0
25–44 years	67.0	56.5
45–64 years	74.0	66.6
65–74 years	78.7	72.6
75 years+ and over	77.1	68.4
Marital status		
Married, spouse present	76.5	69.4
Married, spouse absent	63.9	53.1
Widowed	72.9	62.3
Divorced	69.6	59.2
Separated	60.6	47.4
Never married	60.0	48.9
Education level		
Less than 9th grade	42.3	31.7
9th to 12th grade, no diploma	46.9	35.3
High school graduate or GED	62.6	51.5
Some college or associate's degree	73.1	63.3
Bachelor's degree	80.5	74.2
Advanced degree	84.6	80.3
Annual family income		
Less than $10,000	57.7	41.4
$10,000–14,999	60.9	47.7
$15,000–19,999	62.4	48.8
$20,000–29,999	63.8	51.7

(Continued)

TABLE 15.4 *Continued*

	Citizen VEP Population	
	Reported Registered to Vote (%)	**Reported Voting (%)**
Annual family income		
$30,000–39,999	69.1	58.9
$40,000–49,999	71.9	62.4
$50,000–74,999	77.1	67.6
$75,000–99,999	79.2	71.4
$100,000–149,999	83.6	76.4
$150,000 and over	85.7	80.3
Type of Residence		
Owner-occupied units	74.4	66.9
Renter-occupied units	61.1	48.9
Duration of Residence		
Less than 1 year	69.7	55.0
1–2 years	74.9	63.3
3-4 years	79.3	68.8
5 years or longer	84.5	75.6
Region		
Northeast	70.2	61.6
Midwest	73.5	64.3
South	69.9	60.0
West	68.1	60.7

[a] *VEP, voting-eligible population (citizen population eighteen years and older).*

Source: Compiled from Tables 2.1, 2.3, 2.4, 2.5, 2.6, 3, 5, 7, 8, and 9, Voting and Registration in the Election of 2016, Detailed Tables, https://www .census.gov/data/tables/time-series/demo/voting-and-registration/p20-580.html, retrieved November 14, 2017.

the highest registration and voter turnout of all of the age categories. Only after age seventy-five do the rates begin to decline, but only slightly.

Research indicates that older Americans are more likely to register and to vote than are younger Americans. Classic voting behavior studies concluded that, by and large, young people do not care much about politics.[196] Yet the 2008 election proved to be an exception to the rule, as voters eighteen to twenty-four were the only age group to show a statistically significant increase in turnout. Moreover, Blacks had the highest turnout rate among this group.[197]

Marital Status

A person's marital status affects voting behavior. People who are married and living with their spouses have significantly higher registration and voting rates than do those who are single. Married persons living with spouses are more settled in a community than are individuals who are divorced or have never married. Data from 2016 indicate that this pattern was present in the recent presidential election—married persons living with their spouses voted at a higher percentage, 69.4 percent, than did all of the other marital categories, particularly those who have never been married.

Socioeconomic Status

Research has found that people who have higher educational and income levels, who own their homes, and who reside in the same place for an extended period of time are more likely to register to vote and to vote than are those who have lower educational and income levels, who rent their homes, and who reside in places for shorter periods of time.[198] The data in Table 15.4 demonstrate that as education increases, registration and voting increase as well. In the 2016 national elections, individuals with less than a ninth-grade education registered to vote (42.3 percent) and voted (31.7 percent) significantly less than did those with advanced degrees (84.6 percent registered and 80.3 percent voted).

The same pattern is present in relation to income. Registration and voting increase progressively as income increases. Only 41.4 percent of those making less than $10,000 voted in the 2016 elections, whereas 80.3 percent of those making more than $150,000 voted.

People who own their homes are more likely to register to vote and to vote than are those who rent. In fact, the difference is substantial—74.4 percent of homeowners were registered to vote and 66.9 percent voted in the 2016 elections, whereas 61.1 percent of renters were registered to vote and 48.9 percent voted. Those who own their homes might feel that they have a greater stake in what happens politically than do those who rent and most likely move more often. Moving frequently is complicated by variations in voter registration rules from one location to another.

These factors also contribute to racial differences in registration and voting. Census data from 2016 indicate that whereas almost three-fourths (71.9 percent) of non-Hispanic Whites own their homes, only 41.6 percent of non-Hispanic Blacks, 46.0 percent of Hispanics, 47.6 percent of American Indians and Alaska Natives, and 55.4 percent of Asian, Native Hawaiian and Pacific Islanders own their homes.[199] Coupled with home ownership as a contributing factor to registration and voting is length of residence. Those who live in a residence for an extended period of time are more likely to register to vote and to vote than are those who are more transient. Homeowners are more likely to stay in one place than are renters.

Region

The region in which a person lives can influence registration and voting. People in the Midwest have higher levels of voter registration, 73.5 percent, than do those in other parts of the country and a slightly higher percentage of individuals who voted, 64.3 percent. This might be attributed to the fact that in Idaho, Iowa, Minnesota, Wisconsin, and Wyoming, individuals can register to vote on Election Day, and North Dakota no longer has voter registration.

In past elections, Southerners were less likely to vote than were individuals in other regions of the country. Previous lower voter turnout rates in the South have been attributed to lower economic development in the South, along with lower levels of education and income.[200] In 2016, however, voting by Southerners was on par with that of individuals in the West, and close to that of those in the Northeast.

In summary, these data from 2016 suggest that older people are more likely to vote than younger people, more highly educated people are more likely to vote than less educated people, people from higher-income families are more likely to vote than people from lower-income families, and people who own homes are more likely to vote than people who rent. The gap between non-Hispanic Whites and Blacks disappeared in 2012, but reappeared again in 2016. Also, non-Hispanic Whites are still significantly more likely to vote than non-Hispanic Asians and Hispanics. Black and Latina women are more likely to vote than are their male counterparts, but Asian American women lag slightly behind males in both registration and voting.

The 2016 Presidential Election

The outcome of the 2016 presidential contest was unexpected and counter to virtually every public opinion and tracking poll available, but it was in keeping with the unorthodox and surprise-filled campaign that characterized the election, including the presidential debates. The first debate between the Democratic nominee Hillary Clinton and her Republican counterpart Donald Trump was held on Monday, September 26, 2016, at Hofstra University in Hempstead, New York. Hillary Clinton was clearly substantially more prepared for the debate than was Trump.[201] Clinton dominated most of the exchanges on issues ranging from gender to national security, asserting that Trump did not respect women and warning that he could not be trusted with nuclear codes.[202] Many political commentators agreed that Hillary Clinton scored a decisive victory in the first debate,[203] but some people concluded that Trump won.[204] According to a CNN/ORC poll of voters who watched the debate, 62 percent of voters deemed Hillary Clinton the winner, whereas 27 percent believed Donald Trump prevailed.[205]

Heading into the second debate at Washington University in St. Louis, Missouri, on Sunday, October 9, 2016, Trump's campaign appeared to be coming apart. An audiotape of Trump making vulgar comments about women and bragging about sexually assaulting them had surfaced, causing more than two dozen Republican leaders to disavow their support of the GOP presidential nominee.[206] Although Trump apologized for his grossly inappropriate comments, he brushed his words off as "locker room talk" and denied groping or sexually assaulting women. Hours before the debate, Trump held a press conference with four women who accused Bill Clinton of sexual assault, and during the debate itself, Trump attempted to deflect questions regarding his own assaultive behavior by launching a verbal attack against first Bill and then Hillary Clinton. Trump noted, "If you look at Bill Clinton, far worse. Mine are words, and his was action. His was—what he's done to women, there's never been anybody in the history of politics in this nation that's been so abusive to women . . . Hillary Clinton attacked those same women and attacked them viciously."[207] Although Trump's overall performance in the second debate was a marked improvement from that of the first debate, "Clinton's win in the second debate was decisive."[208] Forty-two percent of voters who watched the debate said Clinton won, including 13 percent of Republicans. Similar to the results of the first debate, only 28 percent of debate watchers believed that Trump won the second debate.

The third and final presidential debate took place at the University of Nevada, Las Vegas, on October 19, 2016, less than three weeks before voters would head to the polls on November 8. As was also the case at the second debate, no handshakes or pleasantries were exchanged before the third debate began.[209] Hillary Clinton presented herself as a well-prepared and experienced politician, and Trump appeared to be a worthy opponent in several ways.[210] Over the course of the debate, both candidates discussed their policy position on a number of important issues, but they also continued to engage in personal attacks and comments on the various scandals that had plagued each other's campaigns.[211] Any gains made by Trump during the first and second debates were reversed when he called Hillary Clinton "a nasty woman" and declined to say whether he would accept the results of the election.[212] Trump later doubled down on his remarks, saying that he would only accept the results if he emerged the winner. Although Trump's comments were shocking, they were not entirely surprising, given that for some time he had been refusing to accept the legitimacy of the election and insisting that the electoral process was "rigged."[213] Overall, the margin tightened following the third debate: 52 percent of debate watchers thought Clinton delivered the better performance, whereas 39 percent believed that Trump won the debate.[214]

Hillary Clinton's primary campaign had largely been overshadowed by the Federal Bureau of Investigation's inquiry into her use of a private email server when she was secretary of state. In the summer, after the conclusion of a full investigation, the FBI announced that it would not recommend filing any criminal charges against Hillary Clinton.[215] The day after the third debate, however, just two weeks before the presidential election, the FBI director James Comey told legislators that the bureau was resuming its investigation[216] as a result of newly discovered email messages found on a laptop seized during a separate criminal investigation of the estranged husband of the Clinton aide Huma Abedin.[217] Comey's letter set off a Republican assault on Clinton, and Trump and his supporters insinuated that the reopening of the investigation indicated that Clinton had, indeed, done something criminal.

On November 6, in a letter addressed to the chairman of the congressional committee, Comey told lawmakers that the FBI upheld their previous findings and stood by their determination that they would not recommend filing charges against Hillary Clinton,[218] issuing the following statement: "Based on our review, we have not changed our conclusions that we expressed in July."[219] Whereas the Clinton campaign welcomed Comey's announcement as a way to finally put to rest concerns about the email scandal, Trump completely rejected it, questioning how it was possible for FBI agents to thoroughly investigate the new emails in such a short period of time.[220] Comey's reopening of the investigation in late October created a firestorm, so his announcement, coming just two days before the November 8 election, was arguably an attempt by the agency to clear "the cloud of suspicion that he had publicly placed" over Clinton's campaign in the last leg of the election.[221] His announcement also renewed skepticism and concern from both Republicans and Democrats about the FBI's handling of the email controversy, however.[222] Although the FBI should remain politically neutral, the organization played a central role in the 2016 presidential election cycle, leading to widespread questions about the agency's integrity.[223]

Clinton appeared to rebound in the polls after the initial dip seen following the release of Comey's October letter. Before the letter's release, early voting had already begun in many states, and by November 8 more than 46 million individuals had already cast their ballots. The projections of which candidate was being helped by early voting were mixed. For example, more than 6 million Florida registered voters voted early but, although Democrats had cast more ballots than Republicans, the number of Democrats was lower than in 2012, which was good news for Trump. The early voting statistics favored Clinton in Nevada, where Latinos turned out in large numbers, and in North Carolina, where Democrats jumped ahead of Republicans. North Carolina was a critical swing state for both Clinton and Trump, as was Nevada for Clinton.

Virtually all of the polls and election models indicated that Clinton was going to win the election and become the first female president of the United States. As the votes began to come in on the evening of November 8, Clinton appeared to be doing well and pulled ahead in several key states, especially Florida. As the night wore on, however, it became clear that although Clinton was leading in the popular vote, the states that had been historically Democratic, her Midwest "blue firewall," were moving in Trump's direction. Three states that had been reliably Democratic in the past—Michigan, Wisconsin, and Pennsylvania—appeared to be leaning toward Trump. Trump ultimately won Wisconsin and its ten electoral votes by about 1 percent of the votes cast, or 27,000 votes.[224] In Pennsylvania, Clinton took Philadelphia and its suburbs by a healthy 635,000 vote margin over Trump, improving on President Obama's margin in the suburban counties in 2012, but falling behind in Philadelphia itself. This was not enough to offset Trump's strength in the rest of the state, however, including three counties that went for Obama in 2012 but flipped to Trump in the 2016 cycle. Trump won Pennsylvania and its twenty electoral votes by 73,224 votes.[225] Trump won Michigan and its sixteen electoral by 11,000 votes, a 0.28 percent difference over Clinton—47.6 percent to 47.33 percent of the total vote. Macomb County, a traditionally Democratic county, went for Trump, whereas heavily Democratic Detroit and Flint, as well as Wayne County, voted for Clinton.[226]

Trump's messages apparently resonated with White voters in rural areas, who believed they have been left behind by the economic recovery.

Seven counties that voted for Obama in North Carolina supported Trump in 2016, primarily because the economic growth experienced by the urban areas has bypassed these counties, many of which have some of the state's highest unemployment rates and lowest incomes. Many of these rural communities have closed factories and most residents have lost their jobs.[227]

Overall, turnout for the 2016 election was the lowest in twenty years (1976), with only 55.8% percent of eligible voters participating. The overall rate in 2012 was 61.8 percent, down from 63.8 percent in 2008. Thus, amid all of the drama and controversy surrounding the 2016 election, fewer voters cast their ballots. Clinton took the majority of the popular vote, 48.1% percent (64,469,963 votes as of November 29, 2016) to Trump's 46.5% percent (62,379,366 votes as of November 29, 2016), but Trump received 306 electoral votes to Clinton's 232.

As Table 15.5 demonstrates, according to the exit polls, Trump took the majority of the White vote (58 percent), whereas Clinton took 88 percent of the Black vote, 65 percent of the Latino vote, 65 percent of the Asian vote, and 56 percent of the vote of those in other categories. Yet, Clinton's margins among these groups was smaller than that of President Obama in 2012, when he received 93 percent of the Black vote, 71 percent of the Latino vote, 73 percent of the Asian vote, and 58 percent of the vote of those in other racial categories.

Clinton needed to carry women in general, and White educated women in particular, in large numbers. She did take the majority of the female vote, 54 percent, but as the exit poll data in Table 15.6 demonstrate, only 43 percent of the White female vote. These percentages are similar to those of Obama in 2012, when he took 55 percent of the female vote, but only 42 percent of the White female vote. Clinton's margin of victory among women came from the votes of Black (94 percent) and Latina women (68 percent). Clinton received 51 percent of the votes of college-educated White women (data not shown), but Trump took 54 percent of college-educated White men, 62 percent of non-college-educated White women, and 72 percent of non-college-educated White men.

We have used the exit poll data for estimates of the voter breakdown, but Edison Research did not poll in all fifty states; only twenty-eight states

TABLE 15.5 2016 Exit Poll Results by Race

% of Voters	Group	Trump	Clinton	Other/NA
70	White	58%	37%	5%
12	Black	8%	88%	4%
11	Latino	29%	65%	6%
4	Asian	29%	65%	6%
3	Other	37%	56%	7%

TABLE 15.6 2016 Vote by Gender and Race

	Vote by Gender and Race		
Total	**Trump**	**Clinton**	**Other/NA**
White men: 34%	63%	31%	6%
White women: 37%	53%	43%	4%
Black men: 5%	13%	80%	7%
Black women: 7%	4%	94%	2%
Latino men: 5%	33%	62%	5%
Latina women: 6%	26%	68%	6%
All others: 6%	32%	61%	7%

were included. As a result, there is debate about the accuracy of Trump's support from Latino and Asian American voters as reported in the exit polls. Edison/ Mitofsy Election System, which conducts the exit polls for a consortium of news organizations, acknowledges that their sampling frame is not ideal to provide estimates of small, geographically clustered demographic groups.

Latino Decisions, a polling organization that specializes in surveying Latino populations, conducted an election eve national survey of Latinos (n = 5,600) and state-level samples in eleven states and interviewed in both English and Spanish. Their data indicate that Clinton received 79 percent of the Latino vote, rather than the 65 percent reported in the exit polls, and Trump received 18 percent rather than 29 percent. According to Latino Decisions, 71 percent of Latino men voted for Clinton compared to 24 percent who voted for Trump, and 86 percent of Latina women voted for Clinton compared to 12 percent for Trump (see Table 15.7). Latinos comprised 7 percent of the electorate in 2000; their proportion increased to 8 percent in 2004, 9 percent in 2008, 10 percent in 2012, and approximately 12 percent in 2016.[228]

Asian American Decisions, a polling group that specializes in surveying Asian Americans, also conducted an election eve national survey of Asian Americans (n = 863), as well as state samples in eight states. Their data indicate that Clinton received 76 percent of the Asian American vote, rather than the 65 percent reported in the exit poll, and Trump received 16 percent, rather than 29 percent. According to Asian American Decisions, 72 percent of Asian American men voted for Clinton compared to 21 percent for Trump, whereas 79 percent of Asian American women voted for Clinton compared to 17 percent for Trump.

There were concerns that the number of Black voters turning out differed from that of 2012 around the country; a comparison of exit polls for both elections suggests this is correct. The Black proportion of the electorate increased from 10 percent in 2000 to 13 percent in 2008; that share was

TABLE 15.7 2016 Latino and Asian American Voters

Total	Vote by Race		
	Clinton	Trump	Other/NA
Latinos	79%	18%	3%
Latino men	71%	24%	4%
Latina women	86%	12%	2%
Asian Americans	75%	19%	5%
Asian American men	72%	21%	7%
Asian American women	79%	17%	4%

Source: Latino Decisions, 2016 Latino Election Analysis; Asian American Decisions, The Asian American Vote in 2016.

maintained in 2012. In 2016, the Black percentage had declined 1 percentage point, to 12 percent. This 1 percent decline might have made a difference for Democrats, but the assumption is, rather, that Black voters chose not to vote. (Table 15.8 illustrates the changes from 2000 in the racial share of the electorate.) What appears to be lost on commentators is the effect the gutting of Section 5 of the Voting Rights Act has had on Black voters in many states that were formerly covered by Section 5. A November 2016 report by the Leadership Conference Education Fund indicated that formerly covered jurisdictions had 868 fewer polling places than in 2012.[229]

North Carolina dealt with many legal battles addressing voter access during the 2016 election cycle. These lawsuits were filed because of concerns about voter suppression tactics that would primarily affect Black voters in the state. On November 4, 2016, a federal court issued a preliminary injunction barring three North Carolina counties from revoking the voting rights of thousands of residents whose voting eligibility had been challenged by Republican activists and political operatives.[230] The ruling held that voters from the three counties—Beaufort, Cumberland, and Moore—whose voter registrations had been canceled in recent months because of the "individual challenge law" must have their voting privileges reinstated.[231] The National Association for the Advancement of Colored People had filed a lawsuit alleging that the three counties had purged voter rolls through a process that disproportionately targeted Black voters. The judge's ruling was based on the National Voter Registration Act, a federal law that prohibits the cancellation or blanket removal of voter registrations in the ninety days prior to an election.[232] In the ruling, the judge noted that "electoral integrity is enhanced, not diminished, when all citizens who are eligible to vote are allowed to exercise that right free from interference and burden unnecessarily imposed by others."[233] The North Carolina State Board of Elections revealed that since the 2014 election, officials had removed from voter registration rolls the names of nearly 6,700 voters registered in eight counties.[234] As previously discussed, in August, the Supreme Court issued a decision preventing the state of North Carolina from implementing a strict voting law during the November election. A lower court had previously established that the law was enacted "with almost surgical precision" to specifically target and disenfranchise Black voters.[235]

Several of North Carolina's counties interpreted the 4th Circuit and Supreme Court decisions to require them to open only one early voting site, with their language of at least one site. Guilford County, for example, which includes Greensboro, opened only one early voting site in the first week of early voting, cutting the number of sites from sixteen in 2012 to just one in 2016—a whopping 94 percent cut. As a result, just 12 percent of the 2016 ballots were cast in the first week compared to those cast during the same period in 2012. This was a very successful voter suppression tactic.[236]

There were many other reports of voter suppression tactics around the country. The responsibility for combatting voter suppression tactics falls on the various election boards or civil rights groups. Often, however, there is not enough time remaining for these groups to go to court and get an injunction against those who are attempting to suppress non-White voters. In Arkansas, for example, a Republican election commissioner was accused of voter intimidation after he harassed individuals who were voting early. In a lawsuit filed against the Republican Party of Arkansas and Jefferson election commissioner Stu Stoffer, Stoffer was accused of yelling at voters, interfering with the voting process, and preventing voters from voting.[237]

In Florida, a political advisory committee known as the Florida Citizens for Honest Elections, placed an ad in newspapers across the state offering a $5,000 cash reward for information that could lead to "the arrest and felony conviction of dishonest persons involved in voter fraud."[238] In Texas, a Republican political consultant promoted an "Election Integrity Tip Hotline"

TABLE 15.8 National Exit Poll Share of the Electorate: 2000–2016

	Share of Electorate 2000	Share of Electorate 2004	Share of Electorate 2008	Share of Electorate 2012	Share of Electorate 2016
VOTE BY RACE					
White	81%	77%	75%	72%	70%
African American	10%	11%	13%	13%	12%
Latino	7%	8%	9%	10%	11%
Asian	2%	2%	2%	3%	4%
Other	0%	2%	2%	2%	3%

Source: Nonprofit Vote. (2012). Nonprofit Voters Increase from 2008. Retrieved October 16, 2018, from http://www.nonprofitvote.org; 2016 data taken from the Exit Poll, http://www.cnn.com/election/results/exit-polls.

our voices

Excerpts from Hillary Clinton's Speech on Donald Trump, the "Alt-Right" Movement, and Mainstreaming Racism[a]

Everywhere I go people tell me how concerned they are by the divisive rhetoric coming from my opponent in this election. And I understand that concern because it's like nothing we've heard before from a nominee for president of the United States, from one of our two major parties.

From the start, Donald Trump has built his campaign on prejudice and paranoia. He is taking hate groups mainstream and helping a radical fringe take over the Republican Party. His disregard for the values that make our country great is profoundly dangerous.

[Just] this past week, under the guise of outreach to African Americans, Trump has stood up in front of largely White audiences and described Black communities in such insulting and ignorant terms. Poverty, rejection, horrible education, no housing, no homes, no ownership, crime at levels nobody has seen. Right now he said you can walk down the street and get shot. Those are his words.

But when I hear them, I think to myself, how sad. Donald Trump misses so much. He doesn't see the success of Black leaders in every field, the vibrancy of Black-owned businesses, the strength of the Black church. . . . He doesn't see the excellence of historically Black colleges and universities or the pride of Black parents watching their children thrive. He apparently didn't see Police Chief Brown of Dallas on television after the murders of five of his officers, conducting himself with such dignity. He certainly doesn't have any solutions to take on the reality of systemic racism and create more equity and opportunity in communities of color, and for every American . . .

Now Trump's lack of knowledge or experience or solutions would be bad enough. But what he's doing here is more sinister. Trump is reinforcing harmful stereotypes and offering a dog whistle to his most hateful supporters. It's a disturbing preview of what kind of president he'd be.

And that's what I want to make clear today. A man with a long history of racial discrimination, who traffics in dark conspiracy theories drawn from the pages of supermarket tabloids and the far dark reaches of the Internet should never run our government or command our military . . .

Maya Angelou, a great American whom I admired very much, she once said, when someone shows you who they are, believe them the first time. Well throughout his career and this campaign, Donald Trump has shown us exactly who he is, and I think we should believe him. When he was getting his start in business, he was sued by the Justice Department for refusing to rent apartments to Black and Latino tenants. Their applications would be marked with a C, C for colored, and then rejected. Three years later, the Justice Department took Trump back to court because he hadn't changed. And the pattern continued through the decades.

State regulators fined one of Trump's casinos for repeatedly removing Black dealers from the floor. No wonder the turnover rate for his minority employees was way above average. And let's not forget that Trump first gained political prominence leading the charge for the so-called Birthers. He promoted the racist lie that President Obama is not really an American citizen, part of a sustained effort to delegitimize America's first Black president.

And in 2015, Trump launched his own campaign for president with another racist lie. He described Mexican immigrants as rapists and criminals. And he accused the Mexican government of actively sending them across the border. None of that is true. . . . I think we all remember when Trump said a distinguished federal judge born in Indiana could not be trusted to do his job because, quote, "he's a Mexican." Think about that. . . . Even the Republican Speaker of the House of Representatives, Paul Ryan, described that, and I quote, as the "textbook definition of a racist comment." . . .

But for Trump, that is just par for the course. This is someone who re-tweets White supremacists online, like the user who goes by the name "White Genocide TM." Trump took this fringe bigot with a few dozen followers, and spread his message to 11 million people. His campaign famously posted an anti-Semitic image, a Star of David imposed over a sea of dollar bills that first appeared on White supremacist websites. The Trump campaign has also selected a prominent White nationalist

---

[a] Excerpted (and edited) version of Hillary Clinton's speech delivered at a campaign rally that was held at Truckee Meadows Community College in Reno, Nevada, on August 25, 2016.

(Continued)

our voices *(Continued)*

leader as a delegate in California, and they only dropped him under pressure.

When asked in a nationally televised interview whether he would disavow the support of David Duke, a former grand wizard of the Ku Klux Klan, Trump wouldn't do it. And only later, again under mounting pressure, did he backtrack. And when Trump was asked about anti-Semitic slurs and death threats coming from his supporters, he refused to condemn them.

Through it all, he has continued pushing discredited conspiracy theories with racist undertones. You remember, he said that thousands of American Muslims in New Jersey cheered the 9/11 attacks. They didn't. He suggested that senator Ted Cruz's father was involved in the Kennedy assassination. . . . Just recently, Trump claimed that President Obama founded ISIS. And he has repeated that over and over again. . . . You know I've stood by President Obama's side as he made the toughest decisions a commander-in-chief has to make. In times of crisis, our country depends on steady leadership, clear thinking, calm judgment, because one wrong move can mean the difference between life and death. I know we have veterans here and I know we have families, mothers, and spouses, and children of people currently serving. The last thing we need in the situation room is a loose cannon who can't tell the difference—or doesn't care to—between fact and fiction. And who buys so easily into racially tinged rumors.

Someone so detached from reality should never be in charge of making decisions that are as real as they come. And that is yet another reason why Donald Trump is simply temperamentally unfit to be president of the United States . . .

He says that children born to undocumented parents in America are anchor babies and should be deported, millions of them. He'd ban Muslims around the world from entering our country just because of their religion. . . . Under Donald Trump, America would distinguish itself as the only country in the world to impose a religious test at the border. Now come to think of it, there actually may be one other place that does that, the so called Islamic State, the territory that ISIS controls. What a cruel irony that someone running for president would equate us with them.

[Trump] hired Stephen Bannon, the head of a right-wing website called Breitbart.com, as [his] campaign's CEO. . . . According to the Southern Poverty Law Center, which tracks hate groups, Breitbart embraces ideas on the extremist fringe of the conservative right. This is not conservatism as we have known it. This is not Republicanism as we have known it.

These are racist ideas, race-baiting ideas, anti-Muslim, anti-immigrant, anti-woman, all key tenets making up an emerging racist ideology known as the alt-right. Now, alt-right is short for alternative-right. The *Wall Street Journal* describes it as a loose but organized movement, mostly online, that rejects mainstream conservatism, promotes nationalism, and views immigration and multiculturalism as threats to White identity.

So the de facto merger between Breitbart and the Trump campaign represents a landmark achievement for this group, a fringe element has effectively taken over the Republican Party. And this is part of a broader story—the rising tide of hard-line, right-wing nationalism around the world. . . . My friends, this is a moment of reckoning for every Republican dismayed that the party of Lincoln has become the party of Trump. It's a moment of reckoning for all of us who love our country and believe that America is better than this.

Twenty years ago when Bob Dole accepted the Republican nomination, he pointed to the exits in the convention hall, and told any racist in the party to get out. The week after 9/11 George W. Bush went to a mosque and declared for everyone to hear that Muslims love America just as much as I do. In 2008, John McCain told his own supporters that they were wrong about the man he was trying to defeat. Senator McCain made sure they knew Barack Obama, he said, was an American citizen and a decent person. We need that kind of leadership again . . .

How many of you saw any of the Olympics? . . . I was—I was so proud I always get carried away every time the Olympics are on. And you look at the diversity of our athletes. Look at our fabulous Olympic team, representing the United States of America. Ibtihaj Muhammad, an African American Muslim from New Jersey, won the bronze medal in fencing with grace and skill. Would she even have a place in Donald Trump's America? And I'll tell you, when I was growing up, in so many parts of our country, Simone Manuel and Katie Ledecky would not have been allowed to swim in the same public pool. And now together on our swimming team, they're winning Olympic medals as teammates . . .

We want to build an America where everyone has a place; where if you work hard and you do your part, you can get ahead and stay ahead. That's a basic bargain of America. And we cannot get to where we need to be unless we move forward together and stand up against prejudice and paranoia, and prove again that America is great because America is good.

offering a $5,000 reward for any fraud-related tips that led to a felony conviction. In response, some Democrats expressed concern that tips about election fraud should go to election officials instead, emphasizing concerns that the hotline was "a systematic and deliberate attempt to suppress votes in the Latino community, specifically targeting the elderly."[239]

American Indians also experienced difficulty in voting in some jurisdictions. The Department of Justice sent election monitors into San Juan County, Utah, which includes a portion of the Navajo Nation. San Juan County has been sued numerous times since 1980 over American Indian voting rights, including brought by the Department of Justice itself. Recently, a federal court ruled in favor of the Navajo Nation in a lawsuit claiming that the county's school districts were drawn in ways that violated the equal-protection clause and that the county had intentionally discriminated against Navajo citizens in setting up commission districts.

San Juan County has a population of 15,000, almost evenly split between Whites and Navajo, yet the county commission has always been majority White. In 2014, the county began to conduct all elections by mail ballot, but many residents of the Navajo Nation do not have street addresses and have to receive their mail at a post office. In some instances, the distance between their home and their post office might be several hundred miles, so getting their mail in a timely fashion is extremely difficult and many of the elderly do not read or write English. If Navajo citizens wanted to vote in person, many had to travel a 400-mile round trip to do so.[240] On Election Day in 2016, there were malfunctioning voting machines and the temporary lack of paper ballots made it difficult for many individuals to vote in San Juan County.

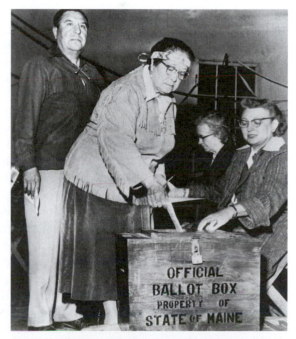

2018 Midterm Elections

Midterm elections are usually not particularly exciting, fewer people turn out to vote in them than in presidential elections, and often there are no controversial issues that generate enthusiasm among voters. Yet, the first election after the inauguration of a new president can generate more attention than a midterm election in the second term of a president. The 2018 midterms have generated lots of attention, primarily because of the chaos of the Trump presidency, both in the White House and in various areas. Trump's racial views—and some consider his views to be racist—attitudes toward women, and the continual lies and convictions and guilty pleas of a number of people that were close to him or in his

American Indians were the last group of Americans to be granted citizenship and obtain the right to vote, which occurred in 1924. But their right to vote was contested by a number of states in the 1960s. American Indians cast their ballots in Maine for the first time in Old Town, Maine, on September 12, 1955. American Indian votes were pivotal to the election of Democratic senators in Montana and North Dakota in 2012.

campaign and the White House have generated a great deal of interest and a backlash against him.

The opening vignette of the election of Democrat Doug Jones as Alabama senator in a 2017 special election foreshadowed the increased primary activity that was to characterize the primary season leading to the 2018 midterm elections. Democrats had big wins in races across the country in 2017 and 2018 elections that were viewed as a referendum on President Donald Trump and his administration. In 2017, Republicans lost the gubernatorial races in Virginia and New Jersey, as well as control of the Washington State Senate. In addition to important wins in gubernatorial races in New Jersey and Virginia, Democrats were able to win hotly contested mayoral races in Charlotte, North Carolina, and St. Petersburg, Florida.[241] Racial and ethnic minorities won many of these primary races and Democrats have attributed their success in the different races across the country to a response from voters who are unhappy with the negative, divisive political climate and an energized base that is opposed to Trump's policies and rhetoric.[242]

The governor's race in Virginia between Democrat Ralph Northam and Republican Ed Gillespie is illustrative of the enthusiasm on the part of Democrats and the weakness on the part of Republicans in finding a message for a state that used to be a Republican stronghold that is now trending toward the middle and Democrats. Gillespie is a moderate Republican tacked to the far right, running on keeping the Confederate Monuments, defunding Planned Parenthood, raising illegal immigrants and immigration as a threat to Virginia, and other Trump hard-right positions. His close primary win is suspected of pushing him in that direction, but his strategy did not pay off. Table 15.9 shows the vote distribution based on Exit Poll data for the election.

The table shows that the majority of White Virginians (57 percent) voted for Ed Gillespie, but the majorities of Blacks and Latinos voted for Northam and non-Whites made up 37 percent of the population that voted in that election. Their votes combined with the 41 percent of Whites provided Northam with a comfortable margin of victory. As with Doug Jones's election in Alabama, the table also shows that Black women played a pivotal role in Northam's election.

Primaries. The Democratic Party had a significantly diverse slate of candidates that advanced to the November ballot.[243] There are several Native American women running for prominent political office in 2018.[244] Democrat Deb Haaland, a member of the Laguna Pueblo tribe, won the primary for New Mexico's 1st Congressional District. Democrat Paulette Jordan, a member of the Couer d'Alene tribe, won the primary for Idaho governor.

Stacey Abrams, the former minority leader of the Georgia House of Representatives, won the Democratic gubernatorial primary in a decisive victory, with more than 75 percent of the vote.[245] Abrams is the first Black woman to be a major party nominee for governor in the United States.[246] In New Mexico, Rep. Michelle Lujan Grisham won the Democratic nomination for governor.

TABLE 15.9 Virginia Governor: Exit Poll Results

WINNER: RALPH NORTHAM (D) – 54%				
Voter Characteristics	**Percentage of Voters**	**Ralph Northam (Democrat)**	**Cliff Hyra (Libertarian)**	**Ed Gillespie (Republican)**
Gender	Male (51%)	48	1	50
	Female (49%)	61	1	39
Age	18–29 years (14%)	69	2	30
	30–44 years (24%)	61	3	37
	45–64 years (42%)	49	1	50
	65+ (20%)	47	0	53
Race	White (67%)	42	1	57
	Black (20%)	87	1	12
	Hispanic/Latino (6%)	67	1	32
	Asian (3%)	N/A	N/A	N/A
	Other (4%)	N/A	N/A	N/A
Gender + Race	White men (36%)	36	1	63
	White women (32%)	48	1	51
	Black men (9%)	81	2	17
	Black women (12%)	91	0	8
Education	College graduates (58%)	60	1	39
	Noncollege graduates (42%)	46	2	52
Party Identification	Democrat (41%)	97	0	3
	Republican (30%)	4	0	95
	Independent/something else (28%)	47	3	50
Ideology	Liberal (27%)	92	2	6
	Moderate (42%)	64	3	33
	Conservative (31%)	9	0	90
Total Family Income (2016)	Under $50,000 (23%)	56	2	43
	$50,000–100,000 (33%)	57	2	41
	$100,000 or more (44%)	54	1	45
Geographic Area	D.C. suburbs (28%)	69	1	30
	Central Virginia (17%)	46	1	53
	Hampton Roads (16%)	61	1	37
	Richmond/South Virginia (19%)	54	1	44
	Mountain (20%)	34	1	64

Source: The Washington Post (2017).
Note: Final exit poll results based on 2,173 interviews of randomly selected voters as they exited polling places across the Commonwealth of Virginia on November 7, 2017.
N/A indicates that not enough data is available to calculate percentages.

Another Native American candidate, Gavin Clarkson, who is a citizen of the Choctaw Nation, lost his bid for the Republican nomination in New Mexico's 2nd Congressional District, securing only 12 percent of the vote. Clarkson is a former Trump administration appointee.

In Minnesota, three Native American women from the Ojibwe tribe were running for lieutenant governor of Minnesota along different party lines—Debra Topping (running with the Independence Party of Minnesota), Donna Bergstrom (running in the Republican primary), and Peggy Flanagan (campaigning for the Democratic Farmer Labor bid).[247] Ray "Skip" Sandman, of the Fond du Lac Ojibwe tribe, was running for Minnesota's 8th Congressional District on the Independence Party ticket.[248] State Rep. Ilhan Omar, a Black Muslim American woman who immigrated to the United States from Somalia as a teenager, won the Minnesota primary on August 14 to fill Rep. Keith Ellison's House seat. Omar, who is projected to win the general election in November, will likely make history and become one of the first Muslim women elected to Congress.[249]

In Kansas, Democratic candidate Sharice Davids narrowly won a six-way primary in her eastern district, enabling her to advance to the November ballot. If she wins the election in November, Davids will become the first gay Native American elected to Congress. Davids, a member of the Ho-Chunk Nation, is a lawyer and activist.[250] Davids is one of approximately 200 LGBTQ candidates who are expected to be on the ballot in races across the country for both state and federal office in the November general election.[251]

In Alaska, Lieutenant Governor Byron Mallot, a member of the Tlingit tribe, ran alongside Gov. Bill Walker on the independent ticket, thereby bypassing the primary elections.[252] Just before the 2018 election, however, Mallot resigned his office and Walker suspended his campaign and endorsed the Democratic candidate for governor, Mark Begich. Debra Call, a member of the Dena'ina tribe, ran unopposed in the Democratic primary for lieutenant governor.[253] Across the country, five Native Americans are running for the office of lieutenant governor, and 13 are seeking statewide executive offices, including governor, secretary of state, and attorney general.

In a stunning upset in the Democratic primary for a New York City congressional seat during the June 26 election, Alexandria Ocasio-Cortez, a 28-year-old Latina activist, defeated Rep. Joseph Crowley (the fourth-ranking House Democrat) to win the nomination, with more than 57 percent of the vote.[254] In the general election in November, Ocasio-Cortez faced Republican Anthony Pappas, a professor at St. John's University. If elected in the general election, Ocasio-Cortez will become the youngest woman ever elected to Congress.[255]

In Michigan, State Rep. Rashida Tlaib won the Democratic primary in the state's 13th Congressional District.[256] If Tlaib wins the November general election, she will become one of the first Muslim women elected to Congress. Tlaib, who dominated in a crowded field of Democratic candidates in her Detroit district during the primaries, will not face a Republican opponent in the general election, but may be opposed by a write-in candidate.[257] Nonetheless, Tlaib was favored to win the November election. On the Republican side, John James, a conservative Black Republican, won the primary to challenge incumbent Democrat Senator Debbie Stabenow in the November election.

In Florida, Tallahassee mayor Andrew Gillum won the hotly contested Democratic primary election for governor.[258] Gillum, who is making history as the first Black Democratic gubernatorial candidate in Florida's history, defeated Gwen Graham, a former member of Congress, as well as former Miami Beach Mayor Philip Levine and businessman Jeff Greene, to win the nomination. Gillum will face Republican Ron DeSantis in the general election in November. DeSantis, a 39-year-old conservative who has received an endorsement from President Trump, faced public backlash after the primaries for comments he made about Gillum during an appearance on Fox News. DeSantis had labeled Gillum as "articulate" and then warned Florida voters not to "monkey this up" when talking about the handling of the economy by his Black Democratic opponent.[259] Some commentators have suggested that DeSantis's remarks were a calculated way for him to gain some traction in the gubernatorial race. The racially charged comment may be a dog-whistle to rally White nationalists to the polls in November.[260] Election forecasters have rated the Florida gubernatorial race as a toss-up between the two candidates,[261] but Gillum's allies have noted that his unusual coalition of young voters, billionaires, racial minorities, members of the LGBTQ community, and White progressives could help him win one of the most important gubernatorial races in the 2018 general election.[262]

In the Democratic primary race in Massachusetts on September 4, Boston City councilor Ayanna Pressley defeated incumbent Rep. Michael E. Capuano with 59 percent of the vote to win the nomination for the U.S. House seat for Massachusetts' 7th District. Rep. Capuano, who has held the seat for 20 years, had been endorsed by almost every major political figure in the Massachusetts Democratic political establishment, including Mayor Martin J. Walsh of Boston.[263] Pressley is poised to become the first Black member of Massachusetts' mostly male congressional delegation; currently, only two of the state's nine House members are women.[264] There is no Republican candidate on the November ballot. Pressley is also among several African American candidates in 2018 who exceeded expectations, and even performed far better than polls had projected, to win nominations during primary races; they include Andrew Gillum of Florida, Stacey Abrams of Georgia, and Ben Jealous of Maryland, who each won the Democratic Party nomination for governor in their respective states.[265]

The September 11 primaries in New Hampshire set up a race in the First Congressional district that will be historic whether the Democrat or Republican wins the seat. Democratic candidate Chris Pappas is openly gay, and the Republican, Eddie Edwards, is a Black former police chief from South Hampton, New Hampshire. This district tends to swing between Democrats and Republicans and is the seat of retiring Democrat Carol Shea-Porter.

In Mississippi, a special election to fill a vacant U. S. Senate seat saw four candidates—two Republicans and two Democrats—on the November 6 ballot in an open primary. The two Republicans are/were Cynthia Hyde-Smith, the person appointed to the Senate seat after the resignation for Senator Thad Cochran, and Chris McDaniel, a state senator. The two Democrats are former Black congressman and former Secretary of Agriculture in the Clinton

Deb Haaland

administration, Mike Espy, and Tobey Bartee, a Naval Academy graduate and an intelligence analyst with the Department of Homeland Security, who is also Black. An interesting twist in Mississippi law on special elections is that the political party of the candidate is not listed on the ballot. The thought is that this will help Espy because of his name recognition and lack of the Democratic label attached to his name. If no candidate receives a majority of the vote, a run-off election between the top two vote-getters will be held on November 27, 2018.

Results

Race and racism played another prominent role in the midterm general election, as President Trump launched an ad about the caravan of Central American asylum seekers moving through Mexico toward the United States that was deemed to be so racist that several networks and social media platforms—CNN, NBC, Facebook, and eventually Fox News—refused to carry the ad. NBC, Facebook, and Fox originally agreed to air the ad, but the backlash and the clearly misleading information led them to decide to stop their airing.[266] Trump began to hype the threat of the caravan as the election drew near, trying to generate fear among his base of voters that the caravan was knocking on the borders of the United States. At the time, the caravan was about a thousand or more miles away. The ad features footage of an undocumented immigrant from Mexico, Luis Bracamontes, who was convicted of murdering two California police officers in 2014 and bragged about his crimes, indicating that he would have killed more. Juxtaposed after the video were images of the caravan overlaid with ominous music,[267] followed by images of the caravan that originated in Central America. The final onscreen message was "Stop the caravan. Vote Republican."[268] The claim of the ad is that Democrats let Bracamontes into the country.

The facts, however, do not back up that claim. Bracamontes originally entered the country illegally in 1992 when Bill Clinton was president, but was arrested three months later in Phoenix by Sheriff Joe Arpaio, who President Trump pardoned after he was convicted of abusing prisoners and was released after he served a four-month sentence. He was arrested again in 1998 by Sheriff Arpaio and again was released. Bracamontes was arrested again in 2001 in Arizona when George W. Bush was president and was deported a total of four times before again returning to the United States and murdering the two California police officers.[269] Nevertheless, the goal of the ad was to drive out Trump's base and others that would be susceptible to fear to vote in the 2018 election. For some populations, the ad and Trump's rallies where he highlighted the caravan worked in several races, but not overall.

On the national level, the turnout rate for a midterm election was the highest in history. Approximately 113 million people voted, for a turnout rate of 49 percent of eligible voters. For comparison, the 2014 midterm election had one of the lowest turnouts, 36.4 percent of eligible voters, in American history.[270] In House races, Democrats held a lead over Republicans in the popular vote of 8.6 million votes, meaning Democrats won 53.1 percent of the votes cast in House races to 45.2 percent for Republicans.[271] The Democrats gained control of the House of Representatives, and the Republicans maintained control of the Senate. The extent of the Democrats' win was not evident on the evening of November 6, and news commentators were saying that the predicted blue wave did not happen. But as the counting of votes continued throughout the days and weeks after November 6, the extent of the Democratic wins became apparent.

On election eve, it looked as if the Democrats picked up possibly 26 seats, which for many was short of a blue wave, but there were 15 seats where a winner had not been determined.[272] As the last of the votes were tallied two weeks after the election, Democrats have captured 40 seats, with the last win being a seat that was called for the Republican incumbent on election eve, but won by the Democrat after all votes were counted. This represents the most seats Democrats have picked up in a midterm election since the Watergate-era election in 1974 when Democrats picked up 49 seats after the resignation of President Richard Nixon.[273]

In the Senate, Democrats were defending 26 seats compared to nine for Republicans. While Republicans have picked up two seats, Democrats flipped the Republican senate seats in Nevada and Arizona, the latter in a state where a Democrat has not been elected to the Senate since 1976. The Florida race between Republican Governor Rick Scott and incumbent Democratic Senator Bill Nelson went through a machine recount and then a hand recount. Nelson was behind by about 12,000 votes, and while he picked up approximately 2,000 votes during the two recounts, he conceded to Scott and

Republicans picked up that Senate seat. The last Senate seat in Mississippi was undecided until a runoff election on November 27, 2018.[274] On November 6, neither Cynthia Hyde-Smith nor Michael Espy received 50 percent of the vote; each received around 41 percent, so a runoff election was held. The race was racially charged. Hyde-Smith made racially insensitive remarks about attending a public hanging, given Mississippi's history of lynching blacks. She did not make things any better by trying to argue that her comments, although recorded on video, were taken out of context and during the one debate before the November 27 election, she apologized and said that she meant no ill will. Hyde-Smith, however, then tried to blame everything on twisting her comments for political purposes. Espy responded that no one twisted her comments, that she said what she said.[275] The polls tightened, but Mississippi is one of the reddest states in the union and Hyde-Smith won besting Espy 53.9 percent to 46.1 percent. This was a far smaller margin than should have been expected.

Overall, nationally, the exit poll data reported by CNN shown in Table 15.10 indicates that White voters, who were 72 percent of those that voted early or in person on Election Day, supported the Republicans 54 percent, compared to 44 percent that supported the Democrats. Blacks, who were 11 percent of the electorate, Latinos, who were also 11 percent of the electorate, and Asian Americans, who were 3 percent, all overwhelmingly voted for the Democrats. As mentioned previously, Democratic House candidates received 7.9 percent more of the vote than did Republican House candidates.[276] Table 15.11 shows that White men supported Republicans (60 percent), while White women supported Democrats and Republicans in equal proportion (49 percent). Black women and men and Latino women and men overwhelmingly supported Democrats. These numbers are the reason why Democrats did so well in House races and were able to retake the House.

For the first time, two American Indian women, Deb Haaland and Sharice Davids, both Democrats, will serve in the House of Representatives. As mentioned previously, Davids is also openly gay. Two Muslim women won seats in the House of Representatives—Ilhan Omar in Minnesota and Rashida Tlaib in Michigan. As expected, Alexandria Ocasio-Cortez of New York and Ayanna Pressley of Massachusetts won their races. In New Hampshire, Democrat

TABLE 15.10 2018 Exit Poll Results by Race

% of Voters	Group	Democrat	Republican	Other/NA
72%	White	44%	54%	2%
11%	Black	90%	9%	1%
11%	Latino	69%	29%	2%
3%	Asian	77%	23%	N/A
3%	Other	54%	42%	4%

TABLE 15.11 2018 Vote by Gender and Race

% of Voters	Vote by Gender and Race		
	Democrat	Republican	Other/NA
White men 35%	39%	60%	1%
White women 37%	49%	49%	2%
Black men 5%	88%	12%	N/A
Black women 6%	92%	7%	1%
Latino men 5%	63%	34%	3%
Latina women 6%	73%	26%	1%
All others 6%	66%	32%	2%

N = 18,778 respondents.
Sources: Edison Research, CNN.

Chris Pappas, an openly gay state representative, won his congressional race against Black Republican Eddie Edwards. A surprise winner was Black Democrat Lucy McBath of Georgia in what used to be a reliably Republican district. Her son, Jordan Davis, was seventeen when he was murdered at a gas station by a white man, Michael Dunn, because the music in the car in which he was riding was too loud. Jordan was unarmed. After two trials, Dunn was found guilty of first-degree murder in 2014 and sentenced to life in prison. McBath became politically active after her son's murder.[277]

Democrats picked up seven governorships. Democrat Michelle Lujan Grisham won her race in New Mexico, becoming the first Latina Democrat to hold the office. She replaces a Latina Republican, Susanna Martinez. In Maryland, Ben Jealous lost his bid to unseat the Republican incumbent, Larry Hogan, and in Idaho, American Indian Democrat Paulette Jordan lost her race against Republican Brad Little. An American Indian woman, Peggy Flanagan, a Democrat, was also elected Lt. Governor of Minnesota. In Wisconsin, Mandela Barnes, a Black Democratic Lt. Governor nominee, won the office when his running mate, Democrat Tony Evers, bested incumbent governor Republican Scott Walker.

The races in Florida and Georgia were more complicated. In Florida, just like the senatorial race, the governor's race also went through a machine recount, but not a hand count. On election eve, DeSantis was ahead and Gillum actually conceded the race, but as balloting continued Gillum took back his concession. At the end of the recount, DeSantis led by approximately 30,000 votes, with 49.6 percent to Gillum's 49.2 percent. Gillum conceded again and the results were certified. Scott's running mate for lieutenant governor was Jeanette Núñez, and she becomes the first Latina elected to a state-wide office.

Republican Brian Kemp, Secretary of State of Georgia, ended the balloting election eve with 50.3 percent of the vote to Stacy Abrams's 48.8 percent. Georgia law says that if no candidate gets 50 percent plus of the vote, it goes to a runoff. Lots of ballots remained to be counted, so Abrams hoped that Kemp's percentage would drop below 50 percent. When all ballots were tallied, Kemp had 50.2 percent to Abrams still 48.8 percent. The results were certified, but Abrams refused to concede as she felt there had been acts of voter suppression by Kemp in his position as Secretary of State. For example, when Abrams went to cast her vote, she was almost denied a ballot as the poll worker told her that she had requested an absentee ballot, so could not cast an in-person ballot. The error was quickly resolved, but it appears that Abrams was not the only person to experience this. Kemp's office also put 53,000 new voter registrations on hold because of there not being an exact match on the name, meaning that even the absence of a period or a hyphen makes the registration invalid.[278] There were other problems in voting as well, not only in Georgia but across the country. Exit poll data showed a very polarized race along racial and gender lines.

Table 15.12 shows that Whites made up 60 percent of voters that voted early or voted on Election Day, and 74 percent of them voted for Kemp. White women also overwhelmingly voted for Kemp—75 percent. (See Table 15.13.) Black Georgians, on the other hand, overwhelmingly supported Abrams.

TABLE 15.12 **2018 Race in Georgia Governor's race**

% of Voters	Vote by Race		
	Abrams	Kemp	Other/NA
White 60%	25%	74%	1%
Black 30%	93%	6%	1%
Latino 5%	62%	37%	1%
Asian 2%	N/A	N/A	N/A
All others 3%	N/A	N/A	N/A

N = 2,493 respondents.

TABLE 15.13 **2018 Vote by Gender and Race in Georgia Governor's Race**

% of Voters	Vote by Gender and Race		
	Abrams	Kemp	Other/NA
White men 28%	25%	73%	2%
White women 32%	25%	75%	N/A
Black men 14%	88%	11%	1%
Black women 16%	97%	2%	1%
Latino men 2%	N/A	N/A	N/A
Latina women 3%	N/A	N/A	N/A
All others 5%	54%	44%	2%

Blacks were 30 percent of the voting electorate and 93 percent voted for Abrams. Black women supported Abrams with 97 percent support, while 88 percent of Black men voted from Abrams. An interesting finding is that 11 percent of Black men voted for Kemp. The meaning of this is not clear at the moment because in Florida Black men voted for Gillum in a higher proportion than did Black women—91 percent to 82 percent.[279] Maybe there is a gender dimension in voting in these races among Black voters, but a definitive explanation cannot be made at the moment.

Conclusion

On July 5, 1852, Frederick Douglass, the great abolitionist leader and former slave, gave a speech at an event celebrating the signing of the Declaration of Independence. Douglass thought it ironic and insulting that he, a former slave now fighting the enslavement of members of his race, was asked to speak at the event. In his famous "The Meaning of July Fourth for the Negro" speech, Douglass saw the Declaration of Independence as a sham because Blacks were enslaved in the land of liberty. Yet Douglass was hopeful that things would change, slavery would be abolished, and the United States would live up to its ideals.

On the evening of November 4, 2008, Barack Obama's election was a manifestation of the nation living up to the ideals Frederick Douglass had felt it capable of more than 150 years earlier. His reelection was an even further ratification of the ideals Douglass thought possible. Although there is still a long way to go on the "long steady march" toward racial equality, the ability of Barack Obama to be elected and then reelected president of the United States in the present electoral system says a lot about the ability of the system to produce outcomes that a majority of the people in the country favor. Moreover, his election highlights the significance of the registration and voting of Blacks, Latinos, Asian Americans, and American Indians. Maybe the country is finally on the path toward "We the People" that Douglass envisioned. With the election of Donald J. Trump as the 45th President of the United States it appears that the promise and accomplishments of President Obama are being reversed. Trump and his administration are also reversing the gains made by Blacks, Latinos, Asian Americans, American Indians, and LGBTQ citizens. We had asked the question in a previous edition if the United States was entering a second Nadir of the political influence of citizens of color? The results of the 2018 midterm elections suggests that the answer to the question is NO!

review **QUESTIONS** _____

1. What are the purposes of elections?
2. How does the Electoral College work?
3. Why has money become so central to presidential campaigns?
4. How do structural inequalities result in differential voter registration and voter turnout rates?
5. Why was President Obama's reelection campaign for the presidency successful?

Check your understanding of Chapter 15.

Flashcard review.

KEY TERMS

Air War p. 485

Bipartisan Campaign
   Reform Act (BCRA) p. 486

Closed Primary p. 470

Debates p. 485

Direct Primaries p. 470

Elections p. 467

General Elections p. 479

Ground War p. 485

Help America Vote Act p. 499

Majority p. 471

National Voter Registration
   Act p. 497

Nomination Petitions p. 477

Open Primary p. 470

Opposition Research
   p. 489

Pledged Delegates p. 468

Plurality p. 471

Political Independents p. 470

Proportional
   Representation p. 480

Public Funding p. 487

Run-off Primary p. 471

Soft Money p. 486

Voting-Age Population
   (VAP) p. 496

Voting-Eligible Population
   (VEP) p. 495

Winner-Take-All p. 480

Need to review key
ideas in greater
depth? Click here.

ADDITIONAL READINGS

McClain, P. D., & Stewart Jr., J. (2014). *"Can we all get along?": Racial and ethnic minorities in American politics* (6th ed.). Boulder, CO: Westview Press.
   This book provides an overview of the history, political attitudes, and behaviors of America's principal racial minority groups.

Mendelberg, T. (2001). *The race card: Campaign strategy, implicit messages, and the norm of equality.* Princeton, NJ: Princeton University Press.
   This book studies the use of race as a campaign strategy and its effect on voters.

Teixeira, R. A. (1992). *The disappearing American voter.* Washington, DC: Brookings Institution.
   This book analyzes the factors that contribute to low voter turnout in the United States.

Verba, S., Schlozman, K. L., & Brady, H. E. (1995). *Voice and equality: Civic voluntarism in American politics.* Cambridge, MA: Harvard University Press.
   This is a landmark study of various aspects of political participation, such as voting and volunteer activities, of the American public.

Walters, R. W. (2007). *Freedom is not enough: Black voters, Black candidates, and American presidential politics.* Boulder, CO: Rowman & Littlefield.
   This is a study of the importance of Black voters to presidential election outcomes.

Lewis-Beck, M. S., Northpoth, H., Jacoby, W. G., & Weisberg, H. F. (2008). *The American voter revisited.* Ann Arbor: University of Michigan.
   This book replicates the approach of the original 1960 *The American Voter* with a focus on the 2000 and 2004 elections.

The Making of Domestic and Foreign Policy: Summing Up American Government in Black and White

Denver police officers arrest a man who sold crack cocaine to an undercover officer, a decoy, during a sting operation. The man took police for a short foot chase, and police officers in the background are looking for money that the suspect ditched. Since the 1980s, prison terms for crack-cocaine offenses have been longer than for powder-cocaine offenses, a policy that has largely affected African Americans. As a result of political pressure, the policy has been changed by bringing the sentences for the two offenses more into balance.

I n 1994, Edward James Clary, a young Black male, was facing federal district court Judge Clyde Cahill in St. Louis, Missouri, to be sentenced after pleading guilty to possession of 67.76 grams of crack cocaine. Federal drug laws required that Clary be sentenced to a minimum of ten years in prison, even though it would take one hundred times the amount of powder cocaine to receive the same sentence. Edward Clary was not the first person to face such a stringent mandatory minimum sentence, and Judge Cahill was not the first federal judge who would regret imposing such an unjust sentence, especially with the disparity between crack-cocaine and powder-cocaine sentences. But this case is remarkable because Judge Cahill was one of the first federal judges who disregarded the federal mandatory minimum sentence. Instead of the mandatory ten-year sentence, he gave Clary only four years.[1]

Judge Cahill, who is African American, wrote a lengthy explanation of his departure from the required sentence. The gist of Judge Cahill's opinion was that because African Americans are more likely than Whites to be arrested and prosecuted for crack cocaine, the sentencing disparities between crack and powder cocaine result in racial discrimination in violation of the Fourteenth Amendment equal protection clause. Judge Cahill's densely researched opinion demonstrated that media hype framed crack cocaine as a "Black problem." This media frenzy frightened the public, which then influenced Congress and the president to respond with harsh criminal sentences against crack-cocaine users. Judge Cahill's opinion also provided convincing quantitative evidence that most crack-cocaine defendants were Black. In short, Judge Cahill attributed the sentencing disparity to unconscious racism among Americans and their political leaders.[2] However, an appeals court reinstated Clary's ten-year prison sentence.[3] Judge Cahill died at the age of 81 in 2004,[4] but the issue of drug criminalization policy and its effect on racial minorities is still salient.

intro

Edward Clary is just one example among thousands of Black males who received disproportionately long prison sentences over the next two decades. A 2010 study demonstrated the overall racial disparities this policy had caused. The average sentence for crack cocaine had been nine years and seven months, whereas the average sentence for powder cocaine had been seven years and three months. Moreover,

79 percent of people sentenced to prison for crack were African American, compared to only 10 percent of whom were White and 10 percent were Latino.[5] As a result of lobbying from a disparate coalition of civil rights organizations, civil liberties organizations, and even judges, Congress passed the Fair Sentencing Act of 2010. The United States Sentencing Commission, which is a federal agency that advises all three branches of government on sentencing policy,[6] reported in 2015 that the Fair Sentencing Act had significantly narrowed the disparities between powder and crack cocaine and halved the number of people sentenced to prison for crack cocaine .[7]

This story illustrates the complexities of policymaking in the United States. Policymaking refers to the actions that the government actually takes. There are two kinds of policies in American government: domestic policy and foreign policy. **Domestic policy** *includes the laws, regulations, and programs that directly affect people living in the United States. It includes economic and fiscal concerns, infrastructure, criminal law, health care, housing, education, civil rights, and civil liberties.* **Foreign policy** *is made up of those laws, rules, and programs that affect the relations of the United States with other nations. It includes diplomatic relations, international trade and economics, human rights, global health, national security, and defense.*

Clary's story also demonstrates that policymaking is a dynamic process that occurs across different stages. Media sensationalism and public hysteria over the dangers of crack cocaine convinced public officials to establish the disparate sentences for possession of crack and powder cocaine. Merely enacting a sentencing policy does not ensure that it will be followed, however, and as this story shows, Judge Cahill refused to implement the mandatory minimum sentence for crack cocaine. Implementation is just one of several stages in the policymaking process. In this chapter, we cover all of the stages of policymaking: the agenda-setting stage; the enactment stage, which includes formulation and adoption; and the postformulation stages of implementation and evaluation.[8] (We define these terms as they appear in the chapter.)

In addition to covering the stages of domestic and foreign policymaking, this chapter ties together the preceding chapters of this book. The framework of American government—that is, the Constitution, federalism, civil rights, and civil liberties—provides the context for foreign and domestic policymaking. Moreover, American political institutions—Congress, the presidency, the bureaucracy, and the judiciary—and each aspect of political behavior—public opinion, the media, social movements, interest groups, political parties, and elections—are relevant throughout the policymaking process.

Although domestic and foreign policymaking encompass a wide variety of areas, many domestic and foreign policies emphasize minority-group politics. Throughout this book, we have shown how minority-group politics intersects with every aspect of American government. Consequently, this chapter focuses on foreign and domestic policies that affect racial and ethnic minorities.

Domestic Policy Laws, rules, and programs that directly affect people living in the United States.

Foreign Policy Laws, rules, and programs that affect the relationship between the United States and other nations.

Agenda-Setting

Agenda-Setting The stage in the policymaking process in which certain issues reach a level of public concern that attracts the attention of government officials.

Agenda-setting refers to the part of the policymaking process in which certain issues reach a level of public concern that attracts the attention of government officials. The term *agenda* carries different meanings, and scholars of public

Agenda Universe All possible legitimate issues that could be brought to the attention of the public and possibly of policymakers.

Systemic Agenda The set of issues that policymakers perceive as worthy of their attention.

Institutional Agenda The set of issues that government officials recognize requires their attention.

Decision Agenda The set of issues that a government body formally resolves to address.

policymaking conceive of agenda-setting on several levels. The **agenda universe** refers to all possible issues that could be brought to the attention of public policymakers. By possible, we mean those ideas that are socially acceptable in American society. For example, even though there are groups that would like to reinstate de jure segregation (e.g., neo-Nazis and the Ku Klux Klan), those goals are not socially acceptable and are therefore not part of the agenda universe.[9]

The next level is the **systemic agenda**, which refers to the issues that policymakers perceive as worthy of their attention and within their authority. Depending on the political and legal climate, issues move from the agenda universe to the systemic agenda. If an issue merits sufficient attention once on the systemic agenda, it proceeds to the **institutional agenda**, where government officials acknowledge that the issue requires their attention. Because government institutions possess finite time and resources, reaching the institutional agenda is an extremely competitive process. In the last stage of the agenda-setting process, the **decision agenda**, a government body resolves to act on an issue.[10]

The key to agenda-setting is to move an issue from the agenda universe to the decision agenda. Many aspects of American politics are important in advancing policies through the agenda-setting process. For example, when political parties include certain issues in their party platforms, those issues are likely to move through the agenda-setting process. The Democratic Party platform in 1948 insisted on ending racial and ethnic discrimination, which engendered a public walkout of Southern Democrats.[11] This dispute between progressives and racists within the Democratic Party certainly highlighted the issue of racial and ethnic discrimination and brought it to the attention of the American public and politicians.

Likewise, the actions of political institutions (Congress, the executive branch, the bureaucracy, and the judiciary) can set the agenda. For example, the problems that Puerto Rico has experienced since Hurricane Maria has revealed the issue of poverty in Puerto Rico, especially given its disadvantaged status as a commonwealth.[12]

Social Movements, Interest Groups, and Agenda-Setting

Social movements and individual interest groups are crucial factors in agenda-setting,[13] especially in minority-group politics. For example, the group Black Lives Matter engages in protests that include music and art to expose injustices that African Americans experience, particularly in the criminal justice system.[14]

Other racial and ethnic minority groups used protests to set the agenda for civil rights policies. In March 1968, Mexican American students at Lincoln High School in Los Angeles staged a student strike that lasted for more than a week, and this action sparked attention to the civil rights concerns of Latinos, especially Mexican Americans in the Southwest.[15] The American Indian Movement (AIM) staged more dramatic protests to highlight the injustices that American Indians experienced. In 1972, members of AIM seized the Washington, DC, headquarters of the Bureau of Indian Affairs, and the following year AIM members engaged in an armed standoff with federal agents at Wounded Knee in the Pine Ridge Reservation in South Dakota.[16] Native Hawaiian movements have highlighted income inequality in Hawaii and the ways in which their traditional culture has been hijacked by Americans since Hawaii became a state.[17]

Interest groups can also set the policy agenda without engaging in protests. For example, many racial and ethnic minority interest groups initiate, finance, and manage litigation when the elected branches of government are not receptive to their claims. By sponsoring this litigation campaign, these groups set the agenda in the federal judiciary. The most significant example of an interest group that litigates is the National Association for the Advancement of Colored People Legal Defense and Educational Fund (LDF), which has set the U.S. Supreme Court's agenda by bringing cases concerning racial discrimination in housing, voting, and, most notably, education.[18] Groups advocating on behalf of other ethnic and racial minorities also set the agenda for the judiciary by sponsoring cases. These groups include the Mexican American Legal Defense and Educational Fund,[19] the Native American Rights Fund,[20] and the Asian Americans Advancing Justice.[21]

Interest groups also play a key role in agenda-setting for foreign policy. Many interest groups are extremely concerned about foreign-policy issues, such as international trade, war, national security, human rights, global health, and relations with particular nations. Some interest groups set the foreign policy agenda on issues that interest racial and ethnic minorities. For example, Amnesty International is a worldwide interest group that promotes human rights throughout the world. Its primary focus is to advocate on behalf of political prisoners throughout the world and against the use of torture. It also supports free expression and opposes the death penalty.[22] Recently, Amnesty International has publicized concerns with President Donald Trump's immigration policies. Although immigration is generally a domestic issue, it does affect people living in other nations, e.g., Mexico and Central America. For example, in April 2018 Amnesty International publicized the Trump administration's plan to use the military to patrol the border in order to set the agenda on this issue.[23] Amnesty International has also set the agenda on other foreign-policy issues that pertain to racial and ethnic minorities. For example, after the African Nation of Uganda passed a law in 2010 that criminalized homosexuality and Uganda's subsequent harsh treatment of its LGBTQ community, Amnesty International has publicized this concern as a civil rights violation.[24]

Assess current debates on free trade.

The Media and Agenda-Setting

The press is another significant influence on agenda-setting. Reporters, editors, and publishers control the content of coverage, and the amount of media exposure that an issue receives determines the extent to which it will advance through the agenda-setting process. Stories that are deemed interesting and profitable will receive extensive media coverage, and the policies involved in those stories will feature prominently on the agenda. Stories deemed unimportant will not receive media exposure, and those issues will be unlikely to attract sufficient public and political attention. Moreover, social media outlets also serve to set the agenda, especially for issues the mainstream media ignores.[25]

The media's coverage of the Civil Rights Movement during the 1960s demonstrates its key role in agenda-setting for domestic policy. As we discussed in Chapter 11, the media's televised coverage of key civil rights events set the agenda for many Americans who were otherwise uninformed about the hardships Blacks endured in the South. In fact, survey evidence demonstrates that Americans viewed civil rights as a more salient issue after the media covered significant events, such as the Montgomery bus boycott, the desegregation of Central High School in Little Rock, Arkansas, the sit-ins of the early 1960s, and the 1963 March on Washington. In 1965, television and newspaper coverage of the police brutality against civil rights activists at the Edmund Pettus Bridge in Selma, Alabama, especially increased public attention to civil rights issues. Nevertheless, many scholars argue that the media's impact on civil rights is overstated. In fact, the media often set the agenda in a way that reinforces negative stereotypes of African Americans.[26]

The media are especially important for bringing issues onto the foreign-policy agenda, especially concerning human rights violations. By disseminating graphic images of people suffering as a result of famine or genocide (and often both), the media help to make Americans aware of a foreign-policy issue about which they otherwise would have remained uninformed. These images often impel the American public to sympathize with the victims and demand that American foreign policy address the problem. For example, during the early 1990s televised coverage of the atrocities that Serbians committed against Bosnian Muslims

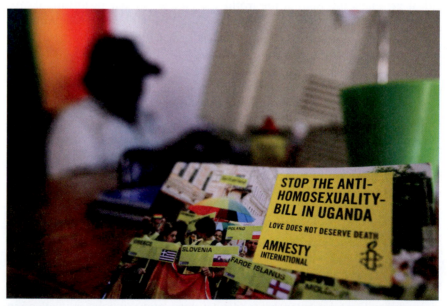

Amnesty International protests against severe anti-LGBTQ discrimination in Uganda. Amnesty International is an interest group that fights against human rights abuses throughout the world, including the human rights violations taking place in Uganda against LGBTQ people.

placed on the agenda the question of whether Americans should economically or militarily intervene on behalf of the Bosnian Muslims.[27] In 1995 President Bill Clinton committed American troops to a peacekeeping mission in Bosnia.[28]

At the same time as the crisis in the Balkans, genocide and a humanitarian crisis were occurring in the tiny African nation of Rwanda, in which close to 1 million people were slaughtered and refugees overwhelmed neighboring countries. This human rights travesty initially received little media coverage in the United States, particularly in comparison to the Balkan region (which is in Europe). Consequently, it was not on the agenda of the American public. Media critic Tim Graham of MediaWatch notes that a lack of televised coverage of the atrocities in Rwanda ultimately led American policymakers to disregard the issue.[29]

Even when the media covers humanitarian crises in Africa, it often presents the issue in terms that are unflattering to Africans and Africa. For example, during the Ebola epidemic in 2014, the media often portrayed the entire African content as plagued with the disease, despite the fact that its effects were concentrated in certain areas. Moreover, the media often depicted African government and institutions as incapable of addressing the Ebola breakouts without help from the West. Consequently, many Westerners assumed all Africans carried the disease, which led to restrictive immigration and tourism policies in many Western nations, including the United States.[30]

Discover how to negotiate agreements with foreign entities.

American politicians and the media also influence the agenda in other nations, which in turn affects U.S. foreign policy. The Our Voices box provides an excerpt from President Obama's 2009 speech at Cairo University in Egypt. Many people have credited this speech for inspiring the Arab Spring, a series of popular uprisings that overthrew Middle East dictators in 2011. However, detractors, such as the late conservative scholar Fouad Ajami, refer to that notion as a "myth."[31] Moreover, despite the deposing of these dictators, struggles still exist. For example, although in 2011, Hosni Mubarak was overthrown in Egypt after three decades of rule, and in 2012, Egyptians democratically elected Mohammed Morsi as president, the nation has still been wrought with problems. Morsi is a member of the controversial Muslim Brotherhood, a group that seeks to enact Muslim religious principles into law, and he tried to expand the power of the presidency and eliminate judicial review, which led to more rioting. After the rioting intensified in early 2013, Egyptian military removed Morsi from power that summer.[32] The group Human Rights Watch, which evaluates nations' human rights records,[33] has excoriated Egypt's government for suppressing civil liberties and using violence, intimidation, and torture against its citizens.[34]

Policy Enactment

Once an issue has captured the attention of government leaders, the next stage in the policymaking process involves political actors considering the range of alternatives to best address the issue. This is the stage at which legislators

our voices

President Obama's 2009 Cairo Speech

American politicians can set the agenda for other nations, which, in turn, can affect U.S. foreign policy. For example, President Obama designed his 2009 speech in Cairo, Egypt, to convince the Muslim world that the United States was not an enemy of Islam, even though it would maintain its vigilant fight against terrorism. To substantiate his point, President Obama highlighted his multiethnic background, and his personal experience with Islam, the first U.S. president who could make that claim. He also emphasized the relevance of Islam throughout American history, and he publicly recognized the mistakes of the Iraq war. Finally, in his speech, President Obama stressed the importance of democracy and self-rule for Muslim nations.

There is some indication that the president's focus on democracy set the agenda in foreign nations because there have been popular uprisings in numerous Arab and Islamic nations. In 2011 citizens of Tunisia, Egypt, and Libya, especially youth, overthrew longtime dictators, in what is now called the Arab Spring. Despite the change in repressive regimes, civil unrest still exists in these nations. Moreover, since 2009, there have also been popular uprisings in Iran and Syria, but those governments successfully, albeit brutally, repressed protests. There is considerable debate over whether this speech is responsible for the Arab Spring, but there is no doubt that President Obama's speech and the foreign press coverage of it helped to set the agenda for the pursuit of democratic reform in that region.

Palestinians in Gaza City watch President Obama's Cairo speech. This speech is credited for helping to inspire the Arab Spring, in which popular protests led to the overthrow of longtime Arab dictators, although the progress toward democracy has been uneven and wrought with setbacks.

Remarks by the President on a New Beginning, Cairo University, Cairo, Egypt, June 4, 2009

. . . We meet at a time of great tension between the United States and Muslims around the world—tension rooted in historical forces that go beyond any current policy debate. The relationship between Islam and the West included centuries of coexistence and cooperation, but also conflict and religious wars. . . . Moreover, the sweeping change brought by modernity and globalization led many Muslims to view the West as hostile to the traditions of Islam.

Violent extremists have exploited these tensions in a small but potent minority of Muslims. The attacks of September 11, 2001, and the continued efforts of these extremists to engage in violence against civilians has led some in my country to view Islam as inevitably hostile to not only America and Western countries, but also to human rights.

I've come here to Cairo to seek a new beginning between the United States and Muslims around the world, one based on mutual interest and mutual respect, and one based upon the truth that America and Islam are not exclusive and need not be in competition. . . . That is what I will try to do today—to speak to the truth as best I can, humbled by the task before us, and firm in my belief that the interests we share as human beings are far more powerful than the forces that drive us apart.

. . . Now part of this conviction is rooted in my own experience. I am a Christian, but my father came from a Kenyan family that includes generations of Muslims. As a boy, I spent several years in Indonesia and heard the call of the azaan at the break of dawn and at the fall of dusk. As a young man, I worked in Chicago communities where many found dignity and peace in their Muslim faith.

. . . I also know that Islam has always been part of America's story. . . . And since our founding, American

Muslims have enriched the United States. . . . And when the first Muslim American was recently elected to Congress, he took the oath to defend our Constitution using the same Holy Koran that one of our founding fathers—Thomas Jefferson—kept in his personal library.

. . . The fourth issue that I will address is democracy. . . . I know there has been controversy about the promotion of democracy in recent years, and much of this controversy is connected to the war in Iraq. So let me be clear: No system of government can or should be imposed on one nation by any other.

. . . That does not lessen my commitment, however, to governments that reflect the will of the people. Each nation gives life to this principle in its own way, grounded in the traditions of its own people.

America does not presume to know what is best for everyone, just as we would not presume to pick the outcome of a peaceful election. But I do have an unyielding belief that all people yearn for certain things: the ability to speak your mind and have a say in how you are governed, confidence in the rule of law and the equal administration of justice, government that is transparent and does not steal from the people, the freedom to live as you choose. These are not just American ideas; they are human rights. And that is why we will support them everywhere.

Source: Adapted from The White House, President Barack Obama. (2009, June 4). *The president's speech in Cairo: A new beginning.* Retrieved July 21, 2018, from https://obamawhitehouse.archives .gov/issues/foreign-policy/presidents-speech-cairo-a-new- beginning.

actually make, or enact, the policy, and it entails two distinct steps. The **policy formulation** stage occurs after the government decides to act on a problem and needs to craft the best solution from the various available alternatives.[35] During the **policy adoption** stage the policy is actually enacted. Government institutions (Congress, the presidency, the bureaucracy, and the courts) play a significant role in policy formulation and adoption, although interest groups, social movements, the media, and political parties are important as well.[36] The policy formulation and adoption stages are especially crucial in foreign and domestic policies that are important to racial and ethnic minorities.

Policy Formulation

After governments decide to act on a problem, they need to craft the best solution from the various alternatives available to them. This policy formation stage takes place for the most part within political institutions and outside of public view. Members of Congress (and their staff) write bills they plan to introduce formally, presidents and key assistants develop executive orders, independent regulatory commissioners craft rules, and federal judges, with the help of lawyers and law clerks, write opinions.

The extent to which formulated policies favor minorities depends largely, albeit not exclusively, on minority representation in the respective institution. For example, a pressing foreign-policy issue concerns the American response to the genocide occurring in the Darfur region of Sudan. People living in the region have been beset with drought and famine, but recently their suffering has been exacerbated by war between Arab Muslim militias backed by the government and non-Arab Africans. More problematic are the numerous

Policy Formulation The stage in the policymaking process in which government actors draft a solution to a problem that they have recognized merits their attention.

Policy Adoption The stage in the policymaking process in which the policy is actually enacted.

Examine the concepts of free trade and protectionism.

Sudanese refugees wait to collect water supplies at a water station in Zamzam refugee camp on the outskirts of the Darfur town of el Fasher, Sudan, April 9, 2010, ahead of the April 11 multiparty general elections in Sudan. American foreign policy has sought to end the conflict and famine in Sudan, and although there had been a promise of peace, conditions have deteriorated.

reports that government-supported gangs have systematically tortured, raped, and murdered thousands of innocent people.[37]

It was African American members of Congress who have taken the lead on formulating American foreign policy to deal with the genocide. The Darfur Genocide Accountability Act of 2005 was introduced into the House of Representatives. The act would not only have provided for sanctions, such as travel restrictions and economic restrictions, against the government of Sudan, but it also would have authorized the president to use military force to stop the genocide. This policy was formulated and introduced by the late African American representative Donald Payne (D-NJ). Four of the other seven members primarily responsible for formulating this policy are also African American. However, the House never passed this specific legislation.[38] Although a peace agreement was reached in Darfur in 2011, the problems there still persist. For example, Human Rights Watch chronicled human rights violations in Darfur in 2017.[39] Moreover, the roots of this conflict have spread to other African nations, most notably Mali. Although the United Nations has peacekeeping forces stationed in Mali, there is still violence among Islamic terrorists, especially ISIS, local militias, and UN troops.[40]

In the area of domestic policy, Latinos and Asian Americans are concerned about immigration and the rights of undocumented immigrants. For example, in 2015 Representative Luis Gutiérrez (D-IL) introduced a bill that would provide the health care benefits of the Affordable Care Act (aka "Obamacare") for undocumented immigrants.[41] This bill had only six cosponsors—two African Americans (Yvette Clarke [D-NY] and Marc Veasey [D-TX]), one Latino (Raúl Grijalva [D-AZ]), one Asian American (Judy Chu [D-CA]), and two Whites (Zoe Lofgren [D-CA] and Janice Schakowsky [D-IL]). Ultimately, the bill died in committee,[42] and it never became law.

Despite the generally closed nature of policy formulation, the public does have input into the process. Political parties, which allow for limited public participation, often try to influence policy formulation by offering in their platforms general outlines of policies the party wants passed. Both party platforms in 2016 outlined foreign and domestic policies that could affect minority-group politics.

On the domestic front, the 2016 Democratic Party platform articulated policies to protect racial and ethnic minorities' voting rights, including keeping early voting, same-day registration, and voting by mail. It also sought to "rectify" the *Shelby County (AL) v. Holder* decision that ended preclearance for regions with a history of voting discrimination (see Chapters 3 and 5). The platform also intended to close the wealth gap between minorities and Whites, financially help the people of Puerto Rico, support statehood for Washington, DC, provide more resources for minority-serving colleges and universities, and end "systemic racism" (the idea that racism is inexorably mixed into American political, economic, and social institutions). An entire section on indigenous tribes addressed enhancing sovereignty and increasing health care. The Democratic platform also endorsed providing a path to citizenship for undocumented immigrants and supported President Obama's policies concerning undocumented immigrants (see Chapter 5). On foreign policy, the Democratic Platform supported more aid for Africa and acceptance of some Muslim refugees from the civil war in Syria.[43] The 2016 Republican Party platform advocated policies that require photo identification to vote and oppose statehood for Washington, DC. It supported statehood for Puerto Rico and sovereignty for indigenous tribes. On the issue of immigration, the Republican platform endorsed policies that would cause undocumented immigrants to leave the United States, build a wall along the border of the United States and Mexico, and oppose so-called "sanctuary cities," in which local law enforcement agencies will not report undocumented immigrants in order to ensure that communities cooperate with law enforcement.[44]

The public can also offer direct input into policy formulation. For example, during the early 1980s Congress created the Commission on Wartime Relocation to investigate the internment of Japanese Americans during World War II and suggest policies to redress that severe injustice. The commission was critical in the passage of the Civil Liberties Act of 1988, which apologized to and compensated the victims of internment. Many Japanese American activists testified before the commission (and even before Congress), and the commission also took essential testimony from the actual victims of the internment. Their testimony helped to shape this important policy in the area of minority-group politics.[45]

Administrative Procedure Act A federal law that requires administrative agencies to publish proposed rules and allow the public to offer comment on them before they go into effect.

Additionally, the **Administrative Procedure Act**, which was first passed in 1946 and has been amended several times since then, requires that any administrative agency seeking to formulate a policy must first promulgate the policy as a proposed rule. Then, for a thirty-day period, the public can comment on the proposed rule. The agency must consider those comments before the rule goes into effect, but it does not need to change the policy in response to public comments or even overwhelming public opposition.[46] Although these opportunities are open to the general public, most people do not avail themselves of this chance to contribute to policy formulation. Instead, well-financed interest groups and corporations usually provide comments.[47]

Think Tanks Interest groups that focus on research and scholarly analysis of issues relevant to the people they represent.

Interest groups can also formulate policies, which are then presented to political institutions. **Think tanks** are interest groups that research, analyze, and design policies to address specific issues, and they play a prominent role in policy formulation. Think tanks are composed of intellectuals and scholars, and, although most think tanks are officially nonpartisan, they do harbor ideological biases. In fact, many think tanks focus on formulating polices that are important to racial and ethnic minority groups. For example, the Joint Center for Political and Economic Studies (JCPES) is a think tank that focuses on issues important to all racial and ethnic minorities, with a special emphasis on African Americans. The JCPES publishes reports that make specific policy recommendations to improve the political and economic life of Blacks and other minorities.[48] In 2012, JCPES published a report that found that health outcomes in heavily African American areas of rural Mississippi were far worse than most other places in the United States. Life expectancy in that region was equal to impoverished nations such as Sri Lanka, Ethiopia, and the Dominican Republic. The report advocated specific policy proposals to improve health, such as providing vouchers to purchase vegetables at farmers' markets, increasing transportation to supermarkets that sell healthy foods, and enhancing opportunities for exercise.[49]

Interest groups also formulate policies in the federal judiciary by sponsoring litigation and submitting briefs. Judges read these briefs and often incorporate them into their decisions. In other words, groups sponsoring litigation not only set the agenda, but through their legal arguments and briefs they also help to formulate judicial policies. Even if groups do not participate directly in a case, they can still influence Supreme Court policymaking through *amicus curiae* briefs. These briefs allow parties that are not directly involved in the case to submit a brief to advocate for a particular outcome or suggest a legal policy for the court to formulate. For example, in the crucial 2003 affirmative action cases *Gratz v. Bollinger* and *Grutter v. Bollinger* (see Chapter 5), 107 *amicus curiae* briefs were filed.[50]

Policy Adoption

Merely formulating a policy does not guarantee its existence. The policy has to be approved by the appropriate government institution(s). Legislatures must pass and executives must sign laws for these policies to take effect, or a majority of appellate court judges must agree on a decision for it to take effect. Recall from the preceding definition that policies are actually enacted at the policy adoption stage, and although many policies are formulated, not all are adopted.

Even though most policy adoption takes place within political institutions, the public is still concerned with exactly what a policy will be when it is passed. Members of the public communicate their views through the activities of social movements, interest groups, and the media. Many controversial policies take a long time to be enacted, so members of the public have ample opportunity to mobilize in opposition to a policy or to compel major changes to it.

The policy adoption process often requires political leaders to compromise. For example, during the 1980s, a key foreign-policy issue concerned the U.S. response to apartheid in South Africa, which inflicted horrendous suffering on Blacks living there. Many Americans, especially African Americans, wanted to enact sanctions against the White-controlled government of South Africa. These sanctions would have effectively ended American economic ties with South Africa by banning imports or exports between the two nations.

By 1986, there was widespread support for a sanctions bill, and a significant sanctions bill was formulated in the House and Senate. But to secure passage of the bill, members of Congress agreed to change the originally formulated bill by exempting grain sales from sanctions because senators from farm states wanted to keep open the grain market. Another change deleted a provision from the bill that would have required the president to sell U.S. gold reserves to lower the price of gold, a key component of the South African economy.[51] The sanctions bill was passed into law, and Congress overrode President Ronald Reagan's veto.[52] The compromises were essential for the policy to be adopted.

Investigate the economy, military, and politics of other nations.

Compromise is even a feature of policy adoption when the U.S. Supreme Court makes policy, which is illustrated in the Court's policy on affirmative action in education. In the 1978 case of *Regents of the University California v. Bakke*, a White applicant to the University of California at Davis Medical School challenged the university's policy of reserving a quota of slots for minority applicants after he was denied admission despite having higher grades and test scores than minorities who were admitted. Four justices believed that public schools should not be allowed in any way to use race as an admission factor, whereas four other justices were willing to uphold the University of California's quota system.

It was Associate Justice Lewis Powell's compromise opinion that became the Court's policy on affirmative action. Powell ruled that quota systems violate the Fourteenth Amendment equal protection clause—a majority of the Court did want to overrule the use of firm quotas for minority applicants. Justice Powell also allowed the use of racial minority status as a benefit in deciding admissions—a majority of the Court was willing to uphold the general use of affirmative action.[53] In 2003, this compromise policy was upheld in *Grutter v. Bollinger*,[54] which concerned the University of Michigan Law School's admission process.

If the policymaking institution is unable to reach a compromise, the policy will not be adopted. For example, recall our discussion of the failed immigration reform policies in 2018. In 2012 President Obama developed the Deferred Action for Childhood Arrivals (DACA) policy, which allowed undocumented immigrants to remain and work or pursue an education in the United States if their parents brought them here when they were children and if they lack a criminal record. In 2017, President Trump reversed President Obama's DACA policy, which he criticized during the campaign. President Trump argued that Congress should develop a broad immigration policy that provides for the DACA recipients and increases security at the border, including appropriating money to build a wall along the border between the United States and Mexico. President Trump actually campaigned on the promise that Mexico would pay for the wall, but predictably, Mexico refused to do so.[55]

In early 2018, Senators Lindsey Graham (R-SC) and Richard Durbin (D-IL) developed a bipartisan compromise bill that would have allowed DACA immigrants to remain in the nation and even become citizens, provided money for border enforcement including building a wall, and limited some legal immigration. Despite initially seeming inclined to support a compromise, President Trump rejected the Graham-Durbin proposal, and during a meeting with the senators, Trump commented that he did not want more immigrants from "shithole countries," referring to Latin American, Caribbean, and African nations. In short, Senators Durbin and Graham's formulated policy was never adopted because the president rejected the bipartisan compromise.[56]

Moreover, single individuals, such as congressional committee chairs, possess unilateral authority to obstruct the policy adoption process. During the 1950s, members of Congress, such as House Rules Committee Chair Howard Smith (D-VA) prevented the adoption of civil rights bills by not reporting them from their committees.[57]

Through executive orders (see Chapter 7), presidents are able to adopt policies unilaterally without having to compromise with other branches. An executive order is a directive that the president issues to subordinates, and many of these orders influence public policy, especially in the area of minority politics. For example, during World War II President Franklin Roosevelt issued two executive orders that greatly shaped the fate of racial minorities. Executive Order 8802 forbade racial and ethnic discrimination in the federal government and in defense companies that contracted with the federal government. Executive Order 9066 established the policy of forcibly removing Japanese Americans to internment camps.[58] Within the first few days of his presidency, President Donald Trump issued Executive Order 13769, which banned immigrants from certain Muslim majority nations and halted the admission of refugees into the United States.[59] During the 2016 campaign, Trump initially proposed banning all Muslims from entering the United States, but the actual policy he initially adopted focused on specific nations. The initial order generated chaos and controversy; therefore, in the fall of 2017, President Trump altered the ban by adding two non-Muslim nations—North Korea and

Senator Dick Durbin (D-IL), left, with Senator Lindsey Graham (R-SC), speaks during a news conference on Capitol Hill in Washington, September 5, 2017, after President Trump ended DACA and challenged Congress to enact a legislative solution. Senators Graham and Durbin formulated a bipartisan compromise, but President Trump rejected their plan. Therefore, the policy they formulated was never adopted.

Venezuela—in addition to Syria, Libya, Chad (which was later rescinded), Iran, Yemen, and Somalia. Opponents challenged the ban, arguing that the president lacked the power to issue the order and that ethnic and religious focus was discriminatory. Nevertheless, in 2018 the U.S. Supreme Court narrowly upheld the ban with a 5–4 ruling.[60]

Although many observers find policy adoption debates to be dry, they can sometimes become heated, especially over controversial issues. There were particularly virulent debates during the process of adopting President Obama's health care reform policy in 2010, especially with many opponents of health care reform focusing on President Obama's race. The Evaluating Equality box examines this issue in more detail.

Postenactment Stages

Despite obstacles in the agenda-setting, policy formulation, and policy adoption stages, the government will often establish policies. The policymaking process does not end there, however. Adopted policies cannot accomplish their goals unless the government and even citizens ensure that the policies are carried out. This stage of the policymaking process is known

evaluating equality

Racial Prejudice and the Public Debate over the Adoption of Health Care Reform Policies

Over the past decade President Obama's health care law, the Affordable Care Act, also known as Obamacare, has generated significant debate. In order to comprehend the politics of the current health care debate, it is essential to understand the debate during the formulation and adoption stages of the Affordable Care Act. In 2009, President Barack Obama and members of Congress formulated different policies to reform the health care system. These policies contained a variety of proposals, such as reducing health care costs, preventing health insurance companies from denying coverage to people with existing illnesses or canceling coverage to people who get sick, limiting lawsuits against negligent doctors, mandating that every person obtain health insurance, and developing a government-run health insurance option for people to obtain coverage. Given the significance and complexity of this issue, the adoption phase for health care reform has been extremely chaotic.

As members of Congress traveled to their districts during the summer of 2009, the debate over the adoption of a specific set of health care reform policies intensified among the American public. Many members of Congress held "town hall" meetings with their constituents to discuss the issue, and interest groups mobilized both supporters and opponents of these reforms to attend these meetings to express their views. Normally,

Formulating and adopting major policy changes, such as health insurance reform, can inflame passions among supporters and opponents of the policy. Here, opponents of the Democratic health care reform proposals attend a protest, with signs lambasting health care reform as well as President Obama. Many anti-health-care-reform protestors have referred to President Obama in nasty and racist terms. The health insurance industry, which strongly opposes reform, has provided the financial backing for these protests.

these town hall meetings are fairly low key, but in summer 2009 these meetings concerning health care reform were extremely boisterous. Initially, opponents shouted down members of Congress who supported health care reform, but then supporters attended meetings to counter these opponents. Vicious shouting matches and occasional violence ensued.

Vigorous public fights over policy are certainly not new to American politics, but the specter of racism emerged in that debate. Because former President Obama is Black and was a major proponent of health care reform, much of the opposition to health care has undertones based on racial prejudice.

There were subtle examples of this prejudice. For example, many protesters at Tea Party and anti-health-care-reform rallies displayed signs or t-shirts with the words "I Want My Country Back," which suggest that these people felt they have lost their country because the president is different from them. Likewise, some health care reform opponents claimed inaccurately that President Obama is not the legitimate president because he was born in Kenya and not Hawaii, again undermining the legitimacy of a duly elected president who happens to be Black.

An extremely disturbing incident occurred on September 9, 2009, when President Obama formally addressed Congress to argue for his health care reform proposals. After the president contended that illegal immigrants would not receive benefits under his plan, Representative Joe Wilson (R-SC) shouted, "You lie." Members of Congress are expected to be extremely respectful to the president during a formal address, even if they disagree with his message. Many people interpreted Representative Wilson's outrageously disrespectful interruption to be based on racial prejudice.

There were even blatant examples of racism. Most notably, in July 2009, Dr. David McKalip, a politically active St. Petersburg, Florida, neurosurgeon and head of the Pinellas County Medical Association, disseminated an email opposing health care reform. His email contained an extremely prejudiced and offensive caricature of President Obama dressed as a stereotypical African witch doctor. After public outcry over the photograph, Dr. McKalip apologized and assumed a much lower profile in the debate, but the offensive message was still clear.

The subtle and blatant racial prejudice underlying the health care reform debate became so controversial that former Democratic President Jimmy Carter directly accused the opponents of health care reform of being racist. Other political leaders disagreed. Former Democratic President Bill Clinton argued that the vitriol against the health care reform proposals would be the same if President Obama were White. Members of the Obama administration, including President Obama himself, downplayed the significance of racism in the debate. The intensity of the debate over health care reform abated by 2011, and although it was not central, the issue of health care still emerged during the 2018 election campaign.

- Research newspaper articles and Internet sites that covered the debate over the adoption and implementation of health care reform policies.
- After conducting this research, debate whether racism motivated the opponents of the president's health care reform proposals.
- How has the debate over health care changed over the past decade, and to what extent is race and ethnicity and still relevant?.

Source: Thompson, S. (2009, July 26). Physician apologizes for offensive Obama image. *Tampa Tribune/Tampa Bay Times*. Retrieved July 21, 2018, from http://www.tbo.com/news/physician-apologizes-for-offensive-obama-image-93254.

as **policy implementation**, the process by which government actors and even private citizens execute a policy that has been adopted.[61]

Furthermore, the policymaking process does not cease once a policy is put into effect. After a sufficient time, the government and private citizens need to ensure that the policy has achieved its desired effect. **Policy evaluation** determines the extent to which those goals have been achieved and suggests ways to improve the policy.[62] It is often the case that policy implementation and evaluation intersect with minority-group politics.

Policy Implementation

During the process of policy implementation, government officials must ensure that money is spent and regulations are enforced. The government agencies and officials charged with implementing policies enjoy considerable discretion; that is, policies are not necessarily implemented according to the

Policy Implementation The stage in the policymaking process in which government actors and even private citizens carry out enacted policies.

Policy Evaluation The stage in the policymaking process in which government actors and private citizens determine whether an implemented policy is achieving its intended effect.

intent of those who formulated and adopted them. Beginning in the 1960s scholars recognized that it was important to examine the extent that policies work according to the intent of the people who enacted them.[63]

Implementation entails the spending of money that has been appropriated or budgeted. Generally, after Congress appropriates money, which is policy adoption, the executive branch and bureaucracy are responsible for laying out the actual expenditures. Occasionally, policy implementation can be affected when money that is targeted to fund a policy is not fully spent. For example, the 2001 No Child Left Behind Act required testing of schoolchildren as a way to increase their performance. By 2004, school districts throughout the nation had adopted the testing mandates, but according to many estimates, the executive branch underfunded the implementation of this policy by about $9 billion. As a result, many schools had to divert money from other crucial programs to pay for the testing, which greatly affected the more impoverished districts containing a large number of racial and ethnic minorities. Representative Robert Scott (D-VA) estimated that the Richmond, Virginia, school district alone lost about $9 million because this policy was not fully funded.[64] In 2011, President Obama announced that some states were exempted from the strict controls in No Child Left Behind because they had enacted their own reforms designed to improve education outcomes.[65]

Moreover, by spending money, the executive branch can shape how a policy actually affects people. For example, the President's Emergency Plan for AIDS Relief (PEPFAR) is a policy designed to spend billions of dollars to treat and prevent HIV/AIDS in Africa and the Caribbean. When Republican President George W. Bush implemented the program, his administration insisted on emphasizing controversial abstinence-only programs as a way to prevent the spread of the disease. However, the Democratic Obama administration embraced all forms of AIDS prevention, including condoms and sex education, but some elements of abstinence promotion remained.[66] President Trump has again reversed course and proposed significantly cutting the funding for PEPFAR altogether.[67]

The executive branch also implements policies by enforcing laws passed by Congress. For example, the Civil Rights Act of 1964 created the Equal Employment Opportunity Commission (EEOC) to enforce civil rights laws, but the chair of the commission, whom the president appoints, possesses discretion in how to enforce these laws. President Ronald Reagan chose conservative Clarence Thomas, now a U.S. Supreme Court justice, to chair the EEOC. Unlike his predecessors, Thomas did not rely on statistical evidence as proof of discrimination, and by declining to act on discrimination complaints he allowed thousands of cases to lapse.[68] Civil rights laws were enforced less vigorously during the 1980s than they had been previously.

Policy implementation is especially important for the Supreme Court. After the Court adopts a policy—that is, issues a ruling—it relies on others to ensure that the ruling is carried out. Lower court judges often implement the Supreme Court's rulings. For example, in 1955 the U.S. Supreme Court adopted a policy in its *Brown v. Board of Education of Topeka, Kansas*, known as

Brown II, decision that required states to desegregate their public schools "with all deliberate speed."[69]

The Supreme Court relied on federal district judges to implement this policy. Although federal district judges are instruments of the national government, they operate entirely within their region and are often subject to local political pressure. When enforcing the "all deliberate speed" mandate, some judges, such as Frank M. Johnson of Alabama, withstood local political pressure from Whites and used their authority to ensure integration in the public schools under their jurisdiction. Other judges, such as T. Whitfield Davidson, who presided over Dallas, Texas, vehemently opposed integration and refused to implement the decision. Consequently, the rate of integration varied throughout the South.[70]

The executive branch is extremely crucial to the implementation of the Supreme Court's policies. After the Supreme Court's *Brown v. Board of Education* opinions, Presidents Dwight Eisenhower and John F. Kennedy used federal military force to ensure that schools were actually integrated. If the president chooses not to enforce a Supreme Court decision, the decision has no effect. For example, in *Worcester v. Georgia*, the Supreme Court in 1832 ruled that a national government treaty with the Cherokee Nation overrode a Georgia law forbidding non-Cherokees from residing on Cherokee land.[71] The decision favored the national government's agreement with the Cherokee Nation over state control, but President Andrew Jackson opposed this decision, and he refused to enforce it.[72]

Local governments often influence policy implementation. For example, after Hurricane Katrina destroyed homes in the Gulf Coast region, FEMA's Individual Assistance Program was adopted to provide temporary trailer housing for displaced people. The policy allowed for trailers to be placed on people's property or in existing trailer parks. The policy also required FEMA to build new trailer parks to accommodate the remaining displaced people. The policy mandates that FEMA search for appropriate places to build the trailer parks and get approval from local governments. Although local government officials understand that the new trailer parks are necessary to house displaced citizens, these officials generally oppose having the trailer parks built in their jurisdictions because the parks have a reputation for increasing crime and lowering existing property values. As a result, wealthy and powerful local governments were able to influence FEMA's implementation of the Individual Assistance Program in a way that avoided trailer parks in their jurisdiction. In fact, a study found that the more Blacks there were in an area, the greater was the chance that a new trailer park would be built.[73]

Variation in implementation also stems from the formulation and adoption processes. If a policy is formulated in detail, then it is more likely to attract opposition and might not be adopted. To ensure adoption, policy designers therefore often formulate broad policies. Broadly constructed policies invite implementers to insert their own biases into the implementation process. As discussed earlier, the U.S. Supreme Court's *Brown II* decision instituted the vague "all deliberate speed" mandate for school desegregation. Supreme Court justices and law clerks recognized that a detailed ruling would decrease the chances of a unanimous opinion and numerous school districts would ignore it. During the justices' conference, Justice Hugo Black remarked, "The less we say, the better off we are." Thus, the broadly formulated policy allowed Chief Justice Warren to secure a unanimous decision, but as a trade-off the broad decision gave tremendous discretion to federal judges in charge of implementing it.[74] As we have discussed, this discretion led to wide disparities in the speed of integration.

Because sentencing people convicted of a crime is a key element of implementation, variations in implementation can also lead to disparate sentences for the same crime. "Measuring Equality: Racial Disparities in the Punishment of Drug Offenders" explains disparate criminal sentencing in more detail.

Policy Evaluation

Assess current debates on Social Security.

The domestic policymaking process does not stop at the implementation stage. Governments, interest groups, and the public need to ensure that the policy has achieved its desired effect, and this stage is known as policy evaluation. Despite the seemingly objective nature of the evaluation task, evaluators enjoy tremendous leeway. Because policymakers are often ambiguous about the objectives of a policy, an evaluator enjoys wide discretion in establishing the goals of a policy. Moreover, the evaluator selects the method to ascertain whether the effects of the policy have met those goals; therefore, the research methodology that evaluators employ can affect how they evaluate policies.[75]

The government evaluates policy through the congressional oversight process (see Chapter 6). Inherent in the lawmaking power of Congress is the authority to make sure that laws are enforced according to congressional intentions and to prevent waste, fraud, or abuse in government. Although oversight often features interbranch disputes, it is largely a partisan process. Committee chairs have tremendous discretion in determining whether to conduct oversight investigations. As a result, Congress is less likely to exercise its oversight power in periods of unified government than in periods of divided government, although the minority party will still engage in oversight as a means of policy evaluation. For example, in 2018 the Democrats on the House Oversight and Government Reform Committee (see Chapter 5) released a report that evaluated the Republican Tax Cut Bill, passed at the end of 2017. Their evaluation suggests that the tax bill costs the average homeowner while increasing money for corporate developers.[76]

Assess current debates on tax reform.

Interest groups, largely through the use of social media, are also engaged in policy evaluation. For example, in 2011 President Obama formulated a policy that sent one hundred U.S. troops to Uganda to track down human-rights abuser Joseph Kony, who had sold young girls into sex slavery and forced young boys to be soldiers in his militia. Although this decision garnered some news coverage at the time, Americans soon forgot about the issue and Kony was not apprehended. In 2012, a group called Invisible Children launched a viral video that highlighted Kony's transgressions and raised awareness on how he had not been caught, despite the president's policy.[77] In the five years between 2012 and 2107, the United States spent $800 million to capture Kony.

measuring equality

Racial Disparities in the Punishment of Drug Offenders

Implementation is crucial to policymaking, and policies can be implemented in a way that creates varying results for different racial or ethnic groups. In particular, the implementation of antidrug policies has negatively affected African Americans and Latinos. Here we explore in more detail the extent to which drug policies affect Blacks and Latinos. Implementation includes enforcement of antidrug laws and sentencing of drug offenders, and we examine the number of inmates in state prison for drug offenses.

We provide two dimensions of this analysis. We compare sentencing among Whites, Blacks, and Latinos, and we compare drug-offense sentences with sentences for other crimes. Specifically, we compare drug crimes to violent crimes (e.g., murder, manslaughter, sexual assault, robbery, and assault), property crimes (e.g., burglary, larceny, fraud, and forgery), public-order crimes (e.g., driving while under the influence, weapons violations, vice, and liquor offenses), and other crimes.

First, we ascertain the percentages of Whites, Blacks, and Latinos incarcerated in state prisons throughout the United States for each offense category. Because some data are missing and because other races are incarcerated (although not reported), these figures do not add up to 100 percent. Therefore, we report the data in Table 16.1 versus a pie-chart format. These data suggest that race matters for drug sentences. Whites make up the plurality of state prisoners for property, public order crimes, and other crimes (i.e., the less serious offenses). However, for more serious crimes—drug and violent crimes—Blacks comprise the plurality of state prisoners, although the Black and White numbers are close. Latinos are the least represented in all types of crimes.

When interpreting these results, remember that Blacks and Latinos comprise a smaller portion of the overall population compared to Whites.

Second, we provide three pie charts, one for each racial group: Whites (Figure 16.1), Blacks (Figure 16.2), and Latinos (Figure 16.3). For each group, we show the percentage of total inmates by type of crime. Because these figures add up to 100 percent (except for small rounding errors), we use pie charts to report these data.

A solid majority (close to 60 percent) of Blacks and Latinos are imprisoned for violent offenses, but for Whites, this figure is only a plurality, not a majority— 47.8 percent. For White inmates, the next highest category is property crimes (25.1 percent), which is then followed by drug offenses (14.1 percent). For Black and

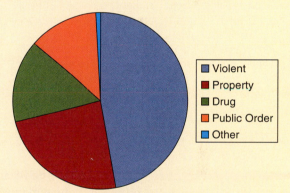

Figure 16.1 Composition of White State Prison Inmates in the United States by Offense Type, 2016

TABLE 16.1 Racial and Ethnic Composition of State Prisoners in the United States by Offense Type, 2016

Crime	White %	Black %	Latino %
Drug	30.9	31.2	19.7
Violent	26.9	35.6	23.0
Property	41.4	27.8	15.3
Public order	36.8	32.1	23.0
Other	39.3	21.3	12.4

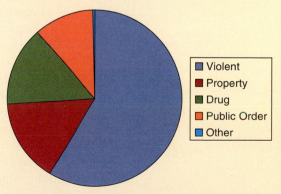

Figure 16.2 Composition of Black State Prison Inmates in the United States by Offense Type, 2016.

(Continued)

measuring equality *(Continued)*

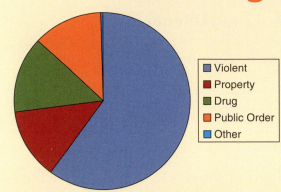

Figure 16.3 Composition of Latino State Prison Inmates in the United States by Offense Type, 2016.

Latino inmates, property crimes and drug offenses are about equal. It is important to note that all three racial and ethnic categories have about the same proportion incarcerated for drug offenses. Nevertheless, unlike White inmates, who are more likely to be serving time for property crimes than for drug crimes, Black and Latino inmates are as likely to be serving prison time for property crimes as they are for drug crimes.

These results show that Whites are incarcerated differently from Blacks and Latinos. There are, however, several ways to interpret these data. First, it is possible that Blacks and Latinos are more likely than Whites to commit violent crimes. In that case, implementation reflects the crimes being committed. Second, it is possible that violent crimes are being committed at an equal level, but that Blacks and Latinos are more likely than Whites to be arrested. In that case then, when police implement antiviolence laws, they would be discriminating against Blacks and Latinos. Third, it is possible that crimes are committed and arrests are made at the same rate, but Blacks and Latinos receive longer sentences than Whites. In this case, the judges implementing the violent crime laws would be discriminating against Blacks and Latinos. Which of the three interpretations is most plausible? What role might property ownership play in the incarceration rates for property crimes? How would you go about conducting further research on these topics?

Sources: Data adapted from Cason, E. A. (2018, January). *Table 13: Number of Sentenced Prisoners Under Jurisdiction of State Correctional Authority, by Most serious Offense, Sex, Race, and Hispanic Origin, December 31, 2015. In Prisoners in 2016.* Washington, DC: U.S. Department of Justice, Bureau of Justice Statistics). Retrieved July 22, 2018, https://www.bjs.gov/content/pub/pdf/p16.pdf.

Although the United States and African forces captured many of Kony's subordinates, Kony remains at large. In 2017 the United States ceased its hunt for Kony, arguing that it had effectively decimated his forces.[78]

The manner in which governments interpret an evaluation can also be biased. Those who initially supported a policy will interpret an evaluation as indicative of success, whereas those who opposed the policy will interpret the same evaluation less favorably. For example, the Personal Responsibility and Work Opportunity Reconciliation Act of 1996 (welfare reform) gave states more authority to distribute aid to the needy, established time limits for receiving aid, and insisted that aid recipients work or attend a training program. In 1999, the federal government collaborated with the Urban Institute—a think tank that focuses on poverty and race—to evaluate this policy, and it reported that welfare rolls had diminished throughout the nation. President Bill Clinton, who willingly signed the act, hailed this evaluation as evidence that the policy was working. Opponents of the law interpreted the study quite differently. Georgetown University law professor Peter Edelman, who had resigned from the Clinton administration because he opposed the welfare reform policy, emphasized that the evaluation showed that many of those individuals who left welfare took menial jobs and would once again return to welfare.[79] In fact, a subsequent evaluation of welfare reform within the state of Wisconsin found that compared to Whites, Blacks and Latinos were disproportionately sanctioned for failing to meet the requirements of the welfare reform program.[80]

Conclusion

Policymaking refers to what government actually does, and it entails several stages. This chapter has traced the policymaking process in both domestic and foreign policies. In the initial agenda-setting stage, an issue is brought to the attention of the American public, largely, albeit not exclusively, through the media, social movements, and individual interest groups.

Next is the policy enactment stage, which includes both formulation and adoption. In policy formulation, political actors actually create the policies. Although formulation is generally dominated by political institutions, the public and interest groups can influence policy formulation. Policy adoption occurs when the formulated policy is formally established, and it often requires compromise.

Finally, there are the postenactment stages, which comprise implementation and evaluation. During implementation, the policy is actually carried out. The actors responsible for implementing policies often enjoy tremendous discretion to alter a policy's desired effect or even refuse to carry out certain policies. In policy evaluation, the policy is assessed to determine whether it has achieved its intended goals. Although the evaluation stage is supposed to be objective, the biases of the evaluators can influence this stage of the policymaking process.

Because the policymaking process entails each of the aspects of government that we have covered throughout this book, this chapter also served to tie together the book's previous chapters. Most notably, this chapter reemphasized our focus on minority-group politics. Minority groups rely on the media, interest groups, and social movements to set the agenda on domestic and foreign policies relevant to racial and ethnic minorities. Minority representation in government institutions is crucial for the formulation of policies favorable to racial and ethnic minority groups, and compromise is crucial for those policies being successfully adopted. The discretion that policy implementers enjoy greatly influences how policies actually affect racial and ethnic minorities, and biases inherent in the evaluation process shape how those policies are assessed.

The story of Edward Clary clearly highlights the intersection between policymaking and minority-group politics. The media hype over crack cocaine, which largely framed the issue as a "Black" problem, set the agenda among the public and then among political institutions that tougher policies against crack cocaine were needed. Accordingly, Congress and the president tremendously increased the penalties for crack cocaine, which resulted in a 100:1 differential between crack- and powder-cocaine sentences. But, during the implementation of the policy, Judge Cahill, an African American, opted not to adhere to the minimum guideline because it negatively affected Black defendants. Although Judge Cahill's departure from the minimum sentence was overturned on appeal, the crack-cocaine policy was eventually evaluated and the disparity has been reduced substantially. Undoubtedly, race played a key role throughout the process.

Check your understanding of Chapter 16.

review
REVIEW QUESTIONS

1. How have various civil rights movements and interest groups set the agenda on domestic and foreign-affairs issues important to racial and ethnic minorities?

2. Do policies in general and those important to racial and ethnic minorities in particular necessarily advance from the agenda-setting stage to the formulation stage? Why or why not?

3. How important is compromise in the policy adoption process, especially for foreign

and domestic policies relevant to racial and ethnic minorities?

4. How does executive branch and bureaucratic discretion in policy implementation affect racial and ethnic minorities?

5. Do interested parties interpret policy evaluations similarly, especially when concerned with issues affecting the people living near or below the poverty line and racial and ethnic minorities?

Need to review key ideas in greater depth? Click here.

terms
KEY TERMS

Administrative Procedures
    Act p. 538
Agenda-Setting p. 529
Agenda Universe p. 530
Decision Agenda p. 530

Domestic Policy p. 529
Foreign Policy p. 529
Institutional Agenda p. 530
Policy Adoption p. 535
Policy Evaluation p. 543

Policy Formulation p. 535
Policy Implementation
    p. 543
Systemic Agenda p. 530
Think Tanks p. 538

Flashcard review.

readings
ADDITIONAL READINGS

Boston, T. D. (Ed.). (1997). *A different vision: Race and public policy* (Vol. 2). London: Routledge.

    This second part of a two-volume edited work focuses on public policies addressing income inequality among Blacks.

Grünfeld, F., & Huijboom, A. (2007). *The failure to prevent genocide in Rwanda: The role of bystanders.* Leiden, the Netherlands: Koninklijjke Brill.

    This book thoroughly evaluates the failures that led to the genocide committed in Rwanda during the 1990s, one of the worst examples of human-rights violations in African history.

Hatamiya, L. T. (1993). *Righting a wrong: Japanese Americans and the passage of the Civil Liberties Act of 1988.* Palo Alto, CA: Stanford University Press.

    This book traces the history of the agenda-setting, formulation, and adoption stages of the legislation that apologized for and

compensated the victims of the internment of Japanese Americans during World War II.

Henry, C. M. (Ed.). (2004). *Race, poverty, and domestic policy.* New Haven, CT: Yale University Press.

    This book, a collection of scholarly essays from the Inner City Poverty Conference sponsored by the Institution of Special and Policy Studies at Yale University, covers a wide range of topics, such as racism, measurement of income inequality, crime and law enforcement, education, family concerns, and welfare.

Provine, D. M. (2007). *Unequal under law: Race in the War on Drugs.* Chicago: University of Chicago Press.

    This book examines how "War on Drugs" policies stem from and exacerbate racism in the United States.

APPENDIX I:
The Declaration of Independence

When in the course of human events, it becomes necessary for one people to dissolve the political bands which have connected them with another, and to assume, among the powers of the earth, the separate and equal station to which the Laws of Nature and of Nature's God entitle them, a decent respect to the opinions of mankind requires that they should declare the causes which impel them to the separation.

We hold these truths to be self-evident, that all men are created equal, that they are endowed by their Creator with certain unalienable Rights, that among these are life, liberty and the pursuit of happiness. That to secure these rights, governments are instituted among men, deriving their just powers from the consent of the governed; that whenever any form of government becomes destructive of these ends, it is the right of the people to alter or to abolish it, and to institute new Government, laying its foundation on such principles and organizing its powers in such form, as to them shall seem most likely to effect their safety and happiness. Prudence, indeed, will dictate that Governments long established should not be changed for light and transient causes; and, accordingly, all experience hath shown, that mankind are more disposed to suffer, while evils are sufferable, than to right themselves by abolishing the forms to which they are accustomed. But when a long train of abuses and usurpations, pursuing invariably the same object evinces a design to reduce them under absolute despotism, it is their right, it is their duty, to throw off such government, and to provide new guards for their future security. Such has been the patient sufferance of these colonies; and such is now the necessity which constrains them to alter their former systems of government. The history of the present King of Great Britain is a history of repeated injuries and usurpations, all having in direct object the establishment of an absolute tyranny over these States. To prove this, let facts be submitted to a candid world:

- He has refused his assent to laws, the most wholesome and necessary for the public good.
- He has forbidden his governors to pass laws of immediate and pressing importance, unless suspended in their operation till his assent should be obtained; and, when so suspended, he has utterly neglected to attend to them.
- He has refused to pass other laws for the accommodation of large districts of people, unless those people would relinquish the right of representation in the legislature, a right inestimable to them and formidable to tyrants only.

- He has called together legislative bodies at places unusual, uncomfortable, and distant from the depository of their public records, for the sole purpose of fatiguing them into compliance with his measures.
- He has dissolved representative houses repeatedly, for opposing with manly firmness his invasions on the rights of the people.
- He has refused for a long time, after such dissolutions, to cause others to be elected; whereby the legislative powers, incapable of annihilation, have returned to the People at large for their exercise; the State remaining in the mean time exposed to all the dangers of invasion from without, and convulsions within.
- He has endeavored to prevent the population of these States; for that purpose obstructing the laws for naturalization of foreigners; refusing to pass others to encourage their migrations hither, and raising the conditions of new appropriations of lands.
- He has obstructed the administration of justice, by refusing his assent to laws for establishing judiciary powers.
- He has made judges dependent on his will alone, for the tenure of their offices, and the amount and payment of their salaries.
- He has erected a multitude of new offices, and sent hither swarms of officers to harass our people, and eat out their substance.
- He has kept among us, in times of peace, standing armies without the consent of our legislatures.
- He has affected to render the Military independent of, and superior to, the civil power.
- He has combined with others to subject us to a jurisdiction foreign to our constitution and unacknowledged by our laws; giving his assent to their acts of pretended legislation:
- For quartering large bodies of armed troops among us;
- For protecting them, by a mock trial, from punishment for any murders which they should commit on the inhabitants of these States;
- For cutting off our trade with all parts of the world;
- For imposing taxes on us without our Consent;
- For depriving us, in many cases, of the benefits of Trial by Jury;
- For transporting us beyond Seas to be tried for pretended offences;
- For abolishing the free System of English Laws in a neighbouring Province, establishing therein an Arbitrary government, and enlarging its Boundaries so as to render it at once an example and fit instrument for introducing the same absolute rule into these colonies;
- For taking away our charters, abolishing our most valuable laws, and altering fundamentally the forms of our governments;
- For suspending our own legislatures, and declaring themselves invested with power to legislate for us in all cases whatsoever.

- He has abdicated government here, by declaring us out of his protection and waging war against us.
- He has plundered our seas, ravaged our coasts, burnt our towns, and destroyed the lives of our people.
- He is at this time transporting large armies of foreign mercenaries to complete the works of death, desolation and tyranny, already begun with circumstances of cruelty and perfidy scarcely paralleled in the most barbarous ages, and totally unworthy the head of a civilized nation.
- He has constrained our fellow citizens taken captive on the high seas to bear arms against their country, to become the executioners of their friends and brethren, or to fall themselves by their hands.
- He has excited domestic insurrections amongst us, and has endeavored to bring on the inhabitants of our frontiers, the merciless Indian savages, whose known rule of warfare, is an undistinguished destruction of all ages, sexes and conditions.

In every stage of these oppressions we have petitioned for redress in the most humble terms; our repeated petitions have been answered only by repeated injury. A prince whose character is thus marked by every act which may define a tyrant, is unfit to be the ruler of a free people.

Nor have we been wanting in attentions to our British brethren. We have warned them from time to time of attempts by their legislature to extend an unwarrantable jurisdiction over us. We have reminded them of the circumstances of our emigration and settlement here. We have appealed to their native justice and magnanimity, and we have conjured them by the ties of our common kindred to disavow these usurpations, which, would inevitably interrupt our connections and correspondence. They, too, have been deaf to the voice of justice and of consanguinity. We must, therefore, acquiesce in the necessity, which denounces our separation, and hold them, as we hold the rest of mankind, enemies in war, in peace friends.

We, therefore, the representatives of the United States of America, in general Congress, assembled, appealing to the Supreme Judge of the world for the rectitude of our intentions, do, in the name, and by the authority of the good people of these colonies, solemnly publish and declare, that these united colonies are, and of right ought to be free and independent states; that they are absolved from all allegiance to the British Crown, and that all political connection between them and the state of Great Britain, is and ought to be totally dissolved; and that, as free and independent states, they have full power to levy war, conclude peace, contract alliances, establish commerce, and to do all other acts and things which independent states may of right do. And for the support of this declaration, with a firm reliance on the protection of Divine Providence, we mutually pledge to each other our lives, our fortunes and our sacred honor.

The Constitution of the United States of America

We the People of the United States, in Order to form a more perfect Union, establish Justice, insure domestic Tranquility, provide for the common defence, promote the general Welfare, and secure the Blessings of Liberty to ourselves and our Posterity, do ordain and establish this Constitution for the United States of America.

Article I

Section 1

All legislative Powers herein granted shall be vested in a Congress of the United States, which shall consist of a Senate and House of Representatives.

Section 2

The House of Representatives shall be composed of Members chosen every second Year by the People of the several States, and the Electors in each State shall have the Qualifications requisite for Electors of the most numerous Branch of the State Legislature.

No Person shall be a Representative who shall not have attained to the Age of twenty five Years, and been seven Years a Citizen of the United States, and who shall not, when elected, be an Inhabitant of that State in which he shall be chosen.

Representatives [and direct Taxes][1] shall be apportioned among the several States [which may be included within this Union, according to their respective Numbers, which shall be determined by adding to the whole Number of free Persons, including those bound to Service for a Term of Years, and excluding Indians not taxed, three fifths of all other Persons].[2] The actual Enumeration shall be made within three Years after the first Meeting of the Congress of the United States, and within every subsequent Term of ten Years, in such Manner as they shall by Law direct. The Number of Representatives shall not exceed one for every thirty Thousand, but each State shall have at Least one Representative; and until such enumeration shall be made, the State of New Hampshire shall be entitled to choose three, Massachusetts eight, Rhode-Island and Providence Plantations one, Connecticut five, New York six,

[1] Modified by the Sixteenth Amendment.
[2] Negated by the Fourteenth Amendment.

New Jersey four, Pennsylvania eight, Delaware one, Maryland six, Virginia ten, North Carolina five, South Carolina five, and Georgia three.

When vacancies happen in the Representation from any State, the Executive Authority thereof shall issue Writs of Election to fill such Vacancies.

The House of Representatives shall choose their Speaker and other Officers; and shall have the sole Power of Impeachment.

Section 3

The Senate of the United States shall be composed of two Senators from each State, chosen [by the Legislature thereof][3] for six Years; and each Senator shall have one Vote.

Immediately after they shall be assembled in Consequence of the first Election, they shall be divided as equally as may be into three Classes. The Seats of the Senators of the first Class shall be vacated at the Expiration of the second Year, of the second Class at the Expiration of the fourth Year, and of the third Class at the Expiration of the sixth Year, so that one third may be chosen every second Year[; and if Vacancies happen by Resignation, or otherwise, during the Recess of the Legislature of any State, the Executive thereof may make temporary Appointments until the next Meeting of the Legislature, which shall then fill such Vacancies].[4]

No Person shall be a Senator who shall not have attained to the Age of thirty Years, and been nine Years a Citizen of the United States, and who shall not, when elected, be an Inhabitant of that State for which he shall be chosen.

The Vice President of the United States shall be President of the Senate, but shall have no Vote, unless they be equally divided.

The Senate shall choose their other Officers, and also a President pro tempore, in the Absence of the Vice President, or when he shall exercise the Office of President of the United States.

The Senate shall have the sole Power to try all Impeachments. When sitting for that Purpose, they shall be on Oath or Affirmation. When the President of the United States is tried, the Chief Justice shall preside: And no Person shall be convicted without the Concurrence of two thirds of the Members present.

Judgment in Cases of Impeachment shall not extend further than to removal from Office, and disqualification to hold and enjoy any Office of honor, Trust or Profit under the United States: but the Party convicted shall nevertheless be liable and subject to Indictment, Trial, Judgment and Punishment, according to Law.

Section 4

The Times, Places and Manner of holding Elections for Senators and Representatives, shall be prescribed in each State by the Legislature thereof; but the Congress may at any time by Law make or alter such Regulations, except as to the Places of chusing Senators.

---

[3] Changed by the Seventeenth Amendment.
[4] Modified by the Seventeenth Amendment.

[The Congress shall assemble at least once in every Year, and such Meeting shall be on the first Monday in December, unless they shall by Law appoint a different Day.][5]

Section 5

Each House shall be the Judge of the Elections, Returns and Qualifications of its own Members, and a Majority of each shall constitute a Quorum to do Business; but a smaller Number may adjourn from day to day, and may be authorized to compel the Attendance of absent Members, in such Manner, and under such Penalties as each House may provide.

Each House may determine the Rules of its Proceedings, punish its Members for disorderly Behaviour, and, with the Concurrence of two thirds, expel a Member.

Each House shall keep a Journal of its Proceedings, and from time to time publish the same, excepting such Parts as may in their Judgment require Secrecy; and the Yeas and Nays of the Members of either House on any question shall, at the Desire of one fifth of those Present, be entered on the Journal.

Neither House, during the Session of Congress, shall, without the Consent of the other, adjourn for more than three days, nor to any other Place than that in which the two Houses shall be sitting.

Section 6

The Senators and Representatives shall receive a Compensation for their Services, to be ascertained by Law, and paid out of the Treasury of the United States. They shall in all Cases, except Treason, Felony and Breach of the Peace, be privileged from Arrest during their Attendance at the Session of their respective Houses, and in going to and returning from the same; and for any Speech or Debate in either House, they shall not be questioned in any other Place.

No Senator or Representative shall, during the Time for which he was elected, be appointed to any civil Office under the Authority of the United States, which shall have been created, or the Emoluments whereof shall have been increased during such time; and no Person holding any Office under the United States, shall be a Member of either House during his Continuance in Office.

Section 7

All Bills for raising Revenue shall originate in the House of Representatives; but the Senate may propose or concur with Amendments as on other Bills.

Every Bill which shall have passed the House of Representatives and the Senate, shall, before it become a Law, be presented to the President of the United States: If he approve he shall sign it, but if not he shall return it, with his Objections to that House in which it shall have originated, who shall enter the Objections at large on their Journal, and proceed to reconsider it. If after such Reconsideration two thirds of that House shall agree to pass the Bill, it shall be

[5]Changed to January 3 by the Twentieth Amendment.

sent, together with the Objections, to the other House, by which it shall likewise be reconsidered, and if approved by two thirds of that House, it shall become a Law. But in all such Cases the Votes of both Houses shall be determined by yeas and Nays, and the Names of the Persons voting for and against the Bill shall be entered on the Journal of each House respectively. If any Bill shall not be returned by the President within ten Days (Sundays excepted) after it shall have been presented to him, the Same shall be a Law, in like Manner as if he had signed it, unless the Congress by their Adjournment prevent its Return, in which Case it shall not be a Law.

Every Order, Resolution, or Vote to which the Concurrence of the Senate and House of Representatives may be necessary (except on a question of Adjournment) shall be presented to the President of the United States; and before the Same shall take Effect, shall be approved by him, or being disapproved by him, shall be repassed by two thirds of the Senate and House of Representatives, according to the Rules and Limitations prescribed in the Case of a Bill.

Section 8

The Congress shall have Power

To lay and collect Taxes, Duties, Imposts and Excises, to pay the Debts and provide for the common Defence and general Welfare of the United States; but all Duties, Imposts and Excises shall be uniform throughout the United States;

To borrow Money on the credit of the United States;

To regulate Commerce with foreign Nations, and among the several States, and with the Indian Tribes;

To establish an uniform Rule of Naturalization, and uniform Laws on the subject of Bankruptcies throughout the United States;

To coin Money, regulate the Value thereof, and of foreign Coin, and fix the Standard of Weights and Measures;

To provide for the Punishment of counterfeiting the Securities and current Coin of the United States;

To establish Post Offices and post Roads;

To promote the Progress of Science and useful Arts, by securing for limited Times to Authors and Inventors the exclusive Right to their respective Writings and Discoveries;

To constitute Tribunals inferior to the supreme Court;

To define and punish Piracies and Felonies committed on the high Seas, and Offences against the Law of Nations;

To declare War, grant Letters of Marque and Reprisal, and make Rules concerning Captures on Land and Water;

To raise and support Armies, but no Appropriation of Money to that Use shall be for a longer Term than two Years;

To provide and maintain a Navy;

To make Rules for the Government and Regulation of the land and naval Forces;

To provide for calling forth the Militia to execute the Laws of the Union, suppress Insurrections and repel Invasions;

To provide for organizing, arming, and disciplining the Militia, and for governing such Part of them as may be employed in the Service of the United States, reserving to the States respectively, the Appointment of the Officers, and the Authority of training the Militia according to the discipline prescribed by Congress;

To exercise exclusive Legislation in all Cases whatsoever, over such District (not exceeding ten Miles square) as may, by Cession of particular States, and the Acceptance of Congress, become the Seat of the Government of the United States, and to exercise like Authority over all Places purchased by the Consent of the Legislature of the State in which the Same shall be, for the Erection of Forts, Magazines, Arsenals, dock-Yards, and other needful Buildings;—And

To make all Laws which shall be necessary and proper for carrying into Execution the foregoing Powers, and all other Powers vested by this Constitution in the Government of the United States, or in any Department or Officer thereof.

Section 9

The Migration or Importation of such Persons as any of the States now existing shall think proper to admit, shall not be prohibited by the Congress prior to the Year one thousand eight hundred and eight, but a Tax or duty may be imposed on such Importation, not exceeding ten dollars for each Person.

The Privilege of the Writ of Habeas Corpus shall not be suspended, unless when in Cases of Rebellion or Invasion the public Safety may require it.

No Bill of Attainder or ex post facto Law shall be passed.

[No Capitation, or other direct, Tax shall be laid, unless in Proportion to the Census or enumeration herein before directed to be taken.][6]

No Tax or Duty shall be laid on Articles exported from any State.

No Preference shall be given by any Regulation of Commerce or Revenue to the Ports of one State over those of another; nor shall Vessels bound to, or from, one State, be obliged to enter, clear, or pay Duties in another.

No Money shall be drawn from the Treasury, but in Consequence of Appropriations made by Law; and a regular Statement and Account of the Receipts and Expenditures of all public Money shall be published from time to time.

No Title of Nobility shall be granted by the United States: And no Person holding any Office of Profit or Trust under them, shall, without the Consent of the Congress, accept of any present, Emolument, Office, or Title, of any kind whatever, from any King, Prince, or foreign State.

Section 10

No State shall enter into any Treaty, Alliance, or Confederation; grant Letters of Marque and Reprisal; coin Money; emit Bills of Credit; make any Thing but gold and silver Coin a Tender in Payment of Debts; pass any Bill of Attainder, ex post facto Law, or Law impairing the Obligation of Contracts, or grant any Title of Nobility.

[6] Modified by the Sixteenth Amendment.

No State shall, without the Consent of the Congress, lay any Imposts or Duties on Imports or Exports, except what may be absolutely necessary for executing it's inspection Laws: and the net Produce of all Duties and Imposts, laid by any State on Imports or Exports, shall be for the Use of the Treasury of the United States; and all such Laws shall be subject to the Revision and Control of the Congress.

No State shall, without the Consent of Congress, lay any Duty of Tonnage, keep Troops, or Ships of War in time of Peace, enter into any Agreement or Compact with another State, or with a foreign Power, or engage in War, unless actually invaded, or in such imminent Danger as will not admit of delay.

Article II

Section 1

The executive Power shall be vested in a President of the United States of America. He shall hold his Office during the Term of four Years, and, together with the Vice President, chosen for the same Term, be elected, as follows:

Each State shall appoint, in such Manner as the Legislature thereof may direct, a Number of Electors, equal to the whole Number of Senators and Representatives to which the State may be entitled in the Congress: but no Senator or Representative, or Person holding an Office of Trust or Profit under the United States, shall be appointed an Elector.

[The Electors shall meet in their respective States, and vote by Ballot for two Persons, of whom one at least shall not be an Inhabitant of the same State with themselves. And they shall make a List of all the Persons voted for, and of the Number of Votes for each; which List they shall sign and certify, and transmit sealed to the Seat of the Government of the United States, directed to the President of the Senate. The President of the Senate shall, in the Presence of the Senate and House of Representatives, open all the Certificates, and the Votes shall then be counted. The Person having the greatest Number of Votes shall be the President, if such Number be a Majority of the whole Number of Electors appointed; and if there be more than one who have such Majority, and have an equal Number of Votes, then the House of Representatives shall immediately choose by Ballot one of them for President; and if no Person have a Majority, then from the five highest on the List the said House shall in like Manner choose the President. But in choosing the President, the Votes shall be taken by States, the Representation from each State having one Vote; A quorum for this purpose shall consist of a Member or Members from two thirds of the States, and a Majority of all the States shall be necessary to a Choice. In every Case, after the Choice of the President, the Person having the greatest Number of Votes of the Electors shall be the Vice President. But if there should remain two or more who have equal Votes, the Senate shall choose from them by Ballot the Vice President.][7]

---

[7] Changed by the Twelfth and Twentieth Amendments.

The Congress may determine the Time of choosing the Electors, and the Day on which they shall give their Votes; which Day shall be the same throughout the United States.

No Person except a natural born Citizen, or a Citizen of the United States, at the time of the Adoption of this Constitution, shall be eligible to the Office of President; neither shall any Person be eligible to that Office who shall not have attained to the Age of thirty five Years, and been fourteen Years a Resident within the United States.

In Case of the Removal of the President from Office, or of his Death, Resignation, or Inability to discharge the Powers and Duties of the said Office, the Same shall devolve on the Vice President, and the Congress may by Law provide for the Case of Removal, Death, Resignation or Inability, both of the President and Vice President, declaring what Officer shall then act as President, and such Officer shall act accordingly, until the Disability be removed, or a President shall be elected.

The President shall, at stated Times, receive for his Services, a Compensation, which shall neither be increased nor diminished during the Period for which he shall have been elected, and he shall not receive within that Period any other Emolument from the United States, or any of them.

Before he enter on the Execution of his Office, he shall take the following Oath or Affirmation:—"I do solemnly swear (or affirm) that I will faithfully execute the Office of President of the United States, and will to the best of my Ability, preserve, protect and defend the Constitution of the United States."

Section 2

The President shall be Commander in Chief of the Army and Navy of the United States, and of the Militia of the several States, when called into the actual Service of the United States; he may require the Opinion, in writing, of the principal Officer in each of the executive Departments, upon any Subject relating to the Duties of their respective Offices, and he shall have Power to grant Reprieves and Pardons for Offences against the United States, except in Cases of Impeachment.

He shall have Power, by and with the Advice and Consent of the Senate, to make Treaties, provided two thirds of the Senators present concur; and he shall nominate, and by and with the Advice and Consent of the Senate, shall appoint Ambassadors, other public Ministers and Consuls, Judges of the supreme Court, and all other Officers of the United States, whose Appointments are not herein otherwise provided for, and which shall be established by Law: but the Congress may by Law vest the Appointment of such inferior Officers, as they think proper, in the President alone, in the Courts of Law, or in the Heads of Departments.

The President shall have Power to fill up all Vacancies that may happen during the Recess of the Senate, by granting Commissions which shall expire at the End of their next Session.

Section 3

He shall from time to time give to the Congress Information of the State of the Union, and recommend to their Consideration such Measures as he shall judge necessary and expedient; he may, on extraordinary Occasions, convene both Houses, or either of them, and in Case of Disagreement between them, with Respect to the Time of Adjournment, he may adjourn them to such Time as he shall think proper; he shall receive Ambassadors and other public Ministers; he shall take Care that the Laws be faithfully executed, and shall Commission all the Officers of the United States.

Section 4

The President, Vice President and all civil Officers of the United States, shall be removed from Office on Impeachment for, and Conviction of, Treason, Bribery, or other high Crimes and Misdemeanors.

Article III

Section 1

The judicial Power of the United States shall be vested in one supreme Court, and in such inferior Courts as the Congress may from time to time ordain and establish. The Judges, both of the supreme and inferior Courts, shall hold their Offices during good Behaviour, and shall, at stated Times, receive for their Services a Compensation, which shall not be diminished during their Continuance in Office.

Section 2

The judicial Power shall extend to all Cases, in Law and Equity, arising under this Constitution, the Laws of the United States, and Treaties made, or which shall be made, under their Authority;—to all Cases affecting Ambassadors, other public Ministers and Consuls;—to all Cases of admiralty and maritime Jurisdiction;—to Controversies to which the United States shall be a Party;—to Controversies between two or more States;[—between a State and Citizens of another State;—][8]

between Citizens of different States;—between Citizens of the same State claiming Lands under Grants of different States, [and between a State,][9] or the Citizens thereof[, and foreign States, Citizens or Subjects].[10]

In all Cases affecting Ambassadors, other public Ministers and Consuls, and those in which a State shall be Party, the supreme Court shall have original Jurisdiction. In all the other Cases before mentioned, the supreme Court shall have appellate Jurisdiction, both as to Law and Fact, with such Exceptions, and under such Regulations as the Congress shall make.

The Trial of all Crimes, except in Cases of Impeachment, shall be by Jury; and such Trial shall be held in the State where the said Crimes shall have been committed; but when not committed within any State, the Trial shall be at such Place or Places as the Congress may by Law have directed.

[8] Altered by the Twelfth Amendment.
[9] Altered by the Twelfth Amendment.
[10] Altered by the Twelfth Amendment.

Section 3

Treason against the United States, shall consist only in levying War against them, or in adhering to their Enemies, giving them Aid and Comfort. No Person shall be convicted of Treason unless on the Testimony of two Witnesses to the same overt Act, or on Confession in open Court.

The Congress shall have Power to declare the Punishment of Treason, but no Attainder of Treason shall work Corruption of Blood, or Forfeiture except during the Life of the Person attainted.

Article IV

Section 1

Full Faith and Credit shall be given in each State to the public Acts, Records, and judicial Proceedings of every other State. And the Congress may by general Laws prescribe the Manner in which such Acts, Records and Proceedings shall be proved, and the Effect thereof.

Section 2

The Citizens of each State shall be entitled to all Privileges and Immunities of Citizens in the several States.

A Person charged in any State with Treason, Felony, or other Crime, who shall flee from Justice, and be found in another State, shall on Demand of the executive Authority of the State from which he fled, be delivered up, to be removed to the State having Jurisdiction of the Crime.

[No Person held to Service or Labour in one State, under the Laws thereof, escaping into another, shall, in Consequence of any Law or Regulation therein, be discharged from such Service or Labour, but shall be delivered up on Claim of the Party to whom such Service or Labour may be due.][11]

Section 3

New States may be admitted by the Congress into this Union; but no new State shall be formed or erected within the Jurisdiction of any other State; nor any State be formed by the Junction of two or more States, or Parts of States, without the Consent of the Legislatures of the States concerned as well as of the Congress.

The Congress shall have Power to dispose of and make all needful Rules and Regulations respecting the Territory or other Property belonging to the United States; and nothing in this Constitution shall be so construed as to Prejudice any Claims of the United States, or of any particular State.

Section 4

The United States shall guarantee to every State in this Union a Republican Form of Government, and shall protect each of them against Invasion; and on Application of the Legislature, or of the Executive (when the Legislature cannot be convened), against domestic Violence.

---

[11] Repealed by the Thirteenth Amendment.

Article V

The Congress, whenever two thirds of both Houses shall deem it necessary, shall propose Amendments to this Constitution, or, on the Application of the Legislatures of two thirds of the several States, shall call a Convention for proposing Amendments, which, in either Case, shall be valid to all Intents and Purposes, as Part of this Constitution, when ratified by the Legislatures of three fourths of the several States, or by Conventions in three fourths thereof, as the one or the other Mode of Ratification may be proposed by the Congress; Provided that no Amendment which may be made prior to the Year One thousand eight hundred and eight shall in any Manner affect the first and fourth Clauses in the Ninth Section of the first Article; and that no State, without its Consent, shall be deprived of its equal Suffrage in the Senate.

Article VI

All Debts contracted and Engagements entered into, before the Adoption of this Constitution, shall be as valid against the United States under this Constitution, as under the Confederation.

This Constitution, and the Laws of the United States which shall be made in Pursuance thereof; and all Treaties made, or which shall be made, under the Authority of the United States, shall be the supreme Law of the Land; and the Judges in every State shall be bound thereby, any Thing in the Constitution or Laws of any State to the Contrary notwithstanding.

The Senators and Representatives before mentioned, and the Members of the several State Legislatures, and all executive and judicial Officers, both of the United States and of the several States, shall be bound by Oath or Affirmation, to support this Constitution; but no religious Test shall ever be required as a Qualification to any Office or public Trust under the United States.

Article VII

The Ratification of the Conventions of nine States, shall be sufficient for the Establishment of this Constitution between the States so ratifying the Same.

The Word, "the," being interlined between the seventh and eighth Lines of the first Page, the Word "Thirty" being partly written on an Erazure in the fifteenth Line of the first Page, The Words "is tried" being interlined between the thirty second and thirty third Lines of the first Page and the Word "the" being interlined between the forty third and forty fourth Lines of the second Page.

Attest William Jackson Secretary

Done in Convention by the Unanimous Consent of the States present the Seventeenth Day of September in the Year of our Lord one thousand seven hundred and Eighty seven and of the Independence of the United States of America the Twelfth In witness whereof We have hereunto subscribed our Names,

G°. WASHINGTON
Presidt and deputy from Virginia

Delaware
Geo: Read
Gunning Bedford jun
John Dickinson
Richard Bassett
Jaco: Broom

Maryland
James McHenry
Dan of St Thos. Jenifer
Danl. Carroll

Virginia
John Blair
James Madison Jr.

North Carolina
Wm. Blount
Richd. Dobbs Spaight
Hu Williamson

South Carolina
J. Rutledge
Charles Cotesworth
  Pinckney
Charles Pinckney
Pierce Butler
Georgia
William Few
Abr Baldwin
New Hampshire
John Langdon
Nicholas Gilman

Massachusetts
Nathaniel Gorham
Rufus King

Connecticut
Wm. Saml. Johnson
Roger Sherman

New York
Alexander Hamilton

New Jersey
Wil: Livingston
David Brearley
Wm. Paterson
Jona: Dayton

Pennsylvania
B Franklin
Thomas Mifflin
Robt. Morris
Geo. Clymer
Thos. FitzSimons
Jared Ingersoll
James Wilson
Gouv Morris

[B] Articles

In addition to, and Amendment of the Constitution of the United States of America, proposed by Congress, and ratified by the Legislatures of the several States, pursuant to the fifth Article of the original Constitution.

(The first ten amendments to the U.S. Constitution were ratified December 15, 1791, and form what is known as the "Bill of Rights.")

Amendment I

Congress shall make no law respecting an establishment of religion, or prohibiting the free exercise thereof; or abridging the freedom of speech, or of the press; or the right of the people peaceably to assemble, and to petition the Government for a redress of grievances.

Amendment II

A well regulated Militia, being necessary to the security of a free State, the right of the people to keep and bear Arms, shall not be infringed.

Amendment III

No Soldier shall, in time of peace be quartered in any house, without the consent of the Owner, nor in time of war, but in a manner to be prescribed by law.

Amendment IV

The right of the people to be secure in their persons, houses, papers, and effects, against unreasonable searches and seizures, shall not be violated, and no Warrants shall issue, but upon probable cause, supported by Oath or affirmation, and particularly describing the place to be searched, and the persons or things to be seized.

Amendment V

No person shall be held to answer for a capital, or otherwise infamous crime, unless on a presentment or indictment of a Grand Jury, except in cases arising in the land or naval forces, or in the Militia, when in actual service in time of War or public danger; nor shall any person be subject for the same offence to be twice put in jeopardy of life or limb; nor shall be compelled in any criminal case to be a witness against himself, nor be deprived of life, liberty, or property, without due process of law; nor shall private property be taken for public use, without just compensation.

Amendment VI

In all criminal prosecutions, the accused shall enjoy the right to a speedy and public trial, by an impartial jury of the State and district wherein the crime shall have been committed, which district shall have been previously ascertained by law, and to be informed of the nature and cause of the accusation; to be confronted with the witnesses against him; to have compulsory process for obtaining witnesses in his favor, and to have the Assistance of Counsel for his defence.

Amendment VII

In Suits at common law, where the value in controversy shall exceed twenty dollars, the right of trial by jury shall be preserved, and no fact tried by a jury, shall be otherwise re-examined in any Court of the United States, than according to the rules of the common law.

Amendment VIII

Excessive bail shall not be required, nor excessive fines imposed, nor cruel and unusual punishments inflicted.

Amendment IX

The enumeration in the Constitution, of certain rights, shall not be construed to deny or disparage others retained by the people.

Amendment X

The powers not delegated to the United States by the Constitution, nor prohibited by it to the States, are reserved to the States respectively, or to the people.

Amendment XI

Passed by Congress March 4, 1794. Ratified February 7, 1795.

Note: Article III, Section 2, of the Constitution was modified by Amendment XI.

The Judicial power of the United States shall not be construed to extend to any suit in law or equity, commenced or prosecuted against one of the United States by Citizens of another State, or by Citizens or Subjects of any Foreign State.

Amendment XII

Passed by Congress December 9, 1803. Ratified June 15, 1804.

Note: A portion of Article II, Section 1, of the Constitution was superseded by the Twelfth Amendment.

The Electors shall meet in their respective states and vote by ballot for President and Vice-President, one of whom, at least, shall not be an inhabitant of the same state with themselves; they shall name in their ballots the person voted for as President, and in distinct ballots the person voted for as Vice-President, and they shall make distinct lists of all persons voted for as President, and of all persons voted for as Vice-President, and of the number of votes for each, which lists they shall sign and certify, and transmit sealed to the seat of the government of the United States, directed to the President of the Senate;—the President of the Senate shall, in the presence of the Senate and House of Representatives, open all the certificates and the votes shall then be counted;—The person having the greatest number of votes for President, shall be the President, if such number be a majority of the whole number of Electors appointed; and if no person have such majority, then from the persons having the highest numbers not exceeding three on the list of those voted for as President, the House of Representatives shall choose immediately, by ballot, the President. But in choosing the President, the votes shall be taken by states, the representation from each state having one vote; a quorum for this purpose shall consist of a member or members from two-thirds of the states, and a majority of all the states shall be necessary to a choice. [And if the House of Representatives shall not choose a President whenever the right of choice shall devolve upon them, before the fourth day of March next following, then the Vice-President shall act as President, as in case of the death or other constitutional disability of the President.—][12] The person having the greatest number of votes as Vice-President, shall be the Vice-President, if such number be a majority of the whole number of Electors appointed, and if no person have a

---

[12] Superseded by Section 3 of the Twentieth Amendment.

majority, then from the two highest numbers on the list, the Senate shall choose the Vice-President; a quorum for the purpose shall consist of two-thirds of the whole number of Senators, and a majority of the whole number shall be necessary to a choice. But no person constitutionally ineligible to the office of President shall be eligible to that of Vice-President of the United States.

Amendment XIII

Passed by Congress January 31, 1865. Ratified December 6, 1865.

Note: A portion of Article IV, Section 2, of the Constitution was superseded by the Thirteenth Amendment.

Section 1

Neither slavery nor involuntary servitude, except as a punishment for crime whereof the party shall have been duly convicted, shall exist within the United States, or any place subject to their jurisdiction.

Section 2

Congress shall have power to enforce this article by appropriate legislation.

Amendment XIV

Passed by Congress June 13, 1866. Ratified July 9, 1868.

Note: Article I, Section 2, of the Constitution was modified by Section 2 of the Fourteenth Amendment.

Section 1

All persons born or naturalized in the United States, and subject to the jurisdiction thereof, are citizens of the United States and of the State wherein they reside. No State shall make or enforce any law which shall abridge the privileges or immunities of citizens of the United States; nor shall any State deprive any person of life, liberty, or property, without due process of law; nor deny to any person within its jurisdiction the equal protection of the laws.

Section 2

Representatives shall be apportioned among the several States according to their respective numbers, counting the whole number of persons in each State, excluding Indians not taxed. But when the right to vote at any election for the choice of electors for President and Vice-President of the United States, Representatives in Congress, the Executive and Judicial officers of a State, or the members of the Legislature thereof, is denied to any of the male inhabitants of such State, being twenty-one years of age,[13] and citizens of the United States, or in any way abridged, except for participation in rebellion, or other crime, the basis of representation therein shall be reduced in the proportion which the number of

---

[13] Changed by Section 1 of the Twenty-Sixth Amendment.

such male citizens shall bear to the whole number of male citizens twenty-one years of age in such State.

Section 3

No person shall be a Senator or Representative in Congress, or elector of President and Vice-President, or hold any office, civil or military, under the United States, or under any State, who, having previously taken an oath, as a member of Congress, or as an officer of the United States, or as a member of any State legislature, or as an executive or judicial officer of any State, to support the Constitution of the United States, shall have engaged in insurrection or rebellion against the same, or given aid or comfort to the enemies thereof. But Congress may by a vote of two-thirds of each House, remove such disability.

Section 4

The validity of the public debt of the United States, authorized by law, including debts incurred for payment of pensions and bounties for services in suppressing insurrection or rebellion, shall not be questioned. But neither the United States nor any State shall assume or pay any debt or obligation incurred in aid of insurrection or rebellion against the United States, or any claim for the loss or emancipation of any slave; but all such debts, obligations and claims shall be held illegal and void.

Section 5

The Congress shall have the power to enforce, by appropriate legislation, the provisions of this article.

*Changed by Section 1 of the Twenty-Sixth Amendment.

Amendment XV

Passed by Congress February 26, 1869. Ratified February 3, 1870.

Section 1

The right of citizens of the United States to vote shall not be denied or abridged by the United States or by any State on account of race, color, or previous condition of servitude.

Section 2

The Congress shall have the power to enforce this article by appropriate legislation.

Amendment XVI

Passed by Congress July 2, 1909. Ratified February 3, 1913.

Note: Article I, Section 9, of the Constitution was modified by Amendment XVI.

The Congress shall have power to lay and collect taxes on incomes, from whatever source derived, without apportionment among the several States, and without regard to any census or enumeration.

Amendment XVII

Passed by Congress May 13, 1912. Ratified April 8, 1913.

Note: Article I, Section 3, of the Constitution was modified by the Seventeenth Amendment.

The Senate of the United States shall be composed of two Senators from each State, elected by the people thereof, for six years; and each Senator shall have one vote. The electors in each State shall have the qualifications requisite for electors of the most numerous branch of the State legislatures.

When vacancies happen in the representation of any State in the Senate, the executive authority of such State shall issue writs of election to fill such vacancies: Provided, That the legislature of any State may empower the executive thereof to make temporary appointments until the people fill the vacancies by election as the legislature may direct.

This amendment shall not be so construed as to affect the election or term of any Senator chosen before it becomes valid as part of the Constitution.

Amendment XVIII

Passed by Congress December 18, 1917. Ratified January 16, 1919. Repealed by Amendment XXI.

Section 1

After one year from the ratification of this article the manufacture, sale, or transportation of intoxicating liquors within, the importation thereof into, or the exportation thereof from the United States and all territory subject to the jurisdiction thereof for beverage purposes is hereby prohibited.

Section 2

The Congress and the several States shall have concurrent power to enforce this article by appropriate legislation.

Section 3

This article shall be inoperative unless it shall have been ratified as an amendment to the Constitution by the legislatures of the several States, as provided in the Constitution, within seven years from the date of the submission hereof to the States by the Congress.

Amendment XIX

Passed by Congress June 4, 1919. Ratified August 18, 1920.

The right of citizens of the United States to vote shall not be denied or abridged by the United States or by any State on account of sex.

Congress shall have power to enforce this article by appropriate legislation.

Amendment XX

Passed by Congress March 2, 1932. Ratified January 23, 1933.

Note: Article I, Section 4, of the Constitution was modified by Section 2 of this amendment. In addition, a portion of the Twelfth Amendment was superseded by Section 3.

Section 1

The terms of the President and the Vice President shall end at noon on the 20th day of January, and the terms of Senators and Representatives at noon on the 3d day of January, of the years in which such terms would have ended if this article had not been ratified; and the terms of their successors shall then begin.

Section 2

The Congress shall assemble at least once in every year, and such meeting shall begin at noon on the 3d day of January, unless they shall by law appoint a different day.

Section 3

If, at the time fixed for the beginning of the term of the President, the President elect shall have died, the Vice President elect shall become President. If a President shall not have been chosen before the time fixed for the beginning of his term, or if the President elect shall have failed to qualify, then the Vice President elect shall act as President until a President shall have qualified; and the Congress may by law provide for the case wherein neither a President elect nor a Vice President shall have qualified, declaring who shall then act as President, or the manner in which one who is to act shall be selected, and such person shall act accordingly until a President or Vice President shall have qualified.

Section 4

The Congress may by law provide for the case of the death of any of the persons from whom the House of Representatives may choose a President whenever the right of choice shall have devolved upon them, and for the case of the death of any of the persons from whom the Senate may choose a Vice President whenever the right of choice shall have devolved upon them.

Section 5

Sections 1 and 2 shall take effect on the 15th day of October following the ratification of this article.

Section 6

This article shall be inoperative unless it shall have been ratified as an amendment to the Constitution by the legislatures of three-fourths of the several States within seven years from the date of its submission.

Amendment XXI

Passed by Congress February 20, 1933. Ratified December 5, 1933.

Section 1

The eighteenth article of amendment to the Constitution of the United States is hereby repealed.

Section 2

The transportation or importation into any State, Territory, or Possession of the United States for delivery or use therein of intoxicating liquors, in violation of the laws thereof, is hereby prohibited.

Section 3

This article shall be inoperative unless it shall have been ratified as an amendment to the Constitution by conventions in the several States, as provided in the Constitution, within seven years from the date of the submission hereof to the States by the Congress.

Amendment XXII

Passed by Congress March 21, 1947. Ratified February 27, 1951.

Section 1

No person shall be elected to the office of the President more than twice, and no person who has held the office of President, or acted as President, for more than two years of a term to which some other person was elected President shall be elected to the office of President more than once. But this Article shall not apply to any person holding the office of President when this Article was proposed by Congress, and shall not prevent any person who may be holding the office of President, or acting as President, during the term within which this Article becomes operative from holding the office of President or acting as President during the remainder of such term.

Section 2

This article shall be inoperative unless it shall have been ratified as an amendment to the Constitution by the legislatures of three-fourths of the several States within seven years from the date of its submission to the States by the Congress.

Amendment XXIII

Passed by Congress June 16, 1960. Ratified March 29, 1961.

Section 1

The District constituting the seat of Government of the United States shall appoint in such manner as Congress may direct:

A number of electors of President and Vice President equal to the whole number of Senators and Representatives in Congress to which the District would be entitled if it were a State, but in no event more than the least populous State; they shall be in addition to those appointed by the States, but they shall be considered, for the purposes of the election of President and Vice President, to be electors appointed by a State; and they shall meet in the District and perform such duties as provided by the twelfth article of amendment.

Section 2

The Congress shall have power to enforce this article by appropriate legislation.

Amendment XXIV

Passed by Congress August 27, 1962. Ratified January 23, 1964.

Section 1

The right of citizens of the United States to vote in any primary or other election for President or Vice President, for electors for President or Vice President, or for Senator or Representative in Congress, shall not be denied or abridged by the United States or any State by reason of failure to pay poll tax or other tax.

Section 2

The Congress shall have power to enforce this article by appropriate legislation.

Amendment XXV

Passed by Congress July 6, 1965. Ratified February 10, 1967.

Note: Article II, Section 1, of the Constitution was affected by the Twenty-Fifth Amendment.

Section 1

In case of the removal of the President from office or of his death or resignation, the Vice President shall become President.

Section 2

Whenever there is a vacancy in the office of the Vice President, the President shall nominate a Vice President who shall take office upon confirmation by a majority vote of both Houses of Congress.

Section 3

Whenever the President transmits to the President pro tempore of the Senate and the Speaker of the House of Representatives his written declaration that he is unable to discharge the powers and duties of his office, and until he transmits to them a written declaration to the contrary, such powers and duties shall be discharged by the Vice President as Acting President.

Section 4

Whenever the Vice President and a majority of either the principal officers of the executive departments or of such other body as Congress may by law provide, transmit to the President pro tempore of the Senate and the Speaker of the House of Representatives their written declaration that the President is unable to discharge the powers and duties of his office, the Vice President shall immediately assume the powers and duties of the office as Acting President.

Thereafter, when the President transmits to the President pro tempore of the Senate and the Speaker of the House of Representatives his written declaration that no inability exists, he shall resume the powers and duties of his office unless the Vice President and a majority of either the principal officers of the executive department or of such other body as Congress may by law provide, transmit within four days to the President pro tempore of the Senate and the Speaker of the House of Representatives their written declaration that the President is unable to discharge the powers and duties of his office. Thereupon Congress shall decide the issue, assembling within forty-eight hours for that purpose if not in session. If the Congress, within twenty-one days after receipt of the latter written declaration, or, if Congress is not in session, within twenty-one days after Congress is required to assemble, determines by two-thirds vote of both Houses that the President is unable to discharge the powers and duties of his office, the Vice President shall continue to discharge the same as Acting President; otherwise, the President shall resume the powers and duties of his office.

Amendment XXVI

Passed by Congress March 23, 1971. Ratified July 1, 1971.

Note: Amendment XIV, Section 2, of the Constitution was modified by Section 1 of the Twenty-Sixth Amendment.

Section 1

The right of citizens of the United States, who are eighteen years of age or older, to vote shall not be denied or abridged by the United States or by any State on account of age.

Section 2

The Congress shall have power to enforce this article by appropriate legislation.

Amendment XXVII

Originally proposed Sept. 25, 1789. Ratified May 7, 1992.

No law, varying the compensation for the services of the Senators and Representatives, shall take effect, until an election of representatives shall have intervened.

Glossary

Abolitionists Nineteenth-century political activists who sought to end slavery.

Administrative Adjudication The quasi-judicial process by which a bureaucratic agency resolves a dispute between the agency and a private citizen.

Administrative Law A type of law pertaining to the rules made by bureaucrats and administrative agencies.

Administrative Procedures Act A federal law that requires administrative agencies to publish proposed rules and allow the public to offer comment on them before they go into effect.

Affirmative Action Corrective policies that attempt to help racial and ethnic minorities (as well as women) achieve equality in education and the workforce by providing them with advantages in college admission, hiring, promotion, and the awarding of contracts.

Agenda Setting The stage in the policymaking process in which certain issues reach a level of public concern that attracts the attention of government officials; also the media's power to influence the importance that the public places on issues.

Agenda Universe All possible legitimate issues that could be brought to the attention of the public and possibly of policymakers.

Air War The part of election campaigns conducted through broadcast media including radio, television, and the Internet.

***Amicus Curiae* (Friend of the Court) Briefs** Briefs filed by parties that have an interest in the outcome of a case but are not directly involved in it.

Antifederalists Opponents of the Constitution during the ratification process.

Appellate Jurisdiction The types of cases in which the Supreme Court reviews legal issues decided by a lower court.

Bicameral Legislature A legislature with two bodies, usually referred to as the upper and lower chambers, or, as is most common in the United States, the House and the Senate.

Bill of Attainder A law passed by a legislative body that punishes specific people without convicting them in a court.

Bill of Rights The first ten amendments to the Constitution, which focus primarily on individual liberties and basic rights.

Bipartisan Campaign Reform Act (BCRA) A campaign finance reform law passed in 2002 that amended the Federal Election Campaign Act of 1971 and strengthened the limits, regulations, and reporting of campaign contributions (also known as the McCain–Feingold Act).

Black and Tan Republicans A wing of the Republican Party that supported civil rights for African Americans.

Black Codes Laws passed in Southern states during the immediate aftermath of the Civil War that singled out African Americans for mistreatment and discrimination.

Block Grants Grants-in-aid from the national government that are general, contain minimal regulations, and give state and local governments considerable discretion on how the money should be used.

Bradley Effect The difference between how Black candidates poll and how they perform at the ballot box (also called the Wilder effect).

Brown v. Board of Education A landmark 1954 Supreme Court case that prohibited government-sponsored segregation as a violation of the Fourteenth Amendment equal protection clause.

Bureaucracy A large, complex organization in which employees work within specific levels of rank and authority to carry out the policies of that organization.

Bureaucrats The employees who work in a bureaucracy.

Cabinet The key presidential aides, each of whom heads an executive branch department, as well as others that the president designates.

Cabinet Departments The major divisions within the executive branch, with each performing a specific function.

Casework Favors and other forms of assistance that members of Congress provide to their constituents.

Catalyst An event that energizes and coalesces a social movement.

Catalytic Leadership Social activists who create or recognize opportunities to galvanize people to organized action.

Categorical Grants Grants-in-aid that contain numerous, detailed provisions on how the states and local governments use the money.

Caucus A method for political parties to select their candidates for office whereby party members convene at local meetings.

Caucuses Informal organizations within Congress.

Central Clearance A requirement that all agency budget requests receive approval from the Office of Management and Budget before the president submits them to Congress.

Chief of Staff A key assistant to the president who coordinates executive branch employees and serves as a link between other presidential advisers and the president.

Civic Virtue The subordination of individualism and individual self-interest to the interest of society.

Civil Law A type of law that pertains to a dispute between two parties, at least one of which is a nongovernmental private party.

Civil Liberties The constitutional freedoms that Americans enjoy and on which the government may not encroach.

Civil Rights The protections against unequal treatment that the government guarantees to all groups.

Civil Rights Act of 1964 A federal law that prevents private businesses from discriminating in service and personnel policies.

Civil Servants Federal bureaucrats who are not political appointees, but instead are hired according to their education and performance on an examination.

Civil Unions Government policies that provided official legal recognition of same-sex couples without sanctioning marriage.

Classical Liberalism A body of Western European political philosophy that is concerned with the freedom of the individual and the role of government in protecting that freedom.

Classical Republicanism A theory that rule by the people ought to be indirect through representatives.

Clear and Present Danger Test A guideline that requires the government to demonstrate that banned expression poses a definite and immediate threat to peace or national security.

Closed Primary A primary in which only registered members of a particular political party can vote in that party's primary election to choose the party's candidate or delegate.

Cloture Vote A procedure in the Senate to stop a filibuster that usually requires three-fifths of the senators (sixty) agreeing to end debate.

Collective Good Any benefit that if available to one member of the community cannot be denied to any other, regardless of whether he or she bore any of the costs of providing it.

Commerce Clause A constitutional provision that gives the national government the authority to regulate commerce among the states, foreign nations, and Indian tribes; it has been used to expand the power of the national government.

Comptroller General The head of the Government Accountability Office.

Concurrent Powers Powers shared by the national government and state governments, such as the power to tax and borrow money.

Concurring Opinion An opinion that agrees with the outcome of a Supreme Court case but for reasons different from those expressed in the majority opinion.

Confederation A system in which states or other types of government units organize a weak central government with limited scope and powers while reserving ultimate power for themselves.

Conference committee A committee composed of members of the House and the Senate that reconciles different versions of the same bill.

Congressional Black Caucus An informal organization consisting of African Americans elected to the United States Congress.

Congressional Record The published record of the official proceedings of Congress.

Congressional War Powers The power granted by the Constitution (in Article 1, Section 8) to Congress to decide when the United States goes to war.

Conservative Individual who believes that government should play a limited role in peoples' lives and that government is not the source of solutions for problems.

Constituency The people who choose a representative to act on their behalf.

Constitution A set of formal written rules and principles governing a state.

Constitutional Democracy A government that derives its authority from a constitution.

Constitutional Law A type of law pertaining to the rules for our government expressed in the Constitution.

Cooperative Federalism A view of federalism in which the national government expands its power and blurs the lines between national and state authority.

County Commissions Representative bodies that make policies that apply to the county.

Coverture A doctrine and system in British common law according to which marriage merged a woman's legal identity with that of her husband.

Criminal Law A type of law that pertains to violations of a code of behavior specified in local, state, and federal statutes.

De Facto Segregation Physical separation of groups that is not legally sanctioned or imposed by the government but instead stems from individual preferences and economic forces.

De Jure Segregation Physical separation of groups that results from laws or official government actions.

Dealignment A period in which voters abandon their ties to the political parties, resulting in a balance of power between Republicans and Democrats.

Debates Important public face-offs between candidates discussing issues in a variety of formats (including traditional question-and-answer sessions as well as town hall forums) and through a variety of media, most important television and more recently the Internet.

Decision Agenda The set of issues that a government body formally resolves to address.

Democracy A system of government in which political power is exercised by the people.

Democratic Party One of the two major political parties, established by Andrew Jackson in the 1820s to champion the interests of commoners.

Democratic-Republicans An early political party that Thomas Jefferson formed to oppose the nationalist policies of John Adams and Alexander Hamilton.

Descriptive Representation The extent to which the characteristics of a representative correspond with the general characteristics of his or her constituency.

Devolution A view of federalism that advocates partially returning power to state and local governments.

Dillon's Rule A principle of local governance in which municipal governments lack independent authority; they can only draw power from their state governments.

Direct Democracy A democracy in which the people are able to participate directly in decision making.

Direct Primaries Elections in which voters select the individual to represent the party in the general election by voting directly for the candidates on the ballot.

Disenfranchisement A government denying a group the right to vote.

Dissenting Opinion An opinion that disagrees with the winning side of a Supreme Court case and explains why.

Divided Government A period in which the president is of one political party and the majority of one or both houses of Congress is of the other party.

Domestic Policy Laws, rules, and programs that directly affect people living in the United States.

Dred Scott v. Sandford A controversial 1857 Supreme Court decision that ruled Congress lacked power to regulate slavery and Blacks had no civil rights.

Dual Federalism A view of federalism in which the national government is limited to a strict interpretation of the powers granted in the Constitution, while states enjoy broad police power to rule within their own territory.

Due Process Clause A specific provision of the Fourteenth Amendment that requires states to use normal judicial and criminal procedures before denying a citizen life, liberty, or property.

Electioneering Working actively on behalf of a political candidate or political party with activities that might include publicly endorsing a candidate, making a campaign contribution, or making phone calls.

Elections The process by which individuals make political choices by voting.

Electoral College The entity that selects the president and vice president, consisting of 538 electors chosen from the fifty states and the District of Columbia.

Emancipation Proclamation, The An executive order issued by president Abraham Lincoln during the Civil War that freed the slaves in the Confederacy.

Eminent Domain A provision in the Fifth Amendment to the Constitution that requires the government to provide compensation when it takes private property for public use.

Enemy Combatants The status given to individuals captured in battle who do not belong to any national military force.

Enumerated Powers Powers of the federal government specifically stated in the Constitution.

Environmental Racism Intentional or unintentional racial discrimination in the enforcement of environmental laws and regulations and in the targeting of racial minority communities for the siting of pollution-producing industries or hazardous waste sites and other related environmentally hazardous entities.

Equal Protection Clause A specific provision of the Fourteenth Amendment that prevents states from passing laws that treat people differently on account of race or ethnicity.

Equal Rights Amendment A proposed, but unratified, constitutional amendment that would have prevented gender discrimination to the same extent that the Fourteenth Amendment prevents racial and ethnic discrimination.

Establishment Clause A provision in the First Amendment to the U.S. Constitution that prevents the government from endorsing religion.

Ethnicity A socially constructed classification of people based on national origin or culture.

Ex Post Facto Law A criminal sanction that applies retroactively and could result in governments charging people for acts committed before they were outlawed.

Exclusionary Rule A judicially created civil liberties protection that prohibits the use of evidence gathered in violation of the Fourth Amendment.

Executive Agreements Agreements between the president and foreign nations that, because they are not treaties, do not need the approval of the Senate.

Executive Office of the President (EOP) A part of the executive branch that is divided into specific offices and contains key advisers who assist the president in managing the executive branch and developing policies.

Executive Orders Directives that the president issues to subordinates in the executive branch and that have the force of law.

Executive Privilege Presidential authority to keep some of the communications among executive branch personnel private and free from Congress, the courts, and the public.

Extradition Clause A provision in the Constitution stipulating that if a person is charged with a crime in one state and flees to another state, then the second state must send the accused criminal back to the first state.

Factionalism Divisions that develop within a movement that may weaken it or cause its demise.

Federal Communications Commission (FCC) An independent regulatory commission that licenses and regulates the content of broadcast radio and television.

Federalism The balance of power between the national government on one side and the state and local governments on the other side.

Federalist Papers, The A collection of the eighty-five articles written by James Madison, Alexander Hamilton, and John Jay in support of the ratification of the Constitution.

Federalist Party An early political party led by John Adams and Alexander Hamilton that supported nationalizing the economy.

Federalists Proponents of the Constitution during the ratification process.

Feudalism A system of landholding involving a network of allegiances and obligations.

Fifteenth Amendment An amendment to the Constitution that prevents states from denying the right to vote on the basis of race or ethnicity.

Fighting Words Derisive, insulting, or offensive words that inflict damage on other people and are therefore not protected by the First Amendment.

Filibuster A parliamentary technique in the Senate that allows senators to delay or block votes by talking endlessly.

Foreign Policy Laws, rules, and programs that affect the relationship between the United States and other nations.

Fourteenth Amendment An amendment to the Constitution that prevents states from denying on the basis of race full citizenship to their residents.

Framing The media's ability to shape how viewers interpret political events and issues.

Franking Privilege The ability of members of Congress to send noncampaign material to their constituents free of charge.

Free Exercise Clause A provision in the First Amendment to the U.S. Constitution that prevents the government from prohibiting people from practicing their religion.

Free Rider A person who profits from the activities of others without participating in those activities.

Fugitive Slave Clause A clause in the Constitution stipulating if slaves escaped from a slave state to a free state the free state must return them to their owners in the slave state.

Full Faith and Credit Clause A constitutional provision requiring states to recognize official documents and records from other states.

Gender Social relations between the sexes and attitudes about how the sexes interact and the roles that society assumes they will play.

Gender Gap The difference between men and women on such crucial issues as partisan identification and voting for certain candidates.

General Elections Elections in which the winner is elected to office and takes office after the end of the term of the current officeholder.

Gerrymandering The practice in which a group, usually a political party, uses redistricting to maximize its chances of winning elections.

Government A social institution that controls the behavior of people; the political and administrative hierarchy of an organized state.

Government Accountability Office (GAO) The part of the legislative branch that is responsible for auditing how bureaucratic agencies spend money appropriated by Congress.

Government Corporations Parts of the federal bureaucracy that charge fees for the services that they provide to the American public.

Grandfather Clause A policy designed to disenfranchise Blacks by exempting Whites, but not Blacks, from literacy tests.

Grants-in-Aid National government expenditures that provide money or property to the states to accomplish a policy goal.

Great Compromise (or **Connecticut Compromise)** Worked out by a committee at the 1787 Constitutional Convention, a compromise that called for membership in the House of Representatives based on population, with states having equal representation in the Senate.

Ground War The part of election campaigns conducted using "pavement-pounding" methods, including candidate public appearances, voter registration and mobilization, fundraising, and public opinion polling, among others.

Hard Money The heavily regulated money that is directly raised by political candidates.

Hatch Act A federal law passed in 1939 and amended in 1993 that restricts federal employees' partisan political activities.

Hate Crime Legislation Laws that enhance criminal penalties for crimes committed out of prejudice toward certain groups.

Hate Speech A form of expression that is hostile toward a particular race, ethnicity, gender, religion, nationality, or sexual orientation.

Help America Vote Act A law passed in 2002 to reform aspects of the voting process that failed in the 2000 presidential election and to increase voter education and turnout.

Home Rule A principle of local governance in which local governments can govern themselves independently of the state governments.

House Majority Leader The second most powerful leader in the House of Representatives; the person who assists the Speaker in passing the majority party's legislative priorities.

House Minority Leader The leader of the minority party in the House of Representatives; the person who articulates the legislative priorities of the minority party and opposes the majority party's priorities but exerts minimal control over the outcome of legislation.

Impeachment The process by which the House of Representatives charges a president, vice president, or federal judge with a high crime or misdemeanor; the Senate can then decide to remove that official from office with a two-thirds vote.

Implementation The day-to-day process by which bureaucrats enforce laws and carry out policies.

Implied Powers Government powers that are inferred from the powers expressly enumerated in the Constitution.

Incorporation The application of the Bill of Rights to state and local governments.

Independent Executive Agencies Parts of the federal bureaucracy with specified functions that are independent from cabinet departments, do not regulate, and do not charge fees for their services.

Independent Regulatory Commissions Government bodies that issue and enforce regulations on specified economic and social interests.

Indirect (or Representative) Democracy A democracy in which people do not participate directly in decision making and instead elect individuals to represent their interests.

Inegalitarianism A tradition of excluding large segments of the American population from participation in the political system despite the language of equality, liberty, and freedom (*see also* Tradition of Exclusion).

Inequality The extent to which one group enjoys more political, social, or economic benefits than another group.

Inequality of Opportunity A form of inequality in which laws or official actions deny specific groups social, political, or economic benefits that are available to other groups.

Inequality of Outcome A form of inequality in which social and demographic forces, not official laws or policies, cause one group to enjoy more political, social, or economic benefits than another group.

Institutional Agenda The set of issues that government officials recognize require their attention.

Interest Group Litigation The practice of interest groups arguing cases before the judiciary as a means of influencing public policy.

Interest Groups Organizations whose members act together to influence public policy to promote their common interests (also known as pressure groups).

Interstate Compact Clause A clause in Article I, Section 10, of the Constitution that requires the approval of Congress when states enter into official agreements with one another.

Iron Triangle A conception of bureaucratic policymaking that is dominated by congressional committees, interest groups, and bureaucratic agencies.

Issue Networks A conception of policymaking as dynamic and not controlled by any particular set of groups or institutions.

Jim Crow Laws The Southern practice of racially segregating all public facilities, such as transportation, schools, libraries, hotels, hospitals, theaters, parks, and cemeteries.

Judicial Activism A conception of judicial review that believes courts should overturn laws or government actions even if there is no clear constitutional directive.

Judicial Restraint A conception of judicial review that believes courts should not overturn laws or government actions unless there is a clear directive in the Constitution.

Judicial Review The power of a court to overturn a law or official government action because it is deemed unconstitutional.

Justiciable The requirement that there must be an actual case or controversy between two parties for the federal judiciary to decide a case.

Latino An ethnic category describing people of Spanish or Portuguese colonial ancestry from the Caribbean, North America, Central America, and South America.

Legislative Veto An act of one or both houses of Congress that overturned an administrative action. The Supreme Court invalidated such acts in 1983.

Libel The publication of written material that damages a person's reputation.

Liberal Individual who believes that government has a role to play in peoples' lives and that government can provide solutions to policy problems.

Lily White Republicans A wing of the Republican Party that opposed civil rights for African Americans.

Line-Item Veto Governors' power to reject specific expenditures and taxes, while allowing the remainder of a bill to stand.

Literacy Tests A form of disenfranchisement in which potential voters need to demonstrate the ability to read as a condition for registering to vote.

Living Constitution A belief that the Constitution should be interpreted to reflect contemporary times.

Lobbying The process by which an individual, a group, or an organization seeks to influence government policymakers.

Logic of Collective Action The view that the costs of large groups collectively organizing are high and the benefits to individual members are relatively low; thus, the appeal to rational members is one of deterrence to organizing collectively.

Logrolling The practice by members of Congress of trading votes or other favors to enhance members' mutual interests.

Lynching The practice of killing people by mob action outside of the formal judicial process. In the United States, lynching was used as an intimidation tactic against Black Americans.

Majority Winning of an election by the candidate who receives at least 51 percent of the vote.

Majority-Minority Districts Legislative districts that contain a population made up of more than 50 percent of a racial or ethnic minority group.

Majority Opinion The opinion reflecting the winning outcome of a Supreme Court case that is signed by at least a plurality of the justices.

Majority Party The political party in the House or the Senate that has more than half of the seats and therefore controls the leadership, rules, and outcome of legislation.

Mandate A president's claim to Congress that his election victory signifies the public's support for his policy preferences.

Mass Media Sources of information, including print, radio, television, and the Internet, that reach a large number of people.

Merit System A system of selecting state judges in which a nonpartisan commission presents the governor with a short list of judicial candidates, out of which the governor selects one name; that judge later appears before the voters in a retention election.

Minor Parties Political parties in a two-party system that are not one of the dominant two political parties.

Minority Party The political party in the House or the Senate that has fewer than half of the seats and therefore does not control the leadership, rules, or outcome of legislation.

Miranda Rights The Supreme Court's requirement that law enforcement must inform criminal suspects of the following: (1) that they have the right to remain silent, (2) that anything they say can be used against them in court, (3) that they have the right to the presence of an attorney, and (4) that if they cannot afford an attorney, then the court will appoint one before the interrogation takes place.

Modern Presidency Since Franklin Roosevelt in 1933, the conception of the presidency, which is characterized by a powerful president who seeks to lead Congress, connects with the American public, and presides over an enormous executive branch.

Monopoly A situation in which one company controls an entire industry.

Mootness An aspect of justiciability that requires that the conflict causing the case must still be germane; it could not have resolved itself on its own.

Municipalities The incorporated districts, usually cities or towns, that comprise the local government.

National Committee The organization responsible for making rules and regulations for a party when the conventions are not in session, raising money for the party, and directing the party's electoral strategy.

National Committee Chair The head of each party's national committee, who is most responsible for directing the party's electoral strategies.

National Government A system of government in which powers are distributed between the central government (federal government) and subunits, such as states.

National Voter Registration Act A law passed in 1993 that provides for voter registration by mail and in departments of motor vehicles (also called the "motor voter" act).

Natural Law Law that comes from nature and is superior to statutory law.

Natural Rights Rights to which every person is entitled, such as life and liberty; rights that are not dependent on government.

Necessary and Proper Clause A clause in Article 1 of the Constitution giving Congress the authority to make whatever laws are necessary and proper to carry out its enumerated responsibilities (sometimes called the elastic clause).

New Deal Coalition The groups that supported president Franklin Roosevelt's policies and as a result made the Democrats the dominant party during the 1930s and 1940s.

New Jersey Plan Drafted by William Paterson of New Jersey at the 1787 Constitutional Convention, a proposal for a system of government that called for the maintenance of a confederation with a unicameral legislature in which all states were represented equally, a multimember executive without the power to veto legislation, and a supreme court.

Nineteenth Amendment An amendment to the Constitution that prevents states from denying women the right to vote because of their sex.

Nomination Petitions The certain number of signatures of registered voters that independent or third-party candidates must collect to qualify for inclusion on a ballot.

Open Primary A primary election in which a voter does not have to declare a political party affiliation but may participate in the primary election of any party.

Opposition Research Campaign activity devoted to undermining the public's confidence in and support of a candidate, a key component of negative campaigning.

Original Intent A belief that the Constitution should be interpreted only according to the intent of its authors.

Original Jurisdiction A defined set of cases that avoids a lower court and goes directly to the Supreme Court.

Parallel Press Newspapers and other forms of media geared toward specific racial and ethnic minority groups.

Partisan Identification The political party an individual most identifies with.

Party Platform A statement a political party produces at its national convention that summarizes the basic policy principles of the party.

Patronage A system of hiring bureaucrats because they supported the winning political candidate, not because they had the skill, training, and experience for their jobs.

Pendleton Act A federal law passed in 1883 that required bureaucrats to be hired and retained according to their demonstrated skill, not their political affiliation.

Penny Press Nineteenth-century newspapers that eschewed coverage of politics and instead focused on human-interest stories.

Peremptory Challenges The right of each side in a legal case to discard a set number of potential jurors without needing to express a reason for doing so.

Pledged Delegates Party members elected or chosen on the state and local levels to support a particular candidate at the party's national convention.

Plessy v. Ferguson A controversial 1896 Supreme Court decision that ruled that under the Fourteenth Amendment, states were allowed to segregate by race.

Pluralism A theory of politics that contends that power is group based and that, because there are multiple points of access within American government, each group possesses an equality of opportunity when competing with other groups for power and resources (also known as interest-group theory).

Plurality Winning of an election by the candidate who receives the most votes (also known as "first past the post" [FPTP]).

Pocket Veto A way for the president to overturn a bill passed by Congress when the president does not act on a bill within ten days of passage (excluding Sundays) and Congress adjourns in the meantime.

Podcast A file that users can download off the Internet and that often features discussions about cultural and political issues.

Police Power A general, unwritten power to regulate health, safety, and morals.

Policy Adoption The stage in the policymaking process in which the policy is actually enacted.

Policy Evaluation The stage in the policymaking process in which government actors and private citizens determine whether an implemented policy is achieving its intended effect.

Policy Formulation The stage in the policymaking process in which government actors draft a solution to a problem that they have recognized merits their attention.

Policy Implementation The stage in the policymaking process in which government actors and even private citizens carry out enacted policies.

Political Culture The attitudes, beliefs, and values that undergird or are at the foundation of a political system.

Political Independents Voters who do not designate a political party affiliation when registering to vote.

Political Party Mass organizations that seek to elect candidates to public office and influence policymaking.

Political Socialization The process through which a person gains political understanding and forms a set of political beliefs.

Politics The conflict, competition, and compromise that occur within a political system.

Poll Taxes Fees that states charged citizens to vote and that disenfranchised the poor and minority citizens.

Pork Barrel Spending Federal money spent on projects that benefit only a specific member's district or state.

Precedent A principle articulated in a previous case that judges use to decide current cases.

Preemption A concept that permits the national government to overturn state and local laws.

Press Conferences Formal question-and-answer sessions that the president or the press secretary holds with the White House press corps.

Press Secretary A member of the president's staff who conducts daily briefings with members of the media.

Primary A method for political parties to select their candidates for office whereby people vote in an election.

Priming The media's ability to influence how the public perceives politicians and candidates.

Prior Restraint A usually impermissible government regulation that prevents the publication of printed material.

Private Law A type of law that concerns disputes between individuals.

Privileges and Immunities Clause A provision in Article IV of the Constitution that prevents states from discriminating against citizens of other states.

Probability Sampling A general term for a sample selected in accordance with probability theory, which ensures that every person in the population has an equal chance of being selected for the sample.

Probable Cause A legal requirement that there be more evidence indicating guilt than indicating innocence before a law enforcement officer can act.

Proportional Representation An election system that uses multi-member districts and in which seats are awarded by political party roughly in proportion to the results of an election.

Public Funding The financing of election campaigns by the American public through tax allocations as distinct from private fundraising by candidates.

Public Good A government policy or action that benefits society as a whole rather than a specific individual.

Public Law A type of law in which the government is a party to the case.

Public Opinion The collective opinions of large segments of the population on an issue, candidate, or public policy on which the public might be much divided and lack a consensus.

Quota Sampling A type of sample in which individuals to be interviewed are selected based on their proportion or quota in the general population being polled.

Race A socially constructed classification of people based on their physical characteristics, especially skin color.

Racial Profiling A law enforcement technique that singles out suspects on the basis of their race or ethnicity.

Realignment Periods when voter allegiances toward the political parties shift for an extended period of time, resulting in one party emerging as dominant.

Reapportionment The process of assigning states a number of representatives to the House of Representatives after each decennial census.

Reconstruction The period from 1865 to 1877 in which former Confederate states were brought back into the Union, often characterized by a military presence in the South and civil rights progress for Blacks.

Redistricting The process by which a state is divided into geographical regions, with each region electing a member of the House of Representatives.

Reparations A concept or tool for providing monetary payments to members of aggrieved groups based on past wrongful actions against them or their ancestors.

Representative A person chosen to make policy decisions on behalf of a defined group of people.

Republican Form of Government A government whose powers are exercised by elected representatives who are directly or indirectly accountable to the people governed.

Republican Party One of the two major political parties, founded in the 1850s by former Whigs who opposed slavery.

Reservations Portions of land set aside for American Indians removed from their ancestral lands by the federal government.

Retention Election A type of judicial election in which voters decide only whether to keep the judge in office; there are no opposition candidates.

Right to Die An extension of the right to privacy that includes an individual's right to refuse life-saving medical treatment but does not include the right to commit suicide.

Rule of Law The predominance of law over discretionary authority.

Rulemaking The process by which bureaucrats issue regulations that have the force of law.

Runoff Primary A second election held in some states if no candidate in the primary election receives a majority of the votes.

Sample A small set of people carefully drawn from a larger population to reflect its overall characteristics.

Sampling Error The degree of expected error in sampling results that comes from estimating the responses of the population from a sample.

School Districts Local government entities that create policies for public schools.

Search Warrant A legal document that allows law enforcement to search someone's person, home, or business.

Sedition Act A 1798 law that criminalized harsh criticism of President John Adams and his policies.

Segregation Physical separation of a dominant group from a subordinate group.

Selective Incorporation The process by which the Supreme Court has gradually incorporated specific liberties deemed absolutely necessary in a free society.

Senate Majority Leader The most powerful position in the Senate; the person who articulates the majority party's legislative priorities and works to pass them.

Senate Majority Whip (also called the assistant majority leader) A majority party leader in the Senate who counts votes, persuades members to vote according to the leadership's wishes, and assists the majority leader in passing the majority party's legislation.

Senate Minority Leader The leader of the minority party of the Senate; the person who articulates the legislative priorities of the minority party and opposes the majority party's priorities but exerts limited control over the outcome of legislation.

Senatorial Courtesy The practice whereby a president consults with senators in his party to find potential lower court vacancies that occur in the senators' states.

Senior Executive Service High-level bureaucrats the president places in different agencies to ensure compliance with his directives.

Separate but Equal Principle A legal principle that allowed states to segregate the races in public facilities, as long as the state provided each race with basic access to the public facility in question.

Separation of Church and State A constitutional principle that prevents the government (federal, state, or local) from interfering with or advancing religion or religious activity.

Separation of Powers The manner in which the Constitution divides power among the three branches of government—the legislature, the executive, and the judiciary.

Sexual Harassment Unwelcome sexual comments or treatment in the workplace or in an educational institution.

Shared Grievances Complaints against the political system (national, state, or local) by a group of people who agree generally on the causes of the complaints.

Signing Statements Presidential declarations issued along with legislative bill signings that express reservations about parts of a bill or announce an unwillingness to enforce aspects of a bill.

Sit-ins A form of protest against segregated restaurants in which Black patrons refused to move from Whites-only sections.

Social Construction of Race The construction of a group of people of various phenotypes, skin colors, and physical characteristics for political and social purposes, such as enslavement and exclusion.

Social Contract Individuals creating government by entering into a contract with it.

Social Movement A sustained challenge to those in power put forth by individuals, acting in concert with others, who have been excluded from the political process or who consider themselves political outsiders.

Soft Money The less-regulated money that is raised by a political party to support and maintain the party.

Solicitor General A high-ranking lawyer in the Justice Department who argues cases before the Supreme Court on behalf of the U.S. government.

Southern Christian Leadership Conference (SCLC) Group designed to be the umbrella organization that would link church-based affiliates throughout the South in the nonviolent struggle for racial justice.

Sovereignty A government policy toward American Indians that allows each tribe to regulate its own people and operate according to its own customs; also complete political power and authority.

Speaker of the House The most powerful position in the House of Representatives; the leader of the majority party; the person who articulates the House's legislative priorities and ensures their passage.

Standing An aspect of justiciability that requires the party bringing the case to show that the policy in question has caused it an injury.

State of the Union Address An annual occasion in which the president speaks before Congress to suggest laws that Congress should pass.

Statutory Law A type of law pertaining to rules made by legislatures, especially Congress.

Student Non-Violent Coordinating Committee (SNCC) Organization of college students dedicated to continuing the campaign for social justice started by the North Carolina A&T students.

Substantive Representation The extent to which representatives advocate policies that benefit their constituents.

Suffrage Movement Large-scale efforts of organizations and activists during the late nineteenth and early twentieth centuries to secure the right to vote for women.

Super PACs Political action committees allowed to raise an unlimited amount of money from any source, including individuals, corporations, labor unions, and interest groups. These committees are then allowed to spend this money in support of or opposition to any political candidate, including people running for president, so long as their activities are not directly coordinated with a campaign.

Superdelegates Delegates to the Democratic National Convention who are not selected by primaries or caucuses but instead are established party leaders.

Supportive Environment An environment receptive to the ideals and demands of a social movement.

Supremacy Clause A clause in Article VI of the Constitution stipulating that the Constitution and national laws are supreme, meaning that when state laws conflict with national laws, national laws take precedence.

Survey Research Administration of questionnaires to a sample of respondents selected from a particular population, useful for making descriptive and explanatory studies of large populations.

Symbolic Representation The extent to which constituents trust and accept their representative and the legislative institution as a whole.

Systemic Agenda The set of issues that policymakers perceive as worthy of their attention.

Tea Party A conservative political movement that advocates for drastically cutting government spending, reducing taxes, and ending most forms of regulations.

Tenth Amendment An amendment to the Constitution that guarantees states powers not given to the national government or forbidden to the states.

Think Tanks Interest groups that focus on research and scholarly analysis of issues relevant to the people they represent.

Thirteenth Amendment An amendment to the Constitution that prohibits slavery throughout the United States.

Three-Fifths Compromise A compromise reached at the Constitutional Convention over how state populations were to be counted for purposes of allocating seats in the House of Representatives; each slave was to be counted as three-fifths of a person for representational purposes.

Tradition of Exclusion A tradition that excludes groups from the political system based on their ascribed traits, such as race, gender, and religion (*see also* Inegalitarianism).

Twelfth Amendment An amendment to the Constitution that requires the president and vice president to be elected on separate ballots.

Two-Party System A government system in which only two political parties compete for elected offices.

Unfunded Mandates Directives the national government issues to state and local governments without compensating them for complying.

Unicameral Legislature A legislature that consists of only one body (rather than two or more).

Unified government A period in which both houses of Congress are controlled by the same party as the president.

Unitary Form of Government A system in which the central government exercises complete control and authority over subunits of government, which means that states or other governmental units do not have autonomous powers.

Veto The president's ability to cancel legislation passed by Congress.

Virginia Plan Drafted by James Madison of Virginia at the 1787 Constitutional Convention, a proposal for a system of government that called for the establishment of a strong central government with three branches: a bicameral legislature, a chief executive chosen by the legislature, and a powerful judiciary.

Voting-Age Population (VAP) The population of both citizens and noncitizens in the United States age eighteen or over.

Voting-Eligible Population (VEP) The population of U.S. citizens age eighteen or over.

Voting Rights Act of 1965 A federal law that significantly curtailed disenfranchisement of racial and ethnic minorities by banning literacy tests and requiring federal supervision of jurisdictions with a history of voting discrimination.

Whigs A political party founded in the 1830s to oppose the politics and policies of President Andrew Jackson.

Whip A legislative leader who assists the party by counting votes and persuading members to vote according to the party leaders' wishes.

Whistleblowers Bureaucrats who publicly expose waste, fraud, or abuse in their agency.

White Citizens Council Formed in 1954 in Mississippi to prevent the implementation of *Brown v. Board of Education*, the council's membership consisted of plantation owners, bankers, doctors, legislators, and others opposed to Black civil rights and determined to maintain segregation.

White House Press Corps Those elite journalists responsible for covering the president and key executive branch officials.

White House Staff The president's personal advisers, who do not need senatorial approval when appointed and provide critical political and policy advice to the president.

White Primary A practice by Southern state Democratic parties in the nineteenth and early twentieth centuries intended to disenfranchise Blacks by preventing them from voting in the crucial Democratic Party primary elections.

Winner-Take-All An election system in which the candidate who gets the most votes in that district wins the election, even if he or she has not received a majority of the votes and has finished only a few votes ahead of the second-place finisher.

Writ of Certiorari A formal legal document filed by the losing party in a lower court case that asks the Supreme Court to hear an appeal.

Yellow Journalism A form of journalism popular during the late eighteenth and early nineteenth centuries that sensationalized stories and distorted facts to sell more newspapers.

Notes

Chapter 1

1 Moyer, J. M. (2016, February 11). Delaware apologizes for slavery and Jim Crow. No reparations forthcoming. *Washington Post*. Retrieved from https://www .washingtonpost .com/news/morning-mix/ wp/2016/02/11/delaware-apologizes-for-slavery-and-jim-crow-no-reparations-forthcoming/.

2 House apologizes for slavery, "Jim Crow" injustices. (2008, July 29). *CNN Politics*. Retrieved July 29, 2008, from http://www.cnn.com/2008/POLITICS/07/29/ house.slavery/index.html.

3 Thompson, K. (2009, June 19). Senate unanimously approves resolution apologizing for slavery. *Washington Post*. Retrieved July 14, 2009, from http://www .washingtonpost.com/wp-dyn/content/article/2009/ 06/18/AR2009061803877.html?noredirect=on.

4 DeMillo, A. (2007, June 5). Gov. questions need for slavery apology. *Washington Post*.

5 States debate formal slavery apologies; arguments question resolutions' necessity. *Grand Rapids Press* (Michigan), p. A5.

6 John Hope Franklin: Apologies aren't enough. (2007, April 18). *Independent Weekly*. Retrieved June 5, 2007, from https://indyweek.com/news/ john-hope-franklin-apologies-enough/.

7 National. *Sun-Sentinel* (Fort Lauderdale, Florida), Broward Metro ed., p. 3A.

8 General Assembly of North Carolina, Resolution 2007–21 (Senate Joint Resolution 1557), April 12, 2007.

9 Johnson, R. (2011, October 28). Graphic: Mapping a superpower-sized military. *National Post*. Retrieved from http://news.nationalpost.com/2011/10/28/ graphic-mapping-a-superpower-sized-military/.

10 King, L. (2012, August 1). Olympics 2012: Title IX made women gold medalists possible at the 2012 Olympics. *Washington Times*. Retrieved from http:// communities.washingtontimes.com/neighborhood/ london-2012-summer-olympic-games/2012/aug/1/ Title-IX-American-women-gold-2012-Olympics/.

11 Acosta, R. V., & Carpenter, L. J. (n.d.). *Women in intercollegiate sport: A longitudinal, national study, thirty five year update. 1977–2012*. Unpublished manuscript. Available at http:// acostacarpenter.org/AcostaCarpenter2012.pdf.

12 Association of Public and Land-Grant Universities. (2012). *The Land-grant tradition*. Retrieved from http:// www.aplu.org/library/the-land-grant-tradition/file.

13 Thomson, S., Osborn, R., Squires, D., & Reed, S. J.. (2011). *International profiles of health care systems, 2011*. New York: The Common Wealth Fund.

14 Curtis, M., Blondel, J., Brown, B. E., Fewsmith, J., Kanet, R. E., Kommers, D., . . . Wright, S. (1997). *Introduction to comparative government* (4th ed.). New York: Longman, p. 13.

15 McClain, P. D., & Stewart Jr., J. (2014). *"Can we all get along?": Racial and ethnic minorities in American politics* (6th ed.). Boulder, CO: Westview Press.

16 Quoted in McDonald, L. C. (1962). *Western political theory: The modern age*. New York: Harcourt, Brace & World, p. 7.

17 Smith, R. M. (1993). Beyond Tocqueville, Myrdal, and Hartz: The multiple traditions in America. *American Political Science Review, 87*, 549–566; Smith, R. M. (1997). *Civic ideals: Conflicting visions of citizenship in U.S. history*. New Haven, CT: Yale University Press, p. 3.

18 McDonald, L. C. (1962). *Western political theory: The modern age*. New York: Harcourt, Brace & World, p. 243.

19 Holmes, S. (1993). *The anatomy of antiliberalism*. Cambridge, MA: Harvard University Press, pp. 3–4.

20 Sellers, M. N. S. (1994). *American republicanism: Roman ideology in the United States Constitution*. New York: New York University Press, p. 47.

21 McDonald, p. 188.

22 Smith, *Civic ideals*, chap. 1.

23 Wilson, J. H. (1976). The illusion of change: Women in the American Revolution. In A. F. Young (Ed.), *The American Revolution: Explorations in the history of American radicalism* (pp. 386–445). DeKalb: Northern Illinois University Press,.

24 Kerber, L. K. (1980). *Women of the republic: Intellect and ideology in Revolutionary America*. Chapel Hill: University of North Carolina Press, p. 23.

25 Rousseau, J.-J. (1957). *Emile* (Barbara Foxley, Trans.). London: J. M. Dent & Sons, p. 322.

26 Kerber, L. K. (1992). The paradox of women's citizenship in the early republic: The case of *Martin v. Massachusetts, 1805*. *American Historical Review, 97*, 349–378.

27 Jordan, W. D. (1968). *White over Black: American attitudes toward the Negro, 1550–1812*. Baltimore, MD: Penguin, pp. 20, 23, 56.

28 McClain & Stewart, *Can we all get along?*

29 Smith, *Civic ideals*.

30 Jefferson, T. (1982). *Notes on the State of Virginia* (William Peden, Ed.). Chapel Hill: University of North Carolina Press. (Original work published 1785)

31 Miller, J. C. (1991). *The wolf by the ears: Thomas Jefferson and slavery*. Charlottesville: University Press of Virginia.

32 Louisiana and North Carolina used the one-sixteenth criterion (one great-great-grandparent). One eighth (one great-grandparent) was the standard in Florida, Indiana, Maryland, Mississippi, Missouri, Nebraska, North Dakota, South Carolina, and Tennessee. Oregon used a one-quarter standard (one grandparent) (McClain & Stewart, *Can we all get along?*, p. 9).

33 Deloria Jr., V., & Wilkins, D. E. (1999). *Tribes, treaties, and constitutional tribulations*. Austin: University of Texas Press, p. 6.

34 Ibid., p. 7.

35 Ibid.

36 Smith, *Civic ideals*, p. 61.

37 Ibid., p. 17.

38 Smith, "Beyond Tocqueville," p. 563, note 4.

39 Kerber, L. K. (1995). A constitutional right to be treated like American ladies: Women and the obligations of citizenship. In L. K. Kerber, A. Kessler-Harris, & K. K. Sklar (Eds.), *U.S. history as women's history*. Chapel Hill: University of North Carolina Press, p. 18.

40 McClain & Stewart, *Can we all get along?*, p. 10.

41 Gulick, S. L. (1918). *American democracy and Asiatic-citizenship*. New York: Scribner's, pp. 55–56.

42 Robinson, D. L. (1971). *Slavery in the structure of American politics, 1765–1820*. New York: Harcourt Brace Jovanovich, p. 86.

43 Ibid., p. 136.

44 Johansen, B. E. (1982). *Forgotten Founders: How the American Indian helped shape democracy*. Boston: Harvard Common Press; Grinde Jr., D. A. (1977). *The Iroquois and the founding of the American nation*. San Francisco: Indian Historian Press.

45 Ibid.

46 Ibid.

47 Ibid.

48 Smith, R. M. (1995). Response to Jacqueline Stevens. *American Political Science Review, 89*, 990–995.

Chapter 2

1 Heil, A. (2018, May 29). ABC cancels Roseanne after its star, Roseanne Barr, went on a vitriolic and racist Twitter rant. *Washington Post*. Retrieved October 19, 2018, from https://www.washingtonpost.com/news/ reliable-source/wp/2018/05/29/roseanne-went-on-a-vitriolic-and-racially-charged-twitter-rampage-now-shes-apologizing/?noredirect=on&utm_term=.85801f250639.

2 Koblin, J. (2018, May 29). After racist Tweet, Roseanne Barr's show is canceled by ABC. *New York Times*. Retrieved October 19, 2018, from https://www.nytimes .com/2018/05/29/business/media/roseanne-barr-offensive-tweets.html.

3 Duster, C. R., Atkinson, C., & Johnson, A. (2018, May 29). Roseanne Barr blames racist Tweet on Ambien after ABC Cancels "Roseanne." *NBC News*. Retrieved October 19, 2018, from https://www.nbcnews.com/ news/nbcblk/roseanne-barr-apologizes-tweet-comparing-obama-adviser-ape-n878171.

4 Selk, A. (2018, May 30). George Soros wasn't a Nazi, Roseanne Barr. He was a 14-year-old Jew who hid from them." *Washington Post*. Retrieved October 19, 2018, from https://www.washingtonpost.com/news/ the-intersect/wp/2018/05/30/unpacking-the-george-soros-was-a-jew-killing-nazi-conspiracy-theory-that-roseanne-barr-spreads/?utm_term=.16e9b1591879.

5 Heil, "ABC Cancels Roseanne."

6 Heil, "ABC Cancels Roseanne."

7 Ohlheiser, A. (2018, March 29). TV Roseanne is a Trump supporter. Real-life Roseanne Barr is already a pro-Trump Internet mainstay. *Washington Post*. Retrieved October 19, 2018, from https://www.wash-ingtonpost.com/news/the-intersect/wp/2018/01/11/ tv-roseanne-will-be-a-trump-supporter-real-life-roseanne-barr-is-already-a-pro-trump-internet-mainstay/?utm_term=.90a6414c3978.

8 Ibid.

9 Duster et al., "Roseanne Barr Blames."

10 BBC. (2018, May 30). Roseanne Barr's Tweet and shelved sitcom sparks debates." *BBC News*. Retrieved October 19, 2018, from https://www.bbc.com/news/ blogs-trending-44300012.

11 Rogers, K., & Cochrane, E. (2018, May 30). Trump responds to fury over "Roseanne," but not to her racist remarks. *New York Times*. Retrieved October 19, 2018, from https://www.nytimes.com/2018/05/30/us/politics/ roseanne-barr-trump.html.

12 Stone, G. R. (2018, May 30). Roseanne Barr and the NFL: What counts as free speech? *Rolling Stone*. Retrieved October 19, 2018, from https://www.rollingstone.com/ culture/news/roseanne-barr-and-the-nfl-what-counts-as-free-speech-w520925.

13 Greene, J. P. (1995). *Understanding the American Revolution: Issues and actors*. Charlottesville: University Press of Virginia, p. 80.

14 Ibid., chap. 5.

15 Bonwick, C. (1991). *The American Revolution*. London: Macmillan, chap. 3.

16 Greene, *Understanding the American Revolution*, chap. 12.

17 Bonwick, *The American Revolution*, chap. 4.

18 Diamond, M. (1976). The American idea of equality: The view from the founding. *Review of Politics, 38*(3), 313–331.

19 Cappon, L. J. (Ed.). (1959). *The Adams-Jefferson letters: The complete correspondence between Thomas Jefferson and Abigail and John Adams* (2 vols.). Chapel Hill: University of North Carolina Press for the Institute of Early American History and Culture, Williamsburg, VA.

20 Jensen, M. (1940). *The Articles of Confederation: An interpretation of the social-constitutional history of the American Revolution, 1774–1781*. Madison: University of Wisconsin Press, p. 126.

21 Ibid., chap. 12.

22 National Archives. (2018). *America's Founding Fathers: Delegates to the Constitutional Convention.* Retrieved from http://www.archives.gov/exhibits/charters/constitution_founding_fathers_overview.html.

23 Vetterli, R., & Bryner, G. (1987). *In search of the republic: Public virtue and the roots of American government.* Totowa, NJ: Rowman & Littlefield.

24 U.S. Census Bureau. (2013). *Congressional apportionment: Historical perspective.* Retrieved from https://www.census.gov/population/apportionment/about/history.html.

25 Borden, M. (Ed.). (1965). *The Antifederalist Papers.* East Lansing: Michigan State University Press, p. x.

26 *McCulloch v. Maryland, 4 Wheat. 316* (1819).

27 Keller, M. (1987). Failed amendments to the Constitution. *The World and I*, pp. 87–93.

Chapter 3

1 O'Dell, R., Sanchez, Y. W., & McGlade, C. (2016, March 24). Lack of polling sites, not Independents, caused Maricopa election chaos. *Arizona Republic.* Retrieved May 2, 2018, from https://www.azcentral.com/story/news/politics/elections/2016/03/23/maricopa-county-presidential-primary-election-chaos-arizona/82174876.

2 United States Census Bureau. (2018). *QuickFacts: Maricopa County, Arizona.* Retrieved May 2, 2018, from https://www.census.gov/quickfacts/fact/table/maricopacountyarizona/PST045216.

3 Slip Opinion, *Shelby County, AL v. Holder*, No. 12–96. Retrieved May 2, 2018, from http://www.supremecourt.gov/opinions/12pdf/12-96_6k47.pdf.

4 Scott, E. (2016, April 5). DOJ Looking into Voter Suppression Claims in Arizona. *CNN Politics.* Retrieved May 3, 2018, from https://www.cnn.com/2016/04/05/politics/justice-department-investigation-arizona/index.html.

5 Frazan, A. N. (2018, February 21). Let my people vote: Adrian Fontes' fight to fix Maricopa County's broken election system. *Phoenix New Times.* Retrieved May 3, 2018, from http://www.phoenixnewtimes.com/news/recorder-adrian-fontes-fighting-voter-suppression-in-arizona-10154527.

6 National Conference of State Legislatures. (2018). *2018 legislative session calendar.* Retrieved May 4, 2018, from http://www.ncsl.org/documents/ncsl/2018_Session_Calendar.pdf.

7 Williams, B. (2018, April 10). *West Virginia moves to single-member districts.* NCSL Blog , National Conference of State Legislatures. Retrieved May 4, 2018, from http://www.ncsl.org/blog/2018/04/10/west-virginia-moves-to-single-member-districts.aspx.

8 *Reynolds v. Sims*, 377 U.S. 84 (1964).

9 *Thornburg v. Gingles*, 478 U.S. 30 (1986).

10 For a brief time during the 1990s, the U.S. president had the line-item veto authority, but in *Clinton v. City of New York*, 524 U.S. 417 (1998), the U.S. Supreme Court ruled that the line-item veto violated the Constitution.

11 Famighetti, C., Melillo, A., & Pérez, M. (2014). *Election Day long lines: Resource allocation.* New York: Brennan Center for Law and Justice at New York University. Retrieved October 12, 2018, from https://www.brennancenter.org/sites/default/files/publications/ElectionDayLongLines-ResourceAllocation.pdf.

12 Bousquet, S. (2012, November 10). Governor Scott defends Florida election, as his chief admits "We could have done better." *Tampa Bay Times.* Retrieved October 12, 2018, from http://www.tampabay.com/news/politics/national/gov-rick-scott-defends-florida-election-as-his-chief-says-we-could-have/1260762.

13 Bousquet, S. (2013, January 18). Scott pushes for more early voting days, sites. *Tampa Bay Times*, p. 1A.

14 Cotterell, B. (2014, March 27). Florida non-citizen voter purge postponed: Elections official. *Reuters.* Retrieved October 12, 2018, from https://uk.reuters.com/article/us-usa-florida-politics/florida-non-citizen-voter-purge-postponed-elections-official-idUKBREA2Q2DH20140327.

15 Wan, W. (2016, November 8). Voting issues in Florida: Intimidation reported at polling places. *Washington Post.* Retrieved May 5, 2018, from https://www.washingtonpost.com/politics/2016/live-updates/general-election/real-time-updates-on-the-2016-election-voting-and-race-results/voting-issues-in-florida-intimidation-reported-at-polling-places/?utm_term=.6b465366c28b.

16 Vasilogambros, M. (2018, February 15). Voting lines are shorter—but mostly for Whites. *Stateline.* Retrieved May 5, 2018, from http://www.pewtrusts.org/en/research-and-analysis/blogs/stateline/2018/02/15/voting-lines-are-shorter-but-mostly-for-whites.

17 For examples of research finding the existence of racially polarized voting, see Davidson C., & Grofman, B. (1994). *Quiet revolution in the South.* Princeton, NJ: Princeton University Press; Grofman, B. Handley, L., &

Niemi, R. (1992). *Minority representation and the quest for voting equality*. Cambridge, UK: Cambridge University Press, 1992; and Lublin, D. (1997). The election of African Americans and Latinos to the U.S. House of Representatives, 1972–1994. *American Politics Quarterly, 25*, 286–296. However, a study of a Los Angeles mayoral race demonstrates that issue voting can trump voting based on race and ethnicity. See Abrajano, M. A., Nagler, J., & R Alvarez, R. M. (2005). A natural experiment of race-based and issue voting: The 2001 City of Los Angeles elections. *Political Research Quarterly, 58*, 203–218.

18 United States Census Bureau. (2018). *QuickFacts New Mexico*. Retrieved May 5, 2018, from https://www.census.gov/quickfacts/NM.

19 National Center for State Courts. (2018). Judicial selection in the states. Retrieved October 12, 2018, from http://www.judicialselection.us. In New Jersey, the state Senate must confirm the nomination. California judges serve a twelve-year term and must run in a retention election to serve another term.

20 Schotland, R. (1998). Comment: Judicial independence and accountability. *Law & Contemporary Problems, 61*, 149–150.

21 For example, see Brace P., & Boyea, B. D. (2008). State public opinion, the death penalty, and the practice of electing judges. *American Journal of Political Science, 52*, 360–372; Hall, M. G. (1992). Electoral politics and strategic voting in state supreme courts. *Journal of Politics, 54*, 427–446; and Hall, M. G. (1995). Justices as representatives: Elections and judicial politics in the American states. *American Politics Quarterly, 23*, 485–503.

22 For a spirited theoretical and empirical justification of judicial elections, see Bonneau, C. W., & Hall, M. G. (2009). *In defense of judicial elections*. New York: Routledge.

23 *Chisom v. Roemer*, 501 U.S. 380 (1991).

24 Goelzhauser, G. (2011). Diversifying state supreme courts. *Law and Society Review, 45*, 761–781.

25 Graham, B. L. (1990). Do judicial selection systems matter?: A study of Black representation on state courts. *American Politics Quarterly, 18*, 316–336; Hurwitz, M. S., & Lanier, D. N. (2008). Diversity in state and federal appellate courts: Change and continuity across 20 years. *Justice System Journal, 29*, 47–70.

26 Luskin, R. C., Bratcher, C. N., Jordan, C. G., Renner, T. K., & Seago, K. S. (1994). How minority judges fare in retention election. *Judicature, 77*, 316–321.

27 United States Census Bureau. (2018). *QuickFacts District of Columbia*. Retrieved May 5, 2018, from https://www.census.gov/quickfacts/DC.

28 Cummings, W. (2015, February 26). Pot now legal in D.C. despite threats from Congress. *USA Today*. Retrieved May 9, 2018, from https://www.usatoday.com/story/news/nation/2015/02/25/dc-marijuana-legalization/24033803.

29 Dye, T. R., & MacManus, S. A. (2009). *Politics in states and communities* (13th ed.). Upper Saddle River, NJ: Pearson Prentice-Hall, p. 150.

30 See, for example, Thompson III, J. P. (2006). *Double trouble: Black mayors, Black communities, and the call for a deep democracy*. New York: Oxford University Press.

31 Stracqualursi, V., & Phelps, J. (2017, September 14). Trump meets with Hurricane Irma respondents and victims in Florida. *ABC News*. Retrieved May 6, 2018, from https://abcnews.go.com/Politics/trump-heads-florida-survey-damage-hurricane-irma/story?id=49821921.

32 Baker, P. (2017, September 30). Trump lashes out at Puerto Rico mayor who criticized storm response. *New York Times*. Retrieved May 6, 2018, from https://www.nytimes.com/2017/09/30/us/politics/trump-puerto-rico-mayor.html.

33 McClain, P. D., & Carew, J. D. J. (2018). *"Can we all get along?": Racial and ethnic minorities in American politics* (7th ed.). Boulder, CO: Westview Press, p. 12.

34 For more on interstate compacts and environmental policy, see Dodson, A. L. (1998). Interstate compacts to bury radioactive waste: A useful tool for environmental policy? *State and Local Government Review, 30*, 118–128.

35 Blaustein A. P., & Zangrando, R. L. (1970). *Civil rights and the Black American: A documentary history*. New York: Clarion, pp. 42–47.

36 United States Census Bureau. (2018). *QuickFacts California*. Retrieved May 10, 2018, from https://www.census.gov/quickfacts/fact/table/CA/AGE135216; *QuickFacts Wyoming*. Retrieved May 10, 2018, from https://www.census.gov/quickfacts/fact/table/WY/AGE135216.

37 Elazar, D. J. (1964). Federal–state collaboration in the nineteenth-century United States. *Political Science Quarterly, 79*, 248–281.

38 For a thorough discussion of the political and economic debates over the Bank of the United States, see Kaplan, E. S. (1999). *The Bank of the United States and the American economy*. Westport, CT: Greenwood Press.

39 *McCulloch v. Maryland*, 17 U.S. 316 (1819).

40 For a more thorough discussion on the importance of this case, see Killenbeck, M. R. (2006). *M'Culloch v. Maryland: Securing a nation*. Lawrence: University Press of Kansas.

41 *Gibbons v. Ogden*, 22 U.S. 1 (1824).

42 For a more thorough discussion of the importance of this case, see Johnson, H. A. (2010). *Gibbons v. Ogden: John Marshall, steamboats, and interstate commerce*. Lawrence: University Press of Kansas.

43 *Prigg v. Pennsylvania*, 41 U.S. 539 (1842).

44 *Dred Scott v. Sandford*, 60 U.S. 393 (1857).

45 McClain & Carew, *Can We All Get Along?* p. 15.

46 Grodzins, M. (1963). The American federal system. In R. A. Goldwin (Ed.), *A nation of states*. Chicago: Rand McNally.

47 For more on the concept of dual federalism, see Corwin, E. S. (1950). The passing of dual federalism. *Virginia Law Review, 36*, 1–24.

48 *United States v. E.C. Knight Company*, 156 U.S. 1 (1895).

49 *Hammer v. Dagenhart*, 247 U.S. 251 (1918).

50 For more on the Second Land Grant Act and HBCUs, see Christy, R. D., & Williamson, L. (Eds.). (1992). *A century of service: American land grant colleges and universities, 1890–1990*. New Brunswick, NJ: Transaction Publishers.

51 *Plessy v. Ferguson*, 133 U.S. 537 (1896).

52 *United States v. Reese*, 92 U.S. 214 (1876).

53 *United States v. Cruikshank*, 92 U.S. 542 (1875).

54 Grodzins, *The American Federal System*.

55 *Palko v. Connecticut*, 302 U.S. 319 (1937).

56 See, for example, *Schechter Poultry Corporation v. United States*, 295 U.S. 495 (1935); *United States v. Butler*, 297 U.S. 1 (1936); and *Carter v. Carter Coal Company*, 298 U.S. 238 (1936).

57 *National Labor Relations Board v. Jones & Laughlin Steel Corp.*, 301 U.S. 1 (1937).

58 *United States v. Darby Lumber Co.*, 312 U.S. 100 (1941).

59 *Wickard v. Filburn*, 317 U.S. 11 (1942).

60 Medicaid.gov: Keeping America Healthy. (n.d.). *Program history*. Retrieved May 12, 2018, https://www.medicaid.gov/about-us/program-history/index.html.

61 U.S. Department of Health & Human Services, Administration for Children & Families, Office of Head Start. (2018). *History of Head Start*. Retrieved May 12, 2018, from https://www.acf.hhs.gov/ohs/about/history-of-head-start.

62 Kovacs, W. L., Johnson, J. M., & Holman, K. W. (2016). *The growing burden of unfunded mandates on the states*. Washington, DC: U.S. Chamber of Commerce. Retrieved May 12, 2018, from https://www.uschamber.com/sites/default/files/documents/files/022879_etra_epa_coercive_federalism_report_fin.pdf.

63 *National League of Cities v. Usery*, 426 U.S. 833 (1976).

64 *Garcia v. San Antonio Metropolitan Transit Authority*, 469 U.S. 528 (1985).

65 For more on the controversy over unfunded mandates, see Koch, E. (1980). The mandate millstone. *The Public Interest, 61*, 42–57; and Kovacs, Johnson, and Holman, *The growing burden of unfunded mandates on the states*.

66 *Brown v. Board of Education*, 347 U.S. 483 (1954).

67 *Heart of Atlanta Motel v. United States*, 379 U.S. 241 (1965); *Katzenbach v. McClung*, 379 U.S. 294 (1965).

68 Slip Opinion, *Shelby County (AL) v. Holder*, No. 12-96. Retrieved October 12, 2018, from https://www.supremecourt.gov/opinions/12pdf/12-96_6k47.pdf.

69 Mann, T. E. & Wakeman, R. L. (2013, June 28). Voting rights after *Shelby County v. Holder*. *Brookings: Up Front*. Retrieved May 12, 2018, from https://www.brookings.edu/blog/up-front/2013/06/25/voting-rights-after-shelby-county-v-holder/.

70 McClain & Carew, *Can We All Get Along?* pp. 308–313.

71 *California v. Cabazon Band of Mission Indians*, 480 U.S. 202 (1987). See also Mason, W. D. (2000). *Indian gaming: Tribal sovereignty and American politics*. Norman: University of Oklahoma Press, 2000; and Rossum, R. (2011). *The Supreme Court and tribal gaming: California v. Cabazon Band of Mission Indians*. Lawrence: University Press of Kansas.

72 *Reed v. Reed*, 404 U.S. 71 (1971).

73 *Roe v. Wade*, 410 U.S. 413 (1973).

74 Phillips, L. (2017, January 24). Nixon's revolutionary vision for American governance. Richard Nixon Foundation, Library, Museum. Retrieved May 12, 2018, from https://www.nixonfoundation.org/2017/01/nixons-vision-for-american-governance/.

75 Pear, R. (1983, January 26). Reagan modifies "New Federalism" plan. *New York Times*. Retrieved May 12, 2018, from https://www.nytimes.com/1983/01/26/us/reagan-modifies-new-federalism-plan.html.

76 Clinton, W. J. (1996, January 23). Address before a Joint Session of the Congress on the State of the Union. In J. Woolley & G. Peters, *The American Presidency Project*. Santa Barbara: University of California at Santa Barbara. Retrieved May 12, 2018, from http://www.presidency.ucsb.edu/ws/?pid=53091.

77 Department of Housing and Urban Development. (n.d.). *Community Development Block Grant Program*. Retrieved May 12, 2018, from https://www.hud.gov/program_offices/comm_planning/communitydevelopment/programs.

78 Department of Health and Human Services, Office of Family Assistance. (2017). *About TANF*. Retrieved May 12, 2018, from https://www.acf.hhs.gov/ofa/programs/tanf/about.

79 For example, see Pavetti L., & Schott, L. (2011, July 14). *TANF's inadequate response to recession highlights weakness of Black grant structure*. Center for Budget Priorities. Retrieved May 12, 2018, from https://www.cbpp.org/research/family-income-support/tanfs-inadequate-response-to-recession-highlights-weakness-of-block?fa=view&id=3534.

80 National Association of Black Social Workers Steering Committee. (2002, October). *Welfare reform*. National Association of Black Social Workers. Retrieved May 12, 2018, from http://c.ymcdn.com/sites/nabsw.org/resource/resmgr/position_statements_papers/welfare_reform.pdf.

81 *South Dakota v. Dole*, 483 U.S. 203 (1987).

82 Mills, K. I. (1995, February 27). Disabilities Act: An "unfunded mandate" too potent to oppose. *AP News* Retrieved May 12, 2018, from https://www.apnews.com/e369ecf20fad4877b5cbea7b072ab2ee.

83 *National Federation of Independent Business v. Sebelius*, 132 S.Ct. 2566 (2012).

84 *Gonzalez v. Raich*, 545 U.S. 1 (2005).

85 Dennis, B. (2013, August 29). Obama administration will not block state marijuana laws if distribution is regulated. *Washington Post*. Retrieved May 12, 2018, from https://www.washingtonpost.com/national/health-science/obama-administration-will-not-preempt-state-marijuana-laws--for-now/2013/08/29/b725bfd8-10bd-11e3-8cdd-bcdc09410972_story.html?utm_term=.bcdf9d1d8d33.

86 Roubein, R. (2017, September 27). Timeline: The GOP's failed effort to repeal ObamaCare," *The Hill*. Retrieved May 12, 2018, from http://thehill.com/policy/healthcare/other/352587-timeline-the-gop-effort-to-repeal-and-replace-obamacare.

87 Pradhan, R. (2018, January 11). Trump paves the way for states to impose Medicaid work requirements. *Politico*. Retrieved May 12, 2018, from https://www.politico.com/story/2018/01/11/trump-medicaid-work-requirements-280969.

88 Zapotosky, M., Horowitz, S., & Achenbach, J. (2018, January 4). Use of legalized marijuana threatened as Sessions rescinds Obama-era directive that eased federal enforcement. *Washington Post*. Retrieved May 12, 2018, from https://www.washingtonpost.com/world/national-security/sessions-is-rescinding-obama-era-directive-for-feds-to-back-off-marijuana-enforcement-in-states-with-legal-pot/2018/01/04/b1a42746-f157-11e7-b3bf-ab90a706e175_story.html?noredirect=on&utm_term=.e4bdba7a7765.

89 Rosenberg, E. (2017, November 21). Federal judge blocks Trump's executive order on denying funding to sanctuary cities. *Washington Post*. Retrieved May 12, 2018, from https://www.washingtonpost.com/news/politics/wp/2017/11/21/federal-judge-blocks-trumps-executive-order-on-denying-funding-to-sanctuary-cities/?utm_term=.3711723954b5; Cummings W. (2018, August 1). "Federal Appeals Court Rules Trump Sanctuary City Order Unconstitutional." *USA Today*. Retrieved October 12, 2018.

90 *United States v. Lopez*, 514 U.S. 549 (1995), at 567.

91 *United States v. Morrison*, 529 U.S. 528 (2000).

92 *Gonzales v. Raich*, 545 U.S. 1 (2005).

93 *Gregory v. Ashcroft*, 501 U.S. 452 (1991).

94 *Planned Parenthood v. Casey*, 503 U.S. 833 (1992).

95 *Swann v. Charlotte-Mecklenburg Board of Education*, 402 U.S. 1 (1971).

96 *Board of Education of Oklahoma City v. Dowell*, 498 U.S. 237 (1991).

97 *Seminole Tribe of Florida v. Florida*, 517 U.S. 44 (1996).

Chapter 4

1 Suarez, C. (2017, February 6). Charlottesville City Council votes to remove statue from Lee Park," *The Daily Progress*. Retrieved May 18, 2018, from http://www.dailyprogress.com/news/local/charlottesville-city-council-votes-to-remove-statue-from-lee-park/article_2c4844ca-ece3-11e6-a7bc-b7d28027df28.html.

2 Spencer, H., & Stolberg, S. G. (2017, August 11). White nationalists march on University of Virginia. *New York Times*. Retrieved May 18, 2018, from https://www.nytimes.com/2017/08/11/us/white-nationalists-rally-charlottesville-virginia.html.

3 Heim, J., Silverman, E., Shapiro, T. R., & Brown, E. (2017, August 13). One dead as car strikes crowd amid protests of White nationalist gathering in Charlottesville; two police die in helicopter crash. *Washington Post*. Retrieved May 19, 2018, from https://www.washingtonpost.com/local/fights-in-advance-of-saturday-protest-in-charlottesville/2017/08/12/155fb636-7f13-11e7-83c7-5bd5460f0d7e_story.html?utm_term=.84f8f2198f5f ; Rankin, S. (2017, December 14). Suspect in Charlottesville car attack faces new first-degree murder charge. *Chicago Tribune*. Retrieved May 19, 2018, from http://www.chicagotribune.com/news/nationworld/ct-james-alex-fields-charlottesville-20171214-story.html.

4 Heim et al.

5 Hamilton, A. (1788). *Federalist Paper No. 84*. Library of Congress. Retrieved May 19, 2018, from https://www.congress.gov/resources/display/content/The+Federalist+Papers#TheFederalistPapers-84.

6 For more on the history of the Bill of Rights, see Schwartz, B. (1992). *The great rights of mankind: A history of the American Bill of Rights*. Lanham, MD, Rowman & Littlefield.

7 *Barron v. Mayor and City Council of Baltimore*, 32 U.S. 243 (1833).

8 *Hurtado v. California*, 110 U.S. 516 (1884). Justice John Marshall Harlan's dissent (pp. 538–558) argued that the due process clause means that the Bill of Rights should apply to the states.

9 *Palko v. Connecticut*, 302 U.S. 319 (1937).

10 For more on the role of the U.S. Government's suppression against opponents of World War I and other activists, see Thomas Jr., W. H. (2008). *Unsafe for democracy: World War I and the U.S. Justice Department's covert campaign to suppress dissent*. Madison: University of Wisconsin Press.

11 *Schenck v. United States*, 249 U.S. 47 (1919), 52.

12 For more on Emma Goldman, see the University of California, Berkeley Library, *Emma Goldman Papers*. Retrieved May 19, 2018, from http://www.lib.berkeley.edu/goldman/index.html. For Emma Goldman's contribution to freedom of expression, see specifically the sections titled, "Emma Goldman and Free Speech," http://www.lib.berkeley.edu/goldman/MeetEmmaGoldman/emmagoldmanandfreespeech.html, and "War Resistance, Anti-Militarism, and Deportation, 1917–1919, http://www.lib.berkeley.edu/

goldman/MeetEmmaGoldman/warresistance-antimilitarism-deportation1917-1919.html.

13 *Brandenburg v. Ohio*, 395 U.S. 444 (1969).

14 *Texas v. Johnson*, 491 U.S. 397 (1989).

15 For more on this history and aftermath of this case, see Goldstein, R. J. (2000). *Flag burning and free speech: The case of Texas v. Johnson*. Lawrence: University Press of Kansas.

16 *Miller v. California*, 413 U.S. 15 (1973).

17 For more on the Supreme Court and pornography cases, see Hixon, R. F. (1996). *Pornography and the justices: The Supreme Court and the intractable obscenity problem*. Carbondale and Edwardsville: Southern Illinois University Press.

18 *Chaplinsky v. New Hampshire*, 315 U.S. 568 (1942).

19 *Cohen v. California*, 403 U.S. 15 (1971). California had initially sentenced Cohen to thirty days in jail after he was convicted of disturbing the peace because he wore a jacket displaying the words "Fuck the Draft."

20 *R.A.V. v. City of St. Paul, MN*, 505 U.S. 377 (1992).

21 *Wisconsin v. Mitchell*, 508 U.S. 476 (1993).

22 *Virginia v. Black*, 538 U.S. 123, 343 (2003).

23 *Walker v. Texas Division, Sons of Confederate Veterans*, 135 S.Ct. 2239 (2015).

24 *New York Times v. United States*, 403 U.S. 713 (1971).

25 *Near v. Minnesota*, 283 U.S. 697 (1931).

26 Wildman, S. (2017, August 17). Why you see swastikas in America but not Germany. *Vox*. Retrieved May 19, 2018, from https://www.vox.com/world/2017/8/16/16152088/nazi-swastikas-germany-charlottesville.

27 *New York Times v. Sullivan*, 376 U.S. 254 (1964).

28 Fabia, J. (2018, January 10). Trump says he'll take a "strong look" at libel laws in response to book. *The Hill*. Retrieved May 19, 2018, from http://thehill.com/homenews/administration/368309-trump-says-hell-take-a-strong-look-at-libel-laws-in-response-to-book.

29 *Federal Communications Commission v. Pacifica Foundation*, 438 U.S. 726 (1978).

30 See *Reno v. American Civil Liberties Union*, 521 U.S. 844 (1997); *Ashcroft v. American Civil Liberties Union*, 542 U.S. 656 (2004).

31 *Everson v. Board of Education Ewing Township*, 330 U.S. 1 (1947).

32 *Engle v. Vitale*, 370 U.S. 421 (1962); *Abington Township School District v. Schempp*, 374 U.S. 203 (1963); *Lee v. Wiseman*, 505 U.S. 577 (1991); *Santa Fe Independent School District v. Doe*, 530 U.S. 790 (2000).

33 Riffkin, R. (2014, September 25). In U.S., support for daily prayer in schools dips slightly. *Gallup*. Retrieved May 19, 2018, from http://news.gallup.com/poll/177401/support-daily-prayer-schools-dips-slightly.aspx.

34 *Zelman v. Simmons-Harris*, 536 U.S. 639 (2002).

35 Green, E. (2018, May 3). Trump creates a not-so-new faith office in the White House. *The Atlantic*. Retrieved May 19, 2018, from https://www.theatlantic.com/politics/archive/2018/05/trump-creates-a-not-so-new-faith-office-in-the-white-house/559574/.

36 Henderson, M. B., Peterson, P. E., & West, M. (n.d.). Results from the 2015 Education Next poll. *Education Next*. Retrieved May 19, 2018, from http://educationnext.org/2015-ednext-poll-interactive/.

37 *Braunfeld v. Brown*, 366 U.S. 599 (1961).

38 *Sherbert v. Verner*, 374 U.S. 398 (1963) and *Wisconsin v. Yoder*, 406 U.S. 205 (1972).

39 *Bob Jones University v. United States*, 461 U.S. 574 (1983).

40 *O'Lone v. Shabazz*, 482 U.S. 342 (1987).

41 *Employment Division, Department of Human Resources of Oregon v. Smith*, 494 U.S. 872 (1990).

42 Santeria is a religion started by African slaves brought to the Caribbean. It combines elements of Catholicism with traditional African and Indian religions, and a major Santeria ritual involves animal sacrifice.

43 *Church of the Lukumi Babalu Aye v. City of Hialeah*, 508 U.S. 520 (1993).

44 *Gonzales v. O Centro Espirita Beneficiente Uniao Do Vegetal*, 126 S.Ct. 1211 (2006).

45 *Equal Employment Opportunity Commission v. Abercrombie & Fitch Stores*, 135 S.Ct. 2028 (2015).

46 *Holt v. Hobbs*, 135 S.Ct. 853 (2015).

47 For more on the exclusionary rule and "good faith" exception, see *Massachusetts v. Sheppard*, 468 U.S. 981 (1984) and *United States v. Leon*, 468 U.S. 897 (1984).

48 *Katz v. United States*, 389 U.S. 347 (1967).

49 *American Civil Liberties Union v. National Security Agency*, 438 F. Supp. 2d 754 (2006)

50 *American Civil Liberties Union v. National Security Agency*, 493 F3d. 644 (2007)

51 Cert. denied, *American Civil Liberties Union v. National Security Agency*, 552 U.S. 1179 (2008).

52 *American Civil Liberties Union v. Clapper*, 785 F.3d. 787 (2015).

53 Diamond, J. (2015, September 7). NSA surveillance bill passes after weeks-long showdown. *CNN.com*. Retrieved May 22, 2018, from https://www.cnn.com/2015/06/02/politics/senate-usa-freedom-act-vote-patriot-act-nsa/.

54 Massie, V. M. (2016, July 11). What Philando Castile's death says about the dangers of "driving while Black." *Vox*. Retrieved May 22, 2018, from https://www.vox.com/2016/7/11/12147878/philando-castile-driving-while-black.

55 Silva, D. (2018, May 21). Border patrol agent detains women for speaking Spanish at Montana gas station. *NBC News*. Retrieved May 22, 2018, https://www.nbcnews.com/news/Latinx/border-patrol-agent-detains-women-speaking-spanish-montana-gas-station-n876096.

56 American Civil Liberties Union. (2004). *Sanctioned bias: Racial profiling since 9/11.* New York: Author. Retrieved May 22, 2018, from https://www.aclu.org/sites/default/files/field_document/racial%20profiling%20report.pdf.

57 *Escobedo v. Illinois*, 378 U.S. 478 (1964).

58 *Miranda v. Arizona*, 384 U.S. 436 (1966).

59 *Gideon v. Wainwright*, 372 U.S. 335 (1963).

60 Sehgal, U., Zelon, H., & Alexander, L. (2014). *State of injustice: How New York State turns its back on right to counsel for the poor.* New York: New York Civil Liberties Union, 2014. Retrieved May 23, 2018, from https://www.nyclu.org/sites/default/files/publications/nyclu_hh_report_FINAL.pdf.

61 Chammah, M. (2016, May 2). *Do public defenders spend less time on Black clients?* The Marshall Project. Retrieved May 23, 2018, from https://www.themarshallproject.org/2016/05/02/do-public-defenders-spend-less-time-on-black-clients.

62 See, for example, *Strauder v. West Virginia*, 100 U.S. 303 (1880); *Swain v. Alabama*, 380 U.S. 202 (1965).

63 *Batson v. Kentucky*, 476 U.S. 79 (1986).

64 Rosen, J. (1992). Jurymandering. *New Republic, 207,* 15–18.

65 Diamond, S. S., Peery, D., Dolan, F. J., & Dolan, E. (2009). Achieving diversity on the jury: Jury size and the peremptory challenge. *Journal of Empirical Legal Studies, 6,* 425–449.

66 *Hudson v. McMillan*, 503 U.S. 1 (1992).

67 *Harmelin v. Michigan*, 501 U.S. 957 (1991).

68 Gerstein, M. (2017, December 28). New law means less prison for repeat drug offenders. *Detroit Free Press.* Retrieved May 24, 2018, from https://www.detroitnews.com/story/news/politics/2017/12/28/michigan-law-drug-offender-parole/108976500/.

69 National Association for the Advancement of Colored People. (n.d.). *Criminal Justice Fact Sheet.* Retrieved May 24, 2018, from http://www.naacp.org/criminal-justice-fact-sheet/.

70 *Wilkerson v. Utah*, 99 U.S. 130 (1878) upheld execution by firing squad, hanging, or beheading. More recently, in *Glossip v. Gross*, 135 S.Ct. 2726 (2015), the Supreme Court upheld the use of midazolam in lethal injection procedures, despite claims that the drug does not sufficiently anesthetize the condemned inmate, which causes intense suffering.

71 Death Penalty Information Center. (2016). *States with and without the death penalty.* Retrieved May 25, 2018, from https://deathpenaltyinfo.org/states-and-without-death-penalty.

72 See, for example, Baldus, D., Woodworth, G., & Pulaski, C. (1990). *Equal justice and the death penalty: A legal and empirical analysis.* Boston: Northeastern University Press.

73 *McCleskey v. Kemp*, 481 U.S. 279 (1987).

74 *Bowers v. Hardwick*, 478 U.S. 176 (1984).

75 *Lawrence v. Texas*, 539 U.S. 558 (2003).

76 *Cruzan v. Director of Missouri Department of Health*, 497 U.S. 261 (1990).

77 *Griswold v. Connecticut*, 381 U.S. 479 (1965).

78 *Roe v. Wade*, 410 U.S. 113 (1973).

79 See *Planned Parenthood of Southeastern Pennsylvania v. Casey*, 505 U.S. 833 (1992).

80 Chappell, B. (2018, June 1, 2018). "Judge Temporarily Blocks Iowa's 'Fetal Heartbeat' Abortion Law." *National Public Radio.* Retrieved October 13, 2018, from https://www.npr.org/sections/thetwo-way/2018/06/01/616136014/court-puts-temporary-stop-on-iowas-heartbeat-abortion-law. .

81 Guttmacher Institute. (2018). *Targeted regulation of abortion providers.* Retrieved May 26, 2018, from https://www.guttmacher.org/state-policy/explore/targeted-regulation-abortion-providers.

82 *Whole Women's Health v. Hellerstedt*, 579 U.S. ___ (2016), Slip Opinion. Retrieved May 27, 2018, from https://www.supremecourt.gov/opinions/15pdf/15-274_new_e18f.pdf.

83 Sanders, L. (2018, January 18). Inside the states with one abortion clinic: Kentucky fights for its last provider in 2018. *Newsweek.* Retrieved May 27, 2018, from http://www.newsweek.com/state-without-abortion-clinic-kentucky-772692.

84 Brown, R., Jewell, R. T., & Rous, J. J. (2001). Provider availability, race, and abortion demand. *Southern Economic Journal, 67,* 656–671.

85 The Henry J. Kaiser Family Foundation. (n.d.). *Reported legal abortions by race of woman who obtained abortion by the state of occurrence: Timeframe 2014.* Retrieved May 27, 2018, https://www.kff.org/womens-health-policy/state-indicator/abortions-by-race/?currentTimeframe=0&sortModel=%7B%22colId%22:%22Location%22,%22sort%22:%22asc%22%7D.

86 Bartowski, J. P. Ramos-Wada, A. I., Ellison, C. G., & Acevedo, G. A. (2012). Faith, race-ethnicity, and public policy preferences: Religious schemas and abortion attitudes among U.S. Latinos. *Journal for the Scientific Study of Religion, 51,* 343–358.

Chapter 5

1 Casas, R. E. (2017). Opinion: American Dreamers. *New York Times.* Retrieved May 27, 2018, from https://www.nytimes.com/interactive/projects/storywall/american-dreamers/stories/fernando-espino-casas; Glauber, B. (2017, September 11). From Milwaukee to Harvard to San Francisco: A dreamer's path suddenly becomes unclear. *Milwaukee Journal Sentinel.* Retrieved May 27, 2018, from https://www.jsonline.com/story/news/local/milwaukee/2017/09/11/milwaukee-harvard-san-francisco-dreamers-life-path-now-has-uncertainow-crossroadsife-amid-uncertaint/647727001/; Peters, A.

(2017, September 6). Young dreamers react to the DACA decision with sadness and determination. *Fast Company*. Retrieved May 27, 2018, from https://www.fastcompany.com/40463026/young-dreamers-react-to-the-daca-decision-with-sadness-and-determination.

2 Glauber, "From Milwaukee to Harvard to San Francisco."

3 Kopan, T., & Fox, L. (2018, February 15). Bipartisan DACA, border security deal fails in Senate, putting immigration bill's future in doubt. *CNN Politics*. Retrieved May 28, 2018, from https://www.cnn.com/2018/02/15/politics/trump-immigration-veto/index.html.

4 Lind, D. (2017, April 25). A judge just opened the door to restarting DACA: Here's what his ruling means. *Vox*. Retrieved May 28, 2018, from https://www.vox.com/2018/4/25/17278644/judge-ruling-trump-end-daca-immigration.

5 Casas, "Opinion."

6 Krogstad, J. M., Passel, J. S., & Cohn, D. (2017, April 27). *Five facts about illegal immigration in the U.S.* Pew Research Center. Retrieved May 28, 2018, from http://www.pewresearch.org/fact-tank/2017/04/27/5-facts-about-illegal-immigration-in-the-u-s/.

7 McClain, P. D., Carew, J. D. J. (2018). *"Can we all get along?": Racial and ethnic minorities in American politics* (7th ed.). Boulder, CO: Westview Press, p. 7.

8 Weaver, C. (2017, May 10). Dwayne Johnson for President! *GQ*. Retrieved May 29, 2018, from https://www.gq.com/story/dwayne-johnson-for-president-cover.

9 For more on the question of whether Judaism is an ethnicity, see Gitelman, Z. (Ed.). (2009). *Religion or ethnicity: Jewish identities in evolution*. New Brunswick, NJ: Rutgers University Press.

10 Blaustein, A. P., & Zangrando, R. L. (1970). *Civil rights and the Black American: A documentary history*. New York: Clarion, pp. 42–44.

11 Ibid., pp. 44–47.

12 *Prigg v. Pennsylvania*, 41 U.S. 539 (1842).

13 Library of Congress. (n.d.). *Primary documents in American history: Northwest ordinances.* Retrieved May 29, 2018, from http://www.loc.gov/rr/program/bib/ourdocs/northwest.html.

14 Library of Congress. (n.d.). *Primary documents in American history: Missouri Compromise.* Retrieved May 29, 2018, from http://www.loc.gov/rr/program/bib/ourdocs/Missouri.html.

15 Library of Congress. (n.d.). *Primary documents in American history: Kansas-Nebraska Act.* Retrieved May 29, 2018, from http://www.loc.gov/rr/program/bib/ourdocs/kansas.html.

16 *Dred Scott v. Sandford*, 60 U.S. 393 (1857).

17 National Archives. (n.d.). *The Emancipation Proclamation.* Retrieved May 30, 2018, from https://www.archives.gov/exhibits/featured-documents/emancipation-proclamation.

18 National Archives. (n.d.). *African American records: The Freedman's Bureau, 1865–1872.* Retrieved May 30, 2018, from https://www.archives.gov/research/african-americans/freedmens-bureau.

19 McClain & Carew, *"Can we all get along?"*, pp. 20–21, 297.

20 McClain & Carew, *"Can we all get along?"*, pp. 20–21.

21 Ferris State University Jim Crow Museum of Racist Memorabilia. (n.d.). *Who was Jim Crow?* Retrieved May 29, 2018, from https://ferris.edu/jimcrow/what.htm.

22 *Plessy v. Ferguson*, 163 U.S. 537 (1896).

23 Nieman, D. G. (1991). *Promises to keep: African Americans and the constitutional order, 1776 to the present*. New York: Oxford University Press, pp. 115–119.

24 *United States v. Cruikshank*, 92 U.S. 542 (1876).

25 Lawson, S. F. (1997). *Running for freedom: Civil rights and Black politics in America since 1941* (2nd ed.). New York: McGraw-Hill, p. 81. African American population figures come from United States Census. *No. 23: Population, By Race, By State 1940 to 1960.* Retrieved June 1, 2018, from https://www2.census.gov/prod2/statcomp/documents/1961-02.pdf.

26 Myrdal, G. (1944). *An American dilemma: The Negro problem and American democracy.* New York: Harper & Brothers.

27 For more on World War II and its economic impact on civil rights, see Kryder, D. (2000). *Divided arsenal: Race and the American state during World War II.* New York: Cambridge University Press.

28 National Association for the Advancement of Colored People. (n.d.). *Oldest and boldest.* Retrieved June 1, 2018, from http://www.naacp.org/oldest-and-boldest/.

29 *Guinn and Beal v. United States*, 247 U.S. 347 (1915).

30 For a good history of the creation of the NAACP Legal Defense and Education Fund, see Greenberg, J. (1994). *Crusaders in the courts: How a dedicated band of lawyers fought for the civil rights revolution.* New York: Basic Books.

31 *Brown v. Board of Education, Topeka, Kansas*, 347 U.S. 483 (1954), 495.

32 Stanford University Martin Luther King, Jr. Research and Education Institute. (n.d.). "Montgomery Bus Boycott." Retrieved October 14, 2018, from https://kinginstitute.stanford.edu/encyclopedia/montgomery-bus-boycott

33 Stanford University Martin Luther King, Jr. Research and Education Institute. (n.d.). Sit-ins. Retrieved June 1, 2018, from https://kinginstitute.stanford.edu/encyclopedia/sit-ins.

34 United States National Park Service. (n.d.). March on Washington for jobs and freedom. Retrieved June 1, 2018, from https://www.nps.gov/articles/march-on-washington.htm.

35 Jones, W. P. (2013, August 23). Five myths about the March on Washington. *Washington Post*. Retrieved June 1, 2018, from https://www.washingtonpost

.com/opinions/five-myths-about-the-march-on-washington/2013/08/23/f760a85e-0a8e-11e3-b87c-476db8ac34cd_story
.html?utm_term=.c82552caa5f9.

36 Stern, M. (1992). Calculating visions: Kennedy, Johnson, and Civil Rights. New Brunswick, NJ: Rutgers University Press.

37 Slip Opinion, *Shelby County (AL) v. Holder*, No. 12–96. Retrieved October 14, 2018, from https://www.supremecourt.gov/opinions/12pdf/12-96_6k47.pdf.

38 Nieman, *Promises to keep*, p. 180.

39 *Swann v. Charlotte-Mecklenburg County Board of Education*, 402 U.S. 1 (1971).

40 Orfield, G., & Frankenberg, E., with Ee, J., & Kuscera, J. (2014, May 15). *Brown at 60: Great progress, a long retreat and an uncertain future*. Civil Rights Project, University of California at Los Angeles. Retrieved June 8, 2018, from https://www.civilrightsproject.ucla.edu/research/k-12-education/integration-and-diversity/brown-at-60-great-progress-a-long-retreat-and-an-uncertain-future/Brown-at-60-051814.pdf.

41 *Board of Education v. Dowell*, 498 U.S. 237 (1991).

42 *Parents Involved in Community Schools v. Seattle School District*, 551 U.S. 701 (2007).

43 Orfield & Frankenberg, *Brown at 60*.

44 U.S. Government Accountability Office. (2016, April). Report to Congressional requesters: K–12 education, better use of information could help agencies identify disparities and address racial discrimination. Retrieved June 13, 2018, from https://www.gao.gov/assets/680/676745.pdf.

45 Carter, S. (1991). *Reflections of an affirmative action baby*. New York: Basic Books.

46 DeSilver, D. (2014, August 23). *Supreme Court says states can ban affirmative action: 8 already have*. Pew Research Center. Retrieved June 13, 2018, from http://www.pewresearch.org/fact-tank/2014/04/22/supreme-court-says-states-can-ban-affirmative-action-8-already-have/.

47 *Regents of the University of California v. Bakke*, 438 U.S. 265 (1978).

48 *Grutter v. Bollinger*, 539 U.S. 306 (2003).

49 U.S. Supreme Court, *Fisher v. University of Texas*, Slip Opinion, October Term 2012. Retrieved June 13, 2018, from https://www.supremecourt.gov/opinions/12pdf/11-345_l5gm.pdf. See also Liptak, A. (2012, February 22). Justices take up race as a factor in college entry. *New York Times*, p. A1.

50 U.S. Supreme Court, *Fisher v. University of Texas*, Slip Opinion, October Term 2015. Retrieved June 13, 2018, from https://www.supremecourt.gov/opinions/15pdf/14-981_4g15.pdf.

51 For more on groups opposing voter ID laws, see, for example, American Civil Liberties Union. (n.d.). Oppose voter id laws – Fact sheet. Retrieved June 14, 2018, from https://www.aclu.org/other/oppose-voter-id-legislation-fact-sheet.

52 Liptak, A., & Wines, M. (2017, May 15). Strict North Carolina voter ID law thwarted after Supreme Court rejects case. *New York Times*. Retrieved June 14, 2018, from https://www.nytimes.com/2017/05/15/us/politics/voter-id-laws-supreme-court-north-carolina.html.

53 Swaine, J., McCarthy, C. (2017, January 8). Young Black men again faced highest rate of US police killings in 2016. *The Guardian*. Retrieved June 14, 2018, from https://www.theguardian.com/us-news/2017/jan/08/the-counted-police-killings-2016-young-black-men.

54 Black Lives Matter. (n.d.). Herstory. Retrieved June 14, 2018, from https://blacklivesmatter.com/about/herstory/.

55 Clemetson, L. (2003, January 22). Hispanics now largest minority, Census shows. *New York Times*. Retrieved June 14, 2018, from https://www.nytimes.com/2003/01/22/us/hispanics-now-largest-minority-census-shows.html.

56 McClain & Carew, *"Can we all get along?"*, pp. 15–16.

57 LULAC. (n.d.). *All for one—one for all*. Retrieved June 15, 2018, from https://lulac.org/about/history/.

58 McClain & Carew, *"Can we all get along?"*, pp. 53–54.

59 U.S. Department of Justice. (n.d.). About Language Minority Voting Rights. Retrieved June 14, 2018, from https://www.justice.gov/crt/about-language-minority-voting-rights.

60 McClain & Carew, *"Can we all get along?"*, p. 16.

61 González-Colón, Honorable J. (n.d.). About: What is the resident commissioner? Retrieved June 14, 2018, from https://gonzalez-colon.house.gov/about.

62 Fox, B., & Coto, D. (2012, November 7). Puerto Rico vote endorses statehood with asterisk. *Yahoo News*. Retrieved June 16, 2018, from https://www.yahoo.com/news/puerto-rico-vote-endorses-statehood-asterisk-205404726.html.

63 Einbinder, N. (2018, May 1). How the response to Hurricane Maria compared to Harvey and Irma. *Frontline*. Retrieved June 16, 2018, from https://www.pbs.org/wgbh/frontline/article/how-the-response-to-hurricane-maria-compared-to-harvey-and-irma/.

64 Bacon, J. (2018, May 29). Hurricane Maria killed more than 4,600 people – more than 70 times the official toll of 64, study says. *USA Today*. Retrieved June 16, 2018, from https://www.usatoday.com/story/news/nation/2018/05/29/hurricane-maria-killed-thousands-puerto-rico/650942002/.

65 Vinik, D. (2018, March 27). How Trump favored Texas over Puerto Rico. *Politico*. Retrieved June 16, 2018, from https://www.politico.com/story/2018/03/27/donald-trump-fema-hurricane-maria-response-480557.

66 Jenkins, N. (2017, October 13). "We want to become a state": Puerto Rico's sole representative in Congress speaks out. *Time*. Retrieved June 16, 2018, from http://time.com/4980934/puerto-rico-statehood-jenniffer-gonzalez-colon/.

67 See, for example, Whalen, C. T., & Vázquez-Hernández, V. (Eds.). (2005). *The Puerto Rican diaspora: Historical perspectives*. Philadelphia: Temple University Press.

68 McClain & Carew, *"Can we all get along?"*, pp. 16–17, 323–324.

69 *Time* Staff,. (2015, June 16). Here's Donald Trump's presidential announcement speech. *Time*. Retrieved October 14. 2018 from http:// time.com/3923128/donald-trump-announcement-speech/.

70 Bierman, N., & Mehta, S. (2018, August 31). Trump backs away from full mass deportations, but his speech packs a slew of hard-line proposals. *Los Angeles Times*. Retrieved June 16, 2018, from http://www.latimes.com/politics/la-na-pol-trump-immigration-speech-20160831-snap-story.html.

71 Kopan, T., Fox, L. (2018, January 11). Trump says some immigrants from "shithole countries" as he rejects bipartisan deal. *CNN Politics*. Retrieved June 16, 2018, from https://www.cnn.com/2018/01/11/politics/daca-deal-obstacles-flake-white-house/index.html.

72 Lind, D. (2018, June 15). The Trump administration's separation of families at the border, explained. *Vox*. Retrieved June 16, 2018, from https://www.vox.com/2018/6/11/17443198/children-immigrant-families-separated-parents; Salama, V. (2018, October 13). "Trump defends separating families at the border." *Wall Street Journal*. Retrieved October 14, 2018, from https://www.wsj.com/articles/trump-defends-separating-families-at-the-border-1539464658.

73 Seitz-Wald, A. (2012, May 22). Rep. Steve King: Immigrants are like dogs. *Salon*. Retrieved June 16, 2018, from http://www.salon.com /2012/05/22/rep_steve_king_immigrants_like_dogs/.

74 Gamboa, S. (2018, February 7). Kelly's "lazy" dreamer comment is racist and obscures truth on DACA numbers, critics say. *NBC News*. Retrieved June 16, 2018, from https://www.nbcnews.com/news/latino/kelly-s-lazy-dreamer-comment-racist-obscures-truth-daca-numbers-n845746.

75 Anti-Defamation League. (2008). *Immigrants targeted: Extremist rhetoric moves into the mainstream*. Retrieved June 16, 2018, from https://www.adl.org/sites/default/files/documents/assets/pdf/civil-rights/immigration/Immigrants-Targeted-UPDATE_2008.pdf.

76 National Archives and Records Administration. (n.d.). *The Chinese Exclusion Act (1882)*. Retrieved June 16, 2018, from http://www.ourdocuments.gov/document_data/pdf/doc_047.pdf.

77 McClain & Carew, *"Can we all get along?"*, p. 18.

78 *Korematsu v. United States*, 323 U.S. 214 (1944).

79 McClain & Carew, *"Can we all get along?"*, p. 19.

80 Japanese American Citizens League. (n.d.). *History*. Retrieved June 16, 2018, from https://jacl.org/about/history/.

81 Chinese American Citizens Alliance. (n.d.). *History of CACA*. Retrieved June 16, 2018, from http://www.cacanational.org/htmlPages/history.html.

82 Chinese for Affirmative Action. (n.d.). *Issue advocacy*. Retrieved June 16, 2018, from http://www.caasf.org/what-we-do/issue-advocacy/.

83 The Cherokee Nation. (n.d.). *A brief history of the Trail of Tears*. Retrieved June 16, 2018, from http://www.cherokee.org/About-The-Nation/History/Trail-of-Tears/A-Brief-History-of-the-Trail-of-Tears.

84 National Archives and Records Administration. (n.d.). *Transcript of Dawes Act (1997)*. Retrieved June 16, 2018, from https://www.ourdocuments.gov/doc.php?flash=false&doc=50&page=transcript.

85 National Archives. (n.d.). *Map of Indian Territory, the Dawes Act, and Will Rogers' enrollment case file*. Retrieved June 16, 2018, from https://www.archives.gov/education/lessons/fed-indian-policy.

86 McClain & Carew, *Can we all get along?*, pp. 15, 307–308.

87 Ibid., p. 56.

88 Fagan, K. (2008, April 20). Casinos riches elude majority of state's Indians; inequities anger many who lobbied for expansion. *San Francisco Chronicle*, p. A10.

89 Francis, R. (n.d.). *The history behind the civil rights amendment*. The Alice Paul Institute. Retrieved June 16, 2018, from http://www.equalrightsamendment.org/history.htm; Free, L. E. (2005). The Seneca Falls Convention. *The encyclopedia of New York State*. Syracuse, NY: Syracuse University Press. Retrieved June 16, 2018, from http://www.syracuseuniversitypress.syr.edu/encyclopedia/entries/seneca-falls-convention.html.

90 See, for example, *Reed v. Reed*, 404 U.S. 71 (1971); *Geduldig v. Aiello*, 417 U.S. 484 (1974).

91 Francis, "The history behind.".

92 Ibid.; McGlen, N. E., O'Connor, K. (1983). *Women's rights: The struggle for equality in the 19th and 20th centuries*. New York: Praeger, p. 380.

93 Library of Congress. (n.d.). *H.J. Res. 51: Removing the deadline for the ratification of the equal rights amendment*. Retrieved June 16, 2018, from https://www.congress.gov/bill/114th-congress/house-joint-resolution/51/text?q=%7B%22search%22%3A%5B%22S.J.Res.+24%22%5D%7D&r=27.

94 Equal Employment Opportunity Commission. (n.d.). *The Equal Pay Act of 1963*. Retrieved June 16, 2018, from https://www.eeoc.gov/laws/statutes/epa.cfm.

95 Celebrities share stories of sexual assault for #MeToo campaign. (2017, October 16). *Vogue*. Retrieved June 16, 2018, from https://www.vogue.com/article/alyssa-milano-metoo-sexual-assault-campaign.

96 ACT UP. (n.d.). *Capsule history.* Retrieved June 16, 2018, from http://www.actupny.org/documents/capsule-home.html.

97 *Lawrence v. Texas*, 539 U.S. 558 (2003).

98 Cloud, D. S., Zucchino, D. (2011, September 21). Military gays celebrate freedom. *Los Angeles Times*, p. A1.

99 *Obergefell v. Hodges* (2016), Slip Opinion. Retrieved October 14, 2018, from https://www.supremecourt.gov/opinions/14pdf/14-556_3204.pdf.

100 Holpuch, A. (2015, April 2). Indiana amends religious freedom bill to put an end to discrimination. *The Guardian*. Retrieved June 18, 2018, from https://www.theguardian.com/us-news/2015/apr/02/indiana-republicans-religious-freedom.

101 Park, H., Mykhyalyshyn, I. (2016, June 16). L.G.B.T. people are more likely to be targets of hate crimes than any other minority group. *New York Times*. Retrieved June 18, 2018, from https://www.nytimes.com/interactive/2016/06/16/us/hate-crimes-against-lgbt.html.

102 Human Rights Campaign. (n.d.). *State maps of laws & policies: Hate crimes.* Retrieved June 18, 2018, from https://www.hrc.org/state-maps/hate-crimes.

103 Blinder, A. (2017, November 4). An embattled North Carolina seeks to overturn a law's bitter legacy. *New York Times*. Retrieved June 18, 2018, from https://www.nytimes.com/2017/11/04/us/north-carolina-transgender-law.html.

104 Terrell, K. (2017, December 14). *The age discrimination law turns 50.* American Association of Retired Persons: Work & Jobs. Retrieved June 18, 2018, from https://www.aarp.org/work/working-at-50-plus/info-2017/adea-age-discrimination-fd.html.

105 Disability Rights Education & Defense Fund. (n.d.). *About DREDF.* Retrieved June 18, 2018, from https://dredf.org/about-us/.

Chapter 6

1 United States Census. (n.d.). *My Congressional District, 115th Congress: Texas, Congressional District 23.* Retrieved June 19, 2018, from https://www.census.gov/mycd/?st=48&cd=23.

2 Congressman Will Hurd: 23rd District of Texas. (n.d.). *About.* Retrieved June 19, 2018, from https://hurd.house.gov/about%20.

3 Five Thirty Eight. (n.d.). Tracking Congress in the age of Trump: Will Hurd. Retrieved June 20, 2018, from https://projects.fivethirtyeight.com/congress-trump-score/will-hurd/.

4 Kopan, T. (2018, June 16). Republican Rep. Will Hurd: Using detained kids as a deterrent policy is "unacceptable." *CNN Politics*. Retrieved June 20, 2018, from https://www.cnn.com/2018/06/16/politics/rep-will-hurd-visit-tornillo-facility/index.html.

5 Five Thirty Eight, "Tracking Congress." 2018 Election results from Politico (n.d.). "House Election Results." Retrieved November 20, 2018, from https://www.politico.com/election-results/2018/house/.

6 As we discussed in Chapter 5, the representative from Puerto Rico is called a resident commissioner, but the position enjoys the same rights and privileges as other nonvoting delegates.

7 Steckelberg, A., & Esteban, C. (2017, September 28). More than 4 million Americans don't have anyone to vote for them in Congress. *Washington Post*. Retrieved June 20, 2018, from https://www.washingtonpost.com/graphics/2017/national/fair-representation/?utm_term=.f4eb1c900820; Ware, N., & Wood, E. (2006, August 24). *Race and the right to vote.* Brennan Center for Law and Justice. Retrieved October 20, 2018, from https://www.brennancenter.org/analysis/race-and-right-vote.

8 U.S. Census Bureau. (n.d.). QuickFacts: District of Columbia. Retrieved June 20, 2018, from https://www.census.gov/quickfacts/DC.

9 To keep the size of the House an odd number, the proponents of the bill wanted to add a 437th seat after adding the new seat from Washington, DC. Utah was next in line to receive another representative after the reapportionment following the 2000 census; therefore, it would receive the extra seat. Redistricting the state would be too complicated, so the seat would be at-large. Moreover, because the DC seat would most likely be filled by a Democrat, proponents of the bill figured that the Utah at-large seat, which would most likely be filled by a Republican, would not change the partisan composition of the House.

10 Bill for D.C. rep put on hold. (2009, March 11). *Bergen Record* (Bergen County, NJ), p. A9.

11 Dinan, S. (2011, January 6). Boehner takes reins of the House. *Washington Times*, p. 1.

12 United States House of Representatives. (n.d.). History, Art, & Archives: Historical highlights 1911 reapportionment. Retrieved June 20, 2018, from http://history.house.gov/HistoricalHighlight/Detail/35159?ret=True.

13 Prokop, A. (2018, March 19). What Pennsylvania's new congressional map means for 2018. *Vox*. Retrieved June 21, 2018, from https://www.vox.com/policy-and-politics/2018/2/21/17032936/pennsylvania-congressional-districts-2018.

14 In 2018 the U.S. Supreme Court declined to rule on the constitutionality of gerrymandering in Wisconsin and Maryland, based on the procedural issue of standing (see Chapter 9). Wheeler, L. (2018, June 21). Supreme Court sidesteps partisan gerrymandering in Wisconsin, Maryland cases. *The Hill*. Retrieved June 21, 2018, from http://thehill.com/homenews/news/392758-supreme-court-rules-against-wisconsin-democrats-in-key-gerrymandering-case.

15 *Wesbery v. Sanders*, 376 U.S. 1 (1964).

16 *Karcher v. Daggett*, 462 U.S. 725 (1983).

17 See *Shaw v. Reno*, 509 U.S. 630 (1993); *Miller v. Johnson*, 512 U.S. 622 (1995); *Bush v. Vera*, 517 U.S. 952 (1996); and *Shaw v. Hunt*, 517 U.S. 899 (1996).

18 For more on these views of representation, see Pitkin, H. F. (1967). *The concept of representation*, Berkeley: University of California Press.

19 For more on the impact of majority-minority districts, see Cameron, C., Epstein, D., & O'Halloran, S. (1996). Do majority-minority districts maximize Black representation in Congress? *American Political Science Review, 90*, 794–812; Hill, K. A. (1995). Does the creation of majority black districts aid Republicans?: An analysis of the 1992 congressional elections in eight Southern states. *Journal of Politics, 57*, 384–401.

20 Kane, P. (2014, August 18). How Jim Jeffords single-handily bent the arc of politics. *Washington Post*. Retrieved June 22, 2018, from https://www.washingtonpost.com/news/the-fix/wp/2014/08/18/how-jim-jeffords-single-handedly-bent-the-arc-of-politics/?utm_term=.e5ed54e1913f.

21 For more on majority party control in the House of Representatives, see Cox, G. W., & McCubbins, M. D. (2007). *Legislative leviathan: Party government in the House* (2nd ed.). New York: Cambridge University Press.

22 Pershing, B. (2011, May 10). Clyburn leadership role a "work in progress." *Washington Post*, p. A15.

23 Korte, G. (2016, January 6). Obama vetoes GOP attempt to repeal Obamacare. *USA Today*. Retrieved June 22, 2018, from https://www.usatoday.com/story/news/politics/2016/01/08/obama-vetoes-gop-attempt-repeal-obamacare/78506800/.

24 Roubein, R. (2017, September 26). Timeline: The GOP's failed effort to repeal ObamaCare. *The Hill*. Retrieved June 22, 2018, from http://thehill.com/policy/healthcare/other/352587-timeline-the-gop-effort-to-repeal-and-replace-obamacare.

25 United States House of Representatives. *History, art, & archives: The Civil Rights Movement and the Second Reconstruction, 1945–1968*. Retrieved June 23, 2018, from http://history.house.gov/Exhibitions-and-Publications/BAIC/Historical-Essays/Keeping-the-Faith/Civil-Rights-Movement/.

26 Congressional Wine Caucus. (n.d.). *About the Wine Caucus*. Retrieved June 23, 2018, from https://winecaucus-mikethompson.house.gov/.

27 Congressional Sportsmen's Foundation. (n.d.). *About*. Retrieved June 23, 2018, from http://congressionalsportsmen.org/about.

28 Congressional Black Caucus. (n.d.). *Criminal justice reform*. Retrieved June 23, 2018, from https://cbc.house.gov/issues/issue/?IssueID=14891.

29 Congressional Black Caucus. (n.d.). *Membership*. Retrieved June 24, 2018, from https://cbc.house.gov/membership/.

30 Congressional Hispanic Caucus. (2018, June 21). CHC chair on GOP immigration bills and Trump Executive Order. Retrieved June 23, 2018, from https://congressionalhispaniccaucus-lujangrisham.house.gov/media-center/press-releases/chc-chair-on-gop-immigration-bills-and-trump-executive-order.

31 Congressional Hispanic Caucus. (n.d.). *Members*. Retrieved June 25, 2018, from https://congressionalhispaniccaucus-lujangrisham.house.gov/members.

32 Congressional Asian Pacific American Caucus. (n.d.). Purpose, mission & goals. Retrieved June 24, 2018, from https://capac-chu.house.gov/about-me/purpose-mission-goals.

33 Congressional Asian Pacific American Caucus. (n.d.). *115th Congress membership*. Retrieved June 23, 2018, from https://capac-chu.house.gov/members.

34 House of Representatives Committee on Rules. (n.d.). *About the Committee on Rules—History and processes*. Retrieved June 24, 2018, from https://rules.house.gov/about.

35 For more on Representative Howard Smith's tenure as chair of the Rules Committee, see Dierenfield, B. J. (1987). *Keeper of the Rules: Congressman Howard W. Smith of Virginia*. Charlottesville: University Press of Virginia; United States House of Representatives. (n.d.). History, art, & archives: The Civil Rights Movement and the Second Reconstruction, 1945–1968. Retrieved June 23, 2018, from http://history.house.gov/Exhibitions-and-Publications/BAIC/Historical-Essays/Keeping-the-Faith/Civil-Rights-Movement/.

36 Calia, M., & Pramuk, J. (2018, January 21). Despite Trump Tweet, McConnell opposes using 'nuclear option' in shutdown battle. *CNBC Politics*. Retrieved June 23, 2018, from https://www.cnbc.com/2018/01/21/mcconnell-opposes-shutdown-nuclear-option-trump-urged-in-tweet.html.

37 Neuman, J. (2007, September 19). The Senate says no to D.C. voice in Congress. *Los Angeles Times*, p. A14.

38 Grunwald, M. (1999, October 23). Missouri Senate race is heating up early: Rejection of judge puts Ashcroft on spot. *Washington Post*, p. A6.

39 Cooper, K. J. (1993, January 6). Hastings joins his accusers. *Washington Post*, p. A10; United States Census. (n.d.). *My Congressional District: Florida Congressional District 20*. Retrieved June 24, 2018, from https://www.census.gov/mycd/?st=12&cd=20.

40 Chaddock, G. R. (2011, January 13). With new oversight powers, House GOP aims to put Obama on defensive. *Christian Science Monitor*. Retrieved October 12, 2018, from https://www.csmonitor.com/USA/Politics/2011/0113/With-new-oversight-powers-House-GOP-aims-to-put-Obama-on-defensive.

41 Memoli, M. (2018, April 27). House Intelligence Committee releases full report on Russia investigation. *NBC News*. Retrieved June 23, 2018, from https://www.nbcnews.com/politics/congress/house-intelligence-committee-releases-full-report-russia-investigation-n869656.

42 Mayhew, D. R. (1974). *Congress: The electoral connection*. New Haven, CT: Yale University Press.

43 Fenno, R. (1978). *Home style: House members in their districts*. Boston: Little, Brown.

44 Fiorina, M. P. (1989). *Congress: Keystone of the Washington establishment* (2nd ed.). New Haven, CT: Yale University Press.

45 Grose, C. R. (2011). *Congress in Black and White: Race and representation in Congress and at home*. New York: Cambridge University Press.

46 United States House of Representatives Committee on House Administration. (n.d.). What is the Frank? Retrieved June 23, 2018, from https://cha.house.gov/franking-commission/what-frank.

47 Foley, E. (2013, October 29). Ileana Ros-Lehtinen supports Democrat-led immigration bill. *Huffington Post*. Retrieved June 25, 2018, from https://www.huffingtonpost.com/2013/10/29/ileana-ros-lehtinen-immigration_n_4173785.html.

48 Fiorina, *Congress: Keystone* also discusses the role that pork barrel spending plays in members' reelection prospects.

49 National Public Radio. (2010, September 8). Origins of bridge to nowhere explained. *All Things Considered*. Retrieved June 25, 2018, from https://www.npr.org/templates/story/story.php?storyId=94481285.

50 Japanese American Citizens League. (n.d.). *History*. Retrieved June 25, 2018, from https://jacl.org/about/history/.

51 League of United Latin American Citizens. (n.d.). *Advocacy*. Retrieved June 25, 2018, from https://lulac.org/advocacy/.

52 Fiorina, *Congress: Keystone*, p. 56.

Chapter 7

1 Clarke, S. (2017, January 17). 10 things you didn't know about Gen. John Kelly. *U.S. News & World Report*. Retrieved June 26, 2018, from https://www.usnews.com/news/national-news/articles/2017-01-17/10-things-you-didnt-know-about-gen-john-kelly; Sacchetti, M. (2016, December 8). General John Kelly: From Brighton to the White House. *Boston Globe*. Retrieved June 26, 2018, from https://www.bostonglobe.com/metro/2016/12/07/son-brighton-nominated-lead-homeland-security/Yifyu8x6bDvufdKhzREaxL/story.html.

2 Nixon, R., & D. Shear, M. D. (2017, July 28). John Kelly, new Chief of Staff, is seen as a beacon of discipline. *New York Times*. Retrieved June 26, 2018, from https://www.nytimes.com/2017/07/28/us/politics/john-kelly-chief-of-staff-donald-trump.html.

3 Alcindor, Y. (2017, October 18). Rep Frederica Wilson on Trump: "That is not what you say to a grieving widow. *New York Times*. Retrieved June 27, 2018, from https://www.nytimes.com/2017/10/18/us/politics/congresswoman-wilson-trump-niger-call-widow.html.

4 King, L. (2017, October 20). Video debunks John Kelly's claim that Frederica Wilson took credit for FBI building funds. *USA Today*. Retrieved June 27, 2018, from https://www.usatoday.com/story/news/politics/onpolitics/2017/10/20/chief-staff-kelly-falsely-accuses-rep-wilson-taking-credit-funding-fbi-building/784456001/; Tatum, S. (2017, October 31). Kelly says he'll "never apologize for comments about Rep. Frederica Wilson." *CNN Politics*. Retrieved June 27, 2018, from https://www.usatoday.com/story/news/politics/onpolitics/2017/10/20/chief-staff-kelly-falsely-accuses-rep-wilson-taking-credit-funding-fbi-building/784456001/.

5 Sanders, L. (2017, October 20). John Kelly's "empty barrel" attack was racist Frederica Wilson says. *Newsweek*. Retrieved June 28, 2018, from http://www.newsweek.com/john-kelly-empty-barrel-attack-was-racist-frederica-wilson-says-689243.

6 Griffiths, B. D. (2017, October 22). CBC Women: John Kelly must apologize to Rep. Wilson. *Politico*. Retrieved June 28, 2018, from https://www.politico.com/story/2017/10/22/black-caucus-wilson-john-kelly-244045.

7 Gamboa, S. (2018, February 7). Kelly's "lazy" dreamer comment is racist and obscures truth on DACA numbers, critics say. *NBC News*. Retrieved June 28, 2018, from https://www.nbcnews.com/news/Latinx/kelly-s-lazy-dreamer-comment-racist-obscures-truth-daca-numbers-n845746.

8 McClain, P. D., & Stewart Jr., J. (2014). *"Can we all get along?": Racial and ethnic minorities in American politics* (6th ed.). Boulder, CO: Westview Press, pp. 153–157.

9 Election of 2008. (1999–2018). In J. Woolley & G. Peters, *The American Presidency Project*. Santa Barbara: University of California at Santa Barbara. Retrieved June 28, 2018, from http://www.presidency.ucsb.edu/showelection.php?year=2008.

10 Election results: Presidential. (n.d.). *CNN Politics*. Retrieved November 16, 2016, from http://edition.cnn.com/election/results/president.

11 Devere, E.-I. (2018, June 11). Inside Obama's secret meetings with 2020 contenders. *Politico*. Retrieved June 28, 2018, from https://www.politico.com/story/2018/06/11/obama-2020-elections-sanders-warren-635165.

12 U.S. Census Bureau. (n.d.). *QuickFacts: New Hampshire*. Retrieved June 28, 2018, from https://www.census.gov/quickfacts/fact/table/nh/PST045217.

13 U.S. Census Bureau. (n.d.). *QuickFacts: Iowa*. Retrieved June 28, 2018, from https://www.census.gov/quickfacts/fact/table/ia/PST045217.

14 Nagourney, A. (2008, January 4). Obama takes Iowa in big turnout as Clinton falters; Huckabee winner. *New York Times*. Retrieved June 28, 2018, from https://www.nytimes.com/2008/01/04/us/politics/04elect.html.

15 Jacobs, J. (2016, February 1). Cruz wins caucuses, beating Trump. *Des Moines Register*. Retrieved June 28, 2018, from https://www.desmoinesregister.com/story/news/

elections/presidential/caucus/2016/02/01/republican-ted-cruz-wins-iowa-caucuses/79625866/.

16 Election of 1876. (1999–2018). In J. Woolley & G. Peters, *The American Presidency Project*. Santa Barbara: University of California at Santa Barbara. Retrieved June 29, 2018, from http://www.presidency.ucsb.edu/showelection.php?year=1876.

17 Election of 1888. (1999–2018). In J. Woolley & G. Peters, *The American Presidency Project*. Santa Barbara: University of California at Santa Barbara. Retrieved June 29, 2018, from http://www.presidency.ucsb.edu/showelection.php?year=1888.

18 *Bush v. Gore*, 531 U.S. 98 (2000).

19 Election of 2000. (1999–2018). In J. Woolley & G. Peters, *The American Presidency Project*. Santa Barbara: University of California at Santa Barbara. Retrieved June 29, 2018, from http://www.presidency.ucsb.edu/showelection.php?year=2000.

20 Election of 2008. (1999–2018). In J. Woolley & G. Peters, *The American Presidency Project*. Santa Barbara: University of California at Santa Barbara. Retrieved June 29, 2018, from http://www.presidency.ucsb.edu/showelection.php?year=2008; Election of 2012. (1999–2018). In J. Woolley & G. Peters, *The American Presidency Project*. Santa Barbara: University of California at Santa Barbara. Retrieved June 29, 2018, from http://www.presidency.ucsb.edu/showelection.php?year=2012.

21 Election of 2016. (1999–2018). In J. Woolley & G. Peters, *The American Presidency Project*. Santa Barbara: University of California at Santa Barbara. Retrieved June 29, 2018, from http://www.presidency.ucsb.edu/showelection.php?year=2016.

22 Struyk, R., & Pearle, L. (2017, May 11). Fact checking Trump's repeated unsubstantiated claim of widespread voter Fraud. *ABC News*. Retrieved June 29, 2018, from https://abcnews.go.com/Politics/fact-checking-trumps-repeated-unsubstantiated-claim-widespread-voter/story?id=45021067.

23 Bradley, T. (2008, December 5). Final fundraising figure: Obama's $750 million. *ABC News*. Retrieved June 29, 2018, from https://abcnews.go.com/Politics/Vote2008/story?id=6397572&page=1.

24 Vogel, K. P., Levinthal, D. & Parti, T. (2012, December 7). Obama, Romney both topped $1B. *Politico*. Retrieved June 29, 2018, from https://www.politico.com/story/2012/12/barack-obama-mitt-romney-both-topped-1-billion-in-2012-084737.

25 For more on the Obama campaign's use of high-tech data mining see, Murphy, T. (2012, September/October). Inside the Obama campaign's hard drive. *Mother Jones*. Retrieved June 29, 2018, from https://www.motherjones.com/politics/2012/10/harper-reed-obama-campaign-microtargeting/.

26 Allison, B., Rojanasakul, M., Harris, B., & Sam, C. (2016, December 9). Tracking the 2016 presidential money race. *Bloomberg*. Retrieved June 29, 2018, from https://www.bloomberg.com/politics/graphics/2016-presidential-campaign-fundraising..

27 Wallace, G. (2016, November 30). Voter turnout at 20-year low in 2016. *CNN Politics*. Retrieved June 29, 2018, from https://www.cnn.com/2016/11/11/politics/popular-vote-turnout-2016/index.html.

28 Krieg, G. J. (2012, August 9). What is a super PAC?: A short history. *ABC News*. Retrieved June 29, 2018, from https://abcnews.go.com/Politics/OTUS/super-pac-short-history/story?id=16960267.

29 Center for Responsive Politics. (n.d.). Super PACs: 2016 cycle. *Open Secrets*. Retrieved June 29, 2018, from https://www.opensecrets.org/pacs/superpacs.php?cycle=2016.

30 Hamilton, A. (2009).*The Federalist Papers, No. 70* (M. Genovese, Ed.). New York: Palgrave Macmillan, p. 199.

31 Neustadt, R. E. (1980). *Presidential power and the modern presidents: The politics of leadership from Roosevelt to Reagan*. New York: Free Press.

32 See Riley, R. L. (1999). *The presidency and the politics of racial inequality: Nation keeping from 1831 to 1965*. New York: Columbia University Press.

33 Stern, M. J. (2017, May 30). Obama's civil rights legacy is crumbling. *Slate*. Retrieved June 29, 2018, from http://www.slate.com/articles/news_and_politics/jurisprudence/2017/05/the_trump_administration_is_dismantling_obama_s_civil_rights_legacy.html.

34 For more on signing statements, see Presidential Signing Statements: Frequently Asked Questions. (1999–2016). In J. Woolley & G. Peters, *The American Presidency Project*. Santa Barbara: University of California at Santa Barbara. Retrieved June 29, 2018, from http://www.presidency.ucsb.edu/signingstatements.php.

35 Savage, C. (2008, February 9). Bush move on Darfur law criticized: Critics say he undercuts law on divestment, president cites policy role. *Boston Globe*, p. A2.

36 The authors counted Obama and Bush signing statements reported for each year in Signing Statements. (1999–2018). In J. Woolley & G. Peters, *The American Presidency Project*. Santa Barbara: University of California at Santa Barbara. Retrieved June 29, 2018, from http://www.presidency.ucsb.edu/signingstatements.php.

37 Donald J. Trump: Statement on signing the countering America's adversaries through sanctions act, August 2, 2017. In J. Woolley & G. Peters, *The American Presidency Project*. Santa Barbara: University of California at Santa Barbara. Retrieved June 29, 2018, from http://www.presidency.ucsb.edu/ws/index.php?pid=126763.

38 McClain, P. D., & Carew, J. D. J. (2018). *"Can we all get along?" Racial and ethnic minorities in American politics* (7th ed.). Boulder, CO: Westview Press, p. 157.

39 Lyndon B. Johnson: Executive Order 11246—Equal Employment Opportunity, September 24, 1965. In J. Woolley & G. Peters, *The American Presidency Project*.

Santa Barbara: University of California at Santa Barbara. Retrieved June 29, 2018, from http://www.presidency.ucsb.edu/ws/index.php?pid=59153.

40 Cohen, T. (2012, June 16). Obama administration to stop deporting some young illegal immigrants. *CNN Politics*. Retrieved June 29, 2018, from https://www.cnn.com/2012/06/15/politics/immigration/index.html.

41 Kopan, T., & Fox, L. (2018, February 15). Bipartisan DACA, border security deal fails in Senate, putting immigration bill's future in doubt. *CNN Politics*. Retrieved June 29, 2018, from https://www.cnn.com/2018/02/15/politics/trump-immigration-veto/index.html.

42 Lind, D. (2017, April 25). A judge just opened the door to restarting DACA: Here's what his ruling means. *Vox*. Retrieved June 29, 2018, from https://www.vox.com/2018/4/25/17278644/judge-ruling-trump-end-daca-immigration.

43 Oreskes, M. (1989, March 10). Senate rejects Tower 53–47. *New York Times*, p. A1.

44 LoBianco, T., Barrett, T., & Scott, E. (2017, February 7). Betsy DeVos confirmed as Education Secretary; Vice President casts historic tie-breaking vote. *Politico*. Retrieved June 30, 2018, from https://www.cnn.com/2017/02/07/politics/betsy-devos-senate-vote/index.html.

45 Everett, B., Palmeri, T., & Levine, M. (2017, February 15). Labor nominee Pudzer withdraws. *Politico*. Retrieved June 29, 2018, from https://www.politico.com/story/2017/02/senate-republicans-tell-white-house-to-withdraw-puzder-nomination-235062.

46 Liptak, K., Diaz, D., & Tatum, S. (2017, August 27). Trump pardons former sheriff Joe Arpaio. *CNN Politics*. Retrieved June 30, 2018, from https://www.cnn.com/2017/08/25/politics/sheriff-joe-arpaio-donald-trump-pardon/index.html.

47 *United States v. Curtiss-Wright Export Corp.*, 299 U.S. 304, 319 (1936).

48 United States Senate. (n.d.). *Treaty of Versailles*. Retrieved June 29, 2018, from https://www.senate.gov/artandhistory/history/common/generic/Feature_Homepage_TreatyVersailles.htm.

49 Thompson, J. (2002, June 14). ABM treaty officially ends after 30 years. *Omaha World-Herald*, p. 5A.

50 *United States v. Belmont*, 301 U.S. 324 (1937); *United States v. Pink*, 313 U.S. 203 (1942).

51 O'Brien, D. (2008). *Constitutional law and politics: Vol. 1. Struggles for power and governmental accountability* (7th ed.). New York: Norton, p. 252.

52 *Hamdan v. Rumsfeld*, 548 U.S. 557 (2006); *Boumediene v. Bush*, 553 U.S. 723 (2008).

53 Miller, G., & Banes, J. E. (2009, January 23). The United States will not torture, Obama says: President says terror war will be won on our own terms. *Baltimore Sun*, p. 1A.

54 Sullivan A. (2018, April 6) "Trump isn't merely tolerating torture – He's celebrating it." *The New York Magazine*,

Retrieved October 16, 2018, from http://nymag.com/daily/intelligencer/2018/04/trump-isnt-merely-tolerating-torture-hes-celebrating-it.html.

55 Zenko, M. (2016, January 12). Obama's embrace of drone strikes will be a lasting legacy. *New York Times*. Retrieved June 29, 2018, from https://www.nytimes.com/roomfordebate/2016/01/12/reflecting-on-obamas-presidency/obamas-embrace-of-drone-strikes-will-be-a-lasting-legacy.

56 Liptak, K., & Gaouette, N. (2018, May 9). Trump withdraws from Iran nuclear deal, isolating him further from the World. *CNN Politics*. Retrieved June 29, 2018, from https://www.cnn.com/2018/05/08/politics/donald-trump-iran-deal-announcement-decision/index.html.

57 Volcovici, V. (2017, August 4). U.S. submits formal notice of withdrawal from Paris climate pact. *Reuters*. Retrieved June 29, 2018, from https://www.reuters.com/article/us-un-climate-usa-paris/u-s-submits-formal-notice-of-withdrawal-from-paris-climate-pact-idUSKBN1AK2FM.

58 Liptak, K. (2018, June 12). Trump's North Korea gamble ends with "special bond" with Kim. *CNN Politics*. Retrieved June 29, 2018, from https://www.cnn.com/2018/06/11/politics/trump-kim-summit-singapore/index.html.

59 Congress.gov. (n.d.). *S. 321 – Indian Preference Act: 101st Congress (1989–1990)*. Retrieved June 30, 2018, from https://www.congress.gov/bill/101st-congress/senate-bill/321.

60 U.S. Senate. (n.d.). Art & History: The State of the Union Address. Retrieved June 30, 2018, from https://www.senate.gov/artandhistory/history/common/generic/News_State_of_the_Union.htm.

61 Office of the Historian and Office of Art & Archives, U.S. House of Representatives. (n.d.). The State of the Union Address. Retrieved June 30, 2018, from http://history.house.gov/Institution/SOTU/State-of-the-Union/; *Historical Highlights: The first televised evening State of the Union Address, January 4, 1965*. (n.d.). Retrieved June 30, 2018, from http://history.house.gov/HistoricalHighlight/Detail/36366?ret=True.

62 Lyndon B. Johnson: Annual Message to the Congress on the State of the Union, January 4, 1965. (1999–2018). In J. Woolley & G. Peters, *The American Presidency Project*. Santa Barbara: University of California at Santa Barbara. Retrieved June 30, 2018, from http://www.presidency.ucsb.edu/ws/?pid=26907.

63 Berenson, T. (2018, January 3). 4 things President Trump wants to accomplish in 2018. *Time*. Retrieved June 30, 2018, from http://time.com/5084907/donald-trump-2018-calendar/.

64 Groppe, M. (2018, January 20). A look at Vice President Pence's first year in office: Key takeaways. *USA Today*. Retrieved June 30, 2018, from https://www.usatoday.com/story/news/politics/2018/01/20/look-vice-president-pences-first-year-office-key-takeaways/1048778001/.

65 U.S. Senate. (n.d.). *Charles Curtis: A featured biography.* Retrieved June 30, 2018, from https://www.senate.gov/artandhistory/history/common/generic/Featured_Bio_Curtis.htm.

66 For more on a comparison between Eleanor Roosevelt and Hillary Clinton, see Chesler, E., & Covert, B. (2011, September 22). *From Eleanor Roosevelt to Michelle Obama, how first ladies can be an asset to the presidency.* The Roosevelt Institute. Retrieved July 1, 2018, from http://rooseveltinstitute.org/eleanor-roosevelt-michelle-obama-how-first-ladies-can-be-assets-presidency/.

67 Clinton Presidential Library. (n.d.). *Heath Care Task Force.* Clinton Digital Library. Retrieved July 1, 2018, from https://clinton.presidentiallibraries.us/collections/show/68..

68 Epstein, J. (2016, June 25). FLOTUS a "huge force" in grassroots outreach. *Politico.* Retrieved June 25, 2018, from http://www.politico.com/news /stories/0912/81800.html; Parsons, C. (2008, February 24). As first lady, Obama takes time to learn: Aware of the perils of a big early agenda, she sets out slowly. *Chicago Tribune,* p. 8.

69 Ruiz, M. (2018, January 9). After nearly a year as first lady, Melania Trump charts an uncertain course. *Vogue.* Retrieved July 1, 2018, from https://www.vogue.com/article/melania-trump-cause-first-lady.

70 Cillizza, C. (2018, June 22). Melania Trump's "I Really Don't Care. Do You?" jacket was no mistake. *CNN Politics.* Retrieved July 1, 2018, from https://www.cnn .com/2018/06/21/politics/melania-trump-jacket-border-visit/index.html.

71 U.S. Department of Interior. (n.d.). *Tribal nations.* Retrieved July 1, 2018, from https://www.doi.gov/tribes.

72 DiClerico, R. E. (2000). *The American President* (5th ed.). Upper Saddle River, NJ: Prentice-Hall, p. 208.

73 Tenpas, K. D. (2014). A curious strategy for the Obama administration's final stretch. In *FixGov: Making government work* [Blog]. Washington, DC: Brookings. Retrieved June 25, 2018, from http://www.brookings.edu/blogs/fixgov/posts/2014/09/15-obama-final-stretch-cabinet-meetings-tenpas.

74 Cook, N. (2018, January 24). Trump sets his cabinet free to shape an agenda. *Politico.* Retrieved July 1, 2018, from https://www.politico.com/story/2018/01/24/trump-cabinet-shapes-agenda-351646.

75 O'Sullivan, J. (2001, November 27). Give Powell credit as peacemaker, but brain behind U.S. war strategy clearly is Rumsfeld. *Chicago Sun-Times,* p. 29.

76 Mazzetti, M., Cooper, H., & Baker, P. (2011, May 3). Behind the hunt for Bin Laden. *New York Times,* p. A1.

77 NBC News Latino. (2016, April 15). Labor Sec. Tom Perez: President has authority on immigration matters. *NBC News.* Retrieved July 1, 2018, from https://www.nbcnews.com/news/latino/labor-sec-tom-perez-president-has-authority-immigration-matters-n556661.

78 Guild, B. (2018, June 18). DHS Secretary Kristjen Nielsen defends family separation in heated White House briefing. *CBS News.* Retrieved July 1, 2018, from https://www.cbsnews.com/news/dhs-secretary-kirstjen-nielsen-defends-family-separation-in-heated-white-house-briefing/.

79 Secretary Cavazos served in both the Reagan and the first Bush administrations.

80 Lee, J. C. (2017, March 10). Trump's cabinet so far is more White and male than any first cabinet since Reagan's. *New York Times.* Retrieved July 2, 2018, from https://www.nytimes.com/interactive/2017/01/13/us/politics/trump-cabinet-women-minorities.html.

81 He spoke these words to the National Association for the Advancement of Colored People during his campaign; see Clinton vows racial accord. (1992, July 12). *Chicago Sun-Times,* p. 16.

82 Parsons, C., & Memoili, M. A. (2013, January 10). Obama cabinet starts looking less diverse. *Los Angeles Times,* p. AA2.

83 Lee, "Trump's Cabinet So Far Is More White and Male."

84 The White House,. (n.d.). The National Security Council. Retrieved July 2, 2018, from https://www.whitehouse .gov/nsc/.

85 Condon, C. (2018, February 24). Mulvaney says that U.S. can outgrow higher spending, debt costs. *Bloomberg.* Retrieved July 2, 2018, from https://www.bloomberg.com/news/articles/2018-02-24/mulvaney-says-u-s-can-outgrow-higher-spending-debt-costs.

86 Associated Press. (2018, April 15). OMB's Raines quits to head Fannie Mae. *Los Angeles Times.* Retrieved July 2, 2018, from http://articles.latimes.com/1998/apr/15/news/mn-39522.

87 *Biography of U.S. Trade Representative Ambassador Ron Kirk.* (2008, August 8). Mission of the United States, Geneva Switzerland. Retrieved July 2, 2018, from https://geneva .usmission.gov/2009/08/08/kirkbi/.

88 Morrow, E. F. (1963). *Black man in the White House: A diary of the Eisenhower years by the Administrative officer for Special Projects, the White House, 1955–1961.* New York: Coward-McCann.

89 Neustadt, R. (1990). *Presidential power and the modern presidents: The politics of leadership from Roosevelt to Reagan.* New York: Free Press.

90 Kernell, S. (1993). *Going public: New strategies of presidential leadership* (2nd ed.). Washington, DC: Congressional Quarterly Press.

91 Devroy, A. (1990, October 23). Bush vetoes civil rights bill. *Washington Post,* p. A1.

92 Clymer, A. (1991, November 8). Civil rights bill is passed by House. *New York Times,* p. A15.

93 Acosta, J., & Holmes, K. (2016, January 8). Obama vetoes Obamacare repeal bill. *CNN Politics.* Retrieved July 2, 2018, from https://www.cnn.com/2016/01/08/

politics/obama-vetoes-obamacare-repeal-bill/index
.html.

94 For more on the comparison between Presidents
Kennedy and Johnson and their abilities to secure civil
rights policies, see Stern, M. (1992). *Calculating visions:
Kennedy, Johnson, and civil rights*. New Brunswick, NJ:
Rutgers University Press.

95 Kernell, *Going public*.

96 Germany, K. (n.d.). *Lyndon B. Johnson domestic affairs*.
Miller Center, University of Virginia. Retrieved July 3,
2018, from https://millercenter.org/president/
lbjohnson/domestic-affairs.

97 See, for example, Dahl, R. A. (1990). Myth of the
presidential mandate. *Political Science Quarterly, 105*,
355–372.

98 Gallup Presidential Approval Center. Retrieved
October 17, 2018, from https://news.gallup.com/
interactives/185273/presidential-job-approval-center
.aspx.

99 United States Senate. (n.d.). *Impeachment: Impeachment
trials in the Senate*. Retrieved July 3, 2018, from https://
www.senate.gov/reference/Index/Impeachment.htm.

100 *United States v. Nixon*, 418 U.S. 683 (1974).

101 *Cheney v. U.S. District Court for the District of Columbia*,
542 U.S. 367 (2004).

102 O'Keefe, E., & Horowitz, S. (2012, June 29). Holder Is
held in contempt of Congress. *Washington Post*, p. A1.

103 Herb, J. (2018, June 29). A tale of two investigations:
Benghazi vs. Mueller," *CNN Politics*. Retrieved July 3,
2018, from https://www.cnn.com/2018/06/29/politics/
benghazi-committee-special-counsel-robert-mueller/
index.html.

Chapter 8

1 National Hurricane Center. (n.d.). Saffir-Simpson
Hurricane Wind Scale. Retrieved July 5, 2018, from
https://www.nhc.noaa.gov/aboutsshws.php.

2 National Oceanic and Atmospheric Administration
Office for Coastal Management. (n.d.). *Fast Facts:
Hurricane costs*. Retrieved July 5, 2018, from https://coast
.noaa.gov/states/fast-facts/hurricane-costs.html.

3 Federal Emergency Management Agency. (n.d.). *About the
agency*. Retrieved July 5, 2018, from https://www.fema
.gov/about-agency.

4 Einbinder, N. E. (2018, May 1). How the response to
Hurricane Maria compared to Harvey and Irma. *Frontline*. Retrieved July 5, 2018, from https://www.pbs.org/
wgbh/frontline/article/how-the-response-to-hurricane-
maria-compared-to-harvey-and-irma/.

5 Mazzei, P., & Armendariz, A. (2018, February 6). FEMA
contract called for 30 million meals for Puerto Ricans,
50,000 were delivered. *New York Times*. Retrieved July 5,
2018, from https://www.nytimes.com/2018/02/06/us/
fema-contract-puerto-rico.html.

6 Bacon, J. (2018, May 29). Hurricane Maria killed more
than 4,600 people – more than 70 times the official toll
of 64, study says. *USA Today*. Retrieved July 5, 2018,
from https://www.usatoday.com/story/news/nation/
2018/05/29/hurricane-maria-killed-thousands-puerto-
rico/650942002/.

7 Einbinder, "How the Response to Hurricane Maria Compared to Harvey and Irma."

8 Acevedo, N. (2018, August 30). Judge gives end date for
Puerto Rican hurricane evacuees in FEMA temporary
housing. *NBC News*. Retrieved October 18, 2018, from
https://www.nbcnews.com/storyline/puerto-rico-crisis/
judge-gives-end-date-puerto-rican-hurricane-evacuees-
fema-temporary-n905111.

9 Acevedo, N. (2018, June 15). New bill pushes for commission to investigate federal response to Puerto Rico
hurricanes. *NBC News*. Retrieved July 5, 2018, from
https://www.nbcnews.com/storyline/puerto-rico-crisis/
new-bill-pushes-commission-investigate-federal-
response-puerto-rico-hurricanes-n883341.

10 Lui, K. (2017, October 2). FEMA chief slammed
for calling Puerto Rico relief efforts the "most logistically challenging event." *Time*. Retrieved
July 5, 2018, from http://time.com/4964574/
hurricane-maria-fema-brock-long-puerto-rico-logistics/.

11 United States Department of Justice, Civil Rights
Division. (n.d.). *About the division*. Retrieved July 6, 2018,
from https://www.justice.gov/crt/about-division.

12 Federal Emergency Management Agency. (n.d.). *About the
agency*. Retrieved July 6, 2018, from https://www.fema
.gov/about-agency.

13 Shields, G. (2006, March 1). Ex–FEMA Chief Witt described as "real deal." *The Advocate* (Baton Rouge, LA),
p. B1; Short Takes: Quick Witt helps. (1996, February 12).
Atlanta Journal and Constitution, p. 8A.

14 Cooper, C., & Block, R. (2006). *Disaster: Hurricane
Katrina and the failure of Homeland Security*. New York:
Times Books; Grunwald, M., & Glaser, S. B. (2005,
December 23). Brown's turf war sapped FEMA's strength;
director who symbolized incompetence in Katrina pre-
dicted agency would fail. *Washington Post*, p. A1.

15 Sherman, A., & Shapiro, I. (n.d.). *Essential facts on the
victims of Hurricane Katrina*. Center on Budget and Policy
Priorities. Retrieved July 6, 2018, from https://www.
cbpp.org/research/essential-facts-about-the-victims-of-
hurricane-katrina?fa=view&id=658.

16 Federal Communications Commission. (n.d.). About the
FCC. Retrieved July 6, 2018, from https://www.fcc.gov/
about/overview.

17 Collins, K. (2018, June 11). Net neutrality has officially
been repealed: Here is how it could affect you. *New
York Times*. Retrieved July 6, 2018, from https://www.
nytimes.com/2018/06/11/technology/net-neutrality-
repeal.html.

18 Le, V. (2017, July 12). *Why net neutrality is a racial justice issue.* The Greenlining Institute. Retrieved July 6, 2018, from http://greenlining.org/blog/2017/why-net-neutrality-racial-justice-issue/.

19 National Hispanic Media Coalition. (n.d.). Net neutrality is inextricably intertwined with fight for racial justice. Retrieved July 6, 2018, from http://www.nhmc.org/net-neutrality-inextricably-intertwined-fight-racial-justice/.

20 *Humphrey's Executor v. United States*, 295 U.S. 602 (1935).

21 U.S. Equal Employment Opportunity Commission. (n.d.). *About: Overview.* Retrieved July 6, 2018, from https://www.eeoc.gov/eeoc/index.cfm.

22 Congressional study says job bias cases are poorly handled. (1988, October 12). *New York Times*, p. A23.

23 Tornone, K. (2017, October 2). Jenny Yang's final days at the EEOC and her hopes for its future. *HR Dive*. Retrieved July 6, 2018, from https://www.hrdive.com/news/jenny-yangs-final-days-at-the-eeoc-and-her-hopes-for-its-future/506222/.

24 McGowan, K. (2017, April 3). EEOC Acting Chair Lipnic skeptical about pay data plan. *Bloomberg Law*. Retrieved July 6, 2018, from https://www.bna.com/eeoc-acting-chair-n57982086113/.

25 Central Intelligence Agency. (n.d.). *About CIA*. Retrieved July 6, 2018, from https://www.cia.gov/about-cia/index.html.

26 Dick, S. J. (n.d.). *Why we explore*. National Aeronautics and Space Administration. Retrieved July 6, 2018, from https://www.nasa.gov/exploration/whyweexplore/Why_We_29.html.

27 U.S. Commission on Civil Rights. (n.d.). *About us*. Retrieved July 6, 2018, from https://www.usccr.gov/about/index.php.

28 MaryFrancesBerry.com. (n.d.). *Mary Frances Berry: About*. Retrieved July 6, 2018, from http://www.maryfrancesberry.com.

29 Reinert, P. (2001, March 10). Critics pounce on Florida: Civil rights panel vows to keep tabs on reform efforts. *Houston Chronicle*, p. A1.

30 Schmidt, P. (2007). Civil Rights Commission pressures law schools on affirmative action. *Chronicle of Higher Education, 36*(2), 36.

31 U.S. Commission on Civil Rights. (n.d.). *About us, commissioners: Catherine E. Lhamon*. Retrieved July 6, 2018, from https://www.usccr.gov/about/bio/Lhamon.php.

32 Blad, E. (2017, July 20). Trump stance on civil rights is "distressing and dangerous," Obama official says. *Education Week*. Retrieved July 6, 2018, from https://www.edweek.org/ew/articles/2017/07/20/trump-stance-on-civil-rights-is-distressing.html.

33 Amtrak. (n.d.). *Amtrak national facts*. Retrieved July 6, 2018, from https://www.amtrak.com/about-amtrak/amtrak-facts/amtrak-national-facts.html.

34 Weisman, J. (2015, May 15). Wreck adds to the debate on Amtrak funding. *New York Times*. Retrieved July 6, 2018, from https://www.nytimes.com/2015/05/16/us/politics/wreck-adds-fuel-to-debate-on-amtrak-funding.html.

35 Office of Personnel Management. (n.d.). *Executive branch civilian employment since 1940*. Retrieved July 6, 2018, from https://www.opm.gov/policy-data-oversight/data-analysis-documentation/federal-employment-reports/historical-tables/executive-branch-civilian-employment-since-1940/.

36 For more on Andrew Jackson and the establishment of the "spoils system," see White, L. D. (1954). *The Jacksonians: A study in administrative history, 1829–1861*. New York: MacMillan.

37 See Erie, S. P. (1988). *Rainbow's end: Irish Americans and the dilemmas of urban machine politics, 1840–1985*. Berkeley and Los Angeles: University of California Press.

38 U.S. Office of Personnel Management. (n.d.). *Our mission, role & history*. Retrieved July 6, 2018, from https://www.opm.gov/about-us/our-mission-role-history/.

39 Moffit, R. E. (1993, July 6). Gutting the Hatch Act: Congresses plan to re-politicize the civil service. *Heritage Research Reports*. Retrieved July 6, 2018, from https://www.heritage.org/report/gutting-the-hatch-act-congresss-plan-re-politicize-the-civil-service-0.

40 *Washington v. Davis*, 426 U.S. 229 (1976).

41 Fesler, J. W., & Kettl, D. F. (1996). *The politics of the administrative process*. Chatham, NJ: Chatham House, pp. 152–153.

42 *Johnson v. Transportation Agency, Santa Clara (CA) County*, 480 U.S. 616 (1987).

43 Department of Homeland Security U.S. Customs and Border Protection. (n.d.). About CPB. Retrieved July 6, 2018, from https://www.cbp.gov/about.

44 Department of Homeland Security U.S Immigration and Customs Enforcement. (n.d.). What we do. Retrieved July 6, 2018, from https://www.ice.gov/overview.

45 Domonoske, C. (n.d.). *What we know: Family separation and "zero tolerance" at the border*. National Public Radio. Retrieved July 6, 2018, from https://www.npr.org/2018/06/19/621065383/what-we-know-family-separation-and-zero-tolerance-at-the-border.

46 U.S. Justice Department Office of the United States Attorneys. (n.d.). 9-27.000 Principles of Federal Prosecution. Retrieved July 6, 2018, from https://www.justice.gov/jm/jm-9-27000-principles-federal-prosecution.

47 Lu, L. D. (2007). Prosecutorial discretion and racial disparities in federal sentencing: Some views of former U.S. attorneys. *Federal Sentencing Reporter, 17*, 192–201.

48 See the Administrative Procedure Act, § 553 Rule Making. Retrieved July 6, 2018, from https://www.archives.gov/federal-register/laws/administrative-procedure/553.html; Bremer, E. S. (2013, May 10). A primer on the informal rulemaking process.

Administrative Conference of the United States. Retrieved July 6, 2018, from https://www.acus.gov/newsroom/administrative-fix-blog/primer-informal-rulemaking-process.

49 Federal Aviation Administration. (n.d.). *FAA regulations & policies.* Retrieved July 6, 2018, from https://www.faa.gov/regulations_policies/.

50 U.S. Environmental Protection Agency. (n.d.). *Regulations.* Retrieved July 6, 2018, from https://www.epa.gov/laws-regulations/regulations.

51 Government Printing Office. (2010, December 28). Federal Housing Finance Agency 12 CFR 1207 RIN 2590-AA28 Minority and Women Inclusion. *Federal Register, 75*(248), 81395–81405.

52 Equal Employment Opportunity Commission. (n.d.). *Facts about mediation.* Retrieved July 7, 2018, from https://www.eeoc.gov/eeoc/mediation/facts.cfm.

53 See, for example, Lowi, T. J. (1979). *The end of liberalism: The second republic of the United States* (2nd ed.). New York: Norton.

54 Heclo, H. (1978). Issue networks and the executive establishment. In A. King (Ed.), *The new American political system.* Washington, DC: American Enterprise Institute, pp. 87–124.

55 Gillman, T. J., & Isensee, L. (2009, January 20). Bush commutes sentences of border control agents. *Dallas Morning News,* p. 1A; Middelstadt, M. (2007, April 26). Rift between border patrol agents, leaders widening. *Houston Chronicle,* p. A7.

56 National Border Patrol Council. (2012, October 26). *Overzealous prosecution results in excessive sentence in Jesus Diaz case.* Retrieved July 7, 2018, from https://bpunion.org/press-releases/overzealous-prosecution-results-in-excessive-sentence-in-jesus-diaz-case.

57 U.S. Office of Personnel Management. (n.d.). Senior Executive Service. Retrieved July 7, 2018, from https://www.opm.gov/policy-data-oversight/senior-executive-service/.

58 Office of Personnel Management. (n.d.). *Federal Equal Opportunity Recruitment Program Report to Congress, Fiscal Year 2016.* Retrieved July 7, 2018, from https://www.opm.gov/policy-data-oversight/diversity-and-inclusion/reports/feorp-2016.pdf.

59 The Obama White House Archives. (n.d.). *The mission and structure of the Office of Management and Budget.* Retrieved July 7, 2018, from https://obamawhitehouse.archives.gov/omb/organization_mission/.

60 Office of the Inspector General, Social Security Administration. (n.d.). *Whistleblower protection history.* Retrieved July 7, 2018, from https://oig.ssa.gov/whistleblower-protection/history.

61 Gorst, I. (2014, August 7). Russia gives Edward Snowden asylum for three more years. *Los Angeles Times.* Retrieved July 7, 2018, from http://www.latimes.com/world/europe/la-fg-russia-snowden-asylum-20140807-story.html.

62 Coleman-Adebayo, M. (2011). *No fear: A whistleblower's triumph over corruption and retaliation at the EPA.* Chicago: Chicago Review Press; Fears, D. (2006, July 10). Coming soon: A tale of whistleblowing at the EPA. *Washington Post.* Retrieved July 7, 2018, from http://www.washingtonpost.com/wp-dyn/content/article/2006/07/09/AR2006070900741_pf.html.

63 Subcommittee on National Security of the House Oversight and Government Reform Committee. (2018, March 22). Hearing: Bureaucratic challenges to hurricane recovery in Puerto Rico. Retrieved July 7, 2018, from https://oversight.house.gov/hearing/bureaucratic-challenges-hurricane-recovery-puerto-rico/.

64 Berry, D. B. (2018, June 6). Hispanic lawmakers call for commission to study reported undercounting of death toll in Puerto Rico. *USA Today.* Retrieved July 7, 2018, from https://www.usatoday.com/story/news/politics/2018/06/06/lawmakers-call-commission-investigate-number-deaths-puerto-rico/676981002/.

65 Hsu, S. S. (2007, July 20). FEMA knew of toxic gas in trailers; hurricane victims reported illness. *Washington Post,* p. A1.

66 U.S. Government Accountability Office. (n.d.). *About GAO.* Retrieved July 8, 2018, from https://www.gao.gov/about/index.html.

67 U.S. Government Accountability Office. (2018, February 28). 2017 disaster contracting: Observations for federal contracting for 4 response and recovery efforts. *GAO-18-335.* Retrieved July 8, 2018, from https://www.gao.gov/products/GAO-18-335.

68 *Immigration and Naturalization Service v. Chadha,* 462 U.S. 919 (1983).

69 *U.S. v. Brignoni-Ponce,* 422 U.S. 873 (1975).

70 Rutcofsky, B S. (2007). The award of attorney's fees under the Equal Access to Justice Act. *Hofstra Law Review, 11,* 307–328.

71 MALDEF. (n.d.). *Protecting immigrants' rights.* Retrieved July 8, 2018, from http://www.maldef.org/immigration/index.html.

Chapter 9

1 California Supreme Court (n.d.). *Associate Justice Goodwin Liu.* Retrieved July 9, 2018, from http://www.courts.ca.gov/15450.htm.

2 Bacon Jr., P. (2010, May 14). Appeals court nomination advances. *Washington Post,* p. A14; Savage, C. (2010, April 13). Appeals court nominee ignites a partisan battle. *New York Times,* p. A15.

3 Richman, J. (2011, May 19). GOP blocks UC Berkeley law professor's vote to bench. *San Jose Mercury News.*

4 U.S. Senate. (n.d.). *Roll call votes 108th Congress*. Retrieved July 9, 2018, from https://www.senate.gov/legislative/LIS/roll_call_lists/roll_call_vote_cfm.cfm?congress=108&session=1&vote=00143.

5 Dolan, M. (2011, September 1). Accolades as justice confirmed. *Los Angeles Times*, p. AA1.

6 Richey, W. (2013, November 21). How new Senate filibuster rules could change balance of power on courts. *Christian Science Monitor*. Retrieved July 8, 2018, from https://www.csmonitor.com/USA/Politics/DC-Decoder/2013/1121/How-new-Senate-filibuster-rule-could-change-balance-of-power-on-courts.

7 Doyle, M. (2017, April 6). Senate Republicans rewrite the rule book to secure Gorsuch Supreme Court nomination. *Miami Herald*. Retrieved July 8, 2018, from https://www.miamiherald.com/news/politics-government/article143085319.html.

8 Abraham, H. J. (1993). *The judicial process: An introductory analysis of the courts of the United States, England, and Great Britain* (6th ed.). New York: Oxford University Press, p. 7.

9 For more on these definitions of the different types of law, consult Banks, C. P., & O'Brien, D. M. (2016). *The judicial process: Law, courts, and judicial politics*. Thousand Oaks, CA: Sage, pp. 13–19.

10 For more on criminal law, consult Banks & O'Brien, *The judicial process*, pp. 196–231.

11 For more on civil law, consult Banks & O'Brien, *The judicial process*, pp. 232–262.

12 28 U.S.C. 1332, Diversity in Citizenship; Amount in Controversy; Costs. Retrieved July 8, 2018, from https://www.gpo.gov/fdsys/pkg/USCODE-2009-title28/pdf/USCODE-2009-title28-partIV-chap85-sec1332.pdf.

13 For more on the Judiciary Act of 1789, see Library of Congress. (n.d.). Primary documents in American history: The Judiciary Act of 1789. Retrieved July 8, 2018, from https://www.loc.gov/rr/program/bib/ourdocs/judiciary.html.

14 United States Courts. (n.d.). U.S. District Courts—Judicial business 2017. Retrieved July 8, 2018, from http://www.uscourts.gov/statistics-reports/us-district-courts-judicial-business-2017.

15 *Brown v. Board of Education*, 349 U.S. 294 (1955).

16 For more on the role of federal district court judges in desegregation, see Peltason, J. W. (1961). *Fifty-eight lonely men: Southern federal judges and school desegregation*. New York: Harcourt, Brace, & World.

17 United States Courts. (n.d.). U.S. Courts of Appeals—Judicial business 2017. Retrieved July 8, 2018, from http://www.uscourts.gov/statistics-reports/us-courts-appeals-judicial-business-2017.

18 For more on the use of judicial review in the states prior to *Marbury v. Madison*, see Treanor, M. W. (2005). Judicial review before Marbury. *Stanford Law Review, 58*, 455–562, 497–517.

19 *Marbury v. Madison*, 1 Cranch. 137 (1803).

20 For more on the legal and political issues surrounding *Marbury v. Madison* and John Marshall, see Graber, M. A., (1998). Establishing judicial review: *Schooner Peggy* and the early Marshall court. *Political Research Quarterly, 51*, 221–239; Knight, J., & Epstein, L. (1996). On the struggle for judicial supremacy. *Law & Society Review, 30*, 87–120; Nelson, W. E. (2000). *Marbury v. Madison: The origins and legacy of judicial review*. Lawrence: University of Kansas Press; O'Fallon, J. (1992). *Marbury. Stanford Law Review, 44*, 219–260.

21 For more on the difference between judicial activism and judicial restraint, see Toobin, J. (2010, May 24). Activism v. restraint. *The New Yorker*. Retrieved July 9, 2018, from https://www.newyorker.com/magazine/2010/05/24/activism-v-restraint.

22 For more on the different approaches to constitutional interpretation, consult Murphy, W. F., Pritchett, C. H., Epstein, L., & Knight, J. (2006). *Courts, judges, and politics: An introduction to the judicial process* (6th ed.). Boston: McGraw-Hill, pp. 539–616.

23 *Brown v. Board of Education*, 347 U.S. 483 (1954).

24 Ibid., footnote 11, p. 494.

25 *Worcester v. Georgia*, 6 Pet. 515 (1832). For more on Jackson's actions after this decision, consult Sundquist, M. L. (2010–2011). *Worcester v. Georgia*: A breakdown in the separation of powers. *American Indian Law Review, 35*, 239–255.

26 *Brown v. Board of Education*, I n15 and II n9.

27 *Dred Scott v. Sandford*, 19 How. 393 (1857).

28 *Wards Cove Packing, Inc. v. Atonio*, 490 U.S. 642 (1989).

29 For a full text of the Civil Rights Act of 1991, see Equal Employment Opportunity Commission. (n.d.). Civil Rights Act 1991. Retrieved July 9, 2018, from https://www.eeoc.gov/laws/statutes/cra-1991.cfm.

30 *United States v. SCRAP*, 412 U.S. 669 (1973).

31 *Lujan v. Defenders of Wildlife*, 504 U.S. 555 (1992).

32 *DeFunis v. Odegaard*, 416 U.S. 312 (1974).

33 *Plessy v. Ferguson*, 163 U.S. 537 (1896).

34 *Brown* I, 492.

35 *Metro Broadcasting v. Federal Communication Commission*, 497 U.S. 547 (1990).

36 *Adarand Constructors, Inc. v. Peña*, 515 U.S. 200 (1995).

37 *Roe v. Wade*, 410 U.S. 113 (1973).

38 Carney, J. (2018, August 21). "Collins" Kavanaugh considers *Roe v. Wade* settled law." *The Hill*. Retrieved October 20, 2018, from https://thehill.com/homenews/senate/402857-collins-kavanaugh-considers-roe-v-wade-settled-law.

39 O'Brien, D. M. (2014). *Storm center: The Supreme Court in American politics* (10th ed.). New York: Norton, p. 34.

40 Supreme Court of the United States. (n.d.). Biographies of current justices of the Supreme Court. Retrieved

July 9, 2018, from https://www.supremecourt.gov/about/biographies.aspx.

41 Binder, S.A and Maltzman F. (2004). "The limits of senatorial courtesy." *Legislative Studies Quarterly* 29:5-22.

42 Abraham, H. J. (1992). *Justices and presidents: A political history of appointments to the Supreme Court* (3rd ed.). New York: Oxford University Press, pp. 255–257.

43 Goldman, S., Slotnick, E., Gryski, G., Zuk, G., & Schiavoni, S. (2007). W. Bush remaking the federal judiciary: Like father, like son? *Judicature, 86,* 304, 308; Goldman, S., Schiavoni, S., & Slotnick, E. (2017). Obama's judicial legacy: The final chapter. *Journal of Law and Courts, 5,* 363–422.

44 Totenberg, N. (2009, April 30). Supreme Court Justice Souter to retire. *National Public Radio.* Retrieved July 10, 2018, from https://www.npr.org/templates/story/story.php?storyId=103694193.

45 Clement M. Haynsworth Jr.: Judge was rejected as 1969 Supreme Court nominee. (1989, November 23). *Los Angeles Times.* Retrieved July 10, 2018, from http://articles.latimes.com/1989-11-23/news/mn-3_1_supreme-court.

46 Anita Hill vs. Clarence Thomas: The back story. (2010, October 20). *CBS News.* Retrieved July 10, 2018, from https://www.cbsnews.com/news/anita-hill-vs-clarence-thomas-the-backstory/.

47 Cohen, A. (2012, December 12). The sad legacy of Robert Bork. *The Atlantic.* Retrieved July 10, 2018, from https://www.theatlantic.com/politics/archive/2012/12/the-sad-legacy-of-robert-bork/266456/.

48 Kelly, A. (2016, March 16). McConnell: Blocking Supreme Court nomination "about a principle, not a person." *National Public Radio.* Retrieved July 10, 2018, from https://www.npr.org/2016/03/16/470664561/mcconnell-blocking-supreme-court-nomination-about-a-principle-not-a-person.

49 Kosoff, M. (2017, April 10). Trump thanks McConnell "for all that he did" to ruin Garland. *Vanity Fair.* Retrieved July 10, 2018, from https://www.vanityfair.com/news/2017/04/trump-thanks-mcconnell-for-all-that-he-did-to-ruin-merrick-garland.

50 Carney, J. (2018, September 10). "More Dems come out in public opposition to Kavanaugh." *The Hill,* Retrieved October 20, 2018, from https://thehill.com/blogs/floor-action/senate/405944-democratic-opposition-builds-against-kavanaugh.

51 Fram A., Mascaro, L., and Daly, M. (2018, October 6). "Kavanaugh sworn to high court after rancorous confirmation." *AP News.* Retrieved October 20, 2018, from https://apnews.com/8234f0b8a6194d8b89ff79f9b0c94f35; Wolf, R., Collins, E., Slack, D., Vanden Brook, T. (2018, September 27, 2018). "Kavanaugh-Ford Hearing: '100 percent certain' vs. '100 percent certain'." *USA Today,* Retrieved October 20, 2018, from https://www.usatoday.com/story/news/politics/2018/09/27/

brett-kavanaugh-christine-ford-assault-hearing-tests-supreme-court-me-too-movement/1434845002/.

52 Wheeler, R. (2013, December 30). Judicial nominations and confirmations: Fact and fiction. In *FixGov: Making government work* [Blog]. Washington, DC: Brookings. Retrieved July 11, 2018, from http://www.brookings.edu/blogs/fixgov/posts/2013/12 /30-staffing-federal-judiciary-2013-no-breakthrough -year.

53 Doyle, M. (2017, April 6). Senate Republicans rewrite the rule book to secure Gorsuch Supreme Court nomination. *McClatchy.* Retrieved October 12, 2018, from https://www.mcclatchydc.com/news/politics-government/congress/article143084409.html.

54 Data adapted from American Bar Association Commission on Women in the Profession. (2017, January). *A current glance at women in the law, January 2017.* Chicago: American Bar Association. Retrieved July 11, 2018, from https://www.americanbar.org/content/dam/aba/marketing/women/current_glance_statistics_january2017.authcheckdam.pdf.

55 Jew-Lim, J. (2010). A brief overview of President Obama's Asian American judicial nominees in 2010. *Asian American Law Journal, 17,* 227–238; Richman, J. (2011, May 10). U.S. Senate confirms Chen to federal bench. *San Jose Mercury News.*

56 Lazo, L. (2009, May 27). Area Hispanics praise selection of Sotomayor. *Richmond (VA) Times Dispatch,* p. A4.

57 Allison, W. (2009, June 7). The buzz on Florida politics: Martinez liking Sotomayor. *St. Petersburg Times,* p. 3B.

58 *Ricci v. DeStefano,* 530 F.3d. 87 (2008); *Ricci v. DeStefano,* 129 S.Ct. 2658 (2009).

59 Allison, W. (2009, May 31). The ruling that has nominee under fire. *St. Petersburg Times,* p. 1A.

60 United States Senate. (n.d.). Supreme Court nominations, present–1789. Retrieved July 11, 2018, from https://www.senate.gov/pagelayout/reference/nominations/Nominations.htm. Senator Edward Kennedy (D-MA) was still in the Senate then, but he did not vote because he was too ill.

61 Federal Judicial Center. (n.d.). Landmark legislation: The judge's bill. Retrieved July 11, 2018, from https://www.fjc.gov/history/legislation/landmark-judicial-legislation-text-document-13.

62 United States Supreme Court. (n.d.). *Frequently asked questions.* Retrieved July 11, 2018, from https://www.supremecourt.gov/about/faq_general.aspx.

63 See Krislov, S. (1963). Amicus curiae: From friendship to advocacy. *Yale Law Journal, 72,* 694–721.

64 For more on the role of oral argument, see O'Brien, *Storm center,* pp. 247–257.

65 For more on the role of conferences and opinion writing, see O'Brien, *Storm center,* pp. 257–289.

66 *Plessy,* Justice Harlan's dissent on pp. 552–564.

67 *Brown* I.

68 See, for example, Farhang, S., & Wawro, G. (2004). Institutional dynamics on the U.S. Courts of Appeals: Minority representation under panel decision making. *Journal of Law, Economics, and Organization, 20*, 299–330; Steffensmeier, D., & Britt, C. L. (2002). Judges race and judicial decision making: Do Black judges sentence differently? *Social Science Quarterly, 82*, 749–764. Steffensmeier and Britt actually unearth some evidence that in certain cases Black judges sentence more harshly than White judges do.

69 Ifill, S. A. (2000). Racial diversity on the bench: Beyond role models and public confidence. *Washington and Lee Law Review, 57*, 405–495.

70 See, for example, Welch, S., Combs, M., & Gruhl, J. (1988). Do Black judges make a difference? *American Journal of Political Science, 32*, 126–136.

71 See, for example, Johnson, S. W., & Songer, D. R., (2009). Judge gender and voting behavior of justices on two North American supreme courts. *Justice System Journal, 30*, 265–279.

72 See, for example, Allen, D. W., & Wall, D. E. (1993). Role orientations and women state Supreme Court justices. *Judicature, 77*, 156–165; Johnson, S. E., Stidham, R., Carp, R. A., & Manning, K. (2008). The gender influence on U.S. District Court decisions: Updating the traditional judge attribute model. *Journal of Women, Politics, and Policy, 29*, 497–526.

73 See, for example, Boyd, C. L., Epstein, L., & Martin, A. D. (2010). Untangling the causal effects of sex on judging. *American Journal of Political Science, 54*, 389–411; Gruhl, J. Spohn, C., & Welch, S. (1981). Women as policy makers: The case of trial judges. *American Journal of Political Science, 25*, 308–322; Segal, J. (2000). Representative decision making on the federal bench: Clinton's district court appointments. *Political Research Quarterly, 53*, 147–150; Songer, D. R., & Crews-Meyer, K. (2000). Does gender matter?: Decision making in state Supreme Courts. *Social Science Quarterly, 81*, 750–762; and Walker, T. G., & Barrow, D. J. (1985). The diversification of the federal bench: Policy and process ramifications. *Journal of Politics, 47*, 596–617.

74 Segal, J. A., & Spaeth, H. J. (2002). *The Supreme Court and the attitudinal model revisited.* New York: Cambridge University Press.

75 See, for example, Salokar, R. (1992). *The Solicitor General: The politics of law.* Philadelphia: Temple University Press; Segal, J. A., & Reedy, C. D. (1988). The Supreme Court and sex discrimination: The role of the Solicitor General. *Western Political Quarterly, 41*, 553–568.

76 United States Supreme Court. (n.d.). *About the Court: Current members.* Retrieved October 20, 2018, from https://www.supremecourt.gov/about/biographies.aspx.

77 O'Brien, *Storm Center,* p. 135.

78 In housing: *Shelley v. Kraemer,* 344 U.S. 1 (1948). See also Vose, C. E. (1959). *Caucasians only: The Supreme Court, the NAACP, and the restrictive covenant cases.* Berkeley: University of California Press. In voting: *Nixon v. Herndon,* 273 U.S. 536 (1927); *Smith v. Allwright,* 321 U.S. 649 (1944). See also Tauber, S. C. (2001). The influence of the NAACP Legal Defense Fund on the U.S. Supreme Court's minority voting rights law. In C. P. Banks & J. C. Green (Eds.), *Superintending democracy: The courts and the political process.* Akron, OH: University of Akron Press.

79 *Brown* I. See also Greenberg, J. (1994). *Crusaders in the courts: How a dedicated band of lawyers fought for the civil rights revolution.* New York: Basic Books.

80 NAACP Legal Defense and Education Fund. (n.d.). *Program areas.* Retrieved July 11, 2018, from http://www.naacpldf.org/program-areas.

81 Mexican American Legal Defense Fund. (n.d.). *MALDEF: The Latino legal voice for civil rights in America.* Retrieved July 11, 2018, from http://www.maldef.org.

82 Native American Rights Fund. (n.d.). *Our work.* Retrieved July 11, 2018, from http://www.narf.org/our-work/.

83 Asian Americans Advancing Justice. (n.d.). *Programs.* Retrieved July 11, 2018, fromhttps://www.advancingjustice-aajc.org/programs.

84 Asian American Advancing Justice. (n.d.). *Advancing Justice: AAJC and MALDEF sue Trump administration, challenging addition of citizenship question to 2020 Census.* Retrieved July 11, 2018, from https://www.advancingjustice-aajc.org/press-release/advancing-justice-aajc-and-maldef-sue-trump-administration-challenging-addition; Mexican American Legal Defense Fund. (n.d.). *MALDEF and Advancing Justice sue Trump administration, challenging addition of citizenship question to 2020 Census.* Retrieved July 11, 2018, from http://www.maldef.org/news/releases/2018_05_31_MALDEF_and_Advancing_Justice_Sue_Trump_Administration_Challenging_Addition_of_Citizenship_Question_to_2020_Census/.

85 Kirkpatrick, D. D. (2005, June 9). Seeing slavery in liberalism: Janice Rogers Brown. *New York Times,* p. A22.

Chapter 10

1 Louis, E. (2018, March 2). Why Americans think Trump is racist. CNN.com. Retrieved from https://www.cnn.com/2018/03/02/opinions/why-americans-think-trump-is-a-racist-louis/index.html.

2 Budowsky, B. (2018, January 12). Defeat Trump's "s---hole" politics of racism in 2018, 2020. *The Hill.* Retrieved from http://thehill.com/opinion/white-house/368704-defeat-trumps-shithole-politics-of-racism-in-2018-2020.

3 Dugan, A. (2018, January 28). Party, ideology and race play key roles in Trump approval. *Gallup News.* Retrieved from http://news.gallup.com/poll/226091/party-ideology-race-play-key-roles-trump-approval.aspx.

4 Pew Research Center. (2017, December 19). Most Americans say Trump's election has led to worse race relations in the U.S. *Pew Research Center: U.S. Politics* *and Policy.* Retrieved from http://www.people-press. org/2017/12/19/most-americans-say-trumps-election- has-led-to-worse-race-relations-in-the-u-s/.

5 Kirby, J. (2017, December 19). A majority of Americans think Trump's election has deteriorated race relations. *Vox.* Retrieved from https://www.vox.com/2017/12/19/ 16798828/ majority-americans-trump-election-worse-race-relations.

6 Swanson, E., & Contreras, R. (2018, February 28). AP-NORC Poll: Most Americans say Trump is racist. *Associated Press.* Retrieved from https://apnews.com/ 9961ee5b3c3b42d29aebdee837c17a11.

7 Ibid.

8 Ibid.

9 Ibid.

10 Quoted in Propaganda in the Civil War. (n.d.). Retrieved July 12, 2009, from http://www.civilwarhome.com.

11 Paludan, P. S. (1007). The better angels of our nature: Lincoln, propaganda, and public opinion in the North during the Civil War. In S. Förster & J. Nagler (Eds.), *On the road to total war: The American Civil War and the German Wars of Unification, 1861–1871.* New York: Cambridge University Press, pp. 362–363.

12 Stevens, D. (2002). Public opinion and public policy: The case of Kennedy and civil rights. *Presidential Studies Quarterly, 32,* 111–136.

13 American RadioWorks. (n.d.). *John F. Kennedy: The Mississippi crisis.* Retrieved July 22, 2009, from http:// americanradioworks.publicradio.org/features/prestapes/ a1.html.

14 Stevens, "Public opinion and public policy," pp. 123–125.

15 See, for instance, Lorell, M. A., & Kelley Jr., C. (1985). *Casualties, public opinion, and presidential policy during the Vietnam War.* Santa Monica, CA: Rand Project Air Force; Schneir, W., & Schneir, M. (1984, May). How the military cooked the books: The uncounted Vietcong. *The Nation, 283,* 570–577; Wirtz, J. J. (1991, Summer). Intelligence to please?: The order of battle controversy during the Vietnam War. *Political Science Quarterly, 106,* 239–263.

16 Becker, E. (2001, November 11). In the War on Terrorism, a battle to shape public opinion. *New York Times,* p. A1.

17 Almond, G., & Verba, S. (1963). *The civic culture: Political attitudes and democracy in five nations.* Princeton, NJ: Princeton University Press.

18 Glynn, C. J., Herbst, S., O'Keefe, G. J., Shapiro, R. Y., & Lindeman, M. (2004). *Public opinion* (2nd ed.). Boulder, CO: Westview Press, p. 8.

19 Pineda, R. D., & Sowards, S. K. (2007, December 22). Flag waving as visual argument: 2006 immigration demonstrations and cultural citizenship. *Argumentation and Advocacy.*

20 http://i.abcnews.com/Technology/story?id=7463348#at, retrieved October 29, 2009.

21 Until 2002, the ANES was conducted every presidential and midterm election year. Currently, the ANES is conducted only during presidential election years.

22 Glynn et al., *Public opinion,* p. 60.

23 Babbie, E. R. (1983). *The practice of social research* (3rd ed.). Belmont, CA: Wadsworth, p. 145.

24 Ibid., p. 143.

25 Ibid., p. 145.

26 Asher, H. (2007). *Polling and the public: What every citizen should know* (7th ed.). Washington, DC: Congressional Quarterly Press, pp. 69–76.

27 Jillesa, G. (2016, June 20). *Does question order affect the type of survey response you receive?* SurveyMonkey blog post. Retrieved from https://www.surveymonkey.com/ blog/2016/06/20/aapor/.

28 Pew Research Center for the People and the Press. (2008, January 31). *The impact of "cells-only" on public opinion polling.* Retrieved October 9, 2018, from http://www.people-press.org/2008/01/31/ the-impact-of-cell-onlys-on-public-opinion-polling/.

29 Shepard, S. (2012, November 18). Gallup blew its presidential polls, but why? *National Journal.* Retrieved February 7, 2003, from http://www.nationaljournal.com/politics/ gallup-blew-its-presidential-polls-but-why--20121118.

30 American Association of Public Opinion Research. (2017, May 4). *An evaluation of the 2016 election polls in the United States.* Retrieved October 9, 2018, from https:// www.aapor.org/Education-Resources/Reports/An-Evaluation-of-2016-Election-Polls-in-the-U-S.aspx.

31 Ibid.

32 American Association of Public Opinion Research. (n.d.). *Poll aggregator.* Retrieved October 9, 2018, from https://www.aapor.org/Education-Resources/Election-Polling-Resources/Poll-Aggregators.aspx.

33 Ibid.

34 Ibid., p. 4.

35 U.S. Census Bureau. (2015, March). *Projections of the size and composition of the U.S. population: 2014–2060.* Table 2. Retrieved June 9, 2016, from http://www.census.gov/ content/dam /Census/library/publications/2015/demo/ p25-1143.pdf.

36 U.S. Census Bureau. (n.d.). *California QuickFacts from the US Census Bureau.* Retrieved June 9, 2016, from http:// www.census.gov/quickfacts /table/PST045215/06.

37 McClain P. D., & Stewart Jr., J. (2014). *"Can we all get along?": Racial and ethnic minorities in American politics* (6th ed.). Boulder, CO: Westview Press.

38 Ayres, I. (2001). *Pervasive prejudice?: Unconventional evidence of race and gender discrimination.* Chicago: University of Chicago Press.

39 Abramson, P. R. (1972). Political efficacy and political trust among school children: Two explanations. *Journal of Politics, 34*, 1243–1275.

40 Gallup Poll. (2015, June 13–July 10). *Race relations*. Retrieved October 9, 2018, from http://www.gallup.com/poll/1687/race-relations.aspx.

41 Kennedy, R. (1997). *Race, crime, and the law*. New York: Pantheon, chap. 4; Warren, P., & Tomaskovic-Devey, D. (2009). Racial profiling and searches: Did the politics of racial profiling change police behavior? *Criminology and Public Policy, 8*(2), 343–369; Fallik, S. W., & Novak, K. J. (2012). The decision to search: Is race or ethnicity important? *Journal of Contemporary Criminal Justice, 28*(2), 146–165; Romero, M. (2006). Racial profiling and immigration law enforcement: Rounding up the usual suspects in the Latino community. *Critical Sociology, 32*(2–3), 447–473; Novak K. J., & Chamlin, M. B. (2012). Racial threat, suspicion, and police behavior: The impact of race and place in traffic enforcement. *Crime and Delinquency, 58*(2), 275–300.

42 Schumann, H., Steeh, C., Bobo, L., & Krysan, M. (1997). *Racial attitudes in America: Trends and interpretations*. Cambridge, MA: Harvard University Press, chaps. 3 and 5; Kinder, D. R., & Sanders, L. M. (1996). *Divided by color: Racial politics and democratic ideals* . Chicago: University of Chicago Press, chap. 6.

43 Hero, R. E. (1992). *Latinos and the U.S. political system*. Philadelphia: Temple University Press; Smith, R. S., & Seltzer, R. (1992). *Race, class, and culture*. Albany: State University of New York Press; Tate, K. (1993). *From protest to politics: The new Black voters in American elections*. Cambridge, MA: Harvard University Press and Russell Sage Foundation.

44 The data sets are the 1984 and 1988 National Black Election Study, the 1993 National Black Politics Study, the 1996 National Black Election Study, the 2004 *CBS News/Black Entertainment Television Monthly Poll*, and the 2008 Joint Center for Political and Economic Studies National Opinion Poll.

45 Tate, *From protest to politics*, pp. 31–32, 38.

46 Hero, *Latinos and the U.S. political system*.

47 de la Garza, R. O., DeSipio, L., Garcia, F. C., Garcia, J., & Falcon, A. (1992). *Latino voices: Mexican, Puerto Rican, and Cuban perspectives on American politics*. Boulder, CO: Westview Press, p. 90.

48 Bobo, L. D., & Johnson, D. (2004). A taste for punishment: Black and White Americans' views on the death penalty and the War on Drugs. *Du Bois Review, 1*, 151–180; Johnson, D. (2008). Racial prejudice, perceived injustice, and the Black–White gap in punitive attitudes. *Journal of Criminal Justice, 36*, 198–206.

49 Bobo & Johnson, "A Taste for Punishment"; Kennedy, R. (1997). *Race, crime, and the law*. New York: Pantheon, chap. 4.

50 Rose, H. M., & McClain, P. D. (1990). *Race, place, and risk: Black homicide in urban America*. Albany: State University of New York Press; Hawkins, D. F. (Ed.). (2003). *Violent crime: Assessing race and ethnic differences*. New York: Cambridge University Press; Kennedy, R. (2001). Racial trends in the administration of criminal justice. In N. J. Smelser, W. J. Wilson, & F. Mitchell (Eds.), *America becoming: Racial trends and their consequences* (Vol. 2). Washington, DC: National Academy Press.

51 United Nations Office of Drug and Crime. (n.d.). *Global Study on Homicide 2013*. Retrieved June 9, 2016, from https://www.unodc.org/documents /gsh/pdfs/2014_GLOBAL_HOMICIDE_BOOK_web.pdf.

52 Andersen, K. (1997). Gender and public opinion. In B. Norrander & C. Wilcox (Eds.), *Understanding public opinion*. Washington, DC: Congressional Quarterly Press.

53 Ibid.

54 Ibid.

55 Kaufmann, K. M. (2006). The gender gap. *PS: Political Science and Politics, 39*, 447–453.

56 Rapoport, R. B., Stone, W. J., & Abramowitz, A. I. (1990). Sex and the caucus participant: The gender gap and presidential nominations. *American Journal of Political Science, 34*, 725–740; Gilens, M. (1988). Gender and support for Reagan: A comprehensive model of presidential approval. *American Journal of Political Science, 32*, 19–49.

57 Kaufmann, "The Gender Gap"; Kaufmann, K. M., & Petrocik, J. R. (1999). The changing politics of American men: Understanding the sources of the gender gap. *American Journal of Political Science, 43*, 864–887.

58 Kaufmann & Petrocik, "The Changing Politics of American Men."

59 Center for the American Woman and Politics. (2005). *The gender gap: Voting choices in presidential elections*. New Brunswick, NJ: Eagleton Institute, Rutgers University.

60 CNN Election Center 2008. (n.d.). *Presidential National Exit Poll*. Retrieved October 9, 2018, from http://www.cnn.com/ELECTION/2008/results/polls/#val=USP00p1.

61 CNN Election Center 2016. (n.d.). *Presidential National Exit Poll*. Retrieved October 9, 2018, from http://www.cnn.com/election/results/exit-polls.

62 Gurin, P. (1985). Women's gender consciousness. *Public Opinion Quarterly, 49*, 143–163.

63 Gilens, "Gender and Support for Reagan"; Klein, E. (1984). *Gender politics*. New York: Cambridge University Press.

64 Cook, E. A., & Wilcox, C. (1989). Feminism and the gender gap: A second look. *Journal of Politics, 53*, 1111–1122.

65 Hutchings, V. L. (2003). *Public opinion and democratic accountability: How citizens learn about politics*. Princeton, NJ: Princeton University Press, pp. 56–57.

66 Kaufmann & Petrocik, "The Changing Politics of American Men."

67 Kaufmann, "The Gender Gap."

68 Verba, S., & Nie, N. H. (1972). *Participation in America: Political democracy and social equality*. New York: Harper & Row, chap. 12.

69 Ibid., chaps. 10 and 12.

70 Philpot, T. (2007). *Race, Republicans, and the return of the party of Lincoln*. Ann Arbor: University of Michigan Press. See also Fauntroy, M. K. (2007). *Republicans and the Black vote*. Boulder, CO: Lynne Rienner.

71 Philpot, *Race*, pp. 47–48.

72 Bump, P. (2016, July 19). There are likely fewer Black delegates to the Republican Convention than at any point in at least a century. *Washington Post*. Retrieved August 13, 2016, from https://www.washingtonpost.com/news /the-fix/wp/2016/07/19/there-are-likely-fewer-black-delegates-to-the-republican-convention-than-at-any-point-in-at-least-a-century/?tid=sm_tw_pp.

73 Ibid.

74 Hutchinson, E. O. (2016, July 17). The 2016 GOP Convention: The Whitest of the Whitest conventions. *Huffington Post*. Retrieved August 13, 2016, from http:// www.huffingtonpost.com /earl-ofari-hutchinson/the-2016-gop-conventionth _b_11028190.html.

75 NBC News. (2016). GOP: At least 133 Latino delegates at Republican Convention. Retrieved August 13, 2016, from http://www.nbcnews.com/storyline/2016-conventions/gop-least-133-latino-delegates-republican-convention-n614376.

76 Frostenson, S. (2016, July 29). Half of the Democratic delegates were people of color. For Republicans, it was only 6%. *Vox*. Retrieved August 13, 2016, from http:// www.vox.com/2016 /7/29/12295830/republican-democratic-delegates-diversity-nonwhite.

77 Philpot, *Race*.

78 Gallup Poll, April 21, 1937; Gallup Poll, April 1981; Gallup Poll, July 13–14, 1998.

79 The News Media/Communications. Polling Report. com, Media Studies Center survey conducted by the University of Connecticut, January 11–18, 1999 (*n* = 1,002 adults nationwide).

80 Pew Research Center for the People and the News. (2012, September 27). *In changing news landscape, even television is vulnerable: Trends in news consumption, 1991–2012.* Retrieved February 7, 2013, from http:// www.people-press.org/2012/09/27/in-changing-news-landscape-even-television-is-vulnerable/.

81 Gallup Poll, July 8, 2013, http://www.gallup.com/poll /163412/americans-main-source-news.aspx.

82 Rasmussen Reports. (2009, March 25). *Nearly one-third of younger Americans see Colbert, Stewart as alternatives to traditional news outlets*. Retrieved February 26, 2012, from http://www.rasmussenreports.com/public_content/lifestyle /entertainment/march_2009/nearly_one_third_of _younger_americans_see_colbert_stewart_as _alternatives_to_traditional_news_outlets.

83 Center of Political Communication, University of Delaware. (2014, November 10). National survey shows public overwhelmingly opposes Internet "fast lanes." Retrieved October 9, 2018, from https://www.cpc.udel .edu/content-sub-site/Documents/UD-CPC-NatAgenda2014PR_2014NetNeutrality.pdf.

84 Public Religion Research Institute and the Brookings Institute. (2014, June 10). *What Americans want from immigration reform in 2014*. Retrieved October 9, 2018, from http://www.brookings.edu/~/media/ research/files/reports/2014/06/10%20immigration%20 reform%20survey/finalimmigrationsurvey%20 %282%29.pdf

85 Pew Research Center: Journalism and Media. (2016, February 4). *The 2016 presidential campaign—a news event that's hard to miss*. Retrieved June 9, 2016, from http:// www.journalism.org /2016/02/04/the-2016-presidential-campaign-a-news-event-thats-hard-to-miss/.

86 Pew Research Center: Journalism and Media. (2015, June 1). Millennials and political news: Social media— the local TV for the next generation? Retrieved June 9, 2016, from http://www.journalism.org/2015/06/01/ millennials-political-news/.

87 Schexnider, A. (1990). The politics of pragmatism: An analysis of the 1989 gubernatorial election in Virginia. *PS: Political Science and Politics*, *23*, 154–156.

88 Hopkins, D. J. (2008). *No more Wilder effect, never a Whitman effect: When and why polls mislead about Black and female candidates*. Unpublished paper.

89 Eicher, D. (1996, September 26). The ABCs of menus: Area schools out of sync with fed plan. *Denver Post*, p. E01; Fritz, S. (2001, July 2). As Bush sinks in polls, he tries new direction. *St. Petersburg Times*, p. 1A.

90 Asher, *Polling and the public*, chap. 9.

91 Ibid.

92 Gallup Poll Presidential Approval Ratings: Truman– Bush. Facsimile copy sent from the Gallup Organization, May 6, 1999.

93 Traugott, M. W., & Lavrakas, P. J. (2000). *The voter's guide to election polls* (2nd ed.). New York: Chatham House, p. 79.

94 Frederick, D. (2008, October 27). John McCain's own polling gives him hope, aide says. *Los Angeles Times*. Retrieved February 5, 2009, from http://latimesblogs .latimes.com/washington/2008/10/john-mccains-ow .html.

95 Clawson, R. A., & Oxley, Z. M. (2008). *Public opinion: Democratic ideals and democratic practice*. Washington, DC: Congressional Quarterly Press, chaps. 10, 11, and 12.

Chapter 11

1 Ewing, P. (2018, February 17). The Russia investigation: Mueller indicts the "Internet Research Agency." *National Public Radio*. Retrieved July 12, 2018, from https://www.npr.org/2018/02/17/586698361/the-russia-investigations-mueller-indicts-the-internet-research-agency; Glaser, A. (2018, February 16). What we know about how Russia's Internet Research Agency meddled in the 2016 election. *Slate*. Retrieved July 12, 2018, from https://slate.com/technology/2018/02/what-we-know-about-the-internet-research-agency-and-how-it-meddled-in-the-2016-election.html.

2 Danner, C. (2018, May 12). More than half of Russian Facebook ads focused on race. *New York Magazine*. Retrieved July 12, 2018, from http://nymag.com/daily/intelligencer/2018/05/more-than-half-of-russian-facebook-ads-focused-on-race.html; Helsel, P., & Ortiz, E. (2016, October 13). Police confirm that Kirk Figueroa, a Boston constable, shot 2 cops. *NBC News*. Retrieved July 12, 2018, from https://www.nbcnews.com/news/us-news/suspect-armed-rifle-killed-after-shooting-2-boston-police-officers-n665516; Penzenstadler, N., Heath, B., & Guynn, J. (2018, May 11). We read every one of the 3,517 Facebook ads bought by Russians: Here is what we found. *USA Today*. Retrieved July 12, 2018, from https://www.usatoday.com/story/news/2018/05/11/what-we-found-facebook-ads-russians-accused-election-meddling/602319002/.

3 Krieg, G. (2016, September 16). 14 of Trump's most outrageous "birther" claims: Half from after 2011. *CNN Politics*. Retrieved July 12, 2018, from https://www.cnn.com/2016/09/09/politics/donald-trump-birther/index.html.

4 For more on the media's role in agenda setting and framing, see Iyengar, S., & Kinder, D. R. (1987). *News that matters: Television and American opinion*. Chicago: University of Chicago Press; Scheufele, D. A., & Tewksbury, D. (2007). Framing, agenda setting, and priming: The evolution of three media effects models. *Journal of Communication, 57*, 9–20.

5 For more on the party press, see Sloan, W. D., (1991). *Perspectives on mass communication history*. Hillsdale, NJ: Erlbaum, pp. 58–73.

6 Sloan, W. D., *Perspectives on mass communication history*, pp. 123–138.

7 Streeby, S. (2002). *American sensations: Class, empire, and the production of popular culture*. Berkeley: University of California Press, pp. 38–77.

8 Nelson, T. (Ed.). (1966). Introduction. In *Documents of upheaval: Selections from William Lloyd Garrison's* The Liberator, *1831–1835*. New York: Hill & Wang, pp. ix–xxii.

9 Washburn, P. (2006). *The African American newspaper: Voice of freedom*. Evanston, IL: Northwestern University Press, pp. 28–36.

10 Nasaw, D. (2000). *The chief: The life of William Randolph Hearst*. Boston: Houghton Mifflin, pp. 79–80.

11 Larson, S. G. (2006). *Media and minorities: The politics of race in news and entertainment*. Lanham, MD: Rowman & Littlefield, p. 110.

12 Kreitner, R., & The Almanac. (2015, March 3). March 2, 1923: The first issue of "Time" Magazine is published. *The Nation*. Retrieved July 13, 2018, from https://www.thenation.com/article/march-3-1923-first-issue-time-magazine-published/; Newsweek Staff. (2007, October 7). History of Newsweek. *Newsweek*. Retrieved July 13, 2018, from http://www.newsweek.com/history-newsweek-103593.

13 Washburn, *The African American newspaper*, pp. 80–100.

14 Kanellos, N., & Martell, H. (2000). *Hispanic periodicals in the United States, origins to 1960: A brief history and comprehensive bibliography*. Houston, TX: Arte Público Press, pp. 3–116; Larson, *Media and minorities*, pp. 125–129.

15 Larson, *Media and minorities*, pp. 115–116.

16 Gugliotta, G. (2017, May 31). How radio changed everything. *Discover*. Retrieved July 13, 2018, from http://discovermagazine.com/2007/jun/tireless-wireless.

17 For more on Roosevelt's fireside chats, see Ryfe, D.-M. (1999). Franklin Roosevelt and the fireside chats. *Journal of Communication, 49*, 80–103.

18 Kierstead, P. (n.d.). News, network. Museum of Television. Retrieved July 13, 2018, from http://www.museum.tv/eotv/newsnetwork.htm.

19 Museum of the Moving Image. (n.d.). 1952: Eisenhower vs. Stevenson. In *The living room candidate: Presidential campaign commercials 1952–2012*. Retrieved July 13, 2018, from http://www.livingroomcandidate.org/commercials/1952.

20 Larson, *Media and minorities*, pp. 171–173.

21 Ibid., pp. 145–192.

22 For more on Black Entertainment Television, see http://www.bet.com; and Pulley, B. (2004). *The billion dollar BET: Robert Johnson and the inside story of Black Entertainment Television*. Hoboken, NJ: Wiley.

23 For more on Noticiero Univision, see https://www.univision.com/shows/noticiero-univision/noticiero-univision.

24 Olmstead, K., Jurkowitz, M., Mitchell, A., & Edna, J. (2013, October 11). *How Americans get TV news at home*. Pew Research Center Journalism & Media. Retrieved July 13, 2018, from http://www.journalism.org/2013/10/11/how-americans-get-tv-news-at-home/.

25 For more on CSPAN, see https://www.c-span.org.

26 Fox Business. (n.d.). *Lou Dobbs*. Retrieved July 13, 2018, from https://www.foxbusiness.com/person/d/lou-dobbs.

27 Beirich, H., & Potok, M. (2006, January 31). CNN's Lou Dobbs refuses to cover anti-Latino racism in anti-immigration activist groups and citizen border patrols. *Southern Poverty Law Center: Intelligence Report*. Retrieved

July 13, 2018, from January 31, https://www.splcenter.org/fighting-hate/intelligence-report/2006/cnn's-lou-dobs-refuses-cover-anti-latino-racism-anti-immigration-activist-groups-and-citizen-border-patrols.

28 Comedy Central. (n.d.). *The Daily Show.* Retrieved July 13, 2018, from http://www.cc.com/shows/the-daily-show-with-trevor-noah.

29 CBS. (n.d.). *The Late Show.* Retrieved July 13, 2018, from https://www.cbs.com/shows/the-late-show-with-stephen-colbert/.

30 TBS. (n.d.). *About Full Frontal with Samantha Bee.* Retrieved July 13, 2018, from http://www.tbs.com/about/full-frontal-with-samantha-bee.

31 HBO. (n.d.). *Last Week Tonight with John Oliver.* Retrieved July 13, 2018, from https://www.hbo.com/last-week-tonight-with-john-oliver.

32 HBO. (n.d.). *Real Time with Bill Maher.* Retrieved July 13, 2018, from https://www.hbo.com/real-time-with-bill-maher.

33 Dawidziak, M. (2009, April 12). Seriously funny: Is this man a jester or journalist? Jon Stewart is blurring the lines. *Cleveland Plain Dealer,* p. E1.

34 Locker, M. (2016, October 31). John Oliver looks at racism and school segregation on *Last Week Tonight.* *Time.* Retrieved July 13, 2018, from http://time.com/4551029/john-oliver-racism-school-segregation-last-week-tonight/,

35 Steinberg, B. (2018, January 24). Samantha Bee's "Full Frontal" visits Puerto Rico for one-hour special. *Variety.* Retrieved July 13, 2018, from https://variety.com/2018/tv/news/samantha-bee-full-frontal-puerto-rico-tbs-1202676289/.

36 https://www.politico.com.

37 https://www.youtube.com/user/whitehouse.

38 Rich, F. (2006, November 12). 2006: The year of the "Macaca." *New York Times,* pp. 4–12.

39 *Our National Conversation About Conversations About Race.* Retrieved July 13, 2018, from https://www.showaboutrace.com.

40 *Native Opinion Podcast: An American Indian Perspective.* Retrieved July 13, 2018, from https://player.fm/series/native-opinion-podcast-an-american-indian-perspective.

41 *They Call Us Bruce.* Retrieved July 13, 2018, from https://theycallusbruce.libsyn.com/website.

42 *Chicago Defender.* Retrieved July 13, 2018, from https://chicagodefender.com.

43 *La Gaceta.* Retrieved July 13, 2018, from http://lagacetanewspaper.com.

44 Mosk, M. (2008, June 28). An attack that came out of the ether: Scholar looks at first link in email chain about Obama. *Washington Post,* p. C1; Silva, C. (2010, June 9). Whoomp!: That is not Obama in music video. *St. Petersburg Times,* p. 1A.

45 See Khamis, S., & Vaughn, K. (2011, Summer). Cyber-activism in the Egyptian revolution: How civic engagement and citizen journalism tilted the balance. *Arab Media & Society, 13.* Retrieved July 13, 2018, from https://www.arabmediasociety.com/cyberactivism-in-the-egyptian-revolution-how-civic-engagement-and-citizen-journalism-tilted-the-balance/.

46 Shearer, E., & Gottfried, J. (2017, September 7). *News use across social media platforms.* Pew Research Center Journalism & Media. Retrieved July 13, 2018, from http://www.journalism.org/2017/09/07/news-use-across-social-media-platforms-2017/.

47 Gottfried, J., & Shearer, E. (2017, September 7). *Americans' online news use is closing in on TV news use.* Pew Research Center Journalism & Media. Retrieved July 13, 2018, from http://www.pewresearch.org/fact-tank/2017/09/07/americans-online-news-use-vs-tv-news-use/.

48 Stephen, B. (2015, October). Get up, stand up: Social media helps Black Lives Matter fight the power. *Wired.* Retrieved July 14, 2018, from https://www.wired.com/2015/10/how-black-lives-matter-uses-social-media-to-fight-the-power/.

49 Holloway, K. (2016, March 16). These are the 10 most racist cities in America according to Twitter. *AlterNet.* Retrieved July 14, 2018, from https://www.alternet.org/media/these-are-10-most-racist-cities-america-according-twitter.

50 Greenberg, J. (2015, November 23). Trump's pants on fire Tweet that Blacks killed 81% of White homicide victims. *PolitiFact.* Retrieved July 17, 2018, from http://www.politifact.com/truth-o-meter/statements/2015/nov/23/donald-trump/trump-tweet-blacks-white-homicide-victims/.

51 Landers, E., & Masters, J. (2017, November 30). Trump retweets anti-Muslim videos. *CNN Politics.* Retrieved July 13, 2018, from https://www.cnn.com/2017/11/29/politics/donald-trump-retweet-jayda-fransen/index.html.

52 Pryne, E. (2009, March 16). Last edition of the Post-Intelligencer set for Tuesday. *Seattle Times.*

53 Yu, R. (2016, May 3). Tampa Bay Times' shuts down rival "Tampa Tribune." *USA Today.* Retrieved July 14, 2018, from https://www.usatoday.com/story/money/2016/05/03/tampa-bay-times-buys-ends-rival-tampa-tribune/83888058/.

54 See http://www.iheartmedia.com.

55 See https://corporate.comcast.com/our-company/businesses/nbcuniversal.

56 See https://www.disneyabcpress.com/disneyabctv/.

57 Lutz, A. (2012, June 14). These 6 corporations control 90% of the media in America. *Business Insider.* Retrieved July 14, 2018, from http://www.businessinsider.com/these-6-corporations-control-90-of-the-media-in-america-2012-6.

58 Matthews, D. (2018, April 3). Sinclair, the pro-Trump, conservative company taking over local news explained. *Vox*. Retrieved July 14, 2018, from https://www.vox.com/2018/4/3/17180020/sinclair-broadcast-group-conservative-trump-david-smith-local-news-tv-affiliate.

59 For a good analysis of journalism as a profession, see Davis, M. (2010). Why journalism is a profession. In C. Meyers (Ed.), *Journalism ethics: A philosophical approach*. New York: Oxford University Press, pp. 91–102.

60 For more on defining what makes someone a journalist, see Black, J. (2010). Who is a journalist? In C. Meyers (Ed.), *Journalism ethics: A philosophical approach*. New York: Oxford University Press, pp. 103–115.

61 MSNBC. (n.d.). Morning Joe: Joe Scarborough. Retrieved July 14, 2018, from http://www.msnbc.com/morning-joe/joe-scarborough-biography.

62 Davis, R. (2001). *The press and American politics: The new mediator*. Upper Saddle River, NJ: Prentice Hall, p. 115.

63 See Sabato, L. J. (2000). *Feeding frenzy: Attack journalism and American politics*. Lanham, MD: Lanham Publishing.

64 American Society of Newspaper Editors. (2017, October 10). Table-H: Percentage of Women Part of the Overall Workforce and Table I: Percent of Men/Women Among Newsroom Leaders and Among All Other Journalists. *Diversity Survey 2017*. Retrieved July 14, 2018, from https://www.asne.org//Files/census/2017%20ASNE%20diversity%20survey%20tables.pdf.

65 For more on priming, see Iyengar & Kinder, *New that matters*; Scheufele and Tewksbury, "Framing, Agenda Setting, and Priming."

66 Larson, *Media and minorities*, pp. 202–228, 237–267.

67 Kornacki, S. (2008, July 23). Media fascination with Obama is no liberal conspiracy. *New York Observer*. Retrieved July 14, 2018, from http://observer.com/2008/07/media-fascination-with-obama-is-no-liberal-conspiracy/.

68 Seelye, K. Q. (2008, May 6). Wright dominated news coverage. *New York Times*. Retrieved July 14, 2018, from https://thecaucus.blogs.nytimes.com/2008/05/06/wright-dominated-news-coverage/.

69 See, for example, Wolf, M. (2011, November 10). Liberal media cues up Cain and friends: All in for Obama while GOP gets snookered. *Washington Times*, p. B1.

70 Waldman, K. (2012, October 25). The problem with Palin's "shuck and jive." *Slate*. Retrieved July 14, 2018, from http://www.slate.com/blogs/browbeat/2012/10/25/shuck_and_jive_meaning_and_history_of_phrase_palin_used_is_it_racist.html.

71 Jacobs, B. (2015, October 7). Rupert Murdoch implies that Obama is not "real Black president" in Tweet praising Carson. *The Guardian*. Retrieved July 14, 2018, from https://www.theguardian.com/media/2015/oct/08/rupert-murdoch-obama-not-real-black-president-tweet-ben-carson.

72 Kiley, E. (2018, January 26). Trump's phony "fake news" claims. *Factcheck.org*. Retrieved July 13, 2018, from https://www.factcheck.org/2018/01/trumps-phony-fake-news-claims/.

73 For more on press secretaries, see Nelson, W. D. (1998). *Who speaks for the president: The White House press secretary from Cleveland through Clinton*. Syracuse, NY: Syracuse University Press.

74 American Urban Radio Networks. (n.d.). *April Ryan*. Retrieved July 14, 2018, from http://aurn.com/april-ryan/.

75 NBC Universal Media Village. (n.d.). NBC news correspondents talent bios: Kristen Welker. Retrieved July 13, 2018, from https://www.nbcumv.com/talent/kristen-welker/bios_read_more.

76 Larson, *Media and minorities*, p. 207.

77 *Near v. Minnesota*, 283 U.S. 697 (1931).

78 *New York Times v. United States*, 403 U.S. 713 (1971).

79 *Cox Broadcasting Company v. Cohn*, 420 U.S. 469 (1975).

80 *Smith v. Daily Mail Publishing Co.*, 443 U.S. 97 (1979); *Globe Newspaper Co. v. Superior Court for the County of Norfolk*, 457 U.S. 596 (1982).

81 *Nebraska Press Association v. Stuart*, 427 U.S. 539 (1976).

82 *Branzburg v. Hayes*, 408 U.S. 665 (1971).

83 *Federal Communications Commission v. Pacifica Foundation*, 438 U.S. 726 (1978).

84 *Denver Area Educational Telecommunications Consortium v. Federal Communications Commission*, 518 U.S. 727 (1996).

Chapter 12

1 Branch, T. (1988). *Parting the waters: America in the King years, 1954–63*. New York: Touchstone, pp. 19–24; Baker, D. P. (2001, March 4). Shame of a nation: The lessons and legacy of the Prince Edward school closings. *Washington Post*, p. W08.

2 Franklin, J. P. (1969). *From slavery to freedom: A history of Negro Americans* (3rd ed.). New York: Vintage, pp. 332–343.

3 Tarrow, S. (1994). *Power in movement: Social movements, collective action, and politics*. Cambridge, UK: Cambridge University Press, p. 1.

4 Adamson, M., & Borgos, S. (1984). *This mighty dream: Social protest movements in the United States*. Boston: Routledge & Kegan Paul, p. 32.

5 Ibid.

6 McCarthy, J. D., & Zald, M. N. (1977). Resource mobilization and social movements: A partial theory. *American Journal of Sociology, 82*, 1214.

7 Adam, B. D. (1995). *The rise of a gay and lesbian movement* (Rev. ed.). New York: Twayne, p. 80.

8 Ibid.

9 Ibid., p. 85.

10 Ibid., p. 89.

11 McCarthy & Zald, "Resource Mobilization and Social Movements," p. 1216.

12 Jenkins, J. C. (1983). The transformation of a constituency into a movement. In J. Freeman (Ed.), *Social movements of the sixties and seventies*. New York: Longman, p. 63.

13 Ibid., p. 64.

14 Janofsky, M. (1995, October 21). Federal parks chief calls "million man" count low. *New York Times*. Retrieved October 23, 2012, from http://www.nytimes.com/1995/10/21/us/federalparks -chief-calls-million-man-count-low.html.

15 Lowi, T. J. (1971). *The politics of disorder*. New York: Basic Books, p. 54.

16 Erskine, H. (1972). The polls: Pollution and its costs. *Public Opinion Quarterly, 36*, 120.

17 Gallup Poll. (n.d.). *Environment—summary data*. Retrieved October 23, 2012, from http://www.gallup.com/poll/1615/environment.aspx#1.

18 Euchner, C. C. (1996). *Extraordinary politics: How protest and dissent are changing American democracy*. Boulder, CO: Westview Press, p. 212.

19 Ibid., p. 218.

20 Howell, S. E., & McLean, W. P. (2001). Performance and race in evaluating minority mayors. *Public Opinion Quarterly, 65*, 231–243; Marschall, M. J., & Ruhil, A. V. S. (2007). Substantive symbols: The attitudinal dimension of Black political incorporation in local government. *American Journal of Political Science, 51*, 17–33.

21 Dobratz, B. A., & Shanks-Meile, S. L. (1997). *White power, White pride!: The White separatist movement in the United States*. New York: Twayne.

22 Ibid., pp. 150–151.

23 Southern Poverty Law Center. (n.d.). *Active hate groups in the U.S. in 2015*. Retrieved July 5, 2016, from https://www.splcenter.org/hate-map.

24 Dobratz & Shanks-Meile, *White power*, pp. 150–151; Southern Poverty Law Center, "Active Patriot Groups."

25 Southern Poverty Law Center. (n.d.). *Hate maps*. Retrieved August 5, 2018, from https://www.splcenter.org/hate-map.

26 Wolff, J. (2015, July 22). The secret agents who stake out the ugliest corners of the Internet. *The Atlantic*. Retrieved July 5, 2016, from http://www.theatlantic.com/technology/archive /2015/07/secret-service-online-threat-president/399179/.

27 Fausset, R., Kovaleski, S. F., & Feuer, A. (2018, August 13). A year after Charlottesville, disarray in the White Supremacist Movement. *New York Times*. Retrieved October 13, 2018, from https://www.nytimes.com/2018/08/13/us/charlottesville-unite-the-right-white-supremacists.html.

28 King, C. W. (1956). *Social movements in the United States*. New York: Random House, p. 27.

29 *Plessy v. Ferguson*, 163 U.S. 537 (1896).

30 Appiah, K. A., & Gates Jr., H. E. (Eds.). (1999). *Africana: The encyclopedia of the African and African American experience*. New York: Basic Civitas Books, p. 442.

31 Harris-Lacewell, M. V. (2004). *Barbershops, bibles, and BET: Everyday thought and Black political talk*. Princeton, NJ: Princeton University Press.

32 *Missouri ex rel. Gaines v. Canada*, 305 U.S. 337 (1938).

33 Appiah & Gates, *Africana*, p. 445.

34 Bunche, R. J. (1936). *World view of race*. Washington, DC: The Associates in Negro Folk Education.

35 McClain, P. D., & Stewart Jr., J. (2010)."Can we all get along?": Racial and ethnic minorities in American politics (5th ed.). Boulder, CO: Westview Press.

36 Branch, *Parting the waters*, p. 193.

37 McClain & Stewart, "Can we all get along?"

38 Appiah & Gates, *Africana*, p. 447.

39 Ibid., p. 449; Branch, *Parting the waters*, p. 271.

40 Appiah & Gates, *Africana*, p. 449.

41 King Jr., M. L. (n.d.). *Letter from Birmingham Jail*. Retrieved July 21, 2009, from http://www.mlkonline.net/jail.html.

42 McClain, P. D. (2000). Foreword. In B. Grofman (Ed.), *Legacies of the 1964 Civil Rights Act*. Charlottesville: University Press of Virginia, p. xii.

43 Appiah & Gates, *Africana*, 451.

44 Ibid.

45 Branch, *Parting the waters*, p. 821.

46 Appiah & Gates, *Africana*, p. 452.

47 Ibid., p. 445; Giugni, M. (1999). How social movements matter: Past research, present problems, future development. In M. Giugni, D. McAdams, & C. Tilly (Eds.), *How social movements matter*. Minneapolis: University of Minnesota Press, p. xiii.

48 King Jr., M. L. (n.d.). *"I Have a Dream" address at March on Washington, August 28, 1963*. Retrieved August 8, 2008, from http://www.mlkonline.net/dream.html.

49 Appiah & Gates, *Africana*, p. 455.

50 Evans, S. M. (1971). *Born for liberty: A history of women in America*. New York: Basic Books, p. 54.

51 DuBois, E. C. (1978). *Feminism and suffrage: The emergence of an independent women's movement in America, 1848–1869*. Ithaca, NY: Cornell University Press, p. 22.

52 Douglass, F. (1848, July 28). The rights of women. *North Star*. Retrieved August 18, 2008, from http://www.iath .virginia.edu/utc/abolitn /abwm03dt.html.

53 Legacy 98. (n.d.). *Living the legacy: The Women's Rights Movement, 1848–1998*. Retrieved August 18, 2008, from http://www.legacy98.org /move-hist.html.

54 Ibid.

55 Guy-Sheftall, B. (1995). *Words of fire: An anthology of African American feminist thought*. New York: New Press, p. 1.

56 Painter, N. I. (1996). *Sojourner Truth: A life, a symbol*. New York: Norton; Guy-Sheftall, *Words of fire*, p. 35.

57 Painter, *Sojourner Truth*, p. 98.

58 Ibid.

59 Hurtado, A. (1989). Relating to privilege: Seduction and rejection in the subordination of White women and women of color. *Signs, 14*(4), 833–855.

60 Guy-Sheftall, p. 35.

61 Dubois, p. 70.

62 Ibid.

63 Ibid., p. 69.

64 Guy-Sheftall, p. 35.

65 Evans, *Born for liberty*, pp. 123–124.

66 Stanton, E. C. (1997). Letter to the National Anti-Slavery Standard, December 26, 1865. In A. D. Gordon (Ed.), *Selected papers of Elizabeth Cady Stanton and Susan B. Anthony.* New Brunswick, NJ: Rutgers University Press, pp. 54–55.

67 Taylor, U. (1998). The historical evolution of Black feminist theory and praxis. *Journal of Black Studies, 29,* 234–253.

68 Evans, *Born for liberty*, p. 153.

69 Taylor, "The Historical Evolution of Black Feminist Theory."

70 Legacy 98, "Living the Legacy."

71 Ibid.

72 Evans, *Born for liberty*, p. 267.

73 Legacy 98, "Living the Legacy."

74 Evans, *Born for liberty*, p. 291.

75 Ibid.

75 Ibid.

77 Legacy 98, "Living the Legacy."

78 Alexander, K. (2012, April 29). Capitol rally aims to reignite Women's Rights Movement. *Houston Chronicle.* Retrieved January 15, 2013, from http://www.chron .com/news/article/Capitol-rally-aims-to-reignite-women-s-rights-3519255.php.

79 Women's March on Washington. (n.d.). *Guiding vision and definition of principles.* Retrieved October 13, 2018, from https://static1.squarespace.com/static/ 584086c7be6594762f5ec56e/t/587ffb31d2b857e5d49dc d4f/1484782386354/WMW+Guiding+Vision+%26+ Definition+of+Principles.pdf

80 Ibid.

81 Przybyla, H. M., & Schouten, F. (2017, January 21). At 2.6 million strong, women's marches crush expectations. *USA Today.* Retrieved from https://www.usatoday .com/story/news/politics/2017/01/21/womens-march-aims-start-movement-trump-inauguration/96864158/.

82 Chira, S. (2018, January 20). The women's march became a movement. What's next? *New York Times.* Retrieved October 13, 2018, from https://www.nytimes .com/2018/01/20/us/womens-march-metoo.html.

83 Women's march 2018: Global demonstrations continue into 2nd day. (2018, January 21). *NBC News.* Retrieved October 13, 2018, from https://www.cbsnews.com/ news/womens-march-2018-global-demonstrations-continue-into-second-day/.

84 Bassett, L. (2018, January 15). "Here's what to know about the 2018 women's march. *Huffington Post.* Retrieved October 13, 2018, from https://www. huffingtonpost.com/entry/2018-womens-march_ us_5a5d14e6e4b03c4189683949.

85 Adamson & Borgos, *This mighty dream*, p. 39.

86 Karson, M. (1958). *American labor unions and politics: 1900–1918.* Boston: Beacon Press.

87 Adamson & Borgos, *This mighty dream*, p. 39.

88 Brooks, T. R. (1971). *Toil and trouble: A history of American labor* (2nd ed.). New York: Delacorte Press, pp. 58–59.

89 Dubofsky, M., & Dulles, F. R. (2004). *Labor in America: A history* (7th ed.). Arlington Heights, IL: Harland Davidson.

90 Tye, L. (2005). *Rising from the rails: Pullman porters and the making of the Black middle class.* New York: Macmillan; Bates, B. T. (2001). *Pullman porters and the rise of protest politics in Black America, 1925–1945.* Chapel Hill: University of North Carolina Press.

91 Giddings, P. J. (2008). *Ida: A sword among among lions.* New York: Amistad, pp. 634–641.

92 Bruinius, H. (2008, February 29). Pullman porters tell tales of a train ride through history. *Christian Science Monitor.* Retrieved July 21, 2009, from http://www .csmonitor.com/2008 /0229/p20s01-ussc.html.

93 Ibid.

94 Hurd, R. W. (1998). Contesting the dinosaur image: The labor movement's search for a future. *Labor Studies Journal, 22,* 5–30.

95 Schiavone, M. (2008). *Unions in crisis?: The future of organized labor in America.* Westport, CT: Praeger.

96 Abraham, S. E. (1996). The impact of the Taft-Hartley Act on the balance of power in industrial relations. *American Business Law Journal, 33,* 341–372.

97 Dubofsky, M. (1994). *The state and labor in modern America.* Chapel Hill: University of North Carolina Press, p. 223.

98 Hurd, "Contesting the Dinosaur Image."

99 Kline, B. (1997). *First along the river: A brief history of the U.S. environmental movement.* San Francisco: Acada Books; Shabecoff, P. (1993). *A fierce green fire: The American environmental movement/* New York: Hill & Wang.

100 Dicum, G. (2006, March 14). Justice in time: Meet Robert Bullard, the father of environmental justice. *Grist: Environmental News and Commentary.* Retrieved July 6, 2009, from http://www.grist.org/news/ maindish/2006/03/14/dicum.

101 Bullard, R. D. (2000). *Dumping in Dixie: Race, class, and environmental quality.* Boulder, CO: Westview Press.

102 Material for this paragraph and the following are taken from Rosenberg, J. (n.d.). Vietnam War. Retrieved January 15, 2013, from http:// history1900s.about. com/od/vietnamwar/a/vietnamwar.htm; Malesky, E. J. (2008). Vietnam War. In W. A. Darity, Jr. (Ed.),

International encyclopedia of the social sciences (2nd ed., pp. 612–617). New York: Thompson.

103 Ibid.

104 Malesky, p. 614.

105 Gettleman, M. E. Franklin, J., & Young, M. (1995). *Vietnam and America: A documented history.* New York: Grove Atlantic, p. 296.

106 Ibid., p. 297.

107 Holsinger, P. M. (1998). *War and American popular culture: A historical encyclopedia.* Westport, CT: Greenwood Press.

108 The Greatest Is Gone. (1978, February 27). *Time.* Retrieved July 6, 2009, from http://www.time.com/time/magazine/article /0,9171,919377,00.html.

109 Farber, D. (1994). *Chicago '68.* Chicago: University of Chicago Press.

110 Ibid., p. 196.

111 Ibid., p. 202.

112 Ibid., p. 204.

113 Gettleman et al., *Vietnam and America,* p. 299.

114 Sutherland, J. (2004). *African Americans at war: An encyclopedia.* Santa Barbara, CA: ABC-CLIO, p. 502.

115 Material for this paragraph and some of the material in the second paragraph are drawn from these sources: Stein, M. (Ed.). (2003). *lgbt: Encyclopedia of lesbian, gay, bisexual, and transgender history in America.* New York: Charles Scribner's Sons/Thomson Gale; Smith, R. (2002). *Gay and lesbian Americans and political participation: A reference handbook.* Santa Barbara, CA: ABC-CLIO.

116 Ibid.

117 Levy, M. (2011). Gay rights movement. *History Channel.* Retrieved February 1, 2013, from www.history.com.

118 Farber, J. (2016, April 20). Before the Stonewall uprising, there was the "sip-in." *New York Times.* Retrieved April 21, 2016, from http://www.nytimes.com/2016/04/21/nyregion/before-the -stonewall-riots-there-was-the-sip-in.html?login =email&_r=0.

119 Levy, "Gay Rights Movement."

120 Janofsky, M. (1999, November 4). Man is convicted in killing of gay student. *New York Times.* Retrieved February 1, 2013, from http://www.nytimes.com/1999/11/04/us/man-is-convicted-in-killing-of-gay-student.html?ref=aaronjamesmckinney.

121 The Leadership Conference. (n.d.). *LLEHCPA 2009-Endorsing Organizations.* Retrieved February 1, 2013, from http://www.civilrights.org /hatecrimes/llehcpa/organizations.html.

122 All of the dates for events in this section come from Stonewall uprising: Timeline: Milestones in the American Gay Rights Movement. (2013). *PBS.* Retrieved February 1, 2013, from http://www.pbs.org/wgbh/americanexperience/features/timeline/stonewall/.

123 Flores, A. R. (2014, November). *National trends in public opinion on LGBT rights in the United States.* The Williams Institute. Retrieved July 4, 2016, from http://williamsinstitute.law .ucla.edu/wp-content/uploads/POP-natl-trends-nov -2014.pdf.

124 McCarthy, J. (2018, May). Two in three Americans support same-sex marriage. Gallup Poll. Retrieved August 5, 2018, from https://news.gallup.com/poll/234866/two-three-americans-support-sex-marriage.aspx.

125 Schwartz, J. (2015, June 26). Highlights from the Supreme Court decision on same-sex marriage. *New York Times.* Retrieved July 4, 2016, from http://www.nytimes.com/interactive /2015/us/2014-term-supreme-court-decision-same-sex -marriage.html.

126 Court overturns DOMA, sidesteps broad gay marriage ruling. (2013, June 26). *NPR.* Retrieved October 13, 2018, from http://www.npr.org /sections/thetwo-way/2013/06/26/195857796/supreme-court-strikes-down-defense-of-marriage-act.

127 Braverman, N. (2016, January 20). At least 11 Alabama counties refuse to comply with marriage equality. *The Advocate.* Retrieved July 4, 2016, from http://www .advocate .com/marriage-equality/2016/1/20/least-11-alabama -counties-refuse-comply-marriage-equality.

128 Phillips, D. (2016, March 24). North Carolina bans local anti-discrimination policies. *New York Times.* Retrieved July 4, 2016, from http://www.nytimes.com/2016/03/24/us /north-carolina-to-limit-bathroom-use-by-birth -gender.html.

129 Minnick, B. (2016, July 4). HB2 changes don't guarantee NBA All-Star game will stay in Charlotte. *WNCN.com.* Retrieved July 4, 2016, from http://wncn.com/2016/07/04/hb2-changes -dont-guarantee-nba-all-star-game-will-stay-in -charlotte/.

130 Sterling, J., McLaughlin, E. C., & Berlinger, J. (2016, May 9). North Carolina, U.S., square off over transgender rights. *CNN.com.* Retrieved July 4, 2016, from http://www.cnn.com/2016/05/09/politics/north -carolina-hb2-justice-department-deadline/.

131 Wojnarowski, A. (2016, July 21). *NBA pulls 2017 All-Star Game from Charlotte, focuses on New Orleans.* Retrieved October 14, 2018, from http://sports.yahoo.com/news/nba-pulls-2017-all-star-game -from-charlotte-focuses-on-new-orleans-190148437.html.

132 Sterling et al., "North Carolina, U.S."

133 Elon University. (2016, April). *Elon Poll: Cooper pulls ahead in N.C. gubernatorial race.* Retrieved July 4, 2016, from http://www.elon.edu/e-web/elonpoll/041916.xhtml.

134 Domonoske, C., & Doubek, J. (2017, March 30). North Carolina repeals portions of controversial "bathroom bill." *NPR.* Retrieved August 5, 2018, from https://www.npr.org/sections/thetwo-way/2017/03/30/

522009335/north-carolina-lawmakers-governor-announce-compromise-to-repeal-bathroom-bill.

135 Berman, M. (2016, April 5). Mississippi governor signs law allowing businesses to refuse service to gay people. *Washington Post*. Retrieved July 4, 2016, from https://www.washingtonpost.com/news/post-nation/wp/2016/04 /05/mississippi-governor-signs-law-allowing-business -to-refuse-service-to-gay-people/?utm_term=.a2fac002eca1.

136 Green, E. (2016, July 1). Why Mississippi's law on religious rights and LGBT discrimination got blocked. *The Atlantic*. Retrieved July 4, 2016, from http://www .theatlantic.com /politics/archive/2016/07/why-mississippis-law-on -religious-rights-and-lgbt-got-blocked/489731/.

137 Muñoz Jr., C. (2007). *Youth, identity, power: The Chicano movement* (Rev. and expanded ed.). London: Verso.

138 This section is indebted to Wilkins, D. E. (2006). *American Indian politics and the American political system* (2nd ed.). Lanham, MD: Rowman & Littlefield.

139 Wei, W. (1993). *The Asian American movement*. Philadelphia: Temple University Press.

140 Wittner, L. S. (1993). *The struggle against the bomb: A history of the world nuclear disarmament movement*. Stanford, CA: Stanford University Press; Wittner, L. S. (2003). *Toward nuclear abolition: A history of the world nuclear disarmament movement, 1971–present*. Stanford, CA: Stanford University Press.

141 Fundamentalism. (2002). In C. Calhoun (Ed.), *Dictionary of the social sciences*. New York: Oxford University Press; Fundamentalism. (2009). In F. L. Cross & E. A. Livingstone (Eds.), *The Oxford dictionary of the Christian church*. New York: Oxford University Press. Retrieved November 6, 2009, from http://www.oxfordreference .com/views//ENTRY.html?subview=Main&entry=t257 .e2750; Withnow, R. (Ed.). (2007). *Encyclopedia of politics and religion*. Washington, DC: Congressional Quarterly Press.

142 McAdam, D. (1999). The decline of the Civil Rights Movement. In J. Freeman & V. Johnson (Eds.), *Waves of protest: Social movements since the sixties* (pp. 325–348). Lanham, MD: Rowman & Littlefield.

143 Libby, R. T. (1998). *Eco-wars: Political campaigns and social movements*. New York: Columbia University Press, chap. 5.

144 Euchner, *Extraordinary politics*, p. 48.

145 Adamson & Borgos, *This mighty dream*, p. 46.

146 Ibid., pp. 47–48.

147 Carlsen, A., & Patel, J. K. (2018, March 22). March for Our Lives: Maps of the more than 800 protests around the world. *New York Times*. Retrieved October 14, 2018, from https://www.nytimes.com/interactive/2018/03/22/us/politics/march-for-lives-demonstrations .html.

148 March for Our Lives highlights: Students protesting guns say "enough is enough." (2018, March 24). *New York Times*. Retrieved October 14, 2018, from https://www.nytimes.com/2018/03/24/us/march-for-our-lives .html.

149 Carlsen & Patel, "March for Our Lives."

150 Hanks, D., & Harris, A. (2018, February 14). Worse than Columbine: This is one of the deadliest school shootings in U.S. history. *Miami Herald*. Retrieved October 14, 2018, from https://www.miamiherald .com/news/local/community/broward/article200180189.html.

151 Peralta, E. (2016, June 12). A list of the deadliest mass shootings in modern U.S. history. *NPR*. Retrieved October 14, 2018, from https://www.npr.org/sections/thetwo-way/2016/06/12/481768384/a-list-of-the-deadliest-mass-shootings-in-u-s-history.

152 Blumberg, J. (2018, February 22). Thousands volunteer, donate to help Mike Bloomberg and Everytown fight gun violence. *CNBC*. Retrieved October 14, 2018, from https://www.cnbc.com/2018/02/22/thousands-help-mike-bloomberg-and-everytown-fight-gun-violence.html.

153 Turning anger into activism: School shooting victims say "never again." *CBSMiami.com*. Retrieved October 14, 2018, from http://miami.cbslocal.com/2018/02/18/turning-anger-into-activism-school-shooting/.

154 Beckett, L. (2018, March 31). Florida school shooting survivors march on unfazed by personal attacks. *The Guardian*. Retrieved October 14, 2018, from https://www.theguardian.com/us-news/2018/mar/31/florida-school-shooting-survivors-march-personal-attacks.

155 Ibid.

156 Garza, A. (2014, October 7). *A herstory of the #BlackLivesMatter movement*. Retrieved October 14, 2018, from http://www.thefeministwire.com/2014/10/blacklivesmatter-2/.

157 Smith. M. D. (2014). How Trayvon Martin's death launched a new generation of Black activism. *The Nation*. Retrieved October 14, 2018, from http://www.thenation.com/article/how-trayvon-martins-death-launched-new-generation-black-activism.

158 Ibid.

159 Zarya, V. (2015, July 19). Founders of #BlackLivesMatter: Getting credit for your work matters. *Fortune*. Retrieved October 14, 2018, from http://fortune.com/2015/07/19/blacklivesmatter-work-credit/.

160 Ibid.

161 Smith, "How Trayvon Martin's Death."

162 Ruffin, H. G. (2016). Black Lives Matter: The growth of a new social justice movement. Retrieved October 14, 2018, from http://www.blackpast.org/perspectives/black-lives-matter-growth-new-social-justice-movement

163 Zarya, "Founders of #BlackLivesMatter."

164 Johnson, K. (2016, May 11). Black Lives Matter finds Canadian voice. *USA Today.* Retrieved October 14, 2018, from http://www.usatoday.com/story/news/world/2016/05/11/black-lives-matter-canada/83827764/.

165 Tamari, S. (2015, October 16). From Ferguson to Palestine, we see us. *Huffington Post.* Retrieved October 14, 2018, from http://www.huffingtonpost.com/sandra-tamari/from-ferguson-to-palestine_b_8307832.html.

166 Henderson, N. (2015, August 18). How Black Lives Matter activists are influencing 2016 race. *CNN.* Retrieved October 14, 2018, from http://www.cnn.com/2015/08 /18/politics/black-lives-matter-2016-presidential-race/.

167 Times Topics: Tea Party movement. (2012, August 12). *New York Times.* Retrieved February 11, 2013, from http://topics.nytimes.com/top/reference/timestopics/subjects/t/tea_party_movement/index.html.

168 Goldstein, J. A. (2011). The Tea Party movement and the perils of popular originalism. *Arizona Law Review, 53,* 831.

169 Ibid.

170 Time Line: Rise of the Tea Party. (2010, November 2). *CNN.* Retrieved February 11, 2013, from http://politicalticker.blogs.cnn.com/2010/11/02/timeline-rise-of-the-tea-party/.

171 Ibid.

172 Fallin, A., Grana, R., & Glantz, S. A. (2013). "To quarterback behind the scenes, third party efforts": The tobacco industry and the Tea Party. *Tobacco Control, 23*(4). Retrieved October 14, 2018, from https://tobaccocontrol.bmj.com/content/23/4/322.

173 "Times Topics, Tea Party movement."

174 Zernike, K., & Thee-Brenan, M. (2010, April 14). Poll finds Tea Party backers wealthier and more educated. *New York Times.* Retrieved October 14, 2018, from http://www.nytimes.com/2010/04/15/us/politics/15poll.html.

Chapter 13

1 Underwood, A. (2018, April 6). What most Americans get wrong about Islamophobia. *Vox.* Retrieved October 14, 2018, from https://www.vox.com/2018/4/6/17169448/trump-islamophobia-muslims-islam-black-lives-matter.

2 Alanis, K. (2017, November 2). Wichita restaurant burns down in what owners believe was a hate crime. *Wichita Eagle.* Retrieved October 14, 2018, from http://www.kansas.com/news/local/article182191451.html.

3 Smith, E. (2017, June 19). Victim of Bronx beating says he was targeted for being Muslim. *CBS New York.* Retrieved October 14, 2018, from http://newyork.cbslocal.com/2017/06/19/bronx-muslim-attack/.

4 Cohen, R. (2017, November 13). *Hate crimes rise for second straight year; anti-Muslim violence soars amid President Trump's xenophobic rhetoric.* Retrieved October 14, 2018, from https://www.splcenter.org/news/2017/11/13/hate-crimes-rise-second-straight-year-anti-muslim-violence-soars-amid-president-trumps.

5 U.S. anti-Muslim hate crimes rose 15 percent in 2017: Advocacy group. (2018, April 23). *Reuters.* Retrieved October 14, 2018, from https://www.reuters.com/article/us-usa-islam-hatecrime/u-s-anti-muslim-hate-crimes-rose-15-percent-in-2017-advocacy-group-idUSKBN1HU240.

6 Council on American-Islamic Relations. (2018). *About us: Vision, mission, core principles.* Retrieved October 14, 2018, from from https://www.cair.com/about_us.

7 Gaillot, A.-D. (2017, January 25). 7 Muslim advocacy groups to support through donations or volunteering. *Bustle.* Retrieved October 14, 2018, from https://www.bustle.com/p/7-muslim-advocacy-groups-to-support-through-donations-volunteering-32913.

8 Reuters, "U.S. Anti-Muslim Hate Crimes.".

9 Ippolito, D. S., & Walker, T. G. (1980). *Political parties, interest groups, and public policy: Group influence in American politics.* Englewood Cliffs, NJ: Prentice Hall, p. 1.

10 National Association for the Advancement of Colored People. (n.d.). *100: NAACP Centennial Celebration.* Retrieved July 9, 2009, from http://www.naacp.org/about/history/, accessed July 9, 2009.

11 National Urban League. (n.d.). History of the National Urban League. Retrieved July 9, 2009, from http://www.nul.org/history.html.

12 Madison, J. (1961). Federalist No. 10. In C. Rossiter (Ed.), *The Federalist Papers.* New York: Mentor Books, p. 78.

13 Ibid., p. 79.

14 Quoted in Mahood, H. R. (2000). *Interest groups in American national politics: An overview.* Upper Saddle River, NJ: Prentice Hall; see also Bentley, A. F. (1995). *The process of government: A study of social pressures* (2nd ed.). New Brunswick, NJ: Transaction Press.

15 Mahood, *Interest groups,* pp. 12–13; Bentley, *The process of government.*

16 Truman, D. B. (1951). *The governmental process: Political interests and public opinion.* New York: Knopf.

17 Mahood, *Interest groups,* p. 15.

18 Dahl, R. A. (1961). *Who governs?: Democracy and power in an American city.* New Haven, CT: Yale University Press.

19 Schattschneider, E. E. (1975). *The semisovereign people: A realist's view of democracy in America.* New York: Harcourt Brace; Mahood, *Interest groups,* p. 17.

20 Schattschneider, *The semisovereign people,* p. 34.

21 Lowi, T. J. (1979). *The end of liberalism.* New York: Norton.

22 Ibid.

23 Ibid.

24 Schlozman, K. L., & Tierney, J. (1986). *Organized interests and American democracy.* New York: Harper & Row, pp. 123–125.

25 Ibid.

26 Ibid.

27 Wilson, J. Q. (1973). *Political organizations.* New York: Basic Books, chap. 3.

28 American Association for Retired People. (n.d.). *About AARP.* Retrieved July 15, 2009, from http://www.aarp .org/about-aarp/.

29 de Tocqueville, A. (1994). *Democracy in America (Vols. 1 and 2)* (H. Reeve, Trans.). New York: Knopf.

30 Mahood, *Interest groups*, p. 28.

31 Ornstein, N. J., & Elder, S. (1978). *Interest groups, lobbying, and policymaking.* Washington, DC: Congressional Quarterly Press, p. 44.

32 Mahood, *Interest groups*, p. 29.

33 Browne, W. B. (1998). *Groups, interests, and U.S. public policy.* Washington, DC: Georgetown University Press, p. 33.

34 U.S. Chamber of Commerce. (n.d.). *About us.* Retrieved May 12, 2009, from http://www.uschamber.com/default.

35 Business Roundtable. (n.d.). *About us.* Retrieved May 12, 2009, from http://www.businessroundtable.org.

36 Browne, *Groups, interests, and U.S. public policy*, p. 32.

37 Sussman, B. (2009, September 25). Associations band together on derivatives fight. *National Journal Online.* Retrieved October 1, 2009, from http:// undertheinfluence.nationaljournal .com/2009/09/ associations-band-together-on.php.

38 U.S. Bureau of Labor Statistics. (2018, January 19). *Union Members — 2017* [News release]. Retrieved October 14, 2018, from https://www.bls.gov/news.release/pdf/ union2.pdf.

39 https://www.opensecrets.org/orgs/list.php.

40 Graham, J. *"Like a slap in the face": Dissent roils the AMA, the nation's largest doctor's group.* Retrieved October 14, 2018, from https://www.statnews.com/2016/12/22/ american-medical-association-divisions/.

41 American Bar Association. (n.d.). *About us.* Retrieved August 9, 2018, from http://www.americanbar.org/ utility/about_the_aba.html.

42 Ibid.

43 NAACP. (2016). NAACP announces 2016 convention theme "Our Lives Matter, or Votes Count." Retrieved July 25, 2016, from http://www.naacp.org/press/entry/naacp-announces-2016-convention-theme-our-lives-matter-our-votes-count; Brock, R. M. (2014). *From the Chairman. All in for justice and equality: NAACP Annual Report.* Retrieved July 25, 2016, from https://www .naacp.org/wp-content/uploads/2018/07/ NAACP2014AnnualReportWEB.pdf; NAACP. (2016). *Our mission.* Retrieved July 25, 2016, from http://www.

naacp.org/pages/our-mission. NAACP Facebook; NAACPConnect Google Plus; NAACP Twitter.

44 National Council of La Raza (NCLR). (2016). *About us.* Retrieved July 25, 2016, from http://www.nclr.org/ about-us/.

45 National Organization for Women (NOW). (2016). *How many members does NOW currently have?* Retrieved July 25, 2016, from http://now.org/faq/how-many-members-does-now -currently-have/; National Organization for Women (NOW). (2016). *Who we are.* Retrieved July 25, 2016, from http://now.org/about/who-we-are/.

46 National League of Cities (NLC). (2016). *About NLC.* Retrieved July 25, 2016, from http://www.nlc.org/ about-nlc.

47 http://www.afscme.org.

48 Mahood, *Interest groups*, p. 40.

49 Libertarians believe that individual liberty is paramount.

50 http://www.cato.org.

51 http://www.pfaw.org/about-us/our-mission-and-vision.

52 Public Citizen. (2016). *About us.* Retrieved July 26, 2016, from http://www.citizen .org/Page.aspx?pid=2306.

53 Ibid.

54 Public Citizen. (2016). *Public Citizen applauds expected release of final silica rule after decades of delay.* Retrieved July 26, 2016, from http://www.citizen.org/pressroom/ pressroomredirect.cfm?ID=5842; Public Citizen. (2016). *Accomplishments.* Retrieved July 26, 2016, from http:// www.citizen.org/Page.aspx?pid=2307.

55 Mahood, *Interest groups*, p. 44.

56 MADD. (2016). *Frequently asked questions.* Retrieved July 26, 2016, from http://www.madd.org/about-us/faqs/.

57 MADD. (2016). *Mission statement.* Retrieved July 30, 2016, from http://www.madd .org/about-us/mission/.

58 MADD. (2016). *MADD's campaign.* Retrieved July 30, 2016, from http://www.madd .org/drunk-driving/ campaign/.

59 Christian Coalition of America. (2016). *About us.* Retrieved July 30, 2016, from http://www.cc.org/about_us.

60 National Council of Churches of Christ. (2016). *About the National Council of Churches.* Retrieved July 30, 2016, from http:// nationalcouncilofchurches.us/about-us/.

61 Milbrath, L. (1963). *The Washington lobbyists.* Chicago: Rand McNally, p. 8.

62 National Public Radio. (2006, January 22). *A lobbyist by any other name?* Retrieved October 14, 2018, from https://www.npr.org/templates/story/story.php?storyId= 5167187.

63 Hrebenar, R. J., & Scott, R. K. (1982). *Interest group politics in America.* Englewood Cliffs, NJ: Prentice Hall, pp. 61–72.

64 Federal Election Commission (FEC). (2009, March 9). *Number of federal PACs increases* [News release]. Retrieved

October 14, 2018, from https://www.fec.gov/updates/number-of-federal-pacs-increases/.

65 Federal Election Commission (FEC). (2016). *Contribution limits for 2015–2016 federal elections*. Retrieved October 14, 2018, from http://www.fec.gov/info/contriblimitschart1516.pdf.

66 Federal Election Commission (FEC). (2017, March 23). *Statistical summary of 24-month campaign activity of the 2015–2016 election cycle*. Retrieved October 14, 2018, from https://www.fec.gov/updates/statistical-summary-24-month-campaign-activity-2015-2016-election-cycle/.

67 Maisel, L. S. (2004, September 17). BCRA's unintended consequences: The 527s controversy. *Central Maine Morning Sentinel*, p. A7.

68 Ibid.

69 Richey, W. (2009, September 8). Supreme Court: Campaign finance overhaul in "Hillary" case? *Christian Science Monitor Online*. Retrieved October 14, 2018, from https://www.csmonitor.com/USA/Justice/2009/0908/p02s01-usju.html.

70 Berry, J. M. (1997). *The interest group society* (3rd ed.). New York: Longman, p. 122.

71 Ibid., p. 123.

72 Ibid., p. 365.

73 Schlozman & Tierney, *Organized interests*, p. 358.

74 *District of Columbia et al. v. Heller*, 554 U.S., 128 S.Ct. 2783, 171 L.Ed. 2d 637 (2008); de Vogue, A. (2008, June 26). Supreme Court shoots down D.C. gun ban. *ABC News*. Retrieved July 9, 2009,, from http://abcnews.go.com/TheLaw/SCOTUS /story?id=5037600.

75 Dolan, M. (2008, June 27). Gun advocates armed for legal fight. *Los Angeles Times*. Retrieved July 30, 2016, from http://articles.latimes.com/2008/jun/27/nation/na-legal27.

76 NRA sues to overturn S.F. gun ban. (2008, June 27). *Associated Press*. Retrieved July 30, 2016, from http://www.nbcnews.com/id/25419519/ns /us_news-life/t/nra-sues-overturn-sf-gun-ban/#.V50tPmWgDiU.

77 Ferraro, T. (2013, December 20). U.S. Senate extends gun ban; rejects bid address 3-D plastic firearms. *Reuters*. Retrieved July 30, 2016, from http://www.reuters.com/article/us-usa-congress-guns-idUSBRE9B900Q20131210.

78 Bradner, E., & Krieg, G. (2016, January 5). Emotional Obama calls for "sense of urgency" to fight gun violence. *CNN*. http://www.cnn.com/2016/01/05/politics/obama-executive-action-gun-control/.

79 Quora question: Why the NRA opposes gun control legislation. (2016, June 25). *Newsweek*. Retrieved July 30, 2016, from http://www.newsweek.com/quora-question-why-nra-opposes-gun-legislation-472955.

80 Stohr, G. (2015, June 8). NRA rejected U.S. Supreme Court on San Francisco gun law. *Bloomberg*. Retrieved July 30, 2016, from http://www.bloomberg.com/news/articles/2015-06-08/

nra-rejected-by-u-s-supreme-court-on-san-francisco-gun-law.

81 Coyle, M. (2008, March 10). Amicus briefs are ammo for Supreme Court gun case. *National Law Journal*. Retrieved July 9, 2009, from http://www.law.com/jsp/article.jsp?id=1205146037339.

82 Bork's nomination pleases some, infuriates others. (1987, October 4). *The Record* (New Jersey), p. O3.

83 Schlozman & Tierney, *Organized interests*, p. 363.

84 Hrebenar & Scott, *Interest group politics*, p. 93.

85 Ibid., p. 94.

86 We Card. (n.d.). *Frequently asked questions*. Retrieved November 4, 2009, from http://www.wecard.org/index.php?option=com_content&task=view &id=16&Itemid=33.

87 http://www.wecard.org.

88 Hrebenar & Scott, *Interest group politics*, p. 96.

89 Kaye, K. (2008, December 15). *Bailout drives search efforts for automakers, advocacy groups*. Retrieved November 4, 2009, from http://www.clickz.com/3632087.

90 Guterman, L. (2002, November 20). Scientists accuse toxicology journal of industry ties, urge disclosure of conflicts of interest. *Chronicle of Higher Education*. Retrieved October 14, 2018, from http://chronicle.com/daily/2002/11/2002112003n.htm.

91 Ibid.

92 Borgardus, K. (2009, March 2). Nonprofits' spending was dominated by card-check. *The Hill*. Retrieved July 9, 2009, from http://thehill.com/business—lobby/nonprofits-spending-was-dominated- by-card-check-2009–03–02.html.

93 Hrebenar & Scott, *Interest group politics*, 197.

94 Ibid.

95 American Civil Liberties Union (ACLU). (2017). *ACLU Annual Report 2017*. Retrieved August 13, 2018, from https://www.aclu.org/other/aclu-annual-report-2017.

96 Strolovitch, D. Z. 92006). Do interest groups represent the disadvantaged?: Advocacy at the intersections of race, class, and gender. *Journal of Politics*, 68, 894–910.

97 Ibid.

Chapter 14

1 Clarke, S. (2017, February 22). 10 things you didn't know about Tom Perez. *U.S. News & World Report*. Retrieved July 17, 2018, from ttps://www.usnews.com/news/national-news/articles/2017-02-22/10-things-you-didnt-know-about-tom-perez; Shabad, R. (2017, February 25). Who is Tom Perez? *CBS News*. Retrieved July 17, 2018, from https://www.cbsnews.com/news/who-is-tom-perez-dnc-chairman/.

2 Easly, J. (2018, February 25). How Perez edged Ellison for DNC chair. *The Hill*. Retrieved July 17, 2018, from http://thehill.com/homenews/news/321210-how-perez-edged-ellison-for-dnc-chair; Gambino,

L. (2017, February 25). Tom Perez is new Democratic Party chair, beating Keith Ellison in tight vote. *The Guardian.* Retrieved July 17, 2018, from https://www.theguardian.com/us-news/2017/feb/25/tom-perez-democratic-chair-keith-ellison-atlanta-ballot.

3 Ibid.

4 Bibby, J. F., & Schaffner, B. F. (2008). *Politics, parties, and elections in America* (6th ed.). Boston: Thomson Wadsworth, p. 21; White, J. K., & Kerbel, M. L. (2012). *Party on!: Political parties from Hamilton and Jefferson to today's networked age.* Boulder, CO: Paradigm Press, pp. 22–24.

5 Bibby & Schaffner, *Politics, parties, and elections in America,* pp. 22–23.

6 Burbank, M. J., Hrebenar, R. J., & Benedict, R. C. (2008). *Parties, interest groups, and political campaigns* (2nd ed.). New York: Oxford University Press, pp. 6–12; Bibby & Schaffner, *Politics, parties, and elections in America,* pp. 22–23.

7 White & Kerbel, *Party on!: Political parties from Hamilton and Jefferson to today's networked age,* p. 81.

8 Bibby & Schaffner, *Politics, parties, and elections in America,* p. 23.

9 Burbank et al., *Parties, interest groups, and political campaigns,* pp. 12–15; Bibby & Schaffner, *Politics, parties, and elections in America,* pp. 23–24

10 See Erie, S. P. (1988). *Rainbow's end: Irish Americans and the dilemmas of urban machine politics, 1840–1985.* Berkeley and Los Angeles: University of California Press.

11 Bibby & Schaffner, *Politics, parties, and elections in America,* p. 25.

12 Burbank et al., *Parties, interest groups, and political campaigns,* pp. 15–18; Bibby & Schaffner, *Politics, parties, and elections in America,* pp. 24–25.

13 Peters, G. (1999–2017). Presidential election mandates. In J. Woolley & G. Peters. *American Presidency Project.* Santa Barbara: University of California, Santa Barbara. Retrieved July 17, 2018, from http://www.presidency.ucsb.edu/data/mandates.php.

14 U.S. House of Representatives. (n.d.). History, art, & archives." "Party divisions U.S. House of Representatives, 1789–present." Retrieved July 17, 2018, from http://history.house.gov/Institution/Party-Divisions/Party-Divisions/.

15 U.S. Senate. (n.d.). History. "Party division." Retrieved July 17, 2018, from https://www.senate.gov/history/partydiv.htm.

16 Burbank, Hrebenar, & Benedict, *Parties, interest groups, and political campaigns,* pp. 18–22; Bibby & Schaffner, *Politics, parties, and elections in America,* pp. 27–30.

17 For more on the issue of partisan realignments see Burnham, W. D. (1970). *Critical elections and the mainsprings of American politics.* New York: Norton; Key Jr., V. O. (1955). A theory of critical elections. *Journal of*

Politics, 17, 3–18; Key Jr., V. O. (1959). Secular realignment and the party system. *Journal of Politics, 21,* 198–210; Paulson, A. (2000). *Realignment and party revival: Understanding electoral politics at the turn of the twenty-first century.* Westport, CT: Praeger; White & Kerbel, *Party on!,* pp. 117–123.

18 Mayhew, D. R. (2002). *Electoral realignments: A critique of an American genre.* New Haven, CT: Yale University Press.

19 McClain, P. D., & Carew, J. D. J. (2018). *"Can we all get along?": Racial and ethnic minorities in American politics* (7th ed.). Boulder, CO: Westview Press, pp. 92–93.

20 Bibby & Schaffner, *Politics, parties, and elections in America,* pp. 30–32.

21 Burbank et al., *Parties, interest groups, and political campaigns,* pp. 22–24.

22 U.S. House of Representatives. (n.d.). History, Art, & Archives. "Party Divisions"; U.S. Senate, History." Party Division."

23 McClain & Carew, *Can we all get along?,* p. 93.

24 Woolley, J., & Peters, G. (1999–2018). Elections: The election of 1948. In J. Woolley & G. Peters. *American Presidency Project.* Santa Barbara: University of California, Santa Barbara. Retrieved July 17, 2018, from http://www.presidency.ucsb.edu/showelection.php?year=1948.

25 McClain & Carew, *Can we all get along?,* p. 93.

26 For more on dealignment, see White & Kerbel, *Party on!,* pp. 123–126.

27 U.S. House of Representatives, History, art, & archives. "Party Divisions"; U.S. Senate, History." Party Division."

28 Woolley, J., & Peters, G. (1999–2018). Elections: The election of 2016. In J. Woolley & G. Peters. *American Presidency Project.* Santa Barbara: University of California, Santa Barbara. Retrieved July 17, 2018, from http://www.presidency.ucsb.edu/showelection.php?year=2016.

29 Bibby & Schaffner, *Politics, parties, and elections in America,* p. 32.

30 Woolley, J., & Peters, G. (1999–2018). Elections: The election of 1968. In J. Woolley & G. Peters. *American Presidency Project.* Santa Barbara: University of California, Santa Barbara. Retrieved July 17, 2018, from http://www.presidency.ucsb.edu/showelection.php?year=1968.

31 See Phillips, K. P. (1969). *The emerging Republican majority.* New Rochelle, NY: Arlington House.

32 See generally, Woolley, J., & Peters, G. (1999–2018). Elections. In J. Woolley & G. Peters. *American Presidency Project.* Santa Barbara: University of California, Santa Barbara. Retrieved July 18, 2018, from http://www.presidency.ucsb.edu/elections.php.

33 Prohibition Party. (n.d.). 2016 party platform. Retrieved July 18, 2018, from http://www.prohibitionparty.org.

34 U.S. Marijuana Party: https://usmjparty.com.

35 Minor/Third Party platforms: Peters, G., & Woolley, J. T. (1999–2018). Populist party platform of 1892. In *American Presidency Project.* Santa Barbara: University of

California, Santa Barbara. Retrieved July 18, 2018, from http://www.presidency.ucsb.edu/ws/?pid=29616.

36 Minor/Third Party platforms: Peters, G., & Woolley, J. T. (1999–2018). Progressive party platform of 1912. In J. Woolley & G. Peters. *American Presidency Project*. Santa Barbara: University of California, Santa Barbara. Retrieved July 18, 2018, from http://www.presidency.ucsb.edu/ws/?pid=29617.

37 Woolley, J., & Peters, G. (1999–2018). Elections: The election of 1912. In *American Presidency Project*. Santa Barbara: University of California, Santa Barbara. Retrieved July 18, 2018, from http://www.presidency.ucsb.edu/showelection.php?year=1912.

38 Felsenthal, C. (2015, April 9). The strange tale of the first woman to run for president. *Politico*. Retrieved July 18, 2018, from https://www.politico.com/magazine/story/2015/04/victoria-woodhull-first-woman-presidential-candidate-116828.

39 Minor/Third Party platforms: Woolley, J., & Peters, G. (1999–2018). Platform of the States Rights Democratic Party. In J. Woolley & G. Peters. *American Presidency Project*. Santa Barbara: University of California, Santa Barbara. Retrieved July 18, 2018, from http://www.presidency.ucsb.edu/ws/?pid=25851; Minor/Third Party platforms: Woolley, J., & Peters, G. (1999–2018). American Independent Party Platform of 1968. In J. Woolley & G. Peters. *American Presidency Project*. Santa Barbara: University of California, Santa Barbara. Retrieved July 18, 2018, from http://www.presidency.ucsb.edu/ws/?pid=29570.

40 Woolley, J., & Peters, G. (1999–2018). Elections: The election of 1948. In J. Woolley & G. Peters. *American Presidency Project*. Santa Barbara: University of California, Santa Barbara. Retrieved July 18, 2018, from http://www.presidency.ucsb.edu/showelection.php?year=1948; and Elections: The election of 1968. Retrieved July 18, 2018, from http://www.presidency.ucsb.edu/showelection.php?year=1968.

41 Bibby & Schaffner, *Politics, parties, and elections in America*, pp. 203–204.

42 Ibid., p. 138.

43 Ibid., pp. 138–141.

44 Ibid., pp. 193–195.

45 Brander, E. (2018, March 10). Democrats' superdelegate debate left unresolved: Will continue into the summer. *CNN Politics*. Retrieved July 18, 2018, from https://www.cnn.com/2018/03/10/politics/democrats-superdelegates-debate/index.html.

46 Bositis, D. A. (2012). Table 8: Black delegates at Republican National Conventions, 1912–2012. In *Blacks & the 2012 Republican National Convention*. Washington, DC: Joint Center for Political and Economic Studies. Retrieved July 18, 2018, from http://jointcenter.org/sites/default/files/Blacks%20and%20the%202012%20Republican%20National%20Convention.pdf; Bositis, D. A. (2012). Table 5: Black delegates at Democratic National Conventions, 1932–2012. In *Blacks & the 2012 Democratic National Convention*. Washington, DC: Joint Center for Political and Economic Studies. Retrieved July 18, 2018, from http://jointcenter.org/sites/default/files/Blacks%20and%20the%202012%20Democratic%20National%20Convention.pdf; Frostenson, S. (2016, July 29). Half of the Democratic delegates were people of color: For Republicans, it was only 6%. *Vox*. Retrieved July 18, 2018, from https://www.vox.com/2016/7/29/12295830/republican-democratic-delegates-diversity-nonwhite.

47 Republican Party platforms: Woolley, J., & Peters, G. (1999–2018). 2016 Republican Party platform. In J. Woolley & G. Peters. *American Presidency Project*. Santa Barbara: University of California, Santa Barbara. Retrieved July 18, 2018, from http://www.presidency.ucsb.edu/ws/?pid=117718.

48 Bibby & Schaffner, *Politics, parties, and elections in America*, p. 88.

49 Ibid., pp. 89–92; Burbank et al., *Parties, interest groups, and political campaigns*, pp. 47–48.

50 Federal Election Commission. (n.d.). Appendix 4: Federal election campaign laws: A short history. Retrieved July 18, 2018, from https://transition.fec.gov/info/appfour.htm#anchor620139.

51 Mears, B. (2012, January 23). Where the money is: A campaign spending primer. *CNN Politics*. Retrieved July 18, 2018, from https://www.cnn.com/2012/01/23/politics/campaign-spending-primer/index.html.

52 *McConnell v. Federal Election Commission*, 540 U.S. 93 (2004).

53 Bibby & Schaffner, *Politics, parties, and elections in America*, pp. 92–96.

54 Burbank et al., *Parties, interest groups, and political campaigns*, pp. 48–49; Jacobsen, L. (2013, May 6). Looking back at Howard Dean's 50-state strategy. *Governing*. Retrieved July 18, 2018, from http://www.governing.com/topics/politics/gov-democrat-howard-deans-fifty-state-strategy.html.

55 Holmes, S. A. (2000). *Ron Brown: An uncommon life*. New York: Wiley.

56 Lipman, L. (2007, October 20). Martinez resigns as Republican chairman. *Palm Beach Post*, p. 10A.

57 West, P. (2009, January 31). Steele elected chair of the RNC: MD's ex-lieutenant governor becomes the first Black head of GOP. *Baltimore Sun*, p. 1A.

58 Preston, M. (2015, January 16). Priebus overwhelmingly elected to third term as RNC chairman. *CNN Politics*. Retrieved July 18, 2018, from https://www.cnn.com/2015/01/16/politics/priebus-reelected-to-third-term-as-rnc-chairman/index.html.

59 Republican National Committee. (n.d.). *Chairwoman: Ronna McDaniel*. Retrieved July 18, 2018, from https://www.gop.com/leaders/chairwoman-ronna-mcdaniel/.

60 Democratic National Committee. (n.d.). *People*. Retrieved July 18, 2018, from https://www.democrats.org.

61 Democratic National Committee. (n.d.). *Our leaders*. Retrieved July 18, 2018, from https://www.democrats.org/about/our-leaders.

62 Republican National Committee. (n.d.). *National leadership.* Retrieved July 18, 2018, from   https://www.gop.com/leaders/national/.

63 Republican National Committee. (n.d.). *GOP groups.* Retrieved July 18, 2018, from https://www.gop.com/groups/.

64 Bibby & Schaffner, *Politics, parties, and elections in America,* pp. 118–120.

65 Burbank et al., *Parties, interest groups, and political campaigns,* pp. 37–44.

66 Ibid., pp. 19–20, 22.

67 *Elrod v. Burns,* 427 U.S. 347 (1976).

68 *Rutan v. Republican Party of Illinois,* 497 U.S. 62 (1990).

69 For more on the supreme Court's role in limiting patronage, see O'Brien, D. M. (2001). Ironies abound in the United States Supreme Court's rulings limiting political patronage. In C. P. Banks & J. C. Green (Eds.), *Superintending democracy: The courts and the political process* (pp. 187–200). Akron, OH; University of Akron Press, 2001.

70 *Smith v. Allwright,* 321 U.S. 649 (1944).

71 Republican National Committee. (n.d.). *State GOP leadership: Minnesota leadership.* Retrieved July 18, 2018, from https://gop.com/leaders/state-chairwoman-jennifer-carnahan-mn/.

72 Association of State Democratic Committees. (n.d.). *Leadership.* Retrieved July 18, 2018, from https://asdc.democrats.org/leadership/.

73 For more on party identification, see the Inter-Consortium for Political and Social Research, University of Michigan. (n.d.). *Party identification.* Retrieved July 18, 2018, from https://www.icpsr.umich.edu/icpsrweb/instructors/setups/notes/party-identification.jsp.

74 Burbank, Hrebenar, and Benedict, *Parties, Interest Groups, and Political Campaigns,* 84–87.

75 Longman, M. (2018, March 23). Millennials really hate Republicans. *Washington Monthly.* Retrieved July 19, 2018, from https://washingtonmonthly.com/2018/03/23/millennials-really-hate-the-republicans/.

76 Pew Research Center U.S. Policy and Politics. (2016, September 13). *Party identification detailed tables.* Retrieved July 19, 2018, from http://www.people-press.org/2016/09/13/2016-party-identification-detailed-tables/.

77 Exit Polls 2016. *CNN Politics.* Retrieved July 18, 2018, from https://www.cnn.com/election/2016/results/exit-polls.

78 Democratic National Committee. (n.d.). *People: Young people and students.* Retrieved July 19, 2018, from https://www.democrats.org/people/young-people-and-students.

79 Republican National Committee. (n.d.). *Young leaders.* Retrieved July 19, 2018, from https://gop.com/groups/gop-young-leaders/.

80 Pew Research Center U.S. Policy & Politics. (2016, September 13). Party identification detailed tables.

Retrieved July 18, 2018, from http://www.people-press.org/2016/09/13/2016-party-identification-detailed-tables/.

81 For a more in-depth analysis of Catholic defection from the Democratic party, see White, S. P. (2012, September 11). The decline and fall of Catholic Democrats. *National Review.* Retrieved July 19, 2018, from https://www.nationalreview.com/2012/09/decline-and-fall-catholic-democrats-stephen-p-white/.

82 Pew Research Center U.S. Policy & Politics, "Party Identification Detailed Tables."

83 Ibid.

84 Exit Polls 2016. (n.d.). *CNN Politics.* Retrieved July 18, 2018, from https://www.cnn.com/election/2016/results/exit-polls.

85 McClain & Carew, *Can we all get along?,* p. 92

86 Ibid., p. 93

87 Ibid., pp. 93–97

88 Muhammad, J. G. (2004, October 28–November 3). Rev. Jesse Jackson: Why Blacks MUST vote for Kerry. *N'DIGO,* p. 4.

89 McClain & Carew, *Can we all get along?,* pp. 97–101.

90 Ibid., p. 100.

91 Ibid., pp. 102–105.

92 Ibid., pp. 105–106.

Chapter 15

1 Seung-Bickley, R. (2017, December 14). Alabama's effort to suppress Black vote couldn't prevent huge turnout. ACLU. Retrieved October 16, 2018, from https://www.aclu.org/blog/voting-rights/fighting-voter-suppression/alabamas-effort-suppress-black-vote-couldnt-prevent.

2 Kamisar, B., & Hagen, L. (2017, December 12). Jones wins Alabama Senate seat for Democrats. The Hill. Retrieved October 16, 2018, from http://thehill.com/homenews/campaign/364547-jones-wins-alabama-senate-seat-for-dems.

3 Pappas, A. (2017, December 13). Alabama Senate election: Doug Jones wins in major upset, Roy Moore won't yet concede. Fox News. Retrieved October 16, 2018, from http://www.foxnews.com/politics/2017/12/13/alabama-senate-election-doug-jones-defeats-roy-moore-fox-news-projects.html.

4 Burns, A., & Martin, J. (2017, December 12). Once a long shot, Democrat Doug Jones wins Alabama Senate race. New York Times. Retrieved October 16, 2018, from https://www.nytimes.com/2017/12/12/us/politics/alabama-senate-race-winner.html.

5 Chandler, K., & Peoples, S. (2017, December 12). Democrat Doug Jones wins Alabama Senate race in stunning upset over Roy Moore. Chicago Tribune. Retrieved October 16, 2018, from http://www.chicagotribune.com/news/nationworld/politics/ct-alabama-senate-race-20171212-story.html.

6 The Editorial Board. (2017, December 12). Roy Moore loses, sanity reigns. New York Times. Retrieved October 16, 2018, from https://www.nytimes.com/2017/12/12/opinion/roy-moore-loss-alabama.html.

7 Chandler & Peoples, "Democrat Doug Jones."

8 Newkirk II, V. R. (2017, December 12). African American voters made Doug Jones a U.S. senator in Alabama. The Atlantic. Retrieved October 16, 2018, from https://www.theatlantic.com/politics/archive/2017/12/despite-the-obstacles-black-voters-make-a-statement-in-alabama/548237/.

9 Levy, P. (2017, December 12). Reports of voter suppression tactics pour in from Alabama election. Mother Jones. Retrieved October 16, 2018, from http://www.motherjones.com/politics/2017/12/reports-of-voter-suppression-tactics-pour-in-from-alabama-election/.

10 Stern, M. J. (2017, December 14). Did Alabama violate federal voting law? Slate. Retrieved October 16, 2018, from http://www.slate.com/articles/news_and_politics/jurisprudence/2017/12/it_looks_like_alabama_violated_federal_law_with_its_inactive_voter_scheme.html.

11 Hayden, M. E. (2017, December 12). Alabama senate election tainted as rights groups allege voter suppression in Black neighborhoods. Newsweek. Retrieved October 16, 2018, from http://www.newsweek.com/alabama-senate-election-allegations-voter-suppression-black-neighborhoods-746190.

12 Lockhart, P. R. (2017, December 13). The Alabama election is the latest example of the political power of Black women. Vox. Retrieved October 16, 2018, from https://www.vox.com/identities/2017/12/13/16772012/alabama-election-black-women.

13 Newkirk, "African American Voters."

14 Naylor, B. (2017, December 13). "Black votes matter": African Americans propel Jones to Alabama win. NPR. Retrieved October 16, 2018, from https://www.npr.org/2017/12/13/570531505/black-votes-matter-african-americans-propel-jones-to-alabama-win.

15 Ibid.

16 Fausset, R., & Robertson, C. (2017, December 13). Black voters in Alabama pushed back against the past. New York Times. Retrieved October 16, 2018, from https://www.nytimes.com/2017/12/13/us/doug-jones-alabama-black-voters.html?hp&action=click&pgtype=Homepage&clickSource=story-heading&module=b-lede-package-region&region=top-news&WT.nav=top-news&_r=0.

17 Maisel, L. S., & Brewer, M. D. (2007). *Parties and elections in America: The electoral process* (5th ed.). Boulder: Rowman & Littlefield, p. 32.

18 Ibid., p. 36.

19 Mayer, W. G. (2009). An incremental approach to presidential nomination reform. *PS: Political Science and Politics, 42*, 65–69.

20 The fourteen Democratic caucus states in 2012 were Alaska, Colorado, Hawaii, Idaho, Iowa, Kansas, Maine, Minnesota, Nebraska, Nevada, North Dakota, Utah, Washington, and Wyoming. The thirteen Republican caucus states were Alaska, Colorado, Hawaii, Idaho, Iowa, Kansas, Maine, Minnesota, Missouri, Nevada, North Dakota, Washington, and Wyoming.

21 Who is running for president? (2016). *New York Times*. Retrieved July 14, 2016, from http://www.nytimes.com/interactive/2016/us/elections/2016-presidential-candidates.html.

22 Frum, D. (2015, January 13). Run, Warren, run. *The Atlantic*. Retrieved July 14, 2016, from http://www.theatlantic.com/politics/archive/2015 /01/run-warren-run/384490/.

23 Healy, P. (2016, February 2). Little separates Bernie Sanders and Hillary Clinton in tight race in Iowa. *New York Times*. Retrieved July 14, 2016, from http://www.nytimes.com/2016/02/02/us/bernie-sanders-hillary-clinton-democratic-iowa-caucus.html.

24 Tupy, M. (2016, March 1). Bernie is not a socialist and America is not capitalist. *The Atlantic*.Retrieved July 14, 2016, from http://www.theatlantic.com/international/archive/2016/03/bernie-sanders-democratic-socialism/471630/.

25 Ibid.; "Who is Running for President?"

26 National Conference of State Legislators. (2016). State primary election types. Retrieved August 22, 2016, from http://www.ncsl.org/research/elections-and-campaigns/primary-types.aspx#closed.

27 Bibby, J. F., & Holbrook, T. M. (1999). Parties and elections. In V. Gray, R. L. Hanson, & H. Jacob (Eds.), *Politics in the American states*. Washington, DC: Congressional Quarterly Press, p. 88.

28 Ibid.; National Conference of State Legislators, "State Primary."

29 Ibid.

30 Ibid.

31 Ibid.

32 Ballotpedia. (2016). Hybrid primary. Retrieved August 22, 2016, from https://ballotpedia.org/Hybrid_primary.

33 National Conference of State Legislators, "State Primary."

34 Ibid.

35 Jewell, J., & Morehouse, S. M. (2001). *Political parties and elections in American states* (4th ed.). Washington, DC: Congressional Quarterly Press, p. 103.

36 National Conference of State Legislators, "State Primary."

37 Jewel & Morehouse, *Political parties and elections*, p. 274.

38 Ibid., p. 106.

39 Maisel, L. S., & Buckley, K. Z. *Parties and elections in America: The electoral process* (4th ed.) Boulder, CO: Rowman & Littlefield, p. 218.

40 Kousser, J. M. (1984, September–October). Origins of the run-off primary. *The Black Scholar*, pp. 23–26.

41 Bialik, C. (2016, March 9). Why the polls missed Bernie Sanders's Michigan upset. *FiveThirtyEight*,. Retrieved September 22, 2016, from http://fivethirtyeight.com/features/why-the-polls-missed-bernie-sanders-michigan-upset/.

42 Lee, M. J., Merica, D., & Zeleny, J. (2016, July 12). Bernie Sanders endorses Hillary Clinton. *CNN.com*. Retrieved September 22, 2016, from http://www.cnn.com/2016/07/11/politics/hillary-clinton-bernie-sanders/.

43 Iowa entrance polls. (2016, February 1). *CNN.com*. Retrieved September 22, 2016, from http://www.cnn.com/election/primaries/polls/ia/Dem.

44 Ohio exit polls. (2016, March 15). *CNN.com*, Retrieved September 22, 2016, from http://www.cnn.com/election /primaries/polls/oh/Dem.

45 Texas exit polls. (2016, March 1). *CNN.com*. Retrieved September 22, 2016, from http://www.cnn.com/election/primaries/polls/TX/Dem.

46 After New Hampshire: Updates, analysis and results. (2016). *New York Times*. Retrieved September 22, 2016, from http://www.nytimes.com/live/new-hampshire-primary-2016-election/.

47 Who is running for president? (2016). *New York Times*. Retrieved September 22, 2016, from http://www.nytimes.com/interactive/2016/us/elections/2016-presidential-candidates.html.

48 Peters, J. W. (2016, July 12). Emerging Republican platform goes far to the right. *New York Times*. Retrieved September 22, 2016, from http://www.nytimes.com/2016/07/13/us/politics/republican-convention-issues.html.

49 Ibid.

50 Ross, J. (2016, February 24). Donald Trump apparently won the Latino vote in Nevada. It doesn't mean Latinos suddenly love him. *Washington Post*. Retrieved September 22, 2016, from https://www.washingtonpost.com/news/the-fix/wp/2016/02/24/donald-trump-apparently-won-the-latino-vote-in-nevada-it-doesnt-mean-latinos-suddenly-love-him/.

51 Damore, D. (2016, April 22). *Nevada Latino voters in the 2016 election*. Retrieved September 22, 2016, from http://www.latinodecisions.com/files/8714/6134/1022/AV_Wave_1_NV_Deck _April_2016.pdf.

52 Ross, "Donald Trump Apparently Won the Latino Vote."

53 Damore, "Nevada Latino Voters in the 2016 Election."

54 Ibid.

55 Ibid.

56 Who's winning the presidential delegate count? (2016). *Bloomberg Politics*. Retrieved August 19, 2016, from http://www.bloomberg.com/politics/graphics/2016-delegate-tracker/.

57 2016 Democratic National Convention: Unpledged delegates—By state. (2016). *Vox*. Retrieved August 19, 2016, from https://cdn1.vox-cdn.com/uploads/chorus_asset/file/6622695/Unpledged_Delegate_List_5.27.16.0.pdf.

58 Why delegates matter in the presidential race. (2008). *CNN.com*. Retrieved July 7, 2009, from http://edition.cnn.com/2008/POLITICS/01/02/delegate.explainer/index.html.

59 Siders, D., & Korecki, N. (2018, August 25). Democrats strip superdelegates of power in picking presidential nominee. *Politico*. Retrieved October 16, 2018, from https://www.politico.com/story/2018/08/25/superdelegates-democrats-presidential-nominee-796151.

60 Cohen, M. (2016, May 9). Donald Trump picks up more unbound GOP delegates. *CNN.com*. Retrieved August 19, 2016,, from http://www.cnn.com/2016/05/09/politics/trump-gop-delegates-unbound/.

61 Silver, N. (2012, February 25). The G.O.P.'s fuzzy delegate math. *New York Times*. Retrieved May 26, 2013, from http://fivethirtyeight.blogs.nytimes.com/2012/02/25/the-g-o-p-s-fuzzy-delegate-math/.

62 CNN Politics. (n.d.). *Election Center*. Retrieved August 19, 2016, from http://www.cnn.com /election/primaries.

63 Ibid.

64 DNC Office of Party Affairs and Delegate Selection. (2016). *2016 Democratic National Convention: Delegate/alternate allocation*. Retrieved August 19, 2016, from https://ballotpedia.org/wiki/images/c/ce/Appendix_B_-_Allocation_Chart _1.29.16.pdf; Republican National Convention. (2016). *About*. Retrieved August 19, 2016, from http://convention.gop/about.

65 Heersink, B., & Milkis, S. M. (2016, July 24). These 2 trends are what produced such a negative Republican National Convention. *Washington Post*. Retrieved August 13, 2016, from https://www.washingtonpost.com/news/monkey-cage/wp/2016/07/24/these-2-trends-are-what-produced-such-a-negative-republican-national-convention/.

66 Election 2016 Primaries + Caucuses. (2016). *CNN.com*. Retrieved August 13, 2016, from http://www.cnn.com/election/primaries.

67 Confessore, N. (2016, July 19). G.O.P. convention day 2 takeaways: A party united, at least for a night. *New York Times*. Retrieved August 13, 2016, from http://www.nytimes .com/2016/07/19/us/politics/republican-national-convention.html.

68 Mason, M. (2016, July 22). A more restrained tone and an appeal to populism: 5 takeaways from Donald Trump's acceptance speech. *Los Angeles Times*. Retrieved August 13, 2016, from http://www.latimes.com/nation/politics/trailguide/la-na-republican-convention-2016-trump-speech-updates -htmlstory.html.

69 Heersink & Milkis, "These 2 Trends Are What Produced."

70 Guevarra, E. C. (2016). Roundup: The Republican National Convention and race (so far). *NPR: North Carolina Public Radio*. Retrieved August 13, 2016, from http://www.npr.org/sections/codeswitch/2016/07/21/486604305/roundup-the-republican-national-convention-and-race-so-far.

71 Breakdown of delegates by race. Black/African American: 18; Hispanic: approximately 133; Asian American: no estimates available.

72 Bump, P. (2016, July 19). There are likely fewer Black delegates to the Republican convention than at any point in at least a century. *Washington Post*. Retrieved August 13, 2016, from https://www.washingtonpost.com/news/the-fix/wp/2016 /07/19/there-are-likely-fewer-black-delegates-to-the-republican-convention-than-at-any-point-in-at-least-a-century/?tid=sm_tw_pp.

73 Ibid.

74 Hutchinson, E. O. (2016, July 19). The 2016 GOP Convention: The whitest of the whitest conventions. *Huffington Post*. Retrieved August 13, 2016, from http://www.huffingtonpost.com/earl-ofari -hutchinson/the-2016-gop-conventionth_b_11028190.html.

75 GOP: At least 133 Latino delegates at Republican convention. (2016). *NBC News*. Retrieved August 13, 2016, from http://www.nbcnews.com/storyline/2016-conventions/gop-least-133-latino-delegates-republican-convention-n614376.

76 Rice, Z. C. (2016, July 22). The RNC was the most flagrant display of GOP racism America has seen in years. *Identities.Mic*. Retrieved August 13, 2016, from https://mic.com/articles/149140/the-rnc-was-the-most-flagrant-display-of-gop-racism-america-has-seen-in-years#.uetHD333I.

77 Ibid.

78 Bump, "There Are Likely Fewer Black Delegates."

79 Guevarra, "Roundup: The Republican National Convention and Race (So Far)."

80 Westfall, J. (2016, January 23). 2016 Democratic Convention to be held right after GOP gathering. *Los Angeles Times*. Retrieved August 13, 2016, from http://www.latimes.com/nation/politics/politicsnow/la-pn-dnc-right-after-republican-convention-20150123-story.html.

81 Election 2016 Primaries + Caucuses. (2016). *CNN.com*. Retrieved August 13, 2016, from http://www.cnn.com/election/primaries.

82 Factbox: The race to the U.S. presidential nominations: How delegates are selected. (2016, February 24). *Reuters*. Retrieved August 13, 2016, from http://www.reuters.com/article/us-usa-election-delegates-factbox-idUSKCN0VY094.

83 Healy, P., & Martin, J. (2016, July 25). Democrats struggle for unity on first day of convention. *New York Times*. Retrieved August 13, 2016, from http://www.nytimes.com/2016/07/26/us/politics/dnc-speakers-protests-sanders.html.

84 Democratic National Convention. (n.d.). Democratic platform drafting meeting concludes. Retrieved August 13, 2016, from https://www.demconvention.com/news/democratic-platform-drafting-meeting-concludes/.

85 Frostenson, S. (2016, July 29). Half of the Democratic delegates were people of color. For Republicans, it was only 6%. *Vox*. Retrieved August 13, 2016, from http://www.vox.com/2016/7/29/12295830/republican-democratic-delegates-diversity-nonwhite.

86 Zezima, K. (2016, August 1). Republicans denounce Trump as confrontation with Muslim parents escalates. *Washington Post*. Retrieved August 13, 2016, from https://www.washingtonpost.com/politics/republicans-denounce-trump-as-confrontation-with-muslim-parents-escalates/2016/07/31/54397028-5722-11e6-9aee-8075993d73a2_story.html.

87 McCrummen, S. (2016, July 31). Khizr Khan responds to the latest from Trump: "Typical of a person without a soul." *Washington Post*. Retrieved August 13, 2016, from https://www.washingtonpost.com/politics/khizr-khan-responds-to-the-latest-from-trump-what-he-said-originally-that-defines-him/2016/07/31/450f78dc-56d6-11e6-b7de-dfe509430c39_story.html.

88 Zezima, "Republicans Denounce Trump."

89 Bibby & Holbrook, "Parties and Elections," p. 89.

90 Office of the Federal Register, National Archives and Records Administration. (n.d.). *A procedural guide to the Electoral College*. Retrieved July 7, 2009, from http://www.nara.gov/fedreg/electcoll /proced.html.

91 Ibid.

92 *Ray v. Blair*, 343 U.S. 214 (1952); Office of the Federal Register, National Archives and Records Administration. (n.d.). *Frequently asked questions on the Electoral College*. Retrieved July 10, 2009, from http://www.nara.gov/fedreg/electcoll/faq.html.

93 Congressional Research Service. (2007, March 12). CRS Report to Congress—The Electoral College: Reform proposals in the 109th Congress.

94 Trygstad, K. (2008, June 26). Obama's 50 State Strategy. *Real Clear Politics*. Retrieved July 9, 2009, from http://www.realclearpolitics.com /articles/2008/06/obamas_50_state_strategy.html.

95 Moore, M. T., & Camia, C. (2015, April 12). Hillary Clinton launches 2016 presidential bid. *USA Today*. Retrieved September 8, 2016, from http://www .usatoday.com/story/news/politics/elections/2015/04/12/hillary-clinton-president-announcement-2016/22018067/; Kreutz, L. (2016, January 8). How Hillary Clinton's campaign has changed in the new year. Retrieved September 8, 2016, from http://abcnews.go.com/Politics/hillary-clintons-campaign-changed-year/story?id=36158940; Binelli, M. (2016, March 9). Hillary Clinton vs. Bernie Sanders: The good fight. *Rolling Stone*. Retrieved September 8, 2016, from http://www.rollingstone .com/politics/news/hillary-clinton-vs-bernie-sanders-the-good-fight-20160309.

96 Chozick, A. (2015, April 12). What Hillary Clinton would need to do to win. *New York Times*. Retrieved September 8, 2016, from http://www.nytimes.com/interactive/2016/us/elections/hillary-clinton.html.

97 Glueck, K. (2016, April 12). The power players behind Hillary Clinton's campaign. *Politico*. Retrieved September 8, 2016, from http://www.politico.com/story/2015/04/hillary-clintons-power-players-116874

98 Miller, Z. J. (2016, June 7). Mismatch 2016. *Time*. Retrieved September 8, 2016, from http://time.com/trump-clinton-mismatch.

99 Hohmann, J. (2016, March 8). The Daily 202: Hillary Clinton is winning with a hyper-local strategy. *Washington Post*. Retrieved September 8, 2016, from https://www.washingtonpost.com/news/powerpost/paloma/daily-202/2016/03/08/daily-202-hillary-clinton-is-winning-with-a-hyper-local-strategy/56de2040981b92a22d7612d7/.

100 Hohmann, The Daily 202."

101 *Hillary for America*. (2016). Retrieved September 8, 2016, from https://www.hillaryclinton.com/issues/.

102 Donald J. Trump for president. (2016). Retrieved September 9, 2016, from https://www.donaldjtrump.com/POSITIONS; Timm, J. C. (2016). A full list of Donald Trump's rapidly changing policy positions. *NBC News*. Retrieved September 9, 2016, from http://www .nbcnews.com/politics/2016-election/full-list-donald-trump-s-rapidly-changing-policy-positions-n547801.

103 Haberman, M. (2016, November 21). Donald Trump calls for surveillance of 'certain mosques' and a Syrian refugee database. *New York Times*. Retrieved September 9, 2016, from http://www.nytimes.com/2015/11/22/us/politics/donald-trump-syrian-muslims-surveillance.html.

104 Lerner, A. B. (2016, June 16). The 10 best lines from Donald Trump's announcement speech. *Politico*. Retrieved September 9, 2016, from http://

www.politico.com/story/2015/06/donald-trump-2016-announcement-10-best-lines-119066.

105 Smith, C. (2016, September 8). Trump campaign announces $90 million fundraising haul in August. *ABC News*. Retrieved September 9, 2016, from http://abcnews.go.com/Politics/trump-campaign-announces-90-million-fundraising-haul-august/story?id=41952316.

106 Narayanswamy, A., Cameron, D., & Gold, M. (2016, February 1). How much money is behind each campaign? *Washington Post*. Retrieved September 9, 2016, from https://www.washingtonpost.com/graphics/politics/2016-election/campaign-finance/.

107 Smith, "Trump Campaign Announces $90 Million Fundraising Haul in August"; Narayanswamy et al., "How Much Money."

108 Smith, "Trump Campaign Announces $90 Million Fundraising Haul in August."

109 Haynes, A. A., & Pitts, B. (2009). Making an impression: New media in the 2008 presidential nomination campaigns. *PS: Political Science and Politics, 42*, 53–58.

110 Warshaw, S. A. (2000). *The keys to power: Managing the presidency*. New York: Addison Wesley Longman, pp. 68–71.

111 Douglass, J. J. (2000, March). The mother's milk of elections. *World and I, 15*, 1.

112 Ibid.

113 Baida, P. (1988, October 24). The legacy of dollar Mark Hanna. *Forbes, 142*, 3.

114 Amount is indexed for inflation during odd-numbered years; Federal Election Commission. (2016, May 13). *Presidential election campaign fund*. Retrieved August 26, 2016, from http://www.fec.gov/press/bkgnd/fund.shtml#search=bcra%202016.

115 Amount is indexed for inflation during odd-numbered years.

116 Center for Responsive Politics. (n.d.). 2016 campaign contribution limits. Retrieved August 26, 2016, from https://www.opensecrets.org/overview/limits.php.

117 Federal Election Commission. (n.d.). Contribution limits for 2013–2014. Retrieved April 14, 2013, from http://www.fec.gov/info/contriblim-itschart1314.pdf; Corrado, A. (1996). The changing environment of presidential campaign finance. In W. G. Mayer (Ed.), *In pursuit of the White House: How we choose our presidential nominees*. Chatham, NJ: Chatham House, pp. 220–253.

118 Key provisions of the McCain–Feingold–Cochran Bill (S. 27). (n.d.). *Public Citizen*. Retrieved January 12, 2009, from http://citizen.org/congress /reform/mcfinkeyprovisions.htm.

119 Ibid.

120 Federal Election Commission. (n.d.). Bipartisan Campaign Reform Act of 2002. Retrieved August 26, 2016,

from http://www.fec.gov/pages/bcra /bcra_update. shtml.

121 Corrado, "The Changing Environment," p. 221.

122 Ibid., p. 227.

123 Wayne, S. J. (2000). *The road to the White House 2000: The politics of presidential selection*. New York: Bedford/ St. Martin's Press.

124 Hirschkorn, P. (2012, September 24). Top super PAC donors giving multimillions in 2012. *CBS News*. Retrieved January 7, 2013, from http:// www.cbsnews.com/8301-250_162-57519344/ top-super-pac-donors-giving-multimillions-in-2012/.

125 Ibid.

126 Center for Responsive Politics (OpenSecrets.org). (2013, February 18). *Super PACs*. Retrieved March 11, 2013, from http://www.opensecrets.org/pacs/ superpacs.php.

127 Ibid.

128 Center for Responsive Politics (OpenSecrets.org). (2013, January 14). *2012 presidential race*. Retrieved March 11, 2013, from http://www.opensecrets.org/ pres12/index.php.

129 Iacob, I. (2016, May 27). The top donors backing Hillary Clinton's super PAC. *Forbes*. Retrieved August 30, 2016, from http://www.forbes.com/ sites/ivonaiacob/2016/05/27/top-donors-hillary-clinton-superpac/#5ed9d7992740.

130 Center for Responsive Politics. (2016). *Hillary Clinton: Candidate summary, 2016 cycle*. Retrieved August 30, 2016, from https://www.opensecrets.org/pres16/ candidate.php?id=N00000019.

131 Iacob, "The Top Donors Backing Hillary Clinton's Super PAC."

132 Schouten, F. (2016, July 20). Hillary Clinton super PAC stockpiles $40 million for Donald Trump attacks. *USA Today*. Retrieved August 30, 2016, from http://www .usatoday.com/story/news/politics/onpolitics/2016/ 07/20/hillary-clinton-super-pac-stockpiles-40-million-donald-trump-attacks /87347474/.

133 Center for Responsive Politics, "Hillary Clinton: Candidate Summary, 2016 Cycle."

134 Schouten, "Hillary Clinton Super PAC Stockpiles $40 Million."

135 Ballhaus, R. (2016, August 20). Hillary Clinton super PAC outpaces Donald Trump groups in July. *Wall Street Journal*. Retrieved August 30, 2016, from http://www .wsj.com/articles/hillary-clinton-super-pac-outpaces-donald-trump-groups-in-july-1471731438.

136 Isenstadt, A., & Vogel, K. P. (2016, July 20). Trump blesses major super PAC effort. *Politico*. Retrieved August 30, 2016, from http://www.politico.com/ story/2016/07/trump-super-pac-donors-225892.

137 Schouten, "Hillary Clinton Super PAC Stockpiles $40 Million."

138 Center for Responsive Politics. (2016). *Donald Trump: Candidate summary, 2016 cycle*. Retrieved August 30, 2016, from https://www.opensecrets.org/pres16/ candidate.php?id=N00023864.

139 Mendelberg, T. (2001). *The race card: Campaign strategy, implicit messages, and the norm of equality*. Princeton, NJ: Princeton University Press, p. 3.

140 Ibid.

141 Kinder, D., & Sanders, L. M. (1996). *Divided by color: Racial politics and democratic ideals*. Chicago: University of Chicago Press, chap. 6.

142 Shaw, G. K., Leusner, J., & Holton, S. 2000, November 15). Uncounted ballots may add up to 180,000. *Orlando Sentinel*.

143 Robles, F., & Dougherty, G. (2000, November 15). Ballot errors rate high in some Black precincts. *Miami Herald*.

144 Mintz, J., & Keating, D. (2000, December 3). Fla. ballot spoilage likelier for Blacks. *Washington Post*, pp. A1, A28.

145 McClain, P. D., & Stewart Jr., J. (2010). *"Can we all get along?": Racial and ethnic minorities in American politics* (5th ed.). Boulder, CO: Westview Press, p. 113.

146 Kinder & Sanders, *Divided by color*, pp. 42–43.

147 CNN Political Unit. (2012, August 29). Two people removed from RNC after taunting Black camera operator. Retrieved January 7, 2013, from http:// politicalticker.blogs.cnn.com/2012/08/29/two-people-removed-from-rnc-after-taunting-black-camera-operator/.

148 Shapiro, A. (2012, August 22). Despite fact checks, Romney escalates welfare work requirement charge. *NPR*. Retrieved January 7, 2013, from http://www .npr.org/blogs/itsallpolitics/2012/08/22/159791065/ despite-fact-checks-romney-escalates-welfare-work-requirement-charge.

149 "Put the White back in the White House" t-shirt spotted at Romney rally goes viral. (2012, October 14). *The Grio*. Retrieved January 7, 2013, from http:// thegrio.com/2012/10/14/put-the-white-back-in-the-white-house-t-shirt-spotted-at-romney-rally-goes-viral/#s:offensive-anti-obama-tshirt.

150 Confessore, N. (2016, July 13). For Whites sensing decline, Donald Trump unleashes words of resistance. *New York Times*. Retrieved September 22, 2016, from http://www.nytimes.com/2016/07/14/us/politics/ donald-trump-white-identity.html?_r=0.

151 Rupar, A., & Dewan, B. (2016, March 1). *Timeline: How Trump took the low road to the top of the Republican Party*. Retrieved September 22, 2016, from http:// thinkprogress.org/politics/2016/03/01/3755255/ donald-trump-super-tuesday-timeline/.

152 Burns, A. (2016, June 16). Choice words from Donald Trump, presidential candidate. *New York Times*. Retrieved September 22, 2016, from http:// www.nytimes.com/politics/first-draft/2015/06/16/

choice-words-from-donald-trump-presidential-candidate/?mtrref=www.nytimes.com.

153 *Trump's bizarre strategy to win back Latino supporters is definitely not working.* (2015, July 11). Retrieved September 22, 2016, from http://thinkprogress.org/immigration/2015/07/11/3679417/donald-trump-joe-arpaio/.

154 Lee, C. (2015, July 11). Arizona crowd welcomes Donald Trump's tough stance on immigration. *Los Angeles Times.* Retrieved September 22, 2016, from http://www.latimes.com/nation/politics/la-na-trump-arizona-rally-20150710-story.html.

155 Donald Trump vs. Univision's Jorge Ramos. (2015, August 26). *CNN.com.* Retrieved September 22, 2016, from http://www.cnn.com/videos/politics/2015/08/26/donald-trump-jorge-ramos-argue-immigration-origwx-bw.cnn/video/playlists/donald-trump-immigration/; Finnegan, W. (2015, October 5). The man who wouldn't sit down. *The New Yorker.* Retrieved September 22, 2016, from http://www.newyorker.com/magazine/2015/10/05/the-man-who-wouldnt-sit-down.

156 Totenberg, N. (2016, June 7). Who is Judge Gonzalo Curiel, the man Trump attacked for his Mexican ancestry? *NPR.* Retrieved September 22, 2016, from http://www.npr.org/2016/06/07/481140881/who-is-judge-gonzalo-curiel-the-man-trump-attacked-for-his-mexican-ancestry.

157 Bever, L. (2016, June 23). "Make America White again": A politician's billboard ignites uproar. *Washington Post.* Retrieved September 22, 2016, from https://www.washingtonpost.com/news/the-fix/wp/2016/06/23/make-america-white-again-a-politicians-billboard-ignites-uproar/.

158 Domonoske, C. (2016, August 5). Former KKK leader David Duke says "of course" Trump voters are his voters. *NPR.* Retrieved September 22, 2016, from http://www.npr.org/sections/thetwo-way/2016/08/05/488802494/former-kkk-leader-david-duke-says-of-course-trump-voters-are-his-voters.

159 Garcia, E. (2016, August 2). Poll shows Louisiana doesn't like David Duke. *Roll Call.* Retrieved September 22, 2016, from http://www.rollcall.com/news/politics/david-dukes-unpopularity-sky-high.

160 Alexander, M. (2016, February 29). Why Hillary Clinton doesn't deserve the Black vote. *The Nation.* Retrieved September 22, 2016, from https://www.thenation.com/article/hillary-clinton-does-not-deserve-black-peoples-votes/.

161 Gearan, A., & Phillip, A. (2016, February 2). Clinton regrets 1996 remark on "super-predators" after encounter with activist. *Washington Post.* Retrieved September 22, 2016, from https://www.washingtonpost.com/news/post-politics/wp/2016/02/25/clinton-heckled-by-black-lives-matter-activist/.

162 Ibid.

163 Kinder & Sanders, *Divided by color,* pp. 42–43.

164 U.S. Census Bureau. (2017, May 10). Voting and registration in the election of November 2016, Table 10. Retrieved October 16, 2018, from https://www.census.gov/data/tables/time-series/demo/voting-and-registration/p20-580.html.

165 Teixeira, R. A. (1992). *The disappearing American voter.* Washington, DC: Brookings Institution.

166 McClain & Stewart, *"Can we all get along?,"* p. 82.

167 Teixeira, *The disappearing American voter,* p. 13.

168 U.S. Election Assistance Commission. (n.d.). *The impact of the National Voter Registration Act on the administration of elections for federal office, 2005–2006.* Retrieved April 15, 2007, from http://www.eac.gov/clearinghouse/docs/the-impact-of-the-national-voter-registration-act-on-federal-elections-2005–2006/attachment_download/file.

169 Federal Election Commission. (n.d.). *Frequently asked questions about election day and voting procedures.* Retrieved July 9, 2009, from http://www.fec.gov/pages/faqvdayeprocedures.htm.

170 Carter, J. (2001, July 31). Election-overhaul panel advises national holiday for voting. *Herald Sun* (Durham, NC), pp. A1, A7.

171 McClain & Stewart, *"Can we all get along?"*

172 Kerr, J. C. (2012, November 2). Farewell lever and punch-card machine. *Seattle Times.* Retrieved January 7, 2013, from http://seattletimes.com/html/politics/2019583491_apushowamericavotes.html.

173 Election Data Services. (n.d.). Nation sees drop in use of electronic voting equipment for 2008 election—A first. Retrieved March 13, 2009, from http://electiondataservices.com/images/File/NR_VoteEquip_Nov-2008wAppendix2.pdf.

174 National Conference of State Legislatures. (2013, January 14). *Voter identification requirements.* Retrieved February 5, 2013, from http://www.ncsl.org/legislatures-elections/elections/voter-id.aspx.

175 Levitt, J. (2014, August 6). A comprehensive investigation of voter impersonation finds 31 credible incidents out of one billion ballots cast. *Washington Post.* Retrieved Octover 16, 2018, from https://www.washingtonpost.com/news/wonk/wp/2014/08/06/a-comprehensive-investigation-of-voter-impersonation-finds-31-credible-incidents-out-of-one-billion-ballots-cast/.

176 Weiser, W., & Kasdan, D. (2012). *Voting law changes: Election update.* New York: Brennan Center for Justice, New York University School of Law.

177 Barnes, R., & Marimow, A. E. (2016, July 29). Appeals court strikes down North Carolina's voter-ID law. *Washington Post.* Retrieved August 1, 2016, from https://www.washingtonpost.com/local/public-safety/appeals-court-strikes-down-north-carolinas-voter-id-law/2016/

07/29/810b5844-4f72-11e6-aa14-e0c1087f7583 _story.
html.

178 Wines, M., & Blinder, A. (2016, July 30). Federal court
strikes down North Carolina voter ID requirement.
New York Times. Retrieved August 1, 2016, from http://
www.nytimes.com/2016/07/30/us/federal-appeals-court-
strikes-down-north-carolina-voter-id-provision.html.

179 Hanna, J., Newsome, J., & de Vogue, A. (2016, July 29).
North Carolina voter ID law overturned on appeal.
CNN.com. Retrieved August 1, 2016, from http://www
.cnn.com/2016/07/29/politics/north-carolina-voter-id/.

180 Gerstein, J. (2016, July 29). Court strikes down North
Carolina voter ID law. *Politico*. Retrieved August 1,
2016, from http://www.politico.com/story/2016/07/
court-strikes-down-north-carolina-voter-id-law-226438.

181 Barnes & Marimow, "Appeals Court Strikes Down
North Carolina's Voter-ID Law."

182 De Vogue, A. (2016, July 20). Appeals court: Texas
voter ID law violates Voting Rights Act. *CNN.com*.
Retrieved August 1, 2016, from http://www.cnn.com/
2016/07/20/politics/texas-voter-id-law/index.html.

183 Ibid.

184 Malewitz, J. (2016, July 20). Texas voter ID law violates
Voting Rights Act, court rules. *Texas Tribune*. Retrieved
August 1, 2016, from https://www.texastribune.org/
2016/07/20/appeals-court-rules-texas-voter-id/.

185 Tamkin, E. (2016). Parts of Wisconsin voter ID law
ruled unconstitutional. *Slate*. Retrieved August 1,
2016, from http://www.slate.com/blogs/the_slatest/
2016/07/30/federal_judge_declares_parts_of_
wisconsin_s_voter_id_laws_unconstitutional.html.

186 American Civil Liberties Union.(2016). *Frank v.
Walker: Fighting voter suppression in Wisconsin*. Retrieved
August 1, 2016, from https://www.aclu.org/cases/
frank-v-walker-fighting-voter-suppression-wisconsin.

187 Wines & Blinder, "Federal Court Strikes Down North
Carolina Voter ID Requirement."

188 Bosman, J. (2016, Octover 15). Voter ID battle shifts to
Kansas. *New York Times*. Retrieved August 1, 2016, from
http://www.nytimes.com/2015/10/16/us/politics/
kansas-voter-id-law-sets-off-a-new-battle-over-
registration.html.

189 Murphy, K. (2016, April 4). ACLU asks federal court
to block Kansas voter ID law. *Reuters*. Retrieved
August 1, 2016, from http://www.reuters.com/article/
us-kansas-voterid-idUSKCN0XB17F.

190 Judge slams Kansas voter ID law's "magnitude of
harm." (2016, May 18). *CBS.com*. Retrieved August
1, 2016, from http://www.cbsnews.com/news/
judge-kansas-rejects-citizenship-proof-to-vote/.

191 Bosman, "Voter ID Battle Shifts to Kansas."

192 Barnes & Marimow, "Appeals Court Strikes Down
North Carolina's Voter-ID Law."

193 Verba, S., Schlozman, K. L., & Brady, H. E. (1995).
Voice and equality: Civic voluntarism in American politics.
Cambridge, MA: Harvard University Press, p. 230.

194 Ibid., p. 252.

195 Mansbridge, J., & Tate, K. (1992). Race trumps gender:
Black opinion on the Thomas nomination. *PS: Political
Science and Politics, 25*, 488–492.

196 Berelson, B. R., Lazarsfeld, P. F., & McPhee, W. N.
(1954). *Voting: A study of opinion formation in a presidential
campaign*. Chicago: University of Chicago Press, p. 91.

197 U.S. Census Bureau News. (2009, July 20). Voter turnout
increases by 5 million in 2008 presidential election.

198 Verba et al., *Voice and equality*.

199 U.S. Census Bureau. (n.d.). *Homeownership rates by race
and ethnicity of householder: 1994 to 2016*. Available at
https://www.census.gov/housing/hvs/files/annual16/
ann16t_22.xlsx.

200 Cassel, C. A. (1979). Change in electoral participation
in the South. *Journal of Politics, 41*, 907–917.

201 J.P.P..

202 Burns & Flegenheimer.

203 Edwards-Levy, A. (2016, September 28). Hillary
Clinton won the first presidential debate, polling finds. *Huffington Post*. Retrieved October 10,
2016, from http://www.huffingtonpost.com/entry/
poll-hillary-clinton-won-first-presidential-debate_
us_57ec15c5e4b082aad9b8be8a.

204 J.P.P. 2016.

205 Agiesta, J. (2016, September 27). Post-debate poll: Hillary Clinton takes round one. *CNN.com*. Retrieved October 10, 2016, from http://www.cnn.com/2016/09/27/
politics/hillary-clinton-donald-trump-debate-poll/.

206 Fact Check: Clinton and Trump debate for
the 2nd time. (2016, October 9). *NPR*. Retrieved October 26, 2016, from http://www.npr.
org/2016/10/09/497056227/fact-check-clinton-and-
trump-debate-for-the-second-time.

207 Keneally, M., Stracqualursi, V., Walshe, S., McGraw, M.,
& Jacobo, J. (2016, October 9). 2nd presidential debate:
11 moments that mattered. ABC News. Retrieved
October 26, 2016, from http://abcnews.go.com/
Politics/presidential-debate-11-moments-mattered/
story?id=42687340.

208 Palmer, A., & Sherman, J. (2016, October 11). Poll:
Hillary Clinton won the second debate. *Politico* Retrieved
October 26, 2016, from http://www.politico.com/
story/2016/10/clinton -trump-debate-poll-229581.

209 Rapperport, A. (2016, October 20). Who won the
debate? Hillary Clinton, the "nasty woman." *New York
Times*. Retrieved October 26, 2016, from http://www
.nytimes.com/2016/10 /21/us/politics/who-won-the-
third-debate.html.

210 Rogers, E. (2016, October 19). Trump won the third
debate. *Washington Post*. Retrieved October 26, 2016,

from https://www.washingtonpost.com/blogs/post-partisan/wp/2016/10/19/trump-won-tonights-debate/?utm_term=.b6d005181f14.

211 Caldwell, L. A. (2016, October 20). 5 major takeaways from the third and final presidential debate. *NBC News*. Retrieved October 26, 2016, from http://www.nbcnews.com/storyline/2016-presidential-debates/5-major-takeaways-third-final-presidential-debate-n669831.

212 Bradner, E. (2016, October 20). Trump always takes the bait and other debate takeaways. *CNN Politics*. Retrieved October 26, 2016, from http://www.cnn.com/2016/10/20/politics/presidential-debate-takeaways/.

213 Caldwell, "5 Major Takeaways."

214 Agiesta, J. (2016, October 20). Hillary Clinton wins third presidential debate, according to CNN/ORC Poll. *CNN Politics*. Retrieved October 26, 2016, from http://www.cnn.com/2016/10/19/politics/hillary-clinton-wins-third-presidential-debate-according-to-cnn-orc-poll/index.html.

215 Schultheis, E. (2016, November 6). FBI Director to Congress: Still no charges recommended after latest Clinton emails reviewed. *CBS News*. Retrieved November 8, 2016, from http://www.cbsnews.com/news/fbi-director-comey-congress-new-letter-hillary-clinton-emails-still-no-charges/.

216 Nakashima, E., Horwitz, S., & Zapotosky, M. (2016, November 6). For FBI, email investigation yields little but criticism. *Washington Post*. Retrieved November 8, 2016, from https://www.washingtonpost.com/politics/fbi-director-comey-says-agency-wont-recommend-charges-over-clinton-email/2016/11/06/f6276b18-a45e-11e6-ba59-a7d93165c6d4_story.html.

217 Gerstein, J. (2016, November 6). Comey says FBI stands by decision to not pursue case against Clinton. *Politico*. Retrieved November 8, 2016, from http://www.politico.com/story/2016/11/fbi-director-comey-says-agency-stands-by-decision-to-not-pursue-case-against-clinton-230842.

218 Edwards, J. (2016, November 7). FBI agents, lawmakers hammer Comey over Clinton emails inquiry. *Reuters*. Retrieved November 8, 2016, from http://www.reuters.com/article/us-usa-justice-comey-idUSKBN1322K6.

219 Bradner, E., Brown, P., & Perez, E. (2016, November 7). FBI clears Clinton—again. *CNN Politics*. Retrieved November 8, 2016, from http://www.cnn.com/2016/11/06/politics/comey-tells-congress-fbi-has-not-changed-conclusions/index.html.

220 Gerstein, "Comey Says FBI Stands by Decision."

221 Apuzzo, M., Schmidt, M. S., & Goldman, A. (2016, November 6). Emails warrant no new action against Hillary Clinton, FBI Director says. *New York Times*. Retrieved November 8, 2016, from http://www.nytimes.com/2016/11/07/us/politics/hilary-clinton-male-voters-donald-trump.html.

222 Nakashima et al., "For FBI, Email Investigation Yields Little but Criticism."

223 Edwards, "FBI Agents, Lawmakers Hammer Comey over Clinton Emails Inquiry."

224 Bosman, J., & Davey, M. (2016, November 11). Republicans expand control in a deeply divided nation. *New York Times*. Retrieved November 1, 2018, from http://www.nytimes.com/2016/11/12/us/republicans-expand-control-in-a-deeply-divided-nation.html?hp&action=click&pgtype=Homepage&clickSource=story-heading&module=b-lede-package-region&region=top-news&WT.nav=top-news&_r=1.

225 Panaritis, M., Purcell, D., Brennan, C., & Couloumbis, A. (2016, November 10). How Trump took Pennsylvania: Wins everywhere (almost) but the Southeast. *Philadelphia Inquirer*. Retrieved November 1, 2018, from http://www.philly.com/philly/news/politics/presidential/20161110_How_Trump_took_Pennsylvania__Wins__almost__everywhere_but_the_southeast.html.

226 Livengood, C., Wayland, M., & Feighan, M. (2016, November 9). Trump narrowly wins in Michigan. *Detroit News*. Retrieved November 1, 2018, from http://www.detroitnews.com/story/news/politics/elections/2016/11/08/michigan-president-election-results/93499404/.

227 Campbell, C., (2016, November 13). 7 rural N.C. counties flip "bloodshot red." *News and Observer*, pp. A1, 8A.

228 Krogstag, J. M. (2016, February 3). 2016 electorate will be the most diverse in U.S. history. Pew Research Center. Retrieved November 1, 2018, from http://www.pewresearch.org/fact-tank/2016/02/03/2016-electorate-will-be-the-most-diverse-in-u-s-history/.

229 The Leadership Conference Education Fund. (n.d.). *The great poll closures*. Retrieved November 1, 2018, from http://civilrightsdocs.info/pdf/reports/2016/poll-closure-report-web.pdf.

230 Wines. "Ruling Preserves Voting Rights of Thousands in North Carolina."

231 De Vogue, A. (2016, November 4). North Carolina counties must restore voters to rolls, judges rule. *CNN Politics*. Retrieved November 7, 2016, from http://www.cnn.com/2016/11/04/politics/north-carolina-naacp-voter-registration/.

232 Judge: North Carolina counties must restore voters removed in "insane" process. (2016, November 4). *Chicago Tribune*. Retrieved November 7, 2016, from http://www.chicagotribune.com/news/nationworld/ct-north-carolina-voter-purge-ruling-20161104-story.html.

233 Ibid.

234 Ibid.

235 Barnes, R.. (2016, August 31). Supreme Court won't let North Carolina use strict voting law. *Washington Post*. Retrieved November 8, 2016, from https://www.washingtonpost.com/politics/courts_law/supreme-court-wont-let-north-carolina-use-strict-voting-law/2016/08/31/b5187080-6ed6-11e6-8533-6b0b0ded0253_story.html.

236 Newkirk II, V. R. (2016, November 8). What early voting in North Carolina actually reveals. *The Atlantic*. Retrieved November 8, 2016, from http://www.theatlantic.com/politics/archive/2016/11/north-carolina-early-voting/506963/.

237 Republican party of Ark., Stu Stoffer respond to lawsuit claims of voter intimidation. (2016, November 3). *KTHV*. Retrieved November 8, 2016, from http://www.thv11.com/news/local/repbulican-party-of-ark-stu-soffer-respond-to-lawsuit-claims-of-voter-intimidation/347245839.

238 Dion, E. (2016, November 2). Group calls for reward for voter fraud tips. *Panama City News Herald*. Retrieved November 8, 2016, from http://www.newsherald.com/news/20161102/group-calls-for-reward-for-voter-fraud-tips.

239 Tinsley, A. M. (2016, October 18). Texas voter fraud concerns prompt hotline offering $5,000 reward for tips. *Star-Telegram*. Retrieved November 8, 2016, from http://www.star-telegram.com/news/politics-government/election/article109027632.html.

240 Bosman, J., & Davey, M. (2016, November 11). Republicans expand control in a deeply divided nation. *New York Times*. Retrieved November 1, 2018, from http://www.nytimes.com/2016/11/12/us/republicans-expand-control-in-a-deeply-divided-nation.html?hp&action=click&pgtype=Homepage&clickSource=story-heading&module=b-lede-package-region&region=top-news&WT.nav=top-news&_r=1.

241 Bradner, E. (2017, November 7). 5 takeaways from the Democrats' big night. *CNN Politics*. Retrieved October 16, 2018, from http://www.cnn.com/2017/11/07/politics/5-takeaways-election-virginia-governor-trump/index.html.

242 Wilkie, C. (2017, November 8). Democrats win big in elections widely viewed as referendums on Trump. *CNBC Politics*. Retrieved October 16, 2018, from https://www.cnbc.com/2017/11/08/democrats-win-up-and-down-the-ballot-in-legislative-mayoral-and-governors-races.html.

243 Beaumont, T., & Hanna, J. (2018, August 8). Gay Native American Democrat busts candidate mold in Kansas. *Associated Press*. Retrieved October 16, 2018, from https://apnews.com/647ba59eff074c52bad0734a5481d85c/Democrats-pick-gay,-Native-American-nominee-in-Kansas-3rd.

244 Ibid.

245 Martin, J., & Burns, A. (2018, May 22). Stacey Abrams wins Georgia Democratic primary for governor, making history. *New York Times*. Retrieved October 16, 2018, from https://www.nytimes.com/2018/05/22/us/politics/georgia-primary-abrams-results.html.

246 Ibid.

247 Trahant, M. (2018, May 24). Mark Trahant: Three Native women are running for top office in Minnesota. *Indian Country Today*. Retrieved October 16, 2018, from https://www.indianz.com/News/2018/05/24/mark-trahant-three-native-women-are-runn.asp.

248 Ibid.

249 Golshan, T. (2018, August 14). Ilhan Omar, a progressive Muslim woman, wins Minnesota primary for Keith Ellison's House seat. *Vox*. Retrieved October 16, 2018, from https://www.vox.com/policy-and-politics/2018/8/14/17689052/minnesota-primary-elections-2018-results-ilhan-omar.

250 Beaumont & Hanna, "Gay Native American Democrat."

251 Ibid.

252 Research before you vote: Educated voters are the key to good governance in Alaska. (2018, August 19). *Daily News-Miner*. Retrieved October 16, 2018, from http://www.newsminer.com/opinion/editorials/research-before-you-vote-educated-voters-are-the-key-to/article_bb6a46a6-a34b-11e8-84cd-e3de1ff7b8c9.html.

253 Ibid.

254 Sullivan, S., & Weigel, D.. (2018, June 25). A top House Democrat loses in upset; Trump extends his winning streak in GOP primaries. *Washington Post*. Retrieved October 16, 2018, from https://www.washingtonpost.com/powerpost/primary-elections-new-york-colorado-oklahoma-maryland-utah/2018/06/25/05bbbc5a-78a2-11e8-80be-6d32e182a3bc_story.html?noredirect=on&utm_term=.f934c98079e8 .

255 Remnick, D. (2018, July 23). Alexandria Ocasio-Cortez's historic win and the future of the Democratic Party. *The New Yorker*. Retrieved October 16, 2018, from https://www.newyorker.com/magazine/2018/07/23/alexandria-ocasio-cortezs-historic-win-and-the-future-of-the-democratic-party.

256 Beaumont & Hanna, "Gay Native American Democrat."

257 Burke, D., & Moorhead, J. (2018, August 8). Michigan Democrat likely to be first Muslim woman elected to Congress. *CNN Politics*. Retrieved October 16, 2018, from https://www.cnn.com/2018/08/08/politics/rashida-tlaib-michigan-13-congressional-district-election/index.html.

258 Scott, D. (2018, August 29). Andrew Gillum wins Florida governor primary in upset victory for the left. *Vox*. Retrieved October 16, 2018, from https://www.vox.com/policy-and-politics/2018/8/28/17793198/florida-primary-results-andrew-gillum-governor.

259 Berman, R. (2018, August 29). "One of the most brutal races in the country" has just begun in Florida. *The Atlantic*. Retrieved October 16, 2018, from https://www.theatlantic.com/politics/archive/2018/08/gillum-desantis-trump-florida-governors-race/568882/.

260 Granderson, L. Z. (2018, August 30). Andrew Gillum is smart not to take Ron DeSantis' "monkey this up" bait. *CNN.com*. Retrieved October 16, 2018, from https://www.cnn.com/2018/08/30/opinions/gillum-wise-not-to-take-monkey-comment-bait-granderson/index.html.

261 Scott, "Andrew Gillum Wins Florida."

262 Ibid.; Stern, M. J. (2018, August 29). How Andrew Gillum can replicate his staggering Democratic primary win in November. *Slate*. Retrieved October 16, 2018, from https://slate.com/news-and-politics/2018/08/andrew-gillum-how-the-democratic-nominee-can-win-floridas-governor-race-in-november.html; Seitz-Wald, A. (2018, August 30). After surprise primary victory, can Andrew Gillum win the Florida governor's race? *NBC News*. Retrieved October 16, 2018, from https://www.nbcnews.com/politics/elections/after-surprise-primary-victory-can-andrew-gillum-win-florida-governor-n904941

263 Seelye, K. Q. (2018, September 4). Ayanna Pressley upsets Capuano in Massachusetts House race. *New York Times*. Retrieved October 16, 2018, from https://www.nytimes.com/2018/09/04/us/politics/ayanna-pressley-massachusetts.html.

264 Bradner, "5 Takeaways."

265 Seelye, "Ayanna Pressley Upsets."

266 Grynbaum, M. M., & Chokshi, N. (2018, November 15). Even Fox News stopped running Trump caravan ad criticized as racist. *New York Times*. Retrieved November 27, 2018, from https://www.nytimes.com/2018/11/05/us/politics/nbc-caravan-advertisement.html.

267 Ibid.

268 Ibid.

269 Fact check on cop killer in campaign video Trump tweeted. (2018, November 2). *CBS News*. Retrieved November 27, 2018, from https://www.cbsnews.com/news/new-trump-campaign-video-luis-bracamontes-ad-cop-killer-immigration-fact-check-trump-tweeted/.

270 De Pinto, J. (2018, November 7). Record voter turnout in 2018 midterm elections. *CBS News*. Retrieved November 27, 2018, from https://www.cbsnews.com/news/record-voter-turnout-in-2018-midterm-elections/.

271 Smith, A. (2018, November 21). Democrats won House popular vote by largest midterm margin since Watergate. *NBC News*. Retrieved November 27, 2018, from https://www.nbcnews.com/politics/elections/democrats-won-house-popular-vote-largest-midterm-margin-watergate-n938996.

272 Martin, J., & Burns, A. (2018, November 6). Democrats capture control of House; G.O.P. holds Senate.

New York Times. Retrieved November 27, 2018, from https://www.nytimes.com/2018/11/06/us/politics/midterm-elections-results.html.

273 Montanaro, D. (2018, November 16). It was a big, blue wave: Democrats pick up most House seats in a generation. *NPR*. Retrieved November 27, 2018, from https://www.npr.org/2018/11/14/667818539/it-was-a-big-blue-wave-democrats-pick-up-most-house-seats-in-a-generation.

274 Burns, A. (2018, November 13). A week after the election, Democratic gains grow stronger. *New York Times*. Retrieved November 27, 2018, from https://www.nytimes.com/2018/11/13/us/politics/midterm-results-democratic-gains.html.

275 Martin, J. (2018, November 20). Cindy Hyde-Smith, in Mississippi Senate debate, addresses "public hanging" remarks. *New York Times*. Retrieved November 27, 2018, from https://www.nytimes.com/2018/11/20/us/politics/mississippi-senate-runoff-debate.html.

276 Bump, P. (2018, November 21). Nine out of 10 incoming Republican House members are White men. *Washington Post*. Retrieved November 27, 2018, from https://www.washingtonpost.com/politics/2018/11/21/nine-out-ten-incoming-republican-house-members-are-white-men/?utm_term=.b5cce6b1b8c2.

277 Capehart, J. (2018, November 20). Lucy McBath: From "cape up" to Congress. *Washington Post*. Retrieved November 27, 2018, from https://www.washingtonpost.com/blogs/post-partisan/wp/2018/11/20/lucy-mcbath-from-cape-up-to-congress/?utm_term=.c2ac18b053ae.

278 Taylor, J. (2018, November 20). Stacey Abrams says she was almost blocked from voting in Georgia election. *NPR*. Retrieved November 27, 2018, from https://www.npr.org/2018/11/20/669280353/stacey-abrams-says-she-was-almost-blocked-from-voting-in-georgia-election.

279 CNN Exit Poll. (2018). Florida governor's race. Retrieved November 27, 2018, from https://www.cnn.com/election/2018/exit-polls/florida.

Chapter 16

1 *U.S. v. Clary*, 846 F. Supp. 768 (1994)

2 *U.S. v. Clary*, 846 F. Supp. 768 (1994); see also Provine, D. M. (2007). *Unequal under the law: Race in the War on Drugs*. Chicago: University of Chicago Press, pp. 1–36.

3 *U.S. v. Clary*, 34 F.3d. 709 (1994); *certiorari* denied, 513 U.S. 1182 (1995).

4 Reid, A. A. (2005, October 6). Judge Clyde Cahill remembered for "character, compassion." *St. Louis American*. Retrieved July 20, 2018, from http://www.stlamerican.com/news/local_news/judge-clyde-cahill-remembered-for-character-compassion/article_eb6e2290-f71e-5014-a940-9d14f8a97037.html.

5 Kurtzleben, D. (2010, August 3). Data show racial disparity in crack sentencing: Obama signed

the Fair Sentencing Act to make punishments
for crack and cocaine more equal. *U.S. News and
World Report*. Retrieved July 20, 2018, from https://
www.usnews.com/news/articles/2010/08/03/
data-show-racial-disparity-in-crack-sentencing.

6 United States Sentencing Commission. (n.d.). *About*.
Retrieved July 20, 2018, from https://www.ussc.gov/
about-page.

7 United States Sentencing Commission. (2015, August).
Report to Congress: On the Fair Sentencing Act of 2010.
Retrieved July 20, 2018, from https://www.ussc.gov/
sites/default/files/pdf/news/congressional-testimony-
and-reports/drug-topics/201507_RtC_Fair-Sentencing-
Act.pdf.

8 For more on the stages of the policymaking process, see
Birkland, T. A. (2015). *An introduction to the policy process:
Theories, concepts, and models of public policy making*
(3rd ed.). London: Routledge; Fischer, F., Miller, G. L., &
Sidney, M. S. (2007). *Public policy analysis: Theory, politics,
and methods*. Boca Raton, FL: CRC Press; Kingdon, J.
(1984). *Agendas, alternatives, and public policies*. Boston:
Little, Brown.

9 Birkland, *An introduction to the policy process*, pp. 170–172.

10 Ibid., p. 172.

11 McClain, P. D., & Carew, J. D. J. (2018). *"Can we all get
along?": Racial and ethnic minorities in American politics*
(7th ed.). Boulder, CO: Westview Press, p. 93.

12 Olivera, G. M. (2017, December 11). Hurricane Maria
exposed the U.S.'s long neglect of Puerto Rico [Blog
post]. Retrieved July 20, 2018, from https://www.aclu
.org/blog/human-rights/hurricane-maria-exposed-uss-
long-neglect-puerto-rico.

13 Birkland, *An introduction to the policy process*, pp. 134–137,
176–177.

14 McClain & Carew, *"Can we all get along?"*, pp. 51–53.

15 Ibid., pp. 53–54.

16 Ibid., pp. 55–56.

17 Ibid., pp. 59–63.

18 In housing: *Shelley v. Kraemer*, 344 U.S. 1 (1948). In
voting: *Nixon v. Herndon*, 273 U.S. 536 (1927); *Smith v.
Allwright*, 321 U.S. 649 (1944). In education: *Missouri
ex. Rel. Gaines v. Canada*, 305 U.S. 337 (1938); *Sweatt v.
Painter*, 339 U.S. 692 (1950); *McLaurin v. Oklahoma*, 339
U.S. 637 (1950); *Brown v. Board of Education*, 347 U.S.
483 (1954). For more on the NAACP Legal Defense and
Educational Fund's work on discrimination litigation,
see Greenberg, J. (1994). *Crusaders in the courts: How a
dedicated band of civil rights lawyers fought for the civil rights
revolution*. New York: Basic Books.

19 Mexican American Legal Defense and Education Fund.
(n.d.). *About MALDEF*. Retrieved July 20, 2018, from
http://www.maldef.org/about/index.html.

20 Native American Rights Fund. (n.d.). *About us*. Retrieved
July 20, 2018, from https://www.narf.org/about-us/.

21 Asian American Advancing Justice. (n.d.). *About*.
Retrieved July 20, 2018, from https://www
.advancingjustice-aajc.org/who-we-are/about-us.

22 Amnesty International. (n.d.). *Who we are*. Retrieved
July 18, 2018, from https://www.amnesty.org/en/
who-we-are/.

23 Amnesty International. (2018, April 3). *USA: President
Trump's plan to militarize the border could cost lives*.
Retrieved July 20, 2018, from https://www.amnesty.org/
en/latest/news/2018/04/usa-president-trumps-plans-
to-militarize-border-could-cost-lives/.

24 Amnesty International. (2014, October 16). *Uganda:
Discriminatory legislation fuels repression and abuse*.
Retrieved July 20, 2018, from https://www.amnesty.org/en/
latest/news/2014/10/uganda-discriminatory-legislation-
fuels-repression-and-abuse/.

25 Birkland, *An introduction to the policy process*, pp. 144–154,
181–183; Iyengar, S., & Kinder, D. R. (1987). *News that
matters: Television and American opinion*. Chicago:
University of Chicago Press; Scheufele, D. A., & Tewksbury,
D. (2007). Framing, agenda setting, and priming: The
evolution of three media effects models. *Journal of
Communication, 57*, 9–20

26 Larson, S. G. (2006). *Media and minorities: The politics of
race in news and entertainment*. Lanham, MD: Rowman &
Littlefield, pp. 145–192.

27 Djordjevich, D. (1993, July). *Bosnia update: The great
debate?* Retrieved July 20, 2018, from https://fair.org/
extra/bosnia-update-the-great-debate/.

28 Anonymous. (1995, December 3). "Clinton Sends First
Troops to Bosnia." *CNN*, Retrieved October 25, 2018,
from http://www.cnn.com/WORLD/Bosnia/updates/
dec95/12-03/clinton/index.html.

29 Price, J. (1994, July 31). Why Rwanda was ignored:
Months of carnage passed before Congress urged aid.
Washington Times, p. A4.

30 Beah, I. (2014, September 19). The West ignores the
stories of Africans in the middle of the Ebola breakout.
Washington Post. Retrieved July 21, 2018, from https://
www.washingtonpost.com/opinions/the-west-ignores-
the-stories-of-africans-in-the-middle-of-the-ebola-
outbreak/2014/09/19/8e151c90-3f49-11e4-9587-
5dafd96295f0_story.html?utm_term=.61fe1f2a421f.

31 Ajami, F. (2012, January 15). 5 myths about the Arab
Spring. *Washington Post*, p. B2.

32 Kirkpatrick, D. D. (2014, July 3). Army ousts Egypt's
president; Morsi is taken into military custody. *New York
Times*. Retrieved July 19, 2018, from http://www
.nytimes.com/2013/07/04/world/middleeast/egypt.html?
pagewanted=all&_r=0.

33 Human Rights Watch. (n.d.). *About*. Retrieved July 20,
2018, from https://www.hrw.org/about.

34 Human Rights Watch. (n.d.). Egypt: Events of 2017. *World
Report 2018*. Retrieved July 20, 2018, from https://www
.hrw.org/world-report/2018/country-chapters/egypt.

35 For more on policy formulation, see Sidney, M. S. (2007). Policy formulation: Design and tools. In F. Fischer, G. L. Miller, & M. S. Sidney (Eds.), *Public policy analysis: Theory, politics, and methods* (pp. 79–87). Boca Raton, FL: CRC Press.

36 Frances Stokes Berry and William D. Berry are two leading scholars of policy adoption. See Berry, F. S., & Berry, W. D. (1994). The politics of tax increases in the states. *American Journal of Political Science*, 38, 855–859; Berry, F. S., & Berry, W. D. (1992). Tax innovation in the states: Capitalizing on political opportunity. *American Journal of Political Science, 36*, 715–742; Berry, F. S., & Berry, W. D. (1990). State lottery adoptions as policy innovations: An even history analysis. *American Political Science Review, 84*, 395–415.

37 Origins of the Darfur crisis. (2008, July 3). *PBS*. Retrieved July 21, 2018, from https://www.pbs.org/newshour/politics/africa-july-dec08-origins_07-03.

38 Library of Congress, Congress.Gov. (n.d.). *H.R. 1424: Darfur Genocide Accountability Act, of 2005*. Retrieved July 21, 2018, from https://www.congress.gov/bill/109th-congress/house-bill/1424.

39 Human Rights Watch. (2018). Sudan: Events of 2017. *World Report 2018*. Retrieved July 21, 2018, from https://www.hrw.org/world-report/2018/country-chapters/sudan.

40 Diarra, S. T. (2018, May 7). Mali ripe territory for ISIS, local militias—and they often clash. *USA Today*. Retrieved July 21, 2018, from https://www.usatoday.com/story/news/world/2018/05/07/mali-isis-islamic-state-militias-violence/546985002/.

41 Gutiérrez, L. (2015, September 30). *Rep. Gutiérrez' new bill expands access to Obamacare to undocumented immigrants*. Retrieved July 21, 2018, from https://gutierrez.house.gov/press-release/rep-guti%C3%A9rrez%E2%80%99-new-bill-expands-access-obamacare-undocumented-immigrants.

42 GovTrack.us. (n.d.). *HR 3659: Exchange Inclusion for a Healthy America Act of 2015*. Retrieved July 21, 2018, from https://www.congress.gov/bill/114th-congress/house-bill/3659/cosponsors.

43 *2016 Democratic Party Platform*. (2016, July 21). In G. Peters & J. T. Woolley, *American Presidency Project*. Retrieved July 21, 2018, from http://www.presidency.ucsb.edu/papers_pdf/117717.pdf.

44 *Republican Platform 2016*. (2016). In G. Peters & J. T. Woolley, *American Presidency Project*. Retrieved July 21, 2018, from http://www.presidency.ucsb.edu/papers_pdf/117718.pdf.

45 For more on the formulation of the policy redressing victims of internment, see Hatamiya, L. T. (1994). *Righting a wrong: Japanese Americans and the passage of the Civil Liberties Act of 1988*. Palo Alto, CA: Stanford University Press.

46 Administrative Procedure Act, "Rule Making," Title 5, Part 1, Chapter 5, Subchapter II, Section 553, *National Archives*. Retrieved July 21, 2018, from https://www.archives.gov/federal-register/laws/administrative-procedure/553.html.

47 Golden, M. M. (1988). Interest groups in the political process: Who participates? Whose voices get heard? *Journal of Public Administration Research and Theory, 8*, 245–270.

48 Joint Center for Political and Economic Studies. (n.d.). *About*. Retrieved July 21, 2018, from http://jointcenter.org/about/about.

49 Joint Center for Political and Economic Studies. (2012, November). *Place matters for health in the South Delta: Ensuring opportunities for good health for all: A report on heath inequities in South Delta, Mississippi*. Retrieved July 21, 2018, from http://www.nationalcollaborative.org/wp-content/uploads/2016/02/PLACE-MATTERS-for-Health-in-South-Delta.pdf.

50 O'Brien, D. M. (2014). *Storm center: The Supreme Court in American politics* (10th ed.). New York: Norton, p. 230.

51 Roberts, S. V. (1986, August 16). Senate votes bill to prod Pretoria, *New York Times*, p. 1.

52 Glass, A. (2010, September 29). House overrides Reagan apartheid veto, September 29, 1986. *Politico*. Retrieved July 21, 2018, from https://www.politico.com/story/2010/09/house-overrides-reagan-apartheid-veto-sept-29-1986-042839.

53 *Regents of the University of California v. Bakke*, 438 U.S. 235 (1978); see also O'Brien, *Storm center*, pp. 298–300.

54 *Grutter v. Bollinger*, 539 U.S. 306 (2003).

55 Romo, V., Stewart, M., & Naylor, B. (2018, September 5). Trump ends DACA, calls on Congress to act. *NPR*. Retrieved July 21, 2018, from https://www.npr.org/2017/09/05/546423550/trump-signals-end-to-daca-calls-on-congress-to-act.

56 Kopan, T., & Fox, L. (2018, January 11). Trump says some immigrants from "shithole countries" as he rejects bipartisan deal. *CNN Politics*. Retrieved July 21, 2018, from https://www.cnn.com/2018/01/11/politics/daca-deal-obstacles-flake-white-house/index.html.

57 For more on Representative Howard Smith's tenure as chair of the Rules Committee, see Dierenfield, B. J. (1987). *Keeper of the Rules: Congressman Howard W. Smith of Virginia*. Charlottesville: University Press of Virginia; United States House of Representatives. (n.d.). History, art, & archives: The Civil Rights Movement and the Second Reconstruction, 1945–1968. Retrieved October 26, 2018, from http://history.house.gov/Exhibitions-and-Publications/BAIC/Historical-Essays/Keeping-the-Faith/Civil-Rights-Movement/.

58 McClain & Carew, *"Can we all get along?"* p. 157.

59 Donald J. Trump: "Executive Order 13769—Protecting the Nation From Foreign Terrorist Entry Into the United States," January 27, 2017. In G. Peters & J. T. Woolley, *American Presidency Project*. Retrieved July 22, 2018, from http://www.presidency.ucsb.edu/ws/?pid=122529; Donald J. Trump: "Executive Order

13769—Protecting the Nation From Foreign Terrorist Entry Into the United States," January 27, 2017. In G. Peters & J. T. Woolley, *American Presidency Project*. Retrieved July 21, 2018, from http://www.presidency.ucsb.edu/ws/?pid=122529.

60 Barnes, R., & Marimow, A. (2018, June 26). Supreme Court upholds Trump travel ban. *Washington Post*. Retrieved July 22, 2018, from https://www.washingtonpost.com/politics/courts_law/supreme-court-upholds-trump-travel-ban/2018/06/26/b79cb09a-7943-11e8-80be-6d32e-182a3bc_story.html?utm_term=.ec0429821fa6.

61 For more on implementation, see Birkland, *An introduction to the policy process*, pp. 266–275; Pülzl, H., & Treib, O. (2007). Implementing public policy. In F. Fischer, G. L. Miller, & M. S. Sidney (Eds.), *Public policy analysis: Theory, politics, and methods* (pp. 89–107). Boca Raton, FL: CRC Press.

62 For more on policy evaluation, see Wollmann, H. (2007). Policy evaluation and evaluation research. In F. Fischer, G. L. Miller, & M. S. Sidney (Eds.), *Public policy analysis: Theory, politics, and methods* (pp. 393–402). Boca Raton, FL: CRC Press.

63 Birkland, *An introduction to the policy process*, pp. 266–275; Pülzl &Treib, "Implementing Public Policy."

64 Wermers, J. (2004, March 23). Education law is faulted: No Child Left Behind is called underfunded, straining poorer schools. *Richmond Times Dispatch*, p. B3.

65 The White House, President Barack Obama. (2011, September 23). *Remarks by the president on No Child Left Behind flexibility*. Retrieved July 22, 2018, from https://obamawhitehouse.archives.gov/the-press-office/2011/09/23/remarks-president-no-child-left-behind-flexibility.

66 Santelli, J., Speizer, I. S., & Edelstein, Z. R. (2013). Abstinence promotion under PEPFAR: The shifting focus for HIV prevention in youth. *Global Public Health: An International Journal for Research, Policy, and Practice, 8*, 1–12.

67 Gramer, R. (2017, December 1). Proposed U.S. cuts to AIDS funding could cause millions of deaths: Report. *Foreign Policy*. Retrieved July 22, 2018, from https://foreignpolicy.com/2017/12/01/proposed-u-s-cuts-to-aids-funding-could-cause-millions-of-deaths-report-world-aids-day-hiv-global-health-pepfar-state-department-trump-one-campaign/.

68 Yarbrough, T. E. (1994). Bush and the courts. In D. M. Hill & P. Williams (Eds.), *The Bush presidency: Triumphs and adversities*. New York: St. Martin's Press, pp. 97–98.

69 *Brown v. Board of Education of Topeka, Kansas*, 349 U.S. 294 (1955).

70 McClain & Carew, *"Can we all get along?"* pp. 192–193.

71 *Worcester v. Georgia*, 6 Peters 515 (1832).

72 For more on Jackson's actions after this decision, consult Sundquist, M. L. (2010–2011). *Worcester v. Georgia*: A breakdown in the separation of powers. *American Indian Law Review, 35*, 239–255.

73 Davis, B. C., & Bali, V. A. (2008). Examining the politics of race, NIMBY, and local politics in FEMA trailer park placement. *Social Science Quarterly, 89*, 1175–1194.

74 O'Brien, *Storm center*, p. 323.

75 Wollmann, "Policy Evaluation and Evaluation Research," pp. 397–398.

76 House Committee on Oversight and Government Reform Democrats. (2018, July 5). *New report details how GOP tax law hurts homeowners and helps wealthy developers*. Retrieved July 23, 2018, from https://democrats-oversight.house.gov/news/press-releases/new-report-details-how-gop-tax-law-hurts-homeowners-and-helps-wealthy-developers.

77 Kron, J., & Goodman, D. (2012, March 9). Online, a distant conflict soars to no. 1. *New York Times*, p. A1; Levy, G. (2013, April 3). *$5 million bounty offered for Joseph Kony*. Retrieved July 22, 2018, from https://www.upi.com/blog/2013/04/03/5-million-bounty-offered-for-Joseph-Kony/2981365016264/.

78 Cakaj, L. (2017, June 28). $800 million later, Joseph Kony is still a threat. *Foreign Policy*. Retrieved July 22, 2018, from https://foreignpolicy.com/2017/06/28/800-million-later-joseph-kony-is-still-a-threat/.

79 Weisman, J. (1999, August 4). Welfare rolls reduced sharply. *Baltimore Sun*, p. 1A.

80 Schultze, S. (2003, March 29). Minority W-2 clients faced more penalties, study says. *Milwaukee Journal Sentinel*, p. 2B.

Credits

Photos

Chapter 1

p. 1: Steve Ruark / AP; p. 4: ©Bettmann / Corbis / AP Images; p. 6: AP Photo / Gerry Broome; p. 13: Universal History Archive / Getty Images; p. 14: ©Bettmann / Corbis / AP Images; p. 14: Hulton Archive / Getty Images; p. 17: Library of Congress Prints and Photographs Division Washington, D.C. 20540 USA; p. 19: AP Photo / The Daily Progress, Dan Lopez; p. 21: Terra Foundation for American Art, Chicago / Art Resource, NY; p. 23: North Wind Picture Archives.

Chapter 2

p. 26: MEGA; p. 30: North Wind Picture Archives via AP Images; p. 32: ©Bettmann / Corbis / AP Images; p. 34: AP Photo; p. 42: North Wind Picture Archives via AP Images; p. 53: Tom Williams / CQ Roll Call via AP Images.

Chapter 3

p. 55: Miguel Otarola via Cronkite News: Arizona PBS; p. 64: AP Photo / Juan Labreche; p. 68: Bill Clark / Roll Call / Getty Images; p. 70: Joshua Komer; p. 70: Patrick Tehan / Bay Area News Group; p. 70: Joseph Geha / Bay Area News Group; p. 79: © Louie Psihoyos / CORBIS; p. 81: Walter Sanders / Time Life Pictures / Getty Images; p. 81: Bettmann / Getty Images; p. 87: Indiana State Police.

Chapter 4

p. 95: Ryan M. Kelly / The Daily Progress via AP; p. 101: Bettman / Getty Images; p. 105: REUTERS / Mario Anzuoni; p. 110: Courtesy John Vachon Collection; p. 113: © Tribune Media Services, Inc. All Rights Reserved. Reprinted with permission; p. 113: LALO ALCARAZ ©2002 Dist. by UNIVERSAL UCLICK. Reprinted with permission. All rights reserved; p. 115: AP Photo / Lou Krasky; p. 123: AP Photo / Manuel Balce Ceneta.

Chapter 5

p. 127: Courtesy of Fernando Espino Casas; p. 133: Russell Lee / Library Of Congress / Getty Images; p. 134: North Wind Picture Archives via AP Images; p. 140: Don Cravens / Time Life Pictures / Getty Images; p. 142: AFP / Getty Images; p. 150: AP Photo / Evan Vucci; p. 155: Library of Congress Prints and Photographs Division Washington, D.C. 20540 USA; p. 156: ©Bettmann / Corbis / AP Images; p. 156: 04-06-06 @ Timothy Swope. Copyright ©2013 iStockphoto LP; p. 160: JEWEL SAMAD / AFP / Getty Images; p. 163: John Sleezer / Kansas City Star / TNS via Getty Images.

Chapter 6

p. 166: AP Photo / Darren Abate; p. 170: National Atlas via Vox; p. 171: Douglas Graham / CQ Roll Call; p. 177: © 2018 CBS Interactive Inc. All Rights Reserved; p. 180: Alex Wong / Getty Images; p. 184: AP Photo / Lawrence Jackson; p. 185: CAMILLE PHILLIPS / ST. LOUIS PUBLIC RADIO; p. 192: Keith Birmingham / Pasadena Star-News.

Chapter 7

p. 199: REUTERS / Yuri Gripas; p. 216 Brennan Linsley / AP; p. 219: Alex Wong / Getty Images; p. 221 ©Bettmann / Corbis / AP Images; p. 224: AP Photo / Pablo Martinez Monsivais; p. 226: Pete Souza / The White House; p. 230: Alex Wong / Getty Images.

Chapter 8

p. 237: PHOTOGRAPH BY DENNIS MANUEL RIVERA; p. 243: Federal Communications Commission; p. 245: Jim Abbott; p. 248: GRANGER / GRANGER — All rights reserved; p. 250: Sari O'Neal / Shutterstock; p. 257: AP Photo / The Sun, Alfred J. Hernandez; p. 260: © Roger Ressmeyer / CORBIS.

Chapter 9

p. 264: AP Photo / Charles Dharapak; p. 276: Franz Jantzen, Collection of the Supreme Court of the United States;

Figures

Index